M000107246

Panorama

A World History
Volume 1: to 1500

The way we once learned history . . .

. . . IS NOW HISTORY

Just as a panoramic image provides a broad view, *Panorama* provides a ground-breaking, broad view of the world's history by reaching across regional boundaries and highlighting large-scale, global patterns. *Panorama's* easily understood chronology, coupled with its innovative, proven digital tools, ensures that learners are always moving forward as they study change and continuity across time, assess knowledge gaps, and mold critical thinking skills. The result is improved course performance through greater understanding of our world's past, its large-scale global trends, and its impact on and relevance to 21st-century students.

Panorama is a program for the 21st Century

McGraw Hill Education |SMARTBOOK™

STUDY SMARTER WITH SMARTBOOK

The first and only adaptive reading experience, SmartBook is changing the way students read and learn. As a student engages with SmartBook and takes its interactive quizzes, the program continuously adapts by highlighting content that the student doesn't know. This helps close specific knowledge gaps and simultaneously promotes long-term learning.

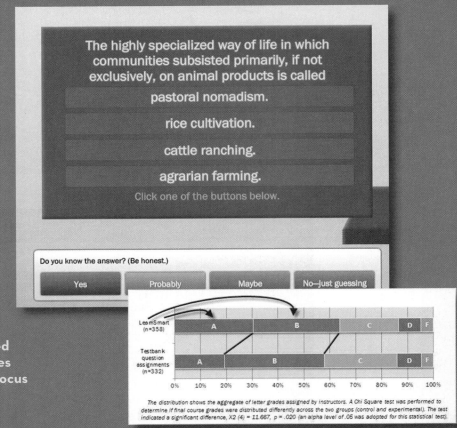

||LEARNSMART®

LEARN BETTER WITH LEARNSMART

LearnSmart is the premier learning system designed to effectively assess a student's knowledge of course content through a series of adaptive questions. LearnSmart intelligently pinpoints concepts the student does not understand and maps out a personalized study plan for success. LearnSmart prepares students for class, allowing instructors to focus on higher-level learning.

THINK CRITICALLY WITH CRITICAL MISSIONS

Critical Missions immerse students as active participants in a series of transformative moments in history. As advisors to key historical figures, students read and analyze sources, interpret maps and timelines, and write recommendations. As part of each mission, students learn to think like an historian, conducting a retrospective analysis from a contemporary perspective.

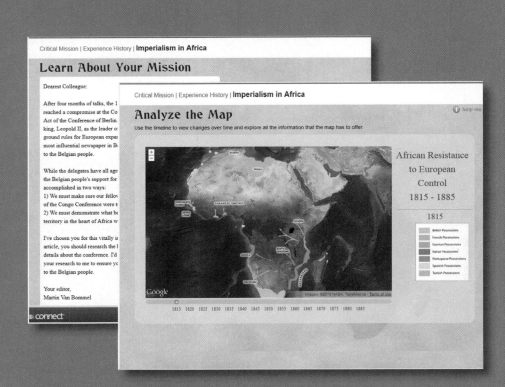

 connect®
|HISTORY

SUCCEED FASTER WITH CONNECT HISTORY

Connect History strengthens the link between faculty, students and coursework. Innovative, adaptive technology aligns the goals of students and faculty, allowing them to work together to accomplish more in less time. It engages students in the course content so they are better prepared, more active in discussions, and able to excel.

Mc Graw Hill Education **Campus**

EASY ACCESS WITH MHCAMPUS

Enjoy Easy Access with MHCampus, which integrates our digital tools into your school's course management system. This integration provides single sign-on access for students and a comprehensive grade book for instructors allowing for easy tracking of students' progress as well as remediation on challenging topics. MHCampus ensures that students will master the learning outcomes and core objectives of their world history course.

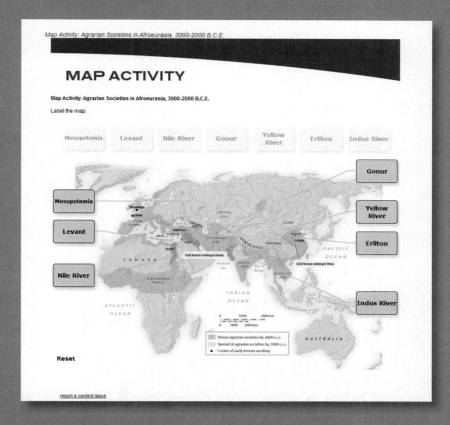

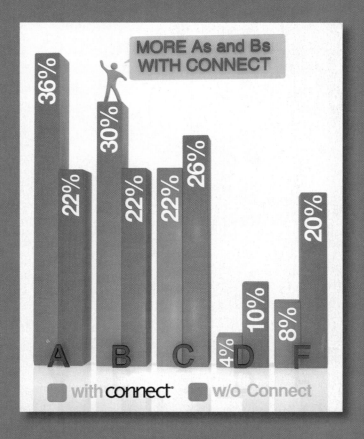

Praise for *Panorama*

"Finally, a world history text that puts human history on world time! Focused on humankind as a whole and its interactions over time, *Panorama* provides a conceptually organized and integrative approach to the human past."

Edmund Burke III, University of California, Santa Cruz

"*Panorama* demonstrates the promise of the 'new world history,' as revealed in the authors' skillful integration of far-reaching global connections with careful attention to the lives of individuals in specific places. Their discussion of peoples who are often found at the periphery of world history, such as Africans, is certain to push world historians and their students to diversify their historical perspectives."

Richard Warner, Wabash College

"This is an excellent text. Dunn and Mitchell's categories of analysis, global research, and their years of experience teaching world history are brilliantly displayed. For those of us who have been in the trenches teaching world history, we finally have a masterful global textbook by world history scholars who have extensive experience teaching such courses."

-Elaine Carey, St. John's University

"I think I've finally found a world history book that is truly 'world' in an intelligent and useful way. It's readable, its coverage is very good, and it has a clear analytical framework. I particularly like its environmental perspective."

-Phyllis Jestice, College of Charleston

"What makes *Panorama* unique is a truly comparative framework that is global in scope within successive eras. It lays a solid foundation for the development of individual societies in the Americas and the Pacific and the cooperative and competitive cultures of Afroeurasia before contact is established in the late 15th century. Then *Panorama* unfolds a gradual and impressive analysis of human interaction across the globe since that pivotal event."

-Ryan Thompson, Cleveland State Community College

"Students want to understand the order of events, but so often world history begins to look like stacked timelines. *Panorama's* format helps to bring global issues and broad themes together in a manageable, chronological way. It also prompts students to think of other examples that they may already be aware of. "

-Erika Briesacher, Worcester State University

"This is a compelling text that makes me eager to teach World History as soon as possible! *Panorama* introduces issues of climate and geography to the human story in a truly profound and innovative way."

-Brian Black, Pennsylvania State University, Altoona

Panorama

A World History
Volume 1: to 1500

ROSS E. DUNN
San Diego State University

LAURA J. MITCHELL
University of California, Irvine

Mc
Graw
Hill
Education

PANORAMA: A WORLD HISTORY

Published by McGraw-Hill Education, 2 Penn Plaza, New York, NY 10121. Copyright © 2015 by McGraw-Hill Education. All rights reserved. Printed in the United States of America. No part of this publication may be reproduced or distributed in any form or by any means, or stored in a database or retrieval system, without the prior written consent of McGraw-Hill Education, including, but not limited to, in any network or other electronic storage or transmission, or broadcast for distance learning.

Some ancillaries, including electronic and print components, may not be available to customers outside the United States.

This book is printed on acid-free paper.

1 2 3 4 5 6 7 8 9 0 DOW/DOW 1 0 9 8 7 6 5 4

ISBN   978-0-07-340704-3 (complete)
MHID   0-07-340704-6 (complete)
ISBN   978-0-07-748232-9 (volume 1)
MHID   0-07-748232-8 (volume 1)
ISBN   978-0-07-748233-6 (volume 2)
MHID   0-07-748233-6 (volume 2)

Senior Vice President, Products & Markets: *Kurt L. Strand*
Vice President, General Manager, Products & Markets:
   Michael J. Ryan
Vice President, Content Production & Technology Services:
   Kimberly Meriwether David
Managing Director: *Gina Boedeker*
Director: *Matt Busbridge*
Brand Manager: *Laura Wilk*
Director of Development: *Rhona Robbin*
Managing Development Editor: *Nancy Crochiere*
Development Editor: *Cynthia Ward*
Map Development: *Robin Mouat*

Brand Coordinator: *Kaelyn Schulz*
Digital Product Analyst: *John Brady*
Executive Marketing Manager: *Stacy Best Ruel*
Director, Content Production: *Terri Schiesl*
Content Project Manager: *Rick Hecker*
Senior Buyer: *Laura M. Fuller*
Design: *Matthew Baldwin*
Cover Image: © *2013 Michael Markieta*
Content Licensing Specialist: *Shawntel Schmitt*
Typeface: *9.75/12 Palatino LT STD*
Compositor: *Thompson Type*
Printer: *R. R. Donnelley*

All credits appearing on page or at the end of the book are considered to be an extension of the copyright page.

The Library of Congress has cataloged the single volume edition of this work as follows

Dunn, Ross E.
     Panorama : a world history / Ross E. Dunn, San Diego State University, Laura J. Mitchell,
The University of California, Irvine.
        pages cm
     Includes bibliographical references and index.
     ISBN 978-0-07-340704-3 (complete : alk. paper) — ISBN 0-07-340704-6 (complete : alk. paper) —
ISBN 978-0-07-748232-9 (volume 1 : alk. paper)—ISBN 0-07-748232-8 (volume 1 : alk. paper) —
ISBN 978-0-07-748233-6 (volume 2 : alk. paper)—ISBN 0-07-748233-6 (volume 2 : alk. paper)
     1. World history—Textbooks. I. Mitchell, Laura Jane, 1963– II. Title.
   D21.D936 2015
   909—dc23

                                                                        2013037646

The Internet addresses listed in the text were accurate at the time of publication. The inclusion of a website does not indicate an endorsement by the authors or McGraw-Hill Education, and McGraw-Hill Education does not guarantee the accuracy of the information presented at these sites.

www.mhhe.com

About the Authors

Ross Dunn

Ross Dunn is Professor Emeritus of History at San Diego State University, where he taught African, Islamic, and world history. In his early career he specialized in North African history, publishing *Resistance in the Desert: Moroccan Responses to French Imperialism, 1881–1912* (1977). Teaching world history inspired him to write *The Adventures of Ibn Battuta, a Muslim Traveler of the Fourteenth Century* (1987). This book is in its third edition. A leadership role in the project to write national standards for world history led to publication, with Gary B. Nash and Charlotte Crabtree, of *History on Trial: Culture Wars and the Teaching of the Past* (1997). In 2000 he edited the essay collection *The New World History: A Teacher's Companion.* He is an associate director of the National Center for History in the Schools at UCLA. In 2012 he received the annual Pioneers of World History award from the World History Association. He was the first elected president of that organization.

Laura J. Mitchell

Laura J. Mitchell is Associate Professor at the University of California, Irvine, where she teaches African and world history. She strives to make sense of early-modern societies in a digital age and to make history accessible to diverse audiences. Her research on colonial southern Africa has been supported by grants from Fulbright, the American Council of Learned Societies, the National Endowment for the Humanities, the UC Office of the President, and the Mellon Foundation. She has collaborated with a wide range of scholars and history educators, serving as president of the Forum on European Expansion and Global Interaction, as a member of the World History Association Executive Council, and as a co-chair of the AP World History Curriculum Assessment and Development Committee. Her book *Belongings: Property, Family and Identity in Colonial South Africa* (2009) won the American Historical Association's Gutenberg-e Prize.

Brief Contents

Contents

Settling the Planet
Beginnings to the First Millennium B.C.E.

part
1

Agrarian Societies and Their Interconnections
1200 B.C.E.–300 C.E.
part 2

An Interview with the Authors of *Panorama: A World History*

Ross Dunn and Laura Mitchell discuss how they came to write *Panorama* and how they believe it contributes to the study of the human past.

Q: Tell us about the unique approach you have taken in *Panorama.*

A: In *Panorama*, we have created a unified narrative of world history, assuming that the primary subject we are investigating is humankind as a whole, and the primary setting of the narrative is the globe. We have organized the chapters chronologically, by consecutive historical periods—never repeating a period from different regional or thematic angles. Our aim is to advance the mission of conceptualizing the human experience in ways that are more holistic and integrated. To do this, we have had to select the very broad developments that define particular historical periods and that we think readers ought to understand.

Q: Why did you choose this approach?

A: We wanted to contribute to the important work of making the history of humankind intelligible, to write a unified narrative that is clear and coherent and that gives readers a sturdy framework for thinking about the global past. We believe we can begin to understand big and rapid changes in the world today only if we have a mental scaffolding of ideas and words for thinking, talking, and writing about the world as a whole. Similarly, we can begin to grasp how the world got to be the way it is only if we have world-scale narratives that help us connect the histories of particular groups—nations, civilizations, religions, corporations—to patterns of change in human society writ large.

Q: How do you balance large historical generalizations with knowledge about particular peoples, places, and events?

A: We know from experience that if the presentation is too broad, abstract, or theoretical, students may have a hard time grasping the generalizations. But if the writing is too loaded with historical details (all of which may be significant at some level), then the big pictures of change tend to get lost in thickets of information about particular societies, individuals, conquests, wars, philosophies, artistic movements, and so on.

Like all writers of world history, we have made choices to leave out a great deal of perfectly useful and interesting knowledge. Only by doing this are we able to keep our sights on the panoramic view and on the unified narrative. We have also, however, aimed to write in concrete, descriptive language, recognizing that history is fundamentally about human beings, individually or in groups, thinking, working, fighting, and creating.

Q: How are you able to combine the telling of "large-scale" history with in-depth, "small-scale" knowledge of people and events?

A: In every chapter, we shift between larger- and smaller-scale narratives, but we aim consistently to relate developments at relatively small scales to those at much larger scales. We cannot understand the Industrial Revolution as the world event it was by studying just one English factory town, but historians might write about such a town as an example of how large-scale changes played out on a local level and affected people's lives.

Q: Does *Panorama* have a central theme?

A: Yes, it does. This theme is the growing complexity of human society from the early era of stone toolmaking to today. Looking over the very long term of history, we see a nearly continuous though by no means inevitable trend toward greater complexity in the relations of human groups with one another and with the earthly environment. This movement from lesser to greater complexity has been manifested across the ages in several nearly continuous trends of growth, even though the rates and dimensions of change in these areas have been uneven:

- Global population (more people and more groups interacting with one another)
- Human use of the planet's energy supply to produce food and other goods
- Human intervention to alter the natural and physical environment
- The intricacy and sophistication of technology and science
- The density and speed of systems of communication and transport

- The density of human networks of interchange, including movement of people, goods, and ideas
- The size of governments and their capacity to manage and control people
- The technical capabilities of weaponry to kill people and destroy property
- The size and elaborateness of systems of belief, including religions, ethical structures, and philosophies

Throughout the book, we pose the same question in different ways: How and why did the world move relentlessly toward greater cultural complexity, despite breaks and unevenness in that trend, for example, short-term drops in global population, periods of economic contraction, or the disappearance of particular languages and local religions?

Q: How did you decide on the topics for each chapter?

A: In aiming to write a unified narrative of history, we followed the basic principle of bringing to the fore historical developments that had (and may still have) an impact on relatively large numbers of people, that is, developments of large scale. We let these big developments generally determine the chronological frame of each chapter, and we investigate them in whatever geographical context seems appropriate for clear discussion of their importance. If most chapters focus in part on developments in a region, it is because a development of large-scale significance happened or started there in that particular period. For example, we devote a primary chapter section to developments in China under the Song dynasties of the eleventh and twelfth centuries because China in those centuries generated exuberant economic innovation and growth, a phenomenon that had effects all across the Eastern Hemisphere.

Q: What is distinctive about *Panorama*'s periodization of the past?

A: As a unified narrative, *Panorama* proposes a plan for dividing the past into specific chunks of time, with the beginnings and endings of those chunks determined by the important historical developments that occurred within them. Our periodization plan is a single chronology, or time-line moving from the remote to the recent past. One way that *Panorama*'s periodization differs from the majority of world history books is its greater attention to very early human history, that is, to the long paleolithic era that preceded the coming of agriculture. The whole paleolithic era (old stone age), which started perhaps 2.5 million years ago, constitutes about 99.6 percent of the history of humankind and its near biological ancestors. Attention to early history encourages readers to think about how and why humans made radical changes in the way they lived—taking up farming, building cities, creating mechanized industries, populating the world

with billions—when they got along without doing these things for hundreds of thousands of years.

Q: You refer to your narrative as "unified"; can you elaborate?

A: One element of our approach to a unified narrative is to conceive of Africa, Asia, and Europe together as a single land mass, a sort of "supercontinent" within which humans interacted, or at least had the physical possibility of interacting, since paleolithic times. As discussed in our Introduction, we refer to this supercontinent as Afroeurasia. For periods of world history up to 1500 C.E., we conceive of the world as divided into four primary geographical regions: Afroeurasia (where the great majority of human beings have always lived—about 86 percent today), the Americas (North and South together), Australia, and Oceania (the Island Pacific). Within these regions, human groups interacted with one another, though with greater or lesser intensity and from different chronological starting points. On the other hand, people did not interact, at least not in any sustained way, between one of these regions and another because wide expanses of ocean and to some extent contrasting climatic conditions prevented or discouraged it. For periods up to 1500 C.E., therefore, we explore developments in these regions in different chapters or sections of chapters, even though we also introduce points of historical comparison between one region and another. Starting in the late fifteenth century, the four regions began to throw out lines of communication to one another, though not all at once. The Great World Convergence, as we call it, began when sea captains established regular transport routes between Afroeurasia and the Americas. For periods after 1500, we treat the entire world as a single zone within which human interrelations became increasingly complex and large-scale developments occurred. From that chronological point to the present, all the chapters are global in scope.

Q: How does *Panorama* cover the significance of individuals—both men and women—in the course of human history?

A: *Panorama* endeavors to take full account of the historical fact that men and women share the planet. Even though much of the narrative is not explicitly gender specific, it aims to be "gender sensitive." This has meant repeatedly asking ourselves as we move from topic to topic how both men and women, whether aristocrats, city workers, peasants, or forager-hunters, acted as agents of change.

In every chapter of this book, the cast of characters is necessarily very large. We aim, however, to remind readers of the importance of individuals as agents of change by introducing a chapter feature titled "Individuals Matter." It presents a biographical sketch of an individual whose life in some way illuminates the period the chapter addresses. In most cases, this individual is a person of public importance, for example, Empress Wu of the Chinese Tang dynasty, or Diego Rivera, the twentieth-century Mexican artist. In a few chapters, however, the individual is an "ordinary" woman or man whose life or deeds illustrate some aspect of the period—for example, Ötzi, the ascribed name of a neolithic traveler in the Alps, or Olga Lisikova, a Russian combat pilot in World War II.

Q: Does *Panorama* incorporate primary sources?

A: Yes. A feature titled "Weighing the Evidence" appears in every chapter—and in the accompanying Connect History program—offering students an opportunity to critically examine a piece of historical evidence relating to the chapter content. The selection is usually a written document (for example, a nineteenth-century Moroccan diplomat's description of France), though in a few chapters a visual artifact (for example, an image of a giant stone head from ancient Mexico) is included. In some chapters, we present two pieces of evidence to compare with each other. "Weighing the Evidence" includes questions that prompt readers to analyze, interpret, and discuss the selection. This feature reminds readers that the *Panorama* narrative rests on the work of thousands of professional historians and other scholars who have examined, authenticated, and interpreted written documents, works of art, fossilized bones, and numerous other kinds of primary evidence.

Q: Is there a theme to your chapter-opening vignettes?

A: Yes. A key element of the trend toward greater complexity in world history has been the development of systems of communication that have allowed humans to move from one place to another and to create networks for exchanging ideas and things in increasingly complicated ways and at faster and faster speeds. To highlight this aspect of human complexity, we open each chapter with a brief story or vignette that has to do with some kind of communication, transport, or movement pertinent to the historical period under study. The subjects of these stories range widely from camel caravans to the profession of telephone operator.

Q: Is *Panorama* available as an e-book?

A: Even better—it is available as a SmartBook, which means not only that students can read it online, but they can quiz themselves after every section. The SmartBook then adapts to their response, highlighting areas in the narrative that they need to study more.

Q: Are any other digital resources available?

A: Absolutely. The Connect History program offers activities with *Panorama*'s maps, primary sources, key concepts and terms, as well as auto-gradable test items and essay questions.

Panorama: A New View of World History

Panorama presents the big picture: a unified chronological narrative of world history that gives students a valuable framework for thinking about the global past.

Panorama's seven parts correspond to seven eras of global history. Within each part, chapters are organized chronologically by consecutive historical periods, never repeating a period from different regional or thematic angles. This organization gives students the mental scaffolding needed to think about the world as a whole. Each part-opening spread previews the major trends of the global era and includes both a time-band placing that period in the larger context of world history and a graph illustrating the era's population growth.

10,000 B.C.E.   8,000 B.C.E.   6,000 B.C.E.

part 3

Shifting Power, Thickening Webs
Afroeurasia, 200–1000 C.E.

I f in the very long term human history has been a story of more and more people sharing the planet, while inventing increasingly complex of ways of organizing themselves, interacting with one another, and exploiting the earth's energy to their own benefit, this trend has not been entirely steady. Within the overall movement toward greater complexity, there have been cycles in which population has declined and recovered, cities have shrunk and flourished again, and economies have contracted and expanded. These cycles may be merely regional in scope, but they have also had interregional or even global dimensions, as we have seen in modern times when business recessions reverberate quickly around the world. The three chapters in Part 3 encompass approximately eight hundred years in the history of Afroeurasia, an era when the demographic and economic trends of the previous millennium temporarily slowed down or even reversed themselves, before accelerating again at an even faster pace.

The third century C.E., where Part 3 begins, represents a jarring break—in some places violent and destructive—in the prevailing pattern of population and economic growth. Between about 200 and 600, the Han, Kushana, Parthian, and western Roman empires all collapsed. These upheavals occurred partly in connection with the aggressive migrations of peoples from the Inner Eurasian steppes into neighboring agrarian lands. Western Europe, North Africa, northern India, and northern China all experienced serious economic turmoil. Disease epidemics that swept around the Mediterranean rim and across Southwest Asia in the sixth century had similar consequences. Conditions of life in several regions became harsh enough that Afroeurasia's overall population declined by several tens of millions between the third and seventh centuries, perhaps the first significant drop since the invention of agriculture.

A terra-cotta camel and rider from the era of the Tang dynasty in China.

246

PART 3: 200 C.E to 1000 C.E.

2,000 C.E.

into deep
...asanid Per-
...d invaders.
...a large part
...thern China,
...y escaped
...ite regional
...n the Inner
...a to South-
...an suffered

...d economic
...rasia:

...China
...dynasties
...f technical
...rowing

...e mid-
...e effect on
...tiles, pep-
...across

■ In western Africa, merchants who discovered the hardy qualities of the dromedary camel set up commercial operations that connected the Mediterranean lands with West Africa. This pioneering enterprise, well under way by the seventh century, lubricated the whole Afroeurasian exchange system with injections of West African gold.

■ Assaults of Eurasian nomads on China, India, and Southwest Asia tailed off. In the steppes new warrior empires arose in the sixth century, but they also stabilized political conditions and recharged silk road commerce. In the late first millennium, Europe endured an incursion of Magyar warriors from the steppes, but these intruders settled down quickly.

■ Finally, invaders from the Arabian Desert, who proclaimed Islam as a new universalist religion, politically united most of Southwest Asia, a region of agricultural and urban productivity that had been divided between rival states for nearly a thousand years. The cities of Southwest Asia had for millennia funneled commercial goods and new ideas along a corridor that connected the Mediterranean basin with the whole expanse of Asia

and eastern Africa. Following unification under Arab leadership, that corridor became more animated than ever before. From Southwest Asia, Arab soldiers, preachers, and merchants introduced Islam along the routes of conquest and trade. This new expression of monotheistic faith drew on the teachings of both Judaism and Christianity, and it put great emphasis on social cooperation and codes of proper ethical and legal behavior. Thus, Islam joined Buddhism and Christianity as a universalist faith offering the promise of community harmony and individual salvation. Together, these three religions reached just about every part of Afroeurasia in the late millennium.

Between 200 and 1000 C.E. migrant farmers, long-distance merchants, conquering armies, and wandering missionaries brought more of Afroeurasia into a single arena of human interchange. This happened without any revolutionary breakthroughs in communication and transport technology, though artisans and engineers tinkered endlessly with ship designs, navigational tools, and more efficient systems of banking and credit. By the end of the millennium, signs of new economic growth and social complexity were abundant. Afroeurasia's overall population climbed nearly back to where it had been eight hundred years earlier. Interlinked commercial networks operated across the breadth of Afroeurasia. China was moving into an era of unprecedented industrial growth. And after suffering a half-millennium of chronic disorder, western Europeans were building a new urban civilization.

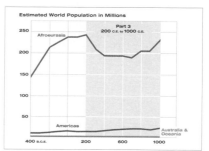

Estimated World Population in Millions

Part 3
200 C.E to 1000 C.E.

250 Afroeurasia

200

150

100

50

Americas   Australia & Oceania

400 B.C.E.   200   600   1000

247

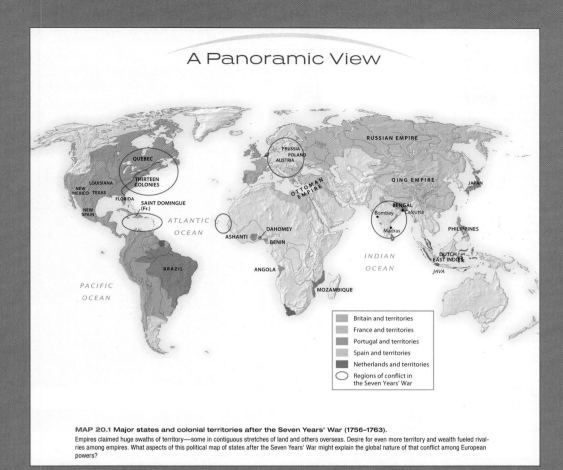

A Panoramic View

Panorama's maps are designed for optimal classroom projection as well as pedagogical clarity (see Map List, pp. xxvii–xxviii). Maps titled "A Panoramic View" at the beginning of each chapter provide a big-picture overview for the narrative. Within each chapter, additional maps zoom into the regional or local level or provide other views. Questions for each map engage students in thinking about geography and history.

MAP 20.1 Major states and colonial territories after the Seven Years' War (1756–1763).
Empires claimed huge swaths of territory—some in contiguous stretches of land and others overseas. Desire for even more territory and wealth fueled rivalries among empires. What aspects of this political map of states after the Seven Years' War might explain the global nature of that conflict among European powers?

Connect History, an online learning tool, offers 28 interactive maps that actively engage students, supporting geographical as well as historical thinking. These dynamic maps allow students to selectively focus on elements of the map. For example, they can examine the spread of specific crops one at a time, then reconstruct the full global process of agricultural diffusion. Other interactive maps enable students to analyze periodization, comparing changing political boundaries or the spread of technology over time.

MAP 13.2 Mongol states and their neighbors, 1300.
What geographical or ecological features might help account for the Chagatai khanate being the economically weakest of the four great Mongol states?

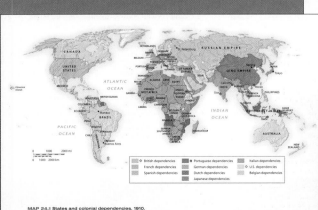

MAP 24.1 States and colonial dependencies, 1910.
On the eve of World War I, western European countries, the United States, and Japan claimed or administered large parts of Africa, Asia, and the island Pacific. Which countries claimed the largest overseas empires?

Each chapter offers students the opportunity to examine historical evidence through a **Weighing the Evidence** selection. The primary sources in these boxed features include public and private documents, visual sources, and material artifacts; sometimes two sources are presented for comparison. A headnote puts the source in context, and a series of questions after the source challenges students to think deeply and analytically about its significance.

Weighing THE EVIDENCE

Frantz Fanon on the Shortcomings of the National Bourgeoisie

One of the most influential texts to emerge from colonial independence movements is Frantz Fanon's The Wretched of the Earth. Fanon (1925–1961) came from a middle-class family on the French Caribbean island of Martinique. During World War II he went to North Africa to join the Free French resistance against the Germans. He was wounded in battle and awarded the Croix de Guerre. After the war he studied medicine and psychiatry in France. There, he became starkly aware of the limits of social assimilation. Though he had grown up in a thoroughly French environment and fought for the country, whites never viewed him as an equal. His interest in the psychological effects of colonialism resulted in his first book, Black Skin, White Masks (1952).

In 1953 Fanon accepted a position at an Algerian psychiatric hospital and gave support to FLN revolutionaries. He became acutely aware, through experiences of his patients, of the violent foundations of French colonial rule. In 1956 the French government expelled him from Algeria. He then moved to Tunisia where he continued his work on behalf of Algerian independence.

Suffering from terminal leukemia, Fanon wrote The Wretched of the Earth in 1961. The book attracted notoriety for its apparent approval of violence as a means to end colonial rule. Fanon recognized, however, that both perpetrators and victims of violence can never escape its psychological effects. In subsequent essays he explained that revolutionary violence must be short lived, or it will destroy all whom it touches.

In the excerpt below, he discusses how the nation (here referring to a body of people with shared political goals) must negotiate the transition from colonialism to independence. Within a general Marxist framework of class struggle, Fanon argues that the indigenous colonial bourgeoisie are ill equipped to lead the nation because they have identified with the values of their capitalist colonial oppressors and lost touch with the masses.

The national middle class which takes over power at the end of the colonial regime is an under-developed middle class. It has practically no economic power, and in any case it is in no way commensurate with the bourgeoisie of the mother country which it hopes to replace. . . .

Seen through its eyes, its mission has nothing to do with transforming the nation; it consists, prosaically, of being the transmission line between the nation and a capitalism, rampant though camouflaged, which today puts on the masque of neocolonialism. The national bourgeoisie will be quite content with the role of the Western bourgeoisie's business agent, and it will play its part without any complexes in a most dignified manner. But this same lucrative role, this cheap-jack's function, this meanness of outlook and this absence of all ambition symbolize the incapability of the national middle class to fulfil its historic role of bourgeoisie. Here, the dynamic, pioneer aspect, the characteristics of the inventor and of the discoverer of new worlds which are found in all national bourgeoisies are lamentably absent. In the colonial countries, the spirit of indulgence is dominant at the core of the bourgeoisie; and this is because the national bourgeoisie identifies itself with the Western bourgeoisie, from whom it has learnt its lessons. It follows the Western bourgeoisie along its path of negation and decadence without ever having emulated it in its first stages of exploration and invention, stages which are an acquisition of that Western bourgeoisie whatever the circumstances. . . . The national bourgeoisie will be greatly helped on its way towards decadence by the Western bourgeoisies, who come to

it as tourists avid for the exotic, for big-game hunting and for casinos. . . . Because it is bereft of ideas, because it lives to itself and cuts itself off from the people, undermined by its hereditary incapacity to think in terms of all the problems of the nation as seen from the point of view of the whole of that nation, the national middle class will have nothing better to do than to take on the role of manager for Western enterprise, and it will in practice set up its country as the brothel of Europe. . . .

If you really wish your country to avoid regression, or at best halts and uncertainties, a rapid step must be taken from national consciousness to political and social consciousness. . . . The battle-line against hunger, against ignorance, against poverty and against unawareness ought to be ever present in the muscles and the intelligences of men and women. . . . There must be an economic program; there must also be a doctrine concerning the division of wealth and social relations. . . . It is only when men and women are included on a vast scale in enlightened and fruitful work that form and body are given to that consciousness. . . . The living expression of the nation is the moving consciousness of the whole of the people; it is the coherent, enlightened action of men and women. . . . No leader, however valuable he may b[e] . . . [illegible] the [illegible] popular will; and the nationa[l] [illegible] itself about international pres[illegible] dignity to all citizens.

Source: Frantz Fanon, The Wretched of [illegible] (New York: Grove Press, 1965), 149, 1[illegible]

Thinking Critically

Why, in Fanon's view, does the national middle class feel a stronger relationship to the colon[illegible] its own country? What do you think Fanon means by saying that the middle class will turn its [illegible] Europe"? What do you think he means by the term "neocolonialism"? What problems must a [illegible] ensure its viability? From this selection, what can you infer about Fanon's views of those tak[illegible] dent countries? In what ways, if any, does the selection reveal the influence of Marxism on F[illegible]

Individuals Matter spotlights women and men— some public figures, others "ordinary" people— whose life or deeds capture an aspect of the period. These biographies remind readers of the importance of individuals as agents of change in world history.

Individuals MATTER

Queen Arsinoe II: Ruler of Ptolemaic Egypt

Coruler, high priestess, and goddess, Queen Arsinoe II (316–270 B.C.E.) was one of the most powerful royal women in Egypt's long dynastic history. Her father was the Macedonian general Ptolemy I, who founded the Ptolemaic dynasty following the death of Alexander the Great. About 300 B.C.E., when Arsinoe was fifteen or sixteen years old, her father arranged her marriage, an entirely political transaction, to Lysimachus, the sixty-one-year-old king who ruled territory on either side of the Bosporus Strait. The couple had three sons in rapid succession, but Agathocles, a child from Lysimachus's previous marriage, stood ahead of them in the line of royal succession. To improve her sons' political positions, as well as her own, Arsinoe accused Agathocles of plotting to kill her father. Consequently, Lysimachus ordered him executed, a vile act that triggered violent uprisings. In 281 B.C.E., less than a year after the murder, the elderly Lysimachus died in battle against Seleucus, ruler of the Seleucid empire of Persia.

When she lost her husband, Arsinoe fled to Macedonia. Once there, she soon accepted a second marriage, this time to her own half-brother Ptolemy Keraunos. Greeks generally regarded marriage between siblings as indecent, but Arsinoe and her new spouse took their cue from Egypt, where such royal unions were customary. Ptolemy Keraunos had

seized part of the dead Lysimachus's territories, and he assured Arsinoe that he would place her sons back in the line of succession as his adopted heirs. He deceived her, however, and fearing these sons as potential threats to his power, murdered the two younger boys, while the eldest escaped. Arsinoe fled once again, this time back to Egypt and the protection of her full brother Ptolemy II (r. 282–246 B.C.E.), who was by this time Egypt's king.

Arsinoe lost no time getting back on her feet and maneuvering for power. She persuaded Ptolemy II that his wife was plotting against him and deserved to be sent into exile. Ptolemy not only complied but also made Arsinoe his new queen. The evidence from surviving texts and images demonstrates convincingly that, although she lived only for another five or six years, she enjoyed equality with her husband-brother as coruler and may have governed more energetically than he did. Historians think she may have helped design the strategy that led to Egypt's victory in a war against the Seleucids for control of territory in Syria. She may also have supervised a major expansion of the Egyptian navy. She appears with her brother on some coins of the period but alone on others, implying her commanding status.

In the years leading to her death in 270 B.C.E. at about the age of forty-five, Arsinoe became not only priestess of her own cult, a typical practice among Egyptian rulers, but also a goddess, worshiped warmly during her own lifetime and for a long time after. A grand shrine was dedicated to her in Alexandria, and towns were named after her in Greece.

Historians, both ancient and modern, have often represented Arsinoe as conniving and power hungry, though these qualities were hardly rare among monarchs of the Hellenistic centuries. She doubtless exercised great political influence during her brief reign, and she offered a model for ambitious Ptolemaic queens that followed her. For example, Cleopatra VII (r. 51–30 B.C.E.), the last of the Ptolemaic rulers, adopted Arsinoe's crown as her own.

Thinking Critically

What political advantages might Arsinoe have gained by encouraging her subjects to worship her as a deity while she shared the throne with her brother?

Arsinoe II strikes a characteristically Egyptian pose, but she sports a Greek hairstyle.

families that lived there adopted an elegant part-Greek, part-Egyptian lifestyle. The city also attracted a large, multi-ethnic merchant population that made money supplying luxuries to the ruling class. The Hellenistic elite liked to think of the city as a kind of outpost of the Greek Aegean, not really *in* Egypt but merely *next* to it. Actually, native Egyptians made up the great majority of the population.

Public life in Hellenistic cities was as patriarchal, that is, as dominated by males, as it generally was in urban societies throughout Afroeurasia. We have some evidence, however, that in the bustling, impersonal climate of the larger cities, upper-class women had somewhat wider scope to pursue private interests than they had in fifth-century B.C.E. Athens, where a tight guard of male relatives kept them close

 178 Chapter 6 | Empire Building and Cultural Exchange from India to the Mediterranean

Focus questions at the beginning of each major section help students focus their reading.

Key terms are defined in the margins as well as in the glossary. They are also listed with other study terms at the end of each chapter.

Change over Time chronologies help students review each chapter's significant events.

The Coming of Farmers: A Peculiar Event

FOCUS Why did humans in several parts of the world take up farming, given that our species had survived without it for 200,000 years?

The activity we call farming refers specifically to the technical process of *producing* food in a systematic way by planting, tending, and harvesting edible plants and by grazing domesticated animals on pasture. These new methods allowed humans to capture and consume much more of the sun's energy, the source of all plant life, than in earlier times. But coaxing food energy and surplus wealth from the soil involved more than tools and techniques. Woven into the activity are social habits, moral rules, and supernatural beliefs. Until the start of the industrial age barely more than 200 years ago, all complex societies were **agrarian societies,** based on farming as the primary way of life. And like the earlier colonization of the world, farming emerged as a consequence of human beings making countless everyday decisions century after century, though no one at the time could see where these experiments might be taking our species.

agrarian society A society in which agriculture, including both crop production and animal breeding, is the foundation of both subsistence and surplus wealth.

Change over Time

1582	Confucian scholars encounter Catholic Christian missionaries in China.
1632	Galileo Galilei offers proof of heliocentric theory of planetary motion.
1639	Russian explorers advancing across Siberia reach the Pacific.
1642–1660	The English Civil War involves temporary abolition of monarchy.
1643–1715	Louis XIV rules France, promoting absolutist principles.
1644	The Qing dynasty comes to power in China, replacing the Ming dynasty.
1648	The Peace of Westphalia proposes principles to guide international relations in Europe.
1652	Khoisan peoples of South Africa encounter Dutch East India Company (VOC) colonizers.
1654–1722	The Kangxi emperor expands China's land frontiers.
1675–1676	Native Americans unsuccessfully rebel against settlers in Massachusetts Bay Colony.
1682–1725	Peter the Great transforms Russia into a major European power.
1687	Isaac Newton publishes *The Principia,* detailing laws of gravity and motion.
1688	The Glorious Revolution in Britain limits the monarchy's power.
1689	China and Russia settle land frontier disputes with the Treaty of Nerchinsk.
1690	John Locke publishes *Two Treatises of Government,* criticizing absolutist government.
1690s	The Austrian Habsburg empire drives Ottoman forces out of Hungary.
1701–1714	The War of the Spanish Succession drains economies of western European states, especially France.
1713–1740	Frederick William I consolidates power in Prussia.
1792	Mary Wollstonecraft publishes *A Vindication of the Rights of Woman,* arguing for equal education for women.
Early 1800s	The Spanish American empire reaches its greatest territorial extent.

Instructor Resources for *Panorama: A World History*

More Primary Sources in Create

The World History Document Collection in McGraw-Hill's Create (www.mcgrawhillcreate.com) allows you to choose from over 100 primary and secondary sources—each with a headnote and questions—that can be added to your print text. Create also allows you to rearrange or omit chapters, combine material from other sources, and/or upload your syllabus or any other content you have written to make the perfect resources for your students. You can search thousands of leading McGraw-Hill textbooks to find the best content for your students, then arrange it to fit your teaching style. When you order a Create book, you receive a complimentary review copy in three to five business days or an electronic copy (eComp) via e-mail in about an hour. Register today at www.mcgrawhillcreate.com and craft your course resources to match the way you teach.

Instructor Resources on the Online Learning Center

The Online Learning Center for *Panorama* at www.mhhe.com/panorama1e contains a wealth of instructor resources, including an Instructor's Manual, Test Bank, and PowerPoint presentations for each chapter. All maps and most images from the print text are included. A computerized test bank powered by McGraw-Hill's EZ Test allows you to quickly create a customized exam using the publisher's supplied test questions or add your own. You decide on the number, type, and order of test questions with a few simple clicks. EZ Test runs on your computer without a connection to the Internet.

CourseSmart e-books

CourseSmart offers thousands of the most commonly adopted textbooks across hundreds of courses from a variety of higher education publishers. It is the only place for faculty to review and compare the full text of a textbook online, providing immediate access without the environmental impact of requesting a printed exam copy. At CourseSmart, students can save up to 50 percent off the cost of a printed book, and gain access to powerful web tools for learning, including full text search, notes and highlighting, and e-mail tools for sharing notes among classmates. Learn more at www.coursesmart.com.

McGraw-Hill Campus

McGraw-Hill Campus is the first-of-its-kind institutional service providing faculty with true single sign-on access to all of McGraw-Hill's course content, digital tools, and other high-quality learning resources from any learning management system (LMS). This innovative offering allows for secure and deep integration and seamless access to any of our course solutions such as McGraw-Hill Connect, McGraw-Hill Create, McGraw-Hill LearnSmart, or Tegrity. McGraw-Hill Campus includes access to our entire content library, including e-books, assessment tools, presentation slides, and multimedia content, among other resources, providing faculty open and unlimited access to prepare for class, create tests and quizzes, develop lecture material, integrate interactive content, and much more.

List of Maps

Acknowledgments

We undertook to write *Panorama* out of a conviction that we must construct holistic, integrated, earth-scale accounts of the past because they will surely help us understand how the world came to be the staggeringly complex place it is today. Such accounts may also help us imagine alternative futures for ourselves as the species that now dominates the earth but that nonetheless faces profound ecological, economic, and social challenges.

Writing a unitary history of humankind has required us to enter an enormous storehouse of historical and social scientific knowledge that other men and women have been filling over many years. We have explored this vast treasury for ideas—sorting, selecting, analyzing, and synthesizing them. A large team of reviewers, editors, designers, cartographers, educational technologists, professional colleagues, and family members have joined us in our mission to transform masses of knowledge into the twenty-eight chapters of *Panorama: A World History*. We offer warm thanks to the numerous instructors, listed separately, who critically and insightfully reviewed, and sometimes reviewed again, the draft chapters.

Our experience working with our editorial, design, and marketing team at McGraw-Hill Education has been nothing short of marvelous. We have worked day by day with a supremely talented publishing and editorial core group—Matthew Busbridge, Nancy Crochiere, Stacy Ruel, Cynthia Ward, Laura Wilk, and Robin Mouat. Their talents have continually amazed us. We would also like to thank Rick Hecker, Danny Meldung, Amy Marks, Kaelyn Schulz, Wes Hall, and Maureen West for their valuable contributions.

We owe warm thanks to the historians who contributed to the project by undertaking research, developing draft materials, and pointing out our errors. We especially thank Nicholas Bomba, Maura Cunningham, Ingrid de Haas, and Ian Kelly. Edmund "Terry" Burke III, a provocative and original world history thinker, read drafts of every chapter and demonstrated an uncanny ability to critique not just sentences and paragraphs but fundamental structures, concepts, and embedded assumptions. Elizabeth Cobbs Hoffman participated in the project for several years and contributed to early iterations of the text.

Ross Dunn writes:

I would never have attempted a project like this were it not for the enduring inspiration of Philip D. Curtin, Marshall G. S. Hodgson, and William H. McNeill, three world history pioneers who, knowingly or not, have shaped my entire teaching and scholarly career. I also thank the members of the San Diego State University history department who encouraged me to introduce a world history course in a decade when deep specialization was the prime qualification for academic success. I remember fondly the band of instructors that first team-taught world history at SDSU (Neil Heyman, William D. Philips, Charles D. Smith, Ray Smith, and Frank Stites). And I appreciate and admire the commitment several members of the department have made, notably under the leadership of Harry McDean and Joanne Ferraro, to perpetuate SDSU's reputation as a center of innovation in global, cross-cultural, and comparative history.

Then there are those colleagues and friends who have profoundly influenced the conceptual foundations of this book by simply feeding me intellectually, and often morally, as I have listened to their lectures and papers, chatted and e-mailed with them, visited their universities and homes, and shared good times. Among many others, these long-time friends and mentors include Terry Burke, David Christian, Bob Bain, Stan Burstein, Bill Cheek, Julia Clancy-Smith, the late Jerry Bentley, Susan Douglass, Tim Keirn, Paul Keeler, Howard Kushner, Craig Lockard, Patrick Manning, Gary Nash, Kevin Reilly, Linda Symcox, John Voll, and Merry Wiesner-Hanks.

The year after I started teaching at SDSU, I married Jeanne Mueller Dunn. My partnership with this remarkable, compassionate, and aesthetically gifted woman has moved into its fifth decade. I could not have written this book without her. Nor would I have undertaken it without the steadfast love and support of our daughters, Jordan and Jocelyn, and their wonderful families.

Laura Mitchell writes:

I have been lucky beyond measure to have joined two history departments that value world history as intellectual inquiry in its own right, and not just as a challenging teaching opportunity. My colleagues, first at the University of Texas in San Antonio and, since 2002, at the University of California, Irvine, have been a consistent source of support, knowledge both arcane and general, inspiration, and good humor.

The University of California Multi-Campus Research Group in World History, spearheaded by Ken Pomeranz and Terry Burke, enabled me to build on my foundation as an Africanist. The collegiality and experimentation of those MRG workshops enabled an assistant professor hired to address just one region of the world to embrace an ever-widening intellectual horizon. A New Directions Fellowship from the Mellon Foundation supported a year devoted to developing new skills working with visual sources, which profoundly shaped my subsequent teaching and research. The many graduate students engaged in world history at UCI have been central to my own development as a scholar and teacher. These pages reflect many robust conversations with them within and beyond the seminar room in Krieger Hall. My engagement with the Advanced Placement program in world history provided another community of exceptional interlocutors. I am grateful for each of these intellectual strands.

I have also been blessed with a joyous and supportive collective of family and friends who have offered encouragement, nourishment, fellowship, and love. You understood when our plans had to change and when I missed dinner. Thank you for putting up with me as I worked on this project and for realizing that a first draft isn't forever. Thank you especially to Graham and Ian, who have borne the intrusions on our family life with grace.

Reviewers and Advisors for *Panorama: A World History*

The authors and publisher would like to express their deepest gratitude to all those faculty members who read the manuscript, consulted on the digital program, did detailed fact-checking, and provided advice on content, images, maps, design, and cover concepts.

Board of Advisors

Carol Bargeron
Central State University

Brian Black
Pennsylvania State University, Altoona

Elaine Carey
St. John's University

Stephanie Field
University of Delaware

Phyllis Jestice
College of Charleston

Hallie Larebo
Morehouse College

Stephanie Musick
Bluefield State College

Ryan Schilling
Mississippi Gulf Coast Community College, Jackson

Ryan Thompson
Cleveland State Community College

Reviewers

Heather Abdelnur
Augusta State University

Jonathon Ablard
Ithaca College

Wayne Ackerson
Salisbury University

Calvin Allen, Jr.
University of Memphis

David Atwill
Pennsylvania State University, University Park

Carol Bargeron
Central State University

Michael Birdwell
Tennessee Tech University

Brian Black
Pennsylvania State University, Altoona

Beau Bowers
Central Piedmont Community College

James Brent
Arkansas State University, Beebe

Michael Brescia
SUNY, Fredonia

Erika Briesacher
Worcester State University

Michael Brose
University of Wyoming, Laramie

Gayle Brunelle
California State University, Fullerton

Edmund Burke III
University of California, Santa Cruz

Stanley Burstein
California State University, Los Angeles

Antonio Cantu
Ball State University

Elaine Carey
St. John's University

Robert Carriedo
U.S. Air Force Academy

Roger Chan
Washington State University

Dana Chandler
Tuskegee University

Mark Christensen
Assumption College

Edward Crowther
Adams State College

Edward Davies
University of Utah, Salt Lake City

Thomas Davis
Virginia Military Institute

Peter Dykema
Arkansas Tech University

David Eaton
Grand Valley State University

Gloria Emeagwali
Central Connecticut State University

David Fahey
Miami University of Ohio, Oxford

Edward Farmer
University of Minnesota, Minneapolis

Alan Fisher
Michigan State University

Nancy Fitch
California State University, Fullerton

Denis Gainty
Georgia State University

Steven Glazer
Graceland University

Steve Gosch
University of Wisconsin, Eau Claire

Gayle Greene-Aguirre
MGCCC Perkinston Campus

Christian Griggs
Dalton State College

Jeffery Hamilton
Baylor University

Casey Harison
University of Southern Indiana

John Hayden
Southwest Oklahoma State University

Linda Heil Wilke
Central Community College

Laura Hilton
Muskingum University

Stephanie Holyfield
University of Delaware

Aiqun Hu
Arkansas State University

Tamara Hunt
University of Southern Indiana

Erik Jensen
Miami University of Ohio, Oxford

Paul Jentz
North Hennepin Community College

Scott W. Jessee
Appalachian State University

Phyllis Jestice
University of Southern Mississippi

Amy Johnson
Berry College

Roger Jungmeyer
Lincoln University

Alan Karras
University of California, Berkeley

Pam Knaus
Colorado State University

Paul Kuhl
Winston-Salem State University

Brian LaPierre
University of Southern Mississippi

Hallie Larebo
Morehouse College

Jonathon Lee
San Antonio College

Anu Mande
Fullerton College

Susan Maneck
Jackson State University

Brandon Marsh
Bridgewater College

Nathan Martin
Charleston Southern University

Tim Mattimoe
Beaufort Community College

Chris Mauriello
Salem State University

Tim May
North Georgia College and State University

Tamba M'bayo
Hope College

Mark McLeod
University of Delaware

Eileen McMahon
Lewis University

Peter Mentzel
University of Utah

Garth Montgomery
Radford University

Jay Moore
University of Vermont

William Morison
Grand Valley State University

Stephanie Musick
Bluefield State College

Catherine Brid Nicholson
Kean University

Jim Overfield
University of Vermont

Alice Pate
Columbus State University

Daniel Pavese
Wor Wic Community College

Ruth Percy
University of Southern Mississippi

Matthew Perry
John Jay College of Criminal Justice

Amanda Podany
California State Poly University, Pomona

Kenneth Pomeranz
University of Chicago

Niler Pyeatt
Wayland Baptist University

Dean James Quirin
Fisk University

Dana Rabin
University of Illinois, Champaign

Stephen Rapp, Jr.
Georgia State University

Joshua Sanbron
Lafayette College

John Thomas Sanders
U.S. Naval Academy

Sharlene Sayegh
California State University, Long Beach

Pamela Sayre
Henry Ford Community College

Bill Schell
Murray State University

Ryan Schilling
MGCCC Perkinston Campus

Robert Scull
Craven Community College

Michael Seth
James Madison University

Munir Shaikh
Institute on Religion and Civic Values

Howard Shealy
Kennesaw State University

Brett Shufelt
Copiah Lincoln Community College

David Simonelli
Youngstown State University

Mary Ann Sison
Mississippi Gulf Coast Community College, Jackson County

Corey Slumkoski
St. Francis Xavier University

Karla Smith
Mississippi Gulf Coast Community College

Adam Stanley
University of Wisconsin, Platteville

Philip Suchma
St. John's University

Mark Tauger
West Virginia University, Morgantown

Ryan Thompson
Cleveland State Community College

Joel Tishken
Washington State University

Sarah Trebanis
Immaculata University

Michael Vann
California State University, Sacramento

Rick Warner
Wabash College

Merry Wiesner-Hanks
University of Wisconsin, Milwaukee

Richard Williams
Washington State University, Pullman

Carlton Wilson
North Carolina Central University

Panorama

A World History

Introduction

The Earth:
World History's Theater

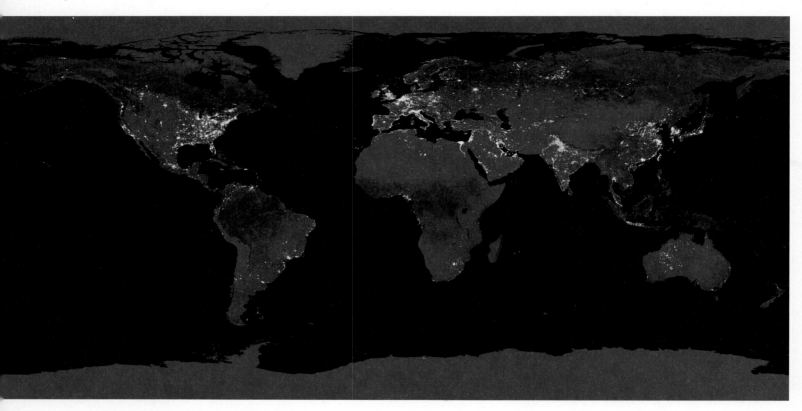

A composite satellite view of the earth at night.

Most of us spend our typical days (when not staring at cell phones or computer screens) in the company of friends, family, or work and school associates. But we are also connected, often unconsciously, to numerous other networks of human relationships that affect the course of daily life. Some of these "communities" may be fleeting (passengers sharing an airplane flying at 30,000 feet), and some may be very large (all members of the Greek Orthodox Church). No individual anywhere in the world is truly isolated from global relationships, not hunters in the Amazon rainforest, not peasants in high Himalayan valleys.

The global nature of change is not simply a matter of one event there (war in the Middle East) affecting some condition of life here (a rise in the price of gas). Nor is it just that products or ideas spread quickly from one place to another. The most striking feature of global interaction is that a significant development occurring in one place is likely to set off a complex chain reaction, disrupting and rearranging numerous relationships over an extensive area. A surge of change in one network of relationships, international trade for example, easily sparks changes in other networks, such as diplomatic negotiations or the migration of workers from one country to another.

As individuals we carry on our daily routines right in the midst of this tumultuous restructuring. We are shielded to some extent from its more jarring effects by our cultural and social bonds, some of them new, some long tested. Even so, all aspects of life are subject to disturbance and revision. The "cultures" that we like to think of as solid and enduring are themselves undergoing ceaseless change.

For how long have peoples of the world been interconnected? Since the Industrial Revolution? Since World War II? A better question might be: How far back in time would we have to go to find a world divided into a collection of separate, self-contained societies, each moving through time along its own track, and unresponsive to wider regional developments? The answer is that we could cast back hundreds of thousands of years and still not find a world of completely atomized societies. Indeed, the earliest history of humankind is a story of long-distance migrations of hunting and foraging bands to all the world's land masses, a process that involved interaction between one group and another and therefore at least small disruptions and surprises wherever such contact occurred. In a sweeping way, then, the history of humanity from remote times is a tale of how groups of men and women connected with one another and how those interactions affected and complicated the lives people lived in different parts of the earth. This challenges us to rethink humanity's history in a more holistic, interconnected way, history that is not only the stories of different nations, civilizations, and regions but also a single story of the species and its development on the spherical earth over the past few million years. Indeed, the history of humankind and the planet are inextricably connected.

We may find it easier to think about human history on a large scale and over the very long term if at the outset we have some familiarity with the planet's geographical "personality," that is, its major land masses, oceans, and large topographical and climatological features. If we consider the whole sphere as the primary "place" where history has unfolded, and keep that context in mind as we investigate the past, we may better grasp the location of particular places and peoples in relation to one another. We may also better

• • •

equip ourselves to make historical connections between one place or group of people and another, to compare historical developments in different places, and to understand large-scale developments that cut across the conventional borders between states, cultural groups, or civilizations.

The Big Land Masses: The Main Stage of History

Most of us think of the earth's surface as the two-dimensional space where ground meets sky. In fact the human drama has unfolded on a stage that has depth as well as length and width. This is the **biosphere,** the zone that shelters all life-forms, including human beings. The biosphere may be visualized as constituting three layers, each one making up part of the whole. On top, as it were, is the atmosphere. About 78 percent of this layer of gasses is nitrogen and about 21 percent oxygen, the substance humans and other higher life-forms need to survive. Second is the hydrosphere, the watery realm, about 97 percent of which is the oceans. Third is the lithosphere, that is, the solid earth, or outer crust of sand, soil, rock, and fossilized organic matter that we recognize as coal, oil, and natural gas. Humans depend for survival on the stability of the biosphere and live in relationship to its sun-powered cycles—photosynthesis, wind, and the evaporation and condensation of water. Our species has a genetic relationship to all living organisms, sharing, for example, a significant portion of our genes with the banana. In short, the arena of history is not just Asia, England, or the Aztec empire, but the "green skin" that envelops the earth.

> **biosphere** The zone of the earth that can support life.

For thousands of years, humans have known how to move across water, which covers about 71 percent of the planet, in various types of boats. Recently, we have mastered air travel and even ventured beyond the atmosphere into space. Nevertheless, our history has played itself out mostly on the surface of the lithosphere, the rocky earth, which we see on the globe as chunks of land, some enormous and some small.

Moving Land Masses

The science of tectonics tells us that the lithosphere is an interlocking puzzle board of sections, or plates. Heat and turbulence in the softer part of the earth's mantle below the lithosphere cause these plates to move. Sometimes they drift apart, sometimes they converge. The seams between the **tectonic plates,** which for the most part lie along the floors of the oceans, are places of volcanic activity and earthquakes. The movement of the plates relative to each other changes the shape and position of the land masses. This phenomenon happens of course in geological time, at the rate of not more than a few centimeters a year.

> **tectonic plates** Irregular blocks of solid rock that make up the earth's lithosphere and that constantly shift and change shape.

About 200 million years ago, one giant land mass, the continent geologists call Pangaea, dominated the earth. Over the succeeding tens of millions of years, it slowly broke

More than 200 million years ago

180 million years ago

65 million years ago

Present

Changes in the earth's plate structure. The land masses that humans inhabit sit atop tectonic plates that are continually in motion. Satellite imagery can accurately detect the tiny distances that continents move in a year's time. On the scale of hundreds of millions of years, patterns of continental drift have affected the ways living species have evolved.

into segments along several lines of seismic upheaval. First it split into two supercontinents, then into several. India, once part of the continent called Gondwanaland, broke off to glide relentlessly northward. It rammed into Eurasia about 30 million years ago, the collision buckling the earth to form the Himalaya Mountains. Because the process of continental drift continues, the land mass configuration that has endured for the past 20 million years or so is only temporary. Africa is heading toward Europe, eventually to close off the Strait of Gibraltar and transform the Mediterranean into an inland sea. Coastal California, part of the Northern Pacific Plate, pushes northward and, to the possible satisfaction of some New Yorkers, might someday separate itself from the rest of North America.

Seven Continents, or Only Five?

Schoolbooks still teach that there are seven primary land masses, or continents: Africa, Antarctica, Asia, Australia, Europe, North America, and South America. In our view this convention needs rethinking. If we accept even a loose physical definition of a continent as a distinct land mass surrounded, or nearly so, by water, Europe and Asia do not separately qualify. No significant waterway or other partition divides the eastern side of Europe from the western side of Asia. Rather, the two places constitute, and have constituted for millions of years, a single great land mass. A little more than a century ago, scholars named this land mass Eurasia. Since then, many have recognized that the standard physical definition of a continent properly applies to it. Logically, then, Europe is a long peninsula at the far western end of Eurasia, that is, a *subcontinent* roughly comparable to South Asia (Bangladesh, India, and Pakistan), a peninsula that juts south.

The precept that Europe is a continent goes back to the ancient Greeks, whose world centered on the Aegean Sea in the eastern Mediterranean basin. They conceived the planet as made up of three parts: Europe was the territory generally north and west of the Aegean Sea (including the Republic of Greece today), Asia was all land to the east and southeast, and Africa (called Libya) lay south and southwest.

In the Middle Ages, European scholars perpetuated the Greeks' three-part scheme, though recognizing that these territories were much larger than the Greeks had known them to be. Europeans came to identify their region with "Christendom," the land where most Christians lived, and they defined Asia and Africa as the continents inhabited mainly by people who were *not* Christians. Therefore, religion, not an ocean or a sea, separated Europe from Asia. This was one way to define what continents were, but this definition was based predominantly on *cultural*, not *physical* distinctions.

But where exactly did Europe leave off and Asia start? In the eighteenth century, a Swedish military officer who traveled to Siberia proposed the Ural Mountains of Russia as a suitable continental boundary.[1] Debates over the proper dividing line continued, but gradually European scholars came to accept the Urals as a "natural" partition, even though those round-topped mountains rise no higher than about six thousand feet and have no compelling significance as a topographical, cultural, or historical boundary. The same may be said of the Bosporus and Dardanelles, the two straits that connect the Mediterranean with the Black Sea and that have served conveniently to demarcate Europe from Asia. But those straits have hardly ever impeded the flow of history, and today one can drive from "Europe" to "Asia" on either of two bridges across the Bosporus. Yet despite the obvious artificiality of the markers, the doctrine of European continent-hood has persisted. European nations came to dominate much of the world militarily and economically in the later nineteenth century. To them, the idea of Europe as a primary world region seemed more natural than ever.

One standard map of the world has reinforced this idea. In 1569, Gerardus Mercator, a Flemish cartographer, devised a flat projection of the world as an aid to sea captains: A straight line drawn between any two points on the map represents a constant true compass bearing. The Mercator map of the world, which until recently served as the standard

An ancient Greek map of the world.
Hecateus of Miletus, a Greek scholar of the fifth century B.C.E., conceived of this circular map of the world. Why do you think Hecateus located the Mediterranean Sea at the center of the map?

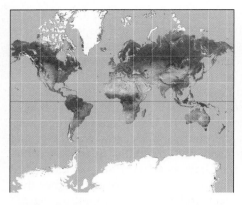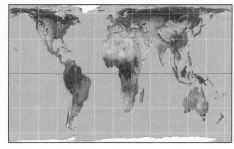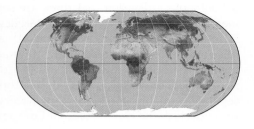

MAP I.1 From left to right: Mercator, Gall-Peters, and Robinson map projections.
The sixteenth-century Mercator world map, which severely distorts the relative size of land masses, was used in school rooms for centuries. In 1973, Arno Peters published an equal area map of the world. It represents the relative size of land areas accurately but distorts their shapes. The Robinson projection, devised in the 1960s, attempts to strike a balance between size and shape distortions. Peters aimed deliberately to correct what he regarded as the Eurocentric bias of the Mercator projection. How do you think the Gall-Peters map accomplishes that aim?

projection, makes Europe look much bigger than it actually is relative to regions that lie farther south. This is because this projection severely distorts the size of land masses toward the poles, so that territories at far northern or far southern **latitudes** appear much larger than they actually are relative to lands nearer the equator. Consequently, Europe, from the southern end of Greece to the northern tip of Norway, looks much bigger relative to South America, Africa, or the Indian subcontinent, for example, than it really is on the round globe.

> **latitude** The imaginary east–west lines that circle the earth and that indicate distance in degrees north and south of the equator, which has the value of 0 degrees.

Mercator maps also sometimes situate Europe in the center of the flat map relative to all four of its edges. That configuration requires pushing the equator to the lower third of the map, which falsely compresses the size of lands in the Southern Hemisphere relative to Europe and the rest of the Northern Hemisphere. Looming as large and conspicuous as it does on this projection, Europe appears as though it might deserve membership in the club of continents.

All flat map projections distort size, shape, distance, or direction in *some* way because the surface of the earth is not flat but curved. Accuracy of all these elements requires a globe, an object impossible to reproduce on a book page. Since the eighteenth century, cartographers have been publishing various equal area maps that rectified Mercator's size perversions. Projections in wide use today, such as Robinson maps, make agreeable compromises between shape and volume of land areas, though they may still somewhat exaggerate size near the poles (see Map I.1).

Afroeurasia

Accepting the idea of Europe as an integral part of geophysical Eurasia, students of global history should find it easier to conceive visually of that entire land mass from the North Atlantic to the North Pacific as a continuous stretch of territory within which humans have lived, migrated, fought, and traded for many thousands of years. But what about Africa? Because it is separated from Eurasia only by the Mediterranean and the Red Seas, it qualifies as a continent by the conventional definition, though barely. Africa also rests on one of the large sections of the lithosphere known as the African Plate. Is it possible, nevertheless, to conceive of Eurasia and Africa together as constituting *one* continent? Look at Map I.2. Cover up the Mediterranean Sea with the thumb of your left hand and place the index finger of your right hand over the Red Sea. Notice that with those two seas covered, it is not hard to see Eurasia and Africa together as a single land mass, and one much bigger than Eurasia alone. Compared to the Atlantic or the Pacific Ocean, the Mediterranean and the Red Seas are merely "lakes." Humans have been shuttling routinely back and forth across them for thousands of years. And it is worth noting that one can *walk* from Africa to Eurasia by crossing the Sinai Peninsula and one of the bridges that spans the Suez Canal.

Because of regular interaction among peoples living around the rims of the Mediterranean and the Red Seas, historical developments in Africa, Asia, and Europe have been intertwined far more intensely than the conventional continental divisions would encourage us to think. In other words, an integrated approach to world history demands that we visualize not only Eurasia as a whole but Africa and Eurasia together (plus adjacent islands or island groups like Japan, the Philippines, and Britain) as a *single space* within which important historical developments have taken place from very early times.

In fact, ancient scholars had no trouble imagining Africa, Asia, and Europe together as constituting a larger interconnected whole. The Romans called it the *Orbis Terrarum,* or "the circle of the world." However, the three-continents scheme, a product of human invention to start with, has become so standardized in schoolbooks as the "right" way to

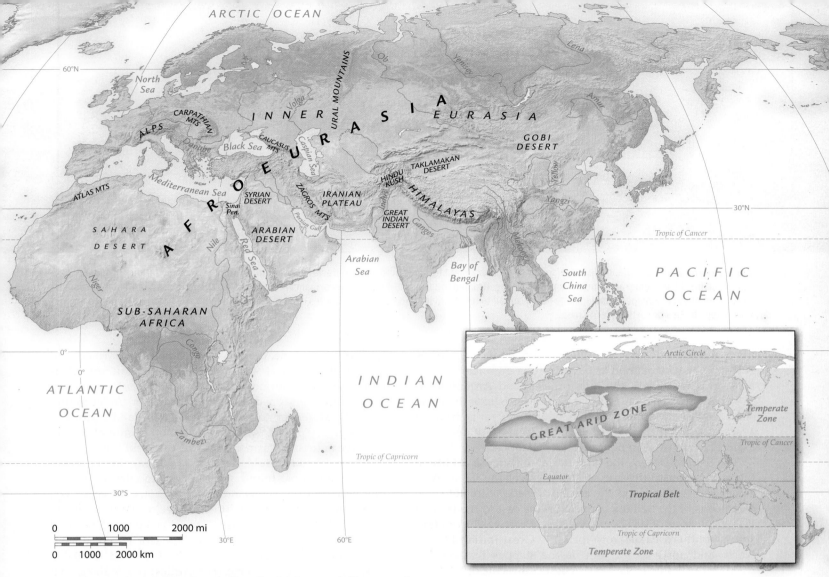

MAP I.2 Major physical and climatic features of Afroeurasia.
What physical features work to connect Afroeurasia as a single geographical unit? Which features support an understanding of this landmass as three continents?

see the world that modern geographers have never settled on a label for all of Africa and Eurasia together. In the sixteenth century the term "Old World" appeared in European languages to distinguish the land masses of the Eastern Hemisphere from the "New World," that is, the Americas. These terms, however, are vulnerable to criticism because the Americas were only "new" to the Europeans who first visited them, not to the people who had been living there for thousands of years. In this book we adopt the single word **Afroeurasia** to express the

> **Afroeurasia** The land masses of Africa and Eurasia, together with adjacent islands, as a single spatial entity.

continuum of lands comprising Africa and Eurasia. It will serve as a convenient geographical tool for discussing large-scale historical developments that cut across the conventionally defined continental boundaries.

Afroeurasia takes up nearly 60 percent of the surface of the earth that is not water. This land mass is not only the biggest one on the planet, it is also where the human species

first evolved (as far as we know), and it has historically been home to most of the humans who have ever lived. Today, about 86 percent of the globe's population inhabits Afroeurasia. To understand the patterns of migration, settlement, exchange, and conquest that unfolded on this land mass, it helps to know its broad physical and climatological features.

The Great Arid Zone

A large part of the Afroeurasian land mass is a belt of dry or semidry country that extends all the way from the Atlantic coast of Africa in a generally northeasterly direction to the northern interior of China. This enormous tract, which we refer to as the **Great Arid Zone,** comprises a chain of

> **Great Arid Zone** The belt of arid and semiarid land that extends across Afroeurasia from the Sahara Desert in the west to the Gobi Desert in the east. It has been home to both pastoral nomadic communities and to farming societies where sufficient water is available.

The Great Arid Zone. Climate in the long band of dry country that stretches across Afroeurasia ranges from extreme year-round aridity to semiarid conditions in which winter rains nourish spring grasses. Dromedaries, or one-humped camels, shown here (left) ambling across the western Arabian Desert, are in several respects biologically better suited to harsh environments than are horses, which for several thousand years have thrived on the grassy steppes of northeastern China.

interconnected deserts, mountains, and semiarid steppes. A steppe may be defined as flat or rolling grassland, equivalent to what Americans call "prairie" and Argentineans call "pampas." The main climatic characteristic of the Great Arid Zone is low annual rainfall, which may range from an average of less than five inches in the bleakest of deserts to twenty inches or so in better watered steppes.

The Sahara Desert, the largest area of intense aridity in the world, constitutes the western end of the Great Arid Zone. The Arabian and the Syrian Deserts, climatological extensions of the Sahara, connect on the east to the Iranian Plateau. A spur of dry country extends eastward from Iran across southern Pakistan to form the Great Indian Desert. North and northeast of Iran lie the steppes that cover a significant part of the huge interior region we call **Inner Eurasia.** Rainfall on the grasslands of western Inner Eurasia, that is, the lands roughly north of the Black Sea, is relatively abundant, as much as twenty inches a year. But further east, Inner Eurasia becomes progressively arid. The Gobi Desert, which overlaps China and Mongolia, marks the eastern end of high aridity, though much of northern China is semiarid.

Inner Eurasia The interior land mass of Eurasia, whose dominant features are flat or rolling regions of grassy steppe or forest, interrupted by deserts and highland areas.

Old Hollywood stereotypes represent the Great Arid Zone as a hellish sea of sand frequented only by camel nomads and French Foreign Legionnaires. Some sections of the belt are indeed infernal and uninhabited, but the movie image is way off the mark. Densely settled farming populations have inhabited dry lands for thousands of years. In fact, the earliest farming societies arose in the Great Arid Zone or on the margins of it. Aridity does not necessarily mean infertility as long as water for crops and pasture is available from rivers or underground sources. The Tigris-Euphrates, Nile, Indus, and Yellow (Huang He) Rivers, which nourished the earliest civilizations, all flow through parts of the Great Arid Zone. Indeed, oases supporting farmers and even great cities have sprung up wherever aquifers (areas under the earth's surface containing significant amounts of water) could be tapped by springs, wells, or underground channels. Moreover, the zone includes highland regions as well as grassy plains. Rainfall and runoff in mountain valleys have nourished farmers from very ancient times.

Where farmers could not make a living in the Great Arid Zone, people found another way to survive. Beginning between four thousand and five thousand years ago, small communities adapted to low precipitation by raising domesticated animals. These stock breeders developed a specialized economy based on herds of sheep, horses, goats, cattle, or camels that could be exploited for meat, milk, blood, hide, and bone. The earliest pastoralists, that is, people whose living depends on pasture, inhabited the semiarid grassy steppes of Inner Eurasia. Stock raisers also adapted long ago to the Sahara, the Arabian Desert, and the Iranian Plateau, in places where seasonal rains and strategically placed wells could keep herds alive. Because herding communities required extensive grazing land, their population densities had to remain low compared to farming societies. Nevertheless, pastoral peoples—hardy, mobile, and often militant—have, as we will see, played a role in world history out of all proportion to their sheer numbers.

The Tropical Belt

South of the Great Arid Zone a broad belt of tropical or subtropical territory runs across Afroeurasia, straddling the equator. In basic geographical terms, the "tropics" is the region bounded by two latitudinal lines: the Tropic of Cancer on the north and the Tropic of Capricorn on the south. The sun shines from directly overhead at least once a year in all areas between these lines. In the west of Afroeurasia lie the humid grassy or wooded savannas and the equatorial rainforests of Africa south of the Sahara. To the east are the woodlands and tropical forests of southern India, the Ganges River plain, Southeast Asia, and southern China. In contrast to the Great Arid Zone, the wet tropics have a short annual dry season and rainfall as high as 430 inches a year. Both plant and animal life are luxuriant and vastly diverse. The earliest human societies made their living hunting and foraging on tropical, sometimes wooded grasslands in eastern Africa. Farming and herding peoples settled the tropical zone of both Africa and Eurasia starting about the second millennium B.C.E., though encountering great ecological challenges owing to nutrient-poor soils and a range of tropical diseases.

The Northern Latitudes of Temperate Climate

Running along the northern tier of the Afroeurasian land mass from the Atlantic to the Pacific is the wide band of temperate climate that was once covered in boreal and deciduous forests. Westerly winds, encircling the earth, blow across northern Eurasia year-round. They create alternating conditions of warm and cold, wet and dry weather, as polar air masses compete for dominance with warm, tropical air. Streaming across the North Atlantic, the westerlies bring high rainfall, mostly in winter, to ocean-facing Europe. But deeper into Eurasia, and especially east of the Ural Mountains, the climate is much drier and winters much colder. From late in the first millennium C.E., the immense hardwood forests of Europe dwindled gradually before the axe and the plow, though east of the Urals and on across Siberia, the taiga, or coniferous forestlands, remained sparsely settled right into modern times.

Sandwiched between the northern forest belt and the Great Arid Zone at the western end of Eurasia is the basin of the Mediterranean Sea, the largest of the "internal" seas of Afroeurasia. Mild, rainy winters and hot summers of almost complete drought characterize the mountains and plains of the Mediterranean basin. Open woodlands once covered much of this temperate region, but in ancient times farmers converted plains and hillsides into wheat fields, olive orchards, and vineyards.

Afroeurasia's Mountain Spine

The regularity of the broad east-to-west climatic zones of Afroeurasia is broken partially by the string of mountains that extends across the land mass. Map I.2 (inset) highlights the mountain chain, which begins in the west with the Atlas Mountains of North Africa and extends eastward to the highlands of southwestern China. Afroeurasia's mountains, where they are high and rugged enough, have frustrated communication between peoples living on either side of their ridges. The Himalaya and Kunlun ranges, for example, were formidable barriers to direct overland communication between China and India. The towering Alps also made travel difficult between the Mediterranean and the forested lands to the north. Indeed, the Alpine wall explains in some

A high pass in the Himalaya Mountains. Merchants have carried goods across high Himalayan passes since ancient times. Only in 1986, however, was a route marked out for trekkers across the 19,500-foot Gondogoro Pass in northern Pakistan.

measure the cultural differences that characterized the development of the southern and northern parts of Christian Europe.

By contrast, Afroeurasia's highland valleys became home to foraging and hunting bands early in human history, later to farmers and herders. The highlands were explored and settled, and ancient trekkers mapped out trails over summer passes. Gaps in even the most foreboding of ranges became channels of slow but regular communication that linked distant peoples in trade. Nomads migrating with their herds and flocks, not to mention great armies of horsemen hellbent on conquest, also crossed high passes of the Atlas, Carpathians, Zagros, or Hindu Kush at different times in history, appearing suddenly out of the hills and plunging down on unsuspecting villagers in the plain below.

The Eleven Seas

A chain of seas also links the extremities of Afroeurasia. Map I.3 identifies the sequence of seas, beginning with the

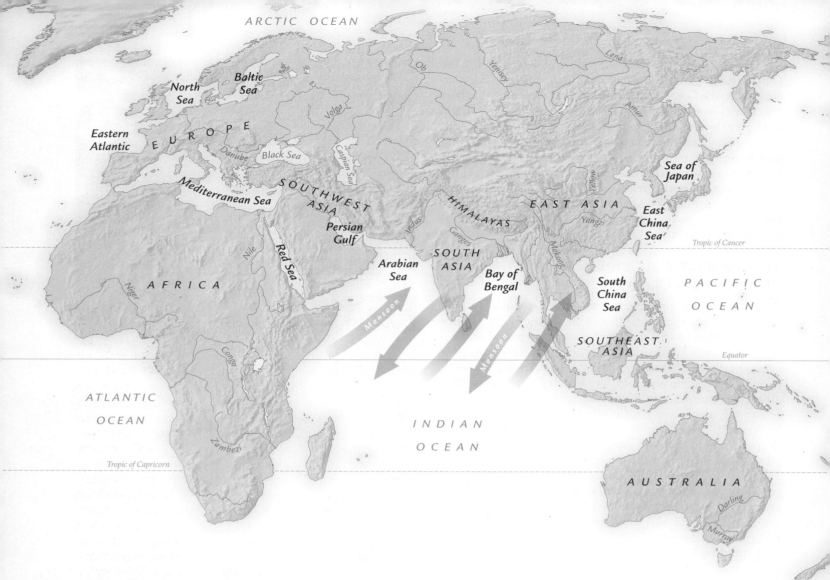

MAP I.3 The eleven seas of Afroeurasia.
How might sea traders sailing across the South China Sea, the Bay of Bengal, or the Arabian Sea in premodern times have benefited from knowledge of the seasonal patterns of the monsoon winds?

Sea of Japan (East Sea) at the far northeastern end of the continent and ending with the Baltic in northern Europe. Straits, more or less narrow, connect several of these seas. The Red Sea and the Persian (Arabian) Gulf are parallel water routes between the Mediterranean and the Arabian Sea. The Red Sea links to the Mediterranean by a short landward passage across the Sinai Peninsula, though the Suez Canal now serves as a human-made strait. Communication between the Mediterranean and the Persian Gulf requires a longer overland passage across Iraq and Syria.

Climate and weather on the eleven seas vary drastically owing to their differing latitudes and wind conditions. However, by the first millennium B.C.E., or in some places much earlier, humans were observing and recording seasonal regularities in weather, wind, and current all along the chain. The largest-scale Afroeurasian wind cycle is the Indian Ocean monsoons, a climatological phenomenon in which the winds over a region reverse direction at particular times of the year. Owing to differences in surface temperature between the Indian Ocean and the Eurasian land mass, winds blow from the northeast in the winter months, passing across Southeast Asia and India toward Africa. Then in the summer months they reverse themselves, blowing from the southwest. In very ancient times, peoples who lived around the rims of the South China Sea, the Bay of Bengal, and the Arabian Sea became aware of the monsoons. Early seafarers soon got the hang of sailing out of port during certain seasons of the year, then back again after the monsoons shifted.

In all the eleven seas, mariners learned how to take advantage of local wind and current to sail out of sight of land with reasonable confidence that they would get where they wanted to go. In time, traders, as well as migrants, pilgrims, and sometimes pirates and seaborne conquerors, regarded the open waters of the eleven seas, not as fearsome voids but as channels of rapid and, compared to overland transport, inexpensive communication. By the end of the first millennium C.E., the entire four-thousand-mile-long corridor of seas was developing into a single network of trade. Individual merchants, even in modern times, have hardly ever carried a cargo from one end of the chain to the other. Rather, groups of traders commonly handed off their shipments to other groups in the commercial ports that sprang up where two seas meet.

Rivers

We may also think of Afroeurasia's great rivers as extensions of oceans, narrow corridors of communication leading deep into the interior of the land mass. The mouths of some major rivers, including the Yangzi (YAHNG-zuh) in China, or the Rhine and Danube in Europe, are broad and deep enough to permit oceangoing vessels to sail directly upriver to inland ports. On other rivers, sandbars, marshes, waterfalls, or shallow deltas block entry from the sea to large craft. Beyond such barriers, however, some rivers are navigable for hundreds or even thousands of miles. For example, the lower course of the Congo River drops precipitately over a series of waterfalls between Central Africa's interior plateau and the Atlantic. Travelers must go around these cataracts by land. Above the falls, however, the river and its numerous tributaries open out to form a network of about 8,700 miles of navigable streams that reach a huge part of equatorial Africa. Many of Afroeurasia's secondary rivers are too short, shallow, or steep to permit useful navigation. The streams that flow from the interior of southern India, for example, fall into that category, and among the dozens of watercourses that empty into the Mediterranean only the Nile and the Rhône provide waterborne access to the deep interior. Rivers of course also mean valleys.

Whether navigable or not, a river may guide travelers along overland routes that parallel its banks, especially where the flow has carved broad bottom land.

Humans began communicating with one another along river valleys, whether overland or in canoes, rafts, and sailcraft, several millennia before they ventured onto the deep oceans. Rivers have partly determined the directions that migrants, merchants, and the carriers of new ideas have taken, and they have shaped the geographical distribution of languages and cultural styles. In Afroeurasia's dry lands, river valleys are typically ribbons of fertility, blessing ancient farmers and city builders with both water and rich soil. Afroeurasia's earliest civilizations all arose in river valleys, where sun, soil, and abundant water created ecological conditions where dense populations could flourish even in the most barren parts of the Great Arid Zone.

Unfortunately, rivers are also among the least stable formations on the earth's surface. Depending on the particular topographical, hydrological, or climatic conditions, rivers may flood unpredictably, change their course abruptly, fill with salts that harm crops, and accumulate alluvial silt that clogs irrigation channels, halts shipping, and creates swamps and marshes. For example, northern China's Yellow River has sustained dense populations, great cities, and boundless wheat lands, but over the centuries periodic floods and channel shifts have also caused millions of deaths and economic disasters severe enough to weaken dynasties.

We cannot, however, blame nature alone for the way rivers behave. Humans began thousands of years ago to clear forests upstream, a practice that invariably increased runoff and with it the risk of flooding and erosion. In modern times, governments have conceived more and more ambitious schemes to put rivers to economic use by rechanneling them, lining them with dikes and levees, and stopping them with mammoth dams, all to uncertain long-term effects. As we explore the past in the chapters to come, we will

Cataracts on the Congo River. This mighty river and its numerous tributaries form the largest network of navigable waterways in Africa. They have served for millennia as avenues of regional commerce. Ships cannot, however, reach this network from the Congo's Atlantic mouth owing to the presence of thirty-two cataracts, or rapids. The lower course of the river drops nearly 900 feet over a distance of about 220 miles.

notice many interconnections between human history and the ever-changing landscapes of rivers and their valleys.

Australia

Geographers continue to argue about Australia. Is it the world's smallest continent or its biggest island? Scholars also recognize "Australasia," that is, Australia plus Tasmania, New Zealand, and sometimes New Guinea, as a distinct world region. A hemispheric view that puts Australia at the center gives it the appearance of a lonely island in the midst of a large sea. But if we focus on the northwestern quadrant of this hemisphere, we can perceive the land mass as the biggest island in an archipelago (chain of islands) that stretches from New Zealand to the Philippines. Only short sea passages separate Australia's northern coast from island Indonesia. And the first humans who set foot "down under" perhaps 60,000 years ago almost certainly arrived there in small boats after a quick trip from some island to the north.

Australia is certainly the most uniform of the great land masses (see Map I.4). It lacks many deep coastal indentations or any large internal lakes or seas. It is also the flattest of all the continents. Most of it consists of boundless plateaus and depressions. Like Afroeurasia, it has a distinctive chain of highlands. The Great Dividing Range runs the length of the continent parallel to the eastern coast. These wooded hills, however, have never impeded human communication since few of the ridges rise more than five thousand feet.

The eastern coastal plains, a narrow strip between the Great Dividing Range and the South Pacific, have adequate water resources because of the southeasterly trade winds that drop Pacific rain as they rise up over the interior hills. But just west of the mountains is the Outback, the uninterrupted dry country that stretches four thousand miles to the Indian Ocean. Australia's own Great Arid Zone of deserts, steppes, and vast fields of sand dunes makes up about two-thirds of the continent. Only the east coast, the far north, and parts of the southern shore receive seasonal rainfall of more than twenty inches a year. Compared to Afroeurasia, Australia is also poor in rivers that may be navigated far inland. The major exception is the Murray River, which originates in the Snowy Mountains of the far southeast and empties into the Indian Ocean.

Australia's distinctive plant and animal life (the eucalyptus tree, the kangaroo, and the duckbilled platypus) is an evolutionary consequence of the continent's physical removal from the once biologically interconnected supercontinent of Gondwanaland (see page I-4). About 200 million years ago, the land masses that are today Australia, Antarctica, Africa, and India went their separate ways. Africa and India moved toward what became Eurasia, but Australia remained farther away. Consequently, the stock of plant and animal life inherited from Gondwanaland continued to evolve along separate lines. In more recent geological ages, however, Australia has exchanged numerous flora and fauna with what is now the Indonesian archipelago.

That exchange included Australia's early human colonization. Throughout almost all of the past 60,000 years,

MAP I.4 Physical features of Australia.

Look at the composite satellite view of the earth at night on page I-2. What geographical factors might help explain the concentration of light along the southeastern and southwestern coasts of Australia?

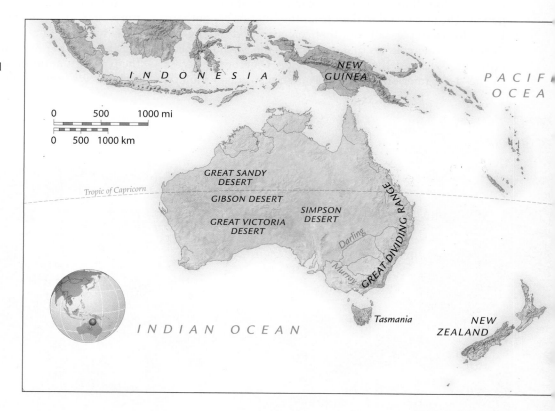

however, the continent's aboriginal societies, which remained small and scattered compared to Afroeurasia's population, lived in isolation, even from the peoples of neighboring Southeast Asia. New colonizers introduced themselves to the continent only a little more than two centuries ago. In 1788, English-speaking Europeans arrived in ships to settle the relatively well-watered eastern coast. From that moment, Australia's native population became firmly connected, whether they liked it or not, to the wider human community.

North and South America

As with any sphere, we can tilt or rotate the globe to get any hemispheric perspective that we like. In other words, we can

> **longitude** The imaginary north–south lines that extend between the North Pole and the South Pole and that run perpendicular to lines of latitude. By international agreement the line with a value of 0 degrees, called the Prime Meridian, passes through Greenwich, England.

bisect the planet along any lines of **longitude** we care to choose. The best known bisection is the one that runs through Greenwich, England, and that we call the Prime Meridian. This line serves as the baseline both for measurement of longitude, that is, distances in degrees east or west of that line, and for marking out the world's standard time zones. The line continues around to the Pacific side of the world as the International Date Line. There is nothing "natural" about this line: A conference of nations meeting in 1884 agreed that it should run through Greenwich, a suburb of London. The vote was twenty-two to one, and France abstained.

No matter what line we choose to bisect the planet, however, schoolbook geography and cultural habit make it difficult *not* to think of Afroeurasia as one side of the world and North and South America as the other side. After all, we call them the Eastern and Western Hemispheres. If we turn a globe on its polar axis so that Afroeurasia faces us, the Americas are on the opposite side and disappear from view. But if we tilt and rotate the earth so that we face the North

The Prime Meridian. These children in their colorful sneakers are straddling a stretch of the Prime Meridian marked on the ground where it passes through Greenwich, England. The line, which marks 0° longitude and runs from North Pole to South Pole, traverses Greenwich because that is where late nineteenth-century European diplomats and scientists decided it should go. How do you think Britain's status as a major world power in that period might have influenced that decision?

Atlantic Ocean, then Europe, Greenland, and Canada all become visible as an almost continuous arc of land bridging the two conventionally defined hemispheres. If we turn the globe again to focus on the North Pacific Ocean, a crescent of nearly connected land stretches from East Asia across Siberia and Alaska to North America. From these northerly angles shown in Map I.5, it is clear that no long oceanic voyage is required for communication between the northerly reaches of Afroeurasia and North America. Vikings figured out how to sail from Europe to Canada more than a thousand years ago, though the connection did not endure. The

MAP I.5 Two northerly views of the earth, one focused on the Atlantic (far left) and one on the Pacific.

What factors do you think might have inhibited humans from traveling regularly between Afroeurasia and North America along these ocean rims for thousands of years?

first humans who crossed from Asia to the Americas thousands of years before that may have blazed a water route along the rim of the North Pacific in rafts or canoes

History, however, does lend some support to the Western Hemisphere–Eastern Hemisphere division because for thousands of years the peoples of both Afroeurasia and Australia lived in virtual isolation from societies in the Americas. No group on either side had the technological or organizational skills to set up regular communication across the Atlantic or the Pacific. From about 12,000 B.C.E. until a little more than five hundred years ago, these two particular halves of the planet were indeed separate "worlds." Only in the late fifteenth century C.E. did European sea captains make transoceanic connections between Afroeurasia and the Americas destined to last. Since that time, advancing transport technology, including air travel over the North Pole, has steadily reduced the historical significance of the physical distinction between the Eastern and Western Hemispheres. In fact, scientists and engineers have formulated plans to dig a sixty-five-mile rail line tunnel under the Bering Strait that would one day link the trans-Siberian railroad to Amtrak.

Connecting the Americas

In the past century, schoolchildren in the United States and most other countries have learned that the Western Hemisphere has two continents, North America and South America. Only the Isthmus of Panama, just thirty miles across at its narrowest stretch, prevents the complete physical separation of the two land masses. Moreover, the isthmus is an area of dense wet tropical forests and mountains that until recent times has significantly impeded overland commer-

Mesoamerica The region comprising southern Mexico plus the seven small Central American states.

cial and cultural exchange between South America and **Mesoamerica.**

On the other hand, North and South America have never been completely disconnected historical worlds. As far as we know, human beings first migrated from North to South America 12,000 years ago or more by advancing along either the isthmus or its coastal waters. Climate, vegetation, and cultural styles in the areas surrounding the Panama neck share more similarities than differences. Also, we do not have to strain our imaginations too much to perceive the Gulf of Mexico and the Caribbean as two internal seas of a single American land mass, much the way we have considered the Mediterranean and the Red Seas as "inside" Afroeurasia. The Caribbean and the Gulf are bounded on three sides by land and on the west by a long string of closely clustered islands. We might then think of a line drawn from Florida along this island chain to the far eastern coast of Venezuela as the eastern edge of a single continent. Indeed, we know from archaeological and linguistic evidence that the peoples who settled Caribbean islands thousands of years ago continued to maintain contacts with mainland societies. This unitary continent—North America, Caribbean islands,

and South America together—could be called simply America, though in this book we also use the more conventional plural term, the Americas.

The Americas' Long *Cordillera*

We can also see on a world map that whereas the long axis of Afroeurasia runs about 8,000 miles east to west, the long axis of the Americas runs nearly 11,000 miles north to south. The northern rim of North America lies within the polar region. Tierra del Fuego at the southern tip of South America is only about 600 miles from Antarctica. In both the Eastern and Western Hemispheres, the high mountain spines extend along a long axis, east–west in Afroeurasia, north–south in the Americas. The Americas' long *cordillera*, or cord, of interconnected ranges extends virtually the entire length of the hemisphere (see Map I.6). It is geologically young and therefore rugged, and it hugs the western side of North and South America. It divides the Americas longitudinally, separating narrow coastal plains on the Pacific side from very broad plains on the eastern side that stretch off toward the Atlantic Ocean. The Appalachian Mountains and the Guyana and Brazilian Highlands of South America interrupt the sweep of the plains on the Atlantic side, but these mountains are much older and more round-topped than the Rockies, Sierra, and Andes ranges.

Most of North America lies in zones of subarctic or temperate climate and shares with Eurasia broad latitudinal bands of tundra, boreal forest, and deciduous forest. Southern Mexico, Central America, and about half of South American regions of Mesoamerica and about half of the continent of South America have tropical or subtropical humid climates similar to Afroeurasia's equatorial zone. South America bulges out to its widest extent in the equatorial latitudes. The Amazonian rainforest plateaus therefore make up a large portion of that continent's mass. This is the largest tropical forest ecosystem in the world. The southern quarter of South America lies across temperate latitudes, but the land mass narrows so much at its "southern cone" that both Atlantic and Pacific sea winds reduce the range of temperature and free the region from the extreme winter cold and summer heat that characterize much of temperate North America.

The climate of the Americas is also complicated by the north–south alignment of high mountains, which skews the flow of oceanic winds on the Pacific side and prevents uninterrupted east–west climatic zones. Neither North nor South America, for example, has a latitudinal belt of dry country comparable to Afroeurasia's Great Arid Zone. Rather, deserts and semiarid prairies lie for the most part in strips running north–south. The starkest of dry lands are found west of the *cordillera* near or bordering the Pacific: the deserts of the southwestern United States and northern Mexico in North America and the coastal deserts of Ecuador, Peru, and Chile in South America. Just east of the *cordillera* are the rain shadows that create long bands of dry or semiarid prairie, notably the Great Plains that run most of the length of North America just east of the Rockies and the Patagonian steppe of Argentina east of the Andes.

Rivers and Seas

In Afroeurasia, as we have seen, the eleven seas have for millennia eased human maritime linkage east and west across the region. The Americas have no comparable belt of usable seas to join people north and south. Though Indian mariners almost certainly paddled canoes along stretches of the Pacific and perhaps Atlantic shores thousands of years ago, the great ocean voids did not invite deep-sea exploration in small boats. On the Atlantic side, water routes give easy access to the far interiors of both continents. The Gulf of Mexico links the North American coastal plains and the Mississippi River valley with tropical Mexico. To the north, Hudson's Bay thrusts deep into North America, and just 275 miles south of it the five Great Lakes make up a complex of inland freshwater "seas" that connect extensive areas of forests and plains.

As in Afroeurasia, several great river systems open the interiors of the two Americas. Indeed, Afroeurasia has no network of navigable streams as extensive as the Mississippi and Amazon watersheds, both of which are accessible directly from the sea. From the Atlantic side, numerous other rivers connect the sea to the deep interiors of both continents. Indian migrants and traders used these rivers for long-distance internal communication, and the Europeans who first arrived at the end of the fifteenth century found them an easy way to extend waterborne colonization from the Atlantic to the Great Lakes, the North American plains, and the far interiors of Brazil and Argentina. By contrast, the Pacific side of the Americas is more like Australia in the poverty of its navigable rivers, owing mainly to the sharp drop from mountain to shore nearly the entire length of the land masses. The two major exceptions are the navigable Columbia, which forms part of the border between Oregon and Washington, and, in the far north, Alaska's Yukon.

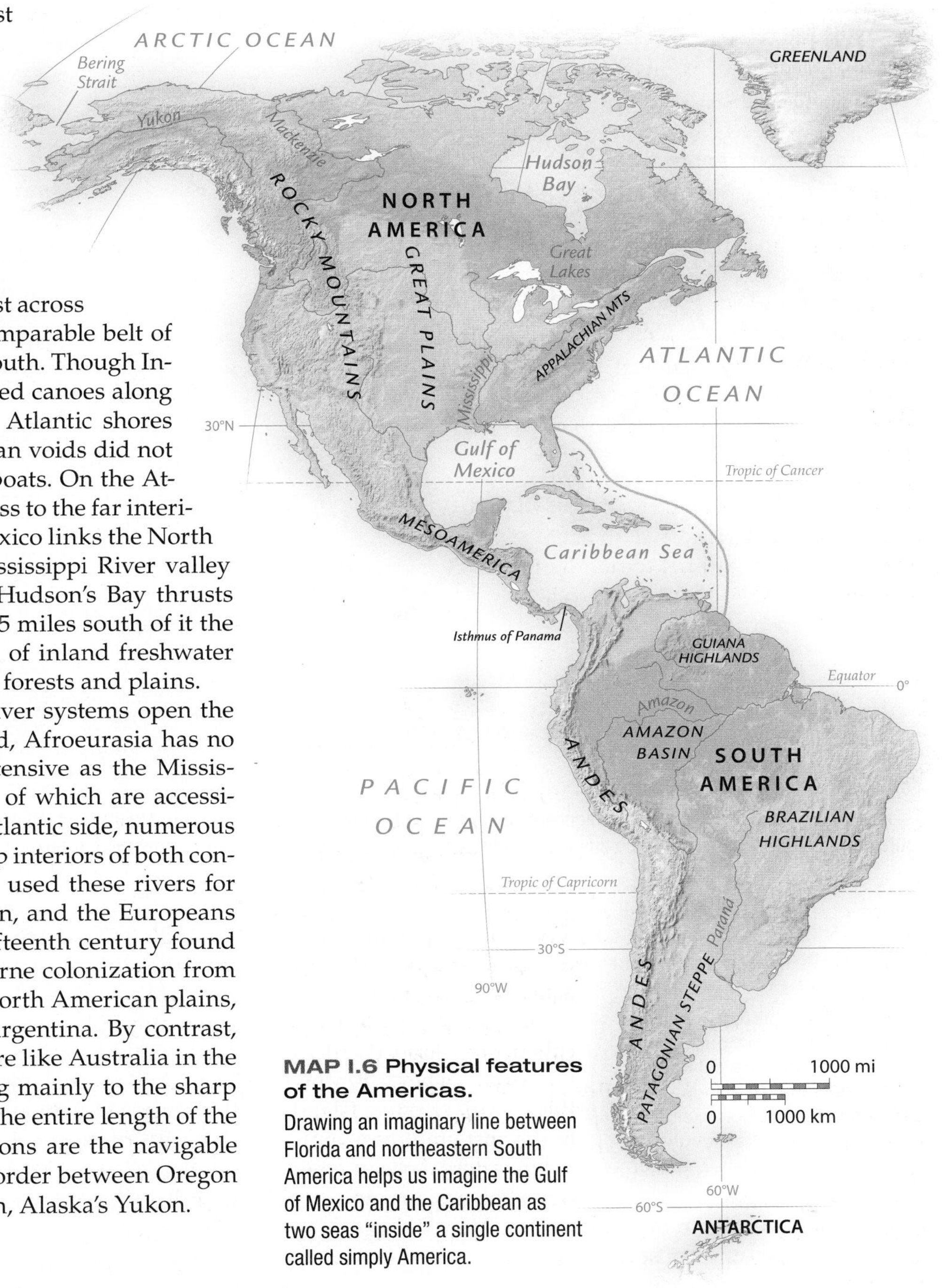

MAP I.6 Physical features of the Americas.

Drawing an imaginary line between Florida and northeastern South America helps us imagine the Gulf of Mexico and the Caribbean as two seas "inside" a single continent called simply America.

The Oceans

Our ancestors may have invented rudimentary watercraft as many as 100,000 years ago and used them to colonize Afroeurasian coastlands and some islands, but human exploration of ocean waters beyond the sight of land is a more recent development. Because of the seasonal regularity of the monsoon winds and the relative serenity of the northern Indian Ocean, valiant mariners of six thousand years ago or more may

monsoon winds
The seasonally reversing winds that governed long-distance sailing in the Indian Ocean and China seas.

have dared to steer primitive sailboats across open stretches of the Arabian Sea or Bay of Bengal. The Atlantic and the Pacific Oceans, however, are so big that they defied human attempts to make roundtrip open-ocean crossings until a little more than five hundred years ago. The Pacific covers a much greater area than the Atlantic. It is fifteen times larger than the United States, the Atlantic less than six and a half times larger. The Pacific, however, has many more islands than the Atlantic, about 25,000 of them. Between

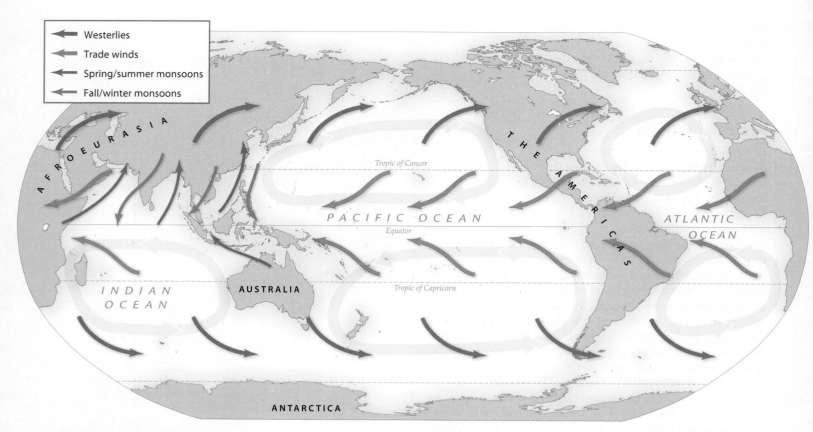

MAP I.7 Ocean wind patterns.

This simplified chart of oceanic winds highlights the giant wind wheels that circulate in the Atlantic and Pacific. Looking at the North Atlantic, what general route do you think Christopher Columbus followed in sailing successfully between Europe and the Caribbean Islands in the late fifteenth century?

Legend (map key):
- Westerlies
- Trade winds
- Spring/summer monsoons
- Fall/winter monsoons

about 1600 B.C.E. and 1000 C.E., Polynesian-speaking mariners, moving generally east and northeast from Afroeurasia, colonized many of these islands, collectively called the Island Pacific or **Oceania.** They reached Rapa Nui (Easter Island) in the vast emptiness of the southeastern ocean, and some Polynesians may even have made landfalls in South America. They did not, however, create a network of sea communication that linked the Pacific's western and eastern rims.

> **Oceania (also, the Island Pacific)** The enormous region centered on the tropical Pacific Ocean and its islands. This definition of the region excludes Australia though not New Zealand.

Not until the fifteenth century C.E. did deep-sea explorers gain sufficient technical skill and geographical knowledge to initiate regular travel *back and forth* across the Atlantic and the Pacific. Success came when sailors figured out that, like the Indian Ocean monsoons, the Atlantic and Pacific winds (and the surface currents driven by those winds) adhere to regular cycles (see Map I.7). Because of a combination of unequal atmospheric pressure and the influence of the earth's rotation, the winds of both the Atlantic and the Pacific flow in a circular, clockwise pattern north of the equator and in the reverse direction south of it. Only in the fifteenth and sixteenth centuries did European navigators begin to map out the Atlantic patterns accurately enough to allow routine roundtrip oceanic voyages. In fact, this four-wheel model of wind and current has numerous local variations and is much more complicated than this introduction suggests. Sea travelers gradually mastered these complexities, however, and by the end of the eighteenth century they were navigating the saltwater passages that connected all the great land masses and most of the world's islands with one another. Only Antarctica remained to be seriously explored.

• • •

Conclusion

This introduction to "big geography"—the large-scale and unifying features of the biosphere—is an important foundation for globe-girdling history. The earth is a single continuum of space, and the events that have mattered most to humankind as a whole have had a cross-cultural or interregional scope. Readers should therefore be ready to range across the whole wide world, considering the achievements, disasters, and dilemmas of the past in whatever context of *space* is most appropriate—whether that context is Afroeurasia, the Atlantic basin, or the rim lands of the Sahara Desert. It is impossible to look at a globe and see the round earth all at once. But fortunately we can encompass the whole in our minds. This is the starting point for a unified history of humankind.

• • •

Key Terms

Afroeurasia I-7	latitude I-6	Oceania (also, the Island Pacific) I-16
biosphere I-4	longitude I-13	tectonic plates I-4
Great Arid Zone I-7	Mesoamerica I-14	
Inner Eurasia I-8	monsoon winds I-15	

part 1

Settling the Planet

Beginnings to the First Millennium B.C.E.

P art 1 of this book sets *Homo sapiens* on the road to complexity. These first four chapters investigate four developments that have successively complicated human society and its relationship to the earth's environment.

The first was human colonization of all the planet's large land masses, a migration that started from eastern Africa. This was the first genuinely global event in our history, and we are the only higher primate species that accomplished it. Settling nearly the whole world required humans to adapt to starkly different ecological conditions. That meant that communities relying on wild food sources had to invent sophisticated ways to adjust to new environments and to long-term changes in world climate. These communities also built networks of exchange with

A wooden carving from the Middle Kingdom shows an Egyptian peasant guiding a plow pulled by two oxen.

one another. They traded not only useful material objects but also technological ideas. The spread of ideas about tools or food-gathering strategies to more communities tended to generate even more clever ways to exploit and manage the natural and physical world.

The second great jump into complexity was the invention of farming. This development got under way about 12,000 years ago, and it happened in several different parts of the world independently. Scholars have reached a broad consensus that this "agricultural revolution" was linked to the coming of the Holocene, the global warming trend that started around 14,000 years ago. Holocene conditions produced more abundant wild grain supplies in some parts of the world. In those places, communities of foragers began to experiment with new ways of nurturing and selecting grains and other edible plants they found appealing, though they had little conscious grasp of the biological causes or potential consequences of what they were doing.

Over many centuries of trial and error, communities found themselves genetically altering certain wild plants and animals to increase their size or otherwise improve their value to humans. This meant that people could settle in permanent and indeed larger communities to grow crops and raise animals. Between about 12,000 and 5,000 years ago, global population surged upward, social relations became more intricate, and networks of exchange became denser. This development happened in several parts of Afroeurasia and the Americas.

The third leap into complexity started about 5,500 years ago, when people in just a few places devised ways to produce large surpluses of food. This happened initially in river valleys where rainfall was low, but where people could generously irrigate fertile soil. These regions could sustain populations of unprecedented size, but people had to live close together to be near water and food. That meant inventing more complex tools, engineering methods, exchange webs, and social organizations. People could do this because the jump in available food energy allowed some individuals to devote full time to finding solutions to the challenges of living in larger, denser communities. Meeting these challenges led to the emergence of "complex societies," that is, societies characterized by cities, occupational specializations, social class divisions, central

governments, sophisticated record keeping, elaborate religious systems, and several other features. Not long after 5,500 years ago, complex societies emerged in both Afroeurasia and the Americas, although for several more millennia the great majority of humans lived in the countryside, not in cities.

Finally, in parts of Afroeurasia's Great Arid Zone, the belt of dry land that extends across the supercontinent, humans invented a third way of life that depended neither on foraging nor on settled farming. Starting as early as the fifth millennium B.C.E., people who raised animals for food, fiber, hides, and other useful products developed technologies and strategies that allowed them to pasture large numbers of cattle, sheep, or horses on seasonal grasslands where arid conditions severely limited farming. In a sense, wild grasses and shrubs became available to humans as food because animals biologically converted these plants into meat, milk, and blood, which humans could digest. People could colonize arid regions in larger numbers. Consequently, mobile herding societies, or pastoral nomads, began to play a much larger part in history.

We start Part 1 by investigating how and why these leaps into complexity occurred. What special endowments allowed humans, alone among animal species, not only to adapt to all but the most extreme environments, but also to transform and manage them in such elaborate ways?

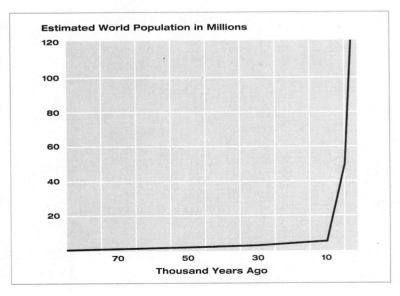

Estimated World Population in Millions

1

The Peopling of the World
7,000,000–10,000 B.C.E.

Some time at least four million years ago our ancestors stood up on two legs and started walking, first in Africa and eventually around the world. A few ancient trekkers even left their footprints. One set is embedded in hardened earth at a site called Laetoli (lie-a-TOE-lee) in a wooded region of northern Tanzania. The scientists who have studied these prints think that one day about 3.6 million years ago three apelike creatures, the biggest of them less than five feet tall, trudged together along a riverbed. They may have been scavenging for the meat of dead or dying animals. As they walked, they pressed their feet into rain-dampened ash, which was spewing out of a nearby volcano. The tropical sun hardened the ash before it blew away, and more layers of it fell to cover the prints. Consequently, the tracks of these individuals endured across the ages. The creatures were bipedal. That is, they walked upright on two legs, one skill among others that distinguishes humans and their forebears—known collectively as hominins—from chimpanzees, gorillas, and other apes.

In 1995 a geologist working at a coastal lagoon near Cape Town, South Africa, discovered another set of ancient footprints pressed into rock. Analysis of the impressions and the surrounding geological formations showed that a small individual walked along this stretch of the Cape coast about 117,000 years ago, leaving two tracks in wet sand, which eventually hardened. The shape of the prints shows that the individual was no remote human ancestor but rather one of our own species, *Homo sapiens*

The footprints of ancient ancestors, found at Laetoli.

("wise human"). The individual was almost certainly anatomically "modern," that is, it exhibited the same fundamental physical characteristics that we do. In fact, these prints are the earliest tracks of *Homo sapiens* so far discovered.

Homo sapiens appeared as a distinct species about 200,000 years ago, and during the following 100,000 years or more of its career, it left evidence of itself only in Africa. Then, starting perhaps 90,000 to 70,000 years ago, it migrated beyond Africa to Eurasia, Australia, and the Americas, and to thousands of islands scattered across the oceans. Among the millions of animal life-forms that trot, crawl, and slither on the surface of the earth, human beings are among the relatively few that made their way around the world and adapted to environments ranging from Arctic to equatorial rainforest. Even our close genetic cousins in the primate family—orangutans, gorillas, bonobos, and chimpanzees—have never left their limited tropical habitats, except in the company of human beings who offered them no choice. The first big story in world history, then, is the peopling of the earth, the story of how and why human beings came to live almost everywhere, not just in eastern and southern Africa.

One of humankind's forebears, the hominin usually identified as *Homo erectus,* preceded our own species out of Africa, migrating as far as Southeast and East Asia. This early traveler, however, took perhaps a million years to get as far east as China, possessed only rudimentary tools, and like all other hominins except us, eventually went extinct. The first part of this chapter introduces briefly the story of these ancestors, whose long but finally doomed sojourn on earth throws into relief the relatively much shorter but, until now at any rate, biologically much more successful history of our own species.

When *Homo sapiens* first left its African cradle to venture north and east, it probably already possessed a biologically modern brain and a much more advanced tool kit than any other hominin species had ever possessed. It had also probably evolved the capacity for self-conscious symbolic thought, expressed through speech, gesture, ritual, and art. On this single talent rested all the astonishing cultural achievements of later millennia. The second part of the chapter surveys the exclusively African evolution of our anatomically modern and intellectually gifted species, an episode that covers something like 60 percent of our history to date.

The third section traces humankind's early colonization of the world, from all regions of Africa, across the breadth of Eurasia, and on to Australia and the far southern reaches of South America. In contrast to the slow and halting movements of *Homo erectus* across Eurasia, bands of foraging and hunting humans advanced to all of the world's major land masses in less than 100,000 years. As they moved and

Chapter Outline

multiplied, they demonstrated their talents for adapting to and altering contrasting physical and natural environments on a much larger scale than any more ancient species had been able to manage.

As human groups fanned out around the world, the pace of invention in toolmaking, shelter building, social organization, symbolic imagery, and techniques for exchanging goods and ideas speeded up as well. Between about 40,000 and 10,000 B.C.E., the era that scholars call the upper paleolithic ("late stone age"), humankind emerged as a species of exquisitely complex culture. The final part of the chapter explores this explosion of technological and artistic innovation, which happened nearly simultaneously in several parts of the world.

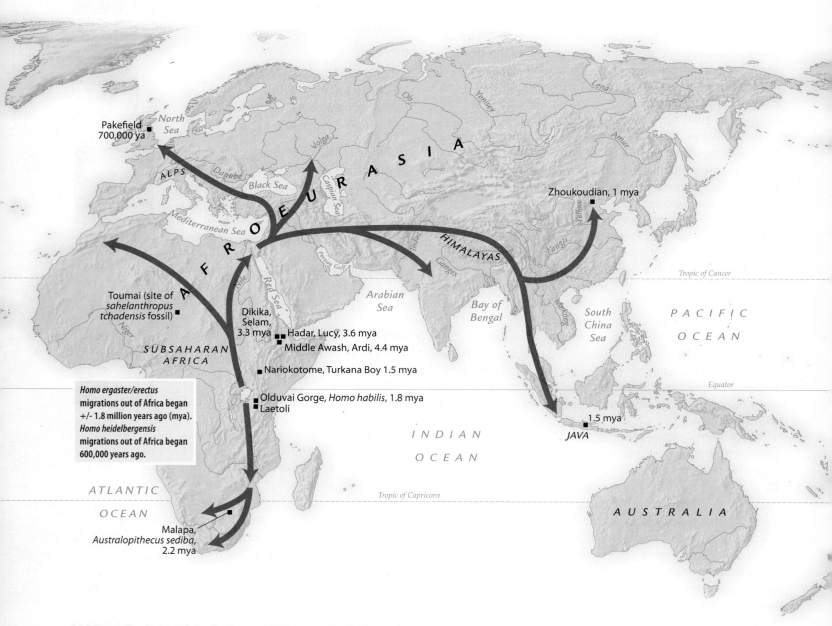

MAP 1.1 Early hominin finds and the spread of *Homo ergaster/erectus*.

The slow spread of *Homo ergaster* and *Homo erectus* from eastern Africa to other parts of Afroeurasia differentiates these species from other primates and from later migrations of *Homo sapiens*. What do the migratory directions of *Homo ergaster* and *Homo erectus* tell us about the success these species had adapting to contrasting climates?

Human Ancestors in Africa and Beyond

FOCUS What types of evidence have scholars used to construct histories of humankind's biological ancestors from 7 million to 200,000 years ago?

The era we investigate in this chapter is a long one, stretching from about seven million years ago, the earliest period

> **hominin** The family of species that includes *Homo sapiens* and its ancestors of the past 6–7 million years.

for which we have evidence of **hominins** as a class of primate separate from the ancestors of chimpanzees and other apes, to about 10,000 B.C.E., when people in some parts of Afroeurasia (the "supercontinent" of Africa, Eurasia, and adjacent islands as a single geographical unit) began to domesticate plants and take up farming. We can, however, tell this long story in just one chapter. One reason is that during most of those seven million years, the ways of life of hominins changed very slowly, especially compared to today, when human society is restructuring itself year-by-year. Key turning points that we can perceive in the fossil or genetic record—for example, toolmaking, control of fire, or the earliest sign of hominins traveling beyond Africa—occurred at widely spaced intervals, perhaps millions of years apart. Nor can we date any of those developments precisely.

A second reason for making a long story short is that the material evidence is scattered sparsely across time and space. The knowledge we possess for constructing hominin history down to 10,000 B.C.E. is miniscule, compared to the data we have about what happened in the world in, say, the first decade of the twenty-first century. The four main types of evidence available to us are human and animal fossil bones, surviving tools and other artifacts (mostly of stone), physical indicators of climatic change that may have affected hominin biological success, and, more recently, genetic material (DNA) from both fossil remains and living men and women. Archaeological and genetic discoveries have been adding new bits of evidence for the deep past just about every month. But as archaeologists have sometimes joked, the number of experts who work in ancient fossil sites exceeds the number of human bones they have so far discovered. Analysis of DNA promises to supply much more knowledge about human evolution and spatial migration, though this class of evidence still has limited uses. The data attesting to our early history are so restricted, and the time gaps between periods for which evidence is available are so long, that we can discern only broad developments. As much as we might like to do it, we cannot write histories about, or even identify, particular communities, leaders, or short-term events.

Early Hominin Evolution

The human species, just one of the millions of plant and animal species that occupy the globe, may be defined simply as a class of individual life-forms capable of interbreeding to perpetuate themselves but incapable of successfully breeding with individuals of other classes. Humans, for example, cannot mate with chimpanzees, and chimpanzees cannot breed with gorillas, even though all three species share between 96 and 99 percent of their genes.

Toumai: The oldest hominin remains. The story of how humans became a species begins with the biological separation of hominins from the ancestors of modern chimpanzees nearly seven million years ago. Evidence for this estimate came in 2001, when French archaeologists working in Chad in west central Africa found a skull bearing hominin characteristics. Dated to that distant time and nicknamed Toumai (TOO-meye), a word meaning "hope of life" in a local language, this individual (*Sahelanthropus tchadensis*) had a brain about the size of a chimp's but remarkably hominin-like facial features, suggesting that a new species genetically different from other primates may have arrived. Scientists are divided on the question of whether Toumai walked upright, but the way the skull appears to have connected to the spine suggests that it did. Just why hominins, in contrast to other primates, evolved a body suited for upright locomotion, including a curved lower spine, knee joints, and a two-footed sense of balance, is a subject of continuing debate among scholars. Hominins definitely had to compete with other animals for food, and perhaps in this game the advantages of full-time bipedalism came to outweigh the disadvantages. **Bipedal** animals faced the danger that large four-legged predators

> **bipedal** Walking upright on two legs, one skill among others that distinguishes hominins from apes.

could outrun them, at least over short distances. On the other hand, upright walkers may have been tall enough to see a predator far out across a grassy plain and so have time to get away from it. Like other primates, bipedal creatures had opposable thumbs for grasping things. By walking on two limbs they had their hands free not only to scurry up trees when they had to, but also to carry food quickly away from rival animals to a place where they could dine in safety. Also, two-legged walkers exposed less surface area of their body to the direct rays of the sun—not their entire back but just the top of their head. They could therefore keep their bodies and brains at efficiently cool temperatures more easily than could animals whose posture was "horizontal" and closer to the ground. That meant they could move around in the midday heat when four-legged animals had to rest in the shade.

Lucy and other australopithecines. While the origins of bipedalism remain speculative, a picture of early bipedal creatures is emerging from the fossil evidence. Until recently, the most famous early hominin was Lucy. In 1975, researchers working in northern Ethiopia found the skeletal remains of at least thirteen **australopithecines** (ah-strah-loh-PITH-uh-seens),

> **australopithecines** Several species of the earliest bipedal hominins, now extinct, whose remains have been found in eastern Africa.

"Lucy." This young, small, and presumably female representative of the species *Australopithecus afarensis* may have looked very much like this reconstruction. Paleoanthropologists and the artists who collaborate with them, however, can only make informed guesses about this species' skin color, hairiness, and nose and lip shape. Modern humans have a large braincase with a small face set beneath the front part of it. Lucy and her australopithecine cousins, by contrast, had a small braincase but a broad, protruding face. In this photo Lucy seems to peer at us with a wistful expression. Might reconstructions like this mislead us into thinking this creature was more "human" than she probably was?

the genus that included a number of early hominin species. One of them was the skeleton, or about 40 percent of it, of a young female. While they were celebrating the discovery in camp, the scientists played the famous Beatles song "Lucy in the Sky with Diamonds." Thus, this fossilized creature got her enduring nickname. Classified as *Australopithecus afarensis* and dated to about 3.2 million years ago, Lucy was only about three feet tall, but she definitely walked upright and could use her flexible thumb and fingers to gather food, perhaps carrying an infant at the same time.

In the past several years, however, Lucy has had to share some of her fame with other Ethiopian fossils. In 2000, **paleoanthropologists** discovered Selam, the nearly complete skeleton of a three-year-old female. This child had been buried in sand and rock for 3.6 million years; perhaps she drowned in a sudden flood. Found at a site in the Dikika region not far from where Lucy lived, Selam had gorillalike shoulders good for tree climbing but also a braincase whose size may not have reached full maturity for an australopithecine adult. This feature points to an extended dependent childhood, a biological trait peculiar to human beings. In 2009, scientists proclaimed more confidently that bipedal australopithecines lived at least 4.4 million years ago. This announcement followed the discovery of a partial skeleton of an adult female creature named *Ardipithecus ramidus,* or Ardi. Analysis of the remains indicates that this individual,

paleoanthropologist A scientist concerned with the study of human evolution and the physical and behavioral characteristics of early humans and their biological ancestors.

who was 1.2 million years older than Lucy, could walk upright, if in a lumbering sort of way. We know that species of australopithecines ranged all the way to the southern tip of Africa. Recently, scientists have been analyzing the skull and several other bones of a creature, named *Australopithecus sediba,* that fell into a deep cave in South Africa nearly two million years ago.

Australopithecines like Lucy, Selam, Ardi, and *Australopithecus sediba* were likely quite intelligent compared to animal competitors, and they may have formed small social bands that cooperated in collecting food and eluding ferocious predators. Even so, this species was a long way from modern humanhood. The australopithecine brain was much smaller than ours—not much larger than a softball. Moreover, we have no evidence that these creatures used even the most rudimentary stone tools. "Despite their human-like posture," one anthropologist has written, "the brain-to-body ratio of Lucy and her friends were such that it is highly probable they could have led full mental and spiritual lives in any municipal zoo."[1] It is possible that one of these varieties of australopithecines was a direct, though very distant ancestor of our own species. But we can only speculate about which one it may have been.

Homo habilis. Less than two million years ago, toolmaking hominins appear in the fossil record. The earliest ones we know of lived near a lake on the Serengeti Plain in modern Tanzania. Discovered in 1960 in Olduvai (OHL-duh-way) Gorge, a region that has yielded a treasury of ancient fossils, this 1.8-million-year-old hominin is the oldest one that scientists have classified as *Homo,* the genus to which we belong. The archaeologists who found the bones of this species named it *Homo habilis,* or "handy person." This species had special attributes, including a larger brain than the likes of Lucy and highly dexterous opposable thumbs, which allowed it to delicately manipulate small objects. It made a number of different tools, including hammers, hand axes, and flakes with sharp edges for chopping or scraping. The evidence available suggests that *Homo habilis* individuals ate plant food as well as meat scavenged from dead animals. Some researchers now argue that a different hominin species living as many as 2.5 million years ago also made tools and that more than one species may have acquired this talent. In any case, the appearance of toolmaking represents the beginning of the **paleolithic,** or "old stone age," an epoch that extended to about 10,000 B.C.E., when the human tool kit became much more sophisticated.

paleolithic Meaning "old stone age," this period dates from approximately 2.5 million years ago, when hominin species first devised stone tools, to about 12,000 years ago, when humans starting experimenting with agriculture.

Well-Traveled Hominins

Perhaps not much later than 1.9 million years ago, a hominin species perhaps to be identified as *Homo ergaster* made its way northward from Africa into Eurasia. During the ensuing million years, small bands of this species, together with its descendant *Homo erectus,* trekked to regions as far apart from one another as western Europe, eastern China, and Indonesia (see Map 1.1). They also extended their range in Africa. Equipped with more complex brains and better tool kits than their genetic ancestors, these species adapted to natural environments very different from those of tropical Africa.

Clever but not quite "us." *Homo ergaster* and *Homo erectus* were tall and full-bodied, not short and slight like australopithecines. They were too heavy to swing through trees but robust enough to stand their ground against formidable animal predators. More important, they had a larger braincase than earlier hominins, suggesting a brain size about three-quarters as large as ours. This bigger skull may have enclosed more complex neural "wiring," a biological advance that permitted more intricate mental processes than earlier hominins could handle. For example, they appear to have fashioned stone tools with some sort of "plan" in their heads for how to use them later.

After millions of years when hominin brain size did not change much, the rather sudden debut of these relatively keen-witted creatures is not easy to explain. We know that *Homo erectus* became omnivorous, eating just about everything that could be eaten, including much larger quantities of meat than its forebears had consumed. The species could never have grown such an ample brain relative to body size, if it had not built up its supply of food energy by consuming meat rich in calories, protein, and fat. *Homo ergaster* and *Homo erectus,* plus a species called *Homo heidelbergensis,* which evolved in Africa perhaps 600,000 years ago, applied their brains to developing diverse, sophisticated tools of chipped and flaked stone, including choppers, chisels, cleavers, scrapers, awls, and hammers, as well as finely fashioned, teardrop-shaped

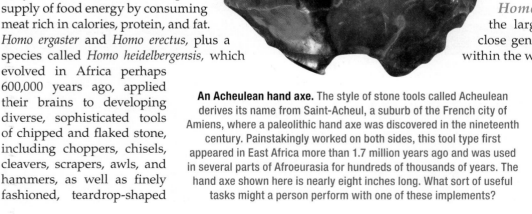

An Acheulean hand axe. The style of stone tools called Acheulean derives its name from Saint-Acheul, a suburb of the French city of Amiens, where a paleolithic hand axe was discovered in the nineteenth century. Painstakingly worked on both sides, this tool type first appeared in East Africa more than 1.7 million years ago and was used in several parts of Afroeurasia for hundreds of thousands of years. The hand axe shown here is nearly eight inches long. What sort of useful tasks might a person perform with one of these implements?

hand axes. Females of the species, who probably spent time every day gathering vegetable foods, almost certainly invented and refined much of this equipment.

The intelligence of the species may have evolved in response to the intellectual demands of daily cooperation in small bands and natural selection favoring individuals with brains capable of complex functions useful in group living. But why would hominins need to work together in groups? A likely factor is that *Homo erectus* mothers, unlike most mammals, gave birth to biologically immature offspring. As with modern humans, the brains of newborns grew gradually in infancy and early childhood, that is, to a fully developed size that was larger than what could have passed through the birth canal. Such offspring had no ability to look after themselves for a long time. Therefore, intensive childcare, including breastfeeding, occupied females for two years or more. This required males and females to find ways to work together routinely to collect food, defend their camp, and chase after toddlers. The species may have been more than intelligent enough to organize some degree of coordination in the hunt. Bands not only killed and ate large, fierce animals from time to time, but also engaged in tactical planning. At one fossil site in Kenya dated to about 480,000 years ago, the configuration of stone hand axes and cleavers, together with the bones of sixty-three baboons, suggests that a band of *Homo ergaster* or related hominins surrounded the primates, then systematically attacked and clubbed them to death.

***Homo* species on the move.** On the largest scale, the history of our close genetic ancestors must be framed within the whole of Afroeurasia. Fossil discoveries at a site near Dmanisi (duh-man-EE-see), a village in the Republic of Georgia, show that tool-using hominins whose forebears almost certainly came from Africa lived in the Caucasus Mountains about 1.8 million years ago. Experts are divided over the

The Turkana Boy: A Distant Ancestor

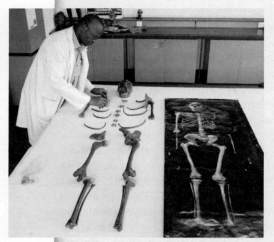

Samuel Muteti, a research scientist at the National Museums of Kenya, displays a replica of the 1.6 million-year-old Turkana Boy (also, Nariokotome Boy).

Human forebears of a million and a half years ago had a good chance of dying young. The Turkana Boy did, falling face down in a soggy marsh where his body decomposed and his skull and bones slowly separated from one another. He was probably between eight and eleven years old when he died. He was walking, maybe running, near a river that lay west of Lake Turkana in what is today northwestern Kenya. His remains show possible signs of spinal disease or injury, and he had inflammation in his lower jaw, which might suggest blood poisoning. He stood well over five feet tall, and he might have reached six feet or more in adulthood, if he had lived. Typical of the Turkana people who inhabit the region today, he had a long, slender body, and his shoulders and hips were narrow. This was a physical type genetically adapted to a hot, tropical environment because it maximized the surface area of the body and therefore its capacity to shed heat. He was certainly a meat-eater, at home on the African savanna because he could run fast and far and hunt in the midday sun.

Some scientists classify Turkana Boy, whose remains lie in boxes in Kenya's national museum, as an early representative of *Homo ergaster.* He probably looked quite like modern humans do, except for his head. He had a protruding face, strong brow, wide nose, and no chin. The small size of his vertebral canal, which encases the nerve-laden spinal cord connecting the brain to the rib cage, suggests that he could not have controlled his breathing in the precise way that we can. He could have made a range of sounds, but, lacking the physical equipment to exhale in a finely modulated way, he could not have strung together nuanced utterances carrying complex meanings. Indeed, his preteen brain was about the size of a modern one-year-old's.

The fossilized bones of a paleolithic hominin rarely give us any sense that they once belonged to a living, moving individual. But with Turkana Boy, stretched out in the mud, we have a kind of stop-action picture of someone on the point of death. The scene invites us to speculate how he died—exhausted from running, badly injured, mauled by an animal, murdered by someone of his own species?

Thinking Critically

Do you think a hominin like Turkana Boy would have been easy prey for other large animal species? Why or why not?

Biological separation of hominins from ancestors of modern chimpanzees (Toumai skull from Chad)

4.4–3 mya: australopithicines, northeastern Africa, Ardi 4.4 mya

| 7 | 6 | 5 | 4 |

Millions of years ago (mya)

Evolution of human ancestors.

question of whether these bones represent *Homo erectus,* but the evidence we have so far tells us that this species made its way, by about 1.5 million years ago, to the tropical island of Java in modern Indonesia and, by about 1 million years ago, to northern China. Flint tools found in eastern England reveal that a species probably descended from *Homo ergaster* lived there about 700,000 years ago, though these hunters may have ventured that far north only during relatively short periods when global temperatures rose temporarily.

Under what conditions did these distant ancestors migrate so far and wide, especially considering that chimps, gorillas, and other African primates did not explore beyond their tropical habitats. One theory has it that the brains of *Homo* species, larger than those of earlier hominins, had great food energy needs. (The brain of modern humans is ravenously hungry, consuming about 20 percent of the body's total metabolic energy.) Therefore, forager (or hunter-forager) bands tended to eat themselves out of one local ecological niche after another, especially when competing with other meat-loving animals that shared the neighborhood. When local resources dwindled relative to the size of the band, some members formed a new band, hived off, and searched for a food niche of its own beyond the next hill. One archaeologist has calculated that if subsistence bands, splitting in this way over and over again, drifted only twelve miles in a generation, they could have covered the distance from eastern Africa to China in a mere 20,000 years.[2] In fact, they likely took much longer than that.

Long-term fluctuations in global temperature may also have propelled migration. About 1.6 million years ago, the planet entered the **Pleistocene** (PLEYES-tuh-seen), an epoch of cycles of cooling and warming, each cycle lasting about 100,000 years over the past million years. Long periods of cooling, or **ice ages,** produced glaciers, that is, great ice sheets that extended from the north polar region southward to cover large areas of northern Eurasia and North America. Glaciers transformed so much saltwater into ice that ocean levels fell, extending coastal zones and exposing land bridges between territories once separated by water. During relatively shorter periods of warming, called **interglacials,** the ice retreated and sea levels rose again. During the past million years, warm periods have lasted only about 10,000 years. Indeed, we have been living in an interglacial, called the **Holocene,** since about 9600 B.C.E. Bands of *Homo erectus* or related species spread across Afroeurasia during the Pleistocene, when temperature cycles produced successive northward and southward shifts in patterns of rainfall and vegetation. Migratory drift across Eurasia may have been linked to these climatic rhythms, with forager bands roving into more northerly areas during interglacials and then having to either adapt or retreat south when temperatures dropped again.

Because these creatures migrated so far and wide, they must have developed tools and social practices rich and flexible enough to adapt to widely varying environments. Learning how to control fire was a key advance. Charred ground found at fossil sites in both eastern and southern Africa suggests that *Homo ergaster* was the first hominin to build fires to keep warm, scare off predators, illuminate murky caves, and perhaps cook food. In 2004 a site in northern Israel yielded evidence of burned chips of flint rock, indicating that hominin bands built campfires some 790,000 years ago. Hominin bands certainly could not have survived in northern climates, even during interglacials,

interglacial A period of global warming and retreating glaciers between ice ages. Our current geological epoch, the **Holocene,** is an interglacial.

ice age Any geological epoch, most recently the **Pleistocene** era (1.6 million to 12,000 years ago), when glaciers covered a large part of the world's surface.

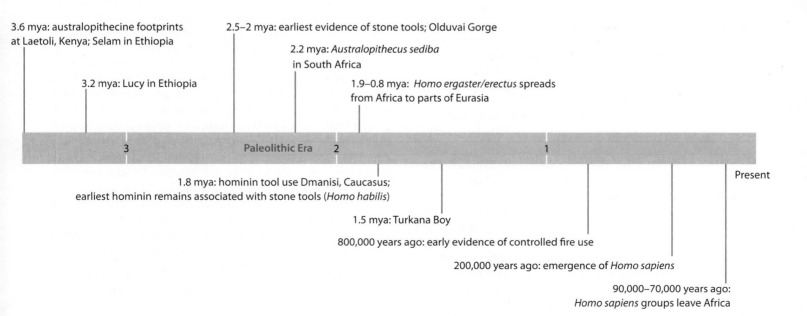

3.6 mya: australopithecine footprints at Laetoli, Kenya; Selam in Ethiopia

2.5–2 mya: earliest evidence of stone tools; Olduvai Gorge

2.2 mya: *Australopithecus sediba* in South Africa

3.2 mya: Lucy in Ethiopia

1.9–0.8 mya: *Homo ergaster/erectus* spreads from Africa to parts of Eurasia

3　　Paleolithic Era　2　　　　　1

1.8 mya: hominin tool use Dmanisi, Caucasus; earliest hominin remains associated with stone tools (*Homo habilis*)

1.5 mya: Turkana Boy

800,000 years ago: early evidence of controlled fire use

200,000 years ago: emergence of *Homo sapiens*

90,000–70,000 years ago: *Homo sapiens* groups leave Africa

Present

without knowing how to use fire. The site at Zhoukoudian (joh-koh-dee-ehn), a town in northern China, reveals that *Homo erectus* individuals occupying a cave there some 300,000 to 400,000 years ago built fires, though scientists continue to dispute the evidence.

A diverse stone tool kit, elemental social organization, and knowledge of fire enabled *Homo erectus* and its like to become a "cosmopolitan" species. This means that it adapted successfully to several contrasting ecological niches. Even so, there is something alien and remote about these creatures. They did not, as far as we know, devise social rules for sharing food, resolving conflicts, or strategizing long-term survival. Fossil and tool sites have so far turned up no evidence that they knew anything of religion or art or even how to build a simple hearth. No wall paintings, no stone carvings, no burial of the dead. In fact, by comparison with the 200,000-year history of our species, the life ways of this species changed remarkably little in the nearly 2 million years that it survived.

Other Traveling Hominins

Starting 200,000 years ago or more, hominin species possessing greater intelligence and more sophisticated tool kits than *Homo erectus* begin to appear in the fossil record. So far, we have evidence of four of them. We know quite a bit about one of these species, the Neanderthals (nee-ANN-duhr-tawls), but not much about two of them, the Floresians and the Denisovans. The fourth one is *Homo sapiens,* the subject of the rest of this book. All four species may be biological descendants of *Homo erectus,* but we cannot demonstrate the lines of descent with certainty.

The Neanderthals. The hominin species known formally as *Homo neanderthalensis* occupied a large part of Europe and Southwest Asia, the region that in modern contexts we call the Middle East. Named after the Neander River valley in northern Germany, where bones were discovered in the nineteenth century, this large-brained species flourished 200,000 years ago, then went extinct about 28,000 years ago. Accumulating scientific evidence has nearly demolished the theory that the Neanderthals are our own direct biological ancestors. More likely, they represent a separate branch descended from an earlier species.

Popular culture has treated Neanderthals harshly, depicting them as ugly, dunderheaded cave-dwellers. This species did live in caves, and they had short, stocky, muscular, strong-jawed bodies. But they were not dimwits. They had brains in the same size range as ours, and they used a complex kit of specialized stone tools. They dressed themselves in warm clothing of fur and skin, controlled fire, and hunted game along the fringes of glaciers. They also buried their dead and placed material objects in the graves, suggesting that they believed the deceased might carry these goods into an afterlife. Fossil remains have also revealed individuals who survived for months or years despite having arthritic or broken bones. Here is a hint that Neanderthal bands cared for sick or aging members of the group rather than abandoning them to die alone. Neanderthals no doubt communicated with one another using both sounds and gestures. Their throat structures, however, may have been ill-designed for stringing together complex sounds, and we have no evidence that they possessed language. Nor did they make art or build even rudimentary houses. But what we know of their behavior suggests that they may have been on the way to acquiring some of these abilities.

Neanderthals had sufficient intelligence and skill to live in a range of climates in Southwest Asia, Europe, and northwestern Africa (see Map 1.2). Within the climatic cycles of the Pleistocene epoch, they probably advanced north during warm, interglacial periods, following the tracks of reindeer and other game. When temperatures dropped and the glaciers spread, however, they retreated southward to friendlier ecological zones. Whatever their adaptive skills, however, they eventually had to face intrusive *Homo sapiens.* We come back to that confrontation later in the chapter.

The Floresians. In 2004, researchers digging in a cave on Flores, an Indonesian island east of Java, announced that they had found what appeared to be a previously unknown hominin species. Scientists reconstructed a partial skeleton, revealing an upright-walking, long-armed adult female barely three feet tall. Her braincase, however, was small, about the size of a chimpanzee's.

The specimen and the excavated materials associated with it presented several puzzles. The shape and size of the face and teeth suggested a species quite close to *Homo sapiens* on the hominin family tree. The interior of the skull indicated lobes and ridges characteristic of the high-powered *Homo sapiens* brain. Stone tools found at the site were small and fine, suggesting more advanced technological skills than *Homo erectus* probably had. Finally, scientists dated the skeleton to only about 18,000 years ago, suggesting that the species far outlived *Homo erectus* and shared tropical Southeast Asia with modern humans, possibly for thousands of years. Scientists named the creatures *Homo floresiensis,* or simply the Floresians, after their island home.

The archaeologists who discovered the fossils have argued that the Floresians are probably not descended from *Homo erectus.* Rather, they represent an entirely different branch of the hominin tree, some members of which migrated from Africa to Southeast Asia either before or after *Homo erectus* did. Other scholars have contended that the cave-dwellers are *Homo sapiens* and that the miniature skull is evidence of a developmental disease. In any case, the skull specimen has impelled scientists to think again about the relationship between intelligence and brain volume. The species that hunted in the island's mountain forests may have had much more complex neural wiring packed into its tiny cranium than other early hominins did.

The Denisovans. Applying new biochemical techniques, scientists have succeeded in the past few years in sequencing the DNA of a young female hominin who spent time in

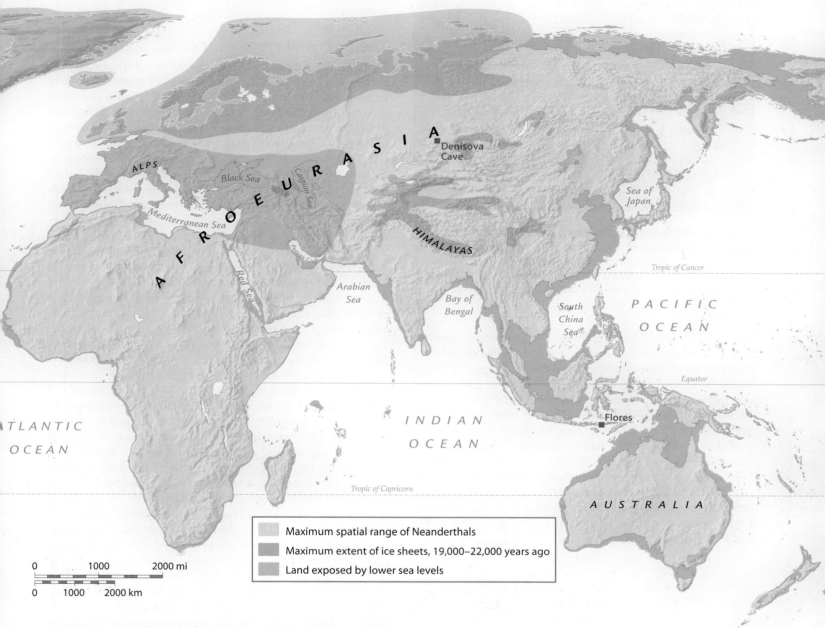

MAP 1.2 Neanderthals and other close human ancestors.

What climatic and geological relationship existed between the expansion of ice sheets and the appearance of land bridges that migrating human ancestors may have crossed?

a cave in southern Siberia as many as 80,000 years ago. Since the 1970s molecular biologists interested in human evolution have been studying the properties of DNA, the main constituent of the human chromosome and the one that carries genes. As DNA flows from one generation to the next, small alterations, or mutations, occur and at a regular rate. This means that over time the genetic differences between individuals sharing a common ancestor increase statistically. The longer two human populations have no contact

with one another, the greater the genetic distance between them will be. Using complex laboratory procedures, scientists can measure the rate of change in genetic material and therefore estimate how long ago in thousands or even tens of thousands of years two hominin groups separated from one another. Analysis of the Siberian girl's genome, that is, her complete set of chromosomes, has revealed that her ancestors separated biologically from *Homo sapiens* somewhere between 170,000 and 700,000 years ago. In other words, she

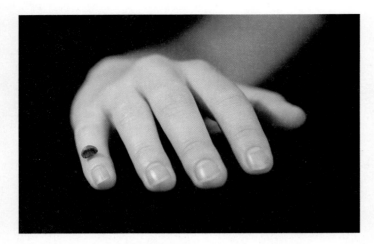

Historical evidence from a pinky finger. Laboratory analysis of undamaged DNA contained in a finger bone fragment from Siberia has revealed that our species probably has a previously unknown cousin. Genetic studies can tell us many things about early human history. What aspects of the past do you think they *cannot* explain?

numbers to colonize the rest of the world until as few as 70,000 years ago.

The Debut of *Homo Sapiens*

The dominant theory of *Homo sapiens'* dispersion contends that our species evolved in eastern and southern Africa. Evidence sustaining this "Out of Africa" theory has been accumulating steadily. Archaeological digs have found the oldest *Homo sapiens* bones only in Africa. In 2005, scientists using new dating technology estimated the age of two partial *Homo sapiens* skulls discovered in southern Ethiopia at about 195,000 years. A fully modern skull from South Africa dated to about 36,000 years ago closely resembles the skulls of *Homo sapiens* individuals who by that era also inhabited far-flung parts of Eurasia, if in small numbers. This similarity suggests that our species evolved fully in Africa *before* venturing to other regions to take up permanent residence.

Genetic research has also supported the Out of Africa theory. In the past few decades, DNA studies have confirmed repeatedly that greater variety exists in the genes of individuals of African descent than among individuals whose ancestors have lived in other regions. This means that the common ancestor of people of African descent in a set of DNA samples, wherever those people live today, existed at an earlier time than the common ancestor of any non-African in the sample. In other words, individuals of African descent in the sample could trace their genetic lineage back to a common ancestor without anyone of non-African descent appearing in it. By contrast, non-Africans in the sample always had at least one African ancestor.

Theoretically then, everyone alive in the early twenty-first century possesses a family tree that goes back to forebears who lived in eastern or southern Africa 150,000 to 200,000 years ago. We all have inherited the DNA (specifically mitochondrial DNA, the type that passes only through women) of distant African ancestors, and from them the genetic branches of the human family tree began to multiply and leaf out. Eventually, humans began to explore other parts of the world, creating more genetic diversity as they drifted in different directions and lost contact with one another. Today, scientists are mapping genetic variations in full detail, a project that will eventually give us a much richer understanding of when and by what routes *Homo sapiens* occupied the world.

The Power of Language

Our fully human ancestors remained exclusively in Africa for a long time, but they made history there by expanding their territorial range over many thousands of miles—from South Africa to Morocco's Mediterranean coast. A large part of Africa lies within the tropical latitudes, but our species nonetheless penetrated a wide range of ecological zones—rainforests, mountain valleys, and semiarid plains, as well as temperate lands in the far north and south where winters required warm shelters. After about 80,000 years

was not a member of our own species, but neither was she a Neanderthal or *Homo erectus*. Rather, she belonged to a hominin species previously unknown.

The Denisova Cave, as it is known, has so far revealed no treasure trove of skeletal parts but only a small bone in one pinky finger and two teeth. The bone yielded such high-quality DNA, however, that scientists have declared confidently that the girl had brown hair, eyes, and skin. They have told us that she was a closer genetic cousin of Neanderthals than of modern humans and that her species inhabited Siberia perhaps tens of thousands of years before *Homo sapiens* arrived in the region. So far, however, we know nothing of the Denisovans' territorial range or the sort of tool kit they used.

Modern Humans in Africa: The First 100,000 Years

> FOCUS What physical and intellectual characteristics distinguish *Homo sapiens* from our species' hominin ancestors?

Homo erectus, Neanderthals, Floresians, and Denisovans all migrated long distances from Africa, but none of them, as far as we know, made their way to Australia, the Americas, or the far-flung islands of the Pacific. That distinction belongs to *Homo sapiens,* which, starting from eastern Africa, colonized all the world's large land masses except Antarctica. Owing to genetic research and fossil finds in recent years, most scholars have come around to the view that people like us evolved exclusively in Africa, emerging about 200,000 years ago. *Homo sapiens* then populated several parts of Africa and may not have moved out from there in significant ago, human forager communities appear to have started multiplying along the belt of wooded and open savanna that runs the breadth of Africa from Ethiopia to the Atlantic Ocean. *Homo sapiens* thus acquired the brain power to adapt to a great variety of environmental niches.

The men and women who originally colonized many parts of Africa probably resembled us fairly closely in an anatomical sense. If a 100,000-year-old *Homo sapiens* were to walk onto a college campus today wearing conventional clothes and sporting an adequate haircut, she would probably attract no more attention than anyone else. If someone tried to speak to her, however, she might have been at a loss for words. This is because humans were only just about then acquiring the gift of language. When they did, the power of humans to work in groups and to manipulate their physical and natural environment swelled dramatically.

Possessing language, people formed social communities that could consciously share, accumulate, and transmit complicated information to offspring. *Homo sapiens* did not have to depend, as all other animals do, on genetic alterations to adapt successfully to changing physical and natural environments. Rather, they had the power to bring about change through the nuanced interaction of many minds. In a word, they acquired the capacity to create culture. And cultural change, by comparison with the sluggish pace of biological adaptation through natural selection, could take place in the blink of an eye. The historian David Christian calls this ability "**collective learning**."[3] Among higher primates like chimps and gorillas, the young learn behaviors related to such things as finding food and avoiding predators by observing and imitating their parents. But the learning largely stops there, and no primate can pass on to its offspring the details of its life experience—"here's what I did a few years ago when this pack of hyenas saw me." In their early months, human babies learn mainly from the sounds and gestures that other family members make, but as they grow older and acquire language, they tap in to vast stores of knowledge communicated not only by their family but also by thousands of other people, as well as by books, radio, television, and the Internet. In turn, these individuals can pass arrays of information to the next generation. Over time, the process of collective learning has led to exponential growth of knowledge, and humans have used it to alter and manage their physical and natural environments in increasingly intricate and powerful ways.

collective learning The process whereby humans accumulate and share complex knowledge and transmit it from one generation to the next.

Symbolic thinkers. All animal species have ways of communicating, but language is another matter. Humans evolved an anatomical sound-making apparatus that could not only pronounce words—that is, individual sounds with meanings assigned to them—but also arrange words in complex clusters of meaning and transmit those meanings from one person to another at a fast rate. This ability to control sounds to convey elaborate, subtle meanings, which people shared with one another, separated even the earliest human language speakers from animals that communicated through grunts, barks, chirps, and screeches.

Underlying the act of speaking is the capacity for symbolic thought, a talent that, as far as we know, only *Homo sapiens* has. The human brain, unlike that of any other animal, has the capacity to transform sensory information coming from the outside world into symbols that represent, or stand for, that information. These symbols take the form of language, and it is language with which we think, that allows us to be self-aware. All animal species monitor and react to the environment outside themselves in one way or another, and they communicate with other members of their species in ways that have evolved biologically. But only humans engage in complex symbolic reasoning regarding the external environment—pondering it, constructing analogies from it, remembering it in detail, or transferring pieces of information from one context to another. Humans can give to things names that symbolically represent those things, talk about things that are not present, and explain technical procedures without having to demonstrate them. They can discuss things that happened in the past, things that are abstract, things that probably do not exist (elves, dragons, sky gods), and things that might happen in the future. Try explaining to a group of friends that you will meet them a week from Thursday at a particular address but only if it is not raining and only if they feel in the mood. Do this, however, using only gestures and sounds that a chimp might make—no speech, pictures, written notes, text messages, or props.

Equipped with language, hunters of 40,000 years ago could huddle together to plan tactics for trapping and slaughtering a herd of zebras. Mothers could explain and children understand why it would be dangerous to go near certain animals. The members of a foraging band could

Early symbols on ochre clay. About 75,000 years ago, someone made these regular marks on a piece of ochre found at the Blombos Cave paleolithic site in South Africa. The marks clearly *stand for something*. The were etched to convey meaning, though we have no idea what the engraver intended to communicate. Why might the production of symbols like this have signaled the early development of spoken language?

make rules to govern social relationships between men and women, create myths to explain how the world began, and express the feelings, desires, affections, and fears that are fundamental to human experience. Language made possible rapid innovation because knowledge of how to construct and use tools could be transmitted from group to group in symbolic form through spoken or pictorial language. For example, a more efficient type of scraping tool could be given a name and classified relative to other tools, and its usefulness could be described.

Body paint and ostrich eggshell beads. *Homo sapiens* appears to have acquired language and culture well before the peopling of the world beyond Africa got seriously under way. An archaeological site on South Africa's Cape coast called Blombos Cave has yielded material dating to between 70,000 and 110,000 years ago. The site includes fragments of human bones having modern anatomical characteristics. The cave has also revealed evidence of decidedly "modern" behavior. The people who lived there manufactured tools that suggest collective sharing of information and intense cooperation. These objects include the world's oldest known tools made of bone, including projectile points and awls (a pointed instrument for piercing holes in skins or other material).

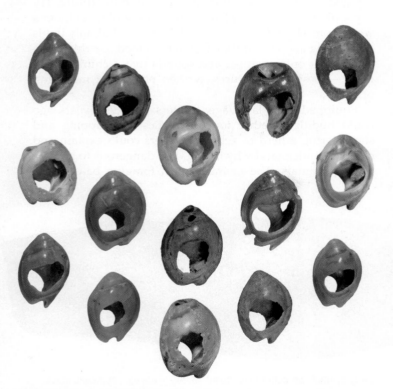

Early jewelry? These perforated shell beads dabbed with red ochre, dated to about 82,000 years ago, come from a site in northeastern Morocco. Can we safely infer that a person strung these shells together to make a necklace or bracelet? Why else might someone have cut holes in shells? What sort of messages do people communicate when they wear jewelry?

Furthermore, the Blombos Cave dwellers made objects that appear to have carried symbolic meaning. They produced pigment of ochre, a red earth that they applied in some way, perhaps as body paint that communicated something about the individual who wore it. Inhabitants also deliberately engraved pieces of ochre with hatched markings. Archaeologists have found tiny seashells intentionally pierced with holes to fashion beads. These objects have been dated to 75,000 years ago, early evidence from southern Africa of humans creating decorative ornaments. Traces of iron oxide pigment on the beads suggest that they were painted. The job of perforating small shells took time and patience, hinting at a division of labor in which at least a few people took on special jobs part of the time rather than finding and preparing food. The owner of a collection of beads worn as a bracelet or necklace likely intended to display it to others. That is, the members of a cohabiting group may have identified themselves to a "foreign" band through distinctive visual signs, or they may have sealed friendly relations with neighbors by symbolic exchange of valuable objects.

Archaeologists have unearthed tantalizing evidence of advanced technological skill and symbolic thinking at other African sites as well. In 2007, scientists working in a limestone cave in eastern Morocco announced the discovery of perforated marine shell beads that they believe are 82,000 years old. These trinkets are covered with red ochre, and some of them show wear patterns suggesting they were suspended from a cord. Other researchers have found beads nearly as old in Algeria and Israel. A site called Twilight Cave in Kenya has revealed ostrich eggshell beads dated to about 40,000 years ago. Men and women appear to have been making and wearing beads—and perhaps talking about them—from South Africa to the shores of the Mediterranean thousands of years before our species ventured to other parts of the world. In the equatorial Congo River valley, researchers have dated finely crafted stone implements, including delicate barbed points, to as many as 80,000 years ago.

Finally, evidence in stone suggests that the world history of material and cultural exchange among human groups had its beginning in eastern and southern Africa. Several digs have revealed objects of particular stone material that does not occur naturally in the area where the items were found. Excavations have turned up many objects of obsidian, a hard volcanic glass used to fashion axes, blades, and projectile points. According to geological evidence, these objects must have been brought to the site from somewhere else, in some cases from locations two hundred miles away. This means that people either carried pieces of obsidian distances significantly greater than the range of a single forager band or, more likely, that networks were being created to relay valuable objects from one band to another. It is possible that these objects were not only practical items of trade but also gifts meant to seal relationships between cooperating bands. The archaeology shows that only a tiny percentage of artifacts found in African sites had to have originated from some distant area. But from about 50,000 years ago, just when humans were migrating to far-flung parts of the planet, material exchange among Africans shows evidence of becoming increasingly voluminous and complex.

The fossils and artifacts that researchers have found in Africa for periods before 40,000 years ago are all subject to multiple and sometimes contradictory interpretations. It seems clear, however, that when humans started leaving that land mass in significant numbers, they already had a well-packed suitcase of mental, linguistic, technical, and social abilities to help them tackle the environmental challenges of new lands.

Colonizing the World

FOCUS What factors contributed to our species' successful colonization of all the world's major land masses (except Antarctica) between about 70,000 and 10,000 years ago?

Among hominin species, only *Homo sapiens* migrated to all the continents and mastered every earthly climate short of the polar ice caps. The story of how this happened is sketchy. So far, we lack the evidence to trace with much precision the routes and timing of the long migrations across Eurasia and on to Australia and the Americas. We do know, however, that between about perhaps 70,000 and 10,000

years ago, a fleeting era in the scale of evolutionary time, humans dispersed to regions as distant from one another as northwestern Europe, southern Australia, eastern Canada, and the far end of South America (see Map 1.3).

The Roads from Africa

We have evidence that as many as 115,000 years ago at least a small number of humans crossed the Sinai Peninsula from the Nile River valley to inhabit an area that is today in Israel. That foray into Southwest Asia, however, appears to have been brief; we have no evidence of movement deeper into Eurasia at that time. Genetic evidence indicates that the pioneers who initiated the sustained colonizing of Eurasia 90,000 to 70,000 years ago may have descended from people who lived along the African coast of the Red Sea in the previous 55,000 years, subsisting partly on shellfish. We cannot demonstrate that communities along that shore had rafts or canoes, but short voyages across the southern Red Sea would have taken them to the Arabian Peninsula. Forager bands making their way eastward from Arabia could have thrived, multiplied, and advanced quite rapidly (on a scale of thousands of years) because they would not have had to face radically varying ecological conditions if they kept to the Asian coastlands. Their diet of edible plants and the fruits of the sea was likely abundant and nutritious. Traces of their

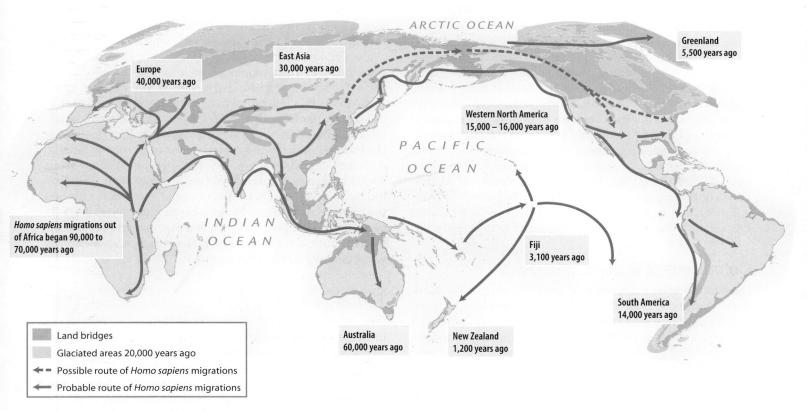

MAP 1.3 Global migrations of *Homo sapiens*.
The dates on the map are approximations. Scholars continue to debate the dates of early human movements, though the sequence and relative chronology of migrations show a fairly rapid peopling of the planet compared to the pace of previous hominin dispersals (see map 1.1). What factors might explain why humans migrating from Africa reached Australia about 20,000 years earlier than they reached Europe?

campsites and boats, however, may now lie deep under water because sea levels rose as the last ice age receded, starting about 18,000 years ago.

South to Australia

Skeletal remains discovered near Lake Mungo in southeastern Australia indicate that the earliest human colonizers reached that continent from Southeast Asia as many as 60,000 years ago. DNA research has supported this hypothesis, marking a genetic separation between Southeast Asians and the native peoples (Aborigines) of Australia 55,000 to 60,000 years ago. Pleistocene conditions in that period locked up polar ice, lowering the sea level in Southeast Asia enough to create land bridges between many of the thousands of islands that make up the Indonesian archipelago. Consequently, small migrant bands might have been able to walk west-to-east across much of the region or to island-hop short distances on log or bamboo rafts. The low sea level also conjoined Australia, New Guinea, and Tasmania into a single land mass, a bygone continent known as Sahul. If migrants reached New Guinea by making a water passage of as little as fifty miles, they could have turned south and continued "down under" on foot. Other pioneers may have followed shortly thereafter, though an initial Australian population of a few dozen men and women would have been enough to jumpstart steady population growth.

When the Pleistocene ice loosened its grip on the world, water flooded in, dividing Australia once again from New Guinea. Sahul no longer existed, but by that time humans had made Australia their own. Most scholars think that people advanced across the immense interior of the continent rather than hugging the shores. Whatever the routes taken, people colonized far southern Australia more than 35,000 years ago. Except on a stretch of the northern coast, where episodic contact between Indonesian mariners and Australians continued, the continent's forager population played out its history in isolation from the rest of the world, until Europeans came ashore in the late eighteenth century C.E.

Colonizers of Europe

Despite the brief occupation of land just east of the Mediterranean more than 100,000 years ago, modern humans did not continue into Europe or any other part of western Eurasia for another 60,000 years or so. If approximate dates now available are correct, people occupied Australia perhaps 10,000 to 20,000 years *before* they entered Europe, even though Europe is much closer to our species' African homeland. Why the long time lag? One theory is that the glacial climate of much of the Eurasian land mass between 80,000 and 40,000 years ago was biologically uninviting to *Homo sapiens*. Our relatively slim, long body type was genetically

Sophisticated tools. These five tools illustrate the remarkable technological advances that appear in the archaeological record between about 40,000 and 20,000 years ago. These implements from Europe—two hand axes, two blades, and a harpoon—are much more finely crafted than the Acheulean tools of earlier times. How might a person of the upper paleolithic equipped with language have explained to someone else the usefulness of a delicately carved barbed harpoon?

unsuited to cold climates as long as people lacked the technology to fashion warm permanent shelters or snugly fitting clothing and footwear. Neanderthals already had the run of ice age Europe, but this species had short, thick-boned bodies that more effectively retained heat.

Between 40,000 and 50,000 years ago, however, an interglacial warming trend set in. Modern humans reestablished themselves in Southwest Asia, which in that age had a greener landscape and more temperate climate than it does today. By then, moreover, their tool kit included finely crafted blades, scrapers, awls, barbed points, and other implements that helped them adapt to novel ecological conditions. In the following 20,000 years, forager bands gradually advanced northward to occupy a belt of temperate land extending from the Atlantic coast of Europe to Siberia. Although global temperatures dropped again after about 30,000 years ago, humans survived the cold with their new tools, weapons, and schemes of social cooperation. When the climate of northern Eurasia became too harsh for survival even with their new inventions, foragers simply retreated south as far as necessary. Nevertheless, *Homo sapiens* was gradually conquering winter.

The American Frontier

Like Australia, the Americas had, as far as the physical evidence shows, no hominin population until *Homo sapiens* showed up. Most experts take the view that bands of *Homo sapiens* arrived in the Americas from departure points in northeastern Asia. As material and genetic evidence has accumulated, however, questions about how and when the peopling of the Americas took place have become more puzzling, not less. For decades, paleoanthropologists conventionally argued that the earliest migrants reached North America by trekking from Siberia to Alaska. Today the Bering Strait, an oceanic passage fifty-three miles wide, separates Eurasia from America. But during the last ice age, a land bridge connected them. Named Beringia by modern geologists, this vanished isthmus supported plant and animal life, especially after global temperatures started going up around 18,000 years ago. The optimum time for forager bands to cross Beringia would have been during the following few thousand years. About 12,000 years ago (10,000 B.C.E.), Beringia surrendered to the rising sea, but by then the first Americans had established themselves and were drifting southward.

Many questions remain about the numbers and precise origins of these colonizers. From a genetic perspective, a single band of migrants including as few as four women of childbearing age could have been the founding ancestors of everyone who subsequently occupied the Americas up to 1492 C.E. However, recent fossil finds and analysis of DNA suggest that more than one wave of colonization may have taken place. Skeletal remains uncovered in Washington state, Nevada, Minnesota, Brazil, and a few other places indicate bone structures different enough from those of later American Indian populations to suggest that groups of migrants originating in different parts of Asia entered North America at different times up to about 12,000 years ago. On the other hand, recent genetic studies have linked living Native American individuals in North, Central, and South America to groups native to Siberia. This evidence suggests that a single group migrating from northeastern Asia to North America is ancestral to all Native Americans.

Peopling the Americas: Overland or by coast? Scholars conventionally have argued that humans who first arrived in Alaska subsequently migrated across the Canadian interior through a habitable corridor of green that opened up between two colossal ice sheets as global temperatures warmed. These hunters and foragers advanced south of the glaciers into thick woodlands and eventually open plains, then fanned out to eventually populate the rest of the

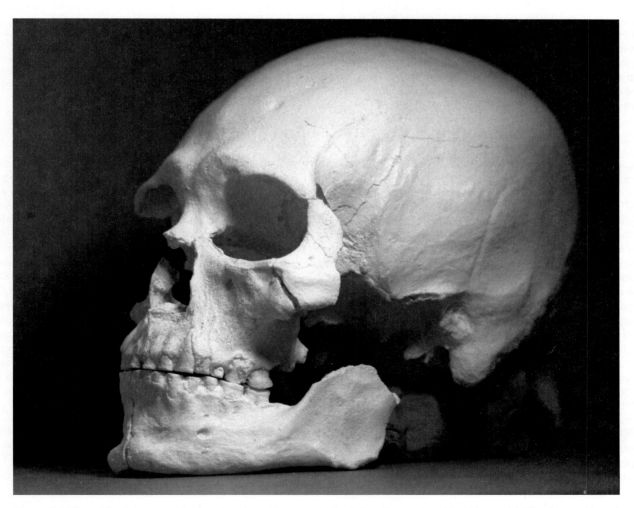

Kennewick Man. This skull, part of the remains of a 9,300-year-old North American male dubbed Kennewick Man, has suggested that humans having different physical characteristics migrated from Asia to the Americas in successive waves. This photo shows a plastic casting of the original skull, which is housed at the University of Washington in Seattle. The Weighing the Evidence box on page 36 addresses the public controversy that the discovery of Kennewick Man has caused.

The Kennewick Man Controversy

In 1996, scientists were startled to learn that a nearly complete human skeleton discovered on federal land in the shallows of the Columbia River near Kennewick, Washington, was about 9,300 years old. Kennewick Man, as he came to be known, exhibited physical features suggesting that American Indians who live in the Pacific Northwest today are not his biological descendants. The Native American Graves Protection and Repatriation Act (NAGPRA) stipulates that Indian remains discovered on federal land must be returned to local tribes for reburial. Paleoanthropologists argued, however, that such ancient bones should be subjected to extensive study. In 2004 a federal court ruled in favor of the scientists. Armand Minthorn, an Umatilla Indian leader, and Robson Bonnichsen, an anthropologist, expressed opposing views on Kennewick Man's appropriate fate.

DOCUMENT 1 Armand Minthorn, Umatilla Indian leader

Our religious beliefs, culture, and our adopted policies and procedures tell us that this individual must be re-buried as soon as possible. Our elders have taught us that once a body goes into the ground, it is meant to stay there until the end of time. . . . Under the Native American Graves Protection and Repatriation Act, tribes are allowed to file a claim to have ancestral human remains reburied. My tribe has filed a claim for this individual and when it is approved, we will rebury him and put him back to rest. . . . If this individual is truly over 9,000 years old, that only substantiates our belief that he is Native American. From our oral histories, we know that our people have been part of this land since the beginning of time. We do not believe that our people migrated here from another continent, as the scientists do. Some scientists say that if this individual is not studied further, we, as Indians, will be destroying evidence of our own history. We already know our history. It is passed on to us through our elders and through our religious practices.

Source: Armand Minthorn, "Human Remains Should be Reburied," Confederated Tribes of the Umatilla Indian Reservation, September 1996, http://www .umatilla.nsn.us/kman1.html. At the time of writing, the author was a member of the Board of Trustees and a religious leader of the Umatilla Confederated Tribes.

DOCUMENT 2 Robson Bonnichsen, anthropologist

A scientist's ability to teach effectively, to write publishable articles, to plan new research projects and to develop and test new theories is dependent upon access to the most up-to-date and accurate information possible. Unfortunately, First Americans researchers like myself are not blessed with an abundance of direct evidentiary data with which to work. Sites and artifacts from the earliest periods of American prehistory are not plentiful, and even less common are well-preserved skeletal remains and other human biological materials. Every new discovery of an early site or human skeleton is important, and each must be investigated as thoroughly and carefully as possible if we hope to ever unravel the mysteries of the peopling of the Americas.

The processes that led to human colonization of the Americas can never be understood without answers to two fundamental questions: who were the first Americans and where did they come from. Sites and artifacts can be informative, but they alone can never provide the definitive answers. People of different biological backgrounds can generate similar sites and artifacts, and people that are closely related biologically can produce very different material cultures. Only skeletal remains and other biological materials can answer questions about biological relationships.

Although the Kennewick skeleton does not date from the time of the first human colonists of the New World, it can provide important data that can be used to develop and test theories about the evolution and development of early New World human populations. The studies of the skeleton that were conducted for the Department of the Interior . . . in 1999 indicate that it does not resemble any of the modern human populations compared in those studies. Measurements and observations reported for the skeleton also indicate that while it is similar in many respects to some of the other early human skeletal remains found in North America, it also differs substantially from some of the others. Such findings, if true, could have important implications for understanding how the Americas were colonized by humans. Among other things, they could indicate that colonization of the New World may have involved multiple colonizing groups and that those groups may have originated in different regions of Eurasia.

Source: United States District Court, District of Oregon, *Bonnichsen, et al.* v. *United States of America, et al.,* Affidavit of Robson Bonnichsen, Nov, 2002. At the time of the affidavit, the author was director of the Center for the Study of the First Americans and professor of anthropology at Texas A&M University.

Thinking Critically

What underlying assumptions do you think informed these two statements, and how do those assumptions differ? Why do you think the bones of a 9,300-year-old man triggered a prolonged public controversy in the late twentieth century?

Americas. In recent years, however, experts have been paying more attention to a potentially much faster route south. Like the discoverers of Australia, the earliest American pioneers had watercraft, perhaps skin-covered boats sturdy enough to make headway along the Pacific coast. Perhaps they did not walk across Beringia at all but paddled along the northeastern coast of Asia and straight on to Alaska and the western Canadian coast. They would have made camps on islands or habitable coastal strips that the ice walls of the interior did not quite reach. Relying on coastal plants and seafood, these men and women might have had to make relatively small changes in their technology and life ways as they advanced from one latitude to the next. However, we have no physical evidence of boat-building on the Pacific coast before 6,000 years ago. Still, the coastal theory remains attractive because it offers plausible answers to perplexing questions about the timing of American colonization. A site rich in stone, bone, and ivory tools excavated in Monte Verde, Chile—10,000 miles from Beringia—has been dated to more than 14,500 years ago. How did humans make their way over such a vast distance in only a few thousand years? One possible explanation is that they migrated down the western coasts of North and South America, at least part of the way in boats.

Researchers have also speculated that humans first reached the eastern side of North America, not by migrating southward through the Canadian interior, but rather by advancing over many generations from the Pacific coast across what is now the southwestern United States to the Gulf of Mexico. From there, they could have moved into the woodlands east of the Mississippi and south of the retreating glaciers. In the last few years, archaeologists have found stone blades, choppers, and projectile points at a complex of sites called Buttermilk Creek in the hills north of Austin, Texas. A dating technique that measures light energy lodged in

minerals in the soil around the artifacts has revealed that people were making tools at Buttermilk Creek as long as 15,500 years ago. The ancestors of these early Texans may have migrated eastward from the Pacific coast. The evidence is controversial, but excavations at Meadowcroft Rockshelter in southwestern Pennsylvania suggest that people lived there as many as 16,000 years ago, cooking meat and fashioning flint blades. A site called Cactus Hill in southeastern Virginia has yielded tools and bits of charcoal hinting that people whose forebears migrated from the west reached a point only about seventy miles from the Atlantic Ocean 15,000 years ago.

Why Did *Homo Sapiens* People the Earth?

Most animal species occupy only certain parts of the world. Humans, by contrast, are biologically cosmopolitan—they live just about everywhere. Why did this happen? We would not be thinking historically if we presumed that people occupied all the continents because human beings have an inherent urge to "explore new lands." Local communities, whether foragers or farmers, historically have tended to live out their lives within a single confined territory as long as they had reasonable security and a sufficient food supply. On the other hand, they have also had to calculate continuously an acceptable balance between the resources their local environment could provide and their prospects for survival. In paleolithic times, periodic shortages, climatic fluctuations, and competition from human or animal predators must have obliged cooperating bands to be ready to move down the coast or over the next hill when they might otherwise have preferred to stay put.

Population growth was almost certainly a key factor in global colonization. Genetic studies suggest that, as recently

Archaeologists at Buttermilk Creek. Researchers working at the Buttermilk Creek complex in Texas have in recent years found a deep level of artifacts suggesting human occupation of the region nearly two and a half thousand years earlier than previously known.

as 70,000 years ago, the total *Homo sapiens* population, all of it in Africa, may have numbered as few as 10,000 individuals. Scientists have theorized that long periods of cold temperatures and arid conditions may have kept humankind on the edge of extinction. Fortunately for us, numbers started climbing again. Estimates vary widely, but total population may have risen to about 300,000 by 30,000 years ago and to perhaps 6 million by 10,000 years ago.

Population growth and human migration were closely interrelated. The very climatic conditions that taxed human ingenuity for survival may have stimulated creative responses to environmental stress, including more effective social cooperation, the invention of new tools, and language development. These improvements permitted groups searching for resources to penetrate lands where conditions were hotter, colder, higher, drier, or in some way different from what could have been tolerated in earlier ages. Also, regional climates continued to fluctuate somewhat, producing ecological alterations serious enough to force communal

bands to abandon deteriorating habitats for new ones offering a better chance of survival. A band of just twenty or thirty men, women, and children required an extensive area within which to hunt, fish, or collect plants. If the group got too big, routines of social cooperation and sharing might break down. One way to avoid social strain was to permit some members of the group to move to another neighborhood to start a new band. As groups divided over and over again, the range of human colonization expanded steadily. Cooperating bands therefore neither wandered aimlessly nor set off on long-distance explorations. Rather, they budded off from one another, advancing into new territory to fulfill very short-term goals to survive and reproduce.

Homo Sapiens:
The Last Surviving Hominin

When *Homo sapiens* started its long journey around the world, did other hominin species still exist? Certainly

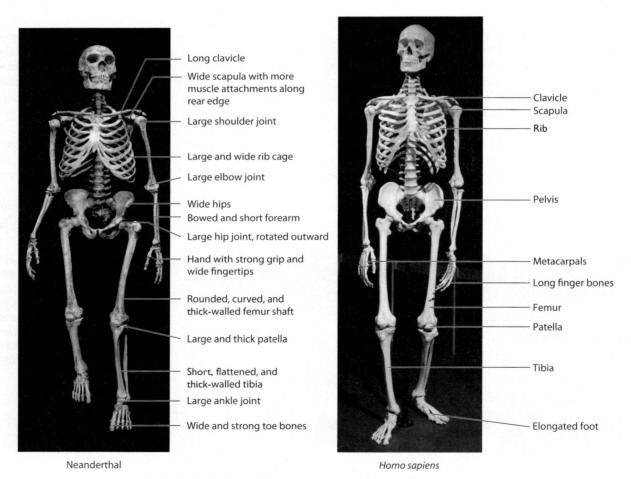

Neanderthal

Long clavicle
Wide scapula with more muscle attachments along rear edge
Large shoulder joint

Large and wide rib cage
Large elbow joint

Wide hips
Bowed and short forearm
Large hip joint, rotated outward

Hand with strong grip and wide fingertips

Rounded, curved, and thick-walled femur shaft

Large and thick patella

Short, flattened, and thick-walled tibia
Large ankle joint

Wide and strong toe bones

Homo sapiens

Clavicle
Scapula
Rib

Pelvis

Metacarpals
Long finger bones

Femur
Patella

Tibia

Elongated foot

Neanderthal and *Homo sapiens* compared. In general, Neanderthals had wider, stockier, shorter bodies than our own species. This physique would have helped them conserve body heat in northern ice age climate. Modern humans were on the whole taller and leaner than Neanderthals, but they also became more proficient at fabricating warm clothes. What factors might explain why we have remains of many more Neanderthal individuals (several hundred of them) than we have of earlier hominin species like *Homo erectus*?

Neanderthals and Denisovans did, probably Floresians, and possibly *Homo erectus*. Recent dating of bones discovered on Java in Indonesia suggests that *Homo erectus* survived, at least in that part of the world, until 50,000 years ago or later. If that is true, our species might have met *Homo erectus* bands and even lived alongside them for a time. At some point *Homo erectus* disappeared, probably because modern humans deployed their amazing mental tools to outwit, outcompete, and outpopulate it.

Scholars generally agree that *Homo sapiens* and Neanderthal groups occupied parts of Southwest Asia and Europe at the same time. The two species had similar stone tool kits for thousands of years, and archaeologists have unearthed tool sites in Europe suggesting that Neanderthals adopted, copied, and even traded for refined tools that modern humans first introduced. Scientists sequenced the Neanderthal genome in 2010, and since then evidence has accumulated showing that humans of non-African origin share as much as 4 percent of their DNA with Neanderthals. This finding indicates that the two species interbred, perhaps in Southwest Asia. These couplings may have occurred rarely, and we have no idea whether they took place in circumstances of friendly intimacy or violent aggression. Some scholars have suggested that since Neanderthals achieved biological adaption to the European disease environment long before *Homo sapiens* arrived there, they may have contributed elements

to our genome that provided immunities against certain cold-climate maladies.

In any case, as *Homo sapiens* bands fanned across Europe in the millennia after 40,000 years ago, they gradually pushed surviving Neanderthals off to the margins of good foraging land. When glaciers advanced and temperatures dropped again about 30,000 years ago, humans proved technologically better equipped than Neanderthals to survive in more northerly parts of Europe. Scientists have also proposed that Neanderthal males and females hunted together and, contrary to humans, never developed a division of labor in which females spent more time gathering plants, hunting small game near camp, and nurturing children, a diversification of activities that may have allowed cooperating bands to grow in size and density. Still another theory argues that Neanderthals had "antisocial" inclinations. They formed small hunting bands that had little to do with one another, whereas human groups, endowed with wagging tongues, interacted more congenially and over longer distances, thereby accelerating the process of collective learning for the species as a whole. Recent tool finds near Gibraltar indicate that the Iberian Peninsula was the last, hopeless refuge of *Homo neanderthalensis*. The species vanishes from the record about 26,000 years ago.

As for the Denisovans, genetic analysis of the Siberian girl's pinky finger demonstrates that this species also mated

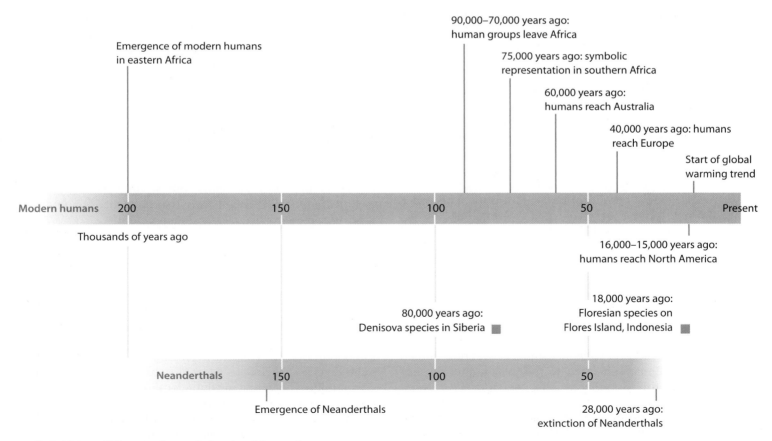

Early history of *Homo sapiens* and close hominin cousins.

with humans. About 3 percent of the genes of people living in Papua New Guinea in Southeast Asia, as well as a much smaller percentage of the DNA of living Chinese, reveal Denisovan ancestry. As in the Neanderthal case, however, scientists can only speculate about where and under what circumstances these sexual episodes took place. And like Neanderthals, the Denisovans vanished. Perhaps archaeological evidence of this species' existence, other than a finger bone and two teeth, will one day turn up.

Why People Look Different

The genes of all human beings are 99.9 percent identical; in fact we share 96–99 percent of our genetic code with chimpanzees. Because of variation within the remaining 0.1 percent, however, all individuals in the world are genetically unique. Our species has evolved in a way that has produced a few broad but observable physical differences between large aggregates of people whose ancestors have lived in different parts of the world and have tended to mate with one another much more often than they have mated with people who live far away. We particularly notice these differences between populations whose forebears lived in starkly different climatic zones. Minor differences in traits, such as skin and hair color, eye shape, nose width, and body type, are the result of either adaptations to particular physical and natural environments or simply random genetic variations. For example, humans who colonized northern Europe evolved skin color lighter than peoples of tropical lands partly because of an ancient and natural deficiency of vitamin D in the basic foods that northerners consumed. Lighter skin allowed greater penetration of the sun's ultraviolet rays, which enhanced the body's own production of vitamin D, thereby decreasing vulnerability to the crippling disease known as rickets. Similarly, the epicanthic fold, that is, an overlap of skin that covers the inner corner of the upper eyelid and is characteristic of people native to northeastern Eurasia, is likely an evolutionary adaptation to northern climate and latitude. Natural selection favored the inner eye fold because it protected people who had it against long summer light, cold, and swirling dust.

Differences like these have in no *biological* way hindered the ability of Sumatrans, Norwegians, Mongols, and Congolese to talk, live, work, and reproduce together. Although the word *race* and its variants are used today to express a variety of social and cultural meanings, respectable scientists and historians have abandoned the notion that separating humankind into a fixed number of separate "races," whether three of them or three hundred, has any useful biological significance. Genetic differences among human groups are minute compared to the total number of our genes. These tiny differences must therefore have developed, not millions of years ago, but in connection with the relatively recent peopling of the world from eastern Africa. As one scientist has put it, "We are all members of a very young species, and our genes betray this secret."[4]

Global Culture of the Upper Paleolithic

FOCUS How may we account for the acceleration of cultural and social change in human societies between about 40,000 and 12,000 years ago?

"We are what we wear," the saying goes. In other words, we send messages about ourselves by the way we drape and decorate our bodies. We paint our faces, wear trousers of a particular cut, and hang golden objects from our ears to communicate to others where we think we fit in the social universe. Humans, we have seen, may have begun to express symbolically their distinctiveness as individuals or as members of groups more than 80,000 years ago by wearing bead necklaces or painting themselves with ochre. This elaboration of human culture is likely to have happened in association with the acquisition of language. In the ensuing tens of thousands of years, human talent for symbolic expression through spoken words, gestures, and visual symbols probably developed gradually, exclusively in Africa at first, then wherever in the world *Homo sapiens* migrated.

Between 40,000 and 30,000 years ago, just when the Pleistocene was heading into its last cycle of extreme cold, the pace of cultural change began to speed up and human society moved in the direction of greater complexity. We know from an ever-growing body of fossil and other material evidence that in the upper paleolithic era (40,000–12,000 years ago) global population rose at a faster rate than ever before, tool kits became more varied and sophisticated, cooperating groups in some regions grew larger and more socially intricate, and symbolic imagery in the form of statues, cave paintings, and abstract designs multiplied. People began to adorn both themselves and the bodies of their dead with necklaces, pendants, bracelets, garment pins, and a multitude of other objects made from stone, bone, shell, or ivory. We will probably never understand much about the symbolic meaning that men and women attached to the decorative objects left to us from the upper paleolithic. But the urge to bedeck and beautify was an elemental part of the emergence of humankind as a species of exquisitely complex culture.

Dawn of a Multicultural World

Because ways of life dependent on gathering, hunting, or fishing had several common elements (limitations on the size of social groups, for example), human culture in the paleolithic had a certain uniformity. However, as global numbers inched upward and people adapted to a wider range of natural environments, cultural expression worldwide became more diverse. The archaeological record makes it clear that communities inhabiting far-flung localities gradually developed distinctively different ways of doing things—designing tools, building houses, or carving animal images in stone.

Owing to the complex collective learning that language made possible, practical ideas for improving tools, shelters, or food sources flowed more widely and rapidly from one group to another. Population growth within a region meant that strangers were likely to live closer to one another and therefore interact more intensively. There is no doubt that encounters between bands sometimes produced rock and spear fights. For example, many of the human remains found in a 14,000-year-old graveyard at Jebel Sahaba (JAH-bahl sa-HAH-bah) on the Nile River show signs of people having been stabbed or clubbed to death. It is also certain, on the other hand, that strangers met together peaceably to share technical information, news about food sources, or hunting and fishing lore.

Regional networks for bartering food, tools, or ornaments also became more elaborate than they had been in their earlier, exclusively African settings. Groups organized exchange networks to barter ivory, seashells, sharks' teeth, high-grade flint, and other practical or ornamental objects. For example, archaeologists digging in upper paleolithic sites in southern Europe have found yellow amber that originated near the Baltic Sea coast hundreds of miles to the north. Forager bands may also have exchanged exotic items as part of rituals to reinforce bonds of feeling and memory among their members, that is, to encourage enduring social relations among people who did not see one another very often. In short, as groups came face to face with new things from far away, they rejected some innovations and accepted or modified others, depending on their own needs and tastes. In these ways, localized populations became more culturally differentiated from their neighbors.

Social and Economic Life

Thirty thousand years ago, all human communities made their livings gathering, hunting, or fishing wild food. A co-operating band typically numbered twenty to thirty individuals but might run to one hundred depending on the local ecosystem. Bands might have been relatively large in western Eurasia where they hunted wild horses, cattle, or bison by driving them over cliffs or into swamps and then slaughtering them in a single operation. This strategy would not work well without a substantial force of men, women, and children to chase, kill, and dress the prey. By contrast, bands that inhabited deserts, high mountain valleys, or other marginally productive regions had to be small enough to maintain a workable balance between local resources and mouths to feed.

The members of a foraging band had to work together intently because upper paleolithic life was too dangerous and unpredictable to permit selfish, go-it-alone behavior. By that era, young men and women of childbearing age almost certainly bonded permanently to produce families. The way animal bones are distributed in some sites in Europe suggests that families within a band shared food with one another. Certainly some men and women stood out as natural group leaders. In fact, evidence dating back at least 25,000 years indicates that communities buried some corpses with especially numerous and refined ornaments or other grave goods. This suggests that certain people had special status and that social differences based on leadership, good fortune, ritual expertise, or spiritual insight were beginning to emerge.

The division of labor within the band, that is, the distribution of economic tasks among members, was uncomplicated. Adult men probably had the job of ranging beyond the immediate neighborhood of the camp to forage or hunt. Women who were pregnant or had small children to look after collected edible plants or small animals close to home. Bands organized work this way, not because males were anatomically larger and stronger than females, but more likely because hunting large animals was hazardous. The death of a woman of childbearing age was in principle a greater threat to the survival of the group than was the death of a man. A hunter also had to move quickly and quietly, something a female carrying a small child could hardly manage. A woman, on the other hand, could gather berries, tubers, and other plants close to home with children in tow.

Certainly, the old cliché of Stone Age Man as macho hunter, killing saber-toothed tigers and dragging them home for the evening meal, is far off the mark. At sites in central Europe, for example, archaeologists have found fragments of pollen and processed vegetable matter suggesting that people ate a remarkably wide variety of plant foods. And small game such as birds, rodents, and even insects may have made up a much larger part of a band's diet than did grizzly bear or giant sloth. Excavations in Europe have also uncovered pieces of clay impressed with crisscrossed strands of fiber. These specimens, dating back more than 25,000 years, hint that women wove nets to catch small game.

The extent to which foragers relied on animal protein depended largely on ecological circumstances. In the cooler latitudes of both Eurasia and North America, for example, a relatively heavy meat diet compensated for the comparatively short plant-producing summers and for the loss of body heat in the cold months. Northern Eurasians especially prized reindeer, which provided hides and antler bone as well as meat. Nearer the end of the upper paleolithic, when temperatures rose again, some western Eurasian peoples turned increasingly to a fish-centered diet. By about 14,000 years ago, communities were forming along rivers or seacoasts where they thrived on salmon and other big fish, using specialized techniques to net, dry, and smoke their catch. This economy encouraged groups to stay in one place a long time and may have permitted relatively larger bands to thrive. On the expansive plains of North America, hunters became expert at following bison herds. By about 11,000 years ago, they were fashioning sharp, finely shaped projectile points and mounting them on long spears. This weapons technology, which is associated with an assemblage of stone tools referred to as Clovis (after a site near Clovis, New Mexico), spread remarkably fast from Canada to Central America.

Humans preyed on reindeer and bison without sending them to extinction, but they may have had a hand in the disappearance of dozens of large animal species from the face of the earth. Mammoths in Inner Eurasia, large marsupials in Australia, and mammoths, horses, camels, and giant ground sloths in the Americas all vanished during the upper paleolithic. Perhaps these doomed species failed to adapt to the globe's climatic warming trend after 18,000 years ago, though numerous temperature cycles had occurred during the previous 2 million years without such fatal consequences for big species. Could skill and social coordination in the hunt have been so ruthless and efficient that people wiped out whole classes of animals in the course of several thousand years? Even if large animals initially had no natural instincts to run away from humans, it seems improbable that hunter bands would have systematically slaughtered certain animals simply because they had the technology to do it. Nevertheless, humans evolved a much greater variety of collective skills and strategies than any other animal species. They were establishing themselves at the top of the food chain and starting to have a noticeable impact on other life-forms, particularly ones good to eat.

Technical Wonders

One of the marvels of the late ice age is that when global temperatures started dropping about 30,000 years ago, humans became more inventive than ever. In northern Eurasia the key to survival was keeping body temperature up. Many communities endured by huddling in ice-free valleys or in caves and rock shelters. In eastern Europe and Inner Eurasia, cohabiting groups built tents of skins fitted over wood or animal-bone frames. Sites uncovered near the Don River in Russia, for example, have revealed hamlets where the residents dug "pit houses," then ringed them with mammoth bones and covered these structures with hides. They kept hearth fires going continuously and preserved meat in "freezers" dug in the cold earth.

Early colonizers of northerly latitudes draped themselves in leather and fur, as their Neanderthal cousins did. Recently, archaeologists have found fibers of flax (the plant from which linen is made) in the Republic of Georgia dating to 34,000 years ago. Some of these strands were twisted and others were dyed, suggesting that the occupiers of the site were fashioning ropes, baskets, or clothing. About 20,000 years ago, some clever individual invented the needle. Made of bone or ivory, this simple device spread quickly and was used to fashion custom-fitted trousers, shirts, parkas, hoods, and boots. Lengths of fiber cord served as thread and also material for snares, nets, tethers, handles, and binders. Upper paleolithic carvings show women wearing string skirts. One scholar argues that the "string revolution" was one of the most important technical breakthroughs of the era.[5]

Keeping warm in the Ukraine.
Shelters fashioned from the bones of mammoths, and probably covered with hides, are among the earliest known built structures. A farmer enlarging the cellar of his house in the western Ukraine in 1965 found a jawbone that led to the discovery of this circular hut. It dates to about 15,000 years ago.

Another key innovation was a "core," or chunk of rock, flint, or other fine-grained stone from which a worker could strike off rough blades. These "blanks" were then fashioned into specialized tools depending on the job at hand. A particular type of carving blade, for example, might be used to fashion bone or antler into an even more specialized device such as a spearhead, fish hook, or harpoon. Hunter-gatherer bands of Inner Eurasia and northern China developed a sophisticated kit of exquisite **microliths,** tiny blades that could be attached to handles and used as spears, scrapers, or knives. Similarly, hunters in North America struck blades off flint cores to make their elegant Clovis spear points.

> **microlith** A small blade of flaked stone used as a tool.

In tropical latitudes, upper paleolithic remains are sparser, partly because warmer, rainier climates provided abundant wood and fiber, an "organic" technology that long ago rotted away and vanished from the historical record. In southern China and Southeast Asia, for example, people continued to use relatively unrefined stone chopping tools for thousands of years. But they probably also invented tools of bamboo, a plant that is superbly suited for making strong, resilient objects, including spears, knives, scrapers, baskets, and even houses and boats. Bamboo may have contributed as much to the growth of human populations in East and Southeast Asia as stone blades did in regions nearer the glaciers.

A World of Symbols

We may define the art of the upper paleolithic fundamentally as the objects or images that women and men made to represent their world symbolically. Art bloomed in myriad styles and materials—paintings on cave and rock shelter walls, carved figures of humans and animals, and geometric patterns etched on bone. Even the sound of music was heard. More than thirty flutelike instruments made of long hollow bone and equipped with finger holes have been found in western Eurasia dated to roughly 37,000 years ago. Wherever people lived, they took advantage of the local materials and opportunities they had at hand. Wall painting, for example, is concentrated heavily in northern Spain and southwestern France where deep limestone caves provided "gallery space" protected from rain and wind. In eastern Europe, by contrast, cave shelters are rare, so people commonly carved small, portable figurines.

Trying to explain the meanings that paleolithic men and women attached to painting, sculpture, stone carvings, or music is always risky because so much depends on the cultural context of the work, about which we know little, and on the presumptions we ourselves bring to the interpretation. The meaning of a piece of twenty-first-century art may be problematic enough, much less the chiseling and daubing of people who lived 20,000 years ago. We can hardly do more than speculate on the aesthetic, social, or spiritual intentions of individuals who drew pictures of bison galloping across rock shelter walls, painted images of human hands, or carved mysterious spiral patterns on pieces of bone. Take, for example, the hundreds of "Venus" figurines found in sites scattered across Eurasia from western Europe to Siberia, one from Germany dating to at least 35,000 years ago. The best-known samples of these have exaggerated breasts and buttocks. Were these female statues sex objects for men? This interpretation used to be popular but has few advocates today. Were the figures symbols of female fertility, and if so, did the symbolic power appeal to men, women, or both? Were they part of a symbolic system by which women shared rituals with one another? Did their meaning vary from one region to another? This debate will continue for a long time.

A panoramic view of upper paleolithic art suggests some general trends. First, as cohabiting bands interacted over increasing distances, artistic forms and styles, as well as the material objects themselves, spread from one region to another. That is, networks of shared symbols became more

Venus of Lespugue. This female figurine dating to between 24,000 and 26,000 years ago comes from a cave in southwestern France. The back view reveals a string skirt attached to a hip belt. Since this is not a very practical piece of clothing, why might an upper paleolithic woman have worn one?

Art in the cave of Chauvet. In 1994 three spelunkers discovered marvelous art like this on the walls of chambers deep in a cave in southern France. Compared with other paleolithic cave art, the Chauvet paintings, dating to about 31,000 years ago, are unusual for their depiction of large wild animals like this rhinoceros and for the artists' use of shading and perspective. What specific artistic features do you notice in this work?

widespread. A second pattern is that art was increasingly important to ritual life, including initiation ceremonies for adolescents, mating rites, funerals, and appeals to supernatural powers to protect the community. For example, one group of nameless folk who lived in southern Europe 15,000 years ago took the trouble to crawl far back into the dark bowels of a cave to carve clay statuettes of bison that hardly anyone was ever likely to see. Surely, there was complex ritual purpose here, not just amusement or "art for art's sake." A third pattern is that people decorated their bodies more and more elaborately to express their social identity, as we do today. Cooperating bands might also have festooned themselves in special ways to signal to other groups whether they were friend or foe. That is, paleolithic decoration was an early expression of ethnic identity.

We have no material artifacts at all to help us know how spoken languages sounded. We may assume that as groups split off and moved apart from one another, the common language they once spoke became in time differentiated in vocabulary and grammatical structure. Consequently, distinct languages, that is, speech systems that were mutually unintelligible, began to multiply. By studying the structural relationships between languages and their distribution in the world today, scholars have formulated theories to explain how and when early forms of those languages, and the people who spoke them, migrated from one part of the world to another. We know, for example, that most American Indian languages may be grouped together in a family known as Amerind and that the relationships and distribution patterns among languages in this family indicate that speakers of them initially migrated from North America to South America, not the other way around. For periods before about 8000 B.C.E., however, conclusions about human movements drawn from linguistic data alone are necessarily sketchy and tentative.

People of the upper paleolithic era clearly communicated in complex, nuanced languages and visual symbols. A material discovery in Southwest Asia in the mid-1990s, however, has shaken conventional theories of just how sophisticated cultural expression had become among foragers in at least one part of the world. On a hill called Göbekli Tepe (goh-behk-LEE teh-peh), overlooking a plain in southeastern

Göbekli Tepe. The site of this astonishingly early stone monument in southeastern Turkey features massive, T-shaped pillars. Because some of the pillars have human limbs carved on them, archaeologists assume they represent human beings, perhaps deities or priests. People deliberately buried the entire complex around 2,000 years after it was built. Why might they have done that?

Turkey, archaeologists have found the site of an elaborate temple complex dating to as many as 12,000 years ago (10,000 B.C.E.). There, people whose identities we will never know constructed a series of stone circles, at least seven of them and perhaps several more, on a twenty-five-acre site. These structures feature stone walls surrounding T-shaped pillars as much as eighteen feet tall ornamented with intricately detailed carvings of animal figures—cattle, lions, leopards, foxes, ducks, snakes, ants, and spiders. Many of the pillars have humanlike shapes, including arms, shoulders, and elbows, though none have faces.

The site has astonished scholars because no construction of such size and complexity appears anywhere else in the world's archaeological record until thousands of years later. Researchers generally agree that Göbekli Tepe had a ritual function. Bones on the site suggest animal sacrifice.

The humanlike pillars indicate representation of gods or goddesses, and the carved animals may have mythic or religious significance. There is no evidence that people who frequented the stone circles practiced agriculture or permanently resided in the vicinity. Rather, foraging groups appear to have converged on the site from many miles around at particular times of the year. This suggests that as many as 12,000 years ago forager populations shared religious beliefs and practices on a regional scale. A religious elite may also have existed because someone must have organized at least several hundred people to haul giant blocks of stone from quarries at least a quarter-mile away from where they were installed. About 10,000 years ago, people abandoned the site and deliberately covered it with soil, as if to suggest that they were finished with the old gods and temples and wanted new ones.

• • •

Conclusion

The peopling of all the great land masses except Antarctica was the first world-scale event in the history of our species. Practical, short-range objectives to find food and secure the survival of the cohabiting group impelled the initial global colonization mile by mile. Humans had no long-range knowledge of where they might be going, nor any consciousness of a destiny to colonize the world. Nevertheless, they accomplished the feat, walking or paddling all the way, in as little as 40,000 years after the first migrants left Africa for points east.

Settling the planet would have taken far longer if our species had not possessed language and the multiplying opportunities for collective learning—accumulating, sharing, and transmitting knowledge—which followed from that special talent. The material record of similarities in tools, shelter construction, and artistic styles within broad regions hints at exchanges among groups on a large territorial scale.

Encounters between strangers took place when a small band split off from a larger one, when a bartering expedition traveled far from home, or when some natural calamity forced migration to uncharted territory. As a result of tens of thousands of such encounters over generations, the "cultural capital" of useful ideas, techniques, symbols, and words generally accumulated for everyone.

Human cultural life appears to have emerged gradually in the past 100,000 years. Then, from about 40,000 years ago, it started to accelerate in its complexity, as we know from the proliferation of symbolic objects and images. Perhaps the stark conditions of the last ice age, whether high-latitude cold or tropical drought, propelled communities to devise ever more ingenious ways to make a living, organize social life, and share ideas. Then the interglacial warming that followed obliged our species to confront a whole new range of environmental perils and challenges.

• • •

Key Terms

australopithecines 23
bipedal 23
collective learning 31
Göbekli Tepe 44
Holocene 27

hominin 23
Homo erectus 21
Homo ergaster 24
Homo sapiens 21
ice age 27

interglacial 27
microlith 43
Neanderthal 28
paleoanthropologist 24
paleolithic 24

Change over Time

7 million years ago	Biological separation occurs between hominins and the ancestors of modern chimpanzees.
4.4–3 million years ago	Evidence of australopithecine species in eastern Africa appears.
2.5–2 million years ago	Evidence of stone toolmaking in eastern Africa appears, initiating the paleolithic era.
2 million years ago	Several hominin species coexist in Africa.
1.9 million–800,000 years ago	*Homo ergaster/Homo erectus* hominin species migrate across Eurasia.
200,000–28,000 years ago	The Neanderthal species flourishes in Europe and Southwest Asia.
200,000–150,000 years ago	*Homo sapiens* (anatomically modern humans) evolves in Africa as a distinct species.
100,000–75,000 years ago	Humans in Africa show evidence of symbolic thought.
90,000–70,000 years ago	Human groups begin to move from Africa into Eurasia.
40,000–12,000 years ago	An accelerating pace of tool invention, artistic creativity, and social experimentation marks the start of the upper (or late) paleolithic period.
14,500 years ago	Human groups reach the southern third of South America.
12,000 years ago	Göbekli Tepe temple complex is constructed in Southwest Asia.

Please see end of book reference section for additional reading suggestions related to this chapter.

Farms, Cities, and the New Agrarian Age
10,000–2000 B.C.E.

Jewelry of gold, carnelian, and lapis lazuli from the Royal Cemetery of Ur, southern Iraq, about 2600 B.C.E.

apis lazuli is an opaque, intensely blue semiprecious gemstone that sparkles with tiny flecks of gold. Polished stones make elegant jewelry, and a powdered form of lapis was the basis of ultramarine, a pigment prized by artists before the advent of synthetic paints. Lapis is mined today in a number of countries, but the most beautiful stone comes from mines in the mountains of northwestern Afghanistan. Trade in lapis dates to the fourth millennium B.C.E. (3999–3000 B.C.E.), if not earlier, and the workings in Afghanistan, together with a site in southwestern Pakistan, may be the oldest continually operating gem mines in history. Lapis was likely an object of gift exchange among early farmers, and by the third millennium B.C.E., it began to appear in the households and burial chambers of the rulers of city-states and kingdoms in Mesopotamia, Egypt, and the Indus River valley. Archeologists excavating the tomb of Pu-Abi, an important woman in the ancient Mesopotamian city of Ur in the twenty-sixth century B.C.E., uncovered a stunning collection of grave goods, including jewelry studded with lapis that could only have come from mines hundreds of miles to the east. Within a few more centuries, a lapis exchange network extended 1,600 miles from the Indus to the Nile.

We saw in Chapter 1 that trade among forager bands had its origins deep in the paleolithic era. But after about 10,000 B.C.E., webs of barter and gift-giving in copper, gold, silver, shells, gemstones, and fabricated products expanded rapidly in several regions of Afroeurasia. This quickening of human exchange happened in association with a sharp upward trend in world population and, in some places, a surge in the size, number, and density of human settlements. The invention of farming made both of these developments possible.

The emergence of a world of farms, cities, and commerce is a recent episode in the history of our species. Anatomically modern humans lived exclusively by hunting and foraging for about 200,000 years, and in *biological* terms, *Homo sapiens* may be best suited to live in tiny communities, eat nutritious food found in the wild, walk a lot, and sit on the ground. During those two hundred millennia, however, our species also acquired the gift of language. With it, humans gained a talent for collective learning, the ability, which no other animal has ever had, to share, accumulate, store, and transmit complex knowledge about themselves and the world around them.

After about 10,000 B.C.E. (12,000 years ago), humans in a few parts of the world began to apply their collective learning skills to the problem of *producing* food rather than merely gathering or hunting whatever nature provided. Over a span of several thousand years, some communities shifted to a way of life that involved deliberately planting, nurturing, and harvesting food crops, as well as confining and protecting animals in order to use them for ritual sacrifice, food, fiber, and bone. This chapter introduces the early era of farming, a startling change in human history, and the spread of this radically new way of living to several regions of the world.

Farming could dramatically increase a community's food supply, offering nourishment for many more individuals than a foraging territory of the same size could provide. Consequently, between 10,000 and 4000 B.C.E., the population in certain parts of the world rose faster than it ever had before, and permanent settlements grew larger and closer together. Social relations among families and settlements became more intricate; leaders emerged who wielded serious authority over the community; technologies increased in sophistication; and trade expanded. The first section of this chapter

Chapter Outline

THE COMING OF FARMERS: A PECULIAR EVENT

Early Farming and the Big Thaw
The Drift toward Domestication
Neolithic Innovations
The Spread of Agrarian Societies
Sunrise over the Village
Super Villages

INDIVIDUALS MATTER Ötzi: A Neolithic Traveler

EARLY COMPLEX SOCIETIES

Irrigation and Complex Society
in Mesopotamia
Complex Society on the Nile

WEIGHING THE EVIDENCE A Pharaoh's Warning
in Stone

Harappan Society in the Indus Valley
Interregional Communication and Commerce
Complex Societies and the Environment

• • •

examines these developments, especially in the region between the Mediterranean basin in the west and South Asia in the east.

From about 4000 B.C.E., the pace of change began to accelerate even faster in farm communities of that broad region. People moved together into settlements that in some places numbered many thousands. Some individuals stopped growing or collecting food altogether in order to specialize in making useful products, supervising other people's work, keeping public order, or communicating with powerful gods to keep them happy and cooperative. The culture of equality that characterized small forager bands or small farm communities gave way to formal social divisions based on wealth, spiritual prestige, special skill, or the power to command armed followers. In the second part of the chapter, we explore the development of complex societies—a new and multifaceted way to organize human communities—which we conventionally call "civilizations." The earliest societies of this type arose between the fourth and third millennia B.C.E. in three river valleys: the Tigris-Euphrates in Mesopotamia (modern Iraq), the Nile in Egypt, and the Indus in modern Pakistan and northwestern India. We investigate these three societies in a comparative frame, focusing on the geographical and ecological conditions under which they emerged and the distinguishing

A Panoramic View

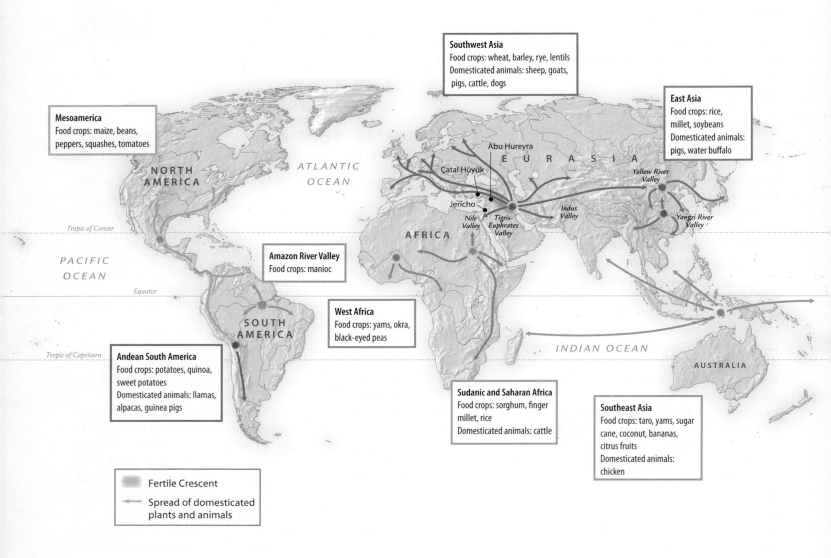

Southwest Asia
Food crops: wheat, barley, rye, lentils
Domesticated animals: sheep, goats, pigs, cattle, dogs

East Asia
Food crops: rice, millet, soybeans
Domesticated animals: pigs, water buffalo

Mesoamerica
Food crops: maize, beans, peppers, squashes, tomatoes

Amazon River Valley
Food crops: manioc

West Africa
Food crops: yams, okra, black-eyed peas

Andean South America
Food crops: potatoes, quinoa, sweet potatoes
Domesticated animals: llamas, alpacas, guinea pigs

Sudanic and Saharan Africa
Food crops: sorghum, finger millet, rice
Domesticated animals: cattle

Southeast Asia
Food crops: taro, yams, sugar cane, coconut, bananas, citrus fruits
Domesticated animals: chicken

Fertile Crescent

Spread of domesticated plants and animals

NORTH AMERICA · ATLANTIC OCEAN · PACIFIC OCEAN · Tropic of Cancer · Equator · SOUTH AMERICA · Tropic of Capricorn · AFRICA · EURASIA · INDIAN OCEAN · AUSTRALIA · Abu Hureyra · Çatal Hüyük · Jericho · Nile Valley · Tigris-Euphrates Valley · Indus Valley · Yellow River Valley · Yangzi River Valley

MAP 2.1 Early domestication and the spread of agriculture.

Humans domesticated food plants and animals independently in several parts of the world. What geographical or climatic factors may have contributed to plant or animal domestication in each of these eight regions?

cultural styles they all developed in their formative centuries. These societies also made trade and cultural connections with one another that affected the histories of them all. Finally, they achieved sufficient size and collective skill to manipulate their natural and physical environments on a much larger scale than humans had ever done before.

The Coming of Farmers: A Peculiar Event

FOCUS Why did humans in several parts of the world take up farming, given that our species had survived without it for 200,000 years?

The activity we call farming refers specifically to the technical process of *producing* food in a systematic way by planting, tending, and harvesting edible plants and by grazing domesticated animals on pasture. These new methods allowed humans to capture and consume much more of the sun's energy, the source of all plant life, than in earlier times. But coaxing food energy and surplus wealth from the soil involved more than tools and techniques. Woven into the activity are social habits, moral rules, and supernatural beliefs. Until the start of the industrial age barely more than 200 years ago, all complex societies were **agrarian societies,** based on farming as the primary way of life. And like the earlier colonization of the world, farming emerged as a consequence of human beings making countless everyday decisions century after century, though no one at the time could see where these experiments might be taking our species.

agrarian society A society in which agriculture, including both crop production and animal breeding, is the foundation of both subsistence and surplus wealth.

The current state of archeological evidence points to Southwest Asia as the site of the earliest communities that grew cereals, especially wheat, barley, and rye, as well as lentils, chickpeas (garbanzo beans), and a few other legumes. At Abu Hureyra (A-boo hoo-RAIR-a) on the Euphrates River in north central Syria, archaeologists have found large, plump seeds of domesticated rye that date to about 12,000 years ago—the oldest known trace of farming in the world. Other agrarian settlements that emerged in the following millennium or two lie along an arc of high country in Southwest Asia, the region traditionally known as the Fertile Crescent.

Early Farming and the Big Thaw

Ten thousand years ago the world had around six million people scattered across Afroeurasia, Australia, and the Americas. Paleolithic bands lived with danger and insecurity, and most people probably died before they reached forty. Nevertheless, foragers ensured themselves of a plentiful, varied food supply, at least much of the time, and they had shorter daily working hours than most humans have enjoyed since farming societies arose. They sheltered themselves adequately in a wide range of climates, and they shared in a rich social and ceremonial life. Why, then, should some groups in certain places take up a strangely different way of life, one that involved hoeing crops in the hot sun, milking animals every day, living in cramped villages, and perhaps handing part of their food supply to local chiefs? Certainly no paleolithic woman suddenly got a flash of brilliance and said to her friends, "Why don't we plant these seeds, care for the young plants, and harvest the food when it's ripe?" Rather, farming evolved as many small groups made small decisions and alterations, many of them unconscious and unintentional. An **agricultural revolution** occurred, but humankind backed into it.

agricultural revolution The transition from collecting food in the wild to domesticating and producing particular plants and animals for human consumption.

Scholars generally agree that early farming was connected in complicated ways to the onset of the Holocene, the global climatic warming cycle that fully set in after about 9600 B.C.E. and that continues today. During the transition from the Pleistocene to the Holocene era, global temperatures increased by fractions of degrees over centuries.

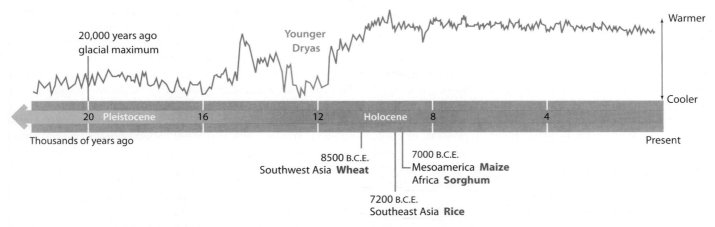

Global temperature change and early farming. The Pleistocene was the long geological era characterized by cycles of climatic cooling and warming. The Holocene is the recent warming, or interglacial, era. The Younger Dryas was a temporary period of colder temperatures lasting about 1,200 years. Does the chronological match between rising global temperature and evidence of agriculture necessarily mean that global warming *caused* people to take up farming?

The retreat of the great ice sheets, warmer seasons, and increased rainfall permitted small animals, marine life, and forests to multiply across the Northern Hemisphere. In some regions, the early Holocene created new ecological niches for various species of wild grass that produced edible and nutritious grains.

The earliest evidence we have of humans systematically collecting and consuming wild grain comes from northeastern Africa between the Nile and the Red Sea (today part of Sudan and Ethiopia). Discoveries of stone blades and grinding implements show that some foragers in that region began between 16,000 and 13,000 B.C.E. to subsist partly on grain, which they roasted or ground into flour to make bread. The idea of grain collecting may well have diffused from the Nile region to the Fertile Crescent around 11,000 B.C.E. Historians have associated this dispersal with an ancient movement of people, perhaps small numbers of them, from Africa to Southwest Asia.

In relatively high and well-watered elevations of the Fertile Crescent, forager bands began to identify and collect wild grains ancestral to einkorn and emmer wheat, as well as barley and rye. Cohabiting groups that found these seeds tasty, nourishing, and easy to harvest with sharp flint blades had good reason to station themselves next to large stands of grain for months at a time. Eventually, they took to husbanding cereal plants by pulling out competing weeds, bringing in water, and scaring away pesky birds and rodents. Because wild cereals contributed an increasing number of daily calories relative to other food sources, some bands settled permanently near abundant stands of the coveted plants. That is, they became sedentary. We know that sedentism was taking place in Southwest Asia from about 11,000 B.C.E. The earliest villages in the Fertile Crescent were no more than little clusters of circular "pit houses" of stone and wood. The residents of these tiny villages ate wheat, barley, or rye boiled, roasted, or ground up for bread. They did not, however, stop foraging for tubers, fruits, and nuts in the neighborhood or hunting gazelles and small game. Farming and foraging economies overlapped for thousands of years.

The Drift toward Domestication

To tend patches of wild grain was one thing. To *domesticate* plants or animals was a more complicated matter. Domestication means that humans changed the genetic makeup of plants and animals by influencing the way they reproduce, thereby making them more appealing in taste, size, and nutrition, as well as easier to grow, harvest, process, or cook. People could not invent new plant species, but they could select plants that possessed certain observable mutations, that is, unusual characteristics that made them desirable.

The marriage of plants and humans. There is no doubt that foragers of the early Holocene knew a great deal about wild plants. They could distinguish between flora that were good to eat and those that were too small, oily, or bitter—or even fatally toxic. At first, however, women and men domesticated desirable plants with no consciousness of what they were doing. They unintentionally disseminated the seeds of plants they liked to eat because waste seeds frequently sprouted near the settlement, especially around latrines and trash heaps. If people looked after desirable plants that were close to the camp, they effectively segregated them from wild plants in the wider neighborhood. Doing this over decades and generations, they unwittingly protected the plants they wanted against genetic contamination from wild ones they did not want. Probably very early in this process, people deduced a connection between seeds that lay on the ground and the later sprouting of new plants. Eventually, they got the hang of broadcasting or sticking in the ground desirable seeds, thereby increasing the yield. Thus, they improved a species further, creating a superior hybrid without knowing they were doing it. Full domestication occurred when humans and their farm products became codependent. That is, the community came to rely for an important part of its food supply on genetically altered plants. The plants, in turn, were so changed that they could no longer grow in the wild.

When we think about world history's first farmers, we should probably picture mostly girls and women. The division of labor in paleolithic bands was informal, but women who had to stay close to camp to breastfeed and look after young children became experts in the locally available food plants. While men were hunting far from camp, women were busy, whether consciously or not, genetically manipulating plants.

Domestication of animals. Humans and animals also domesticated each other unintentionally at first. In Southwest Asia, dogs, which are descended from species of wolves, partnered with humans thousands of years before the advent of farming. A likely scenario is that wolves prowled around forager camps looking for food scraps. Individual animals genetically disposed to be slightly less skittish in the presence of humans tended to stay closer to the camp. Eventually, people captured some of these relatively more placid beasts, perhaps wanting them because they would bark when strangers approached. As canines inclined to tameness interbred with one another in captivity over numerous generations, they gradually transformed themselves into hunting companions and camp guards that could no longer survive in the wild alongside their distant wolf cousins.

Pig bones associated with a human settlement in southeastern Turkey point to domestication of that mammal about 10,000 B.C.E. A recent theory contends that in the early farming era people kept tame pigs, and soon thereafter sheep, goats, and cattle, because they wanted them not for meat or milk but as objects of periodic ritual sacrifice or communal feasting.[1] In time, communities that did this came to recognize the usefulness of these animals as sources of food, hides, hair, wool, and traction (plow-pulling). Humans became more dependent on domesticates than on wild game,

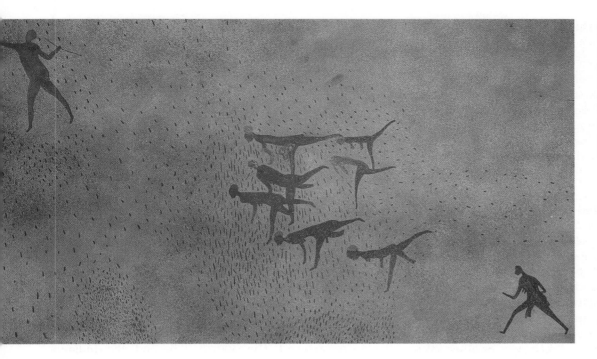

A harvest ballet. The women in this scene painted on rock in the Tassili-n-Ajjer region of southeastern Algeria bend gracefully to gather grain. An artist made the painting between 5000 and 6000 B.C.E., a time when the central Sahara was significantly wetter than it is now.

and, in turn, domesticated pigs, sheep, goats, and cattle genetically acquired tameness, smaller size, and sense organs less adapted to the necessity of alertness or sudden flight. These creatures could no longer live in the wild. Eventually, humans began deliberately to cull and interbreed animals that had desirable qualities, for example, mating sheep that had softer, woolier coats but killing and eating animals that had stiffer ones before they reproduced.

Of the thousands of relatively large animal species in the world, barely a dozen of them have been domesticated as major sources of food, fiber, or traction. These domestications occurred in different parts of the world over a span of thousands of years. For example, horses, camels, water buffalo, and donkeys tied their fates to humans several millennia after the domestication of pigs, sheep, and goats. As for cattle, the world's oldest archaeological evidence of domesticated species comes from the eastern Sahara Desert. Between 9000 and 8000 B.C.E., that region had significantly higher rainfall than it does now, permitting early cattle tamers to herd animals from the banks of the Nile far into the Sahara in winter months when sufficient water was available. About a thousand years later, domesticated cattle appeared in both Southwest Asia and India.

Neolithic Innovations

Farming emerged in several parts of Afroeurasia independently during the early Holocene. Many scholars think this may have happened because the warming trend was irregular rather than steady. About 10,800 B.C.E., global temperatures dove suddenly, an event linked to the surge of cold water from melting glaciers in the North Atlantic. Scientists call this recurrence of cooler, drier weather in the Northern Hemisphere the Younger Dryas after the name of an arctic wildflower (see temperature chart, p. 51). It lasted about 1,200 years, and it likely increased ecological stress on both foragers and early farmers in several regions nearly simultaneously, especially where population was already rising when the cold snap started. This reversal of prevailing weather patterns in turn pushed communities to experiment more urgently with domesticated crops than they would otherwise have chosen to do.

In several regions, groups that had at first shifted to farming without consciously intending to do it eventually recognized the benefits of agrarian life. Food supplies became more secure and predictable. Permanent houses were more comfortable than temporary ones. Community life became more diverse and interesting. Children, the sick, and the aged had their needs met in a more sheltered environment. A sedentary life meant that women could wean children earlier and thus resume ovulation faster. If a woman gave birth more often, more of her children were likely to survive to adulthood and contribute to the family's food needs.

As land cultivation expanded, settlements grew in size and density, obliging their inhabitants to invent clever new tools and techniques. This surge of ingenuity marks the beginning of the **neolithic era,** which we associate with the dawn of farming. Neolithic innovations included finer stone blades (microliths), curved sickles, stone containers and grinders, and houses of sun-dried mud brick. Scholars conventionally date the end of the neolithic to about 4500 B.C.E. in Southwest Asia and Europe, when copper implements came into use alongside stone.

> **neolithic era** The period from about 10,000 to 4000 B.C.E. characterized by refined stone toolmaking and the development of agriculture.

The Spread of Agrarian Societies

The earliest farm communities that we know of appeared in the Fertile Crescent. But given that farming emerged independently in several places, perhaps seven or eight of them, the question of who was first is really beside the point. Agrarian societies appeared on all the inhabited continents except Australia between about 10,000 and 3000 B.C.E. (see Map 2.1). Compared to the paleolithic's 2.4 million years or so of hunting, foraging, and unhurried stone tool development, the agricultural revolution took place practically overnight.

Agriculture from the Mediterranean to India. Several important domesticated plants and animals, and the ideas and technologies connected to them, spread from the Fertile Crescent both east to South Asia (the Indian subcontinent) and west to the lands bordering the Mediterranean Sea. This entire belt of land and sea occupies approximately the same range of latitude: Days and seasons are of a similar length; temperatures, plant populations, animal habitats, and rainfall averages (less than twenty inches a year) are fairly similar. No lofty mountain ranges or other natural obstacles impede communication and travel across the region, and the large bodies of water within it—the Mediterranean, Black, Red, and Arabian Seas, plus the Persian Gulf—link the region from one end to the other.

Most, though not quite all, of the crops and animals that became important in the diets of people along this belt appear to have been domesticated first in either Southwest Asia or northeastern Africa. The staples of the new agrarian economy were wheat (emmer and einkorn), barley, legumes (lentils, peas, chickpeas), sheep, goats, pigs, cows, and flax (for making textiles). All these "founder crops" and domesticated animals were climatically adaptable to most of the region. Indeed, they spread across it within a few thousand years. Some important crops, including cotton and eggplant, were first domesticated in India and then moved westward to Southwest Asia and the Mediterranean basin.

Agrarian ways of life spread in two principal ways. One was by cultural diffusion, that is, the dissemination of *ideas* about how to farm. People probably exchanged information about farming chiefly in connection with regional trade. For example, early peddlers carried products throughout Southwest Asia. Copper from the Sinai Peninsula, shells from Mediterranean shores, salt from the Dead Sea, and obsidian, a dark volcanic glass from mines in Anatolia (modern Turkey), all moved back and forth across the region. These traders probably also took along seeds, animals, and farm tools from one village to another, thus stimulating local farming experiments in new places. Second, farming spread in connection with the migration of people from one locality to another. For example, agriculture centered on wheat, barley, cattle, sheep, and pigs, along with a kit of knowledge and sophisticated tools, probably started moving from Southwest Asia into Europe before 7000 B.C.E. This happened almost certainly as a result of cultivators migrating westward along the Mediterranean coast or into the Balkan Peninsula and the fertile Danube River valley.

Farmers around the world. Beyond the India-to-Mediterranean zone, people took up crop growing and livestock raising in several places independently. One broad region of innovation was northern China, extending from the middle Yellow River (Huang He) southward to the Yangzi (YAHNG-zuh) River. This area of northern China was significantly less arid in the fourth millennium B.C.E. than it is today. People probably domesticated rice and millet (an important grain staple in China today) between about 7000 and 6500 B.C.E. Farmers in the Yellow River region worked light, deep soil known as loess with simple digging sticks. They built hamlets of houses with sunken floors and storage pits, used stone axes and serrated knives, raised pigs and chickens, and laid the dead to rest in cemeteries.

In Africa, the highlands of Ethiopia, the savannas (grasslands) just south of the Sahara Desert, and the wet tropical forests farther south all emerged as distinct centers

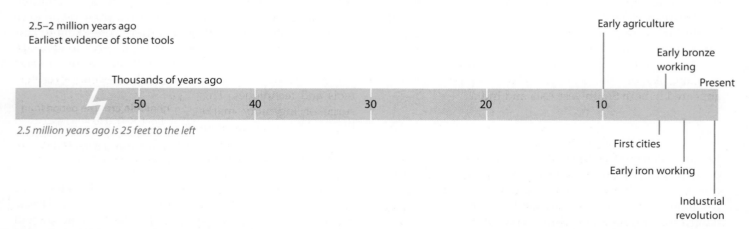

Milestones of technology. Why do you think the pace of technological change accelerated so slowly for about 2.5 million years? Why did it then speed up dramatically from about 10,000 years ago?

of independent domestication between about 10,000 and 5000 B.C.E. Food plants included sorghum, finger millet, yams, and other crops, the choice depending on soil and climate. In Asia's tropical belt, dwellers in what is today Thailand appear to have domesticated rice on their own about 7200 B.C.E. Inhabitants of New Guinea in island Southeast Asia started harvesting sugar cane, yams, and certain species of banana about 7000 B.C.E. Peoples of North and South America definitely invented farming with no stimulus from Afroeurasia. We return to that development in Chapter 4.

Sunrise over the Village

If a group of hardy travelers of 5000 B.C.E. were to tramp 2,600 miles from southeastern Europe to the northwestern frontiers of India (an unlikely journey), they could probably have found refuge almost every night in a village consisting of a few dozen round or rectangular huts of stone, brick, or wood. The resident families would have cultivated small fields of grain and legumes; raised a few pigs, sheep, or cows; and foraged in the surrounding countryside. They would have worn garments of roughly woven wool, animal hair, or plant fiber, as well as skins and furs. Their material inventory would have included an array of stone, bone, and wooden tools, as well as grain and other food.

Households would have had a variety of containers for cooking, storing, and transporting food. The ceramic pot— waterproof, fireproof, and made from readily available clay—was a key development of the neolithic era, not least because it could be used to cook nutritious plant food into soft, mushy gruel that enriched the diets of everyone, including babies and toothless old people. Unlike stone or wood, clay could easily be molded into any of a thousand useful forms and then heated to a high temperature in bonfires, later in furnaces and kilns. "Firing" the clay dried up the water content in it and made it hard. Foragers, not farmers, appear to have brought about the "pot revolution." The oldest potsherds, that is, broken pieces of ceramic, have been found in northern China and dated to as many as 18,000 years ago. Foraging people in Japan began making pots a few thousand years later. On the western side of the hemisphere, the oldest pottery comes from the eastern Sahara Desert, where people began using baked clay utensils to boil wild grain for porridge about 9000 B.C.E. Ceramic containers

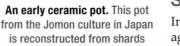

An early ceramic pot. This pot from the Jomon culture in Japan is reconstructed from shards dating to about 12,000 B.C.E.

appeared in farming communities in Southwest Asia two thousand or so years later.

Firing pottery in rudimentary furnaces may have suggested the idea of heating pieces of rock enough to extract beads of molten copper, which could then be cooled, reheated, and hammered into tools or ornaments. Farmers in Anatolia seem to have initiated the era of copper metallurgy about 5000 B.C.E. Within a few centuries, and perhaps in the same region, people figured out the more complicated process of liquefying copper and pouring it into clay molds to fashion bracelets, statues, blades, and many other useful objects. Tools of pure copper, however, did not replace stone. They tended to be too soft or brittle to last very long. But within about two thousand years, societies from western Europe to China either invented copper metallurgy or learned about it from strangers.

In regions where farming became established, social relations invariably became more complicated. The division of labor remained quite simple, and adult men and women probably treated each other with near equality. Both sexes contributed skill and muscle to farming's many tasks and to weaving clothing, nets, baskets, and other essential items from wool, flax, cotton, or reed. But because villages were likely to have several extended families living closely together, leaders inevitably emerged to guide group decisions and mediate personal disputes. Chiefs stood apart because of their physical strength, good judgment, or presumed ability to communicate with the gods. At the same time, permanent settlements and success at farming meant that families had the possibility of storing up wealth. As soon as some villagers accumulated more food reserves than others, the conditions were laid for social inequality. Burial sites in Southwest Asia and other regions of early farming reveal that some people, including children, went to their graves adorned with jewelry and other valuables, while most villagers received more meager interments. These differences suggest that some families gained higher social status than others and that social hierarchy—the ranking of some families and individuals over others—was becoming part of human communal life.

Super Villages

In Southwest Asia, the remains of several agrarian settlements are conspicuous for their size and complexity. One of them is ancient

Jericho, which is also a modern city near the Jordan River. There, about 7000 B.C.E., the inhabitants enclosed their village in a stone wall more than eleven feet high and nearly five feet thick. They also dug a moat and put up a tower. They may have done these things to protect their food, water, or trade goods, though the early inhabitants continued to collect food in the surrounding wild. Building the wall took such a sophisticated level of technical skill and cooperation that the town must have had fairly complex social organization, including distinctions between an elite class of leaders and the rest of the population.

The biggest neolithic center so far discovered is Çatal Hüyük (CHAH-tahl HOO-yook). Located on a grassy plain in south central Anatolia, this site also goes back to about 7000 B.C.E. It covers nearly thirty-two acres, and may at its height have had a population close to ten thousand. The settlement was a solid block of more than a thousand mud-brick houses built so closely together that there was no room for streets. The inhabitants moved from one dwelling to another by scrambling across multilevel rooftops and descending to interiors on wooden ladders. Some dwellings had multiple rooms and upper stories. Domestic activity took place in a large space outfitted with hearth, clay oven, and platforms for sitting and sleeping. Some rooms served as shrines to local deities (about which we know little) and were richly decorated with clay statuary, relief sculptures, and painted walls depicting scenes from daily life.

Çatal Hüyük's inhabitants raised grain, legumes, sheep, and cattle along the banks of a local river. But they also foraged in nearby hills and marshes for almonds, crab apples, and gazelle meat. Material remains suggest a social life centered on clusters of families. Each family appears to have ventured out to farm or forage every morning and then returned to its own "apartment" at nightfall. We do not know why so many people chose to live together in this teeming pile of buildings, but in any case the settlement flourished for one to two thousand years, before falling into ruin around 5400 B.C.E.

About that same time, however, farmers who had planted themselves west of the Black Sea and up the Danube River

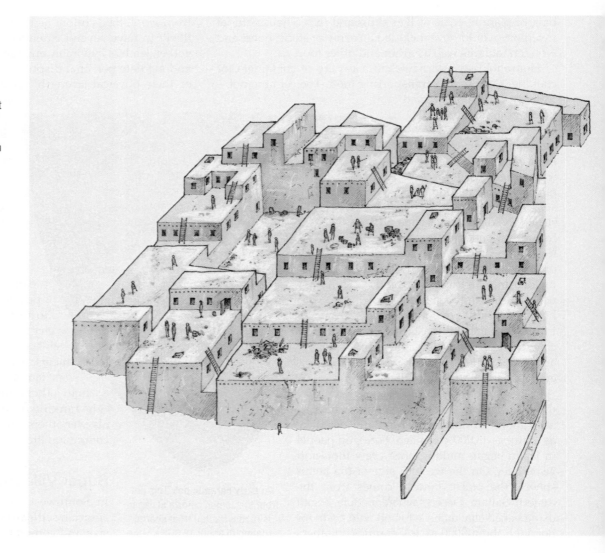

Çatal Hüyük. Historians have debated whether Çatal Hüyük was a town that might in other circumstances have become a city or simply an oversized farming village, doomed to fail because the local area could not produce enough food to sustain its large population. Why do you think the builders made no room for streets or alleys between houses?

Ötzi: A Neolithic Traveler

Farming and village living probably reached western Europe mainly overland from the southeast and was well established by 4000 B.C.E. One remarkable piece of evidence of neolithic life in that region is the body of a man who had been frozen in a glacier for 5,300 years.

In 1991 two German tourists hiking in the Italian Alps near the border with Austria came across a desiccated human corpse. Since then, painstaking analysis of the remains has revealed that this individual died sometime around 3300 B.C.E. Scientists nicknamed the body "Ötzi" after the Ötz valley where he was discovered. Because he became frozen shortly after he died, his corpse remained largely intact. Extensive testing and DNA analysis have allowed scientists to piece together a picture of his life and death. He was probably a herdsman or hunter. He may also have been a warrior or a leader in his community, because he carried a costly item, a finely constructed copper-bladed axe with a yew tree handle.

Ötzi stood about 5 feet 5 inches tall and weighed about 110 pounds. He ate a mixed diet of meat, grains, fruits, and roots. To protect himself against the harsh Alpine climate, he wore clothes made of a variety of skins, tanned and stitched together with animal sinews. The excavation turned up a bearskin hat near his head. Grass stuffed in his leather shoes kept his feet warm. About forty-five years old when he died, he suffered from intestinal parasites and degenerative joint problems. He had more than fifty tattoo marks on his body, made by rubbing charcoal into small incisions. Remarkably, these marks match acupuncture lines, suggesting an early form of this treatment to relieve joint pain.

Objects discovered near his corpse tell us that he carried a variety of weapons on the day he died: his axe, a flint-bladed knife, a bow with arrows, and some unidentified items. He also carried two baskets, which held berries, mushrooms, and a kit for starting fires.

Ötzi was not alone when he died. Researchers originally assumed that he had fallen victim to exposure during a mountain storm, but further analysis of the body has complicated this story. Unhealed cuts and bruises indicate that he was engaged in a violent struggle shortly before his death. A flint arrowhead lodged in his shoulder suggests that someone shot him. He might have died from trauma to his head, though we cannot know whether he fell or sustained a savage blow. Some scientists have speculated that he died when a raiding party he was with attacked an enemy group.

We would like to know much more about Ötzi and the community from which he came. But the information scientists have gleaned from his body and his possessions offer a rare glimpse into the life of an ordinary western European man during the late neolithic age.

Two Dutch artists fashioned this life-sized model of Ötzi based on analysis of the 5,300-year-old mummy.

Thinking Critically

Based on the evidence we have about Ötzi, what generalizations might you propose about the character of society in western Europe around 3300 B.C.E.?

valley started building villages of as many as two thousand houses. These settlements, whose economies were based on wheat, barley, cattle, and sheep, were enclosed in wooden palisades. Some of the dwellings of wood and plaster had multiple rooms and two stories. Archaeologists see a succession of material cultural styles known collectively as "Old Europe," extending from about 5500 to 3500 B.C.E. These related societies, which encompassed most of southeastern Europe, produced elaborately decorated pottery, gold and copper jewelry, and tools such as axes and knives cast from smelted copper. This practice almost certainly indicates the existence of social distinctions. Archaeologists have found female figurines in abundance, probably associated with particular goddesses or spirits venerated in households. Other finds indicate that a network of trade in gold and copper, as well as decorative shells from the Aegean Sea, bound southeastern Europe's farm towns and villages together.

Wherever frontiers of farming advanced in Afroeurasia, populations inevitably grew. Nevertheless, farming technology available between nine thousand and five thousand years ago almost certainly prevented populations from rising above a certain level relative to local food resources. In three parts of the Indo-Mediterranean region, however, a startling transformation began to take place from about

4000 B.C.E. In those places, agricultural production accelerated, population soared, and large, dense clusters of human habitation, that is, cities, started to appear for the first time. That phenomenon began to take place barely six thousand years ago, a time span representing only the most recent 3 percent or so of the years that humans have walked the earth.

Early Complex Societies

FOCUS How did complex societies take shape in the Tigris-Euphrates, Nile, and Indus River valleys, and in what ways did they interact with one another and alter their environments?

complex society A type of society, also called a "civilization," possessing most of the following features: dense population, agricultural economy, cities, complex social hierarchy, complex occupational specialization, centralized state, monumental building, writing, and a dominant belief system.

Complex society, the form of social organization we conventionally refer to as "civilization," first appeared in the Tigris-Euphrates, Nile, and Indus River valleys (see Map 2.2). These societies became "complex" because of the relative size and density of their populations and the intricacy and variety of their social institutions, occupations, technologies, government systems, and forms of creative expression (see Table 2.1). Like farming itself, complex societies emerged as a consequence of humans making countless everyday decisions century after century, no one capable of seeing where these experiments might take them. Village

farmers did not decide to invent complex society because they thought it was a good idea or knew somehow that it was supposed to happen next. Rather, a dynamic interplay among rising population, climate change, and human success at producing food led in a few places to a surge of innovations unlike anything paleolithic hunting bands could have imagined.

Although early complex societies represented a definable type of social organization, the societies of the Tigris-Euphrates (Mesopotamia), the Nile, and the Indus each emerged with a characteristic cultural style expressed in distinctive forms of government, religion, architecture, literature, and so on. These cultural peculiarities reflected underlying differences in the physical and natural environments, the dynamics of interaction among social groups, and simply the flow of historical events. We should not, however, think that these differing styles were innate or remained fixed. The cultural elements that made a complex society culturally identifiable were all susceptible to change because local environmental conditions inevitably changed, social tensions and conflicts occurred among groups within the society, and strangers and strange ideas arrived from outside. Civilizations have never existed as unchanging, self-enclosed cultural packages, and that fact of world history needs to be kept in mind.

Irrigation and Complex Society in Mesopotamia

The three earliest complex societies all arose within the Great Arid Zone, the band of dry country that stretches across Afroeurasia from southwest to northeast (see Map 2.2).

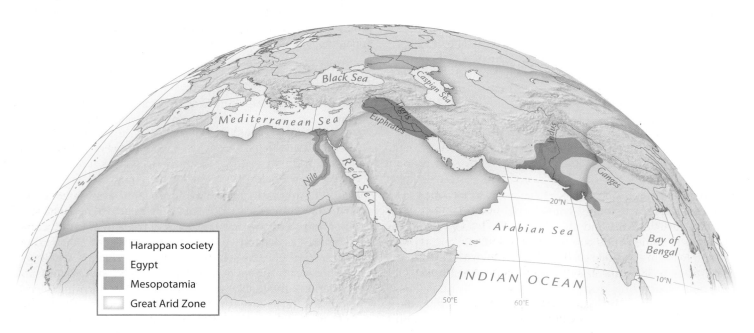

MAP 2.2 The earliest complex societies.
Why do you think the earliest complex agrarian societies arose in arid regions of the world rather than in places with high rainfall?

TABLE 2.1 Types of Societies Compared

Feature Category	Foraging Societies	Early Agrarian Societies	Complex Agrarian and Urban Societies
Economy	Collecting and hunting wild food at subsistence level	Production of domesticated crops and animals at subsistence level, plus collecting and hunting	Production primarily of crops and secondarily of domesticated animals at surplus levels, as well as urban and village manufactures
Settlement	Temporary or semipermanent camps or hamlets	Permanent homesteads, villages, and village clusters	Cities, towns, and villages
Occupations	All members of group forage for food	All members of group raise crops or animals; some members exercise special technical or leadership skills	The great majority engages in farming; minorities in full-time specialized occupations or in urban labor
Social structure	Group is egalitarian; no significant social class divisions; social relations based on kinship	Social class divisions are informal and fluid; certain individuals or families enjoy special status as political and religious leaders; social relations based partly on kinship	Permanent hierarchy of social classes: (a) rulers and aristocrats, (b) skilled artisans, technicians, and professionals, (c) rural farmers and urban workers, (d) in many societies, slaves; social relations based on kinship at local levels and on common obedience to the ruler at the level of the state
Gender relations	Society is egalitarian; simple division of tasks between women and men	Society is egalitarian; more complex division of tasks between women and men	Patriarchal society; most women restricted to the domestic sphere
Political organization	Egalitarian bands generally restricted in size to fewer than 100; informal, fluid leadership	Informal village leadership exercised by individuals, elders, or families with special status	States characterized by central governments, authoritarian rule, hierarchies of officials, and systematic taxation
Laws	Informal, customary rules and prohibitions	More complex customary rules and prohibitions	Complex civil and penal laws, enforced by the state and often organized in written codes
Technological change	Slow pace of technological innovation	Accelerating pace of technological innovation, especially in food production and village manufacturing	Continuous, though often uneven, technological and scientific innovation in a wide range of human activities
Built environment	Shelter in simple, sometimes mobile structures	Permanent dwellings; village construction of shrines, communal granaries, or defensive walls	Dense urban dwelling construction; monumental building of walls, temples, palaces, tombs, and public plazas
Communication	Speech and forms of symbolic expression	Speech and complex symbolic expression	Writing systems and complex symbolic expression; literacy of particular elite groups
Religion	Beliefs and practices associated with local nature spirits and divinities	Beliefs and practices associated with local, natural, and household deities and spirits	Complex systems of belief and practice often associated with central political authority, a class of religious specialists, and written scriptures; centers of development of major belief systems such as Confucianism, Buddhism, or Christianity

Climatologists have theorized that the hot, dry conditions now prevailing in the western Great Arid Zone, that is, from the Sahara to the Great Indian Desert, set in from about 4000 B.C.E., though with periodic cycles of higher or lower temperature and rainfall. Dense concentrations of population were possible in that region only because fresh water flowed from green highlands far away. The Tigris and the Euphrates Rivers originate in the mountains of eastern Anatolia, the Indus River flows from the Himalayas of Tibet, and the Nile has its source in highland Ethiopia and tropical East Africa.

As far as we know, the Tigris-Euphrates River valley is the earliest place where a complex society appeared. Lying largely within what is today Iraq and eastern Syria, the region came to be known by its Greek name, Mesopotamia, or "land between the rivers." From about 7000 B.C.E., farming

settlements flourished on well-watered slopes of the Zagros Mountains, which parallel the Tigris River to the east. As the hill population grew, farmers looking for new land migrated to lower elevations and eventually settled on the valley's alluvial plain. This is the relatively flat, gently sloping area where over the millennia the two rivers deposited layers of alluvium, that is, a mix of silt, clay, sand, and gravel. There, early farmers gradually selected food plants that grew successfully in hot, dry conditions.

In 5000 B.C.E. southern Mesopotamia was a labyrinth of creeks, lakes, and marshes. In the spring, highland runoff inundated the valley, depositing fresh layers of fertile silt. Rain rarely fell in summer, but farmers irrigated fields using simple techniques, and they built mud-brick villages along creeks and lakes. The soil was so rich and easy to work that farms yielded copious crops of wheat, barley, legumes, vegetables, and fruits. Irrigation farming, combined with hunting and fishing in the teeming marshes, gave these settled communities a secure food supply in most years.

The river valley as population trap.

From about 4000 B.C.E., population density in the river valley rose dramatically, a development likely related to a climatic shift toward lower rainfall across Southwest Asia. The spring floods abated somewhat, and lagoons and swamps receded, exposing more acreage for fields, pastures, and settlements. Relatively drier conditions also encouraged people to innovate, for example, building granaries to store food and seeking wider trade relations to acquire a greater variety of products. Villages multiplied, especially along the Euphrates, and "super settlements" that economically dominated neighboring villages began to arise. At some point farmers began to yoke domesticated oxen or donkeys to light wooden plows.

In such conditions of surplus food production and rising population, social changes became a practical necessity. In earlier times forager bands that outgrew local resources had to segment and disperse over a wider territory. The Mesopotamian plain dwellers could not do that because the surrounding lands were much too dry to support the farming they had come to depend on. We might say that the peoples of the plain became "trapped" into creating bigger settlements and more complicated forms of social organization as a result of their own success at producing bounteous crops.

Occupational specialization.

As more people packed into the valley, work had to be organized in more complicated ways. Production of surplus food meant that not everyone had to farm full time. Conversely, population growth raised the demand for men and women who could provide special talents and services as potters, basket weavers, brick masons, stone carvers, coppersmiths, merchants, labor supervisors, soldiers, and religious professionals. Occupational specialization also tended, as it does in modern times, to encourage specialists to experiment with new techniques and products, which generated even more jobs requiring expertise.

Environmental pressures and the first cities.

Archaeology has shown that because water and fertile mud were so abundant in the formative period of Mesopotamian society, large settlements multiplied before there was any need for extensive irrigation of crop land. In time, however, water and soil management became more difficult. For one thing, the region's climatic drying trend continued into the third millennium B.C.E. Wetlands and creeks continued to recede, forcing people to dig canals and ditches to lead water to fields. For another, the spring floods were unpredictable. In some years the rivers carried too little water, in some years too much, though people settled in greater numbers along the Euphrates because its elevation drop was gentler than its twin's. Furthermore, the climate required that spring planting normally take place *before* the flood arrived. These perennial conditions motivated farmers to engineer ways to store water in lakes and ponds and then channel it to fields as needed. As arduous as water management became, there was no going back to simpler days. The valley's population continued to climb, so agricultural productivity had to go up, too. That reality underlay herculean efforts to build dikes, dams, canals, and reservoirs to keep water flowing to fields and pastures that stretched farther and farther from the river banks.

Some settlements in the valley grew larger than others, and when they did they attracted even more people because they offered more opportunities for jobs and trade. These big settlements may be described as cities when they became multifunctional. The residents engaged in many different jobs and professions, not just farming, and they depended for their livings mainly on food imported from outside.

Mesopotamia's early cities emerged in two major clusters (see Map 2.3). The oldest centers appeared sometime after 4000 B.C.E. at the harshly arid southern end of the valley, the region called Sumer (SOO-mehr). There, the alluvial plain bulges out, offering an expanse of potentially arable land to the extent that water could be brought to it. In the early third millennium B.C.E., the southern cluster extended about 150 miles up the valley to encompass Akkad (AHK-ahd), the region near modern Baghdad. The second urban constellation developed in northern Mesopotamia, where winter rains were sufficient to support crops and herds. This region, part of it hill country, extended over a wide area of what is today northern Iraq and eastern Syria. Only in the past half-century have archaeologists discovered that small but flourishing cities began to spring up in northern Mesopotamia from about 3000 B.C.E. and that this phenomenon had little or no connection to the rise of Sumer in the south. In the third millennium B.C.E., however, a growing network of commercial and cultural exchanges knitted the two city clusters permanently together.

Complex society in Sumer and Akkad.

In the centuries after 4000 B.C.E., more than a dozen major cities appeared in southern Mesopotamia. The biggest center was Uruk (OO-rook), which in 3000 B.C.E. had a population of around fifty thousand. Remarkably, the world's oldest cities thrived in a region lacking many natural resources. Other than fertile soil, clay for bricks, poplar trees for wood construction, and marsh reeds for making baskets and small river boats, the southern valley had little to offer. The cities had to trade not only with one another but also with peoples who lived along the Persian Gulf and in the highlands to the north and east. Sumer's continuing urban growth depended on steady importation of timber and stone for construction, copper and tin for bronze making, and an array of precious metals, gemstones, and other luxuries to satisfy urban tastes.

Within each of Sumer's cities, intricate social and occupational relationships, the constant flow of goods in and out, and the relentless upkeep of waterworks demanded vigorous leaders to organize and command the population. Civil peace and order required urban leaders to show a deft mix of public persuasion, group mediation, and threats of punishment. The city's wealth paid for the services of deputies and soldiers to enforce the leaders' will, a condition most city folk accepted in return for a reasonable level of calm and security.

The new forms of power that cities required gave rise to the world's first states. The early state was a type of political organization utterly different from the egalitarian forager band. Decisions became the prerogative of a ruling group and a privileged class of officials backed by armed enforcers. These bosses claimed authority to resolve social conflict, outlaw private vengeance, proclaim public laws, and monopolize the use of violence. Once they achieved enough power to pass it on to their own children, they began to make the case that it was natural and good that power reside permanently with particular families, that this practice encouraged social order and prevented disputes over leadership. Here was the origin of the **dynasty**.

dynasty A sequence of rulers from a single family.

city-state A politically sovereign urban center with adjacent agricultural land.

The early cities of Sumer were **city-states,** centrally governed territories that included a single urban complex and surrounding villages and farmland. For many centuries, the cities of Sumer competed for land and resources, sometimes viciously. Chronic tensions punctuated by intercity wars help explain why ruling elites were able to assert more central authority and why the walls and guard towers that encased cities got progressively taller and thicker.

Religion and the rise of priests. We have ample evidence of a close connection between the emerging state and organized religion. Most scholars agree that as soon as paleolithic humans acquired language, they began to try to "explain the unexplainable" to one another—why the heavenly bodies move across the sky, why rain falls or fails to, why people die and where they go after death. Ritual burials and art from the upper paleolithic tell us that early societies found persuasive explanations for many things in the workings of unseen forces and spiritual beings. There is little doubt that early Mesopotamian farmers regarded the well-being of their communities as dependent on the good will of powerful supernatural entities. People could appeal to these deities, which might be represented in human, animal, or abstract forms, to grant good harvests, help women produce children, or ensure safe passage of the dead into another world. At household shrines and village temples, women and men sought to communicate with deities through ceremonies and sacrificial offerings.

And as Sumerian cities grew, so too did their temples and the power of the gods and goddesses believed to live in them. Each city had its own major divinity, represented in stone

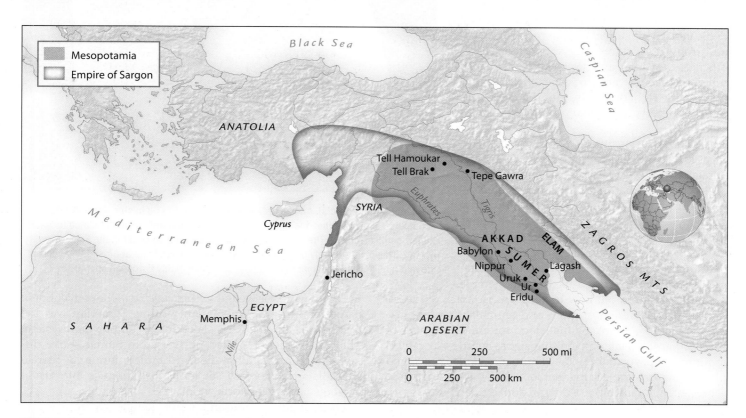

MAP 2.3 Early states in Mesopotamia.
What factors might explain why Sargon's empire expanded in the particular directions it did?

or wooden images. For example, the moon god Nannar (also named Sin) presided over the city of Ur. Inanna, goddess of love, and Anu, the sky god, shared the patronage of Uruk. That city's White Temple, which has remained remarkably preserved to the present, belonged to Anu. It stood atop a brick pyramidal platform that loomed above the city. The temple walls, sheathed in gypsum plaster, shone in the hot white light of the Mesopotamian sun. Temples also served as the headquarters of city-state administration, which took in tax revenues in grain and other commodities, then reallocated it for irrigation works, public construction, war making, famine relief, and other civic purposes.

Every urban temple had its religious personnel, or priests, who had the job of keeping the gods satisfied with continuous rituals, festivals, and sacrifices. The priests, proclaiming that all human labor was dedicated to the service of the deities, monopolized the right to command the city's population and economy. This small minority came to control extensive farmland and to assume powers and privileges that lowlier people did not have. The priests organized the population to work the city's farms and to produce textiles, pottery, and other goods in temple workshops. They dedicated food stores to the resident deity, and from those stores they supported temple officials, servants, and themselves. In short, religious practice came to justify the state, upholding the right of its elite guardians to accumulate property and wield power.

Sounds into symbols. One of the keys to priestly rule was the invention of writing. Foragers of the upper paleolithic had carved abstract signs that might be interpreted as early forms of writing, but the earliest fully developed system emerged, as far as we know, in Mesopotamia sometime before 3000 B.C.E. Complex societies must keep track of a great many things, as our to-do lists and bank statements continually remind us. In Uruk, temple authorities figured out how to keep precise track of the receipt and distribution of grain and animals, first by making distinctive clay tokens that stood for a fixed number of a particular item, later by incising signs on little clay tablets to represent particular goods or numbers. Scribes invented pictograms, or simple signs that looked like the thing being represented, for example, a duck, a donkey, or a house.

Early writers made signs by pushing a stalk of reed with a wedge-shaped end into a tablet of wet clay, which was then dried in the sun or, in later times, baked. From *cuneus,*

A Mesopotamian official. An inscription at the back of this alabaster statue dating to about 2400 B.C.E. identifies the figure as Ebih-II, "the superintendent dedicated to Ishtar Virile," goddess of war. The statue comes from the temple of Ishtar in the Euphrates city of Mari. This man is clearly of high social rank and appears to be at prayer. What sort of life might he have led compared to that of Ötzi, the neolithic European on page 57?

the Latin word for wedge, we get *cuneiform,* the conventional name for early Mesopotamian writing. Sumerian was the first spoken language translated into a complex sign system. The inhabitants of Akkad upriver from Sumer spoke different languages, and in the third millennium B.C.E. literate specialists transformed some of those tongues into visual symbols using cuneiform script.

Over about a thousand years, temple record keepers worked out an elaborate system of signs, some that represented the sound of syllables ("ba," "bo," "ka," etc.) and

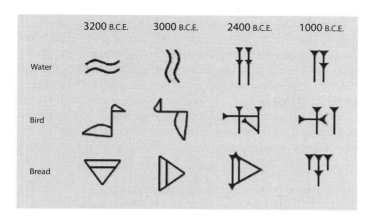

	3200 B.C.E.	3000 B.C.E.	2400 B.C.E.	1000 B.C.E.
Water				
Bird				
Bread				

Early writing in Mesopotamia. The chart shows that the writing system invented in Sumer in the fourth millennium B.C.E. changed considerably over the centuries. Pictograms, signs that look like the things they represent, evolved into abstract logographic symbols. Straight or curved lines were transformed into short lines attached to wedges. Why do you think that Mesopotamian scribes transformed pictograms into abstract signs?

others, called logograms, that represented units of meaning, that is, whole words, or sometimes combinations of words. Logograms stand for particular objects, actions, ideas, or emotions. Modern English is written mainly in an alphabetic, not logographic system, but it still incorporates logograms. For example, we known that the "$" sign stands for the word "dollar," even though it has no sound value to help us pronounce that word. Number signs (1, 2, 3, and so on) are also logograms. They represent meaning but not sounds. The most widespread logographic system in use today is Chinese, though Chinese characters also incorporate signs representing syllables to guide pronunciation.

Most ordinary Mesopotamians remained illiterate, having neither time nor resources to master hundreds of logographic signs. The temple elite no doubt liked it that way because they controlled information other people did not have, and this monopoly contributed to their power. Gradually, however, a larger minority learned to read and write because society found more and more activities to record: royal decrees, government letters, king lists, astronomical observations, merchants' transactions, and eventually myths, hymns, and proverbs.

Monarchy in Mesopotamia.

Despite writing and other tools of power, the authority of the Sumerian priesthood diminished in the mid-third millennium B.C.E. Excavations at several Sumerian and Akkadian cities have uncovered large building complexes that appear to be kingly palaces, not temples. The constant demand for materials and labor to maintain irrigation, the increasingly intricate relations among social and occupational groups, and the periodic wars between city-states combined to force a shift of power from a minority of religious professionals to military rulers.

A cuneiform tablet dating to about 2100 B.C.E. provides a long list of Sumerian kings. Mebaragesi of Kish, who lived around 2600 B.C.E., is the thirtieth name on the list but the first for which we have archaeological evidence that attests to his existence. The ruling dates of many of the early kings are the stuff of myth. The tablet reports that the first eight of them enjoyed reigns ranging from 18,600 to 36,000 years! Gilgamesh, listed among the rulers of the First Dynasty of Uruk, became the subject of legendary tales of heroism, superhuman strength, and flawed ambition that storytellers passed down through the centuries. In the second millennium B.C.E. these yarns were brought together in the Epic of Gilgamesh, the most celebrated work of ancient Mesopotamian poetry. The narrative recounts the king's battles with monsters, his defiance of the gods, and his fruitless search for the key to immortality.

We have substantial evidence from statuary and inscriptions of the reign of Sargon (2340–2284 B.C.E.), a warrior king who founded a state in Akkad. Under his command Akkadian lancers and swordsmen conquered both the city-states of Sumer and territories far up the Tigris and Euphrates valleys. Sargon and his four royal successors, ruling many cities and a linguistically diverse population, should be

Cuneiform tablet. The writing on this small clay tablet probably gives an account of grain distributed from a temple.

empire A type of state in which a single political authority, often identified with a particular kinship, linguistic, or ethnic group, rules over peoples of different ethnic or linguistic identities.

credited with having created the world's earliest **empire.** These rulers also appear to have claimed that their authority derived directly from the gods. For example, statues depicting Naram-Sin, grandson of Sargon, show him sporting a horned helmet previously reserved only for images of deities. Mesopotamian monarchs did not, as far as we know, claim to be heavenly beings, but, as we shall see, god-kings and god-queens became a standard feature of state-building across Afroeurasia in later millennia.

About 2190 B.C.E., the Akkadian empire collapsed, possibly in connection with extended periods of drought, as well as hostile incursions of hill people from the nearby Zagros Mountains. After that event, power shifted back to Sumer. There, a line of rulers in the city of Ur, called the Third Dynasty of Ur, kept southern Mesopotamia united for another two centuries and presided over a new flowering of monumental building and fine art. The kings of Ur also fought nearly continuously with small monarchies and city-states of the Zagros range and the Iranian Plateau east and southeast of Mesopotamia. The brick-walled cities of western Iran, then known as Elam, were strategic prizes because their merchants transshipped copper, tin, lapis lazuli, turquoise, and other valuable metals and gems originating in lands to the east. About 2000 B.C.E., an alliance of Elamite and other western Iranian states captured the last monarch of the Third Dynasty and for the next few centuries dominated the politics of Mesopotamia.

In their third millennium glory days, the rulers of both Sumer and Akkad took steps to build a strong command system, that is, a set of institutions and practices for centrally controlling their subjects and extracting taxes from them. For example, Sargon and his successors appointed military officials to represent royal authority in cities and villages

bureaucracy A hierarchy of officials within a government that carries out the laws, decrees, and functions of the state.

throughout the empire. This way of delegating power constitutes **bureaucracy.** Defined precisely, bureaucrats are more than simply "people who work for the government." Mesopotamian bureaucrats were officials who governed villages, cities, or provinces not in their own right but as formal representatives of the state. Whatever an official said or did publicly was to be understood, not as a personal act, but as one mirroring the ruler's will and backed by the full weight of the state's armed power. A particular official might be relieved of his duties for one reason or another, but the office itself, which usually included special regalia and rituals, remained intact as an instrument of the state. Writing was a potent tool of the bureaucratic command system. It allowed officials to exchange precise messages over many miles and to store accurate records of royal decrees, tax receipts, and military supplies.

Class divisions. The third millennium B.C.E. also witnessed the rise of an aristocracy, or land-owning class. This was a secular elite; its power and prestige rested fundamentally on wealth, not on special religious authority. A small but rich landlord minority emerged as larger areas of irrigated land fell into the hands of private families. In some cities, this elite formed assemblies, which took part in urban governance. At the same time, the economic and social status of ordinary farmers may have declined as more and more

Victory stele of Naram-Sin. This stele, or upright stone slab, commemorates this Akkadian emperor's triumph over a people of the Zagros Mountains. Wearing a horned helmet signifying divinity, Naram-Sin (r. 2260–2223 B.C.E.) marches majestically upward, crushing an enemy soldier under foot as he goes. In front of him, one foe clutches a spear embedded in his neck, another begs the conquering king for mercy. Why do you think the stonecutter included stars twinkling over Naram-Sin's head?

peasants The social and economic class of farmers or herders who hold relatively small amounts of productive land as owners, rent-paying tenants, or serfs bound to a particular estate.

slavery The social institution in which an individual is held by law, custom, or simply coercion in servitude to another individual, a group, or the state.

of them became **peasants,** renting land from affluent families or working as day laborers. Indeed, **slavery** became a significant institution in Mesopotamia. In Mesopotamia most enslaved people originated either as prisoners of war or destitute foreigners, and the great majority of them belonged to the city temple or the ruler. A slave could be bought or sold for about the price of a donkey, but social practice appears to have awarded them some rights to protest publicly if they were abused.

Gender inequality.

Complex society brought not only slavery but also new constraints on women. In Mesopotamia, men came to spend much more time producing food than they had in paleolithic times. They herded sheep, fed pigs, and tilled fields using plows pulled by draft animals. Although men largely took charge of public affairs and warfare, women sometimes held high and powerful positions as priestesses, and they could own property and represent themselves in court. Ordinary women, however, spent less time farming and more time preparing food and weaving cloth, which tied them closer to their homes and villages. Gradually, the social value of female labor diminished relative to that of men. This male "takeover" of early civilization

occurred slowly. Even so, **patriarchy** was on the way to becoming the norm in all known early agrarian civilizations.

patriarchy A society in which males dominate social, political, and cultural life.

Mesopotamian science.

The sheer profusion of human activities in densely populated Mesopotamia demanded more sophisticated methods of computation than any earlier society had required. Sometime before 3000 B.C.E., Sumerian scribes worked out a system of numerical notation in cuneiform script. They devised both base-10 (decimal) and base-60 (sexagesimal) systems. The base-60 method has endured in the ways we keep time (60 seconds to the minute, 60 minutes to the hour) and reckon the circumference of a circle (360°). Mesopotamians used a combination of base-10 and base-60 mathematics, together with geometric concepts for everyday government and commercial transactions as well as to survey land, chart the stars, design buildings, and build irrigation works. Other technical innovations of the age of Sumer and Akkad included the seed drill, the vaulted arch, refinements in bronze metallurgy, and, most ingenious of all, the wheel. This device was probably applied first to pottery making, later to transport and plowing.

Despite class divisions and frequent interurban wars, Mesopotamia achieved remarkable cultural unity expressed in distinctive styles of art, architecture, literature, and science. The southern valley, a productive land hedged on all sides by desert, mountain, or sea, made for a compact cultural world. Ideas and information moved easily from one

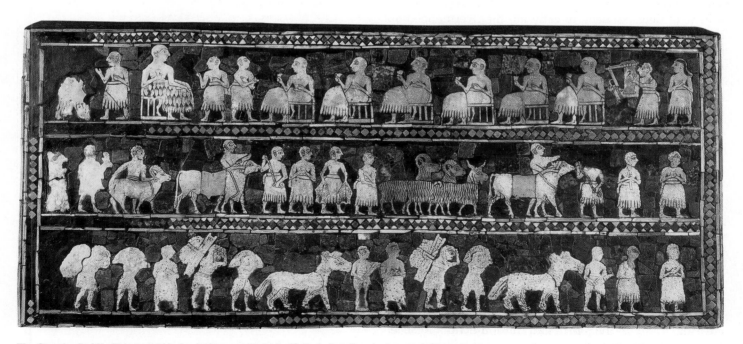

The Standard of Ur. This two-sided wooden panel inlaid with lapis lazuli and other materials comes from a tomb constructed about 2700 B.C.E. in the city of Ur. The pictures on one side of the panel, whose function is not certain, illustrate Mesopotamian class divisions: At the top the ruler and his high officials make merry. In the middle common people bring cattle and other animals to the banquet. At the bottom war prisoners or other foreigners lug various burdens. Can you spot the female companion at the ruler's feast?

city to another by donkey train, wheeled cart, or riverboat. Writing multiplied the possibilities of cultural communication, transforming oral versions of myths, epics, and customary laws that had circulated in the valley for centuries into a fairly standardized literature. In other words, writing hugely broadened the range of collective learning—knowledge that could be shared, preserved, remembered, and passed along.

Complex Society on the Nile

In the Tigris-Euphrates River valley, complex society emerged gradually over two thousand years. In Egypt it came, relatively speaking, all in a rush. The climate of northern Africa gradually dried out starting in the fifth millennium B.C.E., and as it did people who once lived in the Saharan steppes and hill country east and west of the river pushed into the valley, where water was abundant. They brought domesticated cattle from the Sahara and adapted cereals and legumes that had been introduced from the Fertile Crescent. Once farmers began to reap lush harvests twice a year by simply broadcasting wheat or barley seeds in damp Nile mud, the agrarian economy grew fast, especially from about 4000 B.C.E.

The Nile was a fairly efficient hydrological machine. The White Nile, Blue Nile, and Atbara Rivers, the three principal tributaries of the Egyptian Nile, originated in tropical highlands of East Africa and Ethiopia, thousands of miles to the south. Summer rains there produced a gentle but voluminous swelling of the waters, which rolled into Egypt in mid-August. Suspended in these waters were millions of tons of rich sediment. In early fall the river flooded out over the alluvial valley. Then it receded, leaving saturated ground and a thick layer of dark silt. Egyptian farmers needed only simple dikes and ditches to guide the Nile's waters. The black soil produced a cornucopia of wheat, barley, leeks, onions, cucumber, garlic, lettuce, dates, and grapes. Of course there were years when the flood fell short and people went hungry or when it rose too high and swept away villages. Ancient texts show that the Egyptians worried a lot about this. But on the whole the pulse of the river was more predictable than the Tigris-Euphrates.

From the first of several cataracts, or rapids, near the modern city of Aswan, the Nile traced a winding green path about six hundred miles long. Near modern Cairo the river segmented into several channels that fanned out across the coastal plain to form the marshy and immensely fertile Nile delta. Ancient Egyptians visualized their land as divided into two parts, Lower Egypt, which was the delta, and Upper Egypt, which extended upriver more than five hundred miles from the apex of the delta to the First Cataract. Increasing aridity in the fourth and third millennia B.C.E. left Egypt's burgeoning population "caged" within the river valley, as were the populations of the Tigris and Euphrates. Irrigation canals could allow for farming some distance from the river and delta, but farther out only animal herders and

scattered oasis communities could survive. Consequently, Egyptians had no choice but to organize society in drastic new ways, just as the Mesopotamians had done some centuries earlier (see Map 2.4).

The rise of the pharaohs. In contrast to the Sumerians, Egyptians did not respond to the problem of population growth within a rigidly limited space by forming clusters of independent city-states. Rather, strong leaders, known historically as pharaohs, politically unified Upper and Lower Egypt about 3100 B.C.E. This event is associated in Egyptian legend with Narmer (also called Menes), the reputed founder of Egypt's First Dynasty. During the following two millennia, a succession of twenty dynasties ruled the valley. Scholars partition this era into Old, Middle, and New Kingdoms, separated from one another by relatively short Intermediate Periods of disturbance and fragmentation.

In Mesopotamia, rulers took to proclaiming themselves agents of the gods, but the pharaohs went further. Beginning

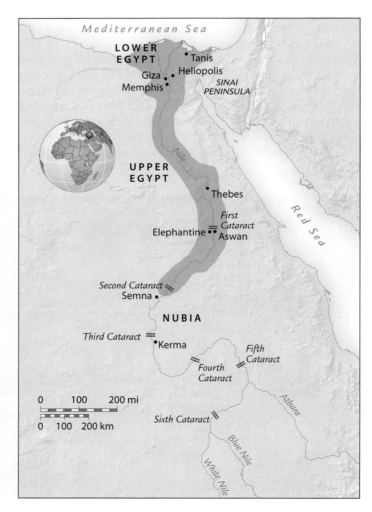

MAP 2.4 Egypt from 3000 to 1000 B.C.E.

The green area represents the maximum territorial extent of the Egyptian state during the Old Kingdom and Middle Kingdom periods. Why is this territory so much wider at the northern end than it is farther south?

TIME PERIODS OF ANCIENT EGYPT

3100–2686 B.C.E.	Early Dynastic Period	Dynasties 1–2
2686–2160 B.C.E.	Old Kingdom	Dynasties 3–8
2160–2040 B.C.E.	First Intermediate Period	Dynasties 9–11 (early)
2040–1652 B.C.E.	Middle Kingdom	Dynasties 11 (late)–13
1652–1540 B.C.E.	Second Intermediate Period	Dynasties 14–17
1540–1070 B.C.E.	New Kingdom	Dynasties 18–20

of the god-king in his palace, whereas the top official, a sort of prime minister, took charge of day-to-day affairs. Meeting the pharaoh's tax demands in grain and other commodities, the rural populace made complex society possible. Indeed, the rich surviving record of sculpture and painting vividly portrays Egyptian villagers at their daily farm routines. Individuals could hold land and sell produce privately, but the pharaoh "owned" Egypt. Ordinary people labored for his pleasure, getting back a share of the riches in famine relief in bad harvest years or in payment for labor on public works projects.

Written words and pyramids. Recent archaeological work in southern Egypt has revealed evidence of writing, including a sequence of abstract symbols and human and animal figures carved into a limestone, dating to about 3250 B.C.E. The Egyptian sign system, called hieroglyphs or "sacred carvings," was at first made up of pictograms, but, as in Mesopotamia, the signs later came to represent both words, or logograms and specific sounds. An aspiring scribe of the pharaoh's court had to master more than seven hundred distinct signs to be considered literate.

Old Kingdom pharaohs spent vast amounts of wealth on temples, monumental sculptures, and paintings, and the bureaucracy mastered the art of mobilizing the population for big civic projects. The most spectacular undertaking was construction of massive royal tombs across the Nile from modern Cairo. The three great pyramids of Giza preserved deep in their cool interiors the remains of three kings of the Fourth Dynasty (2613–2494 B.C.E.). Constructed of millions of blocks of cut limestone brought in by boat from upriver, the pyramids are only the most grandiose of the Old Kingdom's many royal burial sites. In Egyptian religious thought, death was an inevitable event, but

in the era known as the Old Kingdom (2686–2160 B.C.E.), Egyptians accepted their monarchs as incarnations of the hawk-headed sky god Horus. This deity was one of many that controlled the fate of humans and the forces of nature, chief among them Amon and Re, gods associated with the sun. According to Egyptian religious thought, cosmic power underlay the pharaoh's authority, and the prosperity of the valley depended on the ruler's well-being in both life and death. The monarch, in turn, had a moral responsibility to maintain *ma'at,* that is, the essential vitality and balance of the universe, the force that made both the sun and the summer Nile rise. The pharaohs were hardly democratic leaders, but the ideal of *ma'at,* which fundamentally meant "truth," impelled them, at least much of the time, to rule with justice and competence, rather than brutal coercion.

Pharaohs of the five dynasties that encompassed Old Kingdom Egypt maintained their main governing complex at Memphis, near modern Cairo at the apex of the delta. Subordinate centers of command arose in other parts of the valley, as did temple complexes. These places did not, however, grow into densely populated walled cities. On the contrary, most of the population inhabited a strand of hundreds of villages that ran nearly continuously from the First Cataract to the Mediterranean. In the early third millennium B.C.E., this tightly settled corridor was transformed into a highway for government officials and tax collectors.

The term *pharaoh* means "great household," and from the ruler's palace ranks of royal officials marched out to implement the royal will in the countryside. Courtiers, scribes, and servants surrounded the person

Palette of Narmer. Dating to Egypt's first dynasty, this slate ritual object narrates the political unification of the upper and lower Nile valley. The pharaoh Narmer, wearing the white crown of Upper Egypt, commands the scene. Before him, the falcon, symbol of the sky god Horus, sits atop papyrus plants signifying Lower Egypt. What similarities and differences in design and in the representation of figures do you notice on the palette of Narmer compared with the victory stele of Naram-Sin on page 64?

A Pharaoh's Warning in Stone

Pharaohs of the Old Kingdom occasionally sent exploratory missions upriver beyond the First Cataract of the Nile into Nubia, the historic region corresponding today to southern Egypt and northern Sudan. The pharaohs knew the lands at the southern edge of the Sahara Desert to be a rich source of gold, copper, ivory, ebony, cattle, and slaves. Early in the second millennium B.C.E., Sesostris I (also Senusret), a pharaoh of the Twelfth Dynasty, pursued an aggressive policy of expansion into Nubia in order to tap and control trade farther to the south. This king's great-grandson, Sesostris III (r. 1878–1839 B.C.E.), completed a series of forts near the Second Cataract to defend Egyptian territory and to launch campaigns into Nubia. The pharaoh's soldiers, however, faced potentially strong opposition from the African monarchy centered at Kerma, beyond the Third Cataract. This state dated back to the third millennium B.C.E., flourishing partly on Nile trade and partly on farming and herding on grasslands east and west of the river. At the fortress of Semna (Heh) just south of the Second Cataract, Sesostris III had stone markers erected carrying inscriptions that proclaimed Egypt's power in the region and alerting intruders to beware.

The living Horus: Divine of Form; the Two Ladies: Divine of Birth; the King of Upper and Lower Egypt: Khakaure, given life; the living Gold-Horus; Being; the Son of Re's body, his beloved, the Lord of the Two Lands: Sesostris, given life-stability-health forever. Year 16, third month of winter: the king made his southern boundary at [Semna]:

> I have made my boundary further south than my fathers,
> I have added to what was bequeathed me.
> I am a king who speaks and acts,
> What my heart plans is done by my arm.
> One who attacks to conquer, who is swift to succeed,
> In whose heart a plan does not slumber.
> Considerate to clients, steady in mercy,
> Merciless to the foe who attacks him.
> One who attacks him who would attack,
> Who stops when one stops,
> Who replies to a matter as befits it.
> To stop when attacked is to make bold the foe's heart,
> Attack is valor, retreat is cowardice,
> A coward is he who is driven from his border.
> Since the Nubian listens to the word of mouth,
> To answer him is to make him retreat.

> Attack him, he will turn his back,
> Retreat, he will start attacking.
> They are not people one respects,
> They are wretches, craven-hearted.
> My majesty has seen it, it is not an untruth.
> I have captured their women,
> I have carried off their dependents,
> Gone to their wells, killed their cattle,
> Cut down their grain, set fire to it.
> As my father lives for me, I speak the truth!
> It is no boast that comes from my mouth.

As for any son of mine who shall maintain this border which my majesty has made, he is my son, born to my majesty. The true son is he who champions his father, who guards the border of his begetter. But he who abandons it, who fails to fight for it, he is not my son, he was not born to me.

Now my majesty has had an image made of my majesty, at this border which my majesty has made, in order that you maintain it, in order that you fight for it.

Source: Miriam Lichtheim, *Ancient Egyptian Literature, Volume I: The Old and Middle Kingdoms* (Berkeley: University of California Press, 2006), 118–120.

Thinking Critically

Who was likely Sesostris III's intended audience for this inscription? How does Sesostris III describe the Nubians, and what does his description convey about Egyptian attitudes toward them? What qualities in a ruler does Sesostris III emphasize? Based on the inscription, what knowledge might we infer about Egyptian campaigns into Nubia?

---

it might be survived. A pleasant afterlife presumably awaited individuals who had refrained from evil deeds and who made proper preparations for the transition, including the elaborate process of mummifying the body to preserve it for later revival. Almost everything we know about Egypt's culture of death relates to the experience of rich and powerful families, not common farmers. A deceased pharaoh clearly

had to be preserved and safeguarded because the corpse remained inseparable from the immortal soul.

In fact, preparations for a pharaoh's passing became a kind of national industry. Relying on engineering and geometric skill, superb tactical organization, and sheer muscle, the government mobilized thousands of artisans and peasants to build the pyramids. Since the proper entombing of

The pyramids of Giza and a protecting sphinx. This monumental creature with a man's head and a lion's body stands guard before the colossal tomb pyramid of the Fourth Dynasty pharaoh Khafre. The sandstone sculpture, which faces the rising sun, may represent the pharaoh himself. The Old Kingdom's pyramids of Giza loom near the western bank of the Nile opposite modern Cairo. How does the sphinx's pharaonic headdress enhance the visual power of the statue?

the divine ruler was a matter of profound importance to Egypt's well-being, the population went to the task more or less willingly, especially during inactive periods in the agricultural year. Eventually, however, the dynasties of the Old Kingdom scaled down royal burial projects to relatively modest dimensions. Not even the riches of the Nile could provide ruler after ruler with monuments of such stupendous volume.

Harappan Society in the Indus Valley

Complex society emerged along the Indus River just a few centuries later than in Mesopotamia and Egypt. Before British archaeologists started digging in the 1920s, however, the world did not even know that a civilization, named Harappan (huh-RAH-pan) after one of its leading cities, had ever existed. Scholars have so far identified 1,052 ancient Indus settlements, from sprawling cities to modest villages. Their total area embraces most of modern Pakistan and the northwestern corner of India.

The ecological setting. Like the Tigris-Euphrates and the Nile, the Indus transects Afroeurasia's Great Arid Zone. The direct distance between the Tigris and the lower Indus is a little more than 1,300 miles. In neolithic times, farming and herding communities gradually multiplied along this belt of territory, clustering in highland valleys of what are today Iran, Afghanistan, and Pakistan. By around 6000 B.C.E., farmers of the Sulayman Mountains just west of the Indus were raising wheat, barley, sheep, and goats, as well as producing pottery and copper tools. As the highland population grew, it spilled down the Sulayman slopes and onto the Indus River plain much as cultivators spread from Iran's Zagros Mountains to southern Mesopotamia in earlier times.

Plentiful water, rich silt, and a brilliant sun offered farmers higher productivity than the neighboring highlands could provide. Population on the plain grew denser, and as in Mesopotamia and Egypt, early Indus settlers found themselves gradually "trapped" in the valley with no place to go except in the direction of greater social complexity (see Map 2.5).

The Indus and its four major tributaries gush from the great snowy wall of the Himalaya Mountains. These channels converge as they flow across the northern region of the plain, called the Punjab. The rivers conjoin for a stretch, then divide again to form the delta, the region known as Sind, before emptying into the Arabian Sea. The valley's alluvial soil was not only rich but also extended over an area of about 250,000 square miles, twice the arable land area of Mesopotamia or Egypt. The flood season arrived in June, forming numerous natural lakes and ponds on the plain. Farmers planted crops in early fall after the waters receded. In contrast to the hydrological conditions in southern Mesopotamia, these temporary reservoirs saved Indus farmers from having to construct large-scale irrigation works. Monsoon winds flowing from the African land mass across the western Indian Ocean between late spring and early autumn bring rain in varying quantities to South Asia. Recent studies based on evidence from archaeology, geology, and satellite imagery suggest that before about 3000 B.C.E., summer monsoons were powerful, dumping so much rain on the Indus region that annual flooding prevented much human settlement. In the fourth millennium B.C.E., however, the rain-bearing winds weakened gradually over the long term, opening more land to year-round cultivation and encouraging population buildup along the Indus system as well as the Ghaggar-Hakra River and its tributaries east of the Indus.

MAP 2.5 Complex
society in the Indus
valley.

Would early complex soci-
ety in South Asia have been
possible if the Himalaya
Mountains did not exist?

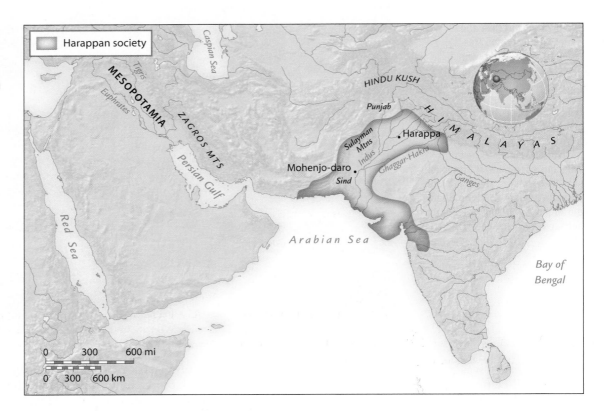

Cities of the Indus.

Between 2800 and 2600 B.C.E., Indus valley dwellers started building cities. As in Mesopotamia, Indus cities developed as dense, distinct settlements separated by village-dotted countryside. One of the biggest centers was Harappa, which arose on the Punjab plain along the Ravi River, an Indus tributary. The city had a circuit of about three miles and a fluctuating population that may have reached as many as eighty thousand when people gathered from near and far to trade in seasonal markets. The largest urban complex so far discovered is Mohenjo-daro, four hundred miles south of Harappa. In contrast to the jumbled maze of lanes and alleys that characterized Mesopotamian cities, the streets of both Harappa and Mohenjo-daro were laid out on a grid pattern, suggesting thoughtful urban design. Houses, stores, and shops of baked brick lined city streets. Subterranean channels brought in fresh water and flushed out sewage. Residents built private homes around a central courtyard, and most of them had toilet and bathing rooms equipped with sewer drains.

Indus city people followed a variety of occupations. Some were specialists at crafts such as masonry, coppersmithing, ivory carving, pottery making, and weaving. Textile production was probably a home industry for every family.

Cities of the Indus valley. If we cast back to the late third millennium B.C.E., we might imagine this straight street in Mohenjo-daro crowded with local residents, shopkeepers, and traders. Why do you think the cities of the Harappan civilization remained unknown to the wider world until the twentieth century?

Many city residents may have been full-time farmers, who trudged daily to the surrounding countryside to tend fields of wheat, barley, peas, dates, sesame, and cotton, or herds of sheep, buffalo, and humped zebu cattle.

Material remains of Indus settlements have so far revealed much less than we would like to know about Harappan society. Recovered treasures include superbly crafted jewelry, masks, seals, ceramics, and figurines. We may assume, therefore, that a minority of men and women were rich. But houses were relatively uniform in size, which hints at a fair degree of social equality rather than a strict division between a land-controlling aristocracy and everyone else. In archaeological sites, baked clay figurines of women often displaying fancy hair styles predominate over male figurines. And ceramic seals carry engravings of female deities. These objects suggest that women could rise to important ceremonial or social positions in Harappan cities, though the evidence is indirect.

Harappan government? The material ruins of Indus society have left no trace of kings, queens, or sprawling palaces. Nor is there any evidence that a single state or even cluster of city-states ever dominated the plain. In stark contrast to Mesopotamia and Egypt, surviving pictorial art shows no warriors capturing people or stabbing and clubbing one another. On the other hand, the rise of cities as impressive as Harappa and Mohenjo-daro suggests some kind of central management. Urban planning and engineering were precise and uniform, suggesting watchful public supervision. Bricks for construction had standard dimensions, main streets were exactly twice as wide as side streets, and artisans dug wells lined with ingenious wedge-shaped bricks that could withstand (and have withstood) centuries of earthquakes. In Mohenjo-daro a cluster of elevated buildings and towers dominated the landscape. These structures, resting on a brick platform of 600,000 square yards, may have served as a fortress or as storehouses for city grain reserves. Although Harappans made figurines and seals that represented deities, no evidence of a temple priesthood has been found. Mohenjo-daro's central complex includes a water

tank nearly forty feet long. People could descend into the tank by either of two sets of stone steps. Many scholars think that the "great bath," as it is called, was a place of ritual cleansing and regeneration, a key element of Indian religious practice as it emerged in later centuries. But no one knows for sure.

The Harappan cultural style. Archaeological work has revealed many similarities from one Indus city to another in urban planning, architecture, pottery, statuary, seals, and jewelry design. This unity of style points to intense cultural intercommunication on the plain and the maturing of a coherent cultural tradition that thrived for more than 500 years. Since we have no evidence of an empire-builder like Sargon of Akkad, we may infer that cultural interchange occurred mainly in association with regional trade, or perhaps with intercity social ties based on kinship or occupation.

Indus society had a written language. Seals, tablets, pottery, and other objects inscribed with a distinctive script have been found in nearly every part of the plain. Unfortunately, linguists have so far been unable to decipher much of the sign system, which dates to as early as 3300 B.C.E. Harappan jottings appear to represent both pictographic and sound symbols, but inscriptions are never more than two lines long. It is likely that only a small minority of the valley's population could read or write because as Indus civilization declined after 1900 B.C.E., the writing system gradually disappeared.

An early yogi? This stone seal from the ancient city of Mohenjo-daro depicts a male deity having three faces and sporting bangles on his arms. He is seated on a throne in *baddha konasana*, the name of a pose familiar to modern practitioners of yoga. He wears an extravagant headdress. On either side of it are signs in the Indus writing system. Why do you think it has been so hard for linguists to decipher the Indus script?

Interregional Communication and Commerce

We should not forget that the populations of early complex societies represented only a small percentage of the world's total in the third millennium B.C.E. Most people around the globe continued to subsist as foragers or as farmers and herders inhabiting small, dispersed settlements. Nevertheless, to the extent that country and city dwellers had knowledge of each other, strong mutual attractions existed between them. Rural people were drawn to the handcrafted goods, precious wares, tools, and technological knowledge that urban centers had to offer. Conversely, the river valley societies reached into the surrounding hinterlands for food, minerals, gems, and timber, as well as live captives to put to work as slaves. As the populations of the three valleys grew, "concentric circles" of exchange around these hubs inevitably grew as well. In time, they overlapped, which brought the valleys into sustained contact with one another. When that happened, products, skills, and knowledge originating in one of the centers began to affect life in the others. Thus, the entire India-to-Mediterranean region emerged as a single zone of communication and exchange (see Map 2.6).

The Mesopotamian network. The oldest intercity trade web emerged in Mesopotamia. In the third millennium B.C.E., canoes, barges, and small sail craft glided up and down the rivers, carrying bulk commodities like barley, hides, and cheap pottery. Donkey pack trains and ox-drawn carts lumbered from the cities to farming villages on the plain and in distant hills. In Sumer, which had few natural resources besides arable land, temple priests controlled most exchange, sending commercial agents far and wide to trade Mesopotamian farm products, as well as textiles, pottery, and other finished goods made in temple workshops for timber, copper, and other commodities. Mesopotamian agents voyaged southeastward along the rim of the Persian Gulf to acquire copper, dates, fish, pearls, and diorite (a hard decorative stone) for Sumerian and Akkadian cities. Trade in the valley grew so much that figuring out the relative value of hundreds of different goods relative to one another became very complicated. Consequently, Mesopotamians began to use units of silver, copper, barley, or other commodities both as units for determining the relative value of other goods and as mediums of exchange. For example, a shekel of silver, which weighed one-third of an ounce, or slightly more than three U.S. pennies, came to serve as a

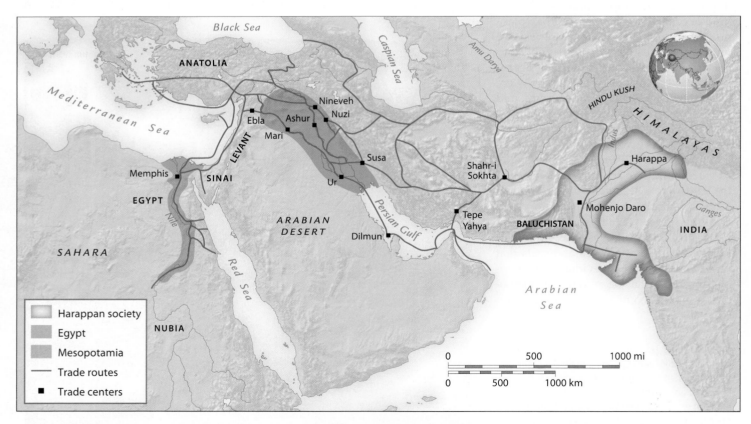

MAP 2.6 Trade in the region from South Asia to the Mediterranean, third millennium B.C.E.
What factors explain why trade was more active between the Indus valley and Mesopotamia than between Egypt and Mesopotamia?

standard to express the value of particular items, say, the price of a slave or a basket of figs.

By about 3000 B.C.E., exchange routes knitting together cities in northern and southern Mesopotamia formed a single network extending from the sources of the Tigris and Euphrates to the Persian Gulf. As this happened, a new breed of trader joined the commercial agents who served temple and palace. These were individuals who trafficked privately and for personal profit—the world's earliest professional merchant class. City-states such as Mari and Ebla near the upper Euphrates River tapped minerals and gems found in Anatolia and northern Iran. Merchants of Assyria, that is, the region centered on the northern Tigris valley, made the city-state of Ashur an important commercial hub. Beginning around 1900 B.C.E., Assyrians penetrated deep into Anatolia, founding twenty or more satellite settlements to deal in gold, silver, and copper, which they shipped throughout Southwest Asia. At a place called Tepe Yahya in southwestern Iran, local artisans began as early as 2800 B.C.E. to manufacture stone bowls of a special style and to ship them more than five hundred miles to Mesopotamia.

Egypt's trade links. We know from archaeological evidence that Mesopotamia had significant commercial and cultural contacts with Egypt by the late fourth millennium B.C.E. For example, archaeologists excavating Egyptian sites have found specimens of lapis lazuli that Mesopotamian traders probably acquired from Afghanistan or Baluchistan (a region that overlaps modern Iran and Pakistan) and carried to the Nile. As Egypt's complex society expanded, however, direct trade with Mesopotamia appears to have remained modest or even shrank. One factor may be that increasing aridity in northern Arabia made overland pack transport directly between southern Mesopotamia and Egypt increasingly expensive and dangerous. The Old Kingdom dynasties also tried to control the movement of goods in and out of the Nile valley, and Egyptian texts of that age make no mention of merchants running private businesses or commercial expeditions.

The pharaoh's commercial agents, however, served the state's interests well. Their main link from the Nile to Southwest Asia was not the desert track to Sumer but shipping routes to ports of the Levant, the eastern Mediterranean coastal region that is today Israel, Palestine, Lebanon, and part of Syria. The Levant's most important export to Egypt was wood, especially large timbers of cedar, pine, and fir from Lebanon's highland forests. Boats could transport timber around the southeastern curve of the Mediterranean in much greater quantity than pack animals could haul it across the Sinai Peninsula.

Like the Tigris-Euphrates, the Nile was a natural highway of north–south trade, though a much longer one. Egyptian

Transport on the Nile. These figures carved from wood crowd onto a boat propelled by rowers. The model, dated to about 1900 B.C.E., comes from the tomb of an Egyptian estate manager. Note the large stern rudder. What uses might a craft like this have had?

agents operated upriver to Nubia to buy gold, slaves, and a variety of exotic products that came from the African tropical latitudes further south. Tomb inscriptions record the trade exploits of Harkhuf, an Egyptian official who held the governorship of southern Egypt between about 2290 and 2270 B.C.E. and who led four commercial expeditions into Nubia. In the inscriptions, he boasts of his success: "I came down [the Nile] bringing gifts from that country in great quantity, the likes of which had never before been brought back to this land. . . . Then his majesty sent me a third time. . . . I came down with three hundred donkeys laden with incense, ebony, . . . panther skins, elephant's tusks, throw sticks, and all sort of good products."[2] Other Egyptian missions traded to the region they identified as Punt, which was most likely the land just west of the Red Sea where the modern states of Eritrea and Ethiopia are today.

Far-flung Harappan trade. In the Indus valley, the inter-urban trade network took shape from about 2400 B.C.E. Pack trains, two-wheeled ox carts, and flat-bottomed boats transported foodstuffs and luxury wares throughout the plain and into the neighboring hills. Merchants who were probably private entrepreneurs, not state agents, traveled west into Baluchistan and southeast toward tropical India in search of metals and gemstones. Harappan colonizers also ventured a thousand miles from the valley to found a trading post in northeastern Afghanistan, probably for trans-shipping gold, silver, copper, and lapis lazuli.

Harappans were among the world's early sea traders, steering rudimentary watercraft from the Indus River delta along the northern edge of the Arabian Sea to the Persian Gulf. Discovery of Harappan artifacts such as weights and seals show that Indus merchants made contact with Mesopotamian counterparts in the gulf, mainly at Dilmun on the island of Bahrain. An inscription of the emperor Sargon tells of ships from Meluhha, which scholars identify with the Indus, docking at Akkad in the twenty-fourth century B.C.E.

Long-distance cultural exchange. The routes linking the three complex societies inevitably carried ideas and information as well as goods. Each of these societies developed profoundly different cultural styles in many respects, but mutual cultural influences were not negligible in the third millennium B.C.E. Mesopotamia was, as far as we know, the world birthplace of a number of key inventions and discoveries, including the wheel, the traction plow, brick-building methods, and bronze metallurgy, plus several major plant and animal domesticates. Several of these ingredients of agrarian culture almost certainly diffused from Mesopotamia to Egypt, India, and lands beyond. Materials and ideas related to food production probably diffused east and west quite rapidly, in part because the climates and seasonal latitudes were similar in all three valleys.

Mesopotamia was also the recipient of innovations. Archeological finds suggest that pottery-making technology spread initially from northeastern Africa to the Fertile Crescent. Around 2000 B.C.E., Harappan farmers began to grow sorghum and pearl millet, both domesticated plants of African origin that probably reached the Indus overland or by way of early Arabian Sea trade. Cotton and several minor food plants are likely to have spread from India westward. The idea of sacred rulership, that is, the belief that chiefs and monarchs possess supernatural powers or even fully divine natures almost certainly spread from the savanna lands surrounding the upper Nile to Egypt—and possibly from there to Mesopotamia. Finally, there is little doubt that Sumerian scribes invented the first full writing system, but Egyptian and Harappan signs have now been dated early enough to weaken the theory that the *idea* of writing necessarily originated in Mesopotamia.

Complex Societies and the Environment

The advent of food production, the crowding of people into dense settlements, and the incessant growth of human numbers worldwide represented a new variable in the continually changing global biosphere. Though neither farmers nor city dwellers were conscious of any but the short-term effects of their behavior, they began to alter the earthly landscape on a scale far beyond the capabilities of paleolithic foragers. Like global society today, they also began to experience unintended and sometimes worrying ecological consequences of settled and urban living.

Agrarian life and infectious disease. One change that accompanied the rise of complex societies, and has been with us ever since, was growing human susceptibility to a host of lethal microorganisms. Paleolithic men and women might die from any number of accidents or calamities long before their fortieth birthdays but not so frequently from infectious disease. When humans began to pack themselves into villages, and then cities, they were obliged to live much closer to their own heaps of garbage and bodily waste—havens for potentially dangerous microbes. Farm people also commonly shared living space with all sorts of animals—sheep, pigs, cows, chickens, and dogs. A number of the maladies that have tormented humankind in the past five millennia, including smallpox, measles, chickenpox, tuberculosis, and flu, started out as pathogens whose hosts were domestic animals. Contagious diseases spread easily among flocks and herds, and some microbes thrived by making genetic adaptations to human bodies. When people transmitted pathogens by coughing, sneezing, touching, defecating, or sharing sleeping mats, they might trigger a citywide epidemic. We do not have much concrete evidence of the larger social effects of these "crowd diseases" on early complex societies. There is little doubt, however, that the first cities were less healthy places to live than foraging camps and that the coming of agriculture permanently transformed the ecological relationships among humans, animals, and disease-producing germs.

Changes on the land. By its very nature, food production required that people deliberately intervene more energetically to alter the physical and natural landscape. To create arable fields, neolithic farmers felled trees or set whole forests on fire. In some regions they practiced shifting agriculture, clearing a field, growing crops on it for a few seasons until the soil became depleted, then moving on with axe and hoe to new ground. If cultivators burned an area repeatedly or permanently grazed animals on it, they might keep woodland from ever regenerating. As early as 5000 B.C.E., for example, neolithic farmers in Britain were already turning large areas of forest into treeless moorland or bogs.

Building complex societies involved more drastic environmental manipulation. In the Tigris-Euphrates, Nile, and Indus valleys, urbanization and intensive farming led to deforestation, calamitous floods, deteriorating soil, and other ecological stresses that seriously affected the directions those societies took. All three civilizations had ravenous appetites for wood for household fuel, construction, and brick making. After depleting local resources, they turned to neighboring areas, and the damage spread. Timber cutters in eastern Anatolia and the Zagros Mountains of western Iran labored to meet Mesopotamia's insatiable appetite for wood but at the cost of deforestation and increased risk of violent flooding and silt buildup downstream on the irrigated plain. In Egypt, forests and marshes receded so fast in the third millennium that by 2200 B.C.E. the populations of elephant, gazelle, giraffe, and rhinoceros that had once flourished there had all but vanished. To the east the Harappans used huge quantities of oven-baked bricks to build their splendid cities. This industry rapidly consumed most of the woodland on the Indus plain, then ate away at the highland forests to the west and north, producing the same problems of erosion and flooding that Mesopotamia faced.

Sumer's special ecological curse was salinization. Because the angle of the alluvial plain was gentle and drainage slow, salts dissolved in river water accumulated gradually in topsoil, poisoning the roots of plants. Sumerian farmers worked endlessly to flush crystallized salts from their fields. But extra irrigation eventually caused water logging, and the salt always returned. Crop yields on salt-infected land dropped slowly, and large areas of once cultivated land had to be abandoned or turned over to animal grazing. By the early second millennium B.C.E. the populations and economies of most of the Sumerian city-states were declining.

Today, wind-swept hillocks in the Iraqi desert mark their ancient locations.

A long drought cycle. Recent climatic research has provided persuasive evidence that all three of the great river valleys, and perhaps much of the Northern Hemisphere, suffered heightened aridity and volatile climatic fluctuations for three centuries beginning about 2200 B.C.E. Relationships of cause and effect between climate change and particular cases of social or economic stress are hard to pin down. But the long-term "dry event" that began in the late third millennium chronologically matches serious crises in the three valleys.

In Mesopotamia the Akkadian empire that Sargon built collapsed about 2190 B.C.E. Aside from extended drought and salinization on the river plain, low rainfall in the deserts east and west of the river valley may have provoked animal-herding peoples to invade farmland close to cities. In the north of Mesopotamia, however, new centers of production and trade sprouted in the second millennium, as we shall see.

In Egypt the Old Kingdom's central authority began to disintegrate about 2134 B.C.E. Political division and civil unrest dragged on for several decades, a time historians call the First Intermediate Period. Scientists studying ancient sediment layers on the Blue Nile in Ethiopia have hypothesized that extended drought severely reduced summer floods on the lower river about the same time that the Old Kingdom fell. This ecological crisis may have triggered famine and social upheaval. Egyptian texts from the era support the theory: "[Grain] has perished everywhere. . . . People are stripped of clothing, perfume, and oil. . . . The dead are thrown in the river. . . . Laughter has perished. Grief walks the land."[3] Nevertheless, strong new leaders united the valley about 2040 B.C.E., ushering in the new era called the Middle Kingdom (2040–1652 B.C.E.).

Harappan civilization peaked around 1900 B.C.E. and then went into permanent decline. Scholars have pointed to an array of ecological stress points, including silt buildup, deforestation in the hill country, excessive flooding, overgrazing, persistent drought, and recurring shifts in the course of the Indus and its tributaries. In the third millennium, weakening summer monsoons appear to have speeded the development of complex society. But as that climatic trend continued, so recent research proposes, farmers in the southern valley experienced increasing water shortages and had to migrate north and east. The Ghaggar-Hakra River network, which was probably fed by monsoons rather than Himalayan glaciers, dried up during part of the year, forcing people to abandon their cities. By about 1500 B.C.E., large-scale complex society no longer existed in the Indus region, though it would return eventually.

• • •

Conclusion

Much of this chapter has focused on the broad region of Afroeurasia between India and the Mediterranean because striking changes in human society occurred there between 10,000 and 2000 B.C.E. Within the fruitful Tigris-Euphrates, Nile, and Indus valleys, population growth and food production reinforced one another in a roughly upward spiral. If those societies were not to burst at the seams, novel social and technological solutions had to be found. Accelerating innovation produced bustling cities, many new occupations, access to exotic goods, grand religious festivals, and conditions of law and order. They also produced iron-fisted rulers, crowded living, infectious diseases, social inequalities, slavery, taxes, and the concentration of public power in the hands of males. Civilization, humans learned early, brought both blessings and vexations.

Meanwhile, the rest of the world by no means stood still. By 3000 B.C.E., agrarian communities were spreading across all the inhabited continents except Australia, transforming landscapes as they advanced. Estimates of total world population growth for such remote times are only educated guesses, but numbers rose from perhaps ten million in 8000 B.C.E., when the agrarian era got seriously under way, to about fifty million by 3000 B.C.E. In that same five thousand years, the number of foragers in the world declined significantly, relative to the total population. Some forager communities saw advantages in turning to farming, but others were displaced or marginalized by cultivators who arrived with their axes, hoes, chiefs, and disease pathogens. By the start of the second millennium B.C.E., where this chapter ends, a fourth complex society was emerging on the floodplains of the Yellow and Yangzi Rivers in northern China. And in temperate Europe, the savanna lands of Africa, tropical Southeast Asia, North America, and the Andes Mountains, men and women were creating more intricate technologies and institutions to meet the demands of farm life and growing populations.

• • •

Key Terms

agrarian society 51	Fertile Crescent 51	neolithic era 53
agricultural revolution 51	Gilgamesh 63	Old Kingdom Egypt 73
bureaucracy 64	Harappan society 69	patriarchy 65
Çatal Hüyük 56	hieroglyphs 67	peasants 65
city-state 61	Jericho 56	pharaoh 66
complex society 58	logogram 63	pictograph 67
cuneiform 62	Mesopotamia 63	slavery 65
dynasty 61	Middle Kingdom Egypt 75	Sumer 72
empire 64	Mohenjo-daro 70	Uruk 60

Change over Time

10,000 B.C.E.	Farming in Southwest Asia marks the onset of the neolithic age.
10,000–3000 B.C.E.	Farming and agrarian societies emerge in several regions in Afroeurasia and the Americas.
7000 B.C.E.	Neolithic settlements are founded at Jericho and Çatal Hüyük in Southwest Asia.
5000 B.C.E.	Copper metallurgy emerges.
4000 B.C.E.	Complex society founded on irrigated farming in Mesopotamia appears.
3500 B.C.E.	Cities appear in Mesopotamia, the largest of them Uruk in the region of Sumer.
3200 B.C.E.	Evidence of hieroglyphic writing in Egypt and of pictographic writing in Mesopotamia appears.
2800–2600 B.C.E.	Urbanization gets under way in the Indus River valley, with large centers at Harappa and Mohenjo-daro.
2686–2160 B.C.E.	Centralized government emerges in Egypt's Old Kingdom period.
2340–2190 B.C.E.	Sargon of Akkad founds the first empire in Mesopotamia.
2200–1900 B.C.E.	Southwest Asia experiences extended drought.
2040–1652 B.C.E.	Political stability is restored in Egypt, ushering in the Middle Kingdom.
1900 B.C.E.	Assyrian merchants establish trade settlements in Anatolia; long-distance trade networks develop from hubs in the Tigris-Euphrates, Nile, and Indus River valleys.

Please see end of book reference section for additional reading suggestions related to this chapter.

3 Afroeurasia's Moving Frontiers: Farmers, Herders, and Charioteers

3000–1000 B.C.E.

The Uluburun vessel rests on the bottom of the Mediterranean near the Turkish coast.

In the summer of 1982 a young man diving for sea sponges off the southwestern coast of Turkey reported seeing oddly shaped metal objects on the Mediterranean floor. A team of underwater archaeologists shortly identified them as part of the wreckage of an ancient ship. Examining fragments of pottery and other datable artifacts, the scientists calculated that the vessel sank sometime around 1306 B.C.E. Excavation at the site 170 feet down yielded thousands of items—commercial goods, pieces of the wooden hull, even personal belongings of crew members.

Because of its rich cargo and great antiquity, the shipwreck of Uluburun, named after a nearby point on the Turkish coast, has become world famous. Scientists have not been able to determine exactly where the ship was going, though some have speculated that it was carrying official gifts from Southwest Asian rulers to the pharaoh of Egypt. Whatever its mission, the vessel's freight came from many different lands. The metal objects the sponge diver spotted turned out to be copper ingots, probably from the island of Cyprus. The hull also contained cobalt blue glass disks manufactured in Mediterranean coastal towns as well as Greek pottery, swords, daggers, and silver jewelry. Some items came from far beyond the Mediterranean: amber from northern Europe, ebony logs from tropical Africa, and tin from as far east as Afghanistan.

Until the late third millennium B.C.E., dense agrarian societies with cities existed only in the Tigris-Euphrates, Nile, and Indus valleys, and, on a smaller scale, coastal Peru. Everywhere else, people lived in either farm villages or forager-hunter camps. The Uluburun discoveries, and the patterns of trade and urbanization they reveal, are just one illustration of how radically the human community changed in the following one thousand years. Farming and herding practices capable of supporting cities, social hierarchies, numerous occupational specializations, and centralized states spread widely in Afroeurasia (see Map 3.1). Many of the inventions and techniques that made accelerating population growth and social complexity possible diffused from the three ancient river valley civilizations to neighboring regions. But in all of the seven or eight places in the world where farming arose independently, men and women devised new ways of producing greater food surpluses, organizing larger numbers of people, and exchanging goods and ideas with strangers. The first part of this chapter explores the emergence in the second millennium B.C.E. of more complex agrarian societies in new regions of Afroeurasia: the Mediterranean basin, western Europe, Central Asia, and, finally, East Asia, where a fourth great river valley civilization arose in the Yellow and Yangzi River valleys.

In the second part of the chapter, we introduce the new and specialized way of life based on animal herding that emerged gradually in several parts of the Great Arid Zone, the wide zone of dry country that extends across Afroeurasia. Crop growing had been intertwined with domestic animal breeding since the beginnings of agriculture. But the practice of large-scale pastoralism, that is, the raising of hoofed animals as a society's *primary* source of food, developed between the fourth and second millennia B.C.E. This type of pastoralism emerged in connection with three fundamental innovations—the domestication of horses, horseback riding, and wheeled wagon transport. These inventions and discoveries allowed people to graze animals over immense stretches of grassland and brushland where crop raising was severely limited. As pastoral populations grew, they began to play an increasingly important role in world history, intruding, peacefully or not, into agrarian and urbanized regions; spreading their languages; and facilitating long-distance trade across Eurasia. Indeed, in the second millennium B.C.E., all the lands from the Mediterranean basin

Chapter Outline

• • •

to China became for the first time incorporated into a single zone of commercial and cultural interchange.

In the third section of the chapter, we shift southward to Afroeurasia's tropical latitudes, where migrations and economic innovations also stimulated population growth and introduced new social and cultural ways, including new languages. In Africa south of the Sahara Desert and in tropical Southeast Asia, peoples with warm-climate crops and in some places cattle herds impinged on lands previously inhabited only by foragers. Sometime in those two thousand years, populations that produced food probably came to

A Panoramic View

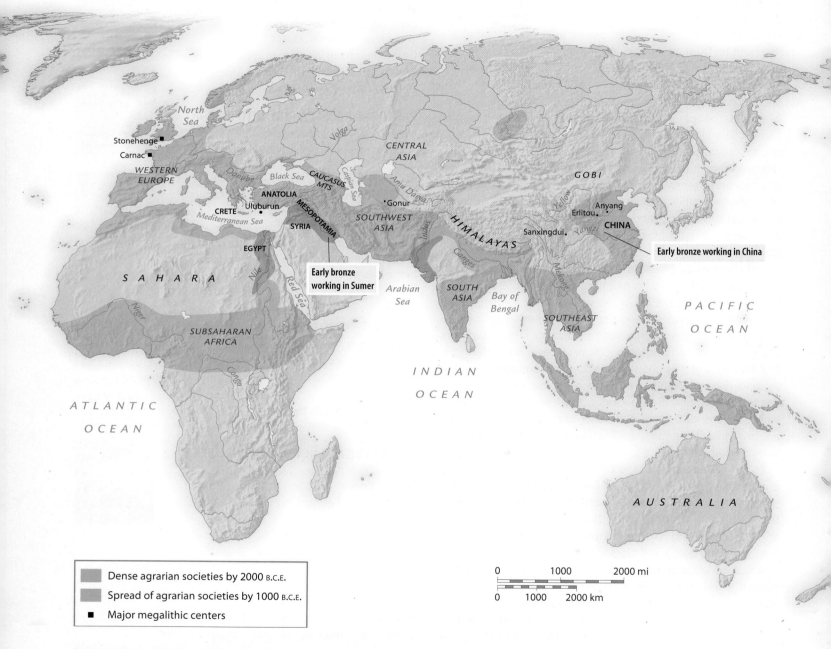

MAP 3.1 Agrarian societies in Afroeurasia, 3000–2000 B.C.E.

People in Southwest Asia and China probably invented bronze technology independently of each other. What geographical or climatic factors might help explain the *absence* of farming in extensive areas of Afroeurasia as of 1000 B.C.E.?

Legend:
- Dense agrarian societies by 2000 B.C.E.
- Spread of agrarian societies by 1000 B.C.E.
- ■ Major megalithic centers

outnumber on a hemispheric scale populations that hunted and gathered it in the wild. In other words, human efforts to alter the face of the earth in increasingly ingenious ways spread far beyond the core lands where food plants and animals were first domesticated to embrace Afroeurasian regions from equatorial rainforests to arid, windswept steppes.

Across Afroeurasia: More Farmers, More Cities

FOCUS What aspects of life during the bronze age in Afroeurasia distinguish it from earlier eras?

Scholars have estimated that the population of the entire world rose from around 6 million in 8000 B.C.E., when the agrarian age was well under way, to about 120 million by 1000 B.C.E.[1] This change in global numbers represents a dramatic upswing in the rate of growth compared to the previous 200,000 years of human history. In the second millennium B.C.E. (1999–1000 B.C.E.), population grew at the fastest rate in Afroeurasia, where farming had the earliest start and continued to expand in every direction. In the Americas, numbers inched upward also, rising fastest in the regions of Mesoamerica and the Andes where crop growing took root. (We examine these developments in Chapter 4.) Nevertheless, the total population of the Americas may have reached no more than about 4.5 million by 1000 B.C.E., less than 4 percent of the numbers in Afroeurasia at that time.[2]

In the world generally, second millennium B.C.E. growth was mostly *extensive,* that is, it took place as small farming and herding communities multiplied across the landscape. By contrast, *intensive* growth took place in areas where technological innovation and surplus farm production allowed a given area of land to support more and more people, in some places in large cities. In this section, we explore four regions that experienced both extensive and intensive growth in the second millennium B.C.E.: the eastern Mediterranean (specifically the shores and islands of the Aegean Sea), western Europe, Central Asia, and East Asia. Keep in mind, however, that as of 1000 B.C.E., city dwellers still accounted for only a small percentage of global numbers.

The Cavalcade of Inventions

Continuing technical innovation was essential to intensive growth in the three early river valley civilizations that we discussed in Chapter 2. Those societies contributed new ideas and tool kits out of all proportion to their share of global population, for example, the wheel, brick making, the closed pottery kiln, hydraulic irrigation devices, star charts, and complex writing and computation systems. In the second millennium B.C.E., much of this technology advanced into other parts of Afroeurasia, all the time undergoing numerous refinements and elaborations. New tools and methods contributed immensely to farming productivity, urban manufacturing, and long-distance communication. Many new techniques, such as glass making, stronger ship design, and lighter wheeled vehicles, spread widely as well. Bronze metallurgy and the traction plow, both invented in the third millennium, were among the most socially significant novelties.

Making bronze. So many thousands of bronze tools, weapons, containers, chariot fittings, and ornaments have been found in Eurasian and northern African archaeological sites from the third and second millennia B.C.E. that scholars have conventionally labeled that period the **bronze age.** Sometime before 3000 B.C.E., metalsmiths discovered that if they mixed copper with

> **bronze age** The era centered on the third and second millennia B.C.E. when bronze making was the most advanced metallurgical technology in the world.

small amounts of arsenic or tin, they could produce a metal alloy far superior to copper alone. These alloys were easier to cast and more durable, and they could hold an edge. Tin bronze gradually became the standard as metallurgists realized that arsenic chronically poisoned anyone who worked with it.

In the Sumerian cities of Mesopotamia, artisans made ornamental and ritual objects of bronze, as well as axes, sickles, chisels, and spears. The technology probably radiated from there to the Nile and Indus valleys. Mesopotamia, however, was not the only center of diffusion. Wherever villagers built kilns to fire pottery, the idea of blending metal alloys at a high temperature in the same oven might plausibly have come to mind. In the third millennium B.C.E., innovators in northern China probably inaugurated bronze working independently. Both southeastern Europe and mainland Southeast Asia are possible candidates for independent innovation. Whatever the source, bronze metallurgy promoted farm productivity and more complex social and political organization across Eurasia and North Africa.

Because of the costs of mining, transporting, and forging, most people could not afford bronze objects. Copper ore occurs quite commonly in nature, but tin does not. The main sources of tin for Mesopotamian and Indus valley bronzesmiths may have been mines in Inner Eurasia. Merchants would therefore have shipped tin hundreds of miles, greatly elevating its cost at the point of final sale. Bronze tools, weapons, and craftwork therefore acquired great social value as symbols of high class

A warrior's bronze helmet. Made in southwestern Iran in the fourteenth century B.C.E., this bronze headgear displays three golden images: a male god in the center and females on either side of him. A bird spreads its wings over these deities. Why might a soldier, certainly one of high rank, want a helmet decorated with divine images?

status or political authority, especially for men. Expanding production of bronze swords, javelins, arrow points, helmets, and body armor made warfare, as well as the power of rulers, possible on a larger scale than ever before. The booming industry also generated a host of new occupations for laboring folk in mining, furnace making, smithing, boat building, and the master crafts.

Plowing the land. A second major innovation of the third millennium B.C.E. was the traction plow, a tilling device pulled by oxen, horses, or mules. To prepare ground for planting, a farmer had to break the soil into particles, aerate it, and kill weeds. Women and men could do this with sticks and hoes, but an animal-powered plow could do it faster with less human energy expended and more arable ground covered. After about 3000 B.C.E., the Sumerians used simple ox-drawn plows to till the light, easily worked soils of the Tigris-Euphrates valley. In the subsequent 1,500 years, farmers gradually applied the new technology to rain-dependent land where soils were sometimes heavier and deeper and therefore resistant to handheld tools.

Farmers who hitched an animal or two to a wooden plow, perhaps one with a bronze tip, often found they could increase grain harvests significantly. This encouraged tillers to drain marshes or clear forests to open more fields and build more villages. Along the belt of territory from India to the Mediterranean, this innovation supported population growth. In some regions, however, plows had little appeal. In the Yellow River valley in northern China, for example, villagers found that their hoes and digging sticks worked well to till the fine, easily aerated soil known as loess. In short, the plow was a useful farm tool only in certain ecological conditions.

Complex Society and Commerce in the Mediterranean Basin

Schoolroom geography tells us that the Mediterranean Sea divides the continents of Africa, Asia, and Europe from one another. But it is also useful to think of the Mediterranean as a sea "inside" the supercontinent of Afroeurasia, a passageway that links peoples all around its rim. Numerous islands and peninsulas within the Mediterranean divide it into several smaller seas that make it relatively easy to navigate. The Aegean Sea in the eastern Mediterranean was especially appealing to ancient mariners. In fact, recent discovery of stone tools on the Aegean island of Crete indicate that foragers crossed water to get there at least 130,000 years ago and perhaps earlier.

After about 3000 B.C.E., farm communities and maritime trade centers multiplied around the eastern Mediterranean rim, notably in the Nile delta and along the seaboard known historically as the Levant, or Levantine coast, today Israel, the Palestinian territories, Lebanon, and western Syria. The same thing happened on the shores and numerous islands of the Aegean Sea. Because that region is mostly mountainous,

farmers had to plant on slopes or small plains. By adopting animal-powered plows, however, they produced bountiful wheat harvests in good years. They also cultivated olive trees and wine grapes, two plants that thrive where terrain is uneven and summers hot and brilliant. Nutritious and calorie rich, olive oil had several uses—for cooking, heating, and lighting, and as an ingredient of fine perfumes. Wine consumption cut down on illnesses from waterborne microorganisms, and no doubt made social life more agreeable. Both commodities, preserved in large earthenware jars and transported readily by ship, became basic staples of Mediterranean trade. As Aegean farmers accumulated surpluses of wheat, oil, and wine (also sheep and goats), inequalities of wealth and social class inevitably appeared. Some individuals were buried with bronze weaponry and other precious grave goods, indicating their special social or political status. Towns began to appear where chiefs or big landowners taxed the local farmers to pay for forts, palatial houses, and artisans' workshops. One of these centers was Troy, a complex of fortifications and dwellings whose third millennium rulers possessed dazzling wealth in bronze, silver, gold, and gemstones.

Minoan society on Crete. A remarkable cluster of small cities also emerged on Crete, the mountainous, 150-mile-long island that marks the southern extremity of the Aegean Sea. Called Minoans after a legendary king named Minos, the islanders started building these centers around 2000 B.C.E. In some of them the main structure was a complex of public or private rooms, spacious courtyards, and storehouses. From these little palaces, an affluent class of aristocrats supervised the village population, which raised olives, grapes, wheat, and sheep. Knossos, the largest center, may have had a second millennium B.C.E. population of about twenty thousand.

Crete's prosperous society may have arisen where it did partly because the island was only a short sailing distance from the culturally weightier societies of the Nile and Southwest Asia. Aspects of Minoan architecture, wall decoration, and religion appear to have originated in Egypt, including adoption of the bull god as a central figure in the Cretan belief system. Cuneiform archives from Mari on the Euphrates River nine hundred miles to the east reveal that that city had contact with Crete. The Minoans also adopted a writing system, perhaps independently but more likely borrowed from one of its mainland neighbors. It is called Linear A, and the governing elite used it to keep track of goods that flowed in and out of the palaces. This script has not been deciphered, nor is anything known of Minoan speech. However, paintings and decorations on the walls of buildings suggest that the population, or at least the aristocratic class, had a remarkably benign view of social life and nature. The ruins have yielded almost no evidence of inter-city warfare, nor any gargantuan statues of glowering god-kings. Minoan art abounds in images of men and women enjoying games and other public activities side by side,

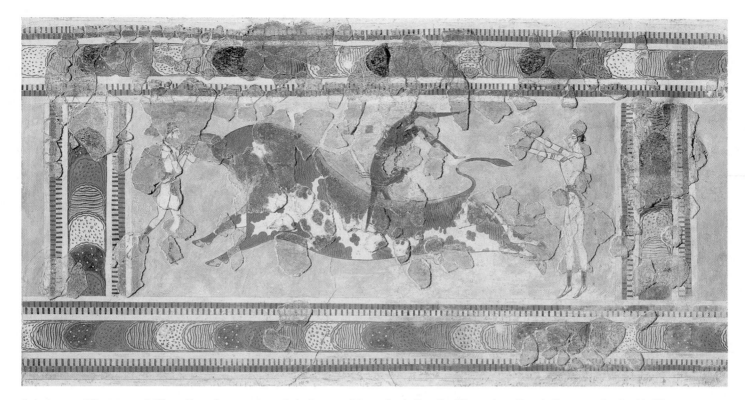

A dangerous Minoan sport. These three figures appear to lack no confidence in challenging this rambunctious bull, a sacred animal in Minoan religion. This reconstructed fresco from the palace of Knossos shows Egyptian influence in the way the faces are drawn and in the rendering of the two female figures on the left and right with lighter skin than the male figure performing the somersault.

suggesting that women had more equality and influence in their communities than was true in the early river valley civilizations. Some historians challenge this interpretation, however, and the physical remains of Minoan culture are too limited to permit firm conclusions.

The expanding trade zone. From the late third millennium B.C.E. onward, towns flourished in several localities around the eastern Mediterranean partly because of sea trade, which was typically cheaper and faster than overland hauls using donkeys and ox-drawn wagons. In effect, this trade represented a widening of the ancient route network that connected the Indus valley, Southwest Asia, and Egypt. The palace centers of Crete benefited from their position as gateways to the Aegean. Minoan traders launched fleets of ships, founded commercial colonies on neighboring islands, and exported Crete's high-grade olive oil and woolen cloth far afield. On the Levantine coast, Byblos and Ugarit flourished as commercial ports. Their merchants profited as intermediaries of trade between greater Southwest Asia and the Mediterranean basin. They sold timber from the hills of Lebanon to wood-starved Mesopotamia and Egypt, and they manufactured bronze goods, cosmetics, and textiles, notably cloths of bright purple.

The Mediterranean trade rarely required heroic voyages far from land. Ships like the sunken wreck found near Uluburun typically tramped from island to island and bay to bay, the crews bartering as they went. When it went down, the Uluburun ship might have been following a counterclockwise circuit of eastern Mediterranean ports. Some daring merchants even set sail for the western horizon, probing their way to Italy or Sicily, where they introduced city wares to rustic farmers. Near the end of the second millennium B.C.E., agrarian societies of the far west, that is, the regions that are today Algeria, Morocco, Spain, and Portugal, joined actively in the trans-Mediterranean commercial system.

The material demands of ruling groups stimulated much trade. To the rising aristocracies of the Aegean region, for example, silver jewelry, fine linens, and bronze ornamental daggers were not simply comforts and amusements. They were also emblems of power and status. They spoke a symbolic language of lavish display that helped validate elite class dominance over humble cultivators. Aristocratic landowners, however, could afford luxury goods only if they collected taxes and **tribute** from ordinary people, persistently rousing them to produce more food, fabric, and handicrafts for export.

> **tribute** Wealth in money or material goods paid by one group to another, often a conquered group to its conquerors, as an obligation of submission or allegiance.

The eastern Mediterranean economy therefore continued to grow, even though driven mainly by the power interests of a small minority of the population.

Developments in Western Europe

In the third and second millennia B.C.E., Europe's climate was probably warmer and wetter than it is now. Dense hardwood forests and dismal marshes covered much of the region, presenting stern challenges to early farmers. Nonetheless, villages multiplied in parts of Europe as cultivators adopted traction plowing and cleared forests for pasture or cropping. When families thought the neighborhood was getting too crowded, they plodded off with their sheep and oxen to found new settlements in the distant reaches of northern and western Europe. The region therefore underwent social and economic changes similar to those that occurred in the Aegean. An upper class of chiefs and property holders appeared, bronze weaponry and handicrafts were traded, and larger population centers sprouted up. These nascent towns usually had walls, ramparts, or ditches, suggesting the need to protect stores of trade goods or artisan workshops. Woodland Europeans also linked themselves into the growing Mediterranean trade net. For example, merchants traded copper mined in central Europe both northward to Scandinavia and southward to the Aegean. The busiest avenue of long-distance trade was probably the Danube River valley, which flowed from the interior of Europe to the Black Sea.

Most of what we know of life in woodland Europe in the third and second millennia B.C.E. comes from scattered finds of pottery, metal ware, earthworks, and other artifacts. The most spectacular material remains are **megaliths,** structures built of massive stone slabs. Concentrated along Europe's Atlantic rim, these constructions took the form of either tombs enclosing multiple burials or circles of huge standing stones that clearly had some ceremonial purpose. Megalithic building began in Europe in the fourth millennium B.C.E. and mostly ended by the second. Stonehenge in southern Britain is the most famous of the megalithic stone circles. Completed between 2400 and 2200 B.C.E., its stones were set up to be astronomical clocks, the slabs arranged to serve as sight lines for charting sun, moon, and stars. We know little about the people who frequented those centers. The erecting of a complex like Stonehenge, however, required so much labor, skill, and organization that an elite class of some sort, perhaps religious specialists, likely directed the work. The recent discovery of the remains of sick and injured individuals buried near Stonehenge in the third millennium B.C.E. suggests that people came to the site in search of supernatural healing.

> **megalith** A large stone sometimes roughly carved and used to build a structure often having religious significance.

Megaliths in France. This famous megalithic site at Carnac on Brittany's Atlantic coast consists of 3,000 standing stones arranged in multiple parallel rows. Dated 4500–2000 B.C.E., Carnac certainly had ritual purpose, but we know nothing of ceremonies performed there. What might we infer about the organization of society from the erection of these stones?

Megalithic sites from Spain to the Orkney Islands north of Britain share enough similarities in technique and design to suggest lively exchange of goods and knowledge all along Europe's Atlantic coast and back and forth across the English Channel. In any case, such interchange did not lead quickly to high social complexity. Thick forests, swamps, and heavy clay soils continued to put limits on productivity and population in northern Europe until well into the first millennium C.E.

The Oxus Civilization in Central Asia

From ancient times to the nineteenth century, the sector of the Great Arid Zone that runs between the Caspian Sea on the west and the snow-capped Himalaya ranges on the east was one of the most important commercial and cultural hinges of world history. Central Asia is the term geographers have given to this region of deserts and semiarid highlands interrupted by green river valleys. It corresponds roughly to the territories of four states that used to be part of the Soviet Union (Kazakhstan, Uzbekistan, Tajikistan, and Turkmenistan), plus northern areas of Iran and Afghanistan. Topographically, Central Asia was a natural corridor of relatively unobstructed communication between Inner Eurasia and the densely populated agrarian lands of the region stretching from India to the Mediterranean.

About 2100 B.C.E., people began to build walled cities in Central Asian river valleys, notably along the Amu Darya River (known to Greek geographers as the Oxus River). Until the 1990s, however, hardly anyone knew about this urban society except for Soviet archaeologists, who published their discoveries only in Russian. Since then, the physical contours and material culture of this "lost civilization" have become better known, and teams of scientists from several countries continue to advance our knowledge. The physical remains of this complex society, known formally as the Bactria-Margiana Archaeological Complex after two ancient regional names, suggest that newcomers, perhaps migrants from drought-stricken hill towns farther south, planned and built several cities quite quickly.

The residents of the Oxus cities, including the carefully excavated site known as Gonur in modern Turkmenistan, erected thick brick walls and high corner towers that commanded the surrounding countryside. In the larger towns, the ruling class, about which we know little, commanded construction of royal bastions and palaces that included temples. At Gonur, canals from a river fed water into the city. In the valley, farmers planted wheat and barley and raised sheep, goats, zebu cattle, and Bactrian (two-humped) camels. The material record of architecture, pottery, clay seals, ivory combs, and bronze work shows clearly that the cities shared a common cultural style and therefore probably intense commercial and social interchange, perhaps including marriage alliances among elite families. Geometric designs on clay seals suggest signs that carried meaning, but there is no evidence of an indigenous writing system.

Uncovering the Oxus civilization. Members of an archaeological team dig at Anau, one of several ancient towns in what is now Turkmenistan in Central Asia. In recent decades archaeologists have uncovered a treasury of information about early urbanization along trade routes that connected Persia with Inner Eurasia and China beyond. Gonur, a city east of Anau, had well-designed streets, sewers, residential neighborhoods, and fortifications. It flourished, however, for only about 300 years.

Oxus artisans and merchants almost certainly initiated Central Asia's historic role as commercial turnstile between Inner Eurasia and the agrarian societies to the south and west. Pot shards, soapstone jars, and other objects of Oxus origin have turned up across Iran, in ports along the Persian Gulf, and in the Indus valley. Oxus artisans made beads of shells that came from both the Indian Ocean and the Mediterranean Sea and also imported gemstones, silver, and gold.

Oxus city building lasted only a few centuries. After 1800 B.C.E. the major towns contracted in size and within two hundred years were abandoned. The cause of decline and collapse is unknown. Deteriorating ecological conditions or intercity warfare may be explanations. The decline also coincides with the arrival of horse-riding, chariot-driving peoples from the steppes to the north, though we do not know whether they came as city-wrecking invaders or peaceful migrants.

Complex Society in East Asia

At the start of the second millennium B.C.E., farming and village life were well established across much of East and Southeast Asia, though foraging communities were still common where food supplies were abundant. In Japan, for example, communities had such plenteous supplies of tubers, nuts, and seafood that they rejected intensive grain farming long after they knew about it, until about 1000 B.C.E. By contrast, complex societies evolved rapidly in the part of northern China extending from the Yellow River valley southward to the Yangzi River, where, as we saw in Chapter 2, people had been cultivating rice and millet since about 7000 B.C.E.

Early urban centers in China. About 2600 B.C.E., people in several localities began building settlements surrounded by walls constructed of earth rammed into wooden forms. Material evidence of walls, as well as graves in which special individuals were buried along with precious objects, indicate that elite groups were emerging in northern China to mobilize and direct the work of others, just as had happened in the Tigris-Euphrates, Indus, and Nile valleys some centuries earlier. Privileged families of warriors and ritual leaders probably appropriated the best land and largest stores of grain and began to collect tribute and labor services from everyone else. Beautifully crafted bronze goblets, cauldrons, animal figures, daggers, and spear points, which first appeared in East Asia about 2000 B.C.E., were closely associated with the needs of chiefs, who took charge of both religious rituals at home and hostile raids on neighbors.

Archaeological evidence shows that, in the Yellow-Yangzi region, fundamental characteristics

of complex society appeared not in just one place but in several starting in the late third millennium B.C.E., significantly later than in the three great river valleys to the west. One important site is at Erlitou (er-lee-toh), a village on the plain just south of where the middle Yellow River flows today. Flourishing between about 1900 and 1500 B.C.E., the Erlitou site reveals evidence of a complex of compounds that archaeologists identify as a palace and therefore perhaps the capital of an early Chinese state. It is not clear whether Erlitou was a bustling town or mainly a ritual and political center, but it had large platforms of pounded earth, bronze foundries, paved roads, and richly equipped graves.

About four hundred miles to the southwest of Erlitou in China's Sichuan (seh-chwan) province, archaeological work since 1986 has uncovered a walled town known as Sanxingdui (sahn-shing-dway). It also flourished in the second millennium B.C.E., but its cultural style was dramatically different from that of Erlitou. Two excavated pits containing sacrificed animals also contained a treasure of bronze, gold, stone, and jade objects, including fifty-seven bronze heads, some with gold masks. Styles of pottery and other objects make clear that large centers in the region projected their cultural and probably political influences outward to smaller settlements. They also developed contacts with one another through trade, gift exchange among rulers, migration, or diffusion of techniques and styles from one center to the next. For example, rulers or merchants organized transport of copper, tin, gold, and jade to workshops sometimes hundreds of miles from where these materials were extracted. In short, the Yellow and Yangzi valleys comprised a single zone of human interconnection well before the first large state arose in East Asia.

The Shang state. Historians identify that first large state with the Shang, a dynasty of kings that exercised power for more than half a millennium, from about 1750 to 1045 B.C.E. Shang rulers supported by an elite warrior class likely started out as one local military state among many in northern China. Over centuries, these kings asserted growing power over their neighbors. Anyang, the largest Shang ritual and royal tomb center so far discovered, sprawled for miles across the Huan River, a tributary of the lower Yellow. The Shang state encompassed only a small part of the territory of modern China, but physical remains, ancient inscriptions, and

Bronze statue from Sanxingdui. Among numerous bronze heads and masks, archaeologists discovered this imposing six-foot-tall figure in a burial pit dating to 1300–1100 B.C.E. The figure has enormous hands that probably once gripped an object, perhaps an ivory tusk. What details of dress and adornment do you notice? Do they suggest anything about the figure's status in society?

chronicles written in later centuries qualify it as the earliest East Asian empire. At the height of their power between the thirteenth and eleventh centuries B.C.E., Shang kings resident in Anyang occupied mansions atop great platforms of compacted earth. The monarch and his officers likely wielded direct authority over a core area, dominated allied monarchs and chiefs in a wider circle, and conducted periodic war campaigns in even more distant regions. The kings organized the state along military lines and required villagers and war prisoners to build tombs, palaces, and perhaps several royal capitals. The Shang therefore initiated a pattern of centralized imperial government that characterized Chinese history down to the early twentieth century.

The kings became patrons of a bronze-centered artistic culture whose influence radiated out across much of northern China. In contrast to Mesopotamia or Egypt, they did not erect giant monuments, so far as we know, but the walls around major towns sheltered extraordinary artisanal skill, notably master work in bronze. At Anyang, archaeologists have unearthed royal tombs containing costly objects, notably from the burial site of Lady Hao, who was likely one of the wives of the Emperor Wu Ding (reigned 1250–1192 B.C.E.) and a military commander in her own right. Her tomb, the only elite Shang grave at Anyang never to have been looted, has yielded hundreds of bronze vessels, bells, and weapons, and numerous items of jade, ivory, bone, and stone. The presence of sixteen corpses in the tomb adds to the ample evidence that the state practiced human sacrifice on a significant scale. According to Shang belief, a deceased king would reside in his tomb and therefore needed to take along with him a select group of nobles, slaves, attendants, and mistresses, as well as horses and other animals. Sacrificial victims usually included even larger numbers of war prisoners, perhaps hundreds of them.

Beginning no later than the reign of Wu Ding, Shang scribes wrote inscriptions on thousands of animal bone fragments known as "oracle bones." The East Asian practice of venerating ancestors originated in neolithic times, as men and women offered grave goods and sacrifices to the spirits of the dead in hopes of receiving protection and favor in return. Shang kings who exercised both political and priestly power ritually communicated with the ancestors of their own royal lineage. These spirits were thought to have sufficient influence to pass on the king's appeals for rain, good harvests, military victories, the birth of healthy sons, and other blessings to Di, the supreme supernatural entity, who might have been associated with the dynasty's ancestor-founder. Monarchs typically made public decisions only after performing ceremonies to reveal the gods' intentions and foretell the future. In one type of divination the king, assisted by **shamans**, asked questions of either ancestors or nature spirits by heating a tortoise shell or cow's shoulder blade bone

shaman A man or woman who the community believes has access to supernatural forces or beings and who can appeal to the spirit world to discern the future, bring good fortune, or perform physical healing.

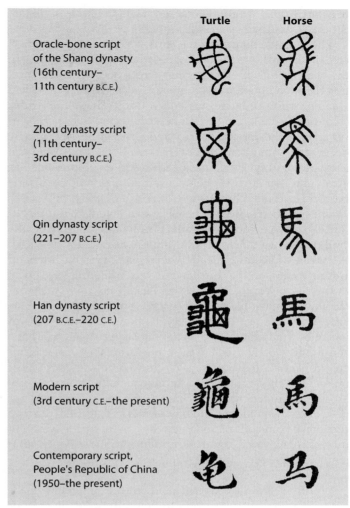

	Turtle	Horse
Oracle-bone script of the Shang dynasty (16th century– 11th century B.C.E.)		
Zhou dynasty script (11th century– 3rd century B.C.E.)		
Qin dynasty script (221–207 B.C.E.)		
Han dynasty script (207 B.C.E.–220 C.E.)		
Modern script (3rd century C.E.–the present)		
Contemporary script, People's Republic of China (1950–the present)		

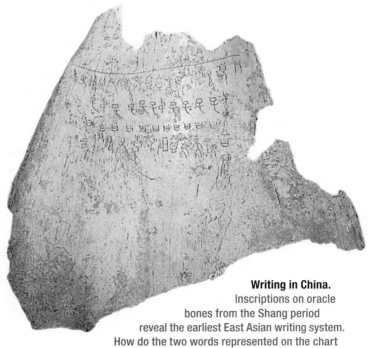

Writing in China. Inscriptions on oracle bones from the Shang period reveal the earliest East Asian writing system. How do the two words represented on the chart show evolution away from pictographic forms?

in a particular way until it cracked. Then the diviners "read" the cracks to discover the response.

These oracle bones are the earliest written "documents" of Chinese history. After diviners analyzed the cracks in the heated bone or shell, scribes wrote questions, interpretations, or commentaries on them using signs that conveyed a combination of meanings and sounds. These characters, as modern scholars figured out early in the twentieth century, were the forerunners of modern Chinese script. By deciphering many oracle-bone inscriptions, linguists have learned not only the names of Shang rulers and towns but also details of such matters as religious practice, warfare, farming lore, and climate.

The northern Chinese very likely invented their own writing system independently of any influence from the civilizations to the west. But this raises a larger question: What role did communication between northern China and westerly lands in the third and second millennia B.C.E. play in the rise of complex society in East Asia? East–west contacts would most likely have occurred by way of Inner Eurasia. Trade goods, technical innovations, and the seeds of wheat or food plants may well have been relayed from one community to another. On the other hand, East Asian farmers probably domesticated pigs, chickens, and two types of millet entirely on their own. Bronze metallurgy very likely arose there independently. One advance of undoubted Chinese origin was the technology of fabricating silk from the cocoons of caterpillars that ate white mulberry leaves. Silk threads discovered on an Egyptian mummy suggest that merchants passed Chinese silk fabric as far west as the Nile as early as 1000 B.C.E.

Within East Asia, economic and cultural interchange advanced rapidly in the second millennium B.C.E. Shang political influence in the Yangzi valley was sporadic, but that region's agrarian population rose steadily owing to cultivation of tropical rice, a cereal probably first domesticated somewhere in southern China. Wheat and millet were well suited to the cool, dry north, rice to the warm, wet south. Already in Shang times traders carried sacks of these cereals between the two regions, laying the foundations for the future economic integration of north and south. Bronzes and other luxury goods of distinctive Shang design have been found all over northern China and in the Yangzi valley. The Shang state was therefore the center of an expanding zone of interaction that in time produced a characteristically Chinese style of culture.

Pastoral Peoples Ride into History

FOCUS Why did pastoral nomadism as a specialized way of life permit accelerating population growth in the steppes of Inner Eurasia between the fourth and second millennia B.C.E.?

Even before complex agrarian society first appeared in Mesopotamia and Egypt, a different way of life began to take form in some parts of the Great Arid Zone where rainfall was too low to sustain farming far from irrigation sources but high enough to support large herds of sheep, goats, cattle, camels, and horses. **Pastoral nomadism,** a highly specialized way of life in which communities subsisted primarily if not exclusively on animal products, allowed humans to reproduce in far greater numbers in arid lands than foraging bands could possibly have sustained (see Table 3.1). Starting around 2000 B.C.E., pastoral peoples of Inner Eurasia precipitated a series of complex migratory and military movements that profoundly altered cultural and political maps, both within the steppe region and eventually in the agrarian lands to the south, west, and east.

> **pastoral nomadism** A type of economic and social organization in which livestock raising is the principal means of subsistence. Pastoral nomadic communities typically migrate seasonally in search of pasture and water.

Horses, Riders, and Wagons

Many scholars agree that an important movement of pastoral peoples from Inner Eurasia to more densely populated agrarian regions originated between the late fourth and third millennia B.C.E. in the grasslands north of the Black and Caspian Seas. Known historically as the Pontic-Caspian steppe (Pontic relates to the Greek name for the Black Sea), this region of temperate to semiarid climate encompasses a large part of what are today southern Russia, Ukraine, and Kazakhstan. Sometime after about 5200 B.C.E., sheep and cattle herding people, probably originating in Southeastern Europe, began to drift around the northwestern curve of the Black Sea and into the Pontic-Caspian grasslands. This long-term event occurred just at the high point of a climatic warming cycle in the region, which encouraged grassy pasture to expand and flourish, supporting the pastoral way of life. Animal herders, who usually also grew some crops, gradually displaced hunting and foraging communities, which either adapted to the new economy or retreated into colder forests to the north. From the fifth millennium B.C.E., pastoral communities gradually populated the Pontic-Caspian region and began spreading farther eastward across the plains in the direction of China.

Three developments particularly favored human adaptation to the steppes. The first was domestication of wild horses, which probably first occurred in the Pontic-Caspian lands around 4800 B.C.E. These animals may have looked something like the small, shaggy Przewalski's horse, the only wild breed that survives in Inner Eurasia today. Horses turned out to be good candidates for an interdependent relationship with humans. Mares, that is, female horses, instinctively bunch together and form a pecking order of leaders and followers, something cats, we can be sure, will never do. A dominant mare, along with a spirited, aggressive stallion, always led the herd, but humans learned that they could also guide and manage docile mares. They also figured out at some point how to identify relatively meek and pliable stallions, then bred mares and stallions that had similarly submissive characteristics. Domesticated horses could outrun most predators, and they acquired heavy coats as protection against frigid steppe winters. Among domesticates, horses also had instincts for finding winter pasture. Cattle and sheep use their noses to move snow out of the way to uncover grass but only if the snow yields easily. Horses, by contrast, use their hooves to plow away crusty snow and to break ice to get at water.[3]

Steppe dwellers probably first exploited horses as meat. In time, they discovered the value of what one scholar of the neolithic era famously labeled "secondary products."[4] These included mare's milk, blood, hair, hides, and bone, as well as horse power for transport and plowing. This "secondary products revolution" allowed communities to depend more on horses and other domesticated animals than on crops if ecological conditions required it.[5] Between the fifth and second millennia B.C.E., domesticated horses multiplied on the Pontic-Caspian steppes by the millions, and in this environment human societies built their mobile way of life around their animals.

A second fundamental ingredient of the pastoral nomadic way of life was mastery of riding. Probably somewhere in the Pontic-Caspian grasslands as early as 4200 B.C.E., a courageous herder climbed on the back of a horse and managed to stay there. Early riders had no saddles or stirrups but learned to control their mounts using their legs and either a nose ring or a bit and reins. From horseback, a single rider could manage a large number of docile domesticated animals. By one estimate, a shepherd on foot, plus a reliable dog, could handle about two hundred sheep. A mounted herder and a dog could control five hundred.[6] Pastoralists on horses could also accumulate larger herds because they could drive animals farther away from water sources and camps and return much faster than if they had to walk. Eventually, horseback riding spread beyond the steppes, for example, across Iran to Mesopotamia, where the earliest images of people sitting on horses appear in the later third millennium B.C.E.

A third tool of the steppe economy was the two- or four-wheeled cart pulled by cattle, oxen, horses, mules, or, eventually, camels. Wagon technology probably reached the Pontic-Caspian steppes sometime between 3500 and 3300 B.C.E., spreading there from Southwest Asia by way of either southeastern Europe or the Caucasus Mountains. Lumbering along on solid wooden wheels, wagons extended the potential range of herders even farther than horse riding allowed. Now, pastoral groups could remain more or less

An uneasy rider. This ceramic mold from Mesopotamia offers evidence of the spread of horseback riding from Inner Eurasia to Southwest Asia, probably through Persia, by the early second millennium B.C.E. The figure on this mount is no horse soldier. He is sitting too far back on the horse's rump to control the animal very well. What technical improvements can you think of that would have contributed to the later development of cavalry warfare?

permanently on the move, transporting food and tools, as well as families with nursing infants, small children, and elderly folk. Wagons equipped with frames and hide or felt covers served as reasonably comfortable mobile homes. Pastoral nomads sometimes left members of the group in camps to grow small amounts of grain; they also ate wild seeds, greens, and a version of the honey-based fermented beverage known as mead. But their main diet remained meat and dairy products.

Pastoral Nomadic Society

Ancient communities of pastoral nomads were almost certainly organized on foundations of **kinship,** the idea that people belonged together, not because they occupied a fixed territory or obeyed a particular ruler, but because they shared descent from a common ancestor. Strangers might also be assimilated into a group by customs of fictional kinship: over time the group deliberately "forgot" that the erstwhile newcomers had not always been part of the extended family. A herding community likely constituted a lineage group, a few generations of people who regarded themselves as blood relatives.

Evidence from graves shows that some individuals and lineages became richer than others and, therefore, achieved

> **kinship** The quality or state of being related by shared genealogical descent or by marriage. Kinship may also be claimed among a group of people for social or cultural reasons even though no biological relationship exists.

TABLE 3.1 Types of Societies Compared

Feature Category	Pastoral Nomadic Societies	Complex Agrarian and Urban Societies
Economy	Production primarily of domesticated animals, sometimes at surplus levels; secondarily of crops	Production primarily of crops and secondarily of domesticated animals at surplus levels, as well as urban and village manufactures
Settlement	Mobile camps and sometimes permanent structures used part of the year	Cities, towns, and villages
Occupations	The great majority engages in herding; a small minority in specialized occupations such as blacksmithing or textile production	The great majority engages in farming; minorities in full-time specialized occupations or in urban labor
Social structure	Social class divisions informal and fluid; minority of individuals and families with special status as political and religious leaders; social relations based on kinship	Permanent hierarchy of social classes: (a) rulers and aristocrats, (b) skilled artisans, technicians, and professionals, (c) rural farmers and urban workers, (d) in many societies, slaves; social relations based on kinship at local levels and on common obedience to the ruler at the level of the state
Gender relations	Society generally patriarchal but women and men share economic tasks, especially animal management	Patriarchal society; most women restricted to the domestic sphere
Political organization	Hierarchy of kinship groups from levels of local lineages to large, and usually temporary, confederations of kin groups; leadership exercised informally by individuals, elders, or families with elite status	States characterized by central governments, authoritarian rule, hierarchies of officials, and systematic taxation
Law	Customary, usually unwritten laws enforced by the consensus of the community or by military leaders	Complex civil and penal laws, enforced by the state and often organized in written codes
Technological change	Generally slow pace of technological innovation; periodic advances, especially in the military sphere	Continuous, though often uneven, technological and scientific innovation in a wide range of human activities
Built environment	Temporary, mobile structures; sometimes fortified camps or towns under pastoral nomad control	Dense urban dwelling construction; monumental building of walls, temples, palaces, tombs, and public plazas
Communication	Most members of society nonliterate; elite use of writing systems	Writing systems and complex symbolic expression; literacy of particular elite groups
Religion	Beliefs and practices associated with local deities and other spiritual forces; local religious specialists who communicate with the supernatural realm; from the first millennium B.C.E., adherence of some pastoral nomad societies to major belief systems	Complex systems of belief and practice often associated with central political authority, a class of religious specialists, and written scriptures; centers of development of major belief systems such as Confucianism, Buddhism, or Christianity

social prestige and political influence. Many of these sites have revealed sacrifice and careful burial of horses, as well as cattle and sheep, signs that the deceased had special social or political status. Horseback riding and wagon technology together allowed especially clever, industrious, or lucky families to acquire enormous herds. The most successful owners could amass more power than ordinary people because they had more animals for exchanging gifts with other leaders, making loans to poorer herders, and hosting funeral sacrifices and public feasts, acts that produced allies and loyal followers. Rich individuals could also marry their daughters into other wealthy families by paying more in bride-wealth, that is, animals presented to the family of the bride in exchange for the loss of her labor when she went to live with her new husband.

The pastoral division of labor. The emergence of elite families, however, did not mean that distinctions between upper and lower social classes became formal and rigid, as they did in dense agrarian societies. Rather, the pastoral economy required the intense and willing cooperation

of everyone in the herding community—men, women, and children. Our knowledge of pastoral societies from later eras shows that fairly egalitarian relations prevailed among adults. The community had to value the skills of women not only as domestic and child-raising experts but also as managers of livestock.

Even so, as pastoral nomadism expanded and herding groups competed more fiercely for choice pasture and water sources, adult men came to revel in a "horse culture" that prized male military skill and bravado. The Pontic-Caspian steppes are the likely birthplace of the mounted warrior and cattle rustler. Burial sites signify that the great majority of elite fighters were men, though in some places archaeologists have also found the remains of women in full military dress. This finding suggests that women sometimes led raids and distinguished themselves on the field of battle.

The horse culture of the steppes was also the likely source of the chariot, a small, two-wheeled vehicle drawn by one or more horses and designed for speed. In the steppes northeast of the Caspian Sea, an ancient site known as Sintashta has revealed graves containing the material vestiges

A Chinese chariot. Shang dynasty burials at Anyang include the remains of horses and chariots. Knowledge of chariot technology spread from Inner Eurasia to northern China by about 1200 B.C.E. Why do you think the graves of Shang rulers included these items?

of chariots and the horses that pulled them. Dated to about 2100 B.C.E., these artifacts mark the start of a period of about a thousand years during which chariotry had great importance in both warfare and political ritual across large parts of Afroeurasia.

The defining characteristics of a chariot are two spoked wheels, rather than heavy solid ones; a small enclosed platform where the driver and perhaps one or two other warriors stand; and harness gear for horses. The chariot was designed for war, intimidation, and the display of power. In combat one fighter usually controlled the animals, while a second threw bronze-tipped projectiles or fired arrows. Sometimes a third warrior held a shield to protect the other two. Well-built defensive walls and towers at Sintashta and neighboring settlements suggest that regional warfare was common, perhaps in response to growing competition for grazing land. Warrior bands may also have competed violently for control of export trade in copper and tin to the Indus and Mesopotamia. Chariots were expensive machines, requiring skilled bending and joining of wood, manufacturing bronze and leather horse gear, and training of horses, drivers, and fighters who could launch spears or arrows from the chariot platform with reasonable accuracy. Consequently, only leaders who could command substantial resources, make alliances, and amass supporters with generous gifts could afford to deploy them. In short,

chariots became weapons of choice of aristocratic warrior groups, not ordinary soldiers. Nevertheless, chariot teams could operate over relatively long distances, permitting more extended military campaigns and encouraging state building on a larger scale than had previously been possible in the steppes.

Encounters Between Agrarian Societies and Migrating Peoples

FOCUS How did the movements of peoples speaking Indo-European languages contribute to political, social, and cultural changes in several parts of Afroeurasia in the second millennium B.C.E.?

Sometime around 3300 B.C.E., pastoral bands began moving beyond the Pontic-Caspian steppes to neighboring regions of Afroeurasia. One explanation for these movements is the occurrence of a cycle of regional climatic drying at the same time that pastoral populations were getting larger and improving their ability to travel long distances. If population exceeded locally available resources, migration offered a potential alternative to chronic dearth or warfare. Whatever the primary triggering factor, the scale of these movements

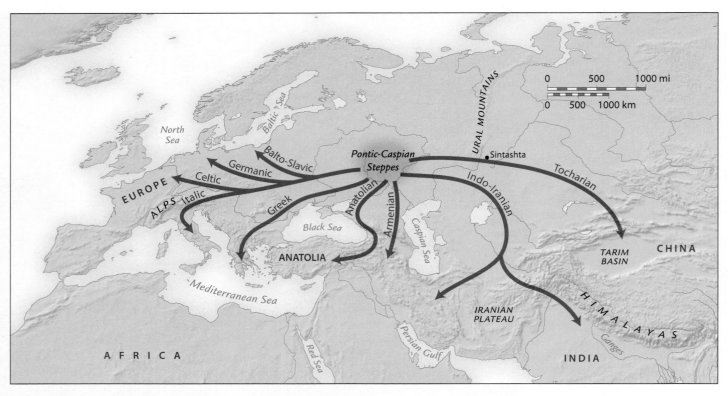

MAP 3.2 Spread of Indo-European languages.
If Indo-European languages or language families spread in particular directions, can we assume that people speaking those languages migrated in those directions as well?

increased in the third and second millennia B.C.E.—southward around the Black Sea to Southwest Asia, westward into Europe, southeastward to Iran and India, and eastward into steppes that today lie within the borders of China. We can only guess at the numbers of people involved, though the process took centuries, and it was spasmodic and fragmented. There was no sudden flood of peoples or a single conquering horde.

The science of historical linguistics has shown us that most of these migrants spoke languages sharing fundamental grammatical elements and word forms. We call this family of related languages Indo-European. All of the many tongues in this family are descended from a distant parent language. Scholars have named this ancestral tongue Proto-Indo-European. Many of them believe that people spoke it in the Pontic-Caspian region between about 4500 and 2500 B.C.E. During the following several millennia, Indo-European languages spread far and wide. Today about three billion people in the world speak languages in this family, which includes English, Spanish, German, Greek, Russian, Persian, Kurdish, Hindi, and many more.

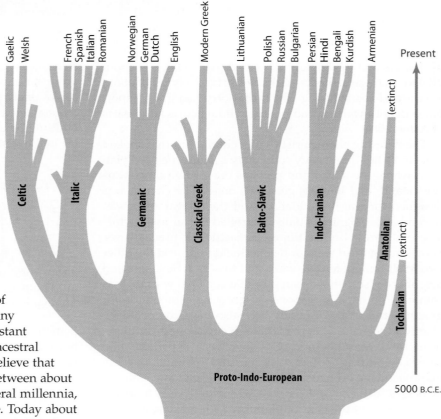

Indo-European languages tree. What are some major languages that do not appear anywhere on this tree?

All languages change over time, and when a population speaking a single language separates into groups that lose regular contact with one another, the speech of those groups invariably diverges. As Proto-Indo-European speakers spread in various directions, the parent language eventually sprouted numerous linguistic branches and twigs, that is, new subfamilies and individual tongues. Groups that spoke Indo-European languages did not *necessarily* share other basic cultural forms, such as way of life or religion, or any sense of common identity. On the other hand, by comparing modern Indo-European languages, scholars have reconstructed a basic vocabulary of ancient Proto-Indo-European. This vocabulary shows that its speakers lived in a temperate climate because the list includes words for beaver, bear, and birch tree. It also includes words for horse, sheep, wheeled vehicle, and plow, suggesting that Proto-Indo-Europeans practiced combinations of stock breeding and farming.

The movement of Indo-European pastoral groups from Inner Eurasia, together with the diffusion of chariot warfare, represented dynamic new elements in the histories of several agrarian lands from western Europe and the Mediterranean basin to South Asia and even China. Relations between densely populated agrarian and pastoral societies played themselves out in a number of different ways: Settled and pastoral groups might engage in mutually beneficial trade and cultural exchange; pastoral bands might advance gradually into agrarian regions, sometimes maintaining their herding way of life, sometimes eventually turning to farming; mounted nomad forces might intrude aggressively into settled and urbanized lands, and sometimes the rulers of agrarian states pushed them back into the steppe or desert; and from time to time pastoral cavalry invaded and overran centralized kingdoms, imposing themselves as a new ruling class.

Indo-European Speakers in Southwest Asia: The Hittite Empire

Migrants from the Inner Eurasian steppes reached Anatolia (modern Turkey) in the third millennium B.C.E. They probably arrived already possessing intimate knowledge of horses and a political culture that stressed alliance building and personal bonds between chiefs and followers. They bred horses and other animals in the grassy highlands of eastern Anatolia, intermingling with existing farming populations. In the sixteenth century B.C.E., the Anatolian group that became known as the Hittites—a word that refers to both the Indo-European language they spoke and the elite warrior culture they practiced—seized control of central Anatolia. There they founded the kingdom of Hatti. Over six centuries the Hittite aristocracy created a well-ordered empire whose monarchs established the rule of law and largely honored the local customs of diverse subject populations.

Archaeologists have excavated the remains of Hattusa, Hatti's impressive capital in north central Anatolia. The city featured a grand palace complex, numerous temples

The Lion Gate at Hattusa. These two fierce beasts, symbolic sentries guarding the Hittite capital, stand seven feet tall at the entrance to the citadel. The lion as defender of royal power was a common motif in ancient Southwest Asia. The face of the lion on the left has recently been reconstructed.

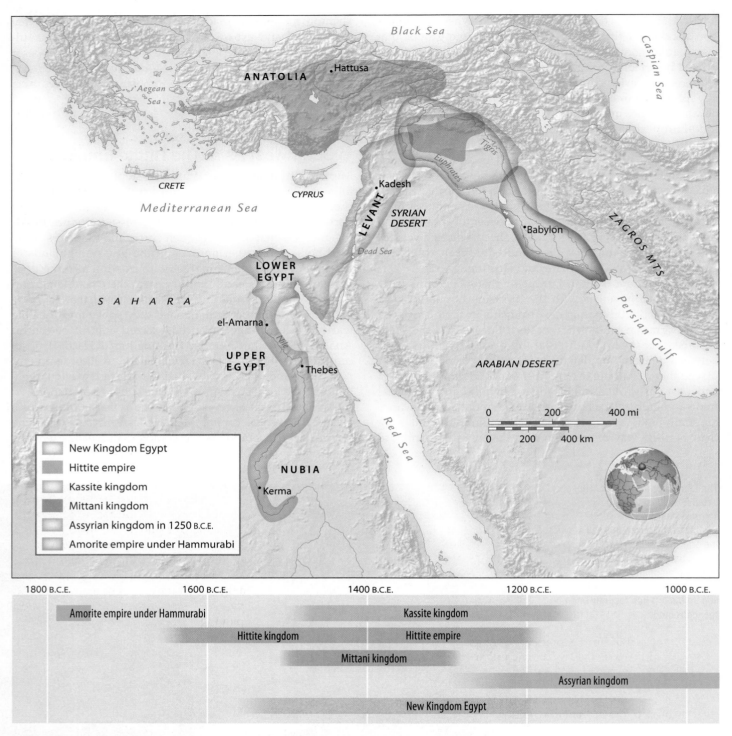

MAP 3.3 Major states of the eastern Mediterranean in the second millennium B.C.E.

What factors might explain why New Kingdom Egypt expanded in a generally north–south direction?

dedicated to the Hittite pantheon of gods and goddesses, imposing fortifications, and an entry gate guarded by two enormous stone lions. Hittite scribes produced thousands of official documents on clay tablets using the Babylonian cuneiform script that originated in Mesopotamia. Surviving tablet fragments dating to about 1900 B.C.E. provide the earliest evidence of inscriptions written in an Indo-European language.

The Hittite kings, like earlier Southwest Asian monarchs, represented themselves as agents of the gods, on whose authority they kept order and defended the land. A class of priests took charge of worship and ritual sacrifice, but the king was the chief priest of the storm-god, the principal deity. According to one cuneiform inscription, "Heaven, earth, and the people belong to the storm-god alone. He has made the . . . king his administrator and given him the entire Land of Hatti. . . . May the storm-god destroy whoever should approach the person of the . . . king, and the borders of (Hatti)!"[7] The monarch typically had several wives, but the Great Queen, or ranking wife, often exerted great influence over the state's internal affairs.

The Hittite economy rested on farmers and stock breeders, the majority of them descended from populations who spoke ancient languages other than Indo-European. Subjects of the king paid a portion of their production to the state to support the administration, army, and royal household. As the kingdom expanded, it also gained control of immensely important Anatolian sources of copper, silver, and tin. The markets for these items in the cities of Mesopotamia, Syria, and Egypt were practically limitless, and those regions reciprocated with linen and woolen textiles and manufactures of silver, lead, and bronze.

After 1400 B.C.E., Hittite armies, perhaps seeking control over a wider circle of commercial routes and cities, overran most of Anatolia and penetrated southward into Syria and the Levantine coast of the Mediterranean. The core of the army was infantry, but chariot squadrons served well to terrorize and scatter enemy forces. Horses put into chariot service required lengthy, expensive training. In the fourteenth century B.C.E., a trainer named Kikkuli dictated a detailed handbook on the proper conditioning of chariot horses. Written on clay tablets in both Hittite and Akkadian, the manual instructs the handler:

> When he lets the horses onto the meadow in the autumn, he harnesses them. He lets them trot 3 miles, but he lets them gallop over 7 fields. But on the way back he has them gallop over 10 fields. Then he unharnesses them, provides for them, and they are watered. . . . Then he gives them mixed together 1 handful of wheat, 2 handfuls of barley, and one handful of hay. They eat this up.[8]

States of Mesopotamia and Syria

In Southwest Asia, the city dwellers of the Tigris-Euphrates River valley had ambivalent relationships, ranging from peaceful commerce to violent conflict, with pastoral communities of neighboring hill country and steppes. In 2191 B.C.E., Akkad,

the world's earliest known agrarian empire (see Chapter 2), collapsed in connection with hostile incursions of people from the Zagros Mountains to the east. Early in the second millennium B.C.E., a much larger-scale pastoral movement emanated from west of Mesopotamia, perhaps from the Syrian-Arabian Desert (see Map 3.3). These steppe herders, known from ancient cuneiform tablets as Amorites, spoke Semitic languages, which were not Indo-European but belong to the large Afroasiatic family that included languages ancestral to modern Arabic and Hebrew. They raised sheep, goats, and cattle but also farmed part of the time. Perhaps because of a long-term drought cycle in Southwest Asia, which started about 2200 B.C.E., Amorite bands intruded bit-by-bit into the irrigated floodplain, competing with villagers for choice land, hiring out to city-states as mercenaries, and, when they felt strong enough, attacking towns. Over the following two centuries, some Amorite leaders gave up their old pastoral ways to become rich landlords and patrons of city culture.

In the eighteenth century B.C.E., Hammurabi (r. 1792–1750 B.C.E.), king of the Mesopotamian city-state of Babylon and descendant of an Amorite herdsman, revived the idea Sargon of Akkad had conceived five hundred years earlier to unite Mesopotamia under one authority. During forty-two years of military campaigning, Hammurabi extended Babylonian rule from the Persian Gulf to the upper Euphrates. Like Sargon before him, he aimed to tax the region's huge agricultural and manufacturing output and make sure that vital raw materials such as timber, copper, tin, and silver flowed into Mesopotamia from neighboring lands. To do this, he created a tightly centralized system of command, personally directing its business and deploying a host of officials up and down the valley to carry out his will. Also, social class distinctions appear to have sharpened because Sargon's regime encouraged private property holding and

Stele of Hammurabi. "If a man has struck a free woman with child, and has caused her to miscarry, he shall pay ten shekels for her miscarriage." This decree is just one of the 282 Mesopotamian legal traditions engraved on a black diorite slab at the orders of King Hammurabi. At the top of the stele, the seated figure of the sun god Shamash offers divine blessing on Hammurabi and his legal code. Why would Hammurabi want these legal precedents carved on a rock stele rather than simply on clay tablets?

commercial enterprise that gave large wealth-gathering opportunities to relatively few.

Cuneiform writing became more important than ever as a tool of state. About 150 of Hammurabi's official letters, written on clay tablets in Akkadian Semitic, have come down to us. The most famous document is Hammurabi's Code, a collection of 282 legal precedents preserved as engraved inscriptions on an eight-foot-high stele, or stone slab. These precedents, which range over such subjects as burglary, property disputes, irrigation management, marriage, trade practices, and personal injury, express the ruler's insistence on orderly government and fairness in dispensing justice. Babylonian judges were expected to be honest in court procedures, which involved hearing witness testimony, weighing evidence, examining contracts, and rendering verdicts.

The strong-willed Hammurabi died in 1750 B.C.E., and the Amorite empire disintegrated shortly thereafter. The various Mesopotamian city-states went their own ways for about a century and a half, though the city-state of Babylon remained the premier custodian of Sumerian and Semitic cultural traditions.

Two other important states arose in Southwest Asia in the mid-second millennium B.C.E. One was a revived Babylonia under the rule of the Kassites, another band of migrant warriors, possibly mountain people from east of the Tigris-Euphrates valley. The Kassites, who probably spoke a Semitic language, took eagerly to chariot warfare. Shortly after 1500 B.C.E., they united southern Mesopotamia, ruling from Babylon on the Euphrates.

The second state was Mittani, founded about that same time in the fertile upper Euphrates valley, territory that is today mainly in Syria. The Mittani military elite, who may have founded the kingdom as chariot-riding invaders, appear to have used an Indo-European language but soon adopted local tongues. For more than two centuries this kingdom dominated the northern Euphrates region and its corridor of trade.

From Middle Kingdom to New Kingdom in the Nile Valley

Off to the southwest, the Old Kingdom of Egypt, which endured more than nine hundred years, ended about 2160 B.C.E. when the central rule of the pharaohs disintegrated (see Chapter 2). Civil strife, known to scholars as the First Intermediate Period, lasted more than a century. About 2040 B.C.E., however, one political faction assembled sufficient military power to reunite Upper Egypt with the bountiful delta (Lower Egypt), ushering in the Middle Kingdom of the eleventh and twelfth dynasties of pharaohs (2040–1786 B.C.E.). These monarchs revived and expanded Egypt's impressive bureaucracy, and irrigation engineers added thousands of acres of cultivable land to the realm. The pharaoh's armies advanced far upriver into Nubia (today southern Egypt and the northern Sudan), pushing the kingdom's power deeper into Africa than at any earlier time. And as the eastern Mediterranean commercial system matured, the kings promoted closer seaborne ties with the Aegean basin, Minoan Crete, and the Levant.

Despite this renewed unity and prosperity, the shadow of armed violence lengthened. In the mid seventeenth century B.C.E., intruders whom the Egyptians called Hyksos, meaning "foreign chiefs," migrated into the delta and then conquered it and part of Upper Egypt. The Hyksos were probably a mix of migrating herders and chariot fighters from Syria and Anatolia, some of them Semitic speakers, others Indo-European. They also appear to have incorporated bands of military mercenaries and outlaws, a type of freelance warrior quite common in Southwest Asia in that era. The Hyksos succeeded in seizing Egypt partly because the Middle Kingdom had already corroded politically and partly because they fielded chariots and bronze weaponry more expertly than the Egyptians did. For two centuries beginning about 1648 B.C.E., Hyksos kings ruled the lower Nile valley, striving to make themselves into legitimate pharaohs and

Akhenaten and his family. The New Kingdom pharaoh Akhenaten is best known for radically departing from traditional Egyptian religion by elevating the god Aten—and Akhenaten himself as Aten's divine servant—above all other deities. The priesthood, and probably most Egyptians, despised him for it, and the new teaching died with the pharaoh. In this limestone relief we see a contented Akhenaten at home with his wife Nefertiti and three of their children. Aten, represented by the sun disk, shines down upon them. What elements do you see in this scene that give it a humane and domestic flavor?

champions of Egyptian culture, neither with very convincing results.

Further upriver in Nubia, a kingdom based at Kerma between the Third and Fourth Cataracts (river rapids) took advantage of the Hyksos invasion to shed Egyptian domination and assert itself as a regional African power. The earliest Nubian state dates to about 2400 B.C.E., and over the centuries it tended to move through successive cycles of expanding and contracting Egyptian political and cultural influence. During the Hyksos period, Kerma flourished on farming and stock raising and on the trade in gold, ivory, ebony, cattle, timber, and slaves that flowed northward toward the Mediterranean.

Then, early in the sixteenth century B.C.E., Egyptian nobles rallied an army that evicted the Hyksos from the valley. This event ushered in the New Kingdom (1540–1070 B.C.E.), an era when Egypt's sphere of power expanded beyond all earlier borders. Pharaohs of the New Kingdom's eighteenth dynasty reasserted their authority far upriver, reducing Nubian rulers to Egyptian dependency once again. To the northeast, they not only chased the Hyksos back into Southwest Asia but also conquered the Levant up to the frontier of Anatolia. Taking lessons from the Hyksos, Egyptian commanders made numerous improvements in chariot technology and tactics.

Notably under the leadership of Thutmose I, Thutmose III, Hatshepsut (coruler with Thutmose and the only female New Kingdom pharaoh), and Akhenaten (inclusive dates 1493–1335 B.C.E.), the empire remained stable and prosperous. Picking up where their Middle Kingdom forebears had left off, these rulers made Egyptian bureaucratic government more efficient than ever. Reigning as divine beings from a splendid complex of palaces and temples at Thebes, they managed the state and closely regulated the economic life of Egyptian peasants with the help of thousands of officials and a professional standing army. They also monopolized foreign trade. As the empire grew, merchants from both the Mediterranean lands and Nubia converged on Egypt, though they had to conduct all their business through the pharaoh's commercial agents. Even so, vast amounts of

Opening of the Mouth Ceremony. This painting on papyrus from the *Book of the Dead*, a collection of spells to help the departed move safely to the next world, depicts a ritual performed for a deceased scribe named Honefer. The mummy's mouth is ritually opened to restore the dead man's senses and faculties. The white stele on the right is engraved with hieroglyphics and at the top is an image of Honefer standing before a seated god. Compare this image to the one on the stele of Hammurabi on page 95. In both, if the deity were to stand up, he would be much taller than the mortal he is facing.

"Here Is the Situation":
The King of Alashiya Writes to the Pharaoh of Egypt

More than 380 clay tablets have preserved correspondence among rulers of Southwest Asia and the eastern Mediterranean in the fourteenth century B.C.E. Scholars first discovered these letters in the late nineteenth century at el-Amarna, an archaeological site in Upper Egypt that was the short-lived capital of the New Kingdom pharaoh Akhenaten (r. 1353–1335 B.C.E.). Now scattered among the collections of several of the world's major museums, the letters brightly illuminate ancient diplomatic, political, and commercial exchange.

The majority of the letters are correspondence sent to Egyptian kings over a span of about thirty years. They are written in Akkadian cuneiform, the language of international diplomacy. Authors of the texts include Southwest Asian rulers, as well as leaders of small states in Syria and the Levant. The letters' concerns range from negotiating marriages to trade relations to political alliances. The international correspondence is generally framed in the language of "brotherhood," signifying that all rulers had equal social status and that in fact royal families commonly intermarried as a way of cementing ties of mutual obligation. Monarchs and princes exchanged gifts but also demanded support from one another in times of need.

This document is part of a letter from the king of Alashiya, a state located on the island of Cyprus in the eastern Mediterranean. This monarchy carried on extensive trade with Egypt, notably copper exports. Referring to the presence of Nergal, a Mesopotamian god associated with disease, destruction, and death, in his realm, the king informs the Egyptian pharaoh of the current situation in Alashiya and seeks to resolve diplomatic and economic issues between the two states.

Say to the king of Egypt, my brother: Message of the king of Alashiya, your brother. For me all goes well. For my household, my wives, my sons, my magnates, my horses, my chariots, and in my country, all goes very well. For my brother may all go well. For your household, your wives, your sons, your magnates, your horses, your chariots, and in your country, may all go very well. My brother, I herewith send my messenger with your messenger to Egypt.

I herewith send to you 500 (*talents*) of copper. As my brother's greeting gift I send it to you. My brother, do not be concerned that the amount of copper is small. Behold, the hand of Nergal is now in my country; he has slain all the men of my country, and there is not a (single) copper-worker. So, my brother, do not be concerned.

Send your messenger with my messenger immediately, and I will send you whatever copper you, my brother, request.

You are my brother. May he send me silver in very great quantities. My brother, give me the *very best* silver, and then I will send you, my brother, whatever you, my brother, request. . . .

Moreover, my brother, men of my country keep speaking with me about my timber that the king of Egypt receives from me. My brother, give me the payment due.

Moreover, here is the situation: a man from Alashiya has died in Egypt, and his things are in your country, though his son and wife are with me. So, my brother, look to the things of the Alashiya people and hand them over, my brother, to the charge of my messenger.

My brother, do not be concerned that your messenger has stayed 3 years in my country, for the hand of Nergal is in my country and in my own house. There was a young wife of mine that now, my brother, is dead. . . .

Moreover, may my brother send to me in very great quantities the silver that I have asked you for. Send, my brother, the things that I asked you for. My brother should do quite everything, and then whatever things you say I will do.

You have not been put (on the same level) with the king of Hatti [the Hittite kingdom] or the king of Sanhar [possibly Babylonia]. Whatever greeting-gift he (my brother) sends me, I for my part send you back double.

May your messenger come to me as of old, and may my messenger go to you as of old.

Source: Letters from Mesopotamia, trans. A. Leo Oppenheim, pp. 122ff. Copyright © 1967 by The University of Chicago. Reprinted by permission of The University of Chicago Press. Diacritical marks have been removed from words in this selection.

Thinking Critically

What particular diplomatic and economic issues does the king of Alashiya want to take up with the ruler of Egypt? From the king's references to the presence of "the hand of Nergal" in his country, what sort of crisis might have been happening in Alashiya? What particular products figure in exchange between the two states? Do you think exchange of gifts between these two rulers might have been important to diplomatic and commercial relations? Why do you think the king of Alashiya mentions the kings of Hatti and Sanhar? What point might he be trying to make by telling the Egyptian king that those rulers are not "on the same level" as him?

wealth poured into the valley in the form of royal trade, tribute from conquered princes, and war booty. The plunder included large numbers of enslaved prisoners from both Nubia and Southwest Asia, who were set to work building colossal temples, among other tasks.

Rivalry and Diplomacy among Militarized Kingdoms

Despite its imperial adventure, New Kingdom Egypt was by no means the only great power in the region. The political arena also included Hatti, the Kassite kingdom of Babylonia, Mittani, and, by the fourteenth century B.C.E., Assyria, a monarchy on the northern Tigris River plain. The spectacle of five large, militarized kingdoms competing with one another for territory, trade, and political advantage was unprecedented in world history. Such grand rivalries were possible, and indeed tempting, because of the rising wealth of Southwest Asia and Egypt, the new war-making technology, and the immense value of interurban trade.

Despite their fierce competition with one another, these large states may have endured as long as they did partly because their aristocratic classes developed methods of diplomacy in order to defuse potential conflicts over territory and trade. Monarchs exchanged ambassadors, lavish gifts, and numerous letters written on clay tablets; they also negotiated treaties and married into one another's families. In 1350 B.C.E., for example, Tadu-Heba, daughter of Tushratta, the king of Mittani, traveled more than six hundred miles from the Euphrates to the Nile to marry Pharaoh Amenhotep III, thereby strengthening cordial relations. In 1284 B.C.E., Egypt signed a formal peace treaty with the Hittites, and shortly after that Ramses II (r. 1279–1213 B.C.E.) married a Hittite princess. Akkadian, the Semitic language written in cuneiform and spoken principally in Babylonia, became a diplomatic *lingua franca* (LING-gwuh FRANG-kuh), a common language that emissaries and officials used to inform and negotiate with one another. Over time, the conventions and protocols governing international relations—for example, rules for the safety of messengers or for proper use of language in letters from one monarch to another—became quite complex. In short, the ruling groups of the whole region from the eastern Mediterranean to Mesopotamia gradually created an international system for engaging in regular political dialogue that encouraged trade and in some measure restrained warfare.

lingua franca A spoken or written language that facilitates commercial or diplomatic communication across cultural frontiers.

The major states of Southwest Asia and the eastern Mediterranean not only exchanged gifts and messengers. They also periodically made war on one another. Most battles took place in Syria or the Levant because that is where frontiers of the Hittite kingdom, Mittani, and Egypt abutted one another. For example, Egypt under Ramses II and the Hittites under Mutawallis II (r. 1295–1272 B.C.E.) clashed at Kadesh in northern Syria in 1275 B.C.E. There, festering disputes over frontier territory escalated into a fight between thousands of archers firing from chariots. Both sides sustained severe losses, but neither army carried the day. The border remained largely as it was, and fifteen years later Egypt and the Hittites signed a peace treaty.

By the late thirteenth century B.C.E., however, the political geography of the region was changing radically. Both Mitanni and the Kassites were finally obliterated by their enemies, and Egypt gave up most of its Syrian territories following the reign of Ramses II. The Hittite empire fragmented amid popular revolts, civil struggles among claimants to the throne, and an extended crisis of drought and famine. In the succeeding century, Assyria became the rising star in Southwest Asia, as we see in Chapter 5.

Early Greeks

Impressive centers of power and wealth also appeared on mainland Greece from about 1700 B.C.E. The most striking material evidence are the well-stocked burial chambers, or shaft graves, that have been excavated at Mycenae in the Peloponnesus, the peninsula that forms the southern part of Greece (see Map 3.4). Carved deep into rock, these tombs contained priceless hoards of gold, silver, and bronze that only an aristocratic class could possibly have accumulated. Citadels protected by thick defensive walls also arose at several locations in the Peloponnesus. Like the Minoan palaces on Crete in an earlier period, these bastions evolved into regional centers of agrarian production and artisanry.

Historians associate the rise of the Mycenaeans (meye-seh-NEE-uhns), as this Aegean aristocracy is known, with the appearance of bands of warriors who spoke an archaic form of Greek, an Indo-European language. Most likely, the earliest Greeks, like the Hittites and Hyksos, started out as loosely organized migrant groups who raised cattle, sheep, and horses supplemented by farming. The *Iliad*, the legendary epic poem recounting a siege of the city of Troy, portrays the Mycenaeans simultaneously as god-like heroes and swaggering pillagers who prized horses, chariots, and stockpiles of bronze weapons. Most historians think that the earliest Greek-speaking people reached the Balkan Peninsula from the north, entering the Aegean Sea region around 2000 B.C.E. By no later than 1450 B.C.E., the Greek language is evident on both Crete and the Peloponnesus in the form of a written script called Linear B.

Around 1500 B.C.E., Mycenaean Greek warriors seized Crete, and Minoan civilization collapsed. Nature may have hastened that development. Sometime in the later seventeenth century B.C.E., a volcano erupted on the little island of Thera (Santorini), which lies about sixty-eight miles north of Crete. The explosion blew apart Thera and very likely caused a tsunami and massive clouds of dust and ash. Some volcanologists, scholars who study eruptions past and present, have hypothesized that the Minoans suffered not only catastrophic destruction but also long-term disruption of agriculture and sea trade.

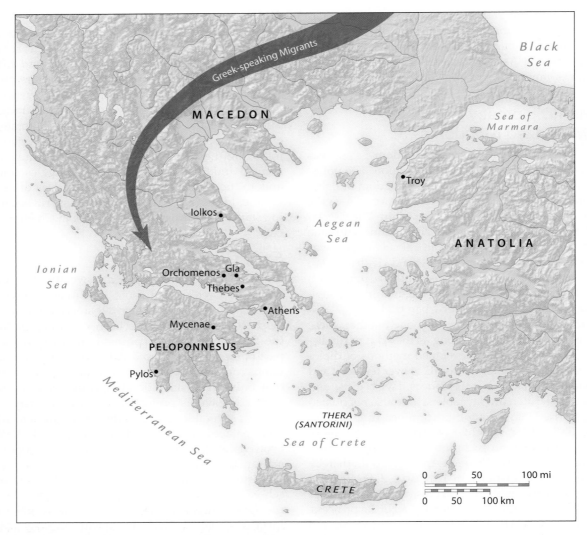

MAP 3.4 Mycenaean centers, second millennium B.C.E.
Mycenaean society included many small settlements in addition to the main palace centers indicated here. Connect this close-up on early Greek movement into the Aegean region with the wider perspective on the spread of Indo-European languages shown in Map 3.2.

The Mycenaean warrior aristocracy that held power between about 1500 and 1200 B.C.E. participated in the larger culture and economy of the eastern Mediterranean. Palace centers around the Aegean came to share a common culture in such areas as pottery design and burial practice. The Mycenaeans also looked to Egypt, the Levant, and Crete for cultural goods and information to help transform themselves from rough-and-ready soldiers into self-assured city elites. In fact, their shaft graves present a microcosm of long-distance commercial connections. Archaeologists excavating these chambers have found ivory from Syria, ostrich eggs from Nubia, lapis lazuli from east of Mesopotamia, and amber from the Baltic Sea. The Mycenaeans exchanged olive oil, wine, and ceramics for these luxuries. Shards of characteristically Mycenaean pottery have been found in Sicily and Italy, a sign that Aegean merchants were venturing far to the west to found settlements. In short, the rise of Mycenaean power represented an extension of complex urban life along the northern Mediterranean rim.

Indo-Europeans in Iran and South Asia

As Indo-European-speaking groups advanced west through Southwest Asia and the Aegean region, other bands migrated east of the Caspian Sea into the semiarid plains and highlands of what are today Turkmenistan, Uzbekistan, and northern Iran. Gradually, these groups diverged from one another in both space and time. So did their speech. Some migrants moved onto the Iranian Plateau, the region of uplands and mountains that encompasses most of modern Iran and parts of Afghanistan and Pakistan. The newcomers there emerged in the first millennium B.C.E. as speakers

Mycenaean dagger. Excavation of a Mycenaean shaft grave revealed this ceremonial bronze dagger with gold work depicting a lion hunt. The decoration has several elements that indicate the artistic influence of Minoan Crete on Mycenaean society. Compare the leaping lion on the dagger with the bull in the Minoan fresco on page 83.

of an ancestral version of Persian (Farsi), as well as several other languages including Kurdish and Pashto. Other groups drifted across Afghanistan into South Asia (the Indian subcontinent). The languages of those herders are classified today as Indic (or Indo-Aryan), an Indo-European subfamily that includes modern Hindi, Urdu, Bengali, and several other tongues.

When Indo-European speakers penetrated the Indus valley, probably beginning about 1700 B.C.E., they almost certainly found the once-great cities of the Harappan civilization in full decline (see Chapter 2). It is likely that a succession of Indic groups filtered through and around the already dilapidated Indus towns over a period of centuries. We have no evidence that they entered the subcontinent in massive numbers. By the later second millennium B.C.E., nevertheless, bands of Indic speakers were advancing eastward along a corridor of grassy plains just south of the Himalayan foothills. Opening before them was the Ganges (GAN-jeez) River, which flowed more than one thousand miles to the Bay of Bengal. In that era the indigenous populations of the valley were either foragers or farmers growing wheat, millet, and, later, rice. They spoke languages of the ancient Dravidian family, perhaps as the Harappan city dwellers had.

The principal source of information on the early period of interaction between Indic speakers and preexisting populations has been the Vedas (VAY-duhs). These are compilations of hymns and prayers that Indic priests presumably recited and passed orally from one generation to the next. From these texts, notably the classic work of Indian literature known as the *Rig Veda*, we may distill a portrait of Indic immigrants as proud militarists who quarreled constantly among themselves and who violently subdued the local population of "dark" demon people. The characters in the *Rig Veda* organized themselves in **clans** led by warrior heroes, and their society was divided into four main social classes: warrior-aristocrats,

priests, common people, and the inferior Dasas, or despised victims of conquest. Historians see in this system the remote origins of the more formal hierarchy of social classes, or castes, that emerged in later centuries. The Indic newcomers also possessed horses, cattle, sheep, bows, metal weapons, and chariots. They worshiped gods of heaven, earth, sun, and fire, notably Indra, ferocious god of war, who rode a celestial chariot and hurled thunderbolts at his enemies.

The *Rig Veda*'s representation of late second millennium B.C.E. India is dramatic, but it is also an idealized origins myth later incorporated into Hindu cultural and religious tradition. The Vedas did not appear in written form until about 400 B.C.E., and other types of historical evidence force us to modify their testimony. For example, the Indic languages absorbed numerous words from the older Dravidian tongue, which might suggest intermarriage and social exchange between Indic speakers and local populations, not just violent domination. The newcomers, moreover, may have had a military culture based on chariots, horses, and bronze weapons, but extremely little material evidence of these things has ever been found on the subcontinent. On the other hand, the Indic languages gradually advanced across the northern and central subcontinent, and Dravidian-speaking populations there virtually disappeared. Today, Indic languages in the Indo-European family are spoken by more than 800 million people.

Indo-Europeans and Chariots from the Far West to the Far East

Indo-European languages also spread to Europe in the second and first millennia B.C.E. in connection with migrations of groups coming from either the Pontic-Caspian steppes or southeastern Europe. With them emerged mixed economies of **pastoralism** and farming, along with horses, wheeled carts, and chariots (which served mainly as symbols of political prestige rather

clan A type of social organization in which a group of people claim shared identity as descendants of a single, usually distant ancestor. Clan organization is common among pastoral nomadic societies.

pastoralism A type of economic and social organization involving the breeding and raising of domesticated hoofed animals, or livestock.

The Beauty of Xiaohe: A Woman of the Steppes

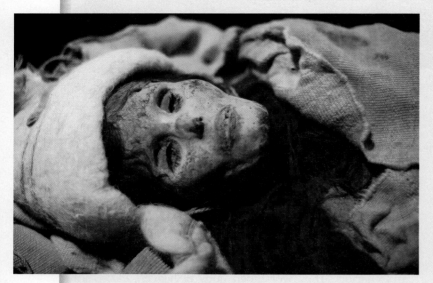

A close look at the "Beauty of Xiaohe" mummy reveals her eyelashes intact.

It must have been cold at the eastern edge of the Taklamakan when the woman died. Those who buried her dressed her for warmth. A fur-lined hat sat atop her long auburn hair, matching the fur-trimmed boots on her feet. She wore a string skirt, and her body was wrapped in a large woolen blanket. Scientists have named her the Beauty of Xiaohe (sh-ih-ow-h-uh) after the cemetery site where she and other human remains were excavated in 2003. She lay in her tomb for nearly four thousand years, reposing beneath a boat of wood and cowhide turned upside down.

In the twentieth century, archaeologists have discovered more than two hundred of these bodies, along with the clothing they wore when they died, in different parts of the Tarim Basin, today China's far western Xinjiang (shin-jyahng) region. Scholars commonly refer to the corpses as "mummies," though their community did not deliberately preserve them with special techniques comparable to ancient Egyptian mummification. Rather, extreme aridity and frigid winters preserved the bodies naturally. Recent DNA testing of human remains, some of which date to about 2000 B.C.E., indicates that these individuals descended from people who migrated into the region from the west and married into local populations. Their forebears may therefore have been speakers of an early Indo-European language who lived in the Pontic-Caspian steppes. If that is the case, the Beauty of Xiaohe probably spoke a Tocharian tongue, though all the languages in this family are now extinct. Many of the mummies exhibit features not typically East Asian, for example high-bridged noses, deep-set eyes, and light-colored hair. Their brightly hued clothing provides another link with peoples to the west. Some of the later mummies wear plaid twills resembling textiles woven by ancestral speakers of the Celtic branch of Indo-European languages who once lived in central Europe.

By four thousand years ago, the lands that fringed the Taklamakan had already become meeting places for people of diverse origins. In her lifetime the Beauty of Xiaohe may have seen caravans of traders moving from one oasis to another, tracing out the "silk roads" that would eventually run along the northern and southern fringes of the great desert, connecting China with Iran and the Mediterranean beyond.

Thinking Critically

Why do you think political controversy over the origins of the Beauty of Xiaohe and other mummies found in the Tarim Basin has arisen in China in recent years?

---

than as war machines). By around 1500 B.C.E., all building of megalithic tombs and ritual centers along Europe's Atlantic rim had come to an end. This suggests the rising cultural dominance of newcomers, though there is no sign that Indo-European movements produced a sudden or violent break in Europe's history. Rather, general trends continued: the population grew, large fortified settlements appeared, chiefly families accumulated great wealth in bronze and gold, and long-distance trade flourished from the Baltic Sea to the Mediterranean and along the Danube River. Gradually, branches and twigs of the Indo-European language trunk appeared all across Europe, including ancestral forms of Latin and Celtic, Slavic, and Germanic languages, including English.

On the eastern side of Inner Eurasia, inhabitants of what are today Mongolia and northwestern China took up pastoral nomadism and a full-fledged "horse culture." Groups speaking Indo-European languages associated with a linguistic branch known as Tocharian moved eastward after about 3500 B.C.E. to occupy the slopes of the Altai and Tien Shan Mountains and eventually the Tarim Basin, location of the enormous Taklamakan Desert.

It seems certain that peoples of the Inner Eurasian steppes came into contact with the Shang dynasty of northern China. Like the older complex societies to the west, the Shang army fielded squadrons of two-horse chariots from around 1200 B.C.E. Chariot technology very likely diffused from Inner Eurasia. The spoked wheels were similar in design to those used in Southwest Asia. Chinese chariotry also carried great aristocratic prestige. Physical remains of vehicles have been found in several Shang tombs along with ritually sacrificed horses.

The chariot was indeed an early example of a single development that affected peoples across Eurasia and northern Africa within the space of a few hundred years. More broadly, by the start of the second millennium B.C.E., if not earlier, the combination of horseback riding, wagon travel, chariotry, and customs and techniques to promote trade permitted the formation of a single network of commercial and cultural exchange that extended from China to Europe and the Mediterranean basin.

Looking across the entire region where militarized, chariot-riding elites took power, historians have also noticed that the mother goddesses and other female deities prevalent in the late paleolithic and neolithic eras gave way in religious worship to ascendant male gods of war and thunder. Evidence from languages, graves, and official documents supports the hypothesis that patriarchal institutions became more entrenched in the second millennium B.C.E. and that the legal and social status of women declined in general. Such correlations suggest at the very least that the migrations and state-building enterprises of male charioteers wielding bows and bronze swords had profound social and cultural effects on a large part of Afroeurasia.

Developments in the Tropical Belt

FOCUS In what circumstances did agrarian societies become more widely established in both Southeast Asia and central and southern Africa between the fourth and second millennia B.C.E.?

Large-scale migrations of a different origin reshaped human landscapes in Afroeurasia's tropical belt in the third and second millennia B.C.E. For the first time, large areas of both Subsaharan Africa and island Southeast Asia became inhabited by people who grew crops and herded animals (see Map 3.5). The fundamental consequence was a more or less steady increase of population and the complexity of society in latitudes near the equator.

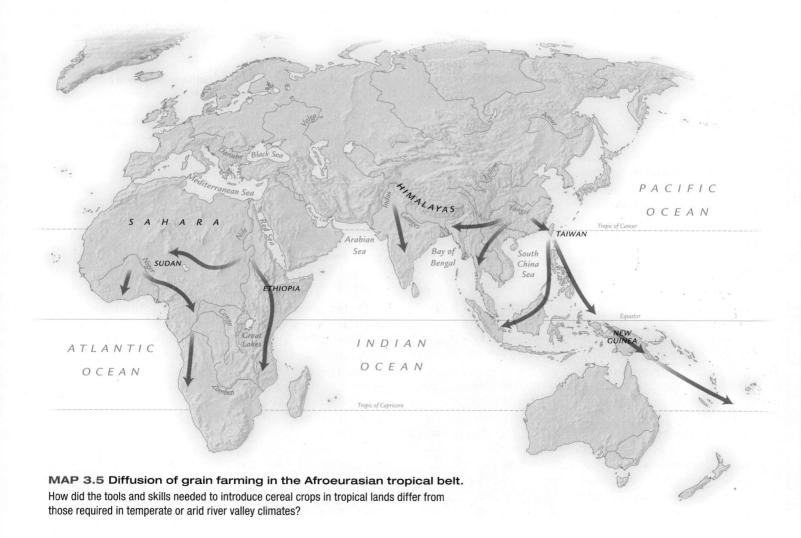

MAP 3.5 Diffusion of grain farming in the Afroeurasian tropical belt.
How did the tools and skills needed to introduce cereal crops in tropical lands differ from those required in temperate or arid river valley climates?

Herders and Farmers South of the Sahara Desert

In tropical Africa, climatic fluctuation was an engine of migration. Six to seven thousand years ago the region that is today the Sahara Desert passed through a long cycle of higher rainfall. Hunters, fishers, and cattle herders flourished on lakeshores, riverbanks, and marshland. By about 2500 B.C.E., however, the wet phase ended. The Sahara, together with the adjacent Arabian Desert east of the Red Sea, moved toward the extreme levels of aridity that characterize these regions today. As that happened, humans progressively retreated from the central Sahara. Some migrated either north toward the Mediterranean or south into the semiarid and grassland zone known historically as the Sudan. Others drifted eastward to the Nile valley to participate in the young civilization blossoming there.

South of the desert, the open or wooded savannas of the Sudan stretched from the Atlantic coast to the mountains of Ethiopia. Saharan cattle-keeping peoples moved into this belt, most of them probably speaking languages belonging to a linguistic family known as Nilo-Saharan. These herding folk shared the region with farming populations already established. Perhaps in response to climatic pressures, farmers of the Sudan domesticated a particularly wide range of nutritious grains, including sorghum, pearl millet, African rice, and, in Ethiopia, the tiny grain called teff.

Migrations into East Africa. Herders who populated the savanna belt could advance only so far southward before reaching tropical forests where their cattle, as well as horses, became susceptible to trypanosomiasis, a lethal disease for most bovine species. This malady, the animal form of sleeping sickness carried by tsetse flies, flourished only where certain kinds of bushes offered cover. On the eastern side of Africa, however, people who practiced a combination of cattle herding and farming were able to move southward along a corridor of highlands inhospitable to tsetse flies. By the third millennium B.C.E., cattle breeders, who used stone tools and made pottery, were advancing toward East Africa's Great Lakes, an upland region of moderate climate and fertile soil. There, and farther south, they gradually assimilated or displaced forager populations, or pushed them deeper into the tropical forests. These older populations spoke languages belonging to the ancient Khoisan (KOI-sahn) family, whose origins may go back to the early days of *Homo sapiens.* The incoming herders and farmers, whose numerous languages belonged to either the Nilo-Saharan or the Afroasiatic families, adopted a variety of Khoisan words. But over the long run, Khoisan languages nearly

Cattle economies in tropical Africa. Long-horned Ankole cattle and related breeds have sustained numerous peoples in East and southern Africa for several millennia.

disappeared in East Africa as agrarian groups spread further and grew larger.

Bantu-speaking farmers. In another theater of migration, farmers who lived in western and central Africa just south of the Sahara also began to advance southward toward the wet forests. Climatic drying was almost certainly a factor in this movement. A second factor was that tropical farmers practiced one form or other of **shifting agriculture.** The nutrient-rich layer, or humus, in tropical soils tended to be thin and to leach away easily under pounding rain.

> **shifting agriculture** A method of crop production in which a farmer clears and cultivates a plot of land until the soil loses its nutrient value, and then moves on to clear and plant a new field, allowing the first one to lie fallow and recover.

The women and adolescent girls who did most of the cultivating therefore had to use hoes and digging sticks, not animal-powered plows. Even if delicately worked, however, humus tended to diminish within two or three years, so fields had to be left to recover over several seasons. The farm family had to move to a new spot to clear and plant again. Consequently, shifting agriculture (sometimes called swidden agriculture) often resulted in slow migratory drift of local populations.

Farmers whose major crop was the yam, a highly nutritious root plant first domesticated in West Africa perhaps about 8000 B.C.E., advanced slowly south and east from a core area of woodland centered on what is today southern Cameroon. The surviving archaeological record shows that they manufactured durable pottery and used both fire and stone axes to clear away forests, opening land to sunlight and yam plots. They also hunted, fished, and produced oil from palm trees.

Scholars have combined archaeology with comparative analysis of languages spoken in Africa today to learn much about the long-distance movements of cultivators into equatorial and southern Africa. They spoke languages classified within the Niger-Congo family and more specifically a subfamily of very closely related tongues called Bantu (BAHN-too). Just as scholars have compared basic vocabularies of living Indo-European languages to reconstruct Proto-Indo-European, linguists have analyzed numerous Bantu languages to recover Proto-Bantu. They hypothesize that it originated sometime after 4000 B.C.E. in Cameroon. The word *Bantu* comes from the root word *ntu*, which means "person," and the plural-forming prefix *ba-*. Linguistic clues tells us that early Bantu speakers built rectangular houses with palm thatch roofs; navigated rivers in boats; made sculptures of wood; and venerated both a supreme creator god, who did not intervene regularly in human affairs, and a range of more accessible deities and ancestral spirits.

In the third and second millennia B.C.E., Bantu-speaking farmers advanced along two major routes. One was southward into the equatorial forests, then upstream along the Congo River (the world's seventh longest) and its numerous tributaries. Some groups settled along the way, others kept moving through the forest belt, emerging eventually into the savannas of the Southern Hemisphere. As centuries passed, paths of migration lengthened, and pioneer farmers colonized a variety of ecological niches. Gradually, therefore, Bantu languages multiplied, and local religious and social practices became more diverse. Foragers who occupied the Congo valley forests before Bantu speakers arrived very likely traded, intermarried, and shared skills with the newcomers. Many must have taken up farming, though some, including ancestors of the Batwa (people known conventionally as Pygmies), remained in the forests to collect and hunt.

Bantu speakers also migrated across the northern savanna zone, then southward into lands around East Africa's Great Lakes. There, they planted cereal crops, notably sorghum and millet. Where the local ecosystem permitted, they also took up herding, which they learned from cattle-keeping people already there. After 1200 B.C.E. the Great Lakes area became one of the most densely populated places in the world's tropical latitudes. In the following millennia, Bantu-speaking farmers and herders occupied nearly the entire southern third of Africa. We come back to this epic story in later chapters.

Austronesian Farmers in Southeast Asia

Paralleling these developments in Africa, farming peoples also moved throughout the tropical lands of maritime Southeast Asia. In terms of sheer geographical scope, this migration was one of the greatest in world history, ultimately extending from Madagascar in the western Indian Ocean to Oceania (the Island Pacific). Both linguistic and archaeological evidence shows that, by the fifth millennium B.C.E., agrarian communities that produced rice, millet, pigs, and chickens were multiplying in the well-watered valleys and coastal plains of both southern China and mainland Southeast Asia, the region that today includes Vietnam, Thailand, and Malaysia. Around 4000 B.C.E., some adventurous farm families crossed the Formosa Strait, which separates mainland China from the large island of Taiwan. These migrants spoke ancient languages of the Austronesian family.

Subsequently, Taiwan became the major dispersal point for further movements of rice-growing farmers southward into the wet tropical islands of the Philippines and Indonesia, as well as to many of the islands that rimmed the western Pacific. (We return to the peopling of Oceania in Chapter 4.) At some point, Austronesian voyagers moving south from Taiwan invented the outrigger canoe. This type of craft has a lateral support float attached to the hull, sometimes one on each side, to add stability to the vessel. A double-outrigger could stay upright in the heaviest of seas. As colonizers sailed from one Southeast Asian island to another, they brought with them an ecological "suitcase" of rice, pigs, chickens, durable pottery, and finely ground stone tools. One factor in their demographic success was the position of maritime Southeast Asia on the "ring of fire," the zone of volcanic activity that arcs around the rim of the Pacific, encompassing both eastern Asia and the western edge of the Americas. Volcanic eruptions in Southeast Asia did (and still do) kill people, but they also deposit layers of fertile volcanic soil, which almost certainly encouraged Austronesian groups to continue to explore and colonize new territory. For example, rice-growing populations became notably dense and productive on Java, an Indonesian island well-endowed with volcanic earth.

Across much of maritime Southeast Asia, Austronesian farming communities replaced forager economies and older languages. This did not, however, happen everywhere. On the great forested island of New Guinea, the much older Papuan-speaking population held its own in the interior regions against Austronesian intruders. The main reason may be that several millennia earlier the Papuans had domesticated varieties of yam, taro, banana, and perhaps sugar cane entirely on their own. Therefore, when Austronesian explorers appeared on New Guinea's shores, they confronted not a scattering of food collectors but relatively dense agrarian societies that were not about to budge.

• • •

Conclusion

Compared to the eight thousand years of the neolithic era, the second millennium B.C.E. was a revolutionary period of population growth, agrarian expansion, and city building across the more northerly latitudes of Afroeurasia. During that millennium, two contrasting trends developed simultaneously. On one hand, as more people adopted either farming or herding (or a combination of the two) and carried those ways of life into regions where they had previously been unknown, languages and numerous other elements of culture proliferated. Also, human adaptation to new ecological conditions, from tropical rainforests to arid grasslands, required continuous cultural innovation and adjustment. In other words, the Afroeurasian map of languages and cultural beliefs and practices became much more complex. Migratory movements, sometimes involving conquest, caused long-enduring communities to split apart, producing new linguistic and cultural offshoots. Indo-European languages multiplied across a territory extending from Europe to India. Austronesian speech became dominant in Southeast Asia from the Indian Ocean to the western Pacific. In Africa, ultimately hundreds of languages in three major linguistic families spread into and beyond the tropical forest zone.

On the other hand, in the same millennium that Afroeurasia was becoming more culturally diverse, intercommunication among communities became more intense and extended over longer distances in connection with migration, trade, conquest, and state building. With the exception of Shang China, no new centers of complex society arose that had quite the cultural weight and density of Mesopotamia, Egypt, or the Indus. However, new kingdoms and ruling groups such as the Hittites, the Mycenaeans, and the builders of the Oxus cities did much to advance regional productivity and interregional commerce for several centuries running. Also, the more that agrarian towns and oases sprang up on the landscape, the faster information tended to circulate from one to the other. Relative to the pace of communication in paleolithic times, the most attractive ideas and inventions spread like wildfire. For example, societies across the breadth of Eurasia and northern Africa adopted the complicated technology of bronze metallurgy within less than a thousand years. Knowledge of chariotry galloped from society to society even faster. By the thirteenth century B.C.E., chariots of a fairly uniform design were in use in places as far from one another as western Europe, Nubian Africa, and China.

This dual process, in which human society became simultaneously more culturally diverse and more firmly interconnected, was not a development unique to Afroeurasia. It also happened, though on a much smaller scale in terms of the number of people involved, in the Americas, Australia, and the Pacific basin. In Chapter 4, we visit these regions, which together encompassed more than half the globe.

• • •

Key Terms

Bantu migrations 105	megalith 84	pastoralism 101
bronze age 81	Minoan civilization 82	shaman 87
clan 101	Mycenaean society 99	Shang dynasty 86
Hittite kingdom 93	New Kingdom 96	shifting agriculture 105
Indo-European migrations 92	Nubia 96	tribute 83
kinship 89	oracle bones 87	Vedas 101
law code of Hammurabi 94	Oxus civilization 85	
lingua franca 99	pastoral nomadism 88	

Change over Time

4200 B.C.E.	People take up horseback riding in the Pontic-Caspian steppes.
4000 B.C.E.	Austronesian-speaking farmers migrate from China to Taiwan, a dispersal point for further migrations into tropical Southeast Asia.
3300 B.C.E.	Indo-European herders begin migrating west, south, and east from Pontic-Caspian steppes.
2400 B.C.E.	Builders in Britain begin constructing Stonehenge, one of many megalithic sites along Europe's Atlantic rim.
2100–1600 B.C.E.	Walled cities emerge in the Oxus civilization in Central Asia.
2000 B.C.E.	Chariots become important vehicles in warfare and political ritual.
2000–1450 B.C.E.	Minoan civilization develops on Crete.
Third and second millennia B.C.E.	Bronze metallurgy spreads across Eurasia and northern Africa (bronze age).
Third and second millennia B.C.E.	Bantu farmers establish agrarian societies in equatorial Africa.
1792–1750 B.C.E.	King Hammurabi expands Babylonian rule in Southwest Asia.
1750–1045 B.C.E.	The Shang dynasty rules over China's first large state.
1700 B.C.E.	Indo-European-speaking herders enter South Asia, a period later mythologized in the *Rig Veda.*
1650–1180 B.C.E.	The Hittite kingdom (Hatti) thrives in Anatolia and Syria.

Please see end of book reference section for additional reading suggestions related to this chapter.

4 Early Odysseys in the Americas, Australia, and Oceania
8000–500 B.C.E.

An outrigger sailing canoe in the southern Pacific, as depicted by an eighteenth-century artist.

I n 1947, the Norwegian adventurer Thor Heyerdahl sailed from the coast of Peru on a balsa wood raft named the *Kon-Tiki*. More than three months later, he and his small crew landed in the Tuamotu Archipelago in the south central Pacific 4,300 miles to the west. Heyerdahl made the voyage as part of a larger project to demonstrate that many centuries ago sailors from South America reached Rapa Nui (Easter Island) and other islands of eastern Polynesia. Heyerdahl's theory never made much headway with scholars, who have argued that the historical record points overwhelmingly to the peopling of the Pacific not from America but from Southeast Asia starting about 10,000 years ago.

Nevertheless, scientists have also generally accepted evidence that a variety of sweet potato domesticated in the tropical Americas spread to the Island Pacific centuries before European mariners first crossed that sea. Perhaps Polynesian seafarers seeking new islands to settle reached the coast of South America and returned home with sweet potatoes. Possibly, an American Indian coastal vessel carrying these tubers drifted westward, eventually to be discovered and planted by Polynesian farmers.

The sweet potato mystery is just one example of rare communication between regions that, after the initial human colonization from Africa, had almost no contact with one another for thousands of years. Peoples of the Americas and Afroeurasia did not interact in any sustained way for about 12,000 years. But we also know that Norse settlers from Iceland or southern Greenland founded a short-lived community on the coast of Newfoundland in eastern Canada around 1000 C.E. The forager (or forager-hunter) population of Australia and the inhabitants of Afroeurasia remained almost entirely isolated from each other from about 6500 B.C.E. to 1788 C.E. Nevertheless, we have evidence that people of New Guinea and some Indonesian islands made sporadic connections with northern Australians during those millennia.

Despite sporadic episodes like these, we can think of the inhabited globe as constituting four distinct macro-regions, four different "worlds" of human interchange, from the neolithic era or earlier up to the past few centuries. Three of these worlds, Afroeurasia, the Americas, and Australia, were continental land masses. Oceania, the fourth, was a universe of islands scattered across the Pacific. The huge majority of humans have always lived in Afroeurasia and its adjacent islands, and beginning in paleolithic times its societies have forged increasingly complex interrelations. Within the other three macro-regions, people also exchanged goods and ideas over long distances, though the numbers involved relative to Afroeurasia were small, even in the Americas. Even so, the early colonizers of those three worlds adapted ingeniously to a wide array of physical and natural environments, and, in the case of the Americas, they created dense agrarian societies.

This chapter explores those three regions, starting with the Americas. There, people in both Mesoamerica ("Middle" America, or the region that is today southern Mexico and Central America) and the Andean Mountain spine of western South America experimented with domesticated crop production only a few thousand years after that process started in Southwest Asia. Maize (or corn) supplemented by other plant foods gradually established itself as a large-seeded grain staple everywhere in the Americas except where summers did not last long enough to sustain it. In the late third millennia B.C.E., farming societies also appeared in the arid region that is today the southwestern United States, in the North American woodlands from the Mississippi to the Atlantic, and in Amazonia (the Amazon River basin). In several regions, such as northern Canada or the California coast, people continued the foraging and hunting way of life because

• • •

crop growing, even if the concept was known, offered no particular advantages as long as fish, game, and wild plants remained plentiful. In a few places, however, farming societies grew large and dense enough to propel more complex forms of social and economic organization, including cities. Such innovations started appearing along the Pacific coast of Peru as early as the fourth millennium B.C.E. and along the gulf coast of Mexico, the site of the Olmec urban civilization, in the second millennium B.C.E.

In the second part of the chapter we zoom across the Pacific to Australia, which our species began to colonize as early as 60,000 years ago, as much as 20,000 years earlier than *Homo sapiens* populated Europe. Despite such a long history of adaptation to a continent that is today about 70 percent arid, all Australians continued to forage and hunt, not plant and hoe, until after the first Europeans arrived barely two and a quarter centuries ago. Nevertheless, research in archaeology, linguistics, and genetic shows that Aboriginal society—Australians whose ancestors populated the continent before Europeans came—experienced long-term historical change as much as peoples of Afroeurasia or the Americas did, even if the population remained consistently tiny compared to both those regions.

A Panoramic View

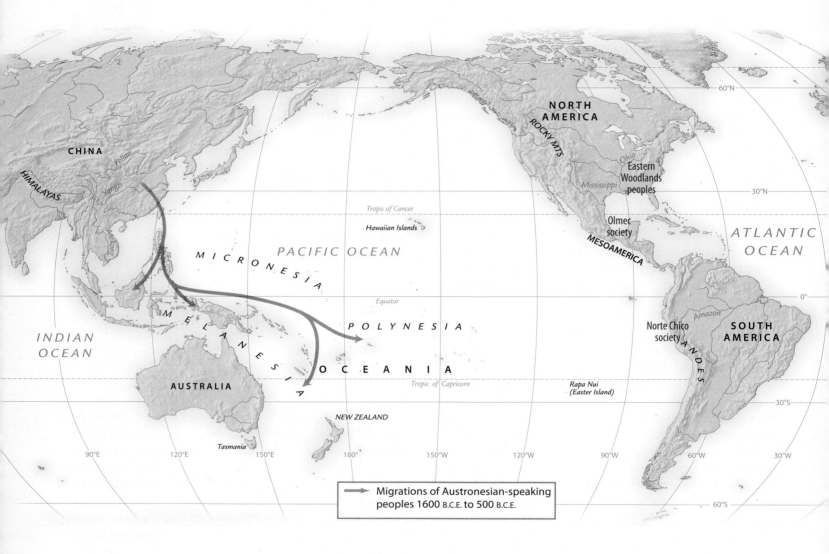

MAP 4.1 The Americas, Australia, and the Pacific Basin to 500 B.C.E.
Permanent contacts among peoples of the Americas, Australia, and Oceania were forged only in the past 250 years. Considering that narrow sea passages separated them, why were contacts between Aboriginal peoples of Australia and the inhabitants of both Southeast Asia and western Oceania so limited before the eighteenth century C.E.?

Until about 3,600 years ago, humans inhabited only far western islands of the Pacific basin. The third section of the chapter describes how, in the ensuing 2,500 years or so, voyagers undertook an astonishing fan-shaped migration far into the sea, hopping, as it were, from island to island. Among the ancient migratory movements that peopled the world, this was the only one accomplished exclusively by boat. As colonization advanced, men and women adapted successfully to contrasting ecological conditions and created different types of societies. Where islands formed archipelagos or were not more than a few hundred miles apart, seaborne trade and cultural exchange took place. But for a few thousand years, Pacific peoples had no sustained contact with the other three inhabited worlds.

Farmers and Platform Builders in the Americas

FOCUS Under what environmental and social circumstances did complex societies emerge in South America and Mesoamerica?

Between 12,000 and 7,000 years ago, people whose genetic ancestors had migrated from northeastern Asia colonized all latitudes of the Americas from tundra to tropical rainforest (see Chapter 1). As of 4000 B.C.E., a time when agrarian societies were spreading rapidly in several parts of Afroeurasia, the Americas had, as far as we know, no full-time farmers. All communities practiced some combination of hunting, foraging, and fishing. Nevertheless, experiments with plant domestication had started much earlier in a few places, as much as 10,000 years ago in southern Mexico.

Around 3500 B.C.E., people along the arid coast of what is today northern Peru planted cotton and food crops to supplement resources from the sea. They also began constructing ritual and residential centers exhibiting characteristics of complex agrarian society. In the following 1,500 years, ceremonial complexes associated with a social class system, including a ruling elite, multiplied in high Andes Mountain valleys in Peru and Ecuador. In Mesoamerica, maize came into use as a staple crop that could support larger concentrations of population. This happened in several localities, notably along the Gulf of Mexico, where the Olmec started building cities about 1350 B.C.E. In the millennium that followed, Mesoamerica and the Andes zone remained the largest centers of population growth and urbanization. A trend toward social complexity, however, also took place in semiarid northern Mexico and the Southwest of the United States, in the eastern woodlands of North America, and, on a smaller scale, in Amazonia.

Native Americans definitely invented agriculture without any cues from the Afroeurasian experience. There is no evidence that what became the principal American food crops—maize, beans, squash, potatoes, peppers, manioc—were grown anywhere in Afroeurasia until after Columbus linked the two hemispheres in the late fifteenth century (see Table 4.1). But despite the absence of sustained contact between human societies from the two hemispheres for at least 12,000 years, they developed in fundamentally similar ways. In both Afroeurasia and the Americas, overall population rose steadily after food production spread, while the proportion of foragers to farmers declined. In both regions, complex societies appeared, characterized by cities, social class divisions, centralized states, writing systems, and streams of technological and scientific innovation. In a sense, humans in Afroeurasia and the Americas provided "control groups" for each other. The two together bore out the hypothesis that wherever in the world crop-growing societies began to produce regular surpluses, greater social complexity followed, including crowded towns, teeming markets, tax collectors, high priests, accumulations of knowledge and skill, and unrelenting alteration of the natural environment.

American Farmer Power

An agricultural revolution took place in the Americas a few millennia later than in several regions of Afroeurasia, but no one in either hemisphere thought they were racing for the title of "First Farmers." As we saw in Chapter 2, forager-hunter communities in Southwest Asia and the Nile River valley experimented with plant and animal domestication, not because they thought life would be better if they became farmers (assuming they could have known what farmers *were*), but because climatic changes and accompanying social and demographic stresses slowly, and in large measure unconsciously, pushed them in that new direction. Under similar conditions of environmental stress, early Americans (a term we will use as synonymous with Native Americans or American Indians) are likely to have selected and sown food or fiber plants they thought had more desirable qualities than others. Farming developed too late in the Americas to be linked to the climatic changes that defined the last Ice Age (Pleistocene) and the onset of the warmer Holocene (see Chapter 2). But in later millennia, regional climatic fluctuations may have produced alternating periods of wet and dry conditions that impelled forager-hunter communities to experiment with crops.

Some of those fluctuations may have been associated with **El Niño Southern Oscillation (ENSO)** events that affected climate over land areas, notably the western coasts of the Americas. Even small-scale efforts to domesticate edible plants offered a potential hedge against disaster when wet and dry years followed one another unpredictably, especially in places where population was growing. Another theory relates to the extinction of several species of large mammals, including mammoths, huge bison, and ancestors of horses and camels, an event that occurred as a result of either climatic changes or relentless human hunting (see Chapter 1). Because of these extinctions, especially in North America, people may have faced more frequent food crises. This obliged them to figure out how to make plant foods more abundant and reliable. As in the Afroeurasian cases of agricultural invention, societies that reached a point where humans and domesticated crops became interdependent and population kept growing would have found it difficult, probably impossible, to return to the old foraging economy.

> **El Niño Southern Oscillation (ENSO)** A warming of ocean surface temperatures that occurs about every five years in the equatorial Pacific Ocean. An El Niño episode produces unusual, sometimes extreme weather in various parts of the world. A Pacific cooling cycle is called La Niña.

American crops and the triumph of maize. As early as 8000 B.C.E., when farming was just getting under way in Southwest Asia, people living in the tropical highland

TABLE 4.1 Examples of Independent Plant Domestication

Twelve Plants Domesticated in the Americas but Unknown in Afroeurasia	Twelve Plants Domesticated in Afroeurasia but Unknown in the Americas
maize (corn)	wheat
squashes	barley
potatoes	rice
manioc (cassava)	lentils
sweet potatoes	cane sugar
beans	coffee
tomatoes	bananas
peanuts	onions
avocadoes	oranges
cacao	grapes
pineapple	coconuts
tobacco	flax

valleys of Oaxaca (wah-HAH-kah) in southern Mexico appear from archaeological evidence to have selected and planted seeds of a particular species of squash. According to one interesting hypothesis, foragers watered and protected wild bottle gourds, then dried them, and used them as containers. Incidentally, some gourd cultivators, quite likely women, found that the plant's seeds toasted on the campfire tasted good. That discovery may then have suggested the food value of the seeds of similar plants, notably wild squashes. From there, people may have started selecting squashes for larger and tastier seeds.

Domestication of a long list of American plants proceeded at a leisurely pace in both North and South America over the ensuing six thousand years. There was no rush to farming because forager bands almost certainly preferred to continue their existing way of life, with its relatively short "work week" of collecting wild food, unless some natural force pressured them to change. It is also likely that in some places people at first consumed domesticated plants as "snack foods" that merely supplemented wild resources. Full-time farming may also have developed slowly because the wild ancestors of wheat, barley, rice, and other relatively large-seeded cereals that formed such productive partnerships with humans in Afroeurasia, did not grow anywhere in the Americas.

The one great exception was maize, a staple grain traded in larger quantities today than any other cereal except wheat and rice. Maize is a highly adaptable plant that flourishes in a wide range of environmental conditions. In the Americas it grows from southern Canada to the southern tip of Chile. It lends itself to endless genetic variation. At present, farmers produce about sixty varieties of maize in Mexico alone. Before the modern era, as many as 30,000 varieties may have existed.

Scholars have not pinpointed the original homeland of maize domestication with any certainty, but the process most likely began in one valley or another of southern Mexico around 7000 B.C.E. Evidence has accumulated indicating that teosinte (TEE-eh-SIN-tee), a wild mountain grass, is probably the genetic ancestor of maize. One may wonder how this could be, since teosinte is a plant with an inch-long "cob" holding about a dozen hard, tiny seeds. People could never have transformed teosinte into large-seeded maize cobs as many as two feet long without a lengthy, painstaking, conscious process of selecting for more desirable plants. Generalizing from later evidence of the division of family labor, we can imagine women in some ancient tropical valley sifting carefully through stands of wild teosinte to find plants with marginally better characteristics, then planting their seeds. They must have repeated this process over and over, perhaps across many generations, until they produced "genetically engineered" plants having kernels large and numerous enough to provide the staple food for an entire village. Early maize ears discovered in caves in southern Mexico's Tehuacán Valley were bigger than teosinte seeds but still six times smaller than the average cob of buttered corn we might eat today.

Maize, however, matures so rapidly, stores so well, and thrives in so many different conditions of soil and climate that farmers kept on experimenting with it. Families

The genetic evolution of maize. Over generations Mesoamerican farmers repeatedly selected and planted maize with desirable characteristics to improve the size of the ear and the size and number of the kernels. On the left is an ear of teosinte, the genetic ancestor of maize. Why do you think Mesoamericans developed not just a few but around sixty different varieties of maize?

also supplemented maize with beans, squash, and other foods that provided additional nutrients. Mesoamerican farmers took to growing crops in a *milpa*, producing altogether a nutritionally complete diet. *Milpa* cultivation may have spread northward across Mexico in association with farmer migrations, reaching what are today Arizona and New Mexico by about 2000 B.C.E.

> **milpa** In Mesoamerica a farm plot created by cutting or burning forest and planted with maize, squash, beans, and other crops.

Maize and potatoes in South America.

Scholars generally agree that people of the Andes Mountains and the adjacent Pacific coastal zone (Ecuador, Peru, Bolivia, and Chile) independently domesticated the white potato and at least a few other edible plants some centuries before they grew maize. Potato consumption definitely contributed to Andean population growth because it is jam-packed with essential nutrients, notably vitamin C, potassium, vitamin B_6, and fiber. Did Andeans also domesticate maize, or did the idea arrive from outside? Even today, direct overland travel between North and South America is difficult because thick marshes, swamps, and dense mountain rainforests straddle the border between Panama and Colombia. Panama's southeastern Darién Province is known as the Darién Gap because this is the one place where the intercontinental Pan-American Highway has never been completed. Nevertheless, most scholars think that maize cultivation diffused from Mesoamerica. Travelers could easily have carried kernels or young plants around the Darién Gap by boat. In any case, maize farming got under way in the northern Andes region sometime around 2200 B.C.E. The Andes diet came to include a nutritionally healthy mix of potatoes, maize, beans, and the seeds of quinoa, a protein-rich grain that in recent years has gained some popularity in the United States.

Until quite recently scholars have misconstrued Amazonia before the nineteenth century as an immense region of forest and grassland where only scattered forager bands lived before modern times. In fact, inhabitants of what is today far western Brazil domesticated the root crop manioc about 2000 B.C.E. In Amazonia, like the equatorial belt in Africa and Southeast Asia, soils tend to be low in nutrient-rich humus content. Forest-dwellers, however, began systematically to build up large tracts of *terra preta*, in which to plant manioc, fruit trees, and other warm-climate crops. They created these fields by partially burning biomass (wood and other plant material) to make charcoal, which they then mixed with soil to enrich it. In this way they improved soil by consciously engineering its chemical characteristics, without knowing the theory involved, of course. This practice had advanced far enough by the start of the Common Era to allow people to build sizable

> **terra preta** A type of nutritionally rich soil that farmers of Amazonia produced by mixing charcoal, organic matter, and pottery shards. Literally "black earth" in Portuguese.

permanent villages. Archaeologists have found remains of some of these settlements in central Amazonia.

The absence of big animal domesticates.

In contrast to Afroeurasia, few large animals presented themselves as suitable candidates for domestication anywhere in the Americas. The mass extinctions of the Ice Age–Holocene transition swept away something like 80 percent of hoofed mammal species, including the cousins of horses and camels that might have been susceptible to taming and selective breeding. Nor did the Western Hemisphere have any sheep, cattle, or pigs. Nevertheless, Native Americans domesticated at least five species: the turkey in Mesoamerica; the llama, alpaca, and guinea pig in the Andes; the Muscovy duck in the tropical latitudes; and the dog, which some people ate, just about everywhere.

Alpacas in the Peruvian Andes. Alpacas and llamas are among the few domesticated hoofed animals native to the Americas. They are biological cousins of the camel, which disappeared in the Western Hemisphere after the last ice age.

The absence of large domesticated mammals made a difference in the capacity of Native Americans, in comparison with peoples of Afroeurasia, to adapt to and manage their environment. Wild game may have supplied abundant animal fat and protein in some regions, but people could not, for example, exploit semiarid grassland environments the way they did in Inner Eurasia. This is because they did not have animals that could be grouped, herded, and ridden and that converted grass or brush into the meat, milk, blood, and hides that humans used. Consequently, the North American prairies and the comparable South American pampas could support no more than thin populations of forager-hunters. Native Americans did not invent either heavy plows or wheels used for anything except toys, but these inventions would in any case have had limited use without horses, mules, cattle, oxen, or camels to pull them. Llamas and alpacas, which adapted to a limited range of territory in Andean South America, provided meat, hair, and hides, but they were not big enough to transport heavy packs and would have cut poor figures trying to pull plows or war chariots. In short, the expansion of agrarian societies in the Americas, which eventually included construction of cities and mammoth public structures, depended fundamentally on human muscle assisted by tools of stone, bone, and wood.

The shortage of big domesticates, however, was not entirely a bad thing. Like humans everywhere, ancient Americans were susceptible to disease. But they do not appear to have suffered the virulent infectious epidemics that raged through Afroeurasian cities. We know that in the Eastern Hemisphere both settled and pastoral populations lived in close proximity to large numbers of animals. We also know that pathogens that originally caused diseases only in animals mutated to afflict their human neighbors with smallpox, chickenpox, measles, and other lethal infections that frequently surged through dense populations (see Chapter 2). None of the few American domesticates either lived in giant herds or outnumbered humans in the confined spaces they shared. Moreover, there is no evidence of a disease microorganism moving from llamas to humans. If the absence of cows, sheep, and pigs deprived Americans of certain advantages, it may also have left them generally less exposed to infectious pathogens than their fellow humans across the oceans.

Platform Builders of Norte Chico

We noted in Chapter 2 that archaeologists first discovered the remains of early Indus valley civilization only in the 1920s. Consequently, that region's ancient history had to be revised radically. Similarly, no one knew anything about America's oldest complex society, a cluster of as many as thirty small cities on the Pacific coast of Peru, until about two decades ago. Since then, archaeological teams have uncovered urban sites whose construction started no later than about 3200 B.C.E. The earliest of these centers, located along a thirty-mile coastal strip known as Norte Chico, predates the

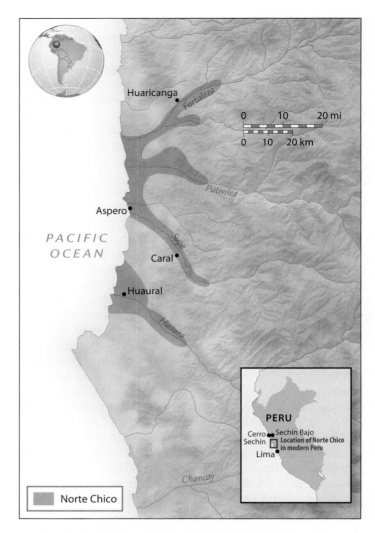

MAP 4.2 Urban centers in the Norte Chico region of Peru.
Did ancient urban societies in Norte Chico and Mesopotamia share any geographical or ecological similarities?

appearance of cities anywhere in the world except Sumer in Mesopotamia (see Map 4.2). They predate the Indus valley cities by at least four hundred years and Egypt's Great Pyramid by more than six hundred years. It would seem, then, that the time lapse between the invention of farming and emergence of the earliest complex society was about three thousand years shorter in the Americas than in Afroeurasia.

Cities of the rain shadows. The Tigris-Euphrates, Nile, and Indus civilizations all arose within Afroeurasia's Great Arid Zone. Their agrarian economies depended on river irrigation, not rainfall. Similarly, the Norte Chico centers sprang up in what might be called South America's great arid zone. In fact, "arid zone" puts it mildly. The narrow belt of contiguous deserts that run along the Pacific coast about 1,500 miles from northern Peru to central Chile are among the driest places on earth. Parts of Chile's Atacama Desert have had no rainfall in recorded history. The scant precipitation that is detectable comes mainly from perennial fog and mist. The region is nearly waterless because it lies between two rain shadows. On the Pacific side, a combination of cold sea current and atmospheric temperature causes trade winds to dump rain offshore, almost never over land. On the east the Andes Mountains, the second highest range after the Himalayas, squeeze the rain out of winds blowing from tropical Amazonia before they reach the coastal strip.

In other respects, however, ecological conditions on the Peruvian coast were quite different from those in the arid Afroeurasian river valleys. Norte Chico's four rivers do not flow across broad fertile plains but pour down out of the snowy Andes, cut across less than fifty miles of bleached desert, and empty into the sea. In Mesopotamia and the Indus valley, farmers struggled constantly against salt contamination of soil resulting from water evaporation in gently flowing irrigation canals. At Norte Chico, by contrast, water gushed along the river courses in spring, flushing out channels and ditches built to irrigate fields of vegetables, fruits, and cotton.

Though shore settlements existed, most of Norte Chico's population clustered some miles up the river valleys where crop irrigation was feasible. We know nothing about the local language or social life, but the society consumed quantities of anchovies, sardines, shellfish, and other marine life, including birds and sea mammals. These species all flourished in the cold Humboldt Current, which even today

nourishes the most bountiful fishing ground on the planet. An economic synergy seems to have developed between upriver and shore settlements. Fishing communities supplied seafood to the valley centers, while irrigation farmers reciprocated with crops and, perhaps just as important, cotton string for making fishing nets. Material clues suggest that the population also produced cotton textiles for clothing and bags. Two items are conspicuous for their absence in the economic repertoire. One is maize, whose cultivation does not appear to have reached that region until around 2000 B.C.E. The other is ceramic pottery. We have evidence that foragers made pottery in eastern Amazonia as early as 6000 B.C.E. and in the Colombia-Panama region about a thousand years later. Norte Chico people no doubt used gourds, bags, and baskets for containers, but, as far as we know, they had no pots.

Faint outlines of Norte Chico society. The population must have had an extended kinship system or other form of social organization because it undertook complex communal projects to build monumental earthen platforms, sunken circular plazas, and a variety of stone buildings in all four of the narrow river valleys. The upriver urban site of Caral, for example, has six platform mounds, one of which rises sixty feet in the air. A large workforce would have been needed to pile up and shape earth for the platforms, move giant stones, and dig irrigation canals. Leaders must have directed these operations, but they may have

A city of Norte Chico. The Supe River, flowing from the high Andes, supported the ancient city of Caral. The ruins of its urban platforms lie near the river's left bank. Looking at this modern photo, why do you think the cultivated area stops short of the city's remains?

been religious figures who organized volunteers, perhaps in groups of kin. Men and women would thus have ratified their membership in the local society by joining work crews and by celebrating public rituals in temples that may once have gilded the tops of the platforms.

In contrast to later South American complex societies, Norte Chico has so far yielded no evidence of a social hierarchy, no class of chiefs, priests, or aristocrats who told other people what to do or collected taxes from them. For example, the sites have revealed no evidence of special tombs or grave goods signifying a privileged elite. Everyone—men, women, and children—got buried the same way. Nor is there evidence of a fighting class or even conflict among the cities. No fortifications or artistic representations of warriors, prisoners, or mutilated bodies have been found. In fact, with the exception of what may have been decorative textiles, Norte Chico has revealed almost no visual art, no stone carving, sculpture, or wall painting. The society probably had no full writing system, but archaeologists have discovered remains of *quipu* (KEE-poo). These are sets of knotted and colored strings that later Andean societies used to record and preserve collective knowledge. Their presence at Norte Chico suggests early experiments to create a system of symbols to convey meanings that at least some members of the community could jointly understand.

Material remains show that Norte Chico people traded with other settlements up and down the Pacific coast and with Andean highlanders to the east. By the third millennium B.C.E., therefore, an Andean zone of commercial and cultural exchange took shape, linking communities that lay at different altitudes and therefore had different goods to barter. Lowlanders, for example, traded salt, cotton, and shells to mountain people in exchange for such items as dyes and obsidian. Another item in demand was mind-altering snuff, which came from Amazonia. Norte Chico is likely to have shared irrigation and architectural technology, as well as cultural practices, with neighboring societies. For example, archaeologists discovered a gourd at Caral carrying the image of a hooded and fanged Staff God. This deity continued to show up in later Andean religious symbolism.

Norte Chico's status as the Americas' earliest urban society may not stand for long. Archaeologists have recently excavated a large stone plaza at Sechín Bajo, a site about two hundred miles farther up the Peruvian coast. It appears to predate Norte Chico construction by a few centuries. In any case the Norte Chico cities went into decline after about 1800 B.C.E. as new centers arose elsewhere along the Andes Mountain spine.

Andean Societies in the Second Millennium B.C.E.

From about 2200 B.C.E., both pottery and maize spread widely across South America. In the ensuing millennium, highland populations rose steadily. Farmers who tilled valley bottoms began to move outward and upward by carving erosion-resistant terraces—green steps marching up hillsides. In Andean Ecuador and Peru, people built dozens of ceremonial and administrative centers, typically focused on stone, mud-brick, and earthen platforms or pyramids. In contrast to the bare walls at Norte Chico, the interior rooms of Andes pyramids and temples displayed elaborate murals featuring deities, warriors, and animals in rich shades of red, blue, yellow, cream, rose, and black. Artisans carved similar motifs in stone. As these centers multiplied, they exhibited distinctively different local cultural styles, and they appear to have remained politically independent of one another. Large centralized Andean states still lay in the future.

Violence at Cerro Sechín. Engraved stones at this Peruvian ceremonial center tell a tale of ritual sacrifice. The warrior armed with a club and wearing plumed headgear bares his teeth. One severed head lies in front of him and a stack of twelve more appear peaceful in death. Why do you think the ruling group at Cerro Sechín would have instructed artists to carve images like this?

As at Norte Chico, leaders in the Andes must have emerged to mobilize men and women for public building, terracing, and irrigation, but practices of that era show little sign of sharp social distinctions. On the other hand, we have more evidence of intercommunal violence than at Norte Chico. Some groups stockpiled great quantities of stones for slingshots, and ominous imagery appeared in public art. For example, on the façade of the enormous U-shaped structure at Cerro Sechín (SER-oh se-CHEEN) in northern Peru, a site dating to about 1300 B.C.E., artisans carved a line of bas reliefs of severed heads, limbs, and torsos, a macabre parade supervised by stone warriors armed with ornate clubs.

Many Andean valleys run north and south rather than east and west, a geographical configuration that may have facilitated the southerly diffusion of maize, pottery, and other technological innovations toward southern Peru, Bolivia, and Chile. Around the shores of Lake Titicaca (tee-tee-kah-kah), located at 12,500 feet above sea level on the modern border between Peru and Bolivia, villagers herded llamas and alpacas and planted potatoes, quinoa, and maize. They also harvested and chewed coca leaves, whose stimulant properties relieved the symptoms of altitude sickness. In that region, communities began to construct platforms and plazas about 1000 B.C.E. As in the northern Andes, leaders having mainly religious functions may have mobilized families and kinship groups to undertake large-scale construction.

The Mesoamerican Zone of Intercommunication

By around 1500 B.C.E. (about when the Shang state was forming in China and the New Kingdom arose in Egypt), pottery-making maize farmers were to be found in nearly every part of Mesoamerica. Agriculture continued to spread *extensively*, meaning that as village populations rose, small pioneer groups trekked off to found new settlements on virgin soil somewhere down the valley or over the hills. Mesoamerica's "pot revolution," which got under way after 1800 B.C.E., enriched settled life by enlarging the technical possibilities of cooking, storage, and transport.

Agrarian society. From the Central American rainforest to the arid Southwest of what is now the United States, men and women built their village dwellings in quite similar styles, suggesting that this whole region formed a single zone of cultural interaction from very early times.

Mesoamerican ball player. This terracotta athlete from Jalisco state in west central Mexico wears a helmet and other decorative sports gear. The sculpture is dated between 200 B.C.E. and 500 C.E.

In the period from 1500 B.C.E. to 150 C.E., villagers typically founded hamlets of ten to twelve dwellings. In time, many of those settlements grew much larger. Dwellings had recessed dirt floors and walls of "wattle and daub," that is, sticks and canes woven together between vertical poles and plastered with mud. Farmers stored maize in bell-shaped underground pits covered with stone slabs. Villages appear to have had a fairly simple division of labor, with women and men working in different parts of the house. Excavations of ancient house floors have revealed needles, spindles, and cornhuskers of bone or ceramic clustered in a part of the dwelling where women presumably sat. Men very likely worked with the stone blades and drills found in different corners.

As the only large-seeded grain staple Mesoamericans had, maize presented one serious drawback. Unlike wheat, barley, or rice, it lacks niacin, an essential human nutrient also known as vitamin B^3. Prolonged niacin deficiency may trigger pellagra, a disease characterized by diarrhea, skin sores, and mental confusion. Early in the agrarian era, however, Mesoamerican women discovered the idea of soaking dried maize in water mixed with white limestone powder, then grinding this mixture into flour. Combining water with lime produced calcium hydroxide (slaked lime), a compound that restored niacin to baked tortillas. Of course no one in those times understood the biochemistry, but families that made tortillas with lime proved less susceptible to pellagra. (Notice that the corn tortillas in your local market are also made with maize, water, and lime.)

From about 1500 B.C.E., Mesoamericans began to create not only beautifully incised and painted ceramic pots but also imaginative figurines of animals and humans. These have turned up in burial remains. For example, the Tlatilco archaeological site is located in the Valley of Mexico, the highland plateau surrounded by mountains and volcanoes where Mexico City now lies. Since the 1940s, researchers at the site have discovered clever sculpted images of animals that people hunted—deer, waterfowl, frogs, turtles, and wild turkeys. Artists also painted scenes of daily life on ceramic ware: women carrying children, men wearing breechcloths, and dancers with rattles strapped to their legs. Excavations have turned up numerous female figurines. These are usually nude, shapely, and adorned with grass skirts, elegant hairdos, body paint, and jewelry. By contrast, images of men are few and comparatively plain. Did female potters wish to portray themselves? Did these figurines serve as dolls? Were they ritual objects in fertility cults? Did they have symbolic significance for communication among women? As in the case of Eurasian "Venus" figurines from the late paleolithic era, we can only guess at their cultural meaning.

At Tlatilco and many other sites, archaeologists have found miniature representations of both athletes and ball courts, an architectural form that became a signature characteristic of Mesoamerican urban society. Figurines of players, both men and women, identify themselves by their gear: a pad on one knee and wrist and a heavy leather belt around the hips to protect body organs. Rules of the game varied from region to region, but typically players tried to hit a hard rubber ball through a center ring. They could use only their hips, knees, and elbows—no hands or feet. Both individuals and teams may have competed. We know from later American Indian sources that the ball game could be both a religious ritual and a high-speed sport involving betting. But we have little knowledge of who made the rules and how they may have changed from one region to another. Ball games may also have contributed to an esprit de corps—a common purpose and identity for people who lived near one another.

The Olmec. Agriculture and the accompanying population growth stimulated greater social complexity in Mesoamerica in the later second millennium B.C.E., just as it had in Andean South America as much as two thousand years earlier. People built big settlements like Tlatilco in the Valley of Mexico, erected ritual structures and defensive walls in the Oaxaca Valley, and designed stone ball courts in southern Mexico's Chiapas (chee-AH-puhs) region. Most impressive of all before 1000 B.C.E. was the society labeled Olmec, which rose up along the Gulf of Mexico's tropical shore south of the modern city of Veracruz (see Map 4.3). In that region of hot, swampy coasts and densely forested uplands, inhabitants of the city called San Lorenzo built a ceremonial platform of nearly 2.8 million cubic yards of rock. They also created a social class system featuring a minority of aristocratic rulers, and probably Mesoamerica's earliest monarchs. We have no idea what these people called themselves. But they made rubber balls, and that suggested "Olmec," which in the Nahuatl language of the later Aztecs refers to "people from the land of rubber." In the sixteenth century C.E., Aztec sages invoked distant memories of this legendary land where

> in a certain era
> which no one can reckon,
> which no one can remember
> . . . there was a government for a long time.[1]

The Olmec heartland curved along the gulf for about 125 miles and extended inland about 50 miles. Moist winds

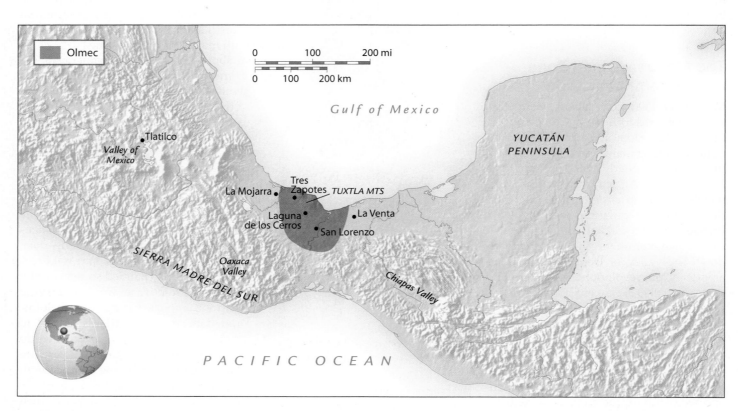

MAP 4.3 Olmec civilization in Mesoamerica.
How might similarities or differences in geography and climate have shaped particular characteristics of Olmec urban society compared to Norte Chico?

The Olmec Heads

The most dramatic Olmec art objects are the exquisitely carved stone heads that have been found in several different places along the gulf coast. Seventeen of these heads, ranging in volume from six to fifty tons, have turned up so far. All the heads, the tallest more than eleven feet high, have individualized faces, leading art historians to hypothesize that the figures represent portraits of Olmec leaders. Some appear quite grim, others benevolent. They all wear headdresses that look like old-fashioned American football helmets, each marked with distinctive insignia that likely indicate the name and identity of the person whom the head depicts.

Carved with stone tools, the volcanic basalt rock for the giant heads came from sites in the Tuxtla Mountains at least forty miles to the west. Some scholars think that workers pushed them on log rollers to a riverbank, transferred them to rafts, floated them downriver, and steered them to their destination on more rollers. Others think the workers slid them the whole distance overland. The hardness of the volcanic basalt rock, which has contributed to the survival of the heads over the millennia, also points to the technical sophistication of the Olmec, since carving the rock without the use of metal tools required considerable skill.

Thinking Critically

What similarities do these heads appear to share? In what ways are they dissimilar? Considering the size and weight of the heads and the distances they had to be moved, what might they suggest, if anything, about the character of Olmec government, the power of an elite group, and the society's artistic and engineering skills? What might the construction and placement of these heads suggest about their function and importance in Olmec society? Some of the heads have gouges and pits that suggest deliberate acts of defacement. Under what circumstances might people have mutilated the heads?

blew in from the gulf, bringing abundant rain in normal years. The earliest farmers in the region probably depended more on shellfish and other aquatic resources than on crops. But along rivers that flowed from the Tuxtla Mountains, which lie not far to the west, farmers cultivated bounteous *milpas* of maize, beans, squash, and numerous other foods.

The region's population grew large enough by about 1350 B.C.E. to support the building of San Lorenzo on a long ridge overlooking a river and an expanse of marshes that stretched forty miles to the coast. A swarm of laborers must have erected San Lorenzo's central platform, an artificial plateau 150 feet high and two-thirds of a mile on each side. They hauled rock from quarries as much as fifty miles away. Atop the big podium, supervisors directed the construction of smaller platforms, more than two hundred of them, as well as courtyards and almost certainly buildings that have long since disappeared.

Archaeologists exploring San Lorenzo and its vicinity in the past several years have gradually shed light on Olmec society. The main center may have had an average population of about 5,500 during its most flourishing period, from about 1200 to 900 B.C.E.[2] An elite class, plus the ordinary men and women who served it, resided in that center. This may indeed have been the earliest place in the Americas where a privileged minority exercised some type of permanent authority over everyone else. Other members of the elite lived in satellite centers. Researchers have found at least nineteen villages and a larger number of single, isolated households in a wide surrounding area. Farmers, artisans, and hunters would have lived in those places, perhaps sending tribute in food or other goods to the ruling group.

Both archaeologists and local residents have found a great number of stone sculptures in the Olmec heartland, including large human and animal sculptures of stone, stele (upright stone slabs bearing carved images), carved altars, and figurines.

The city of San Lorenzo, where ten of the colossal heads have been found, disintegrated about 1200 B.C.E. In fact, many stone sculptures on the site show signs of being vandalized and mutilated. Scholars do not know what happened, perhaps an invasion, a popular uprising, or a famine that forced evacuation of the city. In any case, other Olmec centers arose about that time or later, notably La Venta, Tres Zapotes (TRACE zah-POE-tace), and Laguna de los Cerros. These cities declined only after about 400 B.C.E. While it thrived, La Venta boasted a massive, cone-shaped clay mound rising 110 feet. A grand pavilion, courtyard, and more giant stone heads were associated with it. Many scholars think the clay mound represents a volcano similar to those that rumble away in the Tuxtla Mountains. The Olmec may have regarded one of these volcanoes as the site of creation. La Venta's massive constructions suggest a strong governing authority, even if people did the work voluntarily and for religious motives. San Lorenzo, La Venta, and the other cities appear, however, to have been politically autonomous. There

are no signs of a centralized state exercising authority over the whole Olmec region.

It is clear, however, that the cities were part of a growing Mesoamerican zone of commercial and cultural interchange. We do not know whether people relayed trade items from one village to another or full-time merchants carried goods over long distances. In any case, pottery and other ceramic ware of distinctive Olmec style have turned up in archaeological sites from the Valley of Mexico to Guatemala. Researchers have chemically analyzed the clay composition of pots to demonstrate that communities located hundreds of miles from the gulf coast acquired objects made with clay that originated in Olmec centers. Communities across central and southern Mexico imitated Olmec stone imagery, including representations of the jaguar, the predator that became an emblem of supernatural power throughout much of Mesoamerica. Figurines of chubby infants that play with balls, suck their fingers, and tug at their hair also typify Olmec exports. In the opposite direction of trade, Olmec men and women, perhaps mainly elite families that wished to adorn themselves and their homes, acquired goods from distant parts of Mesoamerica, including obsidian, jade, greenstone, and concave mirrors made of iron oxide.

Experts continue to debate the historical significance of Olmec civilization. The more traditional view is that this complex society should be understood as the "mother culture" from which emanated the foundational elements of all later Mesoamerican urban civilizations. More recently, scholars have tended to regard the Olmec as one of several "sister cultures," including early dense farming societies in the Valley of Mexico, Oaxaca, and Chiapas. According to this theory, all these societies, the Olmec among them, both gave and received goods, ideas, and styles in a complex process of interaction over many centuries. Few doubt that between about 1500 and 400 B.C.E. the Olmec achieved social complexity on an impressive scale. Their centers almost certainly presented the earliest model of societies having a formal social hierarchy headed by a monarch or high priest. In terms of strong elite government, however, later Mesoamerican and South American societies surpassed the Olmec many times over.

North of Mexico

Starting perhaps more than 15,000 years ago, human groups migrated generally from west to east across the temperate latitudes of upper North America (the United States and Canada; see Map 4.4). These forager communities used tools and projectile points broadly associated with a style that scholars call Clovis. Most of them probably spoke ancestral languages in the huge Amerind family of languages, as did all early peoples of Mesoamerica and South America. There were two major exceptions. One was the several peoples in western Canada and Alaska, plus the Navajo in the United States Southwest, who spoke languages in

Harvester Mountain Lord: A Mesoamerican King

The archaeology of the Olmec era reveals almost nothing about individual rulers and their deeds, let alone ordinary women and men. An exception is Harvester Mountain Lord, a boy king born about 144 C.E. in the region that had once been the heartland of Olmec civilization. The knowledge we have of Harvester Mountain Lord's career is carved on a stone stele discovered in 1986 in the Acula River near a village called La Mojarra south of the modern city of Veracruz. The slab, which weighs four tons and stands nearly seven feet tall, displays a carved image of Harvester Mountain Lord wearing an elaborate headdress. It also carries a set of glyphs (graphic figures or characters carved into stone), more than five hundred of them, which scholars have partially deciphered. The text describes several key events of the king's reign, though the decipherment, translation, and interpretation of the glyphs have been fraught with linguistic difficulties.

In Harvester Mountain Lord's time, the great Olmec cities had long deteriorated, but small states still existed along the southern coast of the Gulf of Mexico. According to the writing on the stele, a political faction that supported his rulership triumphed over an opposing one. At about the age of twelve he ascended the throne, following a propitious solar eclipse. The coronation ritual may have featured the new king cutting off the head of an enemy who had challenged his royal birthright.

The engraved text describes the ruler and his aristocratic followers, named "noble war-leader ones," conducting ceremonies, probably to prove their worthiness and ensure the blessing of the gods. These rituals involved the king having his buttocks and penis cut so that drops of his royal blood might be offered to the spirits. As his blood flowed, the king shouted to those around him, "My blood is getting sprinkled for others."[3]

Like monarchs the world over, Harvester Mountain Lord appears to have faced a threat from a person close to the royal court. A sister's husband plotted to overthrow him and seize the throne. The king's supporters, however, killed the conspirator in battle, piercing him with arrows. Then, to demonstrate what happens to brothers-in-law who turn traitor, the

king had his body cut into pieces. Rebels had apparently toppled monuments to Harvester Mountain Lord's exalted reign, but now the king had them set upright again. The text also refers to the ruler's association with a priest, or shaman, and to a trance in which a supernatural animal companion appeared in the king's body. Some time after these events, artisans carved the ruler's image and the glyphs on the stele. No one knows the ultimate fate of Harvester Mountain Lord's kingdom or how long the slab rested on the bottom of the river before its modern recovery.

Harvester Mountain Lord, wearing extravagant headgear and a feathered cape, appears on the left side of La Mojarra stele.

La Mojarra Stele (la moo-hahr-UH STEE-luh) is one of the few examples of Olmec writing so far discovered. Linguists succeeded in deciphering many of the glyphs by starting with the premise that the language they recorded was ancestral to Indian languages still spoken in the region today. The text offers not only scraps of Harvester Mountain Lord's biography but also a glimpse into royal elements of culture—state politics, ceremonial regalia, ritual bloodletting, and beliefs about animal spirits—that prevailed in the gulf coastal lowlands at the start of the first millennium C.E.

Thinking Critically

Do you think La Mojarra Stele should be trusted as historical evidence of the reign of Harvester Mountain Lord? Is it more likely to have been an objective account or a piece of royal propaganda?

the family named Na-Dene, which some linguists have linked to tongues spoken in Asia. The other exception was speakers of Eskimo-Aleut languages, hunters who gradually spread from the Bering Strait region eastward across northern Canada, even as far as the coast of Greenland. As bands moved across upper North America, they and their languages diverged and multiplied. The Amerind family,

for example, spawned several subfamilies, including Ute-Aztecan, Siouan, Iroquoian, and Algonquin.

As of about 2500 B.C.E., all peoples living north of Mexico presumably consumed only wild foods. Foraging and hunting, however, did not necessarily mean continuous wandering. Just as forager bands in Southwest Asia made seasonal camps near stands of wild grain in the centuries before farming, North Americans set up central bases from which they exploited local wild resources for months at a time. When they moved on, they sometimes left behind tools and food, expecting to return to the same place the following year. By the second millennium B.C.E., the rich marine diets of peoples inhabiting the Pacific Northwest and southern Alaska permitted groups to settle in particular ecological niches for long periods and even to build villages with solid rectangular houses of planked timber.

Early North American mound builders.
In the lower Mississippi valley, evidence of settlement without farming extends even further back in time. At a site named Watson Brake, located near the Ouachita (WOSH-i-taw) River in northeastern Louisiana just west of the Mississippi, foragers who lived there about 3400 B.C.E. constructed eleven earthen mounds, the highest rising nearly twenty-five feet. These structures, linked by a ridge to form an oval shape, might just be older than any artificial platform so far discovered in Mesoamerica or even South America. If people settled on the Ouachita floodplain for several months, or even year-round,

they could have built the mounds as a long-term communal project that did not require a big labor force or an elite of chiefs and bosses. We have no evidence that the mounds had anything to do with burials or religious ceremonies. But they were not unique. Other earthworks dating not much later than Watson Brake may be seen in the southern Mississippi watershed.

Poverty Point. Sometime after 1750 B.C.E., people residing about 100 miles east of Watson Brake at the site known as Poverty Point began building a center featuring several mounds and six rows of earthen ridges resembling half an octagon. One of the mounds is conical, others are platforms, and two appear, by a stretch of the imagination, to resemble birds. The Poverty Point people built perishable structures of wood, bark, and mud on top of the ridges, which face toward the Mississippi. They also produced pottery, beads, animal-like figurines, and fine microlithic tools for scraping and cutting. They made long-distance trade contacts, importing shells and copper from the Gulf of Mexico or as far away as the Great Lakes. Perhaps as many as five thousand people lived at Poverty Point some of the time, but we do not know what they did there. Men and women from the surrounding region may have congregated at the site periodically to perform religious rituals. Or, they may have gathered to exchange gifts among kinship groups, meet with distant relatives, or find marriage partners. Some scholars think the mounds and certain pottery styles hint at Mesoamerican influence, perhaps the Olmec, whose centers lay only about 1,200 miles around the curve of the gulf. The evidence is inconclusive.

Farming in the eastern woodlands. Despite its size and complexity, Poverty Point reveals no sign of agriculture. In the eastern woodlands, that is, the lands stretching from the Great Lakes and the Mississippi valley to the Atlantic coast, wild nuts, fruits, berries, and game provided sufficient nutrition to sustain communities as long as some members of the group could break off in times of shortage to find new hunting and gathering grounds not already occupied. Large numbers of upper North Americans *never* took up farming any time before Europeans started arriving just five centuries ago.

Nevertheless, some groups living in the middle Mississippi valley and east from there toward Tennessee and Ohio began to experiment with selective planting of edible seed-producing species by around 2000 B.C.E., that is, as much as six thousand

MAP 4.4 Early farming and mound-building societies in North America.
From a geographical perspective, do you think that cultural contacts in the later second millennium B.C.E. between Olmec society and settlements like Poverty Point in the lower Mississippi valley were likely or not?

The Poverty Point settlement. In this artist's rendering of ancient Poverty Point (1750–700 B.C.E.), smoke rises from houses lined up along the town's six earthen ridges. Archaeological digs on the ridges have revealed hearths, as well as postholes where wooden building posts probably once stood. The largest earthen structure on the site is Mound A, visible in the top center of the picture. Why might the residents have built this semicircle of six ridges?

years later than communities in southern Mexico started planting squash. Woodland dwellers may have tried out plant selection, not because wild resources were giving out, but as a practical hedge against cycles of good and bad years related to modest climatic fluctuations. Some of these may have been related to El Niño episodes, which could affect eastern North America.

As in Mesoamerica, gourds and squashes that yielded tasty seeds may have been the first domesticates. No large-grained plants resembling wheat or barley grew in upper North America, nor did maize, which had not yet reached that far north. Rather, woodland people, probably women and girls, experimented to select the most desirable specimens of small-seeded plants. These flora included the oily seeded sunflower but also plants like goosefoot, marsh elder, and knotweed, which we are unlikely to see in supermarkets today. The tiny seeds of these plants had hard coverings, so domestication involved selecting and nurturing specimens that were marginally more desirable generation after generation. By the second millennium B.C.E., many woodlanders already made pottery, which eased the collecting, storing, and cooking of these grains.

Woodlanders almost certainly became farmers without any stimulus from Mesoamerica. The region qualifies, therefore, as one of the seven or eight places in the world where agriculture emerged independently. For most woodland communities, however, crops like squash, sunflowers, and goosefoot continued to supplement rather than replace wild foods until the Common Era or even much later. Maize farming diffused gradually from Mesoamerica northward but did not become the dominant grain crop in upper North America (as far north as southern Canada) until about 1000 C.E.

Change in Australia

FOCUS Why did all human communities in Australia continue to forage and hunt from the initial colonization of the continent down to modern times rather than adopting farming?

The descendants of foragers who first colonized Australia 60,000 years ago or more (see Chapter 1) spent the following tens of thousands of years spreading across the continent (see Map 4.5). Archaeological evidence points to human occupation reaching as far as Tasmania more than 35,000 years ago, a time when it was attached to the continent, not the island it has been since Holocene sea levels rose. In distant millennia probably the largest forager populations lived either in southern Australia's Murray River region or along the tropical northern coasts facing the Arafura Sea and the Indonesian archipelago beyond. And until about 8,500 years ago, a land bridge connected northern Australia to New Guinea.

We sometimes hear the claim that Australian Aborigines (native peoples) really had no history because until the modern era their way of life never changed. This notion is wrong. Our knowledge of Aboriginal history before the late eighteenth century C.E. depends on archaeology, historical linguistics, Aboriginal oral traditions, and, more recently, genetic analysis. It is therefore difficult to perceive change over short runs of time but not over the long term. On long chronological timelines, scholars have found plenty of evidence of change in migratory patterns, tool making, ceramic technology, settlement construction, and art styles displayed on the walls of rock shelters and caves.

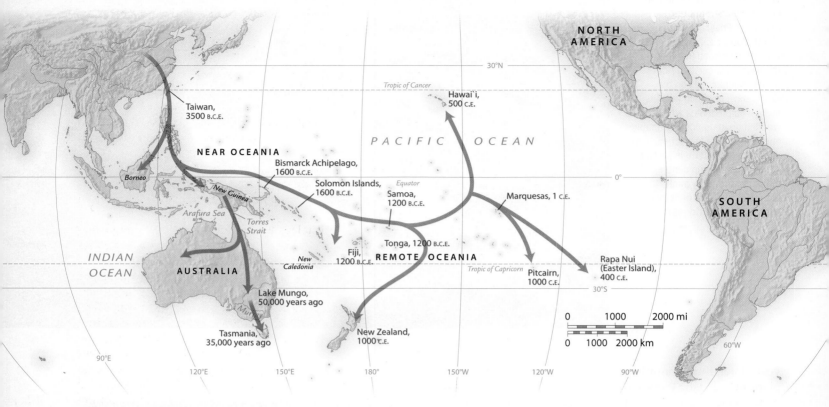

MAP 4.5 Settlement in Australia and Oceania to 1000 c.e.
Agrarian societies became established on Southeast Asian islands in the third and second millennia B.C.E. But farming did not reach Australia until modern times. What geographical factors might account for this long time difference?

The global climatic transition from the Ice Age to the warmer Holocene, which got under way about 16,000 years ago, almost certainly accelerated social change because it affected local environmental conditions for plants and animals. For example, in southwestern Tasmania during the Ice Age, cooperating bands made camps in caves and hunted wallabies (marsupial species smaller than kangaroos). But they appear to have abandoned the region as the Holocene set in because the growth of thick, tangled rainforests made the hunting economy untenable. The inhabitants therefore moved to coastal lands, where they and their descendants successfully switched to a marine diet requiring different technologies and food-gathering knowledge.

Melting glaciers and rising sea levels not only submerged the land bridges connecting both New Guinea and Tasmania to Australia but also pushed back coastlines, forcing shore-dwelling communities to repeatedly abandon their camps, whose material remains now lie under water. Regular human contacts between Australia, New Guinea, and perhaps other islands of the Indonesian archipelago diminished, leaving Australia's foragers and the vastly larger population of Afroeurasia as a whole in separate arenas of interaction. One way of thinking about this development is to note that in the millennia after 8,500 years ago, the inhabitants of the

Indonesian islands became progressively more enmeshed in a greater Afroeurasian web of exchange, while Australians did not.

The isolation between Afroeurasia and Australia was not, however, absolute. People living on the continent's northern coasts had at least sporadic contact with inhabitants of New Guinea. We know this because pottery shards of New Guinean style and certain plants native to Indonesia turned up in Australia after the land bridge disappeared. The wild Australian dog known as the dingo arrived from Southeast Asia about 1500 B.C.E. The Torres Strait separating New Guinea from Australia is only ninety miles across at its narrowest, and most scholars think that at least sporadic trade took place by way of several little islands scattered across the strait. In later millennia, traders of maritime Southeast Asia made frequent landfalls on the coast of Arnhem Land (today Australia's Northern Territory) in search of sea cucumbers, a marine animal regarded as a culinary delicacy.

Change over the Long Term

Occasional contact with Indonesia or not, Australia's history marched on. In some localities, populations continued to grow, nourished by the abundance of game and plant to 8000 B.C.E. in which simple grave goods such as shells, kangaroo teeth, and pieces of ochre (used for body paint) appear to have identified deceased members of a particular community. Excavations also turned up human skulls with elongated shapes possibly formed by binding or massaging the heads of infants to give newborn members of the group a characteristic "look" that people in neighboring groups would not have. Also, as bands migrated throughout the continent, which extends nearly 2,500 miles from east to west, language communities diverged. At the time of European contact, Australians may have spoken more than 250 languages.

Scholars have pieced together enough material evidence to show that, between about 5000 and 6000 B.C.E., groups distant from one another exchanged a number of new ideas for making more delicate and versatile knives, spear points, barbs, drills, adzes (a thin blade attached to a handle), chisels, and grinding stones. In parts of the continent where population densities were relatively high, trade intensified, people from different bands joined in ceremonial gatherings, communities occupied camps along rivers or seashores for longer periods of time, and leaders with special social status started to emerge. Rock and cave art took on more distinctive features from one region to another. In religious life, people across most of Australia shared stories and beliefs about the creator spirit known as the Rainbow Serpent. Some researchers have argued that Aboriginal societies had to keep innovating, at least over the long term, because of the particular instability of Australia's climate. Like the Americas along the Pacific coast, the continent is subject to El Niño cycles, which increases the range of variability between wet and dry conditions over periods of years or decades.

The Rainbow Serpent. In Australia's far northern Arnhem Land, images of the Rainbow Serpent, a potent mythological being linked with bright, variegated color, began to appear on rock walls from about 6000 B.C.E. In Aboriginal tradition this figure is associated with both creation and destruction and with the quest of communities for unity and peace. Some scholars associate the coming of the Rainbow Serpent with long-term social instability and conflict that accompanied coastal flooding at the end of the last ice age.

A Continent without Farmers

Nowhere in Australia, however, did food-collecting strategies lead to plant or animal domestication and full-on agriculture. We have made the point in earlier chapters that in both Afroeurasia and the Americas societies became dependent for survival on domesticated plants and animals, not because they foresaw that farming and village living would turn out to be a great idea, but because they faced social stress related to climatic change, pressure on wild resources, or population growth that obliged them to experiment with ways to *produce* food systematically. Apparently nowhere in Australia did such stresses reach a level critical enough to induce

foods. In those conditions, communities had to create more complex social groupings and rules in order to determine which stretches of territory and its food resources belonged to which cooperating band. As in other parts of the world in paleolithic times, this competition for resources encouraged individual groups to mark themselves out from other bands by adopting distinctive dress, adornments, and perhaps speech habits. In the Murray valley, for example, archaeologists have discovered burial sites dating from 9500 serious efforts to domesticate plants. As for animals, the very large species of marsupials (mammals with pouches for carrying their young) that once roamed Australia all vanished during the Pleistocene as most large mammals did in the Americas somewhat later. Moreover, surviving species of kangaroos and their relatives have never proven susceptible to domestication. Australians did not take to farming even though people near the northern coasts probably knew something about it through contact with New Guinea.

This does not mean, however, that Aborigines never experimented with new ways of finding and processing food. In the southeastern interior, women and men used stones to grind wild seeds into flour as much as 35,000 years ago. In later millennia, groups in the north and east collected wild millet, the sort of activity that in the Fertile Crescent, Egypt, and China eventually led to grain domestication. From very distant times, cooperating bands engaged in what some scholars have called "fire stick farming." They deliberately burned areas of bush or grass in order both to flush out game and to speed the growth of new plants, some of which might be edible. Succulent growth also encouraged herbivorous animals to return, giving hunters opportunities to lie in wait to kill them.

Over tens of thousands of years, trade, migratory wanderings, and intermarriage among bands stimulated innovation in Australia life. But as long as population and wild food resources remained on the whole in balance, change moved at a more stately pace than it did in either Afroeurasia or the Americas. When Europeans first landed down under in 1788, the entire continent may have had a population of no more than 750,000. That number represents about six times fewer people than live in the Sydney metropolitan area today.

Pioneers on the Pacific Frontier

FOCUS How did humans succeed in colonizing many of the islands of Oceania between 1600 B.C.E. and 400 C.E.?

The eastern end of Afroeurasia was the jumping-off point for human colonization of both Australia and the Americas but also of many of the 25,000 islands that dot the Pacific Ocean. Geographers refer to this region of sea and scattered bits of land as Oceania, or sometimes the Island Pacific (see Map 4.5). Australia and the Americas existed as distinct "worlds" of human history for thousands of years partly because the land bridges that connected them with Afroeurasia disappeared. Oceania became a distinct region of settlement because the earliest colonizers migrated across such immense areas of open ocean that they lost touch not only with peoples of Afroeurasia, Australia, and the Americas but also, except where islands lay relatively closely together, with one another. The Pacific Ocean is 10,400 miles wide at the equator

and constitutes nearly a third of the earth's surface. As early explorers advanced in wooden boats eastward from maritime Southeast Asia, they found that the islands they landed on got progressively smaller and the sea gaps between them wider. The most distant frontiers that these migrants reached were the Hawaiian Islands in mid-Pacific and tiny Rapa Nui (RA-pa NEW-ee) in the far southwestern ocean. That crumb of land lies only about 2,600 miles west of Chile.

As European ship captains mapped Oceania in the nineteenth century, geographers categorized the islands into three primary groups—Melanesia, Micronesia, and Polynesia (see Map 4.1). This terminology remains in use, but scholars have also conceived more recently of a two-part division. One is Near Oceania, the islands in the western ocean just south of the equator, which include New Guinea and the Melanesian islands not far east of it. This region has close ecological affinities with maritime Southeast Asia, and humans occupied it sometime between 60,000 and 10,000 years ago. The other region is Remote Oceania, which includes all the rest of the Island Pacific and which humans did not colonize until between about 1600 B.C.E. and 400 C.E.—the end date representing the approximate arrival of seaborne migrants on the Hawaiian Islands and Rapa Nui. Near Oceania, being close to tropical Southeast Asia, has historically exhibited much diversity in plant and animal species. In Remote Oceania, by contrast, that diversity decreased progressively toward the east as the sea gaps between islands widened. Consequently, distant islands offered early settlers relatively meager natural resources or, if fresh water was lacking, no chance of settlement at all.

Colonizers of Near Oceania

By 8000 B.C.E., forager bands occupied Melanesia as far east as the Solomon Islands, which are located about five hundred miles east of New Guinea. The technology of these migrants definitely included seagoing canoes or rafts, though no trace of their design remains. Early Melanesians had a limited tool kit of stone and bone. They also made beads, arm rings, and fishhooks of shell. They set up camps, sometimes under rock outcroppings, of thirty or so people. We have evidence that inhabitants of the Bismarck Archipelago between New Guinea and the Solomons traded obsidian from one island to another. The populations of both New Guinea and the neighboring islands dispersed into numerous localized groups that tended to live in isolation from one another for long periods. We know this because of the extreme diversity of languages classified broadly as Papuan. Today, people in western Melanesia speak about 750 Papuan tongues, and until modern times there were probably more. The grammatical and word relationships among many of these languages are so distant that linguists have categorized them in something like sixty different language subfamilies.

In New Guinea, tropical forest highlanders domesticated bananas, yams, and taro from about 7000 B.C.E., that is, just a little later than Mesoamericans made their first experiments. The archipelagos east of the big island shared generally the same tropical climate and volcanic soils. This may partly explain why inhabitants of those islands, in contrast to the foragers of northern Australia, took up cultivation of New Guinea crops in subsequent millennia.

The coming of the Austronesians. Then, about 1600 B.C.E., a cultural transformation began to take place in Near Oceania. In Chapter 3 we described the long and complex movements of Austronesian-speaking farmers and fishers from China to Taiwan about 4000 B.C.E. and subsequently to the Philippines and Indonesia. Some of these migrants turned east, reaching the coastal lowlands of New Guinea, as well as the nearby Bismarck Islands. They brought with them a trunk load of crops, animals, tools, and ornamental designs previously unknown in Melanesia. This kit included stone adzes, polished chisels, shell decorative styles, dogs, chickens, and pigs. Austronesian speakers settled in larger hamlets than the older Papuan population had done, and they built rectangular dwellings, sometimes erecting them on stilts along the shoreline.

The Lapita people. Most famously, Austronesian speakers introduced distinctive red gloss pottery beautifully embellished with stamped geometric shapes. For archaeologists, this pottery style, called Lapita after a site in Southeast Asia where it was first discovered, came to epitomize the entire cultural complex associated with Austronesian newcomers. On the Bismarck and Solomon Islands and perhaps New Guinea, Lapita-making women and men intermarried with Papuan speakers already there. They also assimilated Papuan tools, ornaments, and crops such as yam and taro, producing, perhaps within decades, a new cultural synthesis having elements of both Papuan and Austronesian origin.

The era of the Lapita style lasted about 1,500 years, to about the first century C.E. During that time, Lapita people migrated farther east, colonizing islands that humans had never reached before, that is, westerly islands of Remote Oceania. Lapita pot shards have been discovered as far east as Samoa and Tonga, which are more than a quarter of the way across the South Pacific.

These mariners have left no material evidence of their boats or navigational lore. Very likely, however, their Austronesian forbearers brought a maritime technology from Southeast Asia including single- and double-outrigger canoes, double canoes, and triangular sails. (See the photo at the beginning of this chapter.) These craft were sturdy enough to inspire sailors to travel out of sight of land for days or weeks in search of new islands. An outrigger, a device presumably invented in Southeast Asia, was a heavy length of wood set parallel to a canoe some feet away from it and firmly attached to it with poles. The outrigger stabilized the canoe by preventing it from tipping either to port or starboard when a wave hit. A double-outrigger provided

A Lapita pot. This piece of Lapita ware, reconstructed from shards, comes from the Pacific island of New Caledonia. How may study of the geographical distribution of a particular pottery style help historians understand the direction and timing of ancient migrations?

even greater stability. Perhaps in outrigger boats equipped with sails and paddles, explorers discovered the Fiji archipelago around 1100 B.C.E. after crossing at least 527 miles of open ocean and most of the time bucking contrary winds and currents.

Maritime historians continue to wonder how these seafarers found their way to landfalls whose existence they could not have known in advance. These voyagers became experts at navigating by sun, moon, and stars, and they also observed the flight of birds, the characteristics of plant matter floating on the sea, and subtle alterations in current, wind, and temperature. Ancient mariners might willingly have taken great risks sailing into the trackless Pacific because their own experience told them that a great sea covered the whole surface of the world and that survival from one generation to the next depended on finding new bits of land that protruded here and there out of the water.

Into Remote Oceania

As sea migrants moved east and southeast to occupy Fiji, Tonga, Samoa, and other islands, they found that local biodiversity narrowed. But they successfully colonized new places because they piled their canoes with Lapita-era cargo, not only pots but also plants and seeds to grow root crops, vegetables, fruits, and nut trees. They also crammed in numerous tools, plus live pigs, chickens, and dogs. If they did not have obsidian, they substituted volcanic basalt, modifying tool designs to make cutters and scrapers from this hard stone. Obviously, both men and women had to travel to uninhabited islands if they intended permanent settlement. Recent genetic research suggests, however, that once a group planted a colony, women mostly remained at home while some males periodically sailed out to neighboring islands to trade or explore.

As colonizers fanned out across the deep, their Austronesian languages changed and multiplied. The western edge of Remote Oceania appears to have been the homeland of the Polynesian subfamily, which evolved into at least thirty-six tongues. Polynesian languages are linguistically closely related, indicating that, similarly to the Bantu languages in Subsaharan Africa, the dispersal of migrating groups from one island to another took place over the course of hundreds, not thousands of years. Recent DNA analysis of tissue samples of living Pacific islanders reveals close genetic relationships among all Remote Oceania's founding populations.

Pacific pioneers adapted ingeniously to a great variety of geographical and ecological settings, from low-lying atolls to towering volcanic islands. They also had to adapt to jarring swings in rainfall resulting from three- to seven-year El Niño cycles of change in Pacific surface temperatures. Remote Oceania did have the advantage of a milder disease environment, with fewer dangerous microorganisms. Colonists created a variety of social and political institutions, living in egalitarian foraging bands on some islands, forming small village communities in others, and, in a few places, including Tonga and eventually Hawaii, creating social hierarchies and chieftaincies.

Wherever they landed, they radically intervened in local environments in ways they did not consciously intend. Their rapidly multiplying pig populations voraciously consumed ground cover. Settlers quickly depleted forests in search of fuel and building material, and they routinely set fires to clear land for planting and grazing. Fire, farming, and deforestation caused chronic soil erosion, and it drove to extinction native plant and animal species that had flourished for eons. When they first arrived, hunters may have swiftly reduced native animal populations to feed themselves while they got their farms established. Studies on the large island of New Caledonia, for example, show

that particular species of crocodile, land snail, and turtle disappeared long ago. Also, the search for islands very likely continued, not because people liked to explore, but because settlers faced combinations of environmental degradation and population growth that forced some families to try to find new places to live. Some succeeded, others undoubtedly perished at sea in a vain search for land. In time, some island communities devised social rules and ritual taboos to protect animal species, slow forest loss, and limit childbirths. Others did none of those things and inevitably suffered.

Colonization of Remote Oceania reached as far east as Fiji, Tonga, and Samoa by about 1100 B.C.E. but then stopped for more than a thousand years. North and east of there, islands and archipelagos were mostly small and farther from each other. Perhaps the Lapita people, who traveled no farther than Samoa, took many centuries to regroup, strengthening their technologies and devising new sailing and navigating methods before daring to push on. At the start of the Common Era, for example, potters stopped making the finely decorated Lapita ware in favor of containers that were thicker, plainer, and more durable. It was also about then that long-distance migrations resumed, leading to the colonization of islands and island clusters farther to the east and northeast. Ironically, no humans reached the two much bigger islands that today comprise New Zealand until close to 1000 C.E.

Except for the mysterious sweet potato connection with South America that we described at the start of the chapter, the inhabitants of Remote Oceania lost all regular contact with the "worlds" of Afroeurasia, the Americas, and Australia. They also became more isolated from one another. No trans-Pacific network of maritime communication took form, and cultural and commercial exchanges between groups occurred within regions where islands were no more than a few hundred miles apart. In short, Remote Oceania did not become an arena of complex interactions of people, goods, and ideas comparable to Afroeurasia, the Americas, or even Australia. Nevertheless, Polynesian-speaking peoples settled the far reaches of the Pacific basin long before any known sailors crossed the much narrower Atlantic.

• • •

Conclusion

If we think of Hawaii, Rapa Nui, and New Zealand as final frontiers of humankind's colonization of the earth, then by the late first millennium C.E., people—unlike most animal species—lived almost everywhere, Antarctica excluded. As human groups starting from the eastern side of Africa girdled the planet, their networks of contact and exchange grew longer, denser, and busier. However, until five hundred years ago or even less, those networks had significant gaps. The world was not yet encased, as it is today, in a single, thick mesh of communication.

In this chapter we described the gaps that until recent centuries separated four macro-regions, four "worlds" of human interchange, from one another for thousands of years. These long-term communication breaks existed for several reasons. One was the disappearance of land bridges as Holocene sea levels rose. A second was that the connecting points between the macro-regions were so far apart as to discourage migration. Few Afroeurasians or North Americans other than locally adapted hunters had much incentive to travel between Siberia and Alaska. The far North Atlantic passage between North America and Europe was also unpromisingly frigid, though Eskimo-Aleut speakers sailed as far east as Greenland, and Vikings later made an abortive attempt to settle Newfoundland. Southeast Asian farmers who might plausibly have colonized northern Australia would have faced tough adaptation to deserts, marshes, and swamps. A third explanation for the gaps was the deficiency of maritime technology. Since the eastern Pacific is nearly devoid of islands, even the most skilled outrigger sailors were unlikely to have reached South America except by a fluke of winds and currents. And only in the fifteenth and sixteenth centuries C.E. did European shipbuilders and navigators figure out how to traverse the Atlantic and Pacific in both directions, and do it routinely.

Because of their mutual isolation for long eras, Afroeurasia, the Americas, Australia, and Oceania offer interesting laboratories for comparing social behavior and historical change.

First of all, it is clear the inhabitants of these four worlds did not come to behave in radically alien ways from one another. They all remained *Homo sapiens,* sharing all but a minute portion of their genes. The cultural and social differences among them became broad and deep but no more so than differences among peoples *within* a single macro-region who had no direct or regular contact with one another—Indonesians and Southwest Africans, for example. In all four worlds, the first colonizers adapted to and altered their environments by hunting and foraging with tools of stone. They all developed institutions of group cooperation to ensure day-to-day survival and to resolve conflict. And in all four, similar processes of linguistic and cultural division occurred as groups split off and migrated away from one another.

In three of the four regions, some people took up farming, though not all. Afroeurasians and Americans domesticated plants and animals independently of each other, though agriculture in the Pacific islands probably diffused entirely from Southeast Asia. After learning how to produce surplus food, Afroeurasians and Americans went on, in several places where ecological conditions permitted, to create complex societies featuring cities, states, social classes, monumental building, and other characteristics of dense living. In Oceania, signs of social complexity began to appear in places like Tonga and Hawaii, though strict limits on island populations prevented innovation on a grand scale. Australians did not become either farmers or city builders because they did not face serious ecological pressures urging them in that direction.

From a bird's-eye view, the most conspicuous difference among the four macro-regions is that Afroeurasia, the physically biggest of them, supported at, say, the start of the Common Era, as much as 95 percent of the globe's population. We return therefore to Afroeurasia in the next few chapters, recognizing that because of its numbers and dense networks of exchange the pace of social, technological, and human-induced environmental change accelerated faster there than in the other three regions.

• • •

Key Terms

Aboriginal society 109
Cerro Sechín 117
Clovis 120
Eastern Woodlands peoples 111
El Niño Southern Oscillation
(ENSO) 111

Lapita 127
milpa 113
Norte Chico 114
Olmec 109
Poverty Point 122

San Lorenzo 118
terra preta 113
Tlatilco 117
Watson Brake 122

Change over Time

The Americas

8000 B.C.E.	Evidence of farming in Mesoamerica appears.
7000 B.C.E.	Maize is domesticated in Mesoamerica.
3400 B.C.E.	Mound construction takes place at Watson Brake, Louisiana.
3200 B.C.E.	City building emerges in Norte Chico region of Peru.
2200 B.C.E.	Farmers in the northern Andes region of South America begin to cultivate maize.
2000 B.C.E.	Evidence of plant domestication in eastern woodlands of North America appears.
1750 B.C.E.	Native Americans construct mounds at Poverty Point, Louisiana.
1500 B.C.E.	Evidence of pottery making in Mesoamerica appears.
1500 B.C.E.–400 B.C.E.	Olmec society flourishes in Mesoamerica.

Australia

60,000–35,000 B.C.E.	Humans colonize Australia and Tasmania.
9500–8000 B.C.E.	Evidence of human burials with symbolic grave goods in southern Australia appears.

Oceania

1600 B.C.E.–400 C.E.	Humans colonize Oceania as far as Hawaii and Rapa Nui (Easter Island).
1500 B.C.E.–1 C.E.	Lapita cultural style develops in Near and Remote Oceania.

Please see end of book reference section for additional reading suggestions related to this chapter.

part 2

Agrarian Societies and Their Interconnections

1200 B.C.E.–300 C.E.

A stone mask from Teotihuacán in Mesoamerica. The color tiles were added some 700 years after the original was carved.

In the late second millennium B.C.E., where we begin Part 2, agrarian societies were well established in several parts of Afroeurasia and the Americas. During the centuries that we explore in the next four chapters, no event transformed humankind's relationship to the natural and physical environment the way farming had done starting about eight thousand years earlier. Even so, the pace of change in the world continued to speed up, and relations among human communities, as well as between humans and the environment, became much more complex. Why did this happen?

A fundamental factor is that both agrarian and pastoral nomadic peoples spread into new parts of the world. And in places where agriculture already thrived in the late second millennium B.C.E., farmers coaxed higher yields from existing fields by selecting new plant hybrids, introducing new crops, and improving irrigation systems. A given acreage of land transformed into fields or pastures could support many more people and much more complex social and economic organization than the same acreage used only for hunting or foraging.

The pace of change also accelerated because societies in much of Afroeurasia, though not until much later in the Americas and Australia, mastered iron metallurgy. This development took place first in both Southwest Asia and East Africa around 1200 B.C.E. Once early users demonstrated how hard, sharp iron tools benefited farming and many other tasks, the technology spread rapidly across Afroeurasia. Wherever iron objects—axes, hoes, wheels, plows, horse gear, boat rigging, arrow points—came into common use, they permitted societies to alter and manage their environments on a larger scale. The coming of iron metallurgy represented a key turning point in the history of

Afroeurasian peoples. Five other major developments of the first millennium B.C.E. signified not sharp breaks with the past, but dramatic boosts in the scale of human activity and organization.

■ First, world population rose by around 137 million between 1000 B.C.E. and 200 C.E., about 23 million more in those 1,200 years than in the previous 7,000. Population growth of that order, most of it in Afroeurasia rather than the Americas, inevitably required more complex social organization and systems of exchange.

■ Second, cities, which had always been arenas of experimentation with class hierarchies, job specialization, government organization, religion, and social relations between men and women, continued to multiply and expand. In 1200 B.C.E., there were probably no cities in the world with more than 50,000 inhabitants. By 100 C.E. there were about thirty-five, the top two rankings going to Rome and Luoyang (China).

■ Third, as cities proliferated, so did routes of exchange. In several regions, cities became vibrant centers of manufacturing, artistry, learning, and finance, and they sent out tentacles of exchange to one another and to their own rural hinterlands. Merchants also linked cities thousands of miles from one another, trading in exotic goods and in the process exchanging technological skills and creative ideas.

■ Fourth, the number of city-states, centralized monarchies, and multiethnic empires in the world multiplied, and some empires became enormous. Leaders who controlled abundant agricultural surpluses invested heavily in soldiers, weapons, and communication systems, deploying them against their neighbors and enriching themselves even more. Several innovations of the first millennium B.C.E., including mass-produced iron weapons and armor, improved road networks, and more tightly organized chains of command, helped rulers build bigger empires.

By definition, empires incorporated peoples of varied languages, customs, social classes, and political interests. Rulers who strove to hold diverse populations together invariably faced uprisings, frontier attacks, and problems arising from massive military and administrative expense. Some empires therefore lasted longer than others. For example, Rome ruled the Mediterranean basin for several centuries, and in Mesoamerica, Teotihuacán endured as a city-state and empire for about 950 years. By contrast, the empire of Alexander the Great lasted just eleven years. Big empires stimulated urban growth, trade, and cultural creativity. They also provoked great violence, exploited slaves, used up forests, and reinforced the social dominance of men over women.

In addition to empires founded on agrarian wealth, pastoral nomadic groups inhabiting the prairies and mountains of Inner Eurasia, where big crop surpluses could not be grown, founded powerful states of their own. Their sources of wealth were giant animal herds, trade with agrarian neighbors, and incessant raiding. It was in late centuries B.C.E. that pastoral nomads began for the first time to field armies of mounted archers mighty enough to threaten large agrarian states of China, India, or Southwest Asia.

■ Fifth, empire building, urbanization, and denser exchange networks all contributed to the emergence of new religions that appealed to men and women across cultural and social frontiers. From the later second millennium B.C.E., monarchs, priestly groups, and merchants began to propagate certain belief systems more widely. Brahmanism, the precursor of Hinduism, advanced across South Asia. Zoroastrianism made gains in Southwest Asia with the encouragement of Persian emperors. In China, the aristocratic land-owning class disseminated Confucianist ethics. After 500 B.C.E., first Buddhism, then Christianity emerged as genuinely universalist faiths, religions that appealed to individuals no matter their language, culture, class, or political loyalties. These two systems served men and women well in a time of increasingly complex interregional exchange because shared standards of worship and morality facilitated cooperation, fellowship, and trust among strangers. In both Mesoamerica and South America, people of different ethnic identities shared particular deities.

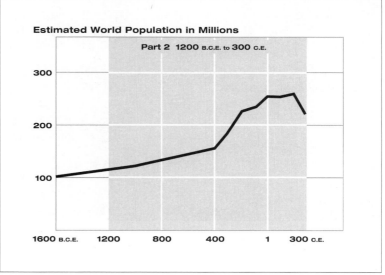

Estimated World Population in Millions

Part 2 1200 B.C.E. to 300 C.E.

300

200

100

1600 B.C.E.　　1200　　　800　　　400　　　1　　　300 C.E.

5 Afroeurasia: Centers of Power, Trade, and New Ideas

1200–600 B.C.E.

Assyrian scribes taking records, royal palace at Nimrud, 730 B.C.E.

Today, about three hundred of the written languages in the world use the Latin alphabet or modified versions of it. Dozens of other languages use different alphabets such as Arabic, Cyrillic, or Bengali. An alphabet is fundamentally a set of signs: characters that correspond to distinct units of sound. The human vocal cords can emit only a limited number of individual sounds. An alphabetic system, therefore, requires no more than a few dozen signs to convert speech into letters written on paper or some other surface. These signs, however, may be combined and arranged in complex ways—into words, sentences, and paragraphs—to represent the nuances of human thought.

The invention of the first alphabets between about 1400 and 1200 B.C.E. represented an immensely important cultural development in world history. Earlier writing systems were much more complicated because they variously included numerous individual signs, some representing single sounds, other standing for syllable sounds, whole words, or even groups of words with a particular meaning. Ancient cuneiform writing, for example, had hundreds of individual signs. Learning such systems involved exhaustive education and great expense. A small child, however, could learn a set of alphabetic characters in a short time. Consequently, in the first millennium B.C.E., more people who did not have wealth or leisure began to learn to write. Literate men and women, though remaining small minorities in all societies, took part in recording knowledge and everyday information and sharing it with others, sometimes over long distances. Over several hundred years, alphabetic writing spread widely from Europe and North Africa across Southwest Asia to India.

This phenomenon was just one indication of accelerating social change and thickening networks of intercommunication in Afroeurasia in the approximate period from 1200 to 600 B.C.E. In the supercontinent as a whole, human population continued to grow at an accelerating pace. This happened as farming societies advanced into new regions, notably into tropical latitudes of Southeast Asia, southern India, and Africa. By contrast, forager bands commanded an ever-shrinking share of global territory. For reasons we will see, the total number of cities in Afroeurasia probably declined in the late second millennium B.C.E., but then began to grow and multiply again, especially in China, northern India, and the Mediterranean lands. On the political landscape, some ruling groups invented new military and organizational techniques for expanding their territories and collecting revenues from larger numbers of people. Small states and self-governing cities also proliferated, and merchant-adventurers founded new seaports that served as nodes of expanding trade networks. In Afroeurasia as a whole, a single trans-hemispheric web of routes gradually took form.

Most of these developments may be connected in one way or another to iron metallurgy, a momentous technological breakthrough that began to spread across Afroeurasia starting about 1200 B.C.E. (see Map 5.1). The first section of the chapter describes early iron making and its growing impact on farming, manufacturing, commerce, and war. We also survey the unintended effects that iron metallurgy began to have on physical and natural environments.

In the second part of the chapter we zoom in on the Mediterranean Sea and the lands around it, including Southwest Asia. Relative to the rest of Afroeurasia, this was a region of particularly intense human interchange associated with several interrelated developments. We first survey the crisis that beset the eastern Mediterranean in the twelfth century B.C.E., when aggressive bands that historians identify as Sea People threw the region, including Egypt, Syria, and the Aegean basin, into turmoil, ending an era of relatively orderly relations among several states. Out of this period of upheaval emerged the Neo-Assyrian empire, the first state to politically unite, at least for a short time, the whole region from the Tigris-Euphrates to the Nile. Also in the aftermath of the Sea People tumult, Hebrew-speaking inhabitants of the southern Levant (the lands along the eastern end of the Mediterranean) put forth the idea, peculiar for that era, that they ought to worship one deity as their protector and moral lawgiver, rather than a crowded hierarchy of gods and goddesses. These Israelites, as they became known, laid the foundations of monotheistic Judaism. Finally, in this part of the chapter we make a sweep around the Mediterranean and outlying regions, exploring the growth of trade and city building in the sea basin, the development of farming societies in Europe, and the rise of a powerful state in the Nile valley south of Egypt.

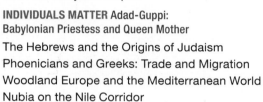

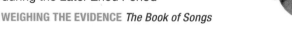

• • •

The third section of the chapter takes us to South Asia, where in the late second millennium B.C.E. the Ganges River valley became the most dynamic center of population growth and urbanization, a process speeded by new iron metallurgy. The 1200–600 B.C.E. period witnessed social and cultural developments fundamental to later Indian civilization. One was formation of a distinctive way of organizing social class relations, known in later times as the caste system. The other was Brahmanism, a complex cluster of religious beliefs and practices that underlay the Hindu tradition of later millennia.

In the final section, we consider developments in East Asia, where at the end of the second millennium B.C.E. the Shang state, a monarchy of unprecedented size and endurance, fell to the Zhou (JOH) dynasty. The Zhou kings then built an even larger state, ruling for more than 250 years, an

A Panoramic View

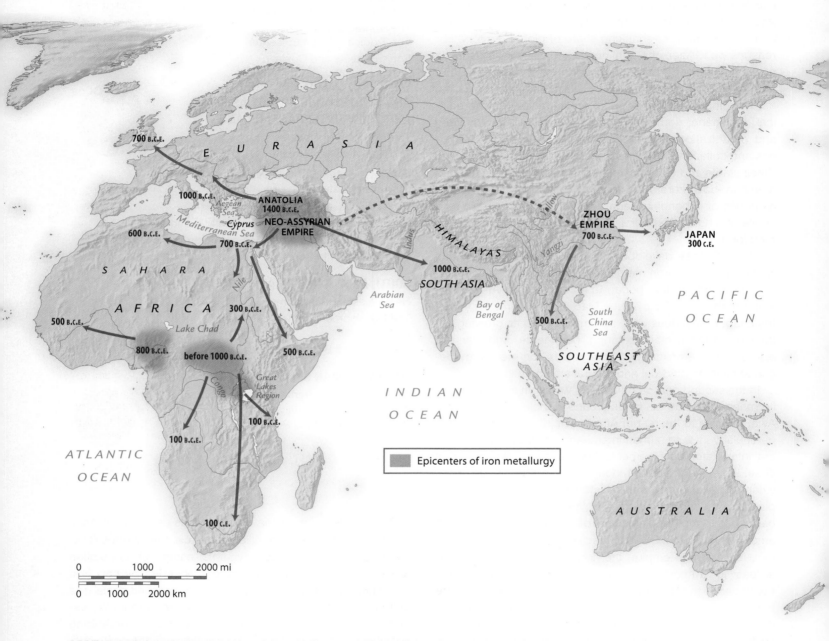

MAP 5.1 Major states and the spread of iron metallurgy, 1200–800 B.C.E.
The dotted line represents the likely route along which iron technology spread to China. What factors may have permitted the spread of iron-making across large distances in many regions of Afroeurasia?

era of population growth in the Yellow and Yangzi valleys related to agricultural innovations, including new iron tools. The trend of demographic and economic growth in China continued after 850 B.C.E., despite the Zhou royal family's loss of all but ceremonial authority over a collection of regional states, which warred with one another off and on for the next 450 years.

The Clang of Iron

FOCUS What part did iron metallurgy play in economic, environmental, or political change in Afroeurasia between 1200 and 600 B.C.E.?

History books have conventionally characterized 1200 to 600 B.C.E. as the "early iron age." This term highlights the initial effects of iron metallurgy on economy and society in Afroeurasia. On the other hand, the label may somewhat overstate iron's importance. For one thing, societies did not suddenly switch from copper and bronze to iron. Rather, both copper and bronze continued in use for a multitude of purposes, including sculpture, jewelry, armor, swords, spears, ship fittings, and numerous other handcrafted objects. Also, ironworking took several centuries to spread from region to region. Basic knowledge of iron metallurgy was one thing, but the creation of iron industries and related cultural changes took time. In every society that learned about the new technology, people had to find iron deposits, figure out ways to haul ore to smelters, tinker continuously with furnace efficiency, train young people for a new type of occupation, enlist merchants to distribute iron goods, convince rulers to buy iron armor and weapons, and persuade skeptical women and men to adopt hoes, knives, pots, pans, and other household tools made of the newfangled metal. Only from around 500 B.C.E. did iron become a primary workaday material in several parts of Afroeurasia. Finally, iron technology was not known in the Americas until the arrival of Columbus or in Australia until the late eighteenth century.

The Spread of Iron: The Southwest Asian Epicenter

The best available evidence indicates that people independently invented iron technology in as few as two places in the world. One of these founding centers was in Southwest Asia, the other in tropical Africa. The earliest evidence of iron smelting comes from eastern Anatolia (modern Turkey) about 1400 B.C.E. There, artisans who probably already possessed skills as bronze makers began to fashion iron ornaments and other objects on a small scale. Within about four hundred years, the Levant and the island of Cyprus became important centers of iron smelting. Subsequently, the new technology spread slowly into neighboring regions. Material evidence shows that both Egypt and the lands around the Aegean Sea began to make ironware on a significant scale by the seventh century B.C.E. Within about another hundred years, Chinese artisans were forging iron, and by the early centuries C.E. the technology reached Japan. Because East Asia had a long history of sophisticated bronze metallurgy, some scholars think that Chinese innovators made the leap to iron independently of developments in Anatolia. Others think the knowledge spread gradually from Southwest Asia eastward by way of routes across Inner Eurasia.

Like copper and tin, iron ore had to be transformed to make the metal useful. Early ironsmiths heated the ore with charcoal in an enclosed space, usually a pit with a facing of clay or stone and one or more pipes or tubes to allow air to reach the lower part of the smelter. The heated mixture produced a "bloom," a spongy mass of iron globules mixed with a slag of impurities. The smith then repeatedly reheated and hammered this substance to separate the iron from the slag and to shape the purified metal into an object of wrought, or "worked," iron. Because of bubbles and impurities, early iron tools cracked or shattered easily. In time, however, craftsmen adopted more exacting techniques, for example, dousing iron objects in cold water after each heating and hammering cycle to strengthen them.

Iron had definite advantages over bronze for a variety of uses. Iron ore is much more commonly available than copper and often lies close to the surface of the ground. Bronze industries also required tin, whose sources were limited and seldom anywhere near copper mines (see Chapter 2). Second, the relative abundance of iron lowered the cost of production and therefore the price of iron tools and weapons relative to bronze. Finally, iron masters learned to produce a metal that lasted longer and held a sharper edge than bronzeware. By experimenting doggedly, artisans found proportions of iron to carbon that produced steel, which had more tensile strength than wrought iron.

Around 700 B.C.E., Chinese artisans pioneered cast iron. That is, they liquefied the metal and poured it into molds to make numerous useful objects, including projectile points, pipes, and bells. Iron melts at 2800°F (1538°C), a temperature much higher than the melting point of copper. To get the desired results, Chinese inventors built larger furnaces with sealed interiors and fashioned bellows to blow air through pipes or shafts to regulate the flow and raise the internal temperature. Cast iron technology became known outside China only several centuries later.

The Spread of Iron: The Tropical African Epicenter

Scholars have firmly established that societies in one or two regions of tropical Africa invented ironworking independently of that development in Southwest Asia. Archaeological digs have revealed smelters in the Great Lakes region of east central Africa by 1000 B.C.E. or earlier and, farther west, in the area between Lake Chad and modern Cameroon by about 800 B.C.E. We do not know whether people in those regions acquired iron skills independently of each other or whether an earlier, so far undiscovered epicenter fed them both. We do know, however, that tropical Africans were making iron some centuries *before* the technology reached Egypt or other parts of northern Africa, so the technology is extremely unlikely to have come from Anatolia.

In contrast to the early metalsmiths in Southwest Asia, African furnace builders did not take any clues from bronze

Iron horse bit from central Europe. Substituting iron for bronze lowered the cost of horse harnesses in the first millennium B.C.E. This set of iron mouthpiece and bridle rings from the sixth century B.C.E. was found in the Czech Republic. Why do you think effective cavalry warfare depended on equipment like this?

making. Copper technology was already known in parts of Africa but not bronze. Tropical Africans simply skipped the bronze age, as it were. There is also evidence that iron masters of the Great Lakes region were the first in the world to design smelters hot enough to produce steel, at least in small amounts, without the additional process of heating, hammering, and quenching.

From the West African and Great Lakes epicenters, iron technology spread gradually throughout most of tropical Africa. In the course of the first millennium B.C.E., the technology advanced from the Cameroon–Lake Chad area westward to other societies of savanna and forest. The Great Lakes region was almost certainly the point from which iron and the numerous economic and social elements associated with it radiated throughout eastern, central, and southern Africa by the early centuries C.E.

The peoples inhabiting the Great Lakes neighborhood, a region that straddles the equator, presented a cultural kaleidoscope. They spoke myriad languages classified in four different major language families, and they practiced various combinations of farming, cattle raising, foraging, and hunting. Then, maybe a century or two after some villagers started experimented with ironworking, a new population arrived on the scene. These were farmers who migrated from the equatorial Congo River lands eastward to the forests rimming the Great Lakes. They spoke languages in the Bantu language group, and they had an agricultural economy based on yams (see Chapter 3).

During the centuries after 1000 B.C.E., the interaction of Bantu speakers with indigenous farming and herding peoples intensified, creating new cultural blends. Bantu farmers adopted local grain-growing methods, house styles,

and iron techniques and tools. They also introduced new religious ideas centered on veneration of ancestors, a musical culture that emphasized polyrhythmic drumming, and a division of labor in which women took charge of both domestic and farm work. By about 400 B.C.E., population pressure on farm and grazing land began to force settled societies just west of the Great Lakes to consider new economic strategies. Some Bantu-speaking communities supplemented their yam crops with sorghum, finger millet, sheep, and cattle. Others, however, set out to find new land, toting their iron axes and hoes with them. These conditions signaled the start of an epic migratory drift that between about 300 B.C.E. and 300 C.E. introduced farming, cattle breeding, iron, and Bantu languages to the entire southern third of the continent. We return to the story of Bantu peoples in southern Africa in Chapter 13.

Iron's Benefits and Costs

In the first millennium B.C.E., people awoke gradually to the amazing utility of ironware—knives, spades, plowshares, swords, arrowheads, nails, wire, wagon wheel rims, keys, hooks, razors, and tubes for blowing glass. Using implements of iron rather than of stone, bone, or wood, workers found they could accomplish numerous specific tasks expending less time and energy. For example, a person could cut and shape hardwoods more economically using an iron axe, saw, and woodworking plane. These advantages also suggested many new uses for wood. Similarly, stonemasons who built temples, palaces, forts, city walls, and ordinary houses worked more efficiently and creatively once they had iron hammers, chisels, and wedges.

A barren hillside on the island of Crete. After farmers began smelting iron and adopting iron tools to expand cultivation, woodlands rapidly contracted throughout the Aegean Sea basin. Much of this deforestation remained permanent.

As smelting technology improved and production costs fell relative to bronze, iron tools came within the reach of ordinary farmers. In China, villagers started using cast iron plowshares as early as the sixth century B.C.E. In many places, rural women became prime consumers of iron pans, skillets, knives, and a host of food-preparing devices. States with armies continued to acquire various types of bronze weaponry throughout the first millennium B.C.E., but iron and steel gradually took precedence. Rulers wealthy and well organized enough to set up their own iron industries could supply their troops with spears, swords, and arrowheads at much lower prices than they had to pay for bronze. Pirates, bandits, and professional mercenaries became similarly equipped. Iron itself in the form of ore, sponge iron (directly from the furnace), bars, rods, and numerous wrought or cast wares became a major item of both local and interregional trade in most of Afroeurasia.

Iron tools permitted cultivators to alter the landscape faster and more extensively than in earlier times. As agricultural production rose in the first millennium B.C.E., so too did the rate at which farmers destroyed trees and other woody plants, the major component of the earth's **biomass.** Humans had been cutting forests since paleolithic times and witnessing the resulting flooding and soil erosion (see Chapter 2). A man or woman swinging iron, however, could fell a tree in a fraction of the time it took to do it using a stone axe. Iron power, combined with techniques of controlled burning, permitted farmers to clear land for planting or grazing more efficiently than ever before. Moreover, the iron smelters that

biomass Plant matter, including wood, brush, straw, and animal waste, used especially as a source of fuel.

multiplied across Afroeurasia devoured enormous amounts of wood and its derivative charcoal. Consequently, wherever iron industries arose, local woodland disappeared in ever-widening circles. For example, in the area around Lake Victoria, the largest of East Africa's Great Lakes, pollen analysis shows that by the late first millennium B.C.E., land clearing combined with iron smelting had already consumed nearly all woodland. Based on a survey of the remains of ancient slag heaps, one scholar has estimated that from as early as the fifth millennium B.C.E., when copper was first liquefied, to the fourth century C.E., smelters in the Mediterranean region consumed fifty to seventy million acres of trees.[1] By 500 B.C.E., the lands around the eastern Mediterranean presented scenes of permanently denuded hillsides. Writing in the fifth century B.C.E., the philosopher Plato lamented the degradation of Greece's forests and soils, though he did not link it to smelting:

There has never been any considerable accumulation of the soil coming down from the mountains, as in other places, but the earth has fallen away all round and sunk out of sight. The consequence is, that in comparison of what then was, there are remaining only the bones of the wasted body, as they may be called, . . . all the richer and softer parts of the soil having fallen away, and the mere skeleton of the land being left.[2]

The scale of biomass eradication in ancient times was small compared to the rate of global deforestation today. Nevertheless, metal technology strengthened human confidence in the idea that the earthly environment was a bountiful, limitless storehouse of resources to be extracted, managed, and transformed.

Warfare, Empire Building, and Trade in Southwest Asia and the Mediterranean Lands

FOCUS What historical developments contributed to increasing commercial and cultural interaction among peoples of Southwest Asia and the Mediterranean basin between 1200 and 600 B.C.E.?

Starting about 1200 B.C.E. and for the next six centuries, iron metallurgy spread from its creative epicenter in Anatolia westward to the Mediterranean and woodland Europe and eastward across Iran to India. The increasing complexity of human interchange that this diffusion involved was especially apparent along the belt of land and sea from the Tigris-Euphrates River valley (Mesopotamia) westward to the Atlantic shore. The peoples of this zone became more intricately meshed together in several ways. For a time in the twelfth and eleventh centuries B.C.E., a prolonged period of military upheaval around the eastern Mediterranean rim depressed trade and city growth, but this decline did not last.

Between the tenth and seventh centuries B.C.E., the rulers of Assyria in the northern Tigris River valley raised the craft of empire building to a new level. Assyrian kings subjugated and ruled more people representing greater linguistic and ethnic diversity than any earlier state had accomplished. In the lands beyond the Assyrian realm, Phoenicians, Greeks, and Etruscans built commercial networks that together extended across the Mediterranean and even reached into the Atlantic. As sea trade grew, more distant peoples of woodland Europe, North Africa, and the Nile River valley became firmly linked into the Mediterranean exchange web.

Twelfth-Century Troubles

Between the sixteenth and thirteenth centuries B.C.E., the cluster of empires and kingdoms occupying the land between the Nile and the Tigris-Euphrates worked out a reasonably practical strategy for getting along with one another. The largest of these states were New Kingdom Egypt, the northern Euphrates valley state of Mitanni, Babylonia and Assyria on the Tigris, and the Hittite empire (Hatti) of Anatolia. These monarchies periodically went to war over territory and resources, but they also invented informal rules for exchanging envoys, negotiating peace, and carrying on trade (see Chapter 3). Then, in the twelfth century B.C.E., this promising system of international relations disintegrated amid widespread violence. For more than a century, Southwest Asia, Egypt, and the Aegean basin experienced upheavals that today's historians, disadvantaged by scanty documentation from the period, continue to struggle to understand.

Mysterious Sea People. Catastrophe descended quite suddenly. In the course of half a century, assailants sacked and burned nearly fifty towns and cities from the Aegean

MAP 5.2 Sites of Sea People attacks, 1200–900 B.C.E.

Does the spatial distribution of the cities that Sea People attacked suggest where these invaders might have originated?

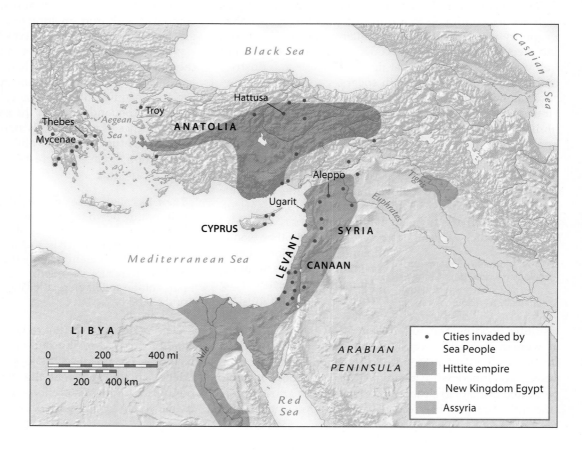

basin to the northern Tigris-Euphrates. We have yet to identify these city burners precisely. One theory argues that usually peaceful farmers and herders of the eastern Mediterranean and its hinterlands went on the warpath owing to drought, famine, or rulers' heavy tax demands.

Another theory highlights new weapons technology. Strong states that deployed well-disciplined infantries and chariot forces usually kept pirates, bandits, hired mercenaries, peasant rebels, and other troublemakers under control or at arm's length. In the mid-second millennium B.C.E., wealthy states had a near monopoly on chariots because vehicles, horses, weapons, and skilled fighters cost a great deal to maintain. Chariot squadrons, together with trained infantry, could usually limit threats from poorly armed brigands and insurgents.

By the thirteenth century B.C.E., however, unruly groups that lived beyond the easy reach of disciplined armies began to adopt a new technology of infantry warfare. It included several elements: tough metal or leather body armor, sturdy round shields, short javelins, and long bronze swords with sharply tapered ends designed for both thrusting and slashing. Fighters who could never afford chariots outfitted themselves as foot soldiers at reasonable cost. Not only did they carry lethal weapons; they also devised new battlefield tactics for surrounding and attacking chariots with javelins and swords. This new war kit appears to have spread around the eastern Mediterranean quite rapidly, though iron weaponry did not replace bronze until later centuries.

This new chariot-challenging weaponry appears to have intersected with another development, the gradual weakening of the established kingdoms and city-states of the region between the Aegean and the Tigris-Euphrates. These states waned under any of a number of possible pressures—food shortages linked to long-term drought, top-heavy and oppressive governments, forced transfer of land from peasants to wealthy classes, or revolts by discontented mercenary solders. Both New Kingdom Egypt and the Hittite empire, for example, had sumptuous royal courts, numerous paid officials, and expensive chariot and infantry forces. The ordinary folk who paid for this magnificence with their taxes and labor had little incentive to support their rulers against sudden intruders.

The throngs that began burning cities around 1200 B.C.E. do not appear to have come from any single direction. Sometimes they moved as large groups of male fighters, sometimes as crowds of women, children, and armored men. In the Aegean, raiding bands attacked Troy, Mycenae, and many other cities. They effectively obliterated the urban Mycenaean society that had flourished for three centuries (see Chapter 3). South of the Mediterranean, seaborne fighters sailed from Libya to Egypt to strike the Nile delta. In Anatolia and Syria, marauders sacked several Hittite cities and brought that once great monarchy to its knees.

Mass bands of swordsmen that historians have named the Sea People, a deliberately vague term reflecting the mystery over their identity and origin, attacked and destroyed at least eighteen cities in Syria and the Levant (see Map 5.2). In a surviving letter on a clay tablet, the king of Alashiya, a state on Cyprus, advised the ruler of Ugarit, one of the leading commercial cities on the Levantine coast, to prepare for an attack: "Where are your troops and chariots? Are they not with you? If not, who will deliver you from the enemy? Surround your cities with walls and bring your troops and chariots into them. Watch out for the enemy and reinforce

A sea battle at the mouth of the Nile. Egyptian forces repelled both Libyan and Sea People incursions into the Nile delta. This relief on a wall of Pharaoh Ramses III's mortuary temple in Luxor commemorates an Egyptian naval victory over Sea People in 1178 B.C.E. In this chaotic scene of shipboard combat, the warrior's horned helmet identifies him as a Sea People marauder. What do we learn from this scene about Sea People weaponry?

yourself well." In reply, Ugarit's ruler exclaimed that attacks had already started: "the ships of the enemy have been coming. They have been burning down my villages and have done evil things to the country."[3] Ugarit was subsequently demolished and not rebuilt for a thousand years.

Raiders who penetrated Southwest Asia appear to have operated in several independent groups. Some Sea People looted and burned cities and villages, then went away. One band of assailants, known from the Old Testament Bible as the Philistines, sacked and burned cities of Canaan, the ancient name for the southern part of the Levantine coast. Those invaders eventually faded from history, though they live on in the regional name "Palestine."

The aftermath. From the smoke and ash of the twelfth-century B.C.E. catastrophe came three important changes. One was a rapid if temporary economic decline in the eastern Mediterranean basin as states fell and bustling ports disappeared. Evidence of shrinking wealth comes from the remains of elite graves in the region. During and after the troubles, a single sword or spear point might accompany a dead aristocrat rather than an assortment of bronzeware and other precious objects. A second change was the decline of the chariot as anything other than a vehicle for racing and royal display. Rulers relied increasingly on well-disciplined foot soldiers equipped with long swords, javelins, and stabbing spears made of either bronze or iron.

A third consequence of the mayhem was a large power void in Southwest Asia. The Egyptian pharaohs withdrew from the Levant and Syria and fell back to the Nile. The Hittite empire gave way to a set of much weaker successor kingdoms. Similarly, Assyria had to defend its Tigris River valley cities against attacks from both mountain people and desert nomads. Assyria, however, held up better than any other Southwest Asian state.

The Neo-Assyrian Empire

Indeed, in the mid-tenth century, Assyria asserted itself as a regional power, in fact as one of the ancient world's greatest empires. One important trend of the first millennium B.C.E. in several parts of Afroeurasia was the effort of rulers to invent more effective ways to organize, integrate, and extract wealth from conquered people. In other words, kings created more powerful and efficient systems of command. Following the Sea People episode, Assyria typified this trend. The Tigris valley, an agriculturally rich and populous region encompassing both rain-watered and irrigated land, supported large military investment. Starting with King Ashur-dan II in 934 B.C.E., monarchs headquartered at Ashur on the west bank of the Tigris (today in northern Iraq) dispatched armies far and wide, filling the Southwest Asian power vacuum (see Map 5.3). Assyrian forces even invaded Egypt and occupied it for about twenty years. For more than a century, it ruled Babylonia in southern Mesopotamia and generally looked to the great city of Babylon for proper standards of art, architecture, literature, and cuneiform writing. As the

Neo-Assyrian empire grew, wealth poured in from plunder, taxation, and interregional trade. These riches fueled an impressive infrastructure of military and political communication and an ever bigger, increasingly ironclad army.

The new era of the horse soldier. Neo-Assyria was also the first major state we know of to deploy horse **cavalry.** Fighters had been launching raids on horseback on the Inner Eurasian steppes since the fourth millennium B.C.E. But only after about 900 B.C.E. did rulers begin to organize units of mounted soldiers that would behave like trained infantry, that is, respond without hesitation to the commands of officers and to maneuver as a team on a field of battle.

> **cavalry** The part of a military force trained to fight mounted on horses or camels.

Cavalry combat became effective, however, only after several innovations were introduced. Charioteers had been fighting with bows and arrows for several centuries, including bows made both lighter and stronger by fusing strips of wood or bone together. Sometime after 1000 B.C.E., artisans began to shorten the length of these composite bows so that horse soldiers could more nimbly swing the weapon around and even fire to the rear of their mount. Arrows and arrowheads were also standardized and made more compact so that every rider could carry dozens of them, permitting well-trained cavalry to fire a blizzard of projectiles. The Assyrian army imported thousands of horses from Anatolia, Iran, and Inner Eurasia and taught riders how to move and fight in coordination with infantry. Even though saddles and stirrups had yet to be invented, mounted troops could travel faster and maneuver with greater alacrity than chariots. The cost of mobile warfare also decreased, and within a few hundred years, cavalry almost completely replaced massed chariots throughout Afroeurasia.

The Neo-Assyrian command system. Neo-Assyria not only grew to enormous territorial dimensions but also achieved remarkable success at politically integrating diverse peoples. Building on earlier models of centralized command in Mesopotamia, the state introduced a number of institutions to concentrate and systematize its power. For example, the kings promoted an elaborate ideology of themselves as possessors of absolute, unquestionable authority over everyone else. They represented themselves as sacred deputies of Ashur, the Assyrian high god, though they did not, in contrast to the Egyptian pharaohs, claim to be deities themselves. They typically took personal charge of planning and leading wars of conquest, extolling themselves as superheroic warriors. They meted out mercy and vengeance as they pleased, and they terrorized their enemies as a policy calculated to encourage negotiation and surrender. Assyrian conquerors treated resistance and disloyalty with all manner of cruelty, piling up decapitated heads and skinning hapless victims alive. The emperors recorded these deeds on numerous stone inscriptions. Concerning an expedition to the Euphrates and the Levant, King

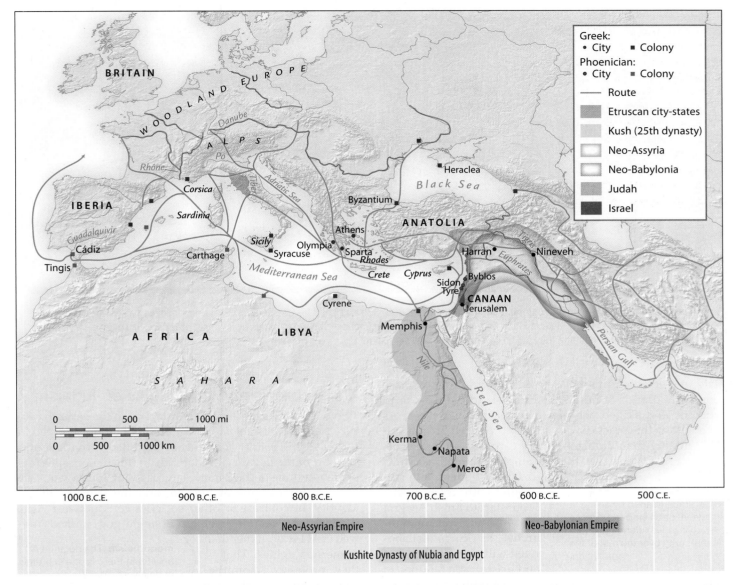

MAP 5.3 States, cities, and trade routes of the Mediterranean region, 1000–600 B.C.E.
Why do you think geographers have described the Mediterranean as many seas rather than one?

Ashurnasirpal II (r. 883–859 B.C.E.) had this boast inscribed: "While I was in the city of Aribua [in Syria], I conquered the cities of the land of Luhutu. I killed many of them [i.e., the inhabitants]. I demolished; I destroyed; I burnt with fire. I captured soldiers alive by hand. I impaled [them] on stakes in front of their cities."[4]

From this authoritarian platform, the emperors organized the expanding empire. They divided it into provinces over which they appointed regional governors and military officers staunchly loyal to the throne. In this way they bypassed to some extent the established land-owning families, who might be tempted to put their own local interests ahead of those of the state. The queens and royal daughters of Assyria did not, so far as we know, hold formal offices, but they controlled immense agricultural estates and on at least a few occasions held the government together in times of internal conflict over the royal succession.

Effective command, as always, depended on good communication. Conscripting laborers from around the empire, the government built a system of roads that unified the Tigris-Euphrates valley and connected the imperial heartland to the urban centers of Syria and the Mediterranean coast. Commodities and luxury goods passed into and through the empire from every direction: textiles and horses from Babylonia, incense and spices from the Arabian peninsula, horses and tin from Persia, silver and iron from Anatolia, timber and glass from the Levant, gold from Egypt.

The Assyrians also tried to integrate the empire by forcefully moving and resettling large numbers of people, mainly from conquered territories to the central region. The

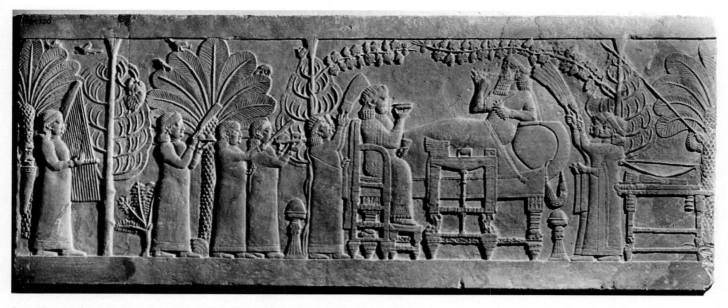

A royal scene from the Neo-Assyrian capital. King Ashurbanipal (r. 668–630 B.C.E.) and his queen relax in a garden following his victory over Teumman, the ruler of the enemy state of Elam. On a tree at left the severed head of Teumman hangs by its nose. How does this palace carving from Nineveh communicate the idea that the king has restored peace to his realm?

state implemented this policy ruthlessly in order to place tens of thousands of military recruits, road builders, farm workers, and skilled artisans where it wanted them. As merciless as this practice was, it likely produced greater cultural mixing than occurred in any earlier large state. This does not mean, however, that the empire's numerous ethnic groups all identified culturally with their rulers. From start to finish Assyria was an **authoritarian monarchy.** Its kings collaborated with loyal lieutenants and aristocratic families to pump revenue from the farming and herding population, and then spent it to augment government power and the elite's extravagant lifestyle. Assyria generally sustained this system of domination for more than three centuries, foreshadowing even mightier empires to follow.

> **authoritarian monarchy** A state, headed by a king, a queen, or an emperor, whose ruling class demands strict authority over the rest of the population.

Under the pressures of frontier attacks and provincial revolts, however, Assyria rapidly declined in the early seventh century B.C.E. The fatal blow came from Babylonia, a state subjugated to dependence on Assyria. In 610 B.C.E., a resurgent Babylonia under the military leadership of King Nebuchadnezzar II (neb-uh-kud-NEZ-er, r. 605–562 B.C.E.) sent forces up the Tigris valley, destroyed the Assyrian capital of Nineveh, and brought down the empire. Nebuchadnezzar then organized a new Mesopotamian state and undertook vigorous conquests of his own to seize nearly all the territories that Assyria once held. This Neo-Babylonian empire, as historians call it, did not, however, last much past Nebuchadnezzar's reign.

The Hebrews and the Origins of Judaism

Two of the states the Assyrians attacked in the seventh century B.C.E. were Israel and Judea, small kingdoms located in the fertile hill country of Canaan, identified with the southern part of the Levant (see Map 5.3). In this region, speakers of Hebrew, one of the Semitic languages of Southwest Asia, laid the foundations of Judaism and the Jewish cultural identity. In contrast to other societies of Southwest Asia, the Hebrews came to worship a single god, named Yahweh (YAH-way), rather than numerous deities. That is, they professed **monotheism,** though Yahweh came to be understood only gradually as God the creator of the universe and humankind, rather than one local deity competing with others for allegiance.

> **monotheism** The doctrine or belief that there is one supreme and universal deity.

Over several hundred years, Hebrew-speaking scholars compiled numerous long books about the origin and early history of their people—chronicles, poems, and the orations of prophets all centered on the often contentious relationship between the Hebrews and Yahweh. This collection of writings, which we know as the Hebrew Bible, or in the Christian tradition as the Old Testament, constitutes a more detailed, vivid historical account than we have of probably any other ancient society. Early Hebrew history, however, remains a challenge for scholars because the Bible is the sole source of almost all we know about it. Only from about the sixth century B.C.E. does evidence independent of the Bible begin significantly to enrich the ancient history of the Jews.

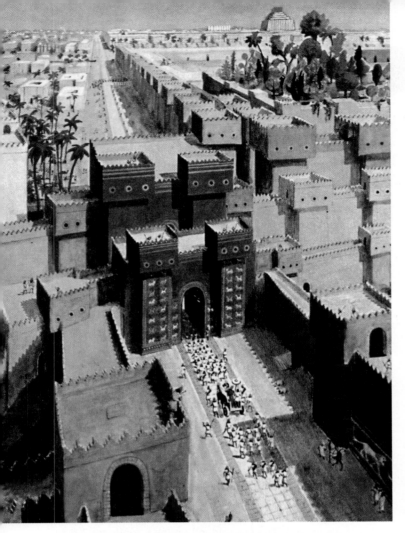

The Ishtar Gate in Babylon. This is a twentieth-century artist's depiction of a ritual procession passing through the Ishtar Gate, one of the entryways to Babylon constructed in the reign of Nebuchadnezzar II. Dedicated to the goddess Ishtar, a reconstructed version of the gate may be seen today in the Pergamon Museum in Berlin. What sources of information could an artist use to render the Babylonian cityscape as it might have looked in the sixth century B.C.E.?

From Hebrews to Israelites. From the Bible, as well as inferences made from other sources, historians have hypothesized that sometime between about 1300 and 1100 B.C.E. the Hebrews emerged as a confederation of extended kinship groups, or tribes, in Canaan. There they became known as Israelites, in the Bible as the Twelve Tribes of Israel. The Hebrew emergence may well be associated with the Sea People invasions, which rid the Levant of Egyptian or Hittite domination and opened the way for local populations to form a number of alliances, small kingdoms, and city-states. However, the biblical account, which begins with the Book of Genesis and Yahweh's creation of the world, explains Hebrew origins in terms of the careers of numerous special individuals—mostly men but some women. These figures struggle to fulfill a covenant with God to obey his commandments and lead exemplary lives of morality and virtue, though some accomplished that task more successfully than others. In fact, it is the narratives of Hebrew leaders backsliding and then redeeming themselves in the eyes of God that give the Hebrew Bible its dramatic force and moral power.

Among the larger-than-life biblical figures are Abraham, the founding patriarch, or father, of the monotheistic tradition. According to Genesis, he was born in the ancient Mesopotamian city of Ur, but Yahweh promised him possession of the Land of Canaan. As Genesis recounts, Abraham started for Canaan with his family and other companions:

> The LORD had said to Abram, "Go from your country, your people and your father's household to the land I will show you.
> I will make you into a great nation,
> —and I will bless you;
> I will make your name great,
> —and you will be a blessing."
> So Abram went, as the LORD had told him; . . . He took his wife Sarai, his nephew Lot, all the possessions they had accumulated and the people they had acquired in Harran, and they set out for the land of Canaan, and they arrived there.[5]

Other biblical luminaries include Joseph, who was sold into slavery by his brothers and taken into Egypt; Moses, who led the Hebrews out of enslavement in Egypt and received from God the Ten Commandments, a set of absolute moral laws; and Joshua, who finally guided the Hebrews into Canaan, conquering that land and dividing the territorial spoils among the Twelve Tribes, from this point known as the Israelites. According to scripture, God promised this chosen people prosperity and large families for generations to come. The Israelites, however, had to abide by God's sacred law, which in time came to include not only the Ten Commandments but also rules for eating, dress, sacrificial rituals, marriage, sex, property inheritance, crime, and other spheres of collective life. Many of these laws echoed the legal systems of early states in Mesopotamia.

Scholars transcribed and edited Hebrew scriptures from oral accounts, a process that went on for hundreds of years. Consequently, the question of who actually formulated the Jewish theology expressed in scripture and when they did it has been the subject of much learned debate. The Hebrew Bible represents God as a person, rather than as an abstract cosmic force. But it also proclaims him to be utterly transcendent, above and beyond nature. This idea of God contrasts strikingly with the religions of ancient Mesopotamia or Egypt, where different elements of nature—sun, moon, rain, lightning—are associated with particular gods or goddesses. For example, in Mesopotamian tradition the sun was the particular deity Shamash, but in Hebrew scripture the sun is merely an instrument of God. In the ancient **polytheistic** belief systems, divine beings

> **polytheism** A belief system that incorporates multiple deities or spirits.

Adad-Guppi: Babylonian Priestess and Queen Mother

This stele is dedicated to the Neo-Babylonian ruler Nabonidus, son of Adad-Guppi. Just to the right of the king's staff is the circular symbol of the moon god Sin.

Nabonidus, the last king of Neo-Babylonia, came to power with the help of his aged mother Adad-Guppi, a priestess devoted to the moon god Sin. This woman lived for more than a hundred years, a remarkable achievement for anyone in the first millennium B.C.E. She witnessed the fall of the Assyrian empire, lived through the forty-year reign of Nebuchadnezzar, and saw her son mount the Babylonian throne when she was in her nineties.

None of the three kings who followed Nebuchadnezzar held power in Babylon for long. They all came and went within six years of his death. However, Nabonidus, the fourth king, enjoyed a longer reign—seventeen full years. When he fell, so did the short-lived empire.

Nabonidus was not a member of the Babylonian royal family. But apparently through the efforts of Adad-Guppi, who had served in the temple of Sin in the Euphrates city of Harran, he held posts in the courts of both Nebuchadnezzar and his son. This career apparently gave him the connections he needed to seize power when the opportunity came. Since the previous king had reigned for only a month, scholars have speculated that Nabonidus had him murdered.

When Nebuchadnezzar's forces seized Harran in 601 B.C.E., the temple of Sin had been destroyed and the statue of the god taken away. Adad-Guppi made it her prime mission in life to see the god restored and the temple rebuilt. Once Nabonidus ascended the throne, he fulfilled his mother's wish.

All that we know about Adad-Guppi comes from two stelae erected at the rebuilt temple, which display what are claimed to be her autobiography, plus a short postscript describing her death. We cannot be sure that she composed the autobiographical text herself, but it may nonetheless express her own experiences and opinions. She recounts her longtime devotion to the gods, particularly to Sin, and to the sacrifices she made after Sin "became angry with his city and his temple and went up to heaven," that is, when the temple was destroyed. By demonstrating her piety, she hoped to convince the deities to return to their temple: "In order to calm the heart of my god and my goddess, I would not wear a fine wool dress, gold or silver jewelry, a new garment, nor would I let perfume or sweet oil touch my body, [but] I wore a torn garment and my clothing was sackcloth."

The inscription recounts that owing to Adad-Guppi's dedication to Sin, the god had chosen her son to lead the Neo-Babylonian empire. In turn, Nabonidus showed his own reverence for Sin by rebuilding the temple in Harran and making it a major religious center. According to Adad-Guppi, "Sin, king of the gods, made me live one hundred and four good years. . . . I myself, the sight of my two eyes is sharp and my comprehension is excellent, my hands and feet are healthy and my words are well chosen, food and drink agree with me, I am in good health, my heart is full."

When Adad-Guppi died in the ninth year of Nabonidus's reign, the text's postscript explains that he led the entire Neo-Babylonian empire in mourning: "He assembled [the people] of Babylon. . . . He [had them] mourn and . . . they made lamentation. They cast [dust] on their heads for 7 days and 7 nights; they murmured; their clothes were cast off. On the seventh day, the people of the entire land cut their hair." Nabonidus ruled another eight years or so after his mother's death. But then Persians invaded Mesopotamia, deposed him, and eliminated the Neo-Babylonian dynasty.

Adad-Guppi's autobiography in stone has transmitted to modern scholars important insights into the influential roles that elite women might play in ancient imperial politics, as well as the complex interplay between political and religious life.

Thinking Critically

What do the inscriptions about Adad-Guppi's long life tell us about the influence of elite women in Neo-Babylonian royal politics?

Source: Mark W. Chavalas, ed., *Historical Sources in Translation: The Ancient Near East* (Malden, MA: Blackwell, 2006), 389–393.

behave unpredictably and indifferently toward human beings. In Hebrew scripture, God cares deeply about his creation and continually uplifts his people in body and spirit.

God's people, however, had to accept full responsibility for the divine covenant, abiding by his moral commandments not just as individuals but also collectively as a society. God governs the universe, but humans must make a choice for social order rather than chaos by upholding God's laws. In the polytheistic systems of the first millennium B.C.E. and later, humans constantly tried to persuade various deities to behave reasonably and not make human troubles worse than they were. By contrast, Hebrew scripture is suffused with the tension between God's promise of protection and prosperity and his people's often-faltering efforts to build a society that deserves God's blessings. This idea of a covenant between God and humankind was to be carried into Christianity and Islam, the other two faiths founded on Abraham's dedication to one god.

A Hebrew seal from Jerusalem. This stone seal dating to the seventh century B.C.E. may have belonged to a Hebrew military officer. He depicts himself as an archer and gives his name in Hebrew characters as Hagab. The decorative style shows strong Assyrian influence.

Phoenicians and Greeks: Trade and Migration

Between 1200 and 600 B.C.E., communication networks stretching from South Asia to the Atlantic Ocean became denser and more tightly interlocked. The Mediterranean basin was a particularly busy zone of commercial and cultural interaction. For the first time, sea travelers connected all the lands around the rims of the Mediterranean and the Black Seas. From ports on those seas, merchants exchanged goods with overland traders, who trekked into the deep hinterlands of Europe and northern Africa.

An important transition also took place in the conduct of trade, notably in the Mediterranean. Since at least the third millennium B.C.E., individuals engaged in commerce typically operated as employees, or agents, of rulers. They also took part in expeditions that rulers organized mainly to obtain luxury goods for temple priesthoods, royal palaces, or wealthy households. New Kingdom Egypt is a classic case of merchants acting as agents of the government, which dispatched and paid for commercial expeditions in the name of the pharaoh.

Unity and expansion, division and exile. From the tenth to the sixth centuries B.C.E., the story of the Israelites was in large part a history of state politics, war, and finally catastrophic defeat. About 1000 B.C.E., the Twelve Tribes united under King Saul. David and Solomon, Saul's successors, led the Israelites in capturing the small hill city of Jerusalem, naming it their capital, building a temple, fielding a chariot army, extending the state's borders, and encouraging trade with neighbors. Owing to unresolved conflicts among the tribes, however, the monarchy split into two following Solomon's death in 922 B.C.E., the kingdom of Judah in the south, which included Jerusalem, and the kingdom of Israel in the north.

In 722 B.C.E., however, the Assyrian army defeated Israel and sent much of its population to other parts of the empire. The Assyrians also invaded Judah, but the Israelite prophet Isaiah assured its ruler Hezekiah that "Jerusalem shall not be given into the hand of the king of Assyria."[6] Indeed, Assyria finally gave up its siege of the city, though Judah paid it tribute. Then, in 610 B.C.E., the reenergized kingdom of Babylonia eradicated Assyria and went on to capture Jerusalem and burn down its temple. The conquerors also exiled the entire Israelite population to Babylonia, ending the first long chapter in the history of the Hebrews, known increasingly from that time as the Jews.

In the early first millennium B.C.E., however, state-managed trade generally declined in importance while private enterprises multiplied. More individuals and small groups of partners traded on their own accounts as entrepreneurs, investing in private ventures with the aim of making personal profit. This change was certainly linked to the rise of both farming and urban populations around the Mediterranean rim. Ordinary people could not afford lapis lazuli jewelry or ivory statues, but they went to the local market to buy imported grain, oil, wine, or cloth. Unlike state commercial agents who served exclusively the consumer needs of the rich, private merchants had potentially much bigger markets. This encouraged them to search for new sources of goods and for new populations to sell them to. In this way, the Mediterranean web of exchange grew in all directions.

Phoenicians and their trading posts. The eastern Mediterranean lands took decades to recover from the twelfth-century B.C.E. city burnings. Assyria's imperial expansion was one sign of that recovery. Another was the commercial revival of ports on the Levantine coast, the strategic interface between the Mediterranean basin and Southwest Asia. A string of towns along the central coast (mainly in what

A Phoenician war galley. This coin from a city on the Levantine coast commemorates Phoenician naval power. In what ways might a vessel powered by rowers be tactically superior to a sailing ship in Mediterranean naval warfare?

Art from Carthage. Phoenician artisans began making terra-cotta masks like this one in the seventh century B.C.E. This grimacing male figure has decorative disks on his forehead and cheeks. Participants in religious rituals or theatrical productions may have worn the masks. Archaeologists have also found them in tombs. Why do you think a person might have wanted to be buried with a mask like this one?

is now Lebanon) somehow escaped the scourge of the Sea People. Their inhabitants, known generally as Canaanites and more specifically as Phoenicians, manufactured and traded textiles, bronzework, pottery, glassware, ivory-inlaid furniture, and other fine wares. The Phoenicians, occupying notably the ports of Tyre, Sidon, and Byblos, spoke a Semitic language closely related to Hebrew (see Map 5.3).

Phoenician merchants extended their lines of trade across the Mediterranean, motivated by both economic recovery and the rise of Assyria as a voracious consumer of metals, timber, and luxury wares. In the ninth and eighth centuries B.C.E., Phoenician vessels sailed far to the west, erecting trading posts on Sicily, Sardinia, and other islands, as well as along the coasts of North Africa and Iberia (Spain). There, Carthage and Cadiz merged as the leading centers. Phoenicians even planted several colonies west of the Strait of Gibraltar, thereby becoming the first traders to link the Mediterranean with nearby Atlantic coastlands. In return for their manufactures, Phoenician merchants shipped tons of silver from mines in Iberia, much of this precious metal reaching Egypt or Assyria. They also transported iron, copper, tin, wine, olive oil, and slaves from

numerous Mediterranean ports. Shipwrights in the Levantine ports, using cedar wood from the mountains of Lebanon, built seagoing vessels big enough to transport bulky, heavy commodities. Powered by large square sails and single or double banks of rowers, these vessels crisscrossed the Mediterranean in the summer months, when seas were usually calm and when the visible sun and stars aided navigation. In winter frequent storms and cloudy skies limited trade except close to shore.

Gradually, the Phoenician ports in the western Mediterranean loosened their ties with the Levant and emerged as independent city-states. By the eighth century B.C.E., Carthage, the key port in North Africa, ruled several satellite towns and a large area of backcountry in what is now Tunisia. The Berber-speaking farming and herding peoples of this hinterland appear to have adapted quickly to the Phoenician newcomers because they also benefited from growing maritime commerce.

The Phoenician expansion may best be understood as an early example of a **commercial diaspora,**

commercial diaspora
Merchants who share cultural identity but who live among alien communities to operate networks of trade.

that is, a scattering of merchants and their trading posts across a region where they made up only a small part of the population. Generally speaking, the members of a diaspora who settled among alien groups fulfilled two related functions. First, they acted as commercial agents for fellow merchants who moved back and forth along the maritime trade routes. These agents offered visiting traders lodging, places to store their goods, loans, up-to-date price information, and local commercial contacts. Second, they served as cultural go-betweens, learning the language, politics, and business etiquette of indigenous people in order to facilitate negotiations with local traders and help close deals. Briefly put, commercial diasporas lubricated exchange between people who otherwise lacked common speech, cultural expectations, or good reasons to trust one another. In time, diasporas took shape in many parts of the world where long-distance trade was important.

Greeks and their colonies. Greek-speaking merchants and migrants also moved out across the Mediterranean. At least partly because of the devastations of Sea People, the early Mycenaean Greek civilization with its mighty citadels and splendid tombs (see Chapter 3) disappeared. From about 900 B.C.E., however, the region bounced back. Its high-quality wine, olive oil, figs, and pottery enjoyed rising demand in the wider Mediterranean world, and Aegean land-owners raised more crops for export. The richest families also led reconstruction of cities, which well-disciplined, sword-wielding militias of local farmers defended. Partly owing to its rugged

coasts, narrow mountain valleys, and numerous islands, the Aegean rim remained politically fragmented. Here and there, however, local kings or alliances of aristocratic families organized strong civic governments. They built walls around their towns, erected temples dedicated to the city's patron god or goddess, and taxed the wealth that farmers of the surrounding countryside generated. The Greeks called this type of state the **polis** (POH-lis), a city-centered community founded on the claim that its citizens were all kin of one another and mutually dedicated to self-rule. From *polis* (plural, *poleis*), we derive the words *politics, political,* and *politician*.

> **polis (plural, poleis)** The ancient Greek term for a sovereign state centered on a single city; a city-state.

As population increased and farmers put more good land to wine and olive production, wheat and other staple foods had to be imported from afar. Moreover, as we have seen, intensive farming and grazing on steep hillsides gradually depleted soil. Unable to make land much more productive, many Aegean city-states organized schemes to resettle groups of citizens on new farms abroad. In the eighth century B.C.E., numerous bands of pioneers moved to eastern Sicily and southern Italy, founding colonies on coastal plains that were broader and more fertile than around the Aegean. Other migrants went farther afield, settling in northern Libya and along the southern coast of what is today France and Spain. To the northeast, Greek farmers colonized coastlands of the Black Sea, a region that from their perspective was a kind of gigantic lagoon

Ruins of a Greek colony. Greek migrants from the Aegean island of Thera (Santorini) founded the colony of Cyrene in northern Libya in the late seventh century B.C.E. It thrived as a Mediterranean commercial center for about a thousand years.

of the Mediterranean reaching deep into the plains of Inner Eurasia.

Greek colonization naturally produced merchants as well as farmers. In the poleis of the Aegean homeland, most traders were noncitizen immigrants or visitors from other regions. Called *metics,* this social class did not have rights to own land or take part in civic life. Partly because of these restrictions, *metics* flourished in trade, creating their own commercial diaspora that, like the Phoenicians, operated in distant parts of the Mediterranean and that knitted the Aegean home city-states and the colonies together.

By the sixth century B.C.E., the number of Greek speakers living and trading outside the relatively small part of southeastern Europe that is today the Republic of Greece probably significantly exceeded the number that lived within it. One important consequence of this dispersion was that a fairly uniform style of Greek urban culture emerged across a large part of the Mediterranean–Black Sea region. We look in more detail at Greek political organization and culture in Chapter 6.

Phoenicians, Greeks, and alphabetic writing. The earliest known alphabets emerged among speakers of Semitic languages in the Levant and Syria in the later second millennium B.C.E. Scribes based in Mediterranean ports experimented with several forms of writing, inventing sound-based signs that drew inspiration from symbols used in both Egyptian hieroglyphic and Mesopotamian cuneiform systems. We associate alphabetic writing especially with the Phoenicians because the particular set of signs they used from about 1200 B.C.E. attracted wide interest. Within two hundred years, the Phoenicians passed their system on to Greek scholars and eventually to the wider Mediterranean world.

As we described earlier (see Chapter 2), both Mesopotamian cuneiform writing and Egyptian hieroglyphics incorporated signs that represented logograms, which are symbols that stand for meanings (one or more whole words). They also included large numbers of signs that stood for syllables. Since humans can make hundreds of syllable sounds by combining different consonants with different vowels, this type of system, especially combined with logograms, required many signs. Modern Chinese, for example, is basically a logographic system with thousands of individual characters that represent whole words (units of meaning rather than units of sound), plus phonetic elements to aid pronunciation. Functional literacy in Chinese requires learning about three thousand distinct characters.

The Phoenician alphabetic system, by contrast, had only twenty-two signs. These were arranged in a particular order, as is our modern alphabet. But this early system included only consonants, not vowels. A reader pronounced a particular word correctly—adding the right vowels—by recognizing the word from the context of words that came before and after it, that is, by the intended meaning of a passage. For example, if the English alphabet did not have

vowels, a reader could still identify the sequence of consonants "frmr" as meaning "farmer" rather than "firmer" by the context of surrounding words. (Today people routinely use text messaging shorthand that omits vowels.) The modern Arabic and Hebrew alphabets, which emerged in the same general region as Phoenician, have no letters for vowels, only special marks that may be inserted to clarify pronunciation. However, when Greek scribes appropriated the Phoenician system, they added two new consonants and six signs for vowel sounds, a system that inspired Latin.

Scribes in the Neo-Assyrian empire composed texts on clay tablets or in stone using cuneiform, but they also wrote documents in Aramaic, which used an alphabet. We have no physical remains of these early Aramaic texts because scribes used perishable writing surfaces. But we know what they were doing from cuneiform tablet descriptions and from pictures of Aramaic scholars at work. Some historians think that Aramaic inspired the alphabet that came into use in northern India to write Sanskrit, the Indo-European language that priests and teachers used. In any case, by 600 B.C.E. alphabetic writing was spreading rapidly from the Mediterranean to South Asia.

Woodland Europe and the Mediterranean World

At the start of the first millennium B.C.E., the most culturally complex societies of inland Europe lay along a belt of heavily forested territory extending from modern Switzerland eastward to Hungary. That region had no centralized states, but people built stout hill forts, buried their chiefs with costly grave goods, and worked expertly in bronze, silver, and gold. Also, farming and cattle-keeping peoples who spoke a number of different languages in the Indo-European family continued to move from western Inner Eurasia to territories west of the Black Sea (see Chapter 3).

Prominent among Indo-European migrants were the ancestral speakers of Italic languages, from which Latin later derived, as well as the Celtic-speaking peoples, who by 600 B.C.E. probably occupied most of western Europe. Celtic clans whose warriors carried bronze weaponry, rode horses and transported their families on lumbering wagons, arrived in Iberia by the seventh century B.C.E. They reached Britain and Ireland on boats or rafts not long after that. These newcomers probably came to politically dominate the earlier populations of western Europe. In time, Indo-European languages displaced all preexisting ones across central and western Europe. The only exception is Basque, an ancient tongue still spoken in the Pyrenees Mountain region between France and Spain.

Once Phoenician and Greek merchants entered the western Mediterranean, the pace of change in Europe accelerated. These sea traders wanted Europe's silver, copper, tin, iron, and lumber, exchanging them for Mediterranean wine, oil, fine ceramics, and finished ironware, which went mainly to the families of woodland clan chiefs. The

Mediterranean network linked to inland Europe along a number of passages, for example the Guadalquivir River in Iberia, the Rhône River in France, high passes across the Alps, and, from very early times, the Danube River, which connected western Europe to the Black Sea. Europe's elite groups, installed in their hill forts, aimed to control the flow of trade across their territories, thereby enriching themselves, elevating their social status, and founding modest kingdoms.

Almost no serious urbanization took place north of the Alps until after 600 B.C.E., but in the plains and river valleys of northern Italy a cluster of impressive city-states emerged as early as the ninth century B.C.E. in tandem with growing commercial activity in the central Mediterranean. Possessing rich mineral and agricultural resources, the Etruscans, a people of the region of Etruria in north central Italy, traded widely by land and sea. From the sixth to the fourth centuries B.C.E., they controlled the trade routes across the Alps. Organized in a loose confederation of city-states, they also competed with both Phoenician and Greek colonies for commercial advantage in the western Mediterranean.

Recent archaeological work suggests that Etruscan society emerged gradually from older populations of Italy. They adopted a variant of the Greek alphabet, which they passed on to the Romans. Etruscan society was remarkably innovative, building efficient iron smelters, crafting exquisite objects in gold and silver, inventing the "Roman arch" before the Romans did, and mastering engineering skills necessary to transform low-lying marshland into productive farms. We also know something about Etruscan daily life from their elite tombs, which display not only numerous grave goods but also wall paintings. These depict people eating together, priests conducting rituals, and women and men socializing casually. The general impression is that Etruscan society, in some respects like the earlier Minoan civilization on Crete (see Chapter 3), allowed greater social freedoms to women than was the case in Greek city-state culture.

Nubia on the Nile Corridor

Looking at a physical map of the Mediterranean and Black Sea regions, we might think of the Nile, like the Rhône or the Danube, as a watery arm of the sea, extending lines of exchange deep inland. The Nile in fact linked the Mediterranean to parts of Africa nearly two thousand miles upriver. Along this avenue, merchants carried an array of wares from the Mediterranean world to Nubia, the region that is today southern Egypt and northern Sudan. The return trade included gold, ivory, ebony, incense, cattle, hides, and slaves.

The Nile was also Main Street of the pharaoh's command system. As a general pattern, when the Egyptian state was strong and secure, the kings pushed their authority upriver. When it weakened or fell into crisis, they retreated closer to the Mediterranean, leaving Nubia alone. Similarly, the influence of Egyptian institutions, elite culture, and hieroglyphic writing on Nubian aristocrats waxed and waned depending on the state of things downriver. During the New Kingdom's imperial expansion between the fifteenth and thirteenth centuries B.C.E., the pharaohs dominated the Nubian state of Kush (see Chapter 3) and dispatched armed expeditions deep into the region. In the twelfth century, however, when the pharaohs were busy fighting Libyans and Sea People, Kush reasserted its independence. Nubian kings moved their capital from Kerma (in the northern part of modern Sudan) another two hundred miles up the Nile to Napata, thus distancing themselves further from meddling pharaohs.

In fact, Kush prospered so well from grain production, cattle raising, and trade that about 735 B.C.E. its armies accumulated sufficient power to turn the tables and invade Egypt. Taking advantage of political conflicts that had plagued that land since the twelfth century B.C.E., Kushite forces overpowered the pharaoh's armies and established what became known as the twenty-fifth dynasty (see

A reclining Etruscan couple. This terra-cotta sarcophagus dating to the sixth century B.C.E. takes the shape of a dining couch. It would have contained the cremated remains of this married couple. What might the representation of the two figures tell us about social relations between spouses in Etruscan society?

Map 5.3). Piye, Kush's conquering monarch (r. 747–716 B.C.E.), had his exploits inscribed on a granite stele (slab or pillar). One passage tells of his seizure of the great city of Memphis located just south of the Nile delta:

> Then he sent forth his fleet and his army to assault the harbor of Memphis; they brought to him every ferry-boat, every cargo-boat, every transport, and the ships, as many as there were, which had moored in the harbor. . . . Then Memphis was taken as by a flood of water, a multitude of people were slain therein, and others were brought as living captives to the place where his majesty was. . . . Then the ships were laden with silver, gold, copper, clothing, and everything of the Northland, every product of Syria, and all sweet woods of God's-land. His majesty sailed up-stream, with glad heart.[7]

For a short time after this, a huge Nile-centered state stretched all the way from southern Nubia to the Mediterranean. Political unity on such a scale must surely have intensified commercial and cultural exchange along the Nile corridor. We know, for example, that the Kushite ruling class, wishing to represent itself as the rightful heirs to New Kingdom glory, adopted Egyptian deities, court rituals, and art forms. The dynasty lasted, however, no more

A Nubian pharaoh. This sphinx in pharaonic head cloth represents Taharqo, the third member of the Nubian dynasty that ruled Egypt for seventy-seven years. Found in the ruins of a temple in Kawa, Sudan, the sphinx stands less than 30 inches high.

than half a century. When the Assyrians attacked the lower Nile valley in 671 B.C.E., Nubian forces had to withdraw. The Kushite defeat apparently taught them at least one good lesson, the effectiveness of iron weaponry. Starting in the late seventh century B.C.E., iron-making industries bloomed along the Nubian Nile, with obvious advantages to farming and trade. Kush thus survived and prospered once again, a story to which we return in Chapter 7.

South Asia: A New Era of City Building

FOCUS How were major historical developments in South Asia between 1200 and 600 B.C.E. similar to or different from developments in Southwest Asia?

In the first millennium B.C.E., iron-making technology almost certainly spread from Southeast Asia to South Asia, as did knowledge of alphabetic writing. However, the network of east–west land routes connecting the two regions remained thinner than the complex of threads integrating Southwest Asia with the Mediterranean basin. One reason for the difference is that the great urban civilization of the Indus River valley withered gradually after 1900 B.C.E. (see Chapter 2). Another was that overland travel involved crossing nearly two thousand miles of deserts, arid plateaus, and rugged mountains, regions of modern Afghanistan and Iran that were not yet heavily peopled or urbanized.

However, within South Asia, population growth, urbanization, and commercial exchange accelerated significantly in the early first millennium B.C.E. After about 1700 B.C.E., herders who spoke Indo-European languages in the Indic subgroup of tongues that includes Hindi, Punjabi, and several other modern languages moved slowly from the Indus valley eastward to the Ganges River plain (see Chapter 3). Northern India's earlier populations were probably speakers of much more ancient Dravidian languages. They were farmers, foragers, and inhabitants of a few small cities that endured following the decline of Harappan civilization. Gradually, most of the Indic-speaking newcomers turned from herding to farming, and they likely intermarried extensively with people already there. After iron-smelting technology arrived, farmers had more durable tools to clear the subtropical forests that flourished in the Ganges valley. Iron axes combined with controlled burning to clear land opened huge expanses of northern India to farming—wheat and barley in the western plains and rice in the moist country along the lower Ganges. More intensive farming and faster population growth in this region had three notable consequences: the emergence of new cities and small states, the creation of a complex social class system, and the development of Brahmanism, the belief system forming part of the foundation of the Hindu tradition.

New Cities and Kingdoms

Between the second and first millennia B.C.E. a general shift took place from the Indus valley to the Ganges as the center of population growth. From about 800 B.C.E., small cities began to spring up on the Ganges plain, a development that coincided approximately in time with the appearance of Phoenician and Greek towns in the central and western Mediterranean (see Map 5.4).

Set behind defensive mud-brick walls, some of North India's new urban centers became the capitals of small monarchies, whose ruling groups accumulated wealth by taxing landholders and collecting customs duties from merchants. With this treasure, they recruited armed forces of infantry and horse soldiers. Despite continuing assimilation between Indic language speakers and older populations, the elite families who organized these states took pride in claiming descent from Indo-European warrior groups that had penetrated the region in earlier centuries. Known as *kshatriyas* (kuh-SHAT-tree-uhs), an Indic word related to "power," these families became the dominant political class of North India. Among the sixteen or so kingdoms that emerged after 800 B.C.E., Magadha in the middle Ganges valley became the most powerful one. According to the *Mahabharata*, India's epic historical poem compiled in later

centuries in Sanskrit, the Magadha capital, located on high ground overlooking the Ganges plain, commanded the allegiance of eighty thousand villages.

The Development of the South Asian Class System

Like complex societies in other parts of the world, those that emerged in South Asia in the first millennium B.C.E. featured a hierarchy of social classes, a small privileged class occupying the top rank. In South Asia, however, class differentiations and rules evolved in particularly elaborate and formal ways. From ancient Indian texts, we learn about the mythology that explains and justifies the social system but not much about how it actually evolved.

According to the *Rig Veda*, the collection of Indic prayers and hymns that was transmitted orally for hundreds of years and first transcribed in Sanskrit about 400 B.C.E., the primal Cosmic Person (*Purusha*) generated four classes of Indians in descending order of intrinsic purity. The purest was the priestly class called Brahmins. Their principal functions were to protect and preserve fundamental cultural values, to transmit those values to the young, and to perform sacrificial rituals essential to honor and satisfy numerous deities. Second in the hierarchy were the Kshatriyas, or governing and fighting class of Indic warrior heritage. The Kshatriya class collaborated with the Brahmins, upholding their ritual and teaching authority and sharing with them much agricultural wealth. Members of the third-ranked

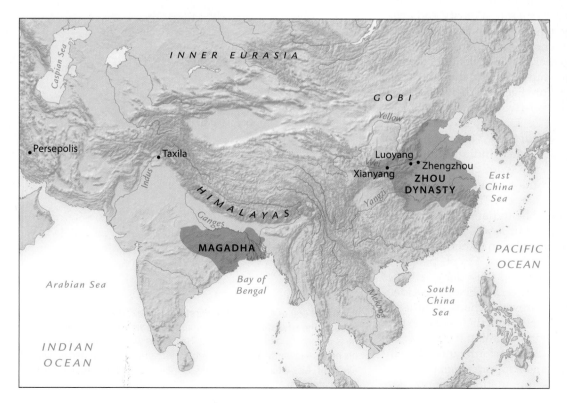

MAP 5.4 States of South and East Asia, 800–600 B.C.E.

Why do you think direct overland trade between China and the western side of South Asia remained less important in premodern centuries than exchange by the much longer maritime route between the South China Sea and the Bay of Bengal?

class were Vaishyas (VEYES-yuhs), the farmers, herders, merchants, and artisans who produced the food, fiber, manufactures, and commercial institutions that society required. The Shudras (SHOO-druhs), the fourth and least pure class, were destined to serve the other three groups as menial laborers. The Brahmins sanctioned this hierarchy, which stipulated that membership in one of the four classes was divinely ordained and determined by birth. A fifth segment of society also emerged, called Panchamas, or "fifths." It may have originated among foraging and hunting peoples that Indic-speaking newcomers regarded as hopelessly barbaric and therefore wholly unclean. Brahmin teaching declared this group to be "untouchable," its members consigned to living apart from the rest of society and to carrying out the most polluted tasks such as cleaning latrines and moving corpses.

In the course of the first millennium B.C.E. and later, Indian society established numerous social rules to ensure each of the four classes followed its dharma (DHUHR-muh), the ritual duties, occupations, privileges, and daily behavior specifically assigned to it. All formal relations among classes and the boundaries between them came to be expressed in the language of ritual purity and impurity. Depending on their class affiliations, individuals were born relatively polluted or unpolluted, but they could pollute themselves more, at least temporarily, by failing to fulfill their class duties or by physical contact with people of lower rank. For example, at some point Brahmins determined that they should not wear footwear or other clothing made of leather because leatherworking occupations involved dead animals and blood. The effort to maintain purity and avoid pollution came to determine who should have which occupations, who should marry whom, and who should be allowed to eat or socialize together. As time went on, the four major class divisions split into numerous smaller groups, or *jatis,* based mainly on occupation. Each *jati* then subscribed to its own customs and taboos relative to other groups.

caste A social class more or less rigidly separated from other classes by distinctions of heredity, occupation, wealth, or degree of ritual purity.

In the sixteenth century C.E., Europeans who visited India began to use the word *caste* to describe the social system they observed. That term came to be firmly associated with India. The Indian social structure there became increasingly rigid, but it was only relatively less flexible than social pecking orders in other premodern complex societies. In Southwest Asia or Egypt, people of high rank would likely have defended their domination of the rest of the population in similar terms: Fixed class identity promotes social order and prevents chaos in times of change, it ensures that people know what their social expectations are, all social classes are important in the eyes of the gods in terms of the functions they perform, and all members of society enjoy solidarity and support *within* their own group. In an era of expanding population, urbanization,

and commerce, India's developing social system, in which all men and women knew their proper place in society and how to behave toward one another, was fundamentally rational, even though it was unbending, discriminatory, and repressive from a modern democratic perspective.

Brahmins and Brahmanism

Closely linked to the ideology of social class, Brahmanism emerged as a cluster of religious teachings and practices across northern India after 1000 B.C.E. Formulated by the Brahmin class, this belief system developed as a complex blending of Indic and ancient indigenous beliefs, some of them perhaps associated with the earlier Harappan civilization of the Indus valley (see Chapter 2). Brahmins assumed authority over religious routines, including both devotional rituals and the supervision of the duties and prohibitions for all social groups. Among thousands of gods and goddesses that South Asians venerated, certain divinities acquired

Indra, the god of rain and thunderstorms. The *Rig Veda* describes Indra as the king of the gods and courageous warrior. In this painting he is covered with all-seeing eyes. He carries weapons in three of his hands—swords and a thunderbolt. Indra is often depicted on his elephant, Airavata. How might images of Indra, Vishnu, and other gods have communicated ideas about Hindu beliefs?

multifaceted qualities and rose to prominence in the religious imagination. Vishnu (VIHSH-noo), preserver of the world, and Shiva (SHEE-vuh), creator and destroyer of the world, emerged as dominant, though they had a variety of names and manifestations. The Brahmanic religious tradition took on varying forms from one part of South Asia to another and readily incorporated numerous local religious ideas. It had neither a centralized religious organization nor a specific set of doctrines that adherents were expected to follow.

Nevertheless, this dense thicket of beliefs and devotions gradually incorporated a concrete body of teachings that gave deeper meaning to daily rituals. Early Brahmanic theology is known to us mainly from the *Upanishads* (oo-pah-NIH-shuhds), a collection of sacred texts composed in Sanskrit. These texts, which emerged between about 800 and 500 B.C.E., expounded the idea of Brahman, the infinite, sublime essence of the universe. Brahman is the divine principle of all being, the tradition proclaims, and this transcendent "all-ness" includes the soul of every individual. Brahman is god but may nonetheless appear in innumerable personal manifestations, including incarnation as Vishnu, Shiva, or any other deity.

For South Asians, performance of rituals and duties became one dimension of the supreme quest to achieve oneness with divine reality. Spiritual fulfillment, however, required obedience to the moral law of the universe, which, like class duties, was also called dharma. Success or failure at living in harmony with dharma determined how many times an individual might be subjected to death and rebirth as a being of higher or lower social rank or even as an animal. Progress was governed by karma, the principle that the right deeds done in a lifetime conditioned an individual's happiness in the next one. Reincarnation (*samsara*) became fundamental to the Brahmanic tradition. So too did the moral imperative to escape this illusory world with all its pain and disappointment by eventually attaining spiritual salvation in unification with Brahman.

Brahmanism, though extremely diverse in thought and devotional practice, was the earliest belief system to exhibit at least some characteristics of a "world religion." In contrast to the Israelite faith, that is, early Judaism, as well as to most local religions in ancient times, Brahmanic ideas attracted people across a wide spectrum of linguistic and class groups as a foundation for social relations, shared moral expectations, and spiritual hope. That is, Brahmanism was not limited to a group claiming a particular ethnic identity. We should not, however, equate the Brahmanic tradition with Hinduism (related to the word *Indus,* thus to *India*). Most historians assert that Indian religious experience linked historically to Brahmanism remained extremely diverse until the modern era.

The East Asian Sphere

FOCUS What evidence documents the expansion of complex agrarian society in China in the era of the Zhou dynasty?

The East Asian lands centered on the Yellow and Yangzi River valleys grew steadily in population and agrarian wealth during these centuries, despite great political and military commotion (see Map 5.4). The Shang dynasty emerged about 1600 B.C.E. as the first monarchy to exercise power over a large part of northern China (see Chapter 3). The Shang expired, however, between 1050 and 1045 B.C.E., when the nobles of a small vassal state called Zhou attacked and dethroned their Shang overlords. Sima Qian, the illustrious Chinese historian of the second century B.C.E., wrote about the Shang collapse nearly a thousand years after it happened. He may have worked through layers of mythology about those distant times, but he claims that the last Shang king lost all support because he oppressed his people, committed moral offenses, and had opponents roasted alive.

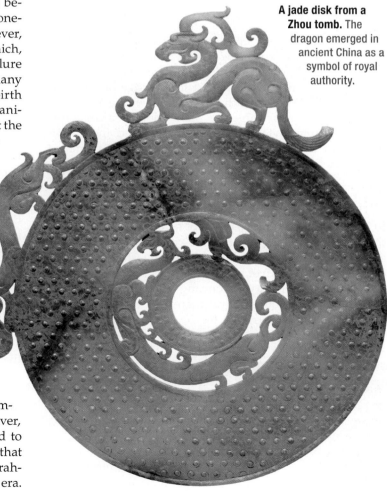

A jade disk from a Zhou tomb. The dragon emerged in ancient China as a symbol of royal authority.

The Era of the Western and Eastern Zhou

The Zhou dynasty (1045–256 B.C.E.), whose homeland was somewhere west of the Shang capital, proclaimed that it rightfully seized power because the emperor had lost the Mandate of Heaven. This was the concept that royal authority derived from a supreme moral force, called *tian* (TEE-ehn), or "heaven," which governed the universe. By being just and fair, a ruler demonstrated to his subjects that he possessed the Mandate of Heaven. If he was despotic and mean, he risked losing that mandate, a failing that would lead to natural disasters and social crises. In such circumstances, people were entitled to rise up in rebellion to replace an oppressive or incompetent monarch with someone more virtuous. From Zhou times onward, the idea that the monarch (the Son of Heaven) had public moral obligations sanctioned by cosmic power became part of the fabric of Chinese political culture. Whether they behaved virtuously or not, however, most rulers reigned until they died and passed on their power to a son or other male relative. Nonetheless, the Chinese ideal of moral worthiness tended to curb the worst excesses of kings and, on occasion, served as popular justification for rebellion against a despot. This ideal of the virtuous ruler was a key element of the moral and ethical doctrines of Confucianism, which we explore in Chapter 7.

In the ninth and eighth centuries B.C.E., at the same time that Assyria was expanding across Southwest Asia, Zhou infantry and charioteers built a state even larger than the Shang realm, pushing northwest to the edge of the Inner Eurasian steppes and south to the valley of the Yangzi. In contrast to the Assyrians, the Zhou adopted a decentralized governing style. The monarchs divided the empire into about fifty territories, appointing family members, loyal lieutenants, or local chiefs to govern them. These lords owed the Son of Heaven tribute and military service, but they kept their own armies and lands.

This system worked quite well for nearly three centuries. In 771 B.C.E., however, a coalition of rebellious vassals killed the king, terminating what is known as the Western Zhou state. The royal family fled from Xianyang (shan-yahng), its capital on the Wei River, about 700 miles east to a new center near the modern city of Luoyang. The dynasty survived, but the Eastern Zhou, as it was thereafter known, ruled directly only a small territory. By the fifth century B.C.E., the more powerful of regional princes no longer bothered to acknowledge even the ceremonial sovereignty of the Zhou monarch. From then until the late third century B.C.E., East Asia experienced the Warring States period (475–221 B.C.E.), when these regional rulers fought periodically with one another for territory and resources.

Destruction and Innovation during the Later Zhou Period

A general pattern noticeable in world history is that intense rivalry among several states in a region has often tended to stimulate rather than stifle technical innovation. East Asian rulers who competed with one another experimented with new tools and weapons to gain advantage over their rivals. Like the Assyrians, Chinese commanders gradually abandoned the chariot in favor of infantry and mounted archers. Cavalry troops almost certainly acquired equestrian skills from the pastoral nomads who inhabited the arid steppes northwest of the Wei and Yellow Rivers. In the seventh century B.C.E., iron-smelting industries spread across northern China, gradually supplementing bronze weaponry with iron swords and projectiles.

Along with these new destructive capabilities, which no single state could monopolize, came productive strategies for building alliances, thereby preventing endless conflict. In the aftermath of the Zhou decline, Chinese regional states created something of an "international" system similar to the one that came together in Southwest Asia in the late second millennium B.C.E. Ruling families intermarried with one another, exchanged envoys, and negotiated truces.

The tumultuous times prompted new approaches to class relationships as well. Especially after the eighth century B.C.E., rulers needed to conscript large numbers of people of the farming class, which was most of the population, to build defensive walls, fight as massed infantry, or otherwise provide military labor. One consequence was that ambitious rulers had to recognize more than in earlier times the needs and aspirations of ordinary men and women. In the Shang era, a form of **serfdom** had been common. In the Zhou period, this institution declined gradually.

> **serfdom** A system of labor in which farmers were legally bound to work for and pay fees to a particular landlord in return for protection and rights to cultivate land.

More farmers became independent land-owners or offered their labor services on the open market, a trend that surely contributed to rising productivity and improved living standards. On occasion, rulers also looked beyond the elite class for bureaucratic and military talent, recruiting at least some of their officers and administrators for their intelligence and loyalty rather than merely for their aristocratic birth.

Economic growth and innovation accompanied the constant fighting of later Zhou times. Arable land in the Yellow

ZHOU DYNASTY	
1050–1045 B.C.E.	Zhou state overthrows Shang dynasty
770 B.C.E.	Western Zhou state falls; Eastern Zhou period begins
475–221 B.C.E.	Warring States period
256 B.C.E.	End of Zhou dynasty

The Book of Songs (Shijing)

One of the most precious sources we have of the lives of ordinary women and men in the Zhou era is The Book of Songs (Shijing), *a collection of 305 poems and hymns compiled over several centuries. The earliest of the poems dates to about 1000 B.C.E. The contents of* The Book of Songs *range from poems lauding the achievements of early Zhou rulers to folk songs outlining the daily routines of rural peasants. Many of the verses describe and celebrate farming life, in the purposeful seasonal routines that continued no matter the rise and fall of emperors. Though the origins of the poems are unclear, one traditional explanation is that the Western Zhou imperial court sent officials to newly conquered territories to record the lyrics of popular songs. When the Zhou king received these songs, he read them to try to understand the hearts and minds, as well as the daily lives, of the people he ruled.*

They clear away the grass, the trees;
Their ploughs open up the ground.
In a thousand pairs they tug at weeds and roots,
Along the low ground, along the ridges.
There is the master and his eldest son,
There the headman and overseer.
They mark out, they plough.
Deep the food-baskets that are brought;
Dainty are the wives,
The men press close to them.
And now with shares so sharp
They set to work upon the southern acre.
They sow the many sorts of grain,
The seeds that hold moist life.
How the blade shoots up,
How sleek, the grown plant;
Very sleek, the young grain!
Band on band, the weeders ply their task.

Now they reap, all in due order;
Close-packed are their stooks [piles of cut grain ready for
   threshing]—
Myriads, many myriads and millions,
To make wine, make sweet liquor,
As offering to ancestor and ancestress,
For fulfillment of all the rites.
"When sweet the fragrance of offering,
Glory shall come to the fatherland.
When pungent the scent,
The blessed elders are at rest."
Not only here is it like this,
Not only now is it so.
From long ago it has been thus.

Source: Arthur Waley, trans. and Joseph R. Allen, ed., *The Book of Songs (Shijing): The Ancient Chinese Classic of Poetry* (New York: Grove Press, 1996), pp. xxi, 304.

Thinking Critically

Who is mentioned as involved in farming in this poem? What are the relationships among those taking part in the work? What lines do you see in the poem that connect the harvest with religious belief? What religious ritual is mentioned? What sense of time and place do you think are conveyed in the final three lines? According to a traditional Chinese adage, "The sky is high and the emperor is far away." How might you link this saying to the sentiment expressed in this poem?

. . . .

and Yangzi River valleys increased dramatically as a result of marsh draining, use of iron tools, and farming by **freeholders,** who had strong incentives to increase their yields of millet, wheat, or rice. By the sixth century B.C.E., Chinese farmers were turning the soil with sturdy plows tipped with cast iron and pulled by oxen. They planted crops in neat rows that could be tended more easily and weeded fields with cast iron

freeholders Farmers who own the land they cultivate.

hoes. None of these methods was known outside of East Asia until centuries later. Increasing use of bronze coins of various shapes also signaled an expanding market economy in which sellers and buyers needed a convenient medium of exchange to supplement bartering of goods. In cultural life, artisans of the Zhou era continued to make exquisite objects of bronze, jade, and ceramic. Scholars achieved new refinements of the Chinese writing system, and the earliest known works of poetry and history appeared.

Conclusion

In the period this chapter has explored, interaction among human communities across Afroeurasia grew more intense and complicated than in the previous millennium or in fact in any period before that. More complex networks of interchange followed directly from accelerating population growth. Afroeurasia's numbers grew on average 3 percent faster per century in the first millennium B.C.E. than in the previous two thousand years. The world's population, most of whom lived in Afroeurasia, may have nearly doubled during that millennium, rising to about 250 million.[8] What we call *extensive* population growth took place when people who grew crops or herded animals spread across a large region, raising its population fairly evenly across space. In the 1200–600 B.C.E. period, this phenomenon was especially noticeable in central and southern Africa, the Inner Eurasian steppes, and woodland Europe. In other places, by contrast, growth was *intensive,* meaning that numbers increasing dramatically in relatively limited areas where farming and trade could support more and more people. Population density continued to rise in the older river valley centers of Mesopotamia, Egypt, and northern China. But new clusters of intensive growth also appeared, for example, in the Ganges valley, the Aegean Sea basin, Italy, Nubia on the Nile, East Africa's Great Lakes region, and tropical Southeast Asia. In some places intensive growth involved urbanization (see Map 5.5). One compilation of estimates suggests that, in 1200 B.C.E., the world's sixteen largest cities ranged in population from 24,000 to 50,000. By 650 B.C.E., the populations of the twenty largest cities varied from 30,000 to 120,000, totaling 894,000 inhabitants.[9]

As we have seen, technical and intellectual developments of the period facilitated the growth of exchange networks. Iron metallurgy animated farming and therefore both population growth and incentives for commerce. Across Afroeurasia, smelters turned out thousands of new products of wrought or cast iron, stimulating local and long-distance trade. The invention of alphabetic scripts made it easier for scholars to share knowledge and for manufacturers and merchants to exchange business information over long distances. Diasporas of merchants who shared language, business customs, and trust lubricated the wheels of commerce, notably in the Mediterranean basin. Equestrians continually experimented with horse breeding and riding gear, which contributed to the advent of cavalry warfare and wider use of horses to move goods and transmit information.

To be sure, the Afroeurasian exchange web was in an early stage of development. Trade across the Inner Eurasian steppes was still thin and tentative. The Sahara Desert remained a forbidding deterrent to links between the Mediterranean and tropical Africa. Indian Ocean mariners continued to fear sailing too far from land. Foragers or farmers living in small communities in far southwestern Africa, the Arctic north, deep tropical forests, or high mountain valleys remained isolated from more than local routes of trade. In the following several centuries, however, people impelled by commerce, conquest, or the search for land strengthened more weak links and filled more voids.

• • •

Key Terms

authoritarian monarchy 144	Hebrew Bible 144	polis (plural, poleis) 149
biomass 139	Judaism 144	polytheism 145
Brahmanism 154	Kush 151	Sea People 140
caste 154	Magadha 153	serfdom 156
cavalry 142	Mandate of Heaven 156	The Book of Songs (Shijing) 157
commercial diaspora 148	metics 150	Upanishads 155
early iron age 137	monotheism 144	Warring States period 156
Etruscan city-states 151	Neo-Assyrian empire 142	Zhou dynasty 156
freeholders 157	Phoenician trading posts 147	

Change over Time

1400–1200 B.C.E.	The first alphabets are invented.
1200 B.C.E.	Iron metallurgy starts to spread across Afroeurasia (early iron age).
1200 B.C.E.	Sea People begin widespread attacks in the eastern Mediterranean.
1045–256 B.C.E.	The Zhou dynasty rules in China; its rulers claim the Mandate of Heaven.
1000 B.C.E.	An Israelite state is established in the Levant, laying the foundations of monotheistic Judaism; Brahmanism develops across northern India.
934–610 B.C.E.	The Neo-Assyrian empire unites the whole region from the Tigris-Euphrates to the Nile.
9th century B.C.E.	Etruscan city-states emerge in Italy and control trade routes across the Alps.
9th–8th centuries B.C.E.	Phoenician merchants erect trading posts along the Mediterranean coast; Carthage, among other ports, emerges as an independent city-state.
8th century B.C.E.	New cities emerge in the Ganges River valley in India; the largest is Magadha.
747–671 B.C.E.	Monarchs of Kush rule Nubia and Egypt as the Twenty-Fifth dynasty.

Please see end of book reference section for additional reading suggestions related to this chapter.

Empire Building and Cultural Exchange from India to the Mediterranean

600–200 B.C.E.

The Greek voyager Pytheas may have sailed northern European seas on a ship resembling this gold model from an ancient hoard found in northern Ireland.

Near the end of the fourth century B.C.E., a Greek-speaking official named Megasthenes traveled more than two thousand miles on a diplomatic mission from the Seleucid (sih-LOO-sid) empire in Southwest Asia to the court of the king Chandragupta in northern India. The ambassador settled for a time in the royal capital, where he carefully observed Indian society and politics. Later, he compiled his observations in a literary work titled the *Indika*. The surviving fragments of this text constitute the only eyewitness record we have of life in India during that period.

About the same time that Megasthenes traveled east, a Greek navigator named Pytheas boarded a sailing vessel at Massalia (Marseilles) on the Mediterranean coast of what is today France. He and his crew sailed west through the Strait of Gibraltar to the Atlantic, then north to Britain. Perhaps he aimed to trade with Celtic-speaking people in northern Europe. After circumnavigating Britain, he returned to Massalia to write a report of his travels. In his account he described an island called Thule Ultima, possibly Iceland, where midsummer days lasted twenty hours. He also included practical information on such subjects as the position of the North Pole and the correlation between tides and the phases of the moon.

The careers of Megasthenes and Pytheas vividly illustrate the far-flung activities of Greek-speaking people between the sixth and third centuries B.C.E. Greeks (known as "Hellenes" in the ancient world) were on the move, strengthening colonial settlements along the shores of the Mediterranean and Black Seas, plying long-distance trade, and offering their skills abroad as scholars, artisans, and soldiers. In the Aegean Sea basin, the Hellenic city-states of Athens, Sparta, and several others achieved impressive economic and military power.

The explosion of Greeks onto the world scene was one sign of intensifying human communication across Afroeurasia as a whole. Population continued to grow, more cities appeared, and migrating farmers and herders moved into new territories in Inner Eurasia and the tropical latitudes of Africa and Asia. The greatest concentrations of both cultivators and city dwellers were to be found in two regions: in the zone from the Ganges River valley to the lands rimming the eastern Mediterranean and in northern and central China. Throughout most of those four hundred years, China continued on a long trajectory of technological advancement and commercial growth but remained politically fragmented. We come back to East Asia in Chapter 7.

• • •

This chapter opens on the rise of the Achaemenid (uh-KEE-muh-nid) empire of Persia, the largest state in both territory and population that the world had so far seen. On the Iranian plateau east of Mesopotamia, people speaking Persian (Farsi) founded the Achaemenid dynasty around 550 B.C.E. Persian horse troops and infantry seized the territories of the former Assyrian and Babylonian empires, and for several decades in the sixth and fifth centuries, Achaemenid governors ruled provinces stretching from northwestern India to Libya west of the Nile. For the first time in history, the three great river valleys—Tigris-Euphrates, Nile, and Indus—were incorporated into a single state, if only briefly. With this

A Panoramic View

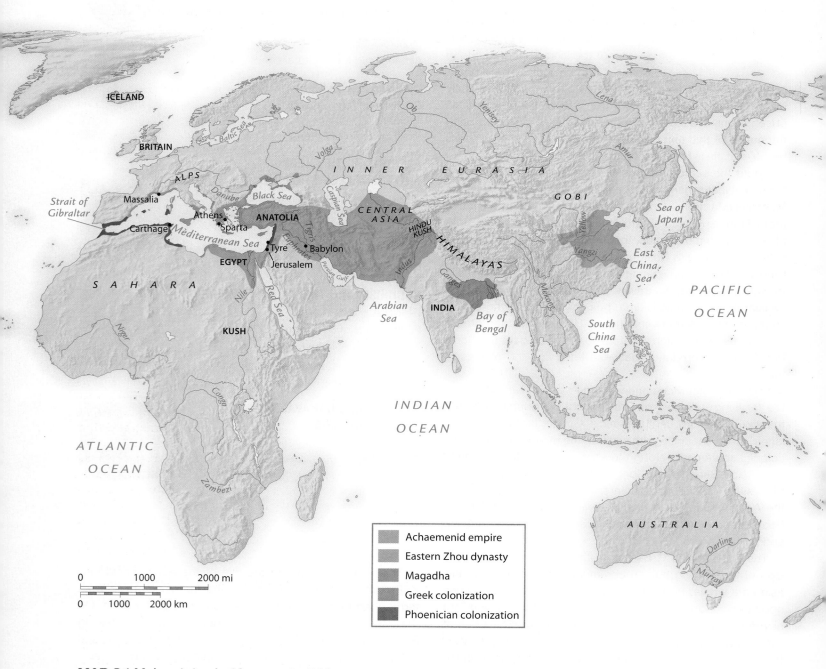

MAP 6.1 Major states in Afroeurasia, 500 B.C.E.

The voyages of Phytheas to the north Atlantic and Megasthenes to India suggest Greek speakers were interested in the world far beyond their Mediterranean homeland. Would educated Greeks of the Mediterranean in the fourth century B.C.E. likely have had more knowledge of India or of Britain?

Legend:
- Achaemenid empire
- Eastern Zhou dynasty
- Magadha
- Greek colonization
- Phoenician colonization

integration, more farmers, artisans, and merchants entered into the interregional web of exchange.

Early in the fifth century B.C.E., the Achaemenids tried to bring the Greek poleis (city-states) of the Aegean into submission. In the second part of the chapter, we turn to that region in the period after the Persian threat receded, a time when several poleis participated in a remarkable flowering of science, literature, philosophy, art, and architecture. Athens shone brightest in this firmament of ideas. For about a century and a half, that city and a few others also experimented with novel institutions of government centered on the idea that a sovereign state may be founded on the collective will of a body of citizens rather than on the decrees of a monarch claiming divine authority.

In the later fourth century B.C.E., the political landscape of Southwest Asia and the eastern Mediterranean changed dramatically. In the third part of the chapter, we introduce Alexander the Great, the young ruler of the Balkan kingdom of Macedon who conquered the Aegean, Egypt, and Southwest Asia. With Alexander, both Athenian democracy and the colossal Achaemenid empire came to an end. After Alexander's death in 323 B.C.E., Greek-speaking monarchs continued to rule from the eastern Mediterranean to India as late as the first century B.C.E. During that era, Greek-inspired ideas and styles radiated far beyond the Aegean.

In the fourth part, we shift to South Asia. The monarchs of the Maurya (MORE-yuh) dynasty, the first to unite northern and central India under one authority, arose nearly simultaneously with the Hellenistic states that succeeded Alexander's empire. The Maurya established diplomatic ties with those states, a policy that also encouraged east–west trade. The empire reached its zenith under Ashoka Maurya, who warmly embraced the teachings of the Buddha, the moral sage who had lived more than two hundred years earlier. Consequently, Ashoka advanced Buddhist thought and practice in India, to some extent at the expense of the older Brahmanist (early Hindu) religion.

In the final section of the chapter, we return to Inner Eurasia, where the growing population of pastoral nomads, valley farmers, and city merchants began to have a more serious impact on developments in neighboring agrarian and urbanized lands than in any earlier time. Around 500 B.C.E., Inner Eurasian chieftains began to organize larger alliances of clans and tribes capable of attacking towns and cities to the south and east. But even as tensions grew between pastoral and settled peoples along the edges of the steppes, traders busied themselves developing Inner Eurasia's town markets, caravan trails, and commercial institutions, thereby pushing pastoral and agrarian societies into greater mutual dependence.

Persia Ascending

FOCUS In what ways did the Achaemenid empire of Persia contribute to increasing commercial and cultural exchange in Afroeurasia?

Since at least the third millennium B.C.E., trade routes have crisscrossed historic Persia, whose central regions roughly coincide with the modern Republic of Iran. As exchanges on Afroeurasia's long-distance land and sea routes became progressively busier, warrior groups with territorial conquest in mind became increasingly aware of Persia's strategic importance as an east–west funnel of trade. The region might be likened to the narrow stem of an hourglass, a conduit of routes wedged between the Caspian and Arabian Seas (see Map 6.1). Along these trails, goods, people, and ideas moved between the eastern and western expanses of Afroeurasia. No wonder that starting in the first millennium B.C.E., ambitious conquerors made Persia the core of one empire after another. Some of these rulers in fact pushed their armies beyond Persia—northward to Central Asia, eastward to India, and westward to Mesopotamia, Syria, and even Egypt—in order to absorb more routes, cities, and taxable populations.

Empire Building on a New Scale

The Achaemenid dynasty founded the first Persia-centered empire in the sixth century B.C.E. The rise of this state represented a regional power shift in Southwest Asia from the Tigris-Euphrates valley to the Iranian plateau, the arid region that stretches from the Zagros Mountains to Afghanistan. Near the end of the second millennium B.C.E., pastoral peoples speaking Indo-European languages migrated from the Inner Eurasian steppes across Central Asia to the Iranian Plateau. Two of these groups, the Persians and the Medes (meeds), took up mixed farming and herding on the western plateau. In the eighth or seventh century B.C.E., they founded modest monarchies. Compared to fertile Mesopotamia, Iran might have seemed an unlikely place to build a state that required revenue from agriculture. Much of the land is barren, including vast expanses of salt desert. Nevertheless, the slopes and valleys of the mountain ranges that nearly ring the plateau supported numerous villages and irrigated farms.

Persian conquests. In the mid-sixth century B.C.E., Persian forces, probably responding to the weakening condition of the Babylonian empire in Mesopotamia, launched an offensive. Advancing northwestward along the Zagros range, they overpowered their rivals the Medes. Under the leadership of Cyrus II (r. 559–530 B.C.E.), a brilliant strategist and head of a clan named the Achaemenids, Persian horse archers and infantry, joined by defeated Medes and other fighters, seized northern Mesopotamia, then advanced westward all the way across Anatolia to the Aegean Sea, destroying the kingdom of Lydia and converting its capital, Sardis, into an Achaemenid royal center. Other Persian troops moved northeastward across Central Asia, where they occupied the fertile Amu Darya (Oxus) River valley and the commercial towns that bordered Inner Eurasia. By the end of the century, Babylonia, the major Syrian cities, and the coastal ports of the Levant were all in Persian hands. Reaping huge agrarian revenues from Mesopotamia, the imperial government financed even wider conquests, occupying Egypt upriver to the borders of Nubia (525–523 B.C.E.) and, far to the east, a large part of the Indus valley (518 B.C.E.).

Battles in the Aegean. The Achaemenids also muscled their way into the Mediterranean, occupying Cyprus and launching warships from Levant ports in collaboration with the Phoenicians. Having gained control of the interior of Anatolia and its rich metal deposits, Persian soldiers subjugated the small, prosperous Greek poleis of Ionia, the coastland facing the Aegean Sea.

Larger and militarily stronger Hellenic poleis, however, lay across the sea on mainland Greece. When the Ionian poleis rose in rebellion against their Persian governors, Athens sent ships to support them. This provocation convinced King Darius I (r. 522–486 B.C.E.) that if Persia were to dominate the Aegean basin and its commerce, it must attack mainland Greece. In 490 B.C.E. the Athenian army fought the Persians on the plain of Marathon northeast of Athens

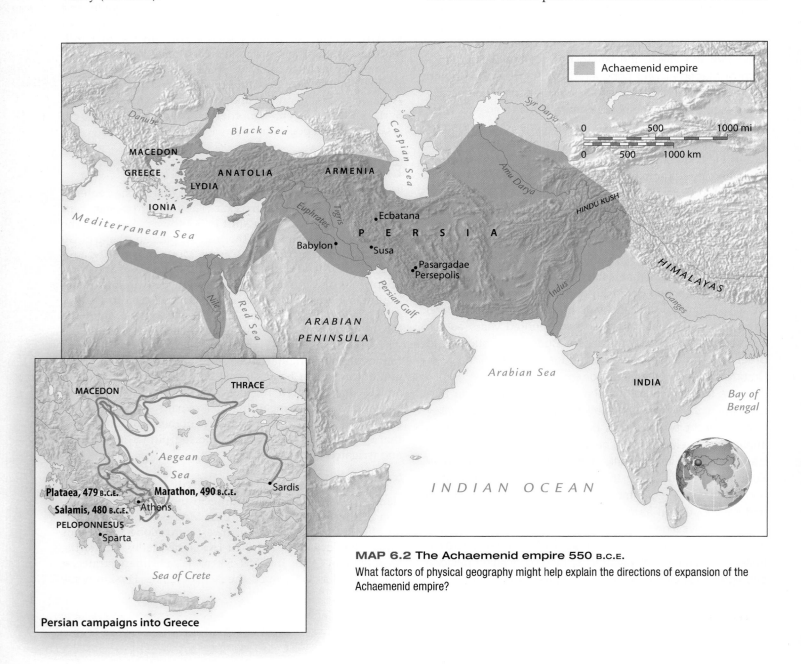

MAP 6.2 The Achaemenid empire 550 B.C.E.

What factors of physical geography might help explain the directions of expansion of the Achaemenid empire?

and turned them back. A decade later, the emperor Xerxes (r. 486–465 B.C.E.) invaded Greece, but a Hellenic navy of 370 warships defeated a larger Persian fleet off the island of Salamis. Greek victory in a land battle (Plataea) followed in 479 B.C.E. Fighting between Greeks and Persians continued for decades but sporadically and with no conclusive victory for either side.

The Achaemenids as "Universal" Rulers

The Assyrians and Babylonians provided the Achaemenids with a model of how to organize an empire in the Mesopotamian tradition of state building developed over the previous three thousand years (see Map 6.2). The Persians, however, enlarged on the possibilities of power. The emperors promoted an ideology suitable for a state of great ethnolinguistic diversity. In both royal inscriptions and architectural imagery, the emperors explicitly represented themselves as the custodians of a prosperous society whose diverse peoples happily joined together in service to the sovereign. Indeed, the Persian state claimed the right to bring all peoples into its orbit. More insistently than earlier Southwest Asian states, it proclaimed a "universal" mission to rule the world. As Darius I declared in a royal inscription, "I am Darius the Great King, King of Kings, King of countries containing all kinds of people, [king] of this great earth far and wide. . . ."[1] The sheer technological limitations of the first millennium B.C.E. made any imperial claim to global rule, or anything close to it, a practical absurdity. Since the Achaemenids, however, many regimes have claimed the mantle of universal empire.

universal empire A multiethnic state whose ruler claims a right to authority over all of humankind.

Persian nobles, drawn from families proud of their heritage as conquering warriors, served the emperor's government. This class of aristocrats, a tiny minority of the population, held key positions as royal court officials, provincial governors, and high army officers. Following the Assyrian model, however, the emperors systematically stripped their nobles of special powers and rights, transforming them into political servants of the state. They rewarded aristocratic families generously for loyal service with titles, gold, horses, estates, and royal daughters in marriage. But officials branded as corrupt, incompetent, or treasonous might expect to be summarily fired or even gruesomely executed. Darius I

satrapy An administrative unit of the Persian empire under the authority of a satrap, or provincial governor.

devoted much effort to bureaucratic organization, creating approximately twenty large provinces known as **satrapies** (SAY-trap-eez). Each provincial governor, or satrap, had the job of keeping order, provisioning garrisons, and, most important, collecting taxes from the population and forwarding them to the royal treasury.

The empire had no single capital. Rather, the emperors and their royal entourage moved regularly between

An Achaemenid official on state business. The figure facing backward in this model chariot of gold is probably a satrap, or Achaemenid governor. The horses represent a stout Iranian breed. The model comes from a site in the upper Amu Darya valley in Central Asia, the empire's far northeastern corner. A protective image of the Egyptian god Bes is stamped on the front of the chariot. What might that detail suggest about cultural exchange within the Achaemenid realm?

Ecbatana, Susa, Pasargadae, and Persepolis in western Iran and Babylon on the Euphrates. The palace center at Persepolis, which Darius started building about 515 B.C.E., occupied a giant platform commanding spectacular views of the countryside in three directions. The complex included military quarters, an imperial treasury, royal residences, and a vast throne room, whose seventy-two marble pillars supported a cedar wood ceiling nearly sixty-five feet high. Thirteen of those pillars still stand in the sprawling ruins that amaze visitors today.

The vast majority of the empire's subjects were farmers or herders. There were also minority classes of merchants, artisans, scribes, office holders, and priests, plus a large population of slaves, most of whom lost their freedom as prisoners of war. Many slaves labored in affluent households, craft shops, or temples. Others worked on imperial construction projects under harsh, life-shortening conditions. We do not know much about the daily lives of women, but the record of inscriptions suggests that the Achaemenid government had a more open-minded view of females in public life than earlier Southwest Asian states had. Some high-ranking women attended the emperor at court and owned their own landed estates. Moreover, because powerful families used marriage to tighten their political alliances, aristocratic mothers and wives exerted considerable public influence from within their houses.

The Achaemenid palace at Persepolis. Artisans decorated the walls and staircases of this royal center with reliefs of nobles, tribute bearers, and, in this view, imperial guards moving in stately procession.

The Persian Empire as Communication Hub

The Achaemenid communication network was essential to effective government over territories that at the imperial zenith extended east to west nearly 2,500 miles. Much of Southwest Asia already had an infrastructure of roads and trails connecting major cities and ports. The Achaemenids, however, extended this network, broadening highways and equipping them with forts and way stations. People working for the emperor had travel priority, though trade caravans certainly used the roads as long as they had government permission. Imperial officers, diplomats, and spies moved incessantly along the routes, monitoring regional political conditions, checking on the loyalty of local leaders, and suppressing any sign of rebellion.

The Achaemenids commanded the central zone of the growing India-to-Mediterranean trade web. They not only built roads but also encouraged sea trade between the Indus and the Persian Gulf, sponsoring maritime expeditions to gather information on the routes across the Arabian Sea. Persia functioned as a kind of

An Achaemenid coin. This gold Daric from fifth-century B.C.E. Persia depicts the emperor, perhaps Xerxes, carrying a bow and a spear.

economic pump, sucking in products from neighboring lands near and far, and discharging city-made luxury goods in all directions. The emperor Darius I completed construction of the first "Suez canal" linking the Mediterranean to the Red Sea, a project that an Egyptian pharaoh had started earlier. To promote commerce, Achaemenid officials introduced both gold and silver coins of standardized weight, adapting the idea of metal money, which appears to have originated in the Anatolian kingdom of Lydia.

On the periphery of this exchange system were the oasis cities that the Achaemenids dominated in Central Asia and the Greek city-states of the Aegean. Both benefited from their position, however, because they linked the Persian center to immense, mostly rural commercial hinterlands. The towns of Central Asia fronted the Inner Eurasian steppes, and the Aegean cities connected Persia with the whole Mediterranean, the Black Sea, and continental Europe. Products that flowed from those outer regions toward the Achaemenid center included iron, gold, silver, gems, grain, timber, wool, and livestock.

The Achaemenids and the Teachings of Zoroaster

The Persian emperors declared themselves to be worshipers and devout agents of the Ahura Mazda, supreme creator of the world, the Lord of Wisdom. According to an inscription from the reign of Darius I, "A great god is Ahura Mazda, who created this earth, who created yonder heaven, who created man, who created welfare for man, who made Darius king, one king of many, one lord of many."[2] In their early days on the Iranian Plateau, the Persians had very likely made ritual sacrifices to deities of sky and earth, as did other pastoral peoples. The emergence of Ahura Mazda as supreme god and guardian of all that is good, peaceful, and just in the universe is associated with the teachings of the prophet Zoroaster (the Greek version of the name Zarathustra).

The puzzle of Zoroaster. If we know less than we might like about the lives of the Buddha or Jesus, we know even less about Zoroaster. He may have been born anywhere from Iran to the Inner Eurasian steppes and lived anytime between the thirteenth and sixth centuries B.C.E. Priests preserved hymns that embodied Zoroaster's teachings by ritually transmitting them orally for many generations. In their expressive language, these hymns have much in common with the *Rig Veda*, the sacred songs and prayers of early Indo-European peoples of northern India (see Chapter 3). Only in the early centuries C.E., however, did scholars put in writing the seventeen hymns (the *Gathas*) attributed to Zoroaster plus other sacred traditions. This compilation, titled the *Avesta*, recounts that Ahura Mazda appointed Zoroaster, a member of a priestly family, to preach a divine message to a world that had become chaotic and brutal. The prophet's own society would not listen to him (a typical fate of religious reformers), so he wandered abroad and eventually attracted disciples.

Zoroastrian beliefs. Like the ancient Israelites, Zoroaster and his followers preached a monotheistic conception of deity, that is, one, universal God exclusively deserving of worship. The *Avesta* acknowledges the existence of a limited number of other divinities but conceives of them as dependent emanations of Ahura Mazda. Zoroaster also taught that evil operates in the world as Angra Mainyu, the "hostile spirit," which wars against Ahura Mazda for domination of the cosmos. At the End of Time, Ahura Mazda will defeat Angra Mainyu, and universal good will triumph. In the meantime, human beings must make moral choices between good and evil in their everyday lives. If they consistently dedicate themselves to the good, they will ascend at death to the presence of Ahura Mazda. If they behave wickedly, they risk being pitched into hell, where Angra Mainyu awaits them. Zoroaster's vision of moral living did not require renunciation of the world and its pleasures but demanded honest, just, and compassionate dealings with others. Scholars commonly characterize Zoroaster's teachings as "dualist," describing a universe in which humans have a choice of allegiance between good and evil, light and dark, the truth and the lie. This idea of a cosmic conflict in which God will inevitably prevail had a great impact in later centuries on both Christianity and Islam, monotheistic faiths that nonetheless acknowledged the stark power of evil. The Persian term *daeva*, which Zoroaster associated with malign spirits allied with Angra Mainyu, is derived from the same Indo-European root as the English *devil*.

Zoroastrian beliefs and rituals appear to have gained gradual acceptance among the Achaemenid elite class. Zoroaster commanded his followers to pray to Ahura Mazda five times a day and always in the presence of light from the sun or from fire. These were the prime agents of human purification and the focus of thanks to God. We have abundant archaeological evidence that "fire temples," where priests performed rites dedicated to Ahura Mazda, began to be built in Persia during the Achaemenid era. Only several centuries later, however, did Zoroastrian beliefs and rituals take form as the codified and coherent belief system known as Zoroastrianism (zohr-oh-ASS-tree-ahn-ism), a faith that exists today among minorities, mostly in South Asia.

Achaemenid Multiculturalism

From at least the time of Darius I, the Achaemenid emperors claimed the right to rule on the grounds that Ahura Mazda put monarchs on the earth to ensure social order and justice. Both Darius and his successor, Xerxes, had these words inscribed: "By the favor of Ahura Mazda I am of such a kind that I am a friend to what is right. . . . It is not my wish that the weak is . . . hurt because of the mighty, that the mighty is hurt because of the weak."[3] The idea that the emperor must govern all his subjects fairly shared similarities with the political ideology emerging in China about the same time (see Chapter 5). That is, the ruler's enjoyment of divine blessing, whether the Mandate of Heaven or the endorsement of Ahura Mazda, depended on his commitment to justice for all.

In this spirit the Achaemenid emperors generally encouraged their provincial officers to honor local customs and religious practices in return for loyal obedience and cooperation. King Cyrus, the Achaemenid founder, claimed to have seized the great city of Babylon in 538 B.C.E. amid "acclamation and rejoicing" and to have bowed before Marduk, the city's patron deity. "My numerous troops marched peacefully through Babylon. . . . All its cult centers I maintained in well-being."[4] Conceiving of Ahura Mazda as a boundless cosmic presence, the Achaemenids had little trouble thinking of him as the force animating all local deities, whether Marduk or the Israelite god Yahweh. Indeed, Cyrus permitted Israelites who had been deported from Judea to Mesopotamia by the Babylonian king Nebuchadnezzar a half-century earlier (see Chapter 5) to return to Jerusalem to rebuild their sacred temple. Some did go back, though by that time the prophet Jeremiah had successfully

The emperor at court. King Darius holds audience in the ceremonial complex at Persepolis. Behind him stands his son Xerxes, the royal heir. Who do you think the figures on the left and right of the relief might be?

preached that Yahweh was the god of all humankind, not just the Israelites' territorial deity, and that they could justly worship him wherever they lived. It was in the Achaemenid era that Israelites, shortly to be known as Jews (*Yuhudi*, or people of Judea), began to form communities throughout much of Southwest Asia and the Mediterranean basin, creating the Jewish diaspora.

The dispersion of Jews was just one example of the complex social and cultural cross-fertilization that took place in the Achaemenid empire. The Persian army grew into a diverse assortment of soldiers drawn from all the imperial lands. The armies that invaded Greece constituted a motley ethnic mix, including numerous Greeks who fought on the Achaemenid side. Visitors to urban marketplaces or imperial audience halls heard a cacophony of languages. The Persian warrior class originally spoke an ancient form of Farsi, the main language of Iran today. The Achaemenids, however, also promoted Aramaic, the Semitic language already widely spoken and written in Southwest Asia, as a medium of imperial administration and diplomacy. When an emperor built a new palace, his agents looked far and wide to find engineers, artisans, laborers, and construction materials. In an inscription praising the construction of a royal center at Susa in southwestern Iran, Darius captured the rich multicultural character of the Achaemenid realm:

> The silver and the ebony were brought from Egypt. The ornamentation with which the wall was adorned, that from Ionia was brought. The ivory, which was worked here, was brought from Kush (Nubia), and from India and from Arachosia [Afghanistan]. . . . The goldsmiths who worked the gold, those were Medes and Egyptians. The men who worked the wood, those were Sardians [from Anatolia] and Egyptians. The men who worked the baked brick, those were Babylonians. The men who adorned the wall, those were Medes and Egyptians. . . . At Susa a very excellent [work] was ordered.[5]

Inventive Greeks

FOCUS What factors contributed to the emergence of Greek city-states as important centers of political and cultural innovation from the sixth century B.C.E.?

As we have seen, Persian armies failed to subjugate the poleis of mainland Greece or most of the Hellenic cities and settlements of the Black Sea basin. In fact, many Greek cities enjoyed an economic boom in the sixth and fifth centuries B.C.E. Those cities took a leading part in the expanding market networks of the Mediterranean and Black Sea basins. This was economic activity in which private traders and shippers sought personal profit by looking for new products to sell and new populations to buy them. Greek farmers found that by selling olive oil, wine, pottery, and other products abroad, they could afford to import much-needed grain, timber, and iron. Greek city artisans also turned out painted ceramic vessels, silver jewelry, and other luxury merchandise that commanded markets in growing Mediterranean ports and among the affluent urban elites of Egypt and Southwest Asia. Agricultural and commercial prosperity, together with proud victories over the formidable Persians, gave the poleis a new political confidence. Wealth and independence also permitted some of the cities, especially Athens, to encourage creative citizens to devote themselves to literature, art, and philosophical speculation. For about 150 years, that single city emitted extraordinary waves of cultural energy.

Government and Society in Greek City-States

If we situate Greece in the very long term of history, we see that most of the time from the second century B.C.E. to the nineteenth century C.E., it was a colonial territory within one

A temple at Delphi. A sanctuary dedicated to the goddess Athena occupies the smaller of two shrine complexes at the spectacular site of ancient Delphi. This circular building, whose purpose is not known, dates to the fourth century B.C.E.

empire or another. In that long-term perspective, the existence of hundreds of self-governing city-states, separated from one another by mountains and rugged coastlines, was a distinctive circumstance of just a few centuries. Most poleis, which included both a city and surrounding agricultural lands and villages, had ten thousand or fewer inhabitants. These centers typically had defensive walls and an imposing temple dedicated to a patron deity in the manner of Mesopotamian cities. The poleis traded, exchanged emissaries, and fought with one another, forming political alliances that grew, changed, and fell apart from one decade to another. In the sixth and fifth centuries B.C.E., Greek identity was based on shared cultural bonds, not political unity.

Foremost among the elements that set Greeks apart from non-Greeks was a common alphabetically written language, which embraced many dialects. Greeks also generally shared the same household of gods and goddesses with numerous local variations; reverence for mythic heroes of the past, especially the military champions in the *Iliad* and the *Odyssey,* the epic narratives attributed to the eighth-century B.C.E. poet Homer; and participation in religious

ceremonies at the holy centers of Delphi, Delos, and Olympia, where, from 776 B.C.E., male Greeks from many cities took part in competitive games.

Governments in the poleis took a variety of forms. In some of them, the citizens chose a single individual to govern; in others, a small minority of aristocrats, that is, rich and influential men, ruled as an **oligarchy.** Before about 600 B.C.E., only the wealthiest land-owning males, most of them of aristocratic birth, could decide who would lead and participate in government. In the following two centuries, however, several poleis gradually broadened their laws to allow nonaristocratic and less advantaged men into the political process, granting them the rights and responsibilities of full citizenship.

> **oligarchy** A political system in which a relatively small number of individuals or families control the government.

Militaristic Sparta. Occupying a broad plain in the Peloponnesus (pell-uh-puh-NEE-suhs), the peninsula at the southern end of mainland Greece, Sparta was one of the largest city-states. Its male citizens created a government and social system unlike that found in any other polis. The duties of citizenship included full-time army training from age seven. Men typically married at eighteen, but they lived and ate together in barracks until they were about thirty. While girls in other poleis occupied themselves with textile weaving and other domestic chores, Spartan girls undertook tough physical training, presumably to prepare them to produce strong, healthy sons. In fact, Sparta had the character of a permanent army base. When its forces conquered the neighboring state of Messenia, they reduced most of its inhabitants to the status of servile laborers (*helots*). Understandably, the oppressed classes, which came to constitute a majority of Sparta's population, periodically rose in rebellion and had to be repressed. In the sixth century B.C.E. the city-state coerced all the poleis on the Peloponnesus into submission. Consequently, the city-state's harsh military culture could never be relaxed.

Athenian democracy: direct and limited.

In striking contrast to the Spartans, the inhabitants of Athens and some other city-states established governments founded on *demokratia,* meaning "rule of the people." The "people" here did not mean everyone but only adult male citizens who had rights to vote and hold office. In the sixth and fifth centuries B.C.E., Athens instituted a type of collective government in which as many as 60,000 men out of a total population of about 350,000 could legally participate. In a world of divinely anointed monarchs, this system was remarkable, though direct democracy in one form or another was not unique to the ancient Aegean. For as far back in history as we have any record, farming communities and herding bands, probably in all parts of the world, made decisions by group consensus. Like Athens, these communities defined which members of the group had the right to take part and which did not.

In Athens beginning in the late seventh century B.C.E., a succession of judicious leaders, notably Solon, Cleisthenes, and Pericles, engineered political and legal reforms that extended rights to vote and own property, as well as the privilege of speaking in the popular assembly, to all adult, native-born, free (not enslaved) males. The authority to govern was vested in this citizenry, not in a monarch. By drawing lots, citizens took turns serving on civil juries and on the Council of Five Hundred, which managed the city's day-to-day affairs. In practice, the wealthiest Athenian families continued to have great influence over daily affairs, a limitation on democracy that should not surprise us.

A Greek worshiper. This woman standing before an altar emblazons a vase from the sixth century B.C.E. Oil stored in this flask may have been used in religious rituals.

Male citizens professed equality among themselves, responsibility for the welfare of the polis, and the right to primacy over women, children, and all noncitizen residents. Free women did not have public rights, but despite their formal exclusion from government, they contributed a great deal to the city-state's economy and cultural life. The wives and daughters of free men not only managed domestic economies but also did farm work, wove textiles for market, labored in craft shops, and ran small businesses. They played important roles in religious sacrifices, processions, and festivals dedicated to one or another of the numerous deities that Greeks worshiped, including Athena, the patron goddess of the city. Some cults and festivals, which Athenians regarded as vital to the city-state's well-being, were reserved for women only.

Slavery and slave trade grew in tandem with economic expansion in the whole Mediterranean basin. In the fifth century B.C.E., slaves in Athens probably ran to the tens of thousands, though this number would have been small relative to the servile population of the Achaemenid empire. Most slaves reached Greece as prisoners of war or as captives of pirates, though impoverished or debt-ridden men and women sometimes offered themselves as slave laborers in order to survive. Slaves might serve as domestic servants, scribes, tutors, artisans, construction workers, or prostitutes. The silver and lead mines of Attica, the peninsula that was part of the Athenian state, consumed slaves at a voracious rate. According to Athenian law, an owner could physically assault slaves but not kill them wantonly.

Aside from a few restrictions, slaves had no legal rights. Rather, they were **chattels,** comparable in status to domestic animals. As the Greek philosopher Aristotle wrote, "A slave is a living possession."[6]

chattel slavery A type of slavery in which the bonded individual has the social and sometimes legal status of a unit of property and therefore no formal rights or privileges in law.

In the aftermath of the wars with Persia, Athens emerged as probably the biggest and richest polis. The farm production of Attica plus imports of grain from the Black Sea and northern Africa fed the urban population. Attica's mines swelled the city's treasury and financed a powerful navy. Foreigners (*metics*) flocked to the city, energizing craft industries, banking, and overseas trade. The fortified port of Piraeus, located five miles southwest of the city, swarmed with sailing ships that exported wine, oil, figs, pottery, and other goods and brought in grain, fish, timber, and numerous exotic wares from lands near and far.

Greek military prowess. The evolution of self-governing city-states was linked to military changes initiated in late eighth century B.C.E. In Chapter 5, we described how, after the twelfth century B.C.E., infantry progressively replaced chariot riders in Southwest Asia and the eastern Mediterranean. As Greek city-states multiplied, their inhabitants organized infantry militias. All male citizens trained and fought to defend the polis or to enlarge its territory at the expense of neighbors. Consequently, when farmers and artisans joined their city's army or navy, they had good cause to demand citizenship rights and duties equal to men who were wealthy and well born.

Except in Sparta, militia service was typically part time but also a basic duty of citizenship. Soldiers outfitted themselves with bronze helmets and body armor; they carried round wooden shields and spears designed for close-in fighting. Massing together shoulder-to-shoulder and shield-to-shield six-to-eight ranks deep, these fighters, or *hoplites* (from *hoplon,* a Greek word for shield) marched into battle in close formation. This ingenious tactical formation, called a **phalanx,** was designed to charge, smash into, and crush an enemy force. As long as a phalanx maneuvered on level ground and maintained its cohesion, it could wreak havoc on any opposing force that was deployed more loosely or that tried to stop an advancing wall of shields by firing arrows from a distance. On the political and social sides, the phalanx also

phalanx A military formation in which soldiers march and fight in closely packed, disciplined ranks.

fostered civic solidarity within the polis because military success depended absolutely on intense physical and psychological cooperation. Cohesion, however, did not necessarily extend beyond a city-state's frontiers. On the contrary, the more unified a polis perceived itself to be, the more it might be inclined to attack other cities.

The Flowering of Athens

Athens in fact attacked cities near and far. After the Persian threat receded, the city's leaders continued to invest lavishly in its citizen navy. The prime weapon was the trireme, a fast, quick-turning ship powered with three ranks of rowers and designed to ram enemy vessels head on. Young citizens, not slaves, powered the ships. The trireme fleet freed many poleis from Persia but then made them into tax-paying dependencies of Athens. Under the leadership of Pericles (495–429 B.C.E.), Athens reduced former military allies to the status of tribute-paying dependent states. The navy also took control of the major Aegean Sea passages, including the Bosporus, the strait leading to the Black Sea. On the Greek mainland, however, Sparta and its dependencies remained powerful rivals.

Whenever in world history a country has displayed great cultural creativity, wealth and labor have been marshaled to pay for it. In the case of Athens, riches pouring in from the seaborne empire, including slave labor, financed a period of intense intellectual and aesthetic innovation that began about 480 B.C.E. and lasted nearly a century and a half. As the Athenian empire grew, artisans, builders, and scholars converged on the teeming capital. Athenian wealth, funneled through the public treasury and the most affluent

The Acropolis. The Parthenon and the other public buildings on the fortified hill that dominates Athens display the city-state's wealth and power in the decades following Greek victory over Persian invaders. Athens obliged its allied cities to contribute generously to the lavish beautification of the Acropolis.

families, financed an ambitious building program, notably construction of a complex of temples, statues, and public spaces on the Acropolis, the hill that commanded the city. The crowning glory was the Parthenon, an exquisitely proportioned temple dedicated to the cult of Athena. The polis also patronized artists and thinkers, who dedicated themselves to painting, sculpture, architectural design, music, drama, history, philosophy, mathematics, and science.

The Athenian cultural inheritance.
This burst of ingenuity was not entirely self-generated. The inventive people who lived and worked in Athens were all heirs to the stream of ideas that had been emanating from Southwest Asia and the Nile valley during the previous three thousand years. Much of this accumulated knowledge became available to Greek thinkers, and they took great interest in it. The philosopher Aristotle, for example, contended that "it was in Egypt that the mathematical arts were first formed" thanks to the scientific work of its priestly class in earlier millennia.[7]

Despite the wars with the Achaemenids, Persia also contributed significantly to Athenian cultural achievement. Greeks spoke of the Persian elite as barbarians (mainly because they did not speak Greek) and expressed contempt for their extravagant lifestyle. Even so, the wars did not prevent Persian luxury goods—gems, jewelry, textiles, gold ware—from arriving in Greek ports. Athens sent envoys to the Achaemenid court, and Greeks in substantial numbers resided in the empire's western provinces as political exiles, mercenaries, artisans, and scribes. Herodotus (484–425 B.C.E.), the Greek historian who wrote the classic account of the Persian Wars, traveled extensively in the empire, including Egypt. Affluent Athenians took warmly to Persian finery, clothing styles, and other status symbols, for example, using slaves in the Achaemenid manner to carry parasols, fans, and fly-whisks.[8]

Servants attend an affluent woman. Scenes of everyday life decorate this loutrophoros, a water container used in marriage and funeral rituals. Made in Greek style in a polis in southern Italy, the vase depicts a status symbol borrowed from Persian custom—the subordinate parasol carrier. What factors help explain the diffusion of Persian cultural practices as far west as Italy?

Religion and philosophy.
The citizens of Greek poleis participated in rituals and sacrifices to win favor from the gods and goddesses believed to reside on Mount Olympus in northern Greece. Religious life, however, was also diverse and jarringly incoherent. The Greeks had no sacred scripture or set of doctrines comparable to either the Hebrew Bible or the moral teachings of Zoroaster. Various cults to cure illnesses, ensure fertility, and predict the future flourished. The most influential individuals in Greek urban communities were secular, or nonreligious, civic leaders, rather than priests, who enforced codes of belief and behavior. This relatively open-minded religious climate is likely to have encouraged adventuresome thinkers to engage in wide-ranging speculation about nature, the human condition, and cosmic truth. Moreover, the civic culture of some poleis, especially Athens, stimulated remarkably open debate among free male citizens on questions of public duty, moral justice, and proper community behavior.

In the sixth century B.C.E., Greek scholars inhabiting cities of Ionia on the eastern Aegean shore led the way in formulating a method of scientific and moral inquiry that became known as **natural philosophy**. This discipline was founded on the idea that just as the polis thrived because citizens subscribed to underlying laws, so fundamental rules might also govern nature, including human action. These laws might even transcend the will of the quarreling, unreliable gods on Mount Olympus, who offered little help in making sense of the world. Natural laws, rather, might be discovered through the exercise of human logic and reason and, at least for some philosophers, careful observation of the external world.

natural philosophy A method of scientific and moral inquiry founded on the idea that fundamental laws governing nature, including human behavior, may be discovered through the exercise of logic, reason, or careful observation.

The Ionian tradition of abstract speculation bloomed in Athens in the fifth century B.C.E. Scientific work focused on mathematics and on the natural constitution of the earth and heavens. Cultural and psychological studies aimed to fathom the universal principles underlying moral and political behavior. Drama, which got its start in festivals dedicated to Dionysus, the god of wine, explored the complex relationships between individuals, society, and the gods. Sculptors and architects sought to find universal principles to represent harmonious order and symmetry, especially in the human body. Greek intellectuals heartily disagreed with one another over questions of moral truth, the proper ranking of social classes, and whether democracy was a good idea or not. They founded their speculations on the premise that humans might achieve the good life by using their reasoning power to discover natural explanations for things, rather than merely waiting helplessly while the gods bullied, seduced, and played tricks on them.

Socrates (470–399 B.C.E.), the earliest of the great philosophers, set the agenda for human action founded on reason with his celebrated declaration that "the unexamined life is not worth living." Plato (428–347 B.C.E.), who tells us almost everything we know about Socrates, and Aristotle (384–322 B.C.E.), Plato's student, wrote on a colossal range of subjects. Plato was the idealist, interested in metaphysics, that is, speculation on the "first causes" of things. He argued that the world we see with our senses is merely a flickering silhouette of perfect reality. Among many other implications, this idea led Plato to imagine the ideal political state, which in his view would not be a democracy but a system ruled by Guardians, or philosopher-kings.

In contrast to Plato, Aristotle was an empiricist, a seeker of concrete, observable knowledge about humankind and the world. Beyond that, he sought to understand the fundamental interconnectedness and coherence of all phenomena. In the process he produced a huge body of work on politics, economics, mathematics, logic, poetry, astronomy, chemistry, and biology. The ideas of Socrates, Plato, Aristotle, and numerous other Greek thinkers endured, probably less because of the theories they formulated and observations they made than because of the questions they asked. As Socrates reputedly said, "All I know is that I know nothing." This was certainly an invitation to inquiry. Greek philosophers had no monopoly on logical reasoning or high-flying speculation about the nature of reality. But the questions they posed continued to intrigue and confound thoughtful people in the succeeding centuries and indeed down to our own time.

Alexander the Great and the Hellenistic Era

FOCUS To what extent did societies within the region from northern India to the eastern Mediterranean embrace Greek-style cultural and political forms between the fourth and second centuries B.C.E.?

In the fifth century B.C.E., Greek warriors defended themselves against the Persian empire. In the last third of the fourth century, Greek and Macedonian soldiers destroyed it. The conquests of Alexander (r. 336–323 B.C.E.), the young king who led that campaign, figure among the most extraordinary military adventures in history. Marching from Greece to the Indus valley, Alexander carved out an empire even bigger than the Achaemenid state. He succeeded only fleetingly, but his conquests led to a drastic rewriting of the political map of Southwest Asia and the eastern Mediterranean (see Map 6.3). Following the conqueror's withdrawal from India, the Maurya dynasty, a third large state, united the Indus and Ganges River valleys for the first time in history. The existence of these and several smaller monarchies, most of them under the authority of Greek-speaking elites, stimulated more than two centuries of intense commercial and cultural interchange from India and Central Asia to the Mediterranean.

Alexander's Short, Brilliant Career

In the Aegean the rise of the Athenian sea-based empire sparked more than one hundred years of inter-polis conflict, starting with the Peloponnesian War (431–404 B.C.E.). Athens, Sparta, and the powerful city-state of Thebes took turns dominating the scene. Within the cities, land-owning and commercial minorities continued to accumulate wealth at the expense of ordinary people, causing bitter alienation between rich and poor. To the east, the Achaemenid empire also showed signs of stress. Imperial leadership deteriorated, rebels pushed the Achaemenids out of Egypt for fifty-seven years, and the Indus valley's subject populations reasserted their independence.

Amid these unstable circumstances, Macedon, one of a number of woodland kingdoms on the Balkan Peninsula north of Greece, arose to regional power. A small class of warrior-aristocrats who spoke Macedonian, which may have been either a dialect of Greek or a language closely related to it, ruled a population of mostly farmers and herders. Athens and the other culturally sophisticated city-states to the south tended to regard Macedon as a useful source of timber, gold, and horses but otherwise as a wild frontier. In 358 B.C.E., however, Philip II ascended the Macedonian throne and initiated a vigorous program to strengthen his kingdom, obliging the Greek poleis to take him seriously. He had no use for Athenian-style democracy, but he "Hellenized" his royal court, adopting Greek ceremonies and cultural refinements and hiring Greek artists and intellectuals to model proper standards of civilization. On the military side, he expanded his cavalry of heavily armored aristocrats, and he trained Balkan peasants to fight in a phalanx eighteen thousand strong. He armed these foot soldiers with the *sarissa*, a bronze-tipped pike fifteen to eighteen feet long. Macedon's enemies therefore faced a massed infantry bristling with spears.

In 339–338 B.C.E., Philip advanced south, crushing the disunited poleis, including Athens, and proclaiming himself supreme leader of a unified Macedonian and Greek federation. Within the city-states, the ideal of citizenship endured, but the brief era of Athenian democracy came to an end. Philip planned to cross the Aegean and attack western Anatolia, where thousands of Greeks still lived under Persian rule. In 336 B.C.E., however, a bodyguard, who might have been the tool of an aristocratic conspiracy, assassinated him.

Alexander's campaigns. The kingship then passed to Philip's son Alexander, who was barely twenty years old. Philip had given this bright boy a Greek education, Aristotle serving for a time as the lad's tutor. When the king was killed, Alexander moved with great speed to carry forward his father's plan. In 334 B.C.E., he invaded Anatolia at the head of an army of thirty-five thousand Macedonians and Greek allies. During the next eleven years, he blazed a trail of conquest nearly three thousand miles to the east. From 334 to 330 B.C.E., he fought his way to the heart of Persia,

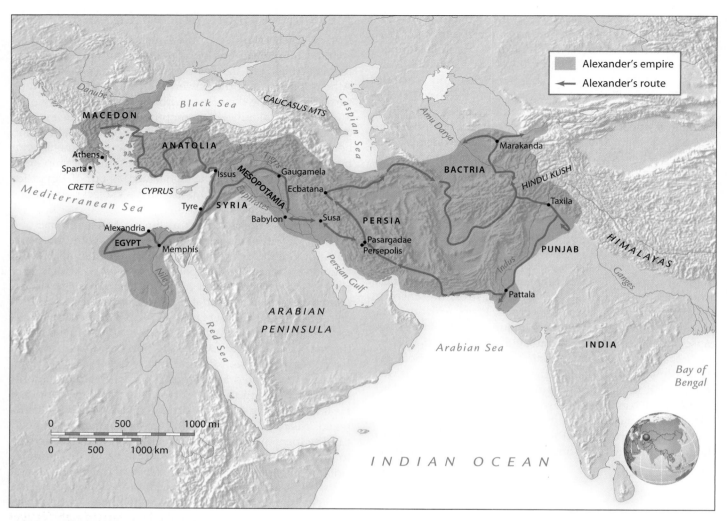

MAP 6.3 Alexander's empire, 325 B.C.E.

Compare this map with Map 6.2 of the Achaemenid empire. What similarities and differences do you notice in the directions of conquest? Why do you think the conquered territories on the two maps overlap to such a great extent?

subduing Anatolia, Syria, Egypt, and Babylonia along the way. He engaged Achaemenid armies in three great battles, brilliantly deploying both cavalry and phalanx infantry, and he won every time against unfavorable odds. He forced the emperor Darius III (r. 336–300 B.C.E.) to flee for his life, occupied the great Persian capitals, and seized the imperial treasuries.

Marching onward to the northeastern Achaemenid provinces, Alexander led his army over an eleven-thousand-foot pass of the Hindu Kush mountains to Central Asia and the populous Amu Darya River valley. As if destruction of the Persian empire were not enough, he then pushed his exhausted troops back over the Hindu Kush and across Afghanistan to the Indus valley, where in 326 B.C.E. he routed the army of a local king. At this point even Alexander's toughest warriors refused to go farther. Relenting, he returned west, crossing the deserts of southern Iran to reach

Babylon in 325 B.C.E. In the final period of his career, from 325 to 323 B.C.E., he applied himself to organizing his empire. But before he could do much, he died suddenly after falling ill in the extreme heat of a Mesopotamia summer— and possibly after a night of heavy drinking with his officers. With no provision for a successor, his leading generals gave him a glorious funeral, then set quickly to fighting one another for his throne.

In thirteen years, Alexander created an empire larger than any state in history. He was personally charismatic and a phenomenal military tactician. Like most warlords of that era, he was also ruthless—terrorizing, killing, and enslaving countless numbers of people from Greece to India. For example, when the leaders of the Greek city of Thebes challenged his authority, he assaulted the city and razed every building except the temples and the house of a famous poet. He then sent most of the population into slavery. In Alexander's attack on the Mediterranean port of Tyre, his forces killed six thousand defenders, then had two thousand more crucified on the beach.

What did Alexander want? Alexander almost certainly aimed to create a state centered on Mesopotamia and Persia, not on Greece. He conceived of himself as ruler of a transformed Persian empire that would one day incorporate the entire Mediterranean and Black Sea basins. He introduced elaborate Persian rituals to his royal court and held audience there dressed in the flowing robe and sash of an Achaemenid potentate. Moreover, he linked his authority to Egyptian and Mesopotamian notions of divine monarchy, which were foreign to Greek tradition. After occupying Egypt, for example, he accepted the pharaoh's crown, in effect making himself a god.

Yet Alexander also assumed that the members of his governing class, whatever their ethnic origin, would accept the Greek model of culture, the only one he knew. He ordered new cities built in the Greek style, twenty-five or more of them in eastern Persia alone. These towns were to serve as military and administrative colonies and as regional economic centers. Army veterans, as well as civilian settlers drawn partly from crowded Aegean cities, formed a privileged elite over local non-Greeks, though Alexander permitted the new towns varying degrees of local self-government. Thousands of Greeks settled across the empire, facilitating Greek cultural diffusion into parts of Afroeurasia where such influences had previously been unknown.

Alexander at war. This detail from a mosaic that decorated a house in Pompeii, Italy, in the first century C.E. illustrates Alexander in combat. The mosaic commemorates his victory over the Persian emperor Darius III at the Issus River in Anatolia in 333 B.C.E. What sort of impression of Alexander do you think the artist might be trying to make?

Foundations of the Hellenistic World

The term *Hellenistic* refers to the political and cultural developments that occurred across much of the India-to-Mediterranean region in the three centuries following Alexander's death. The Hellenistic Age describes the period when Alexander's successors ruled much of this region and when Greek speakers interacted with peoples of diverse ethnolinguistic identity—Persians, Mesopotamians, Syrians, Arabs, Egyptians, Central Asians, North Indians—creating novel cultural amalgamations.

> **Hellenistic** Relating to the interaction between Greek language and culture and the languages and cultural forms of peoples of Southwest Asia, the Nile valley, the western Mediterranean, and the Black Sea region.

For about fifty years after Alexander's death, Macedonian commanders competed brutally for domination of the conquered lands. The unitary empire broke up but did not simply disintegrate. Rather, three of Alexander's former generals founded regional monarchies and established governments whose highest officials had Macedonian or Greek backgrounds, forming a Greco-Macedonian ruling class. The largest and richest of these new states was the Seleucid empire (312–64 B.C.E.), named after the former Macedonian officer Seleucus I (r. 305–281 B.C.E.). This monarchy embraced the greatest cities of Southwest Asia and the overland routes from the Mediterranean to Central Asia and India. Roughly speaking, it overlay the defunct Achaemenid domain. A second Hellenistic state emerged in Egypt under Ptolemy I, another of Alexander's generals. The Ptolemaic (TAWL-oh-may-ihk) dynasty (305–30 B.C.E.) endured for 275 years, dominating at the height of its power the Nile valley plus the island of Cyprus and parts of Libya, Anatolia, and Syria. The Macedonian officer Antigonus the One-Eyed took control of Philip's original Balkan kingdom, but this third state (the Antigonid dynasty) lost control of the Greek poleis, which once again formed their own alliance leagues. Far to the northeast in Central Asia, Greek commanders broke away from the Seleucid empire about 240 B.C.E. and founded the kingdom of Bactria. In short, Greek-speaking ruling groups continued to dominate an immense range of territory long after Alexander's empire had broken apart (see Map 6.4).

Hellenistic governments. Like the Achaemenids before them, the Seleucid and Ptolemaic monarchs regarded their authority as theoretically absolute. To them, monarchy existed chiefly to pump revenue from ordinary people to enrich the ruling elite, defend the imperial territories, and, when the opportunity arose, extend them by war. Hellenistic rulers also took responsibility for rituals that had to

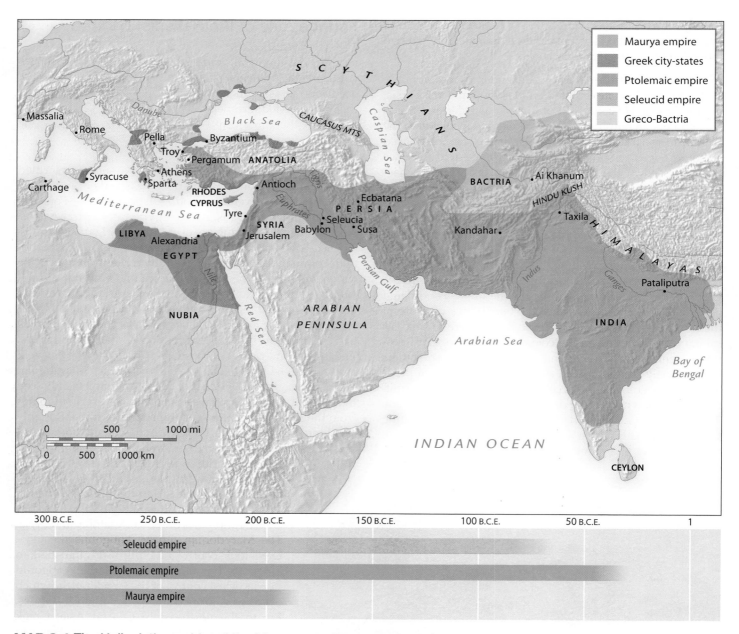

MAP 6.4 The Hellenistic world and the Maurya empire, ca. 300–200 B.C.E.

Which of the states on this map is likely to have had the greatest volume of trade passing through its cities?

be performed to appease the gods in order to avert bad harvests and other disasters. The statecraft of the Seleucids and Ptolemies centered on massive displays of military might and quick repression of any outbreak of popular opposition.

Hellenistic monarchs ruled in association with an intimate circle of friends, advisors, and high officers, most of them from Greek or Macedonian families. The Seleucid realm numbered about thirty million people, and the road network the Achaemenids had built enabled state officials to collect taxes and administer justice with remarkable efficiency. The Ptolemaic government was even better organized. It had the advantage of ruling a core population (about seven million) tightly concentrated in the Nile valley and fully accustomed to taking orders from the top. Hellenistic rulers collaborated with local village elders, nomad chiefs, and religious leaders, relying on them to help keep order in return for political and economic privileges. Both the Seleucids and the Ptolemies went to great lengths to inspire awe in their subjects, ordering construction of giant statues and temples in their honor.

In the Ptolemaic state, which became particularly good at managing economic life, a hierarchy of Egyptian officials, clerks, and secretaries supervised by Greco-Macedonian bosses regulated farming, irrigation, artisanry, commerce, and prices. They also monopolized the manufacture and trade of numerous products, including papyrus, linen, oil, and beer. This centralized economic management generally inhibited private economic initiative. The rulers expended revenue mainly on military procurement, payments to officials, regal pomp, and self-aggrandizing monuments. Conversely, the living standards of ordinary men and women appear to have declined steadily during the third century B.C.E.

Like the pharaohs before them, the Ptolemies sponsored commercial expeditions up the Nile to Nubia. In the third century B.C.E., they also sent seaborne trade missions to the southern end of the Red Sea, partly to purchase Indian goods coming across the Arabian Sea. Egyptian agents cultivated relations with local African traders and hunters as far south along the East African coast as modern Somalia. The commodity they most wanted was elephants, which they transported back to Egypt on ships specially designed to carry them. When Alexander invaded northwestern India, he learned the value of tamed elephants as weapons of war—ancient tanks, as it were. Subsequently, both the Seleucids and the Ptolemies traded in battle elephants, incorporating them into their armies.

Hellenistic society. Because of the ambitious building program started by Alexander, the number of cities in the lands his empire encompassed rose dramatically in the fourth and third centuries B.C.E. (see Map 6.4). Some of these cities, including Alexandria in Egypt, Antioch in Syria, Seleucia on the Tigris, and Pergamum in Anatolia, became large sprawling hubs of manufacture, trade, and cultural interchange. Others were no more than modest military colonies. Like Alexander, the Hellenistic rulers wanted their cities to conform to Greek cultural ideals in layout, architecture, and ornamentation. A new center should have a temple, theater, marketplace, gymnasium for athletic training and education, and comfortable villas on a neat grid of streets. New towns as far from Greece as Ai Khanum in northwestern Afghanistan resembled the cityscapes of Athens and Thebes.

The populations of these cities varied greatly from one region to another. Though thousands of Greek migrants and visitors poured into Seleucid cities, the majority of inhabitants were local people. In the bigger towns, a floating, polyglot populace of soldiers, merchants, artisans, and scholars came and went incessantly. We know little about everyday society in these places. Ethnic neighborhoods may have been a feature of some of them, but recent archaeology has turned up no general evidence that different language communities lived in isolation from one another. Excavations at Susa east of the Tigris show that houses inhabited by Greeks and other groups stood side by side, suggesting that men and women of different origins mingled freely in daily life.

The Ptolemies built few new cities, but they transformed Alexandria on the Nile delta into the greatest metropolis anywhere in Afroeurasia in the third century B.C.E. The city surpassed all other Hellenistic centers in population, wealth, and concentrated intellectual achievement. The Greek and Macedonian elite

A war elephant. The baby trailing its parent softens this image of an African elephant carrying soldiers into battle. The fighting tower may have been a Greek invention. This terra-cotta plate, dated to the third century B.C.E., comes from southern Italy.

Queen Arsinoe II: Ruler of Ptolemaic Egypt

Coruler, high priestess, and goddess, Queen Arsinoe II (316–270 B.C.E.) was one of the most powerful royal women in Egypt's long dynastic history. Her father was the Macedonian general Ptolemy I, who founded the Ptolemaic dynasty following the death of Alexander the Great. About 300 B.C.E., when Arsinoe was fifteen or sixteen years old, her father arranged her marriage, an entirely political transaction, to Lysimachus, the sixty-one-year-old king who ruled territory on either side of the Bosporus Strait. The couple had three sons in rapid succession, but Agathocles, a child from Lysimachus's previous marriage, stood ahead of them in the line of royal succession. To improve her sons' political positions, as well as her own, Arsinoe accused Agathocles of plotting to kill his father. Consequently, Lysimachus ordered him executed, a vile act that triggered violent uprisings. In 281 B.C.E., less than a year after the murder, the elderly Lysimachus died in battle against Seleucus, ruler of the Seleucid empire of Persia.

When she lost her husband, Arsinoe fled to Macedonia. Once there, she soon accepted a second marriage, this time to her own half-brother Ptolemy Keraunos. Greeks generally regarded marriage between siblings as indecent, but Arsinoe and her new spouse took their cue from Egypt, where such royal unions were customary. Ptolemy Keraunos had

Arsinoe II strikes a characteristically Egyptian pose, but she sports a Greek hairstyle.

seized part of the dead Lysimachus's territories, and he assured Arsinoe that he would place her sons back in the line of succession as his adopted heirs. He deceived her, however, and fearing these sons as potential threats to his power, murdered the two younger boys, while the eldest escaped. Arsinoe fled once again, this time back to Egypt and the protection of her full brother Ptolemy II (r. 282–246 B.C.E.), who was by this time Egypt's king.

Arsinoe lost no time getting back on her feet and maneuvering for power. She persuaded Ptolemy II that his wife was plotting against him and deserved to be sent into exile. Ptolemy not only complied but also made Arsinoe his new queen. The evidence from surviving texts and images demonstrates convincingly that, although she lived only for another five or six years, she enjoyed equality with her husband-brother as coruler and may have governed more energetically than he did. Historians think she may have helped design the strategy that led to Egypt's victory in a war against the Seleucids for control of territory in Syria. She may also have supervised a major expansion of the Egyptian navy. She appears with her brother on some coins of the period but alone on others, implying her commanding status.

In the years leading to her death in 270 B.C.E. at about the age of forty-five, Arsinoe became not only priestess of her own cult, a typical practice among Egyptian rulers, but also a goddess, worshiped warmly during her own lifetime and for a long time after. A grand shrine was dedicated to her in Alexandria, and towns were named after her in Greece.

Historians, both ancient and modern, have often represented Arsinoe as conniving and power hungry, though these qualities were hardly rare among monarchs of the Hellenistic centuries. She doubtless exercised great political influence during her brief reign, and she offered a model for ambitious Ptolemaic queens that followed her. For example, Cleopatra VII (r. 51–30 B.C.E.), the last of the Ptolemaic rulers, adopted Arsinoe's crown as her own.

Thinking Critically

What political advantages might Arsinoe have gained by encouraging her subjects to worship her as a deity while she shared the throne with her brother?

families that lived there adopted an elegant part-Greek, part-Egyptian lifestyle. The city also attracted a large, multi-ethnic merchant population that made money supplying luxuries to the ruling class. The Hellenistic elite liked to think of the city as a kind of outpost of the Greek Aegean, not really *in* Egypt but merely *next to* it. Actually, native Egyptians made up the great majority of the population.

Public life in Hellenistic cities was as patriarchal, that is, as dominated by males, as it generally was in urban societies throughout Afroeurasia. We have some evidence, however, that in the bustling, impersonal climate of the larger cities, upper-class women had somewhat wider scope to pursue private interests than they had in fifth-century B.C.E. Athens, where a tight guard of male relatives kept them close to home. Elite Hellenistic women engaged more openly in commercial and financial affairs, sought more education, and in some cases took up careers as poets or artists. In Egypt, the Ptolemaic monarchs sometimes married their sisters in order to keep the Macedonian dynasty free of foreign blood. Queen Arsinoe II (316–270 B.C.E.), for example, married her brother Ptolemy II (r. 282–246 B.C.E.) and shared the throne with him for five or six years.

Cultural Trends

The power of the Hellenistic states, the multiplying of cities, and expansion of long-distance trade all worked together to intensify cultural interchange among peoples of different languages and ethnic identities from the Mediterranean to India. By the sixth century B.C.E., the Greek language, as well as Greek religious, political, literary, and artistic ideas, had become known in Southwest Asia. But following Alexander's campaigns, these ideas and styles imposed themselves quite suddenly on the consciousness of numerous other peoples who had previously heard nothing about them. The conqueror and his successors built numerous cities as islands of Hellenistic culture, projects that required Greek merchants, artisans, architects, scholars, poets, and musicians to move to these new centers to implant civilized standards.

In the early third century B.C.E., a person could journey across Southwest Asia without ever losing the company of Greek speakers. Koine (common tongue), a dialect of Greek that developed in the Hellenistic world and incorporated vocabulary from other, mostly Semitic languages, became the premier medium of trade, business, and intellectual conversation wherever Greco-Macedonians dominated society. Like Aramaic in the Persian empire, Koine served as a *lingua franca,* facilitating diplomacy and business across

cultural and linguistic frontiers. A traveler in Southwest Asia would also see temples and homes reminiscent of Athens, painted pottery made in the Aegean, Greek statuary, Greek plays performed in Greek-style amphitheaters, and silver and gold coins bearing Greek inscriptions and the likenesses of Greek rulers and gods.

It is hard to know to what extent local people who lived under Greco-Macedonian rule accepted Hellenistic culture. Certainly only a small minority became fully converted to Greek ways. This group included local elites, notably political climbers who voluntarily cloaked themselves in Greek habits and styles to improve their chances of entering the charmed circles of influential men and women. Also, Greco-Macedonian army veterans and male civilian settlers typically severed personal attachments when they migrated to distant cities. Instead, they wedded local women, and the children of these mixed marriages usually had Greek names, spoke Greek, and grew up in a Hellenistic cultural milieu.

Philosophers and scientists. Literate residents of Hellenistic cities were likely familiar with the utterances of Socrates, Plato, Aristotle, and other Greek thinkers. For example, archaeologists have found faint physical traces of a treatise on Aristotle's philosophy as far from Athens as Ai Khanum in Afghanistan. On the other hand, the Hellenistic centuries also inspired new philosophical movements concerned with the practical problems of living a calm and stable life in cities characterized by social flux, commercial hubbub, and authoritarian governments. Cynicism, Epicureanism, and Stoicism were three of these movements. All of them focused on ethical choices individuals must make to find peace in an unpredictable and perplexing world. All of them extolled human reason as the proper guide to the

Hellenistic Philosophies

Philosophical School	A Key Idea	Key Thinkers	Quotation	Modern Use of Related Words
Cynicism (Cynics)	Individuals should seek freedom and self-reliance to the point of repudiating material possessions, social ties, and yearnings for pleasure.	Antisthenes (d. 350 B.C.E.) Diogenes of Sinope (d. 323 B.C.E.)	"I would rather go mad than enjoy myself." —Antisthenes	*Cynical:* distrustful of human motivations, sincerity, or honesty
Epicureanism (Epicureans)	Reality has no ultimate sense or structure, so the individual should strive to avoid pain by pursuing pleasure grounded in tranquility, self-control, and moderation practiced in the company of loyal friends.	Epicurus (d. 271 B.C.E.)	"Pleasure is the beginning and end of a happy life" —Epicurus	*Epicurean:* an individual fond of sensual enjoyment, especially in eating and drinking
Stoicism (Stoics)	Individuals have a fundamental duty to accept the role nature has assigned them. Neither pleasure nor pain is of any account, only the practice of virtue, which comes naturally by living in accordance with nature.	Zeno of Citium (d. 262 B.C.E.)	"Our individual natures are part of universal nature. Hence the chief good is life according to nature." —Zeno, after Diogenes Laertius (third-century C.E. biographer)	*Stoic:* an individual who is able to suffer pain or misfortune without complaining or revealing personal feelings

art of living. Though their founders all lived and worked in Athens, these schools attracted followers in the wider Hellenistic world.

Hellenistic intellectuals who studied mathematics, physics, and astronomy worked from the premise that general theories could be formulated to explain how the universe worked. Like Aristotle, they observed, measured, and classified rather than simply speculated. Some of their findings were way ahead of their time. For example, Aristarchus (d. ca. 230 B.C.E.) proposed a heliocentric solar system in which the earth turned on its axis and revolved around the sun, a theory that gained general world acceptance only two thousand years later. Eratosthenes (d. ca. 195 B.C.E.) used an ingenious geometric procedure to measure the circumference of the earth, coming up with a figure only fifteen miles off the mark. Euclid (d. ca. 270 B.C.E.) synthesized geometric knowledge whose axioms and theorems schools teach

today. Archimedes (d. 212 B.C.E.) pioneered the geometry of cylinders and spheres and calculated the value of pi more precisely than any earlier scholar had done. He is also said to have invented a screw device for raising irrigation water from one level to another.

Athens remained intellectually lively in the fourth and third centuries B.C.E., and new centers of learning blossomed in Pergamum and on the Mediterranean island of Rhodes. Alexandria in Egypt attracted intellectuals from near and far. The leading institution was the Museum, a kind of government-sponsored think tank for scientific, literary, and philosophical research. Next to it, the Ptolemies built a library that came to house nearly half a million books, probably the largest concentration of accumulated knowledge anywhere in the world. Among Hellenistic cities, Alexandria was undoubtedly the most cosmopolitan, a "world city" that had both a diverse population and an educated class

Egyptian and Greek representations of Isis. The goddess Isis was associated with nature and magic and revered as an ideal mother and wife. On the left, an Egyptian tomb mural from the fourth century B.C.E. shows Isis carrying an ankh, a symbol of eternal life, in one hand and a scepter, an emblem of dominion, in the other. On the right, the statue of a Hellenistic Isis dated to the second or first century B.C.E. holds a cornucopia, a Greek symbol of fertility. What other artistic elements in the two images would you characterize as distinctively Egyptian or Greek?

that shared philosophical, scientific, and aesthetic ideas with similarly minded people scattered in other cities.

Cultural cross-currents. Despite the influence of Greek language and cultural forms thousands of miles from Athens, the immense region exposed to them remained a complex cultural stew. Koine Greek gradually became the dominant language in Anatolia, but this did not happen in Syria or Egypt. In the Seleucid domain, Aramaic appears to have remained as important as Greek for government and commerce. Cultural forms not of Greek origin also gained importance within the Hellenistic zone. For example, Greco-Macedonians abroad adopted Egyptian or Persian gods into their pantheon by associating them symbolically with Hellenic divinities having similar character traits. The Egyptian goddess Isis took on a quasi-Greek identity and became popular in the Seleucid lands. Worship of deities like Isis sometimes metamorphosed into religious cults devoted to secret rituals, spiritual fellowship, and exercises to achieve union with the divine. Several of these mystery religions, as they are known, spread widely in the Hellenistic world and became popular among people of all classes. Among cultural fashions, rich Hellenistic families acquired tastes for female slaves of South Asian origin. These women fetched attractive prices because their exotic origins and looks elevated their value as servants in the households and bedchambers of the wealthy.

Jewish communities continued to multiply across Southwest Asia and the eastern Mediterranean between the fourth and second centuries B.C.E. The Jewish population in Alexandria rose to around 180,000, as much as a third of the city's total. Thousands learned to speak Greek, rather than Hebrew or Aramaic, as their first language. Jewish intellectuals produced a substantial body of religious, philosophical, and dramatic literature in that language. In the third century B.C.E., Ptolemy II sponsored translation of the Hebrew scriptures into Greek, a work known as the Septuagint. Greek-speaking Jews who were losing their knowledge of Hebrew needed this new edition, and non-Jews now had greater opportunity to become familiar with Jewish belief and practice. On the other hand, many Jews either resisted Hellenistic culture or had little contact with it, notably in Jerusalem and its vicinity. Some educated Jews studied Greek philosophical ideas but as worshipers of one God had nothing to do with the deities on Mount Olympus.

Buddhism and the Maurya Empire in India

FOCUS In what circumstances did Buddhist beliefs and practices achieve success among growing numbers in South Asia between the fifth and third centuries B.C.E.?

The first state to unify much of South Asia arose nearly simultaneously with the Seleucid and Ptolemaic empires. In 321 B.C.E., two years after Alexander died, the young warlord Chandragupta seized Magadha, the most powerful of a cluster of kingdoms along the Ganges River. He subdued several neighboring states and then advanced to the Indus River, where about 303 B.C.E. he defeated Greco-Macedonian occupiers, forcing them out of most of northwestern India. Ashoka, Chandragupta's grandson and the third ruler in the Maurya dynastic line, conquered more of India (see Map 6.4) and tried to create more efficient and orderly centralized government founded on a set of moral principles. He derived these precepts from the teachings of Buddhism, which was just then emerging in India as a popular religious movement.

Foundations of Buddhism

We saw in Chapter 5 that Brahmanism took root in northern and central India in the later second millennium B.C.E. Brahmanism was an intricate lacework of metaphysical ideas, sacred sacrifices, and social rules. In its spiritual dimension, it offered the individual hope of eventual release from earthly tribulation and endless cycles of rebirth. It involved worship of numerous gods and goddesses (Shiva and Vishnu chief among them), all of these deities manifestations of Brahman, the transcendent essence of the universe. This multisided religion gave the individual a spiritual anchor through the medium of daily rituals, whose performance varied from one locality to another.

The Brahmins, or male members of the privileged priestly class, aspired to define and regulate the religious and social conduct of all social groups, including the ruling warrior families. As their ritual power grew, Brahmins tended to neglect the longings of ordinary people for spiritual salvation. Instead, they devoted themselves to elaborate animal sacrifices and magical practices on which, they insisted, the well-being of the universe depended. Salvation was possible to those of low station, but only if they worked their way up the ladder of ritual purity to the Brahmin level, a process likely to require multiple rebirths, perhaps thousands of them. The sign of advancement was purer karma, the principle that good deeds done in a previous lifetime determined an individual's status in the present one. The Brahmins, however, defined good deeds mainly as scrupulous attention to ceremony and unquestioning acceptance of the rules that ritually separated the social classes, known in modern times as castes, from one another in matters of occupation, social relations, marriage, and physical contact.

The Buddha's message. Whereas Brahmins collaborated with aristocratic warriors (the Kshatriya class) to maintain the hierarchy of social inequality, teachers and preachers began to offer alternative paths to moral living and divine salvation, sometimes denouncing Brahmin dogmatism. One of these sages was Siddhartha Gautama, known to his followers as the Buddha, or Enlightened One (ca. 563–ca. 483 B.C.E.). He was born into a Kshatriya family in what is

The great stupa at Sanchi. According to tradition, when the Buddha died, his cremated remains were placed in eight earthen burial mounds, or stupas. The emperor Ashoka later redistributed the ashes among more than 60,000 stupas. To house some of the ashes and other relics of the Buddha, Ashoka also built monumental stupas, including an early form of this celebrated shrine at Sanchi in central India. Pilgrims replicate the Buddha's exodus from the world by entering the stupa's stone enclosure through one of four gates. Then they walk clockwise around the spherical structure, whose vault represents the dome of the cosmos.

today Nepal. He gave up family wealth and power to become an ascetic, an individual who renounced worldly cares and pleasures for a life of self-denial and spiritual reflection. Accompanied by a growing body of followers, he preached a message of moral renewal and the possibility of freedom from suffering.

All men and women, the Buddha taught, are responsible for right living, not mainly by acting out rituals but by giving up material desire, greed, and all conduct that kept them enslaved to pain and distress. In his best-known sermon, he expounded the Four Noble Truths: first, that earthly life is inevitably unfulfilling; second, that this suffering is a consequence of our cravings for transient things and experiences; third, that the way out of suffering is renunciation of craving; and fourth, that the only course of action is to walk the Eightfold Path, a plan for attentive, decent, meditative living. This commitment included *ahimsa* (uh-HIM-suh), or the practice of nonviolence, on the principle that all life-forms are sacred and cosmically interrelated. At the end of the Eightfold Path lies nirvana, a limitless, indescribable

state where the self is extinguished and thereby released from the cycle of rebirth and suffering. Many historians have noticed similarities between Buddhist thought as it evolved from the fifth century B.C.E. and Hellenistic philosophical movements that offered moral designs for living in harmony with the cosmos.

The Buddha's words and acts, first put in writing long after his death, originated from the Brahmanist tradition, not in opposition to it. He accepted the validity of rebirth and karma, and he did not preach social revolution against the rigid class hierarchy. He associated karma, however, with day-to-day righteousness, not ritual conformity. People of all social ranks could escape from suffering if they fulfilled the demands of the Eightfold Path. The quest, however, required great dedication.

In the centuries following the Buddha's passing, the new religion germinated mainly in self-contained communities, or monasteries. There, early devotees gathered to work, meditate, and perform charitable works. Laypeople, those who stayed "in the world" and did not become monks, also flocked to Buddhism by frequenting the monasteries or materially supporting them. Brahmanism categorized women as having essential roles in society but nonetheless as innately inferior and a source of ritual pollution to men. The Buddha, however, admitted after much consideration that both women and men could achieve nirvana and that women should be admitted to monasteries. He did not, however, preach equality between the sexes, and except in Tibet female monasteries never took root. The archaeological record shows that between the fifth and third centuries B.C.E., Buddhist *stupas*, structures in which holy relics associated with the Buddha or other saintly individuals were placed, multiplied across northern India. By the time of the Maurya empire, Buddhist practice was well established among urban mercantile and professional classes in much of the subcontinent.

Jainism. Numerous schools of philosophical thought flourished in India in the Buddha's time, but among these only Jainism (JEYEN-ism, from a Sanskrit word meaning "saint") endured as a significant religious movement into the modern era. The founding teacher, Mahavira (the "Great Hero," ca. 540–468 B.C.E.), left his warrior class family to seek enlightenment, just as the Buddha had done. Both of those worthies taught that self-centered material desires obstructed the individual's path to salvation—the attainment of a state of pure bliss. But, in contrast to the Buddha, Mahavira recommended a life of self-denial so strict that only the most zealous monk could hope to meet its demands. The members of Jain monasteries were prohibited from owning property, having sexual

relations, or killing any life-form. Monks often carried brooms to brush away insects before sitting down, and they hired people outside the monastery to harvest their crops since no devotee could do that without murdering, as it were, tiny animals. Mahavira himself is reputed to have set the highest standard by going naked and eventually starving himself to death. In contrast to the Buddhist way, Jainism did not spread beyond South Asia before modern times. But there it grew into a significant religious minority, categorized by some as a sect within Hinduism.

The Reign of Ashoka Maurya

Buddhist teachings had wide impact in India during the reign of Ashoka (273–232 B.C.E.), who commanded an empire of about fifty million people employing many of the bureaucratic methods of the earlier Achaemenids of Persia. Pataliputra, Ashoka's capital in the middle Ganges valley, was reportedly nine and a half miles long and defended by mammoth timber walls. Here, the emperor received diplomatic missions, dispensed justice, and coordinated the work of his ministries, which regulated taxation, commerce, and agriculture. He launched his reign as an autocratic conqueror, but in a moment of regret over a particularly bloody military campaign, he repudiated repression and cruelty and formulated a philosophy of moral government. The key concept in his ideology, which drew heavily from Buddhist teachings, was *dhamma* (or dharma). For the emperor this meant commitment to nonviolence, political moderation, family

Pillar with a lion capital. The emperor Ashoka had this pillar erected at the town of Vaishali north of the Ganges River to commemorate the day the Buddha preached his last sermon. The use of the lion icon as an emblem of royalty points to Persian cultural influence on Ashoka's India.

Rock Edicts of the Emperor Ashoka

Most of Emperor Ashoka's rock edicts were written in a South Asian script that later fell out of use. While later generations knew about the inscriptions, they were unable to read the texts. Instead, people passed on oral legends about what the stone markers were thought to say. These legends claimed that Ashoka had erected the rocks at important Buddhist sites to commemorate people or events, so that pilgrims passing by would be aware of the locations' significance. As Buddhism waned in India over several centuries, people forgot the connection between Ashoka and the rock inscriptions altogether.

It was not until 1837 that the British scholar James Prinsep deciphered the ancient script and read the edicts. Only then did their subject matter become known. Prinsep did not realize that Ashoka was the author of the texts because the emperor referred to himself on the known inscriptions only as the Beloved of the Gods. Although other scholars suspected that the edicts were Ashoka's, they confirmed this only in 1915, when an inscription with the emperor's name in it was finally discovered.

The texts here are short selections from rock edicts in which Ashoka sought to explain how to rule justly and to spread Buddhist values in the empire.

ROCK EDICT 1

Formerly, in the kitchen of Beloved-of-the-Gods, . . . hundreds of thousands of animals were killed every day to make curry. But now with the writing of this Dhamma edict only three creatures, two peacocks and a deer are killed, and the deer not always. And in time, not even these three creatures will be killed.

ROCK EDICT 5

In the past there were no Dhamma Mahamatras [officials who looked after the spiritual and material needs of people], but such officers were appointed by me thirteen years after my coronation. Now they work among all religions for the establishment of Dhamma, for the promotion of Dhamma, and for the welfare and happiness of all who are devoted to Dhamma. They work among the Greeks, the Kambojas, the Gandharas, the Rastrikas, the Pitinikas and other peoples on the western borders. They work among soldiers, chiefs, Brahmins, householders, the poor, the aged and those devoted to Dhamma—for their welfare and happiness—so that they may be free from harassment. They (Dhamma Mahamatras) work for the proper treatment of prisoners, towards their unfettering, and if the Mahamatras think, "This one has a family to support," "That one has been bewitched," "This one is old," then they work for the release of such prisoners. They work here, in outlying towns, in the women's quarters belonging to my brothers and sisters, and among my other relatives. They are occupied everywhere.

ROCK EDICT 6

Beloved-of-the-Gods . . . speaks thus: In the past, state business was not transacted nor were reports delivered to the king at all hours. But now I have given this order, that at any time, whether I am eating, in the women's quarters, the bed chamber, the chariot, the palanquin, in the park or wherever, reporters are to be posted with instructions to report to me the affairs of the people so that I might attend to these affairs wherever I am. And whatever I orally order in connection with donations or proclamations, or when urgent business presses itself on the Mahamatras, if disagreement or debate arises in the Council, then it must be reported to me immediately. This is what I have ordered. I am never content with exerting myself or with dispatching business. Truly, I consider the welfare of all to be my duty, and the root of this is exertion and the prompt dispatch of business. There is no better work than promoting the welfare of all the people and whatever efforts I am making is to repay the debt I owe to all beings to assure their happiness in this life, and attain heaven in the next.

Sources: "The Edicts of King Ashoka," an English rendering by Ven. S. Dhammika (Kandy, Sri Lanka: Buddhist Publication Society, 1993).

Thinking Critically

What does the passage from Edict 1 infer regarding Ashoka's conversion to Buddhism and the effect it had on his actions? According to Edict 5, how did the Dhamma Mahamatras spread the value of compassion in their work? How did their efforts transcend social class barriers? Why do you think Ashoka was inclined to publish an edict about the importance of conducting imperial business promptly? What particular moral qualities does Ashoka think a good Buddhist monarch should have? How would you compare Ashoka's approach to kingship with that of Alexander the Great and other Greco-Macedonian rulers?

harmony, toleration among social groups, and dedication to the well-being and prosperity of all imperial subjects. Ashoka did not aim to reform the Indian social hierarchy, but he encouraged his subjects to accept social responsibilities for one another beyond the boundaries of class and ethnicity. We know quite a bit about his conception of *dhamma* because he had proclamations inscribed on rocks and pillars near population centers and along well-traveled roads. In one of his rock edicts, he described the event that set him on a new path, referring to himself in the third person as the Beloved of the Gods:

> Beloved-of-the-Gods, . . . conquered the Kalingas eight years after his coronation. One hundred and fifty thousand were deported, one hundred thousand were killed and many more died (from other causes). After the Kalingas had been conquered, Beloved-of-the-Gods came to feel a strong inclination towards the Dhamma, a love for the Dhamma and for instruction in Dhamma. Now Beloved-of-the-Gods feels deep remorse for having conquered the Kalingas.[9]

As "Beloved of the Gods," Ashoka, like monarchs to the west, claimed universal authority over humankind and vowed to rule justly. However, he seems to have differed from the Greco-Macedonian rulers of his era in his explicit appeal to his subjects to behave toward one another in a spirit of toleration and generosity. He appointed special officials to travel the provinces, spreading Buddhist teachings on moral behavior. Putting into practice the Buddhist precept of *ahimsa*, he also preached against the killing of animals, promoted vegetarianism, and admonished the Brahmins to halt bloody animal sacrifices.

Ashoka's philosophy was almost certainly calculated to address real problems of social conflict in a time of rapid economic change. Agricultural production in the two great river valleys was rising. Cities were mushrooming, and artisans were forming guilds to organize an array of urban industries such as metalworking, textile manufacturing, and banking. This commercialization no doubt aggravated social tensions. Although merchants and crafts workers were becoming more prosperous, the Brahmin and warrior classes generally treated them as inferiors. Consequently, many productive members of society patronized Buddhist monasteries, which practiced social egalitarianism and offered brighter hopes of salvation. Buddhism also appealed to farmers and laborers (Shudras) for the same reasons.

Dhamma as a philosophy of government did not outlast Ashoka, but it nonetheless had important long-term consequences. The emperor tried to achieve his aims of social integration partly by developing South Asia's infrastructure of communication and transport. He improved the great trunk road that ran from the city of Taxila in the upper Indus valley to Pataliputra on the Ganges, accommodating travelers with shade trees, wells, and rest houses. Other tracks stimulated exchange of foodstuffs and manufactures between the northern grain-growing plains and the tropical forests of the

far south. Long after the Maurya dynasty vanished, the road network expedited trade and cultural interchange across South Asia. Ashoka also appears to have had his edicts carved into rocks and pillars as a way of building social consensus across class lines regarding the aims of *dhamma*. We have no idea how well these messages worked as mass communication, but edicts that survive represent precious historical evidence of developments in India 2,300 years ago.

A second major consequence of Ashoka's reign was that Buddhism became for several centuries the most dynamic religious force in India. The tenets embodied in *dhamma*, extensive conversions among merchants and artisans, and the improved communication network all facilitated the spread of this faith. For several centuries Buddhism competed vigorously with Brahmanism as an alternative vision of cosmic truth and righteous living. Ashoka himself propagated Buddhist teachings by sending missionaries far and wide. Ancient sources report that he dispatched one of his sons to broadcast *dhamma* on the island of Ceylon, where Buddhism became firmly established. To the northwest his messengers carried *dhamma* into Afghanistan. A rock edict located near the Afghan city of Kandahar is inscribed, not in Prakrit, the Indic language of the Maurya state, but in both Greek and Aramaic, as if Ashoka were deliberately reaching out to peoples of the west.[10] Yet despite Buddhist success in South Asia and beyond, the Brahmin class continued to dominate the yearly cycle of sacrifices and festivals in the rural villages. And after a few centuries, Buddhism gradually declined in the land of its birth, though flowering elsewhere in Eurasia, as we see in later chapters.

When Ashoka died after a forty-two-year reign, the *dhamma* experiment ended abruptly. Succeeding Maurya kings possessed little of his energy and none of his moral vision. Revolts broke out on the edges of the empire, and the imperial bureaucracy decayed. Within a few decades South Asia's first universal empire collapsed. The next great enterprise to unify India would not appear for another six hundred years.

Cavalry and Caravans in Inner Eurasia

FOCUS How did dense agrarian societies from the Mediterranean to China change as a result of developments in Inner Eurasia in the 600–200 B.C.E. period?

Monarchs from India to the Mediterranean, as well as rulers in China, kept a watchful eye on peoples of Inner Eurasia, the northerly land of steppes, forests, mountains, and deserts that stretches nearly five thousand miles across Afroeurasia. As their numbers grew, Inner Eurasia's pastoral nomadic groups began to organize politically on a larger scale than merely local chieftaincies. At the same time, trade across the region grew busier. Dusty trails connected

Inner Eurasian societies both with one another and with the densely populated, urbanized lands to the south and east.

Nomad Power

On the Inner Eurasia steppes, pastoral communities organized themselves in extended kinship groups, a social system suited to societies that moved from pasture to pasture as the seasons changed rather than inhabiting a fixed territory year round. That is, people expressed their social identity not primarily in terms of *where* they lived but in terms of *who* their shared paternal ancestors were, their grandfathers, great grandfathers, and so on. A group that interacted regularly in daily life and that claimed descent from a forebear who lived a few generations back constituted a lineage (see Chapter 3). Lineages were typically embedded in larger social groups, numbering hundreds or even thousands of living men and women, that we may call "clans." All the lineages constituting a clan claimed descent from a common ancestor that lived in the more distant past. On an even larger scale, several clans might regard themselves as genealogically related, constituting a **tribe.** Clan and tribal identities did not have much significance in daily life. Rather, leaders called on loyalties at those levels mainly when large numbers of people had to be mobilized for defense or war.

tribe The largest social group in a region whose members claim shared descent.

From about the eighth century B.C.E., we have some evidence of clans and tribes forming large military coalitions led by elite families. These allied bands of mounted archers took advantage of technological innovations, including improved leather and metal horse harness, the riding saddle (though without stirrups), iron as well as bronze weaponry, and, perhaps most important, the light but powerful composite bow (see Chapter 5). Pastoral and agricultural communities regularly traded with one another, but some herding societies built up enough destructive potential to entertain ideas of attacking farm settlements, cities, or even densely populated agrarian regions. In the first millennium B.C.E., therefore, a recurring theme in world history appears: persistent political tensions and periodic warfare between mounted nomads and their settled neighbors.

Ancient texts identify Inner Eurasian warrior alliances under a variety of names—Scythians, Cimmerians, Sakas, Sarmatians, and several others. From the eighth century B.C.E., mounted bands harried the northwestern frontiers of China, and in the following century a throng of Cimmerian archers attacked the Assyrian empire in northern Mesopotamia. Of all these marauders, we know most about the Scythians. Herodotus, the Greek historian of the fifth century B.C.E., described them in detail, and archaeologists have uncovered elite Scythian tombs

littered with worked gold and other precious grave goods. Scythians inhabited the Pontic-Caspian steppes north of the Black Sea, and they spoke one or more Indo-European languages. From the sixth century B.C.E., Scythians established commercial links with Greek settlements around the rim of the Black Sea, trading grain, furs, livestock, honey, and slaves for Mediterranean commodities and manufactures. Affluent Scythian families acquired tastes for Greek wine and olive oil. Some groups added Greek gods and goddesses to their own collection of deities and displayed Greek ceramic ware in their tents.

Near the end of the seventh century B.C.E., Scythian cavalry crossed the Caucasus Mountains to pillage farms and towns from Syria to Iran. According to Herodotus, Scythian archers took part in the final destruction of the Assyrian state. These warriors, Herodotus reports, were particularly disposed to headhunting:

> As for the actual skulls—the skulls of their enemies, that is, not all skulls—they saw off the bottom part of the skull at

Scythian warriors. The two hardy-looking men on this vessel of Greek workmanship hold long spears.

the level of the eyebrows and clean out the top bit. A poor Scythian then wraps a piece of untanned cowhide tightly around the outside of the skull and puts it to use like that, while a rich Scythian goes further: after wrapping it in cowhide he gilds the inside and then uses it as a cup. Also, if a Scythian falls out with one of his relatives, they fight to the death in the presence of their king, and the winner treats the loser's skull in the way I have just described. When he has important visitors, he produces these skulls and tells how they had once been his relatives, and how they made war on him, but he defeated them.[11]

Ancient legends about Amazons, or ferocious women fighters, probably originated with the Scythians. According to one Greek text, "Their women ride horses and shoot arrows and hurl javelins from horseback and they fight in campaigns as long as they are virgins."[12] A significant number of graves excavated on the Pontic-Caspian steppe have revealed the skeletons of women in full battle gear.

The rulers of agrarian states eventually understood they had to push back at pastoral intruders. For example, in both Central Asia and on the plains west of the Black Sea, Achaemenid armies campaigned aggressively against the Scythians and other nomads. The Persians demonstrated that a strong centralized state with ample agrarian resources, many soldiers, and the skills to build walls and forts could turn the tables, challenging militarized herders on their own territory. But by the late first millennium B.C.E., pastoralists were discovering ways to organize even larger military alliances and hold them together longer.

Early Times on the Silk Roads

Trade across Inner Eurasia became significant from at least the late third millennium B.C.E., when a cluster of small walled cities sprang up in Central Asia (see Chapter 3). These cities became key centers for transshipping goods of high value and low bulk—silk, gems, furs, metalwork, ceramics—overland between East Asia and westerly lands. An unbroken chain of Inner Eurasian trails, known by the modern term "silk roads," gradually formed. There were several alternate routes not just one, and their locations tended to shift over time. Some goods might have been relayed very long distances. For example, archaeologists have discovered strands of East Asian silk on the mummy of a woman who lived in Egypt about 1000 B.C.E.

We know little about commercial organization in the early silk road centuries. Associations of merchants, guides, packers, and armed guards likely banded together temporarily to share costs and risks and, if they reached their destination safely, to sell their merchandise at a profit. If we can infer from later times how this trade worked, merchants who shared common language, culture, and business customs likely set up their own associations to facilitate trade, much as the Phoenicians and Greeks established diasporas, or scatterings of merchants and commercial agents across the Mediterranean. The silk roads therefore became regular channels of human interchange, not only for material goods but also for "cultural capital" of all kinds—new technologies, religious teachings, and artistic styles.

Why did the silk roads become busier in the first millennium B.C.E.? One factor is certainly the continuing agrarian and urban expansion taking place in the agrarian lands from China to the Mediterranean, a growth that generated rising demand for products that could not be produced locally. Inner Eurasia's population also grew steadily in that millennium. This happened mainly because the specialized economy of pastoral nomadism, together with farming in river valleys here and there, allowed relatively more people to inhabit these dry latitudes. Most herding societies wanted to encourage ties with the villages and cities that lay along the edges of the steppes in order to trade grain, livestock products, metals, and furs for goods they could not make themselves. Moreover trade moved not only east and west on the silk roads but also north and south across contrasting climatic and ecological zones. To the north, foragers and hunters of the temperate Siberian forests joined the commercial web, trading furs to pastoral peoples for wares that in some cases originated in distant cities to the south. In short, Inner Eurasia was by no means a vacant land that caravans scurried across to get from one civilization to another. Rather, it became a locus of both military and economic power, exerting a huge impact on neighboring regions of much denser population.

• • •

Conclusion

The political ascendancy of Alexander the Great and his Greco-Macedonian successors over a large piece of Afroeurasia lasted less than two hundred years in some places and no more than three hundred anywhere. Even so, we can only marvel that the young son of the king of a modest Balkan state instigated a run of conquests that reached from the Nile to the Indus. Alexander, together with the Achaemenid emperors who came before him, demonstrated that by the later first millennium B.C.E. the technology of overland transport, road building, army supply, and weaponry reached a level of sophistication that permitted a determined conqueror to subjugate populations numbering in the tens of millions. The Greco-Macedonian and Indian rulers who came after Alexander also showed that many millions of subjects could actually be organized, made answerable to royal laws, and taxed. In the era of the Hellenistic kings and the Maurya emperors, authoritarian governments supported construction of dozens of new cities and the expansion of farming and trade. Wealth piled up in splendid capitals as never before, and class divisions between rich minorities and ordinary people remained rigid or became more so, and long-distance communication intensified not only across the India-to-Mediterranean lands but also in lesser measure between that region and China by way of the emerging silk roads.

By the late third century B.C.E., the Afroeurasian political map was changing in significant ways. To the east the Maurya dynasty disintegrated and for the next six centuries smaller states competed for power in South Asia while also battling invaders from the steppes. The Greco-Macedonian rulers of Persia progressively lost territory, some of it to Inner Eurasian horse archers. The Athenians' lively experiment with direct democracy proved to be, not a new trend, but a political oddity. In the far west, Rome, a modest city-state on the west side of Italy, gradually rose to regional dominance. Far to the east, the leaders of the Qin and Han dynasties united much of northern and central China after several centuries of rivalry among several regional kingdoms. A new era of grand empire building was about to begin.

• • •

Key Terms

Achaemenid empire of Persia 161	Jainism 182	Scythians 185
Alexander the Great's empire 173	Maurya empire 181	Seleucid empire 175
Athenian empire 171	natural philosophy 172	silk roads 187
Buddhism 181	oligarchy 169	Sparta 169
chattel slavery 170	Peloponnesian War 173	tribe 185
dhamma (dharma) 183	phalanx 171	universal empire 165
Hellenistic 175	Ptolemaic dynasty 178	Zoroastrianism 167
Iliad and *Odyssey* 169	satrapy 165	

Change over Time

9th–4th centuries B.C.E.	Scythian pastoral society flourishes north of the Black Sea.
8th–4th centuries B.C.E.	Self-governing Greek poleis dominate the Aegean Sea region.
ca. 563–483 B.C.E.	Siddhartha Gautama, the Buddha, lives.
550–330 B.C.E.	The Achaemenid empire centered on Persia proclaims a universal mission to rule the world.
6th century B.C.E.	Achaemenid rulers adopt Zoroastrian beliefs and rituals.
ca. 540–468 B.C.E.	Mahavira, founding teacher of Jainism, lives in India.
480 B.C.E.	The Greek naval victory over Persia at the Battle of Salamis thwarts Persian expansion farther west.
470–399 B.C.E.	Greek philosopher Socrates teaches in Athens.
ca. 461–429 B.C.E.	Pericles leads in Athens and the Athenian maritime empire rises.
431–404 B.C.E.	Greek city-states engage in Peloponnesian War.
336–323 B.C.E.	Alexander the Great conquers and rules the largest state in world history to this point.
321–185 B.C.E.	Northern and central India are united under the Maurya empire, which reaches its zenith during the reign of Ashoka Maurya.
312–64 B.C.E.	The Seleucid empire, the largest and richest of the Hellenistic states, dominates Southwest Asia.
305–30 B.C.E.	The Ptolemaic dynasty rules a Hellenistic state in Egypt.

Please see end of book reference section for additional reading suggestions related to this chapter.

Bactrian camels in the Gobi Desert, Mongolia.

amel raising is a demanding occupation. The species will breed only once a year, and during this short time it may behave badly—biting, kicking, or spitting at anyone who comes near. Males find copulation an awkward business and sometimes require assistance from their human handlers to make a go of it. When mating is successful, a camel's pregnancy lasts thirteen months. A female gives birth rarely more often than once every two years. Despite these vexations, patient camel breeders of the third millennium B.C.E. gave the ancient world one of its most versatile domesticates.

Camels, along with cattle, sheep, goats, and horses, allowed humans to build herding economies in arid regions of Afroeurasia where intensive farming was not possible. Camels provided pastoral societies with meat, milk, hides, and bone. And because they have wide-spreading feet for easy walking on sand or snow, double rows of eyelashes for protection against blowing sand, and a biological constitution that allows them to forego water for more than two weeks, camels were well suited to moving people and cargo across arid terrain. In the first millennium B.C.E., pastoral nomads and merchants rode Bactrian (two-humped) camels or hitched them to wagons to cross the steppes, deserts, and mountains of Inner Eurasia. From northern India to the Sahara Desert, the dromedary (one-humped species) became the animal of choice for transport across dry country. The harnessing of camels was one of the developments that contributed to intensified exchange across Afroeurasia in the period from 300 B.C.E. to 300 C.E.

This chapter investigates how and why Afroeurasia's regional zones of intercommunication not only grew larger but also joined more firmly to one another. The chapter explores this phenomenon in connection with the rise of several new states—a few of them gigantic—that formed a nearly continuous chain of polities stretching across Afroeurasia. Each of these states provided a political framework for channeling revenue from their populations to their treasuries, while also refining the communication systems that tightened cultural and economic bonds. And because each state bordered, or nearly bordered, one or more of the others, tentacles of exchange reached out to connect one network with another. This process could be interrupted by wars. Nevertheless, it was in these centuries that a system of land and sea routes running continuously, if still somewhat tentatively, across Afroeurasia first took shape.

Human interchange became particularly intense around the Mediterranean Sea. In the first part of the chapter, we focus on the rise of Rome, which grew to encompass the entire Mediterranean rim, all of its islands, and deep hinterlands in western and central Europe. The spatial core of the empire was the sea itself, an expanse crossed easily by sailing ships and oar-powered galleys except in stormy winter months. Rome's seaborne thoroughfares conducted troops and officials thousands of miles from Italy and made possible the diffusion of a distinctively Hellenistic style of intellectual, religious, and artistic culture to cities as far apart from one another as northern England and the edge of the Sahara Desert.

In the second part of the chapter, we zoom to the opposite end of Afroeurasia, where the Qin (chin) and Han dynasties successively ruled a state that mirrored Rome in its size, population, and military might. The heart of the empire was not a central sea but the Yellow and Yangzi River valleys, which sustained the millions of farmers whose taxes largely paid for the imperial bureaucracy and army. In the Han centuries, from 206 B.C.E. to 220 C.E., Confucianism and Daoism

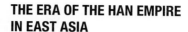

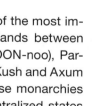
• • •

(DOW-ism), two belief systems originating in the fifth century B.C.E., became major shapers of Chinese society and culture.

The third part of the chapter surveys five of the most important states that occupied Afroeurasian lands between Rome and Han China: the Xiongnu (SHEE-OON-noo), Parthian, and Kushana empires of Asia, and the Kush and Axum kingdoms of Africa. Like the two giants, these monarchies embodied the hemispheric trend toward centralized states capable of amassing great wealth and military power.

In the chapter's final section, we turn to developments made possible by this new chain of states in Afroeurasia. First, we investigate the marked intensification of long-distance commerce, especially exchange on the Inner Eurasian silk roads and on the tropical southern seas. Second, we survey the growth of Buddhism and Christianity, two belief systems that transcended identification with any particular region or ethnolinguistic group and that spread far beyond their natal lands.

A Panoramic View

MAP 7.1 Major states and empires in Afroeurasia, 100 B.C.E.
A string of large states stretched across Afroeurasia in 100 B.C.E. What geographic and climatic features did these seven states share?

Rome and Mediterranean Unification

FOCUS How did the Romans, whose history began as the inhabitants of a modest city-state, succeed in subjecting peoples all around the Mediterranean rim to their rule?

In long-term historical perspective, it is useful to view the Mediterranean Sea, not as a watery barrier separating three continents from one another, but as an internal sea of Afroeurasia, binding together people all around its rim from very ancient times (see Map 7.1). This domain of intercommunication also included the Black Sea, the Mediterranean's big "lagoon" to the northeast. The agricultural, mineral, and marine wealth of the sea basin was potentially immense. Prospects of exploiting that wealth impelled Phoenicians, Greeks, Etruscans, Egyptians, and Persians to try at different times in the first millennium B.C.E. to dominate parts of the basin by controlling strategic points—islands, ports, and narrow sea passages.

republic A type of government in which supreme power rests with a body of citizens possessing rights to vote to approve laws and to select public officials and representatives.

In the third century B.C.E., Rome, a **republic** and the dominant state on the Italian peninsula, emerged as a new Mediterranean power. Unlike its predecessors, however, Rome kept expanding until it encircled the sea. At its zenith around 100 C.E., the empire embraced a population of fifty to sixty million and land area more than half the size of the continental United States. Like Achaemenid Persia and other earlier empires, it aspired to universal rule, that is, to sovereignty over the whole world.

This section of the chapter encompasses two major periods of Roman history. The first was the Republic (509–27 B.C.E.), when the Romans conquered Italy and most of the Mediterranean basin. In that period, republican government meant, as it generally did in the Greek city-states, that all adult males possessing citizenship had rights and obligations in public life. The second period was the Principate (27 B.C.E. to the later third century C.E.), when individual rulers achieved autocratic command of an enormous multiethnic state. In both periods, episodes of political instability, social upheaval, and provincial revolt disturbed the long-term pattern of imperial unity.

Rome the Republic

When Rome emerged as a republican city-state in the late sixth century B.C.E., the peoples of Italy were mostly farmers. The early Romans spoke an ancient form of Latin, a tongue in the Indo-European subfamily known as Italic. Their modest city on the lower Tiber River lay between two more sophisticated spheres of urban life. To the north were the Etruscan city-states (see Chapter 5). Kings of Etruscan origin ruled Rome throughout much of the seventh and sixth centuries B.C.E. To the southeast were numerous cities that Greek-speaking colonists had established on Sicily and along the southern Italian coast.

The Romans borrowed elements of culture from both of these neighbors. The Etruscans contributed ideas of city planning, gold and bronze metallurgy, particular gods and goddesses, arch-building technology, the Greek alphabet in modified Etruscan form, and, we should add, the toga. Greek influences on Rome were even greater. When the Romans threw off Etruscan domination about 509 B.C.E., they set up a government patterned basically on Greek-style republicanism. Rome's aristocratic land-owners fell under the spell of Greek philosophy, medicine, drama, and art. The Romans also adopted many Greek deities. These Hellenistic influences washed over Rome in successive waves: in the fourth century B.C.E., when Romans admired the Greek cities of southern Italy from afar; in the third century, when they conquered those cities and made them junior allies; and in the second century, when Rome's legions invaded Greece itself. Thereafter, Rome became the major center from which Hellenistic culture radiated out across the western Mediterranean and Europe.

Republican government and society.

When Rome became a republic, that is, a state founded on the collective authority of all land-owning male citizens, social tension no doubt already existed between the society's two principal classes. One was the aristocratic minority known as the patricians. The wealthy and privileged families who constituted this class sat in the Senate, an elective and advisory body. The other group, making up the great majority of the citizen population, was known collectively as the plebs. In early republican days, the patrician families tried to keep a tight hold on power. But plebeian leaders gradually won legal equality for all citizens, a written set of laws (the Twelve Tables), and the privilege of forming an assembly

A patrician of Rome. Like aristocratic classes in all ancient agrarian societies, the Roman elite put great value on quality of their family pedigree. This gentleman displays the busts of two of his venerable ancestors.

called the Plebeian Council. This body had authority to enact laws, hold trials, and elect officials called tribunes to look after plebeian interests. Between the fifth and second centuries B.C.E., the plebs gained additional rights and responsibilities. In the long term, this trend helped defuse social class conflict.

Elected officials, or magistrates, managed Rome's internal and foreign affairs. At first the Republic had only two magistrates, called consuls, who were elected to one-year terms and who supervised civil affairs and military campaigns. As Rome grew, however, several new public offices had to be created to oversee such affairs as public works, commerce, and military supply. Eventually, plebeians gained the right to hold high offices, including the consulship, and to take seats in the Senate, a governing body of about three hundred males who served for life. Senators managed the Republic's finances, wars, diplomacy, and provincial administration. Male citizens could vote in one of the popular assemblies that passed laws to regulate property, commerce, slavery, duties of officials, and other spheres of social life. These bodies were the Plebeian Council, plus the Curiate and Centuriate Assemblies, which included both plebeians and patricians. Roman leaders generally honored the rule of law, the precept that legislation represented the will of the citizenry and should be enforced equitably and consistently.

As in the Greek city-states, the majority of the Republic's population was excluded from the major rights and responsibilities of citizenship. Foreign immigrants and slaves (many of them captured as war prisoners) had no citizenship rights, though freed slaves could become citizens with certain restrictions. Rome usually offered generous political terms to peoples that it conquered on the Italian peninsula but granted them citizenship only incrementally over several centuries. Free women could attain citizenship but with serious restrictions. They could not attend assemblies or serve as either elected or appointed officials. On the other hand, free women could make wills, sue for divorce, circulate in public quite freely, and hold certain priestly offices. Wives and mothers in wealthy families might exert great informal influence on public decisions. Upper-class women gradually achieved rights to buy and sell property, though they remained legally subordinated to fathers, husbands, or other guardians.

The Republic's political institutions operated to perpetuate the collective government of the Roman people and to prevent any single individual from accumulating too much power. Citizens voted frequently in their assemblies, but the system was only narrowly democratic. In contrast to the assembly in Athens in the fifth century B.C.E., for example, the Roman assemblies had no provision for citizens to debate proposals. Rather, they simply voted yes or no. Citizens gathered in the forum at the center of the city or on the nearby Field of Mars to vote as members of either "centuries" (divisions of the population based on wealth) or "tribes" (territorial divisions). Each century or tribe had just one collective vote. Moreover, the richest families effectively stage managed the popular assemblies most of the time to get the decisions they wanted. Plebeians who took advantage of the Republic's prosperity to accumulate wealth tended to ally themselves not with poorer plebeians but with patrician families. In its politics, Rome remained an oligarchy, a state dominated by a small minority with power founded fundamentally on wealth.

Rome did almost all its public business through networks of patrons and clients. That is, rich and powerful individuals (patrons) sought loyal supporters from among the relatively poorer and weaker classes (clients), offering them jobs, money, physical protection, favors, or marriage alliances. In return, they expected favorable votes in the assemblies, public demonstrations of support, and a variety of personal services. **Patron–client systems** formed into hierarchical webs, with the clients of the richest and most powerful patrons acquiring clients of their own. This process replicated itself down the line to the level of people so poor and politically weak they could become no one's patron. Put another way, until quite late in its history the Roman empire did not have a strong bureaucracy, that is, a system in which officeholders were entrusted to carry out their duties as impersonal agents of the state, rather than as personal dependents or allies of someone higher up the chain of command.

> **patron–client system** A vertical social and political system in which individuals possessing relative degrees of power, wealth, or social status offer protection or economic benefits to other individuals in return for personal loyalty and services.

Rome's early imperial conquests. The Republic deployed a formidable army of citizen-soldiers. As in the fifth-century Greek city-states, property-owning farmers who paid for their own swords and other weapons constituted the core of the army. At first, infantrymen grouped in large Greek-style phalanxes, but eventually commanders cut the size of combat units to improve their speed and maneuverability. The army also formed cavalry divisions, armed auxiliaries from conquered peoples, and a corps of engineers who built roads, bridges, walls, and forts. Citizen-soldiers were expected to embody the Republic's military culture of steadfast service and manly virtue, though the promise of loot and land also motivated war service. Military campaigns provided a safety valve for social class tensions over land and income because the state awarded farm plots in conquered territories to both soldiers and poor citizens. At the same time, rich landlords got war prisoners for slave labor on their giant estates.

Rome's nearly continuous drive to expand got under way in the fourth century B.C.E. when the Republic's legions (military divisions) conquered central Italy. In the following century, the army subjugated the rest of the peninsula plus Sicily (see Map 7.2). In 264 B.C.E., Rome went to war against the Phoenician maritime empire that from Carthage, its

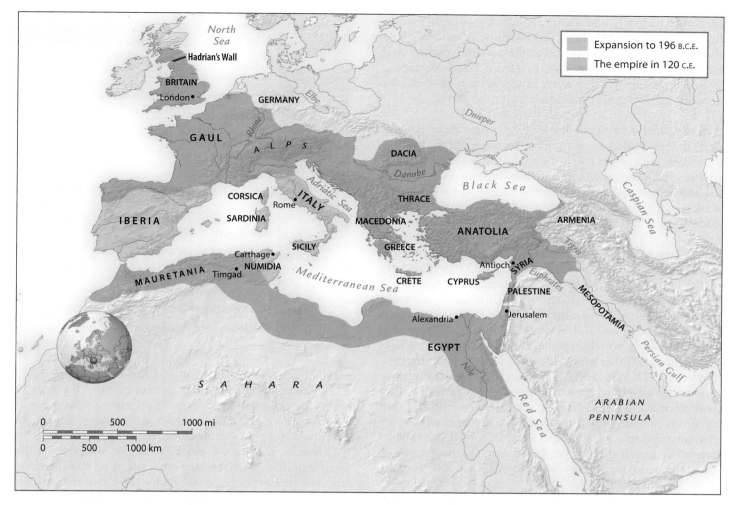

MAP 7.2 Roman imperial expansion, to 300 C.E.
What factors of physical geography may have shaped the directions of Roman conquest?

capital on the coast of what is today Tunisia, dominated the ports, trading posts, and routes of the western and central Mediterranean. Rome constructed a powerful navy, and over the span of 119 years the two states fought three wars, known as the Punic Wars (from the Latin word *Punicus*, meaning Phoenician). The second war (218–202 B.C.E.) featured the Carthaginian general Hannibal leading an army that included brightly painted African war elephants from Spain over high Alpine passes to Italy—though most of the beasts soon died in Italy. The invaders came close to attacking the city of Rome, but after supply and reinforcement lines dried up, Hannibal had no choice but to withdraw. In the long run, the Republic could mobilize people and resources that Carthage could not match. In 146 B.C.E., Roman troops obliterated the city of Carthage, thereby securing full control of Sicily, southern Iberia (Spain), and a long stretch of North African coast. Consequently, the empire gained thousands of square miles of wheat land in those regions, as well as a windfall of silver from Iberian mines.

After Rome's victory over Carthage, the Senate adopted a more aggressive strategy of empire building around the Mediterranean. Macedonia and Greece were absorbed, and from there, soldiers crossed the Aegean Sea to Anatolia, as Alexander the Great had done two hundred years earlier. In the first century B.C.E., a large part of both Anatolia and Syria, territories that had been part of the Hellenistic Seleucid empire, fell to Rome. In 30 B.C.E., Egypt, the other major Greek-ruled kingdom in the eastern Mediterranean, surrendered to Rome following a naval victory over Queen Cleopatra, the last monarch of the Ptolemaic dynasty.

In Iberia and Gaul (the ancient name for the region centered on modern France), legions pushed back Celtic warriors. Within another century the imperial frontiers reached to the Danube River and central Britain. On the southern shores of the Mediterranean, Romans advanced westward from Carthage across North Africa, progressively annexing the Berber-speaking peoples that inhabited what are today Tunisia, northern Algeria, and Morocco. In the first century C.E., Rome had about 250,000 troops under arms, including a navy of galleys and sailing ships that plied the Mediterranean transporting soldiers and supplies and clearing out pirates. The state drafted a large percentage of Roman males into the army at age seventeen, typically keeping them in service for seven years.

The Republic falters. Ironically, the republican institutions that propelled the empire to greatness did not survive its success. In the first century B.C.E., the regime of collective, elected government teetered slowly, then collapsed under the colossal weight of imperial might and wealth. The wars of conquest generated vast riches in tribute, plunder, trade profits, and slaves, which poured into Rome. As this happened, the Senate became increasingly fixated on internal struggles for choice military commands, governorships, and commercial deals. To fight distant wars, citizen-soldiers had to leave their farms for longer periods, putting women, children, and slaves in charge of much of Italy's agrarian economy. Meanwhile, wealthy citizens bought up the lands of absentee farmers and consolidated them into estates, called *latifundia*, which exploited huge slave gangs to produce grain and other commodities for commercial markets. Somewhat like African slave labor in the Americas in early modern times, large concentrations of chattel slaves on Roman plantations increased the likelihood of rebellion. Slave uprisings in Sicily in 135 B.C.E. and in Italy under the slave gladiator Spartacus from 73 to 70 B.C.E. forced the state to expend large sums to keep enslaved workers under control. As the empire grew, cities mushroomed but also became

THE RISE OF ROME	
509 B.C.E.	Romans oust Etruscan kings and found republican city-state
272 B.C.E.	Armies complete conquest of Italy
146 B.C.E.	End of the Punic Wars and destruction of Carthage
146 B.C.E.	Conquest of Greece
83–82 B.C.E.	Civil war in Rome
73–70 B.C.E.	Slave rebellion led by Spartacus
63 B.C.E.	Capture of Jerusalem
51 B.C.E.	Conquest of Gaul completed
49–31 B.C.E.	Civil war in Rome
30 B.C.E.	Egypt annexed to Rome
27 B.C.E.	Start of Principate under Augustus Caesar
27–180 C.E.	*Pax Romana*, when empire reaches greatest extent
43 C.E.	Emperor Claudius invades Britain
44 C.E.	Mauretania (Algeria and Morocco) annexed to Rome
106 C.E.	Conquest of Dacia (Romania)

socially less stable. Ex-farmers and their families migrated to the city of Rome and other centers by the tens of thousands. The state had to support this underemployed population with free grain distribution, while the gulf between urban rich and poor stretched wider.

Continuous military expansion coupled with the shrinking availability of citizen-farmers, convinced the Senate to eliminate property qualifications for service in the legions. Ambitious commanders such as Julius Caesar exploited this new policy to recruit virtually private armies, offering pay, war booty, and free farms to landless men in return for personal allegiance. Thus, professional fighters replaced citizen-soldiers, and imperial wars became occasions for commanders to beef up their personal political influence.

Rome the Empire

In the first century B.C.E., Rome's problems reached a tipping point. Italian groups that had been denied citizenship rebelled, and factional fighting and intrigue periodically paralyzed the capital. From 49 to 31 B.C.E., a ferocious civil war pitted the mightiest generals—Julius Caesar, Pompey, Mark Anthony, and Octavian—in a deadly competition for power that might have spelled the breakup of the empire. However, Octavian, a gifted politician, emerged triumphant and restored public order against overwhelming odds. Under the name Augustus ("the August One"), he ruled single-handedly, though with Senate compliance, from 27 B.C.E. to 14 C.E. He named himself First Citizen, or *Princeps*, inaugurating the era of the Principate, which lasted until the end of the third century C.E.

Pax Romana, **or not.** From then on, Rome had the typical characteristics of an authoritarian monarchy and virtually

A Roman slave tag. The message in Latin on this iron slave collar offers a reward of gold to anyone who returns the wearer to his master. What might you infer about slavery in Rome from the use of tags like this one?

Extinguishing rebellion. The emperor Titus celebrated his army's suppression of the Jewish rebellion in Palestine (66–70 C.E.) by erecting a triumphal arch in Rome. In this relief on one of the arch's walls, Roman troops parade through the streets of the capital carrying plunder from the temple in Jerusalem. The soldiers exult in their victory by holding aloft the temple's menorah, or candelabrum, a sacred symbol of Jewish faith.

no resemblance to a republican city-state. The citizen population, war-weary and disenchanted, accepted the new autocracy without much complaint. The empire's high period of order and prosperity, known as the *Pax Romana,* or Roman peace, extended until nearly the end of the second century C.E.

The imperial frontiers reached their greatest extent in the reign of Trajan (98–117 C.E.). He conquered more territory in eastern Europe (Dacia, or modern Romania), the northwestern fringe of the Arabian Peninsula, Armenia to the slopes of the Caucasus Mountains, and both the upper and lower Tigris-Euphrates valleys. However, his successor Hadrian (r. 117–138 C.E.) retreated from the last three of these distant Southwest Asian territories (the Tigris River was more than two thousand miles from Rome). Rather, he gave his attention to stabilizing the remaining and still enormous empire, deploying an army of 300,000 soldiers to defend the frontiers (including Hadrian's Wall across north central Britain) and to suppress rebellions.

Despite the advantages of Roman security, millions of people around the Mediterranean did not want to be absorbed into the empire as tax-paying subjects. Numerous peoples first resisted imperial invasion and later rose against military occupation. The army forged the empire amid great violence and held it together by coercion. Resistance fighters and rebels sometimes won battles though usually lost their struggles in the end. In Palestine, for example, much of the Jewish population, provoked by tensions between Jews and Greeks, Roman misrule, and onerous taxation, rose up in 66 C.E. The rebellion spread across Palestine,

but in the year 70, Roman forces led by a son of the Emperor Vespasian besieged and captured Jerusalem, sacking it and burning down the holy temple. Flavius Josephus, the first-century Jewish historian, described the seizure of the city, already in a desperate state owing to lack of food:

> When [the Roman soldiers] went in numbers into the lanes of the city with their swords drawn, they slew those whom they overtook without and set fire to the houses whither the Jews were fled, and burnt every soul in them, and laid waste a great many of the rest; . . . they ran every one through whom they met with, and obstructed the very lanes with their dead bodies, and made the whole city run down with blood.[1]

The imperial political system. Rome retained some of the forms and symbols of republican government, such as the Senate, long after its emperors centralized their power. But in a shift away from republican symbolism, rulers beginning with Augustus willingly associated themselves with an imperial cult. He allowed Romans to venerate his "life force"—the word is *genius* in Latin. And after Augustus's reign, the Senate began to issue decrees awarding divine honors, that is, deification, to deceased rulers. People revered the ruler by dedicating temples and altars to him and by displaying his image in processions and festivals. Imperial cult worship first became popular in the eastern empire, where rulers had long cultivated this tradition. The practice spread west, though in Rome itself, memories of the Republic provoked some private skepticism about making dead monarchs into gods. Moreover, despite imperial

Individuals MATTER

Boudica: British Rebel Leader

A bronze statue of Boudica stands near Westminster Bridge in London.

In 43 C.E. the Emperor Claudius, mainly to overcome a perception in Roman political and military circles that he was weak and dim-witted, ordered an army of forty thousand troops to invade Britain. The island was then a patchwork of Celtic-speaking British kingdoms and clans. The Romans suppressed initial resistance, made dependent clients of several British kings, and started building new towns, including London (Londinium). Just seventeen years into the occupation, however, the government faced a massive revolt under the leadership of Boudica, queen of the British people called the Iceni.

Little is known about Boudica prior to her rebellion, though she was the wife of Prasutagus, the Icenian king. The Roman chronicler Cassius Dio, writing more than a century after Boudica's death, offers a description of her: "In stature she was very tall, in appearance most terrifying, in the glance of her eye most fierce, and her voice was harsh; a great mass of the tawniest [sandy-colored] hair fell to her hips."[2] Dio's depiction may be a figment of his imagination, but this description has persisted down through history, probably because it nicely conjures up the image of how a "warrior queen" might appear.

The Iceni avoided direct Roman control by allying themselves voluntarily with the invaders as soon as they arrived. Prasutagus believed he had an agreement with the Romans to pass his authority as a client king to Boudica and the couple's two young daughters after his death. The Iceni elite, however, had grown wealthy mining and selling salt, and the Romans wanted that revenue. The historian Tacitus described what happened to the Iceni about 60 C.E., when Prasutagus died:

> Kingdom and household alike were plundered like prizes of war, the one by Roman officers, the other by Roman slaves. As a beginning, his widow Boudica was flogged and their daughters raped. The Icenian chiefs were deprived of their hereditary estates as if the Romans had been given the whole country. The king's own relatives were treated like slaves.[3]

In response to this treatment, Boudica vowed to avenge her family's humiliation. She assembled a rebel army in league with neighboring people also frustrated by Rome's oppressive rule. Boudica led her troops to three decisive victories over Roman units, sacking and burning the southern British cities of Colchester, London, and St. Albans, which the imperial army had left poorly defended. In a fourth battle, however, Boudica's rebels lost to a much smaller but better disciplined Roman force. The insurgents scattered, and both Boudica and her two daughters shortly died, perhaps from either illness or suicide. Nevertheless, Roman officials feared more outbreaks. To pacify the country, the occupiers changed their tactics, seeking to conciliate and compromise with local leaders rather than repress them harshly.

Cassius Dio and Tacitus, both men born long after the uprising took place, composed the only accounts we have of Boudica's revolt. Their narratives leave many gaps, and we have no archaeological evidence of the queen's short reign. Like the Egyptian monarch Cleopatra, Boudica remains a historically intriguing figure as much for the legend she generated as for her actual exploits. In the nineteenth century, when British global power was at its height, Boudica served as a symbol of national strength and determination. Queen Victoria (r. 1837–1901) invoked the memory of Boudica the warrior queen as an example of a female determined to defend the rights of her ancient British people. She remains today one of Britain's semimythical folk heroes.

Thinking Critically

Since Britain was itself an imperial power in the nineteenth century, conquering peoples in Africa and Asia, why would British citizens wish to honor as a folk hero an ancient woman who resisted a foreign invasion?

---

autocracy, the Roman legal system, which grew increasingly complex, remained vital. The worthiest emperors collaborated with jurists and legal scholars to enforce laws fairly.

The Republic's style of governing through networks of patrons and clients carried over to the empire. In many regions, emperors preferred to collaborate personally with dependent kings and princes rather than annex territory outright. Provincial governors appointed to office often brought along their own male family members, friends, and other clients to help them with their duties. Since governors typically held office for only one year, even the most dedicated appointees moved quickly to enrich themselves and their entourage by skimming revenue or trading gifts and favors with local people of means.

Cities of the empire. Rome ruled its provinces mainly from cities, which grew in size and number along with conquered territory. From a collection of villages on a cluster of hills near the Tiber River, Rome burgeoned into a metropolis of nearly a million people by the second century C.E. Augustus and his immediate successors expanded and beautified it, constructing new public forums, temples, theaters, arches, and statues. The great amphitheater called the Coliseum, which opened in 80 C.E. in the reign of Titus, could hold about fifty thousand spectators for games and dramatic performances. The elite minority lived in magnificent houses built around grand open-air courtyards, while hundreds of thousands of ordinary folk crowded into multistory apartment buildings, about a fifth of the population surviving on public handouts of grain.

The eastern Mediterranean rim had long been urbanized. But many eastern cities grew bigger because of the presence of Roman garrisons and demand throughout the empire for the fine wares their artisans manufactured. Alexandria in Egypt and Antioch in Syria, for example, reached populations of more than 100,000. In the western provinces, that is, in North Africa and in western Europe beyond Italy, pre-empire towns were scattered and typically small. Roman rule, however, stimulated urbanization to meet the need for garrisons, administration, and trade. In frontier regions, the state often awarded free land to immigrant settlers.

One remarkable example is the city of Timgad, which lies in modern Algeria nearly one hundred miles inland from the Mediterranean. The Timgad region was home to Berber-speaking herders and farmers who had mostly lived beyond the reach of Roman legions until the first century C.E. The emperor Trajan had Timgad built from the ground up to serve as a military colony on the southern imperial frontier. As it became a grain- and cattle-producing center, architects adorned it with Hellenistic temples, theaters, baths, palatial homes, and a triumphal arch.

Cultural Romanization. Timgad's urban refinement illustrates the spread of a distinctly imperial style of culture around the Mediterranean rim. In all ancient empires, cultural standardization took place in some measure, especially among elite classes. Rulers usually expected local aristocrats and chieftains to imitate the tastes, fashions, and refined ways practiced at the royal court. Contrariwise, local elite families in conquered territories often rushed to mimic imperial culture in order to display their allegiance and enhance their social prestige.

Romanization involved a complex intermeshing of imperial Roman and local ethnic and linguistic ideas and customs. Hellenistic influences were paramount, displayed notably in public architecture and naturalistic sculpture and painting. Greek

> **Romanization** The spread within the Roman empire, especially among elite classes, of a style of social and cultural life founded on practice in Roman Italy.

Rome's far southern frontier. The sprawling ruins of Timgad, a city built in the early second century C.E., protected imperial territory in North Africa from the incursions of Berbers who inhabited the nearby Aurès Mountains. In what other ways might a distant frontier town like this one have served the empire?

remained the most prestigious language in the eastern provinces, and throughout the empire affluent Roman families obliged their children to learn it. Latin, however, became the language of imperial administration and the primary medium of literature, law, rhetoric, and science in the western regions.

Generally speaking, Romanization transformed the western empire more than the eastern, the cities more than the countryside, and affluent elites more than ordinary people. In western Europe and North Africa, local kings and clan leaders who spoke Berber, Celtic, Germanic, and other local languages often worked hard to transform themselves into bona fide Romans by learning Latin, donning togas, and building Italian-style villas decorated with ceramics and statuary. Cities in Gaul, Iberia, and other western lands arose as much smaller versions of Rome, complete with temples, amphitheaters, baths, and arenas for chariot races.

Ordinary men and women, especially in rural areas, tended to cling steadfastly to their local customs. Romanization reached them in some measure, however, because they visited provincial towns, had contact with Roman colonists, and used imperial coinage, which circulated widely as the empire grew. Numerous and varied religious ideas also circulated, and new ones tended to attract followers among all social classes. For example, worshipers of Isis, the Hellenistic spirit derived from the Egyptian fertility goddess, built temples for her in Rome. The cult of Mithras, a god of Persian origin linked to the sun, gained popularity among Roman soldiers, who bore it to all corners of the empire. Romanization never came close to homogenizing the empire, but the Mediterranean basin attained a level of cultural integration that, once Rome fell, was never to be seen again.

A Persian god in northern England. The ruin of this little temple dedicated to the deity Mithras lies next to Hadrian's Wall, the complex of walls, forts, towers, and gates Roman soldiers built across the width of England in the second century c.e. to defend imperial towns against Celtic marauders. The cult of Mithras, imported from Southwest Asia, gave spiritual solace to soldiers posted on the empire's far northern edge.

The Era of the Han Empire in East Asia

FOCUS As the Han and Roman empires developed between about 200 B.C.E. and 200 C.E., what similarities and differences emerged in their political, social, religious, and economic systems?

For several hundred years, political developments in the Mediterranean basin and East Asia followed a fairly similar trajectory. At both ends of Afroeurasia, population, urbanization, and economic production accelerated in the late first millennium B.C.E. In both regions a single state gained ascendancy over several states between the fourth and third centuries B.C.E. In East Asia the forces of Shi Huangdi, founder of the Qin dynasty (221–207 B.C.E.), united a large part of China at approximately the same time that Rome fought and won its second war against Carthage (218–210 B.C.E.). The Qin state had only two rulers, but the Han dynasty that immediately followed it lasted for nearly 450 years (206 B.C.E.–202 C.E.), a period corresponding to Rome's most vigorous centuries. The Qin and Han dynasties together mark the beginning of a Chinese tradition of centralized, bureaucratic government that lasted with only one interruption down to the early twentieth century. Stretching about three thousand miles east to west, the Han empire at its zenith exceeded Rome in territory. Both empires encompassed peoples of diverse languages and ethnicity, but both also facilitated commercial integration and cultural interchange over large regions (see Map 7.3).

The Qin Dynasty and the First Emperor

The Qin state appeared in the fourth century B.C.E. as a minor agrarian kingdom located in the upper Wei River valley. Gradually, it gained dominance over its neighbors, emerging victorious from the Warring States period, two and a half centuries (475–221 B.C.E.) of political fragmentation and conflict in northern China. Shi Huangdi, or First Illustrious Emperor, managed during a reign of eleven short years (221–210 B.C.E.) to set up a centralized government more elaborate than that of any earlier Chinese state. He organized the empire into forty provinces, each headed by an appointed governor and army commander, who replaced

QIN AND HAN DYNASTIES	
475–221 B.C.E.	Warring States period
221–206 B.C.E.	Qin dynasty, founded by Shi Huangdi, First Illustrious Emperor
206 B.C.E. –220 C.E.	Han dynasty, founded by Liu Bang
188–180 B.C.E.	Reign of Empress Lu
141–87 B.C.E.	Reign of Han Wudi; empire reaches greatest extent

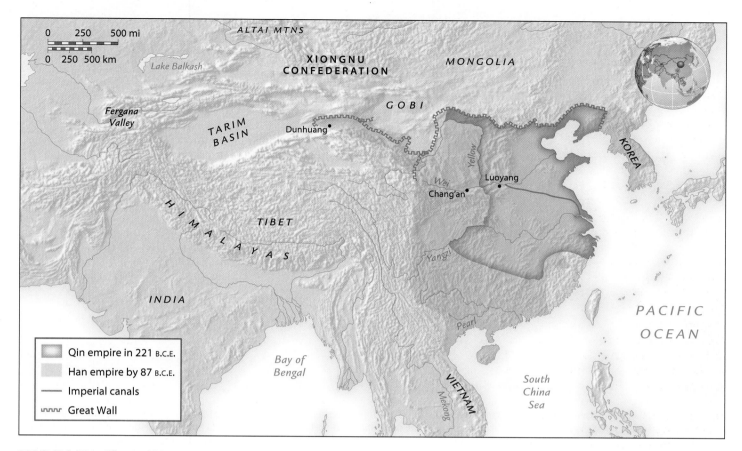

MAP 7.3 The Qin and Han empires.

Why do you think the Han state incorporated the long tongue of land that extends to the northwest?

once powerful regional lords. He then subdivided these provinces into numerous local administrative districts. He conscripted young men into his army, encouraging enthusiastic service by allowing common soldiers who killed many enemies to rise in the ranks. He also drafted peasant men and women to build roads, dikes, canals, and palaces. Earlier rulers had erected barriers of pounded earth to defend China's northwestern land frontiers against attack. Shi Huangdi ordered labor gangs to extend and connect these barricades. In this way the Great Wall first took shape, though later rulers added most of the stone wall construction that survives today.

The First Emperor's vision of an efficient authoritarian state rested on a Chinese school of thought known as Legalism. This austere philosophy asserted that human nature was fundamentally corrupt, obliging the state to closely regulate people's lives. Legalist scholars argued that laws and punishments should apply equally to everyone, whether aristocrats or peasants. State officials, furthermore, should be appointed for their ability to get the job done, not for their moral character or high social status.

Because Legalist ideology demanded standard regulations and procedures, Shi Huangdi aimed to rationalize not only politics but also economic and cultural life. He standardized weights and measures and reduced the several different coinages circulating in China to one. Perhaps most important for China's later cultural development, he instructed scholars to standardize and simplify Chinese writing, an evolving logographic system that included thousands of individual signs, not a simple alphabet. Policies that promoted uniformity meant that even though East Asian peoples continued to speak many different languages and Chinese dialects, officials, scholars, and merchants throughout the empire could now better understand one another in writing.

Since the First Emperor's time, scholars have been ambivalent about his record. In accord with Legalist principles, he and his officials praised farmers and artisans, not the aristocratic class, as the moral backbone of the state. Peasants may generally have honored him because he kept order and insisted on equality before the law. On the other hand, he severely punished all who defied him, encouraged his subjects to spy on one another, and ordered burning of books that he did not think served the interests of the state. According to one tradition, he took vengeance on several hundred disobedient scholars by burying them alive. He spent colossal sums on his own tomb near Chang'an (modern Xian) in north central China. Undergoing excavation

An army of clay. Rank upon rank of soldiers equipped with crossbows, swords, and spears and accompanied by horses and chariots guard the excavated burial chamber of the First Emperor Shi Huangdi. Artisans made the terra-cotta warriors from molds but added distinctive features to each face. The twenty-one-square-mile complex near modern Xian contains close to 8,000 life-sized figures. What sentiments might have motivated the emperor to order such a grandiose project?

since the 1970s, this astonishing mausoleum, with its army of life-sized terra-cotta soldiers and horses, each one unique, is regarded as both a marvel of the ancient world and a testament to the efforts of the ordinary folk who were obliged to construct and embellish it.

The Han State and the Ascendance of Confucianism

When the First Emperor died, his empire nearly collapsed. Within a few years, Liu Bang (r. 206–195 B.C.E.), a man of peasant origins who built up a military following, pulled the state back together under the dynastic name Han, a word that also came to refer to Chinese-speaking people in general. Liu Bang and the monarchs who followed him succeeded partly by retaining many of the Legalist laws and regulations of the Qin dynasty and by developing a hierarchy of officials reaching from the royal palace down to the village. At its height, the Han government may have employed twenty times more officials than Rome ever did.[4] The period of greatest stability and prosperity extended from the rule of the Empress Lu (188–180 B.C.E.) through the long reign of Han Wudi (141–87 B.C.E.).

Confucian ethics and the Han empire. Under Han Wudi, the set of moral and ethical ideas associated with

the sage Confucius, who had died nearly 340 years earlier, were incorporated into Han imperial ideology. Confucius (551–479 B.C.E.) was born into a minor noble family known as Kong. The name the world knows him by is derived from the Chinese *Kong Fuzi,* meaning "Master Kong." He served at a princely court for a time but then took to wandering from one kingdom to another, gathering disciples eager to discover ways to improve Chinese society and government. Like other moral teachers of that era, he sought a path out of the violence and disorder that afflicted China in the era of the Eastern Zhou (770–256 B.C.E.), a dynasty that lost almost all real authority over violently competing regional lords.

In the two and a half centuries after Confucius died, political mayhem in northern China became worse—the tumultuous Warring States period. Nevertheless, scholars and reformers continued to gain inspiration from his *Analects,* the collection of his sayings transmitted orally from one generation of students to another. Scholars such as Mencius (ca. 370–300 B.C.E.) elaborated on Confucian ideas and continued to appeal to kings and princes to exchange their greed and power-hunger for righteous and responsible government. The Qin First Emperor appears to have publicly represented himself as a righteous ruler of the sort Confucians would have admired. But it was only after 140 B.C.E., when Han Wudi came to the Han throne, that Confucianism became closely identified with the Chinese state and its governing class.

Many scholars characterize Confucianism as a path of moral and ethical enlightenment rather than as a religion. Confucius and his disciples affirmed the existence of the supernatural universe, but they had little to say about gods, the afterlife, or the workings of the divine. In the Han era, Confucian thinkers espoused four central ideas. The first was that all people share a common bond of humanity and should behave respectfully toward one another, displaying charity, courtesy, and sympathetic understanding. Second, the ideal individual was the gentleman or gentlewoman who embodied maturity, confidence, and refinement, never rudeness, vanity, or cruelty. Third, ethical principles should uplift the state. Rulers should govern righteously and prudently because when they do, they enjoy the trust and loyalty of their subjects. By acting with benevolence and compassion, the monarch demonstrates that he possesses divine approval, or the Mandate of Heaven, the moral concept that first emerged in the Zhou period several centuries earlier.

Fourth, peace in society requires propriety, that is, dedication to thinking and doing the right thing as mapped out by custom and tradition. Harmony in the family is the key to harmony in the world, and the greatest expression of propriety within the family is **filial piety.** "In serving your father and mother, you may gently admonish them," Confucius declared in one of the *Analects.* "But if you see they have no intention of listening to you, then be respectful as before and do not disobey them. You might feel distressed but should never feel resentful."[5] Decorous behavior should guide all relationships, parent to child, friend to friend, subject to sovereign, and sovereign to subject. Rules of conduct expressed in proper ritual should shape all social and political relations. Confucian ideology categorized women as appendages of their husbands, brothers, and fathers. As in Rome, however, women of wealthy families had some latitude to realize talent and exercise power. Empresses and wives of officials exerted political influence, and some educated women produced Confucian literary works.

Founding an academy of Confucian studies, the Emperor Wudi established the model of the scholar-bureaucrat—the literate, humane official who devotes his life to gentlemanly, evenhanded management of the empire. The Han state continued the First Emperor's strategy of centralizing power by shifting local authority from aristocratic landlords to imperial appointees organized in a pyramid of authority

filial piety The quality in children of showing respect and care for their parents and all ancestors.

Lady Dai's funeral banner. Modern scholars have learned an astonishing amount about Lady Dai, a Han noblewoman who died about 168 B.C.E. In 1972 archaeologists working in Hunan province discovered Lady Dai's tomb, her wondrously preserved body encased in four nested coffins and twenty layers of cloth. A t-shaped silk banner covered the innermost coffin. The painting on the silk illustrates ancient Chinese conceptions of heaven, earth, and the underworld. In the lower half of the banner, Lady Dai herself stands before two kneeling attendants. The figure at the top of the banner seated on a snake may represent Lady Dai's ascendance into the heavenly realm.

extending from the imperial palace to local districts. Wudi appointed intelligent commoners to office, not just aristocrats, and wrapped official activity in layers of ceremony. Generally, Han government relied more on the moral character and talent of officials and on their loyalty to the bureaucratic system than on personal ties between powerful officeholders and their clients and retainers, which turned the wheels of government in Rome.

Daoism: a different way. Probably all of the world's major cultural traditions have displayed two parallel tendencies in their moral and religious systems. One has been to exhort individuals to commit themselves to firm rules of moral conduct in their relations with one another as the foundation of community order. The other has been to urge detachment from the world's social complexities and to seek meaning and fulfillment in private meditation, study, or simple living.

Early Confucian philosophers argued for public moral commitment and activism to ensure stability at all levels of society. In the same centuries, however, other truth-seekers contended that individuals should not try to confront the world's greed, disorder, and violence but to disengage from society and to live quietly and privately in harmony with the cosmos. This philosophy had similarities to Stoicism in the Hellenistic world. People should seek oneness with the Dao, or Way—the invisible, indefinable, transcendent principle underlying all reality. All phenomena in the universe exist in relationship to one another, including forces that seem to be opposites (*yin yang*). Human efforts to organize, regulate, or change the world, rather than accepting the eternal flow of the Dao, lead ultimately to mayhem and confusion.

The complex set of beliefs and practices that came to be known as Daoism probably had roots in ancient Chinese ideas about ancestral and nature spirits. The earliest Daoist scripture dates from at least the fourth century B.C.E. and is associated with the sage named Laozi. This five thousand word collection of sayings, the *Daodejing* (DOW-DAY-JIHNG), or the *Classic Text of the Way and Virtue,* expresses the concept of *wuwei* (woo-WAY), the achievement of harmonious being through the paradox of "actionless action." As the *Daodejing* instructs:

> Whoever mean to take this realm and rule it—
> I see them failing to attain that end.
> For this realm below, a sacred vessel,
> Never may be subject to such rule.
> They ruin it who try,
> Lose it who hold on.[6]

Skepticism about all absolutes, that is, anything claiming to be unconditionally good or bad, beautiful or ugly, encouraged Daoist thinkers to meander along many different philosophical and spiritual byways. In time these included speculative explorations of medicine, diet, magic, martial arts, alchemy, quests for immortality, and *feng shui,* the art of living in harmony with one's physical and natural environment.

Daoist masters criticized Confucians for their vain struggles to organize and manage society. Confucians reproached Daoists for passively ignoring social responsibility. In fact, however, no titanic clash of belief systems occurred. Rather, in the Han era these multifaceted modes of thought emerged as two general tendencies in Chinese cultural life, overlapping and blending in many ways, for example, in their commitment to individual moral behavior and use of ritual. The most dedicated Confucian magistrate might, as it were, engage in Daoist meditation and study at home over the weekend.

Han economy and society. From the cosmopolitan capitals of Chang'an and, later, Luoyang, Han officers ruled a population that in the first century C.E. numbered about sixty million, probably slightly more than in the Roman empire. The productivity of Chinese farmers was clearly on the rise. Because many peasants owned land, people bought and sold it freely. Because sons inherited property in equal shares, individual holdings were likely to get smaller with each new generation. Peasants therefore had good reason to farm more efficiently and open new land to cultivation where opportunity presented itself.

Wheat, millet, and rice farmers, who increasingly used iron tools, made several important technological advances. These included the wheelbarrow, the seed drill, and the animal breast strap. Until the third century B.C.E., horses and oxen were harnessed with a throat-and-girth device that choked them if the load they had to pull was too heavy. The new breast strap, later perfected as the cushioned collar harness, transferred the load pressure from the horse's throat to its chest, allowing it to haul several times more weight. Another Chinese invention was the cast iron plow, which

Papermaking. A Han artisan raises a mesh screen from a vat of pulp. The thin layer of pulp remaining on the screen will be left to dry, forming a sheet of paper. What advantages might paper have had over silk, wooden tablets, or bamboo strips as a writing surface?

had a curved plate that pushed overturned soil to one side, burying cut weeds and forming furrows that drained excess water from the field. Iron plow technology extended the range of intensive agriculture in China, especially in the rainy, rice-growing south. The silk industry grew rapidly when farm women learned how to produce long, strong strands of fiber from the boiled cocoons of silkworms fed exclusively on mulberry leaves. Finally, paper made from rags, hemp, flax, or mulberry bark first appeared in the Han era, eventually replacing bamboo strips as a writing surface.

The Confucian conception of social hierarchy placed scholars and educated officials on top, farmers and artisans in the middle, and merchants on the bottom. Members of the commercial class, scholars argued, deserved this low station because they made their living buying and selling rather than producing anything useful. Even so, trade flourished in the Han era, and many new towns sprang up. Luoyang, the dynasty's second capital, reached a population of something like 500,000 at the start of the Common Era, making it probably the largest city in the world after Rome.

Han expansion. The territorial growth of the Han state, which got seriously under way in the second century B.C.E. under Han Wudi, had military, demographic, and cultural dimensions. The huge Chinese army, wielding swords, axes, and powerful crossbows, moved out in all directions, pushing the empire's borders south of the Yangzi River as far as the northern reaches of Vietnam and northeastward to Manchuria and the Korean peninsula. Most of the conquered peoples spoke languages other than Chinese. As the state expanded, merchants and land-hungry Chinese peasants followed voluntarily. In the first two centuries C.E., somewhere between five and ten million farmers migrated to the Yangzi valley and further south. As these cultivators penetrated the subtropical latitudes, they switched from northern grain crops, especially wheat and millet, to wet-field rice. Once southern lands came under the Han military umbrella, Chinese officials moved in to organize society and transmit tax revenue to the capital.

Sinification The spread within East Asia, especially among elite classes, of a style of social and cultural life founded on practice in China.

Han expansion and Chinese migration encouraged a process of cultural **Sinification** (from the Greek word *sino*, meaning "Chinese") comparable to the Romanization that occurred about the same time in the Mediterranean basin. Standardization of the writing system, the spread of Confucian values, the trade in Han luxury goods, and the installation of bureaucrats in new provinces combined to promote a relatively more uniform style of Chinese cultural life over a much larger part of East Asia, at least at elite social levels.

Starting in 129 B.C.E., Han Wudi also ordered campaigns of conquest deep into Inner Eurasia, the habitat of oasis dwellers and pastoral nomads. Deteriorating relations and chronic fighting between Chinese forces and the powerful pastoral nomadic state known as the Xiongnu partially motivated this expansion. We come back to the Xiongnu in the next part of the chapter. Han Wudi also saw financial benefit to the state in pushing imperial control out along the silk roads leading to Central Asia, South Asia, and Iran. Chinese infantry and cavalry seized key oasis towns on the trade routes on both the northern and southern edges of the arid Tarim Basin. To acquire superior mounts for his army, he sent expeditions all the way to the well-watered Ferghana valley, which overlaps modern Kyrgyzstan (kuhr-gi-STAHN), Tajikistan, and Uzbekistan. Chinese officials already knew of this region's reputation for "heavenly horses," a breed larger and stronger than the animals raised on arid steppe grasses. The advance into this valley meant that for a short time only about 1,600 miles separated the far western arm of the Chinese empire from the most eastern territories of Rome. Emperors who succeeded Han Wudi attempted to maintain control of these western lands, but in the first two centuries C.E., troubles multiplied in the very heart of the empire, a story we pick up in Chapter 9.

States Between Rome and China

FOCUS What part did wealth from commerce play in the growth of the Xiongnu state, Parthian Persia, Kushana, Kush, and Axum?

At the start of the Common Era, the chain of states that ran across the temperate and northern tropical latitudes of Afroeurasia numbered in the hundreds—from city-states and small kingdoms to empires almost as large, if not nearly as populous, as Rome and Han China. States next to one another or more distant typically engaged in diplomatic and mercantile relations, which stimulated exchanges of ideas and technological novelties that might in particular cases have a significant effect on society and economy. Here, we highlight five of these states—the Xiongnu, the Parthian and Kushana empires, and the African states of Kush and Axum. All five affected, in one way or another, broad patterns of change in Afroeurasia in the period 300 B.C.E.–300 C.E. All five were monarchies, though the power of the central government over local aristocrats or tribal groups varied considerably from one case and period to another.

The Xiongnu and Their Relations with Han China

In the first millennium B.C.E., pastoral nomadic groups that inhabited the Inner Eurasian steppes typically supplemented their wealth in livestock by trading with neighboring farmers and town dwellers. They also learned, however, that violent raiding of settled societies might be more profitable than peaceful commerce whenever they had sufficient armed strength and good opportunity to make war. As early as the eighth century B.C.E., peoples that circulated with their herds on the eastern steppes adjacent to China began to organize alliances of otherwise independent clan and tribal groups and to launch cavalry attacks on villages and towns in the upper Yellow River region to amass loot and prisoners. Or, they might simply threaten to attack if their settled neighbors refused to pay tribute—nomad blackmail, as it were. As Inner Eurasian pastoral societies continued to grow, talented leaders had increasing success assembling larger and longer lasting tribal coalitions. The earliest known steppe alliance to transform itself into a durable state lasting several decades was the Xiongnu confederation.

The horse-breeding people who became the core of the Xiongnu steppe empire inhabited the region where the Yellow River makes a great loop across China's northwestern frontier. They may have spoken a language ancestral to Mongolian. In the late third century B.C.E., Maodun (r. 210–174 B.C.E.), a charismatic and ruthless warrior, rallied a following of mounted archers owing personal loyalty to him, rather than to their families and clans. After murdering his own father to seize leadership, he led his cavalry, ranked in a disciplined hierarchy of military units, to victory over several other steppe peoples. As Xiongnu power grew, it drew on the riches of several ecological zones: the fur-rich forests of Siberia to the north, the metals-producing Altai Mountains, the grasslands of Mongolia, and numerous oasis towns. Xiongnu fighters, like other nomads before them, also enriched themselves raiding into China.

Early in the second century B.C.E., a Xiongnu host defeated a Chinese army on the northwestern frontier. Following this debacle for the Han, the imperial government decided prudently to recognize the Xiongnu state as a political equal and to send bountiful annual "presents" of grain, wine, and silk. They also firmed up relations by negotiating marriages between nomad aristocrats and young women of the Han royal family, who had, in effect, to live on the steppe as hostages. Chinese bureaucrats calculated that paying off the Xiongnu was cheaper than fighting them, and ceremonial gift exchanges strengthened Maodun's prestige. That made it easier for him and his successors to redistribute wealth to other warrior chiefs who in return dispatched archers to the Xiongnu army. The Xiongnu promised not to invade China and instead subjugated both pastoral and oasis communities far to the west, forging a territorially huge state in the second century B.C.E. Maodun also created a Chinese-like government hierarchy, the top rung occupied by him as supreme commander, or khan.

The negotiated agreements between China and the Xiongnu, however, did not permanently stabilize relations. Persuaded that the empire remained under threat, Emperor Han Wudi ordered a massive and costly offensive in 129 B.C.E., not only to propel Han authority out along the silk roads but also to bring the Xiongnu to heel. Several campaigns forced the nomads to accept Chinese overlordship, and the weakened Xiongnu state fell into civil war, then broke into southern and northern federations, one subordinated to the Han, the other confined to the steppes beyond the Chinese horizon.

The Parthian and Kushana Empires

Like the Xiongnu, the founders of the Parthian and Kushana states originated as Inner Eurasian steppe warriors. Unlike the Xiongnu, they conquered and ruled dense agrarian populations and large cities.

Parthian conquests. The Seleucid dynasty, founded in the late fourth century B.C.E. by Greco-Macedonian successors of Alexander the Great, ruled the Iranian Plateau, Mesopotamia, and neighboring regions in the late fourth and the third centuries B.C.E. But from about 240 B.C.E. it suffered a string of reversals. The Greek-speaking governor of Bactria threw off Seleucid authority and formed a Bactrian monarchy. To the west, a huge Seleucid army attempted to invade Greece, but Roman legions expanding eastward defeated it in 191 B.C.E. and forced the Seleucids to abandon Anatolia. Finally, the Parni, a band of nomad fighters from somewhere in Inner Eurasia, seized the Seleucid province of Parthia east of the Caspian Sea. In the mid-second century B.C.E., Mithridates I (r. 171–138 B.C.E.), the Parthian king, captured Babylon, the Seleucid capital on the Euphrates. Within another thirteen years, the Seleucid empire was all but gone and the Parthians on the ascendant from Mesopotamia to Central Asia.

Remains of Ctesiphon. Parthian rulers founded Ctesiphon on the northeast bank of the Tigris River as a winter capital. The city fell into ruin after a Roman army sacked it in 165 C.E. But the great arch, called the Taq-i-Kisra, somehow survived.

An empire loosely organized. Following the model of the Seleucids and the Persian Achaemenid dynasty before them, the Parthian conquerors expected the farmers and herders of Mesopotamia and the highlands around the Iranian Plateau to support the empire, especially its large mounted army. Boasting the title "King of Kings" to evoke past Achaemenid glory, the Parthians dominated Iran and Mesopotamia for more than four hundred years. This was a remarkable feat because in contrast to the Han in China they showed little talent for centralized bureaucratic government. Rather, they orchestrated with varying success a fluid federation of tribal groups and small kingdoms, depending on local aristocrats to send taxes and tribute to the capital and to supply troops when needed. Using horses bred specially for size and endurance, their heavy cavalry—both rider and horse swathed in bronze, iron, and leather—overpowered enemy foot soldiers or more lightly armed riders.

Like the Seleucids, the Parthians ruled over an ethnically diverse population. And much like affluent Romans, the Parthian elite class adopted Hellenistic models of refined art and court ceremony. Parthian kings built a series of Greek-looking royal cities, including Ctesiphon on the Tigris River. All that remains of that city today is a 121-foot-high vaulted arch, part of an ancient palace. Literate Parthians wrote Pahlavi, an Indo-European language, but Aramaic and Greek remained popular languages of learning and commerce. The government appears to have taken a tolerant view of their subjects' religious practices.

The royal household and aristocratic families tended to favor the supreme god Ahura Mazda and beliefs and rituals of Zoroastrianism.

Parthians and Romans. Parthian cavalry advanced to the Tigris-Euphrates valley about the same time that Roman legions first crossed the Aegean to campaign in Southwest Asia. The gap between the two imperial frontiers narrowed steadily, and in 53 B.C.E. a Parthian army routed a larger Roman force in Southeastern Anatolia. (The victors severed the head of the Roman general Crassus and, according to the historian Plutarch, presented it to the Parthian royal court while they were watching a Greek play!) For the next 250 years, Parthians and Romans fought repeatedly along a fluctuating Tigris-Euphrates frontier without decisive victory for either side. The Parthians lacked sufficient armed force to drive the Romans out of Southwest Asia, but Rome found campaigning far to the east logistically difficult and too expensive to sustain permanently.

The Kushana empire. East of Parthian territory, the Kushana (or Kushan) state arose after 45 C.E. to dominate an immense area extending from Inner Eurasia to northern India. Knowledge of Kushana has come hard because few texts have survived, and the state left behind few inscriptions, sculptures, or architectural remains. So far, their history is best illuminated by their skillfully made silver and gold coins stamped with texts and images that tell us something about their rulers, their religious beliefs, and their cultural relations with their neighbors.

Kushana coin. King Vima Kadphises (r. ca. 75–100 C.E.) appears on this gold coin holding a club in his right hand. Flames, a symbol of royal legitimacy, leap from his right shoulder. Oesho, the Kushana god of the wind and of high places, appears on the reverse side. Why do you think coins are often important sources of historical evidence?

Like the Parthians, the founders of Kushana started out as Inner Eurasian nomads, a tribal group known as the Yuezhi. In the mid-second century B.C.E., the Xiongnu, then at their peak of power on the eastern steppes, forced the Yuezhi to migrate westward. They settled in Bactria and about 80 B.C.E. extinguished the Greco-Macedonian state that had ruled there. Shortly after that, leaders of the Kushana, a group within the larger Yuezhi, organized a military confederation that began conquering in every direction. In addition to their great livestock herds, Kushana warriors tapped farm and artisan wealth from the Amu Darya and Syr Darya River valleys of Central Asia, as well as collecting duties on trade that flowed through the region's urban hubs. At the start of the reign of King Kanishka (ca. 129–152 C.E.), Kushana embraced not only Central Asia and Afghanistan but also much of northern India, which had been politically fragmented since the fall of the Maurya empire in the third century B.C.E. At the farther reaches of its vast territory, Kushana kings, like the Parthians, lacked the personnel and communication technology to do more than monitor an often unruly collection of tribal groups and independent-minded cities, relying mainly on local princes to keep order and ensure revenue flow. A succession of four talented kings held the state together into the third century C.E., when, as we shall see, new empire builders arose to supplant it.

The Kushana ruling class adapted remarkably to the empire's great cultural diversity, taking a many-sided view of religion, art, and royal symbolism. Drawing nearly equally on Indian, Persian, and Hellenistic styles, Kushana coins depicted the gods and the royal titles and insignia from all those civilizations without discrimination. King Kanishka even took as one of his titles the Roman title *kaisara*, or Caesar.

The African Kingdoms of Kush and Axum

In northeastern Africa, the monarchy of Kush (whose name has no connection to Kushana) first emerged in the second millennium B.C.E. along the stretch of the Nile River that encompasses Nubia, the region corresponding today to the Republic of the Sudan. Kush thus formed a bridge of exchange between the Roman Mediterranean and tropical Africa. Trade also flowed from Kush eastward to the Red Sea, where in the first century C.E. the kingdom of Axum arose as a powerful commercial state linking the Mediterranean world to the Arabian Sea (see Map 7.4).

Kush shifts upriver. Following several decades of rule over both Nubia and Egypt in the eighth and seventh centuries B.C.E., Kush's royal court moved from the Nile city of Napata to a new capital farther upriver at Meroë (MER-oh-ee), near where the great river divides into its Blue and White branches. This location was far enough south of the Sahara Desert to sustain grain and cotton farming from rainfall. And the savannas, or grassy plains, that stretched west and east of the two Niles supported plentiful herds of cattle and wild game. Sometime in the seventh century B.C.E.,

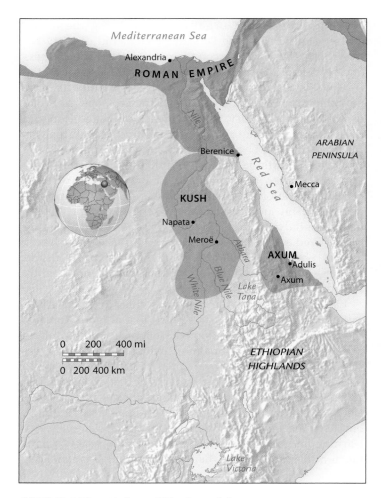

MAP 7.4 The states of Kush and Axum.
How did the geographical locations of Kush and Axum contribute to their commercial prosperity?

knowledge of iron making reached Nubia, probably having spread from East Africa's Great Lakes region to the south, one of the early centers of iron metallurgical invention. A flourishing smelting industry later developed around Meroë, where both iron ore and timber resources were apparently abundant. Giant slag heaps that have survived to today are dramatic proof of this ancient enterprise.

Meroë's distinctive culture. When Kush's center of gravity shifted upriver from Napata to Meroë, cultural interchange with Egypt weakened. Egyptian influences faded somewhat, and art, architecture, religion, and other aspects of elite culture took on more distinctively local features. In earlier times Nubians had connected their supreme god associated with the sky to the Egyptian deity Amun. In Meroë, however, the focus of worship turned to Apedemak, a Nubian god depicted in stone as a lion. Kings of Meroë had themselves buried under small pyramids, keeping alive an architectural form that the Egyptians had given up centuries earlier. In state politics both the senior wife and mother of the king played prominent political roles, much more so than in Egypt. Residents of Meroë and its region probably spoke a number of different languages. Around 300 B.C.E., officials and religious specialists developed a writing system for Meroitic, probably a language in the Nilo-Saharan family. This system was alphabetic, made up of twenty-three signs. Derived from Egyptian hieroglyphs, the alphabet had both consonants and vowels and, as far as we know, no relationship to the Phoenician system that inspired Greek and Latin. Unfortunately, linguists have not so far deciphered much of it.

Kush and Rome.
Kush's prosperity after 300 B.C.E. was almost certainly connected to its brisk trade with Hellenistic Egypt and later Rome. Nubian merchants shipped ironware, cotton textiles, war elephants, gold, ivory, ebony, and slaves downriver, importing Mediterranean wine, olive oil, ceramics, and precious metalwork. Following occupation of Egypt in 30 B.C.E., Rome sent forces upriver to control a longer stretch of the Nile trade and force Kush into dependency. The Nubians, however, fought back, finally convincing Rome to agree to mutually profitable relations. Consequently, stronger Mediterranean cultural winds reached Nubia. For example, the ruins of temples and palaces in Meroë and other towns dating from the early centuries C.E. reveal an eclectic mix of local, Egyptian, and Hellenistic influences.

By the fourth century C.E., Kush went into full decline. Rome's mounting political troubles hurt the Nile-to-Mediterranean trade. Prolonged drought in Nubia may have driven pastoral nomads in the region to attack Nile towns. Finally, the kingdom of Axum dealt a lethal blow in the 340s C.E., sacking Meroë and bringing Kush's long history to a close.

Axum between Kush and the Red Sea.
The kingdom of Axum (also Aksum) first appears in the historical record at the start of the Common Era, when trade was growing busier on the Red Sea corridor. Sometime in the late first millennium B.C.E., merchants founded a cluster of ports at the southern end of the Red Sea on both the Arabian and the African shores. From these ports, they shipped products that included frankincense and myrrh, both locally grown aromatic tree resins of immense value for incense, perfume, and medicine. Dromedary camel caravans also carried goods on the south–north land route that paralleled the Red Sea, connecting southern Arabia to Syria.

A temple of Kush. This small structure in the ruins of Naqa, a city east of the Nile, testifies to the flow of cultural influences along the valley. The temple, probably dedicated to the popular goddess Hathor, displays a blend of Egyptian, Hellenistic, and Roman influences. The Egyptian lintel over the entranceway is inscribed with cobras. The Corinthian capitals on the columns are of Greek inspiration, and the side arches are Roman. How might knowledge of Corinthian column design have reached Nubia?

Trade in the African Port of Adulis

Traders in the ancient world who sailed between Roman Egypt and India might have either compiled or consulted a document called a periplus. This is a type of report that helped ships' crews navigate by listing ports in the order that sailors encountered them, describing important landmarks, and estimating distances between one port and another. Sometime between 40 and 70 C.E., a Greek merchant composed the Periplus of the Erythraean Sea. *Although "Erythraean Sea" could be taken narrowly to mean the Red Sea, traders of the Roman era used it as a general term that encompassed the Red Sea, the Persian Gulf, the Arabian Sea, and the wider Indian Ocean. In this selection from the* Periplus, *the author lists commodities found in and around Adulis (or Adouli), the major port of the Axumite kingdom on the Red Sea. This account offers information on the range of products traded and the distances they were transported before reaching Adulis. Other sections of the* Periplus *offer comments on the characteristics of the people that mariners were likely to encounter in different ports. Rather than an explicitly personal account of one trader's journey between Egypt and India, the* Periplus *is a sort of instructional manual or guidebook for sailors wanting knowledge of the Indian Ocean trade network.*

Adulis [is] a port established by law, lying at the inner end of a bay that runs in toward the south. Before the harbor lies the so-called Mountain Island, about two hundred stadia [an ancient Greek unit of length] seaward from the very head of the bay, with the shores of the mainland close to it on both sides. Ships bound for this port now anchor here because of attacks from the land. . . . Opposite Mountain Island, on the mainland twenty stadia from the shore, lies Adulis, a fair-sized village, from which there is a three days' journey to Coloe, an inland town and the first market for ivory. From that place to the city [Axum] of the people called Auxumites [sic] there is a five days' journey more; to that place all the ivory is brought from the country beyond the Nile through the district called Cyeneum [probably in the modern Republic of the Sudan], and thence to Adulis. Practically the whole number of elephants and rhinoceros that are killed live in the places inland, although at rare intervals they are hunted on the seacoast even near Adulis. . . .

There are imported into these places, undressed cloth made in Egypt for the Berbers; robes from Arsinoë [modern Suez]; cloaks of poor quality dyed in colors; double-fringed linen mantles; many articles of flint glass, and others of murrhine [probably agate or carnelian], made in Diospolis [probably Thebes]; and brass, which is used for ornament and in cut pieces instead of coin; sheets of soft copper, used for cooking utensils and cut up for bracelets and anklets for the women; iron, which is made into spears used against the elephants and other wild beasts, and in their wars. Besides these, small axes are imported, and adzes and swords; copper drinking-cups, round and large; a little coin for those coming to the market; wine of Laodicea [on the Syrian coast] and Italy, not much; olive oil, not much; for the King, gold and silver plate made after the fashion of the country, and for clothing, military cloaks, and thin coats of skin, of no great value. Likewise from the district of Ariaca [on the northwest coast of India around the Gulf of Cambay] across this sea, there are imported Indian cloth called *monaché* [fine quality cotton] and that called *sagmotogene* [probably tree cotton], and girdles, and coats of skin and mallow-colored cloth, and a few muslins, and colored lac [a resinous insect secretion used to make shellac]. There are exported from these places ivory, and tortoise-shell and rhinoceros-horn. The most from Egypt is brought to this market [Adulis] from the month of January to September.

Source: Wilfred H. Schoff, ed. and trans., *The Periplus of the Erythraean Sea: Travel and Trade in the Indian Ocean by a Merchant of the First Century* (New York: Longmans, Green, 1912), 22–24.

Thinking Critically

Create a list of broad categories into which you might divide the goods listed in this selection. Does the trade focus on practical objects, luxury items, or a mixture of the two? Which source of imports listed in the selection is farthest away from Adulis? Why do you think people in Axum wanted to buy the imports mentioned? What goods could Axumites offer that Romans did not have? What are some conditions that sailors and merchants had to take into account as they planned a voyage to or from Adulis?

The rise of Axum, situated in what are today Eritrea and northern Ethiopia, represented a consolidation of political power on the African side of the Red Sea. The early Axumite monarchs established a capital, also called Axum, in the Ethiopian highlands, which stretched west and south from the coast. Farmers herded livestock or grew millet, sorghum, wheat, and teff (a tiny grain characteristic of Ethiopian cuisine today) on mountain slopes and ridges. Axum's rulers also developed the port of Adulis to serve as an exclusive **entrepôt** (ON-truh-poh). In the process, they paid customs duties to the Axumite authorities.

> **entrepôt** A port or other urban center where merchants of different origins exchange goods and ship them onward.

We know little about the identity of the kings of Axum or the sort of government they organized. Their capital blossomed into a thriving city, the rulers adorning it with temples, a palace, and stone pillars (obelisks, or stelae) that marked the burial chambers of rulers or aristocrats. Some of these monuments, the tallest of which rose more than one hundred feet, were elaborately carved with false doors and windows. There is some evidence that the monarchs appointed provincial governors and other officials, though they may have done little more than collect tribute from rural village and clan leaders. The principal language of town dwellers, governors, and merchants was Ge'ez, a Semitic language related to Arabic and Hebrew and written with an alphabetic script.

Flourishing trade through Adulis encouraged Axum's rulers to launch campaigns to corral more routes, ports, and market towns within their sphere of influence. From the second to the sixth centuries C.E., Axumite forces advanced north along the Red Sea shore and periodically invaded South Arabia in order to control ports on both coasts. To the west, Axum may well have speeded Kush's decline by seizing territory and diverting trade in ivory and other tropical goods from the Nile route to the Red Sea. The glory of Kush had long since faded when Axum's King Ezana dispatched an army against Meroë in the mid-fourth century C.E. Fragments of stone inscriptions found at Meroë boast of Ezana's triumph over his enemies:

I fought with them on the Takkaze [River east of the Nile]. . . . Thereupon they took flight and would not make a stand. And I followed after the fugitives for twenty-three days, killing some and making prisoners of others, and capturing spoil wherever I stopped. . . . My soldiers carried off [the country's] food, and its copper, and its iron, and its brass, and they destroyed the statues in their houses, and the treasuries of food, and the cotton trees, and cast them into the River Seda [probably the Nile]. Many people died in the water; I do not know their number.[7]

After Ezana despoiled Kush, the Axumite state reached its greatest territorial extent, though control as far west as the Nile may not have lasted long. Between the fourth and sixth centuries C.E. Axum remained a wealthy and powerful state, and, as we see in Chapter 9, it became a Christian one.

Bridges Across Afroeurasia

> **FOCUS** What similarities and differences were there in the way that Buddhism, Christianity, and Confucianism emerged as large-scale belief systems in the period 300 B.C.E.–300 C.E.?

In the first and second centuries C.E., Rome, Kush, Axum, Parthia, Kushana, and Han China were all prosperous and reasonably stable states. Not accidentally, this was also a period in which long-distance commerce and cultural exchange across Afroeurasia grew significantly. In this period, private merchants handled an ever-increasing volume of interregional trade. Instead of sponsoring their own commercial expeditions, governments put more effort into ensuring conditions of security and opportunity in which private merchant operations might flourish. They did this, for example, by investing in roads, canals, and harbors, combating pirates and bandits, and granting hub cities varying degrees of self-government. High-cost luxury goods flowing to affluent classes or as gifts from one ruler to another continued to be the bread and butter of long-distance trade. By the start of the Common Era, however, merchants added to their shipments bulky, relatively cheaper wares, such as cotton textiles, everyday pottery, and glass beads.

Afroeurasia's commercial cities traded in ideas as well as merchandise, including ideas about god, compassion, salvation, ritual, and righteous behavior. In the six hundred years that this chapter addresses, Buddhism and Christianity, religions that broadcast their message universally, that is, to anyone who would listen, spread widely from their place of origin to other parts of Afroeurasia and attracted millions of adherents of diverse identity. Except for the Hellenistic tradition, which included a complex jumble of religious and philosophical ideas, Buddhism and Christianity were the first belief systems to achieve interregional scope.

East–West Interregional Trade

Ancient states invested in communication networks primarily to move armies, officials, and vital information where they were needed. State builders also understood that allowing private merchants, local farmers, slave dealers, and traveling scholars to use roads, trails, and navigable rivers helped integrate the state and increase its wealth. When the Roman empire arose, Mediterranean sea trade was already extensive. The Romans, learning from both Greeks and Etruscans, also began constructing a system of roads and bridges early in the republican centuries. This system in effect extended communication from Mediterranean shores into deep hinterlands. Engineers devised new techniques for building hard surface roads that would hold up under the weight of horses, wagons, and massed infantry. At its maximum extent in the second century C.E., the Roman empire may have had about 55,000 miles of

A road made to last. A stretch of the Appian Way near Itri in central Italy was part of a highway that connected Rome to Brindisi, a port on the Adriatic Sea coast.

highways. At the other end of the hemisphere, the Qin and Han rulers also built a highway system that radiated out from Chang'an and Luoyang, the successive royal capitals. The Qin emperor Shi Huangdi started the work, ordering that both road beds and wagon axles have standard widths to increase transport efficiency.

The Inner Eurasian silk routes. The silk roads that threaded across the steppes and mountains of Inner Eurasia, ultimately connecting the Han Chinese and Roman networks, were trails and paths, not stone-paved roads (see Map 7.5). Merchants sometimes hitched oxen or Bactrian camels to wagons, but pack trains of donkeys, horses, or camels were more suitable for crossing deserts and mountain passes. On routes in Southwest Asia, North Africa, and the Sahara, traders came to prefer dromedary camel and other animal pack trains almost exclusively. In the early centuries C.E., wheeled vehicles virtually disappeared from those regions.

Goods moved along the silk roads between China and the western lands in relay fashion. That is, groups of merchants, usually united by shared language and customs, operated along a particular segment of trails, towns, and oases. Then they sold their goods to other traders who carried them on the next stretch. In the late first century C.E., Gan Ying, a commercial envoy commissioned by the governor of a western Han province, traveled from China to somewhere in Southwest Asia, possibly Mesopotamia, on a not-quite-successful mission to make contact with the Roman empire. He was a notable exception because individual merchants rarely made such long trips. In the Han era, Chinese merchants set up operations along the silk roads both north and south of the Tarim Basin and as far west as the Ferghana valley. Conversely, the Han government encouraged caravaners from Kushana territory to visit western China.

Silk routes of the sea. Despite the growing importance of the silk roads, probably a much greater volume of long-distance trade flowed along the chain of interlinked seas that extended from East Asia to the Mediterranean (see this book's Introduction). From a commercial standpoint, merchants could move goods in larger quantities and at lower unit cost by ship than by caravan. In the tropical **southern seas,** seasonal winds, or monsoons, drove sailing ships forward. Differences in atmospheric temperatures between the Eurasian land mass and the Indian Ocean cause winds to blow generally from eastern Eurasia toward tropical Africa in the winter months. This is the northeast monsoon. In the warm months the winds reverse course, blowing from Africa toward Eurasia.

southern seas The China seas and the Indian Ocean, including the Arabian Sea and the Bay of Bengal.

We know that sailors took advantage of the monsoon cycle from ancient times, but they introduced new ship and sail designs in the first millennium c.e. that more efficiently capitalized on the alternating breezes. Malay mariners who traded among the islands of Southeast Asia may have been the first to develop a sail that could be set in a fore-and-aft position, meaning that the sail was aligned parallel with the sides of the ship rather than perpendicular to them. This design allowed a vessel to "tack," that is, to sail at a fairly sharp angle to the direction from which the wind was blowing and to zigzag back and forth against the wind to stay on course. Several types of fore-and-aft sails came into use in the southern seas, notably a triangular rig called the lateen sail. Maneuverability in monsoon conditions gave captains greater confidence to sail out of sight of land and allowed them to calculate with rough accuracy the time it might take to sail from one port to another.

Malay mariners appear to have carried much of the Indian Ocean exchange. A cluster of ports associated with Funan, a rice-growing state (or federation of small states) on the Gulf of Thailand in what is today southwestern Vietnam and Cambodia, served as key entrepôts linking the South China Sea to the Bay of Bengal. A remarkable example of long distance relay trade was the westward movement of cloves, nutmeg, and mace. Inhabitants of islands in the Moluccas group, part of the Indonesian archipelago, harvested cloves from one tree and nutmeg and mace (the kernel and covering of a single fruit) from another. In the late centuries b.c.e., Malay merchants began to sell these aromatic spices at high markups in Indian and Chinese ports. By the first century c.e., small quantities of them periodically reached the spice market in Rome, nine thousand miles from where they were harvested.

Tropical African products also entered the southern seas market. Ivory, tortoise shells, leopard skins, rhinoceros horn, ebony wood, and other goods found ready buyers in India and the Roman and Parthian empires. No later than the first century c.e., a port known as Rhapta arose on the East African coast, probably in what is today Tanzania. Rhapta's residents included local Bantu-speaking farmers, artisans, and traders, as well as maritime merchants from South Arabia and Axum. Although Rhapta appears to have declined from the fourth century c.e., other East African ports later took its place, playing a strategic part in the trans-hemispheric commercial system.

Roman merchants in the southern seas. It was a measure of Roman power that its rulers could supply affluent men and women with exotic goods from distant lands, including much prized gemstones, spices, incense, ivory, aromatics, and silk originating far to the east. In that age, Chinese farmers were the only people in the world who practiced sericulture, that is, the production of silk thread and yarn from silkworm cocoons. Chinese weavers also made most of the silk cloths sent to other parts of Afroeurasia. The enormous influx of gold and silver into Rome from conquests and mining inspired wealthy Romans to invest in expensive trade ventures between the Mediterranean and the southern seas. Moreover, Rome's conquest of

Egypt and part of Southwest Asia beginning in the late first century b.c.e. opened the way to the Red Sea and the Indian Ocean beyond. Some Asian products also reached Rome overland through territory of the Parthian empire.

Roman subjects of Greek, Arab, Hebrew, Aramaean, or Egyptian origin handled most of the southern seas trade, and Greek served as a commercial *lingua franca* around the Arabian Sea rim. In that era, South Asian ports were emerging rapidly as the turnstiles of trans-hemispheric commerce. Consequently, Roman merchants had great incentive to reach ports on both the western and the eastern shores of India and on the island of Ceylon (Sri Lanka) in order to traffic with Asian merchants established there. In ports in northwestern India, merchants from the Kushana-ruled lands of the Indus valley, Afghanistan, and Central Asia met their Roman counterparts. According to the *Periplus of the Erythraean Sea*, the Greek shipping manual written in the first century c.e. (see "Weighing the Evidence"), Roman ships arriving at the port of Barbaricum near the Indus River unloaded "a great deal of thin clothing . . .; figured linens, topaz, coral, storax (an aromatic resin), frankincense, vessels of glass, silver and gold plate, and a little wine." In exchange, Kushana merchants offered such products as lapis lazuli, turquoise, silk yarn, and indigo (a blue dye).[8] In southern India, Romans bought Indian cotton textiles, black pepper, cinnamon, pearls, and Southeast Asian spices. Chinese documents record that in 166 c.e. a group of Romans, probably merchants, reached Luoyang, the Han Chinese royal capital. Nothing came of this initiative, however, and Romans had no stake that we know of in trade east of India.

Since Rome seems to have had a much greater hunger for Asian products than Asians had for Mediterranean manufactures, Roman merchants carried quantities of gold and silver coins to pay for purchases. Archaeologists have found several large hordes of Roman money in India, where natural deposits of these metals were scarce. Some Roman leaders worried about a drain of the empire's bullion supply to the east, but in fact the value of coin exports remained modest relative to the commercial wealth circulating *within* the empire.[9]

The First Missionary Religions

Why, we may ask, did Buddhism and Christianity, among a few other religions, grow into interregional, ultimately worldwide movements, when such a phenomenon had never occurred earlier? Like all religions in varying ways, these faiths answered to the individual's search for consolation, hope, and spiritual meaning in a world fraught with inexplicable events and everyday troubles. But why "big" religions? One possibility is that by the late centuries b.c.e. continuing world population growth, coupled with intensified interaction among communities, required spiritual and moral codes that might strengthen bonds among people otherwise divided by language, culture, and class. As these religions attracted followers beyond the confines of a single region, they became foundations for cultural communication and

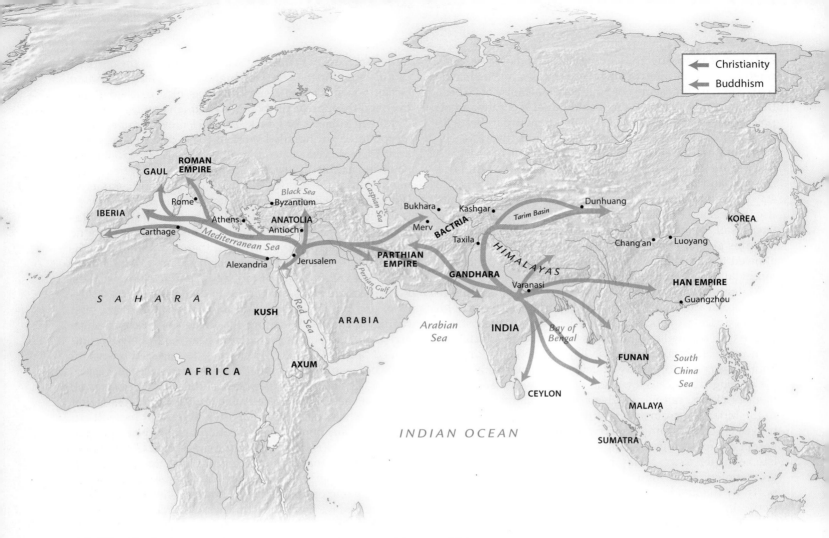

MAP 7.5 The growth of Buddhism and Christianity, 200 B.C.E.–300 C.E.
What geographic factors might help explain why Christianity and Buddhism spread in the particular directions they did from their founding areas?

mutual trust among strangers who met to exchange information, do business, or, in any of countless ways, cooperate with one another. Buddhism and Christianity each offered a distinctive moral and spiritual path. But both religions transcended association with any particular state, ruling class, or ethnolinguistic group, thereby uniting people in shared belief and practice whoever they were and wherever they lived (see Map 7.5).

Buddhism beyond India. In the two hundred years after the death of the Buddha (ca. 483 B.C.E.), his message of hope and compassion to suffering humanity spread across South Asia (see Chapter 6). Around 250 B.C.E., a council of monks, meeting at the behest of Ashoka, king of the Maurya state, proclaimed that the Buddha's followers should actively broadcast his teachings to the world. In the following centuries, Buddhist missionaries advanced northwestward to Persia, Bactria, and Inner Eurasia, east to Burma, and south to Ceylon. Buddhist scholars also generated sacred texts (*sutras*) that introduced both teachings

attributed to the Buddha and enlightened commentaries on those doctrines.

Many Buddhist converts became monks, joining monasteries and taking up lives of self-denial, meditation, and study. Wherever clerics founded new monastic communities, they worked to copy, translate, and disseminate religious writings. Other Buddhist converts, both men and women, remained "in the world," supporting the work of the monasteries but living in their village and town communities. Buddhism's message of freedom from suffering for people of all social ranks, combined with its emphasis on personal moral responsibility, attracted large numbers of artisans and traders. Buddhist merchants who carried goods long distances helped spread the new faith beyond India.

Buddhism had an early flowering in Gandhara, the region of the upper Indus valley that is today northern Pakistan. Greek-speaking kings of Bactria ruled that region in the second century C.E. from the thriving commercial city of Taxila. After Buddhist monks and merchants started arriving, Gandhara became a lively cultural meeting ground.

One striking consequence was the flowering of a Buddhist art style that gracefully combined Greek and Indian elements. In the second and third centuries C.E., Kushana kings, noted for their cultural tolerance and cosmopolitanism, welcomed Buddhists. From Kushana territory, missionaries introduced the faith to Iran under Parthian rule and to the oasis towns strung out along the silk roads north and south of the Tarim Basin. The first Buddhist missionaries reached China as early as the first century B.C.E. We come back to that story in later chapters.

As Buddhist belief and practice took hold beyond India, several schools of thought emerged, each offering somewhat different approaches to belief and practice. The Mahayana school attracted the largest following. Its early disciples favored incorporating new scriptural ideas into the Buddhist canon of texts, notably the idea that individuals might seek total enlightenment (nirvana) without committing themselves to monastic life. Probably originating in silk road towns rather than in India, the Mahayana way taught that beings who possessed power to bestow grace on sincere seekers might help them gain spiritual illumination. These divines were of two sorts. First were saints, or *bodhisattvas* (BOH-dih-SAT-vuhs), holy individuals believed to have postponed their own enlightenment in order to aid others along the sacred path. Second was the Buddha himself, whom Mahayana viewed not only as the great teacher but also as a personal savior. Mahayana Buddhists celebrated compassion as the cardinal virtue and introduced new doctrines, rituals, and expressions of sacred art.

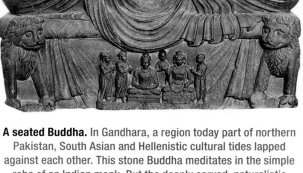

A seated Buddha. In Gandhara, a region today part of northern Pakistan, South Asian and Hellenistic cultural tides lapped against each other. This stone Buddha meditates in the simple robe of an Indian monk. But the deeply carved, naturalistic folds of the garment tell us that local or immigrant artisans also appreciated Hellenistic styles.

Jesus and the beginnings of Christianity. Roman rulers generally tolerated the welter of religious and philosophical ideas that circulated in their empire, for example, recognizing Judaism as a "legal religion." Large numbers of Jews lived in Palestine (the southern Levant), but communities of the diaspora inhabited many cities in the Mediterranean basin, Mesopotamia, Iran, and Central Asia (see Chapter 5). Jews did not proclaim a universalist mission to convert others but rather sought to preserve and vitalize Jewish law and worship.

After Roman forces seized Jerusalem in 63 B.C.E., their relations with the Jewish population deteriorated steadily. As monotheists, many Jews expressed their abhorrence for both foreign rule and Rome's plethora of gods and goddesses. In return, the Romans, notably with the collaboration of their local client king Herod (r. 37–4 B.C.E.), ferreted out Jewish resisters and imposed heavy taxes. The Jewish revolt that broke out in 65 C.E. festered for eight years before Roman authorities finally stamped it out.

During those decades of tension, Jesus, a Jewish carpenter who lived in the small Palestinian city of Nazareth, began about 27 C.E. to preach a message of peace and divine salvation through brotherly and sisterly love. He attracted a following and eventually traveled to Jerusalem, where he taught in the temple. Nearly everything he said had deep roots in the spiritual and moral teachings of Hebrew scripture. He seriously disagreed with Jewish leaders, however, over the practice of distinguishing between people who were holy, righteous, and ritually pure, and those who were not. Jesus taught that God loved all his creation, regardless of their status or circumstance, and that humans should reflect that love in their relations with one another. Like Mahayana Buddhists, he preached compassion as the key human virtue. Unlike them, he proclaimed one God, the Father of all, as the sole source of compassion. He taught that by God's grace humans receive his love, share it with others, and prepare themselves for eternal salvation. To the alarm of some pious Jews, Jesus associated freely with criminals, outcasts, and prostitutes, and he went about healing people without presuming who was worthy and who was not.

Jesus preached for just three years before the Roman authorities, advised by some Jewish leaders that he was a troublemaker and potential rebel, had him crucified for treason. The earliest records we have of this event, and everything else about Jesus' life and teachings, are found in the Gospels, the books attributed to the disciples Matthew, Mark, Luke, and John. These texts, written a generation after Jesus' time, form the first part of the Biblical New Testament. According to the Gospels, God raised Jesus from the dead; shortly thereafter, he ascended into heaven. Precisely how he perceived his own relationship to God became a matter

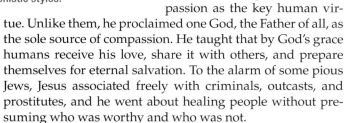

of great dispute among the Christian congregations that arose in succeeding generations. Nevertheless, the authors of the Gospels and the other books of the New Testament clearly regarded him as the Christ, a word of Greek origin meaning the "anointed one" or messiah. Jewish doctrine already embraced the idea that a messiah would one day appear. This redeemer would serve as the instrument of God's judgment of all humankind and lead the Jews to freedom. Early Christians declared that the spirit of Christ continued to live among them and that Jesus would shortly return to proclaim the kingdom of God on earth.

For a short time, Christians formed a small group within the Jewish fold. But owing primarily to the initiative of Paul, a Jewish scholar from Anatolia who lived in Jesus' time but did not know him, Christian groups began to share their message of the resurrected Christ with Gentiles, that is, non-Jews. Paul and other preachers argued that Christians had no obligation to observe Jewish law, such as dietary restrictions that would have prevented Christians of Jewish and Gentile background from eating together. By about 100 C.E., Gentiles took over leadership of the movement, and Christianity emerged as a **universalist religion** in its mission to evangelize, that is, to bring the "good news" of the Gospel, to the world at large.

universalist religion A religion whose doctrines and practices aim to appeal to all people irrespective of their language, ethnicity, social class, or political affiliation.

Christ as shepherd. This is an early depiction of Jesus Christ (second or third century C.E.) on the wall of a catacomb, or underground cemetery in Rome. Jesus supports a goat on his shoulders. What do you think the animals (two birds, two goats, and a sheep) in this fresco collectively signify?

Christianity beyond Palestine. Paul, who had the privileged status of a Roman citizen, took advantage of the imperial roads and sea lanes to travel widely in the eastern Mediterranean, preaching to both Jews and Gentiles, helping Christian groups found churches, and finally settling in Rome. In the two and a half centuries after Jesus preached, the same centuries when Buddhism was spreading along the silk roads to China, Christians founded communities in many eastern Mediterranean cities and in a few large centers in the west, including Rome. Leaders also created an increasingly sophisticated organization of churches with a hierarchy of officers headed by bishops based in different cities.

Several factors help explain the success of Christianity in those 250 years. One was the fierce devotion of Christians impelled by expectations of eternal life and of Jesus' imminent return to earth. Another was the warm welcome early Christians gave newcomers without regard to their social or political status, including the urban poor and women. Early Christian converts of elite Roman origin appear to have been predominantly women, and some took energetic roles in missionary and organizational work. A third factor was persecution, which Christians experienced episodically in different parts of the empire. Roman authorities prosecuted and executed Christians, including Paul, not so much for what they believed about Jesus but for refusing to take part in public cult rituals that invoked Rome's numerous deities. The martyrdom of Christians had the principal effect of strengthening faith and resolve within communities and attracting the admiration and sympathy of potential converts.

At the end of the third century C.E., a period when official persecution became more systematic and severe, Christian groups formed not only in the Mediterranean basin but also in Mesopotamia, Iran, and the western coast of India. At that time, Christians may have numbered no more than about 10 percent of the Roman empire's population. But that percentage soared in the following centuries, and Christianity became the imperial religion.

. . .

Conclusion

In the six centuries we have considered in this chapter, men and women had a variety of motives for traveling long distances and encountering strangers. One was trade. On the local level, people bought and sold basic commodities such as grain, fish, coarse textiles, and ironware. Merchants hauled bulk goods from one neighboring region to another but seldom on long interregional routes. Long-distance traders, by contrast, carried mainly goods of high value and low bulk, that is, costly merchandise such as silk cloth, glassware, fine ceramics, gemstones, and spices. The profits merchants could amass moving such wares across seas and mountains provided motive enough to cooperate with one another across ethnolinguistic borders.

The process of state building also impelled people to spin more complex webs of communication. We have seen that imperial transport networks built in the first instance to move soldiers and officials also carried merchants, artisans, scholars, and missionaries—people who introduced products, skills, and ideas from one place to another. The Han road and river networks, for example, facilitated the spread of Confucian morals and ethics in China. Roman roads and ships carried Christian proselytizers. Buddhists trekked along trails that Kushana authorities made secure. Literate scholars introduced new societies to Greek, Latin, Aramaic, Sanskrit, and Chinese writing systems, all of them associated with powerful states or new religions.

Some corners of Afroeurasia still had only tenuous links to interregional networks because rugged topography isolated them, their populations were sparse, or their locations were geographical cul-de-sacs—on the way to nowhere. This was the situation for hunting communities living in far northern parts of Europe, Russia, and Siberia. Japan had been inhabited for thousands of years, but human contacts with the East Asian mainland remained weak throughout most of the first millennium B.C.E. Only in the Han period did exchange, mainly by way of the Korean Peninsula, start to quicken. In far southwestern Africa, iron-using farmers were just beginning to advance to regions that faced the empty Atlantic.

Peoples of Afroeurasia had no sustained contact with the other three "worlds" of human habitation. Except intermittently along Australia's northern edge, the foragers of that continent had no connections to Afroeurasia. The same was true of the communities scattered out across the Island Pacific. The Americas was also a separate realm, but in contrast to Australians and Pacific Islanders, ancient Americans built cities and empires of their own. In Chapter 8 we turn to developments there.

• • •

Key Terms

Analects 202	Han empire 200	Qin dynasty 200
Axum 205	Kush 205	republic 193
Christianity 211	Kushana empire 205	Roman empire 194
Confucianism 202	*latifundia* 196	Romanization 199
Daodejing 204	Legalism 201	Sinification 204
Daoism 204	Parthian dynasty 205	southern seas 212
entrepôt 211	patron-client system 194	universalist religion 216
filial piety 203	*Pax Romana* 196	Xiongnu empire 205

Change over Time

6th–4th centuries B.C.E.	The kingdom of Kush prospers, with its center at Meroë.
ca. 563–ca. 483 B.C.E.	Siddhartha Gautama, the Buddha, preaches in northern India.
551–479 B.C.E.	The Chinese philosopher Confucius lives.
509–27 B.C.E.	The Roman Republic expands Mediterranean power with a republican form of government.
ca. 250 B.C.E.	Buddhism begins to spread beyond South Asia.
247 B.C.E.–**224** C.E.	The Parthian dynasty, founded by steppe warriors, succeeds the Seleucids in Persia and battles Rome along the Tigris-Euphrates frontier.
221–207 B.C.E.	The Qin dynasty in China establishes an efficient authoritarian state based on Legalism.
210–174 B.C.E.	The Xiongnu steppe alliance becomes an empire under Maodun as khan.
206 B.C.E.–**220** C.E.	The Han dynasty in China establishes the Chinese tradition of centralized bureaucratic government.
2nd century B.C.E.	Trade on Inner Eurasian silk roads intensifies.
141–87 B.C.E.	Han Wudi incorporates Confucian ideas into the Han imperial ideology.

Please see end of book reference section for additional reading suggestions related to this chapter.

8 American Complexities
900 B.C.E.–900 C.E.

Numbers on this inscription give the accession date of a ruler of Palenque, an ancient Maya city-state in Chiapas, Mexico.

When we do everyday arithmetic, we may never think about the fact that we are using a numerical system based on the ingenious concept of positional notation, also called place-value notation. In the long run of history, humans have tried a variety of systems for counting, calculating, and measuring. Positional notation is just one of them, though it is used nearly universally today. In the past three thousand years, only three societies appear to have invented a positional system independently. In Afroeurasia, Babylonians did it in Mesopotamia about 2000 B.C.E. and South Asians in the Ganges valley around 500 C.E. In the Western Hemisphere, sages somewhere in southern Mexico or Guatemala invented it in the late centuries B.C.E.

Our modern system, which the South Asian scholars passed on to us, is a base-ten counting method that uses only ten integer (whole number) signs, that is, 1 through 9 plus 0. The value of a number is determined by its position relative to other numbers in a row. Each number, reading from right to left, represents a higher power of ten. Thus, when we write 999, the 9 in the far right position signifies the value of 9. The 9 in the next position means 90, and the 9 on the left means 900. Thus we get 900 + 90 + 9, but all we have to write is 999.

In ancient Mesoamerica, Maya scholars fully developed a positional notation system, though it looked different from our modern one. The Maya used a base-twenty rather than base-ten counting method, with certain exceptions. They showed the value of numbers, not by arranging them in a positional sequence on a line from right to left but on a column of rows from bottom to top. The bottom row represented a number between 1 and 19, the next one up a multiple of 20, the third a multiple of 400 (20 × 20), and so on. The Maya used combinations of dots and bars to signify numbers, one dot representing "1" and one bar representing "5." The number 999 would therefore be expressed like this:

2 { • • } meaning 2 x 400 = 800

9 { ••••• } meaning 9 x 20 = 180

19 { ••••• } meaning 19 x 1 = 19

The very existence of the Maya number system speaks of a society of great complexity. The Maya and several other agrarian civilizations that emerged in the Americas after about 900 B.C.E. had no known contact with peoples of Afroeurasia (see Map 8.1). But two generalizations about long-term change appear to apply to both Afroeurasia and the Americas before modern times. First, human groups that succeeded well enough at farming to produce significant surpluses of food were likely to grow in numbers at accelerating rates. That growth in turn required new forms of social organization, usually manifested in social class divisions, occupational specializations, centralized states, city building, and indeed elaborate methods for keeping accounts and calendars. Such complexity developed in both Afroeurasia and the Americas, even though neither hemisphere borrowed or adapted any ideas or technologies from the other.

Second, in no premodern complex society anywhere in the world did a particular state, empire, or ruling class last indefinitely. All of them eventually collapsed or withered away, though the reasons for decline varied from one case to another. The American societies that we investigate in

• • •

this chapter all proved finite, their governing classes failing at some point to solve mounting ecological, political, or social problems. They abandoned once dazzling cities, leaving them to crumble. In both the Americas and Afroeurasia, however, the general trajectory toward greater complexity continued on. For every political and cultural system that faltered and fell, another one arose to take its place, in some cases on top of the old ruins.

The first part of this chapter explores developments in North America, chiefly in the region that geographers call Mesoamerica, or Middle America. (We extend the chronological range of this chapter about six hundred years longer than the other chapters in Part 2 in order to respect political and cultural continuities.) This area corresponds generally to the tropical southern half of Mexico and the Central American states of Guatemala, Belize, Honduras, and El Salvador. It is the region in which a number of complex urban societies developed starting in the late second millennium B.C.E. (see Chapter 4). Several Olmec cities from that period flourished far into the first millennium B.C.E., and they may finally have declined mainly because new centers in other parts of Mesoamerica attracted more people, skilled artisans, and commerce. In this section of the chapter, we highlight peoples who achieved social complexity on relatively large physical scales: the state centered on the city of Teotihuacán (tay-oh-tee-wa-KAHN) in the Valley of Mexico, the Zapotec city

A Panoramic View

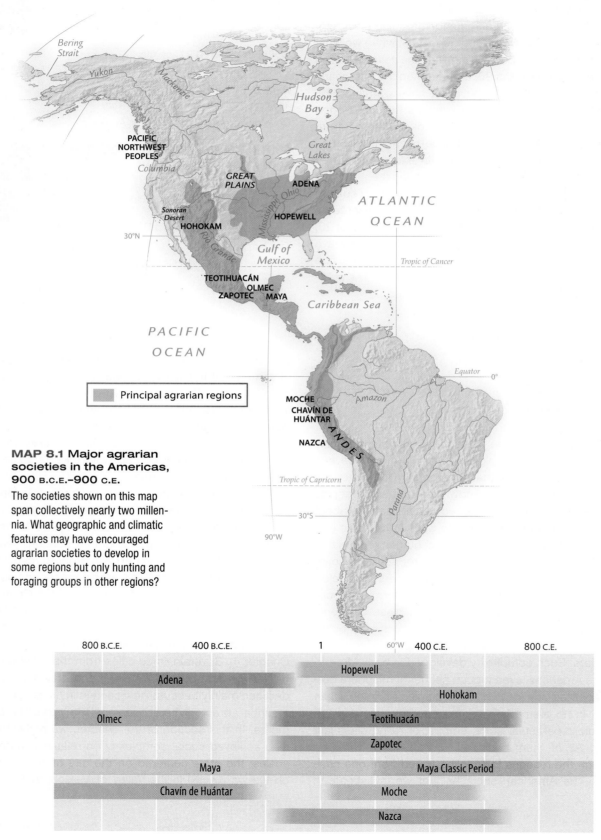

MAP 8.1 Major agrarian societies in the Americas, 900 B.C.E.–900 C.E.

The societies shown on this map span collectively nearly two millennia. What geographic and climatic features may have encouraged agrarian societies to develop in some regions but only hunting and foraging groups in other regions?

Principal agrarian regions

800 B.C.E.	400 B.C.E.	1	400 C.E.	800 C.E.
		Hopewell		
Adena				
			Hohokam	
Olmec		Teotihuacán		
		Zapotec		
Maya		Maya Classic Period		
Chavín de Huántar		Moche		
		Nazca		

builders in the Oaxaca valley, and the Maya of southern Mexico and Central America. We then move to upper North America (northern Mexico to the Arctic), where in several places agrarian societies became more complex, though on a much smaller material scale than in Mesoamerica. These North Americans included peoples of the Pacific coast, the Sonoran Desert of northwestern Mexico and the southwestern United States, and the temperate woodlands that stretch from the Mississippi River to the Atlantic.

In the second part of the chapter we turn to South America, where societies scattered along the Pacific coastal plain and the Andean highlands began to construct remarkable ceremonial centers as early as the fourth millennium B.C.E. (see Chapter 4). Here, we focus on the large-scale building and numerous technical innovations associated with the ceremonial center of Chavín de Huántar in the northern Peruvian highlands, the Pacific coastal states of Moche (moh-CHEE), and the relatively small but artistically spectacular center known as Nazca.

The Spread of Complex Societies in North America

> **FOCUS** What factors may explain differences in the development of political, social, and economic systems in agrarian societies in Mesoamerica and upper North America between 200 B.C.E. and the late first millennium C.E.?

All of Mesoamerica lies within the earth's northern tropical latitudes. But its ecological profile is extremely complex, owing to dramatic gradations of altitude, temperature, and rainfall, from the slopes of Pico de Orizaba, the third highest mountain in North America, to the lowland marshes of the Yucatán Peninsula. The Olmec built Mesoamerica's earliest urban society, starting about 1350 B.C.E., in the wet tropical plains and river valleys that parallel Mexico's southern Gulf coast. But even as Olmec civilization ascended, several other centers of dense agrarian settlement began to take shape in different regions and ecological conditions (see Map 8.2).

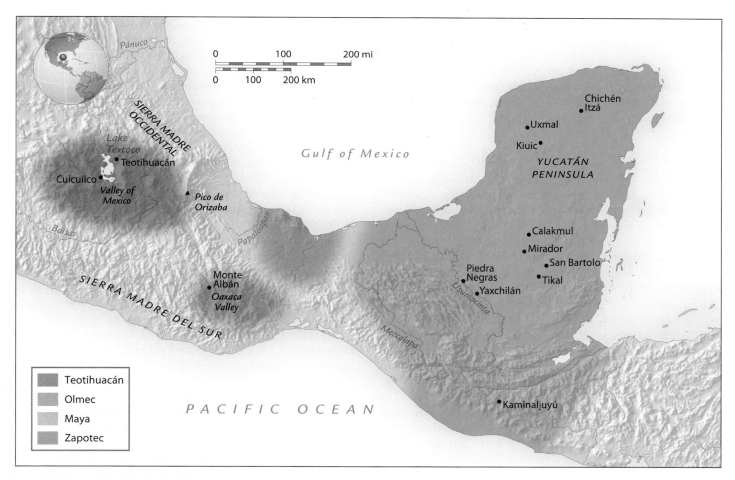

MAP 8.2 Major states in Mesoamerica, 500 B.C.E.–800 C.E.
What geographic features would likely have either facilitated or impeded travel among the states of Mesoamerica?

One of these centers arose in the Valley of Mexico, the highland basin that includes modern Mexico City. A second appeared in the fertile Oaxaca valley in the rugged mountains of southern Mexico. A third emerged in the low-lying Yucatán Peninsula and adjacent upland areas of modern Mexico, Guatemala, Belize, and Honduras, where the population spoke mainly languages in the Maya family. Archaeologists have uncovered ample material evidence to show that in the first millennium B.C.E. and thereafter all of these centers regularly exchanged goods, ideas, and techniques with one another and with neighboring rural peoples of mountain, forest, and desert. In other words, Mesoamerica as a whole became a zone of dynamic intercommunication. Despite great variety in language and cultural style, this interaction is evident in similarities in such aspects of life as architecture and religious practice.

The intensity of exchange gradually tapered off to the north (northern Mexico and the southwestern United States), where rainfall was generally much lower and farming populations smaller and more widely dispersed. On the southern frontier of Mesoamerica, cultural contact between Mayan-speaking societies and peoples of the Isthmus of Panama or South America beyond appear to have been irregular. In the 1,800 years or so that this chapter addresses, people did not, as far as we know, migrate in significant numbers or conduct long-distance trade between Mesoamerica and South America by way of Panama or its coastal waters. On the other hand, certain cultural innovations, notably knowledge of how to work gold and silver into useful objects, may have diffused from South America, reaching the Maya lands in the first millennium C.E.

Empire Builders of Teotihuacán

In the period this chapter explores, the centralized states that rose and fell in Mesoamerica were for the most part geographically small. We might think of them as city-states, that is, temple and civic centers from which monarchs and aristocratic elites controlled surrounding agricultural lands. They were similar in scale to the ancient Greek city-states in the Aegean Sea region. In Mesoamerica the single great exception to this pattern was Teotihuacán, a monarchy that started out as a city-state but later came to dominate a large part of Mesoamerica. In the process it disseminated its cultural style far and wide. Teotihuacán endured as a sovereign state from about 200 B.C.E. to 750 C.E., rising like Rome from city-state to empire and lasting about as long, approximately 950 years.

City of the gods. Twenty-two hundred years ago, Teotihuacán was a small city occupying a corner of the Valley of Mexico, an extensive highland plateau surrounded by mountains and active volcanoes that rise to 16,000 feet. The ancient basin, now the site of greater Mexico City and its more than twenty-two million people, had a mild climate, several large lakes, and a blanket of fertile volcanic soil.

Farmers drew on lake and spring water to irrigate fields of maize, squash, beans, nopal cactus (prickly pear), and numerous other crops. By 400 B.C.E., some people lived in large villages and towns. The biggest of these in the early period may have been Cuicuilco, a temple center of perhaps five thousand inhabitants. But about 50 B.C.E., a nearby volcano erupted in a spectacular display of fire and ash, spewing molten lava across Cuicuilco's fields, canals, and ceremonial buildings. The explosion buried the city and no doubt part of its population under thick debris. With Cuicuilco destroyed, people streamed into neighboring Teotihuacán. By 100 C.E., that town may have sheltered about 60,000 people, and by 600 C.E., more than 150,000. At that time it was probably one of the top ten largest cities on the planet.

Urban planning and the Pyramid of the Sun. Teotihuacán's rulers erected a magnificent capital whose sprawling ruin near Mexico City continues to amaze visitors. We do not know what the inhabitants called the city or even what language they spoke. In later centuries local people who spoke Nahuatl (the language of the Aztecs) named it Teotihuacán, meaning "Abode of the Gods," or "Where Men Became Gods." It is easy to understand why. Laid out on a grid with formal streets, the city occupied about eight square miles. It enclosed temples, palaces, a government center, single-story apartment blocks, workshops, plazas, markets, canals, lakes, and outlying neighborhoods of cheap housing. In the early centuries C.E., architects divided the city core into four quarters. A central thoroughfare, now called the Avenue of the Dead, ran four miles north to south. A second major road crossed the avenue at a right angle. Using astronomical measurements, the builders aligned this grid with particular stars and nearby sacred mountain peaks.

Teotihuacán functioned primarily as a center of religious worship and ritual. The Pyramid of the Sun, its largest monument, loomed over the city to a height of two hundred feet. Its base dimensions rivaled the largest pyramid at Giza in Egypt, though it rose less than half as high. The Egyptian pyramids served as tombs, and once they were built no one had special reasons to climb to the top of them. Excavations at Teotihuacán have uncovered burials in both the Pyramid of the Sun and the smaller Pyramid of the Moon north of it. Like pyramids throughout Mesoamerica, however, these structures also had staircases leading to their summits, where rulers erected shrines for performance of religious rituals in full view of the crowd gathered below. Archaeologists have found a tunnel connecting to a natural cavern within the Pyramid of the Sun. Some have suggested that the city's population believed this cluster of chambers to be the "house" of the storm god, an important deity, or the place where the gods created the sun and moon.

Teotihuacán society. The great majority of people who lived in Teotihuacán and surrounding villages cultivated the land. Farmers who resided in the city "commuted" to outlying fields during the day. Artisans and their apprentices

Teotihuacán. A view of the city from the Pyramid of the Moon. The Avenue of the Dead extends south. The Pyramid of the Sun, the highest structure in the city, is on the left.

made up perhaps 5 to 10 percent of the urban population. Stone carvers fashioned blades, spear tips, and fine objects of obsidian. Potters made both exquisitely decorated ceramics and everyday vessels. Other craftspeople produced sandals, baskets, building stone, and wall plaster from burnt limestone. Material objects or artistic styles that originated in other parts of Mesoamerica point to distinct urban quarters where foreigners lived, probably traveling merchants, commercial agents, or immigrant artisans. For example, archaeologists have discovered pottery, obsidian tools, and architectural forms in these neighborhoods, which suggest that people originating in the Maya region hundreds of miles to the southeast lived there. Direct evidence is scant, but there must also have been a class of officials who worked as administrators, clerks, and police. An elite minority of aristocrats, military officers, and religious specialists surely supervised these civil servants, though we know very little about Teotihuacán's urban government. There is no doubt, however, that the splendid city could not have been built without mobilizing and directing many thousands of workers.

Dwellings in the city likely fit the social status of their inhabitants. The structure called the Citadel, a complex of buildings surrounding a square 1,300 feet long on each side, almost certainly served as a center where aristocratic families lived. Other palace-like structures along the Avenue of the Dead presumably also housed elite families. One typical villa had forty-five enclosed rooms, a central courtyard with an altar in the center, and seven smaller courts and patios.

After about 250 C.E., builders knocked down plain adobe huts in the central part of the city and replaced them with more than two thousand flat-roofed apartment complexes of varying sizes. Most of the city's inhabitants apparently lived in these well-designed flats, made chiefly of a type of concrete of volcanic rock, gravel, clay, and mortar. Excavations of some of these compounds have revealed kitchens, clay braziers, sleeping quarters, wells, floor drains, and polished plaster walls. Domestic trash dumps show that families dined on maize, beans, squash, pumpkin, tomatoes, and avocados. Deer, dog, cottontail rabbit, and turkey meat added fat and protein to the diet. Apartments had no windows, but courtyards and patios allowed in light and air. Artisans painted colorful murals on the interior walls of almost all houses, as well as temples and palaces. These works portrayed gods, religious ceremonies, warriors, and jaguars but also images of men and women playing, singing, and chasing butterflies through irrigated fields. The repetition of patterns suggests that some artists may have used stencils, a type of mass-produced art that would have allowed people of ordinary means to have their walls decorated. Some wall painting also includes signs, or **glyphs** that indicate the names or titles of individuals whose images are shown. Scholarly efforts to decipher these glyphs continue, though so far we have

> **glyph** A graphic figure or character that conveys information, often a symbol carved or incised in relief.

no evidence that the Teotihuacanos created a full writing system.

The city appears to have been the fount of religious ideas that eventually permeated much of Mesoamerica. The personalities and functions attached to particular gods and goddesses changed from one society to another, but deities whose influence spread far beyond Teotihuacán included the storm god (or rain god), whose ancestry as an image may stretch back to the were-jaguar spirit (part man, part animal) that the Olmec had worshiped in earlier times. Other Teotihuacán deities of lasting importance were Quetzalcoatl (keht-zahl-koh-AHTL), or feathered serpent deity, and the female divinity sometimes called the Great Goddess. We have no archaeological evidence that Teotihuacán's rulers and priests practiced human sacrifice on a large scale. But it did apparently happen. For example, digs at the city's Pyramid of Quetzalcoatl have revealed that, around 200 C.E., priests consecrated this monument by killing and ritually burying about two hundred young men.

What sort of empire? Starting around 150 C.E., Teotihuacán began to expand its political sway beyond the Valley of Mexico. It is difficult to determine the precise form this influence took in different localities, because the historical record is limited mostly to material artifacts. Teotihuacano armies appear to have conquered or at least intimidated many of their neighbors, ruling some groups directly and others through submissive local clients, just as the contemporaneous Romans did. Merchants and perhaps migrating colonists also disseminated Teotihuacán's religious ideas and artistic styles, introducing them to distant rulers eager to boost their own prestige by associating themselves with the great city's culture. We should remember, however, that in contrast to Afroeurasian empires of the same era, no Mesoamerican state had large transport animals or cavalry. Moving big armies long distances and regularly supplying garrisons far from the capital had to rely entirely on the walking or running speed of troops and porters. This limited direct imperial rule on the scale of the Romans, Persians, or Han Chinese.

Nevertheless, archaeological finds shows that warriors from Teotihuacán intruded into the affairs of cities hundreds of miles away. One example is Kaminaljuyú, a ceremonial center in highland Guatemala nearly 650 straight-line miles southeast of the Valley of Mexico. Kaminaljuyú's ruins have revealed so much Teotihuacáno influence in urban layout, temple

A mural in Teotihuacán. Frescos decorated the walls of Tepantitla, an apartment compound in the great city. This detail is part of a larger mural portraying a deity interpreted by some scholars as the Great Goddess. These tiny figures in the mural appear to be going about their daily business. How might you interpret the curved shapes extending upward from the faces of the two figures on the far left?

construction, and manufactured objects that some scholars have argued for a full armed takeover, which would have happened about 300 C.E. Archaeologists have discovered tombs full of luxury wares of Teotihuacán origin, indicating sustained contact. A second example of Teotihuacán's long reach is its relations with Tikal (Mutal), one of the largest cities in the Yucatán Peninsula. In 378 C.E., Teotihuacáno soldiers appear to have engineered the overthrow of the Maya ruler of Tikal. They replaced him with a man whose name glyph identifies him as Curl Nose. Tikal subsequently became a more powerful city-state, perhaps because it was an ally, if not a colonial dependency, of Teotihuacán.

We do not know exactly *why* Teotihuacán embarked on three and a half centuries of expansion, but if its population climbed to 150,000 or more, the demand for food, textile fiber, stone, and luxury wares must have far exceeded local resources. The need to make sure the flow of goods into the city never stopped may have motivated an aggressive foreign policy. Some of these goods probably arrived as tribute from subordinate towns and cities.

Uninterrupted long-distance exchange required a growing network of communication radiating out from Teotihuacán. This trade and tribute web was no doubt thicker toward the densely populated south and southeast than toward the drier lands to the north. The busiest route, named by modern scholars the Teotihuacán Corridor, connected the Valley of Mexico with the Olmec and Maya lowland regions. From there traders brought cacao beans, rubber, salt, honey, tropical bird feathers, pottery, and jade. Other merchants carried Teotihuacán's fine manufactures far and wide, including green obsidian blades, clay figurines, and ceramic ware. It is possible that Teotihuacán seized Kaminaljuyú in order to control distribution of the cacao that farmers grew in quantity along Guatemala's Pacific coast. Cane sugar was unknown in the Americas before 1492, but Mesoamericans blended cacao with water, honey, chilies, and other spices to make a chocolate drink used in rituals or for the pleasure of men and women who could afford an expensive brew.

The empire's decline. In the late fifth century C.E., Teotihuacán's commercial and cultural influence on southern Mesoamerica began to fade, and in about 650 C.E., assailants ravaged the city, plundering and burning the great temples and pyramids along the Avenue of the Dead. By this time Teotihuacán must have been so weakened that it could no longer effectively defend itself, something it had not had to do for centuries. Most scholars agree that several forces contributed to the city's fall. One factor may be that the ruling class became increasingly rigid and oppressive, inciting popular discontent and perhaps insurgency from within the city. A second may be that Teotihuacán's success at stimulating Mesoamerican trade had the unintended consequence of advancing the prosperity and power of other cities, which then refused to pay tribute to their former imperial master, or even attacked it. Third, there is little

A soldier far from home. This figure wears the costume and carries the shield of a Teotihuacano warrior, but he appears on the side of a stele in Tikal, a Maya city more than 600 miles to the southeast. The precise nature of the political relationship between the two cities is not known.

doubt that Teotihuacán voraciously consumed local forests for construction, household fuel, and production of plaster, which required burning large quantities of limestone. Deforestation would have caused erosion and leeching of arable soil on the slopes of the surrounding hills, eventually reducing the urban food supply. Climatological research shows that a drying cycle occurred in Mesoamerica in the mid-first millennium C.E. Extended droughts would have put even greater pressure on the city's elite to prevent chronic hunger, which, if it could do little to respond, might have led to insurgency and war. As many as forty thousand people continued to live in Teotihuacán for another century or so after 650 C.E., but its high civilization never recovered. Rather, the City of the Gods deteriorated into the splendid ghost town it is today.

Zapotec Civilization in the Oaxaca Valley

Teotihuacán was the largest urban center in Mesoamerica in the first millennium C.E., but the city of Monte Albán in the Oaxaca valley two hundred miles to the southwest rivaled it in architectural grandeur. Oaxacan farmers harnessed water from numerous rivers and streams to irrigate fields of maize, beans, and squash in the valley bottom and up the slopes of the surrounding mountains. At some point cultivators invented an irrigation method that involved digging shallow wells at regular intervals along the borders of long rectangular fields, then pouring pots of water from these boreholes onto individual plants. Oaxacans still use this technique today.

Around 500 B.C.E. the pace of change in the valley began to speed up. Population growth accelerated, villages multiplied, artisans took up new specializations, and several small states emerged. Within another four hundred years, the region's elite class began to use a writing system, though it has not been deciphered fully. People probably spoke languages ancestral to modern Zapotec, the name of a set of closely related Mesoamerican tongues.

Monte Albán. One of the valley's states founded a ceremonial center on a ridge in the valley, and from around 200 B.C.E., its rulers either defeated the other states or formed a federation with them. In the following centuries, this city, whose site is known as Monte Albán, expanded across two other ridges and became the capital of a much larger, centralized Zapotec state. Ruins of fortifications and stone depictions of prisoners, some of them bound and looking dejected, others mutilated and dead, suggest long periods of fighting among Zapotec groups in the valley and campaigns of conquest some distance beyond it.

Monte Albán's ruling class consisted of aristocratic families whose lords claimed both hereditary authority and descent from the gods. We know little about the Zapotec government, but the ruling elite, like the leaders in Teotihuacán, clearly had power to mobilize huge labor gangs. Amazingly, these crews sheared off the tops of Monte Albán's ridges and reshaped them into broad, flat plazas. Mammoth platforms, temples, palaces, and an astronomical observatory line the most expansive of these civic and ceremonial squares, which occupies fifty-five acres. The aristocracy no doubt lived on the great plaza, but, as in Teotihuacán, thousands of farmers and artisans

Ball court and players. This court with sloping sides is located on Monte Albán near the great temple plaza. The two ball players portrayed on a stone altar from the late eighth century C.E. are Maya rulers. Does the shape of the court or the action of the two figures suggest what the rules of the ball game might have been?

occupied apartment compounds. These residential areas were divided into wards, or urban neighborhoods, each with its own temples and other civic buildings. At its zenith in the sixth century C.E., the center had a population of about 24,000.

In earlier centuries, the Olmec of the Gulf coast had established the tradition of playing a ritual ball game on specially designed courts. Teotihuacán has revealed no evidence of a ball court, but Monte Albán had one of the earliest so far discovered. It was a rectangular space flanked on two sides by high sloping walls covered in plaster and painted red.

Oaxaca's external links. The material evidence of art, architecture, and everyday goods shows that the Zapotec took part in the trade and cultural exchange of greater Mesoamerica. As early as the second millennium B.C.E., obsidian blades and other objects of Olmec origin reached the Oaxaca valley; conversely, mirrors made from pieces of iron ore mined in Oaxaca turned up on the Gulf coast. The Zapotecs shared various gods and goddesses with Teotihuacán and other Mesoamerican peoples, including the storm god, the maize god, and Quetzalcoatl. We have no evidence that in its centuries of imperial expansion Teotihuacán ever attacked Oaxaca. In fact, beginning about 300 C.E., people from Oaxaca settled in Teotihuacán and founded a neighborhood

community. Material remains of what archaeologists call the Oaxacan Barrio indicate that these residents adapted to Teotihuacán's culture in everyday life. But they also designed tombs in Oaxacan fashion and equipped them with pottery, incense burners, and other objects either imported from Oaxaca or made by Teotihuacán's Zapotec community. We have pictorial evidence that ambassadors or other visitors traveled from Teotihuacán to Oaxaca. Carved stones in one of the great platforms at Monte Albán tell a tale of eight individuals in Teotihuacano headdresses (but carrying no weapons) leaving a place with temples in that city's style and then arriving at another location where an aristocrat in Zapotec headdress greets them. Another stone slab depicts two men, one from each city, in jaguar costumes. Accompanying glyphs seem to indicate that the two were engaging in some sort of diplomatic meeting, perhaps to keep relations between the two states running smoothly.

Monte Albán started to lose population and decay materially around 700 C.E., just a little later than Teotihuacán did. A process of political decentralization appears to have taken place in the Oaxaca valley as aristocratic groups built several new but also smaller centers in other parts of the valley. Monte Albán may have waned partly because Teotihuacán's earlier decline had a negative commercial impact on other Mesoamerican cities. Or, perhaps Oaxaca no longer needed a big government and large army once all threat from Teotihuacán had evaporated. Food production might also have suffered, as it did in the Valley of Mexico, from relentless deforestation and cycles of drought.

The Innovative Maya

The ancient Maya may be characterized fundamentally as people who spoke a number of closely related Mesoamerican languages. The most widely spoken language may have been Yucatecan, a forerunner of one of the thirty or so Mayan languages heard today. In the first millennium C.E., Classic Mayan emerged as a written medium of religious, political, and intellectual communication among priests, aristocrats, and other literate individuals, much as Sanskrit, Greek, and Latin did in Afroeurasia. The Maya writing system, combined with numerous other refined ideas and practices, infused the region, and especially its aristocratic and priestly class, with a distinctive cultural style in buildings, art, literature, and ritual.

This style, however, never coincided with a single Maya state. Rather, between 200 to 800 C.E., the era scholars call the Classic Period of Maya civilization, more than fifty independent city-states competed for territory and resources. These states variously flourished and declined, their size, wealth, and longevity

A meeting of two strangers? This drawing replicates a carved stone slab known as the Lápida de Bazán. The artist has added a hypothetical rendering of the slab's missing upper left corner. The figure at center right represents an individual of Oaxaca. The one on the left is wearing clothing characteristic of Teotihuacán.

MAYA STYLE PERIODS	
1100 B.C.E.–200 C.E.	Preclassic Period
200–800 C.E.	Classic Period
800–1200 C.E.	Maya collapse

depending in large part on their resources in water and soil and their access to strategic goods such as salt or obsidian. As in the ancient Greek Mediterranean, Maya city-states joined in political and military alliances, which formed and reformed with changing circumstances. In some periods, particularly powerful states, for example, Tikal and Calakmul, forged regional alliance blocs and reduced weaker neighbors to political dependency. Some states lasted only a few hundred years before falling into ruin, others longer. Tikal experienced political ups and downs but carried on for as many as eight centuries.

Farmers and cities of the Maya heartland.

The ancient Mayan-speaking region extended across three broadly defined geographical zones: the Pacific coastal plain in the far south, the interior highlands that include active and extinct volcanoes, and the lowlands of northern Guatemala, Belize, and the Yucatán Peninsula. The Maya built most of their cities in the lowlands, where the natural cover is tropical forest and the soil rests on a monolithic plate of white limestone. Rain falls mainly between April and October, with more of it in the southern half of the lowlands than in the northern half. Farmers began to settle the region around 1100 B.C.E. These cultivators built villages, made pottery, and planted *milpas,* or fields where maize, beans, manioc, avocadoes, and other crops grew side by side. The lowland population continued to grow, and large-scale urban building got under way about 500 B.C.E. Mirador, whose ruins lie near Guatemala's northern border with Mexico, arose sometime after 150 B.C.E. as one of the largest early cities. In the following eight hundred years, the populations of Tikal and Calakmul reached perhaps fifty thousand each.

As numbers multiplied, the ecology of water became increasingly critical. Farmers had to find ways to access and store water during the dry season from November to March. Nor could the summer rains always be expected because extended drought cycles were both inevitable and unpredictable. The Usumacinta River flows six hundred miles across the southern lowlands to the Gulf of Mexico, but the wider region has few rivers. The water in lowland swamps, lakes, and natural sinkholes (where the limestone collapsed) tends to be too saline to drink or even to use for irrigation. In the face of these challenges, ancient farmers innovated cleverly. They excavated cisterns to collect water during the rainy season, fashioning aprons of plaster around them to catch and direct the water. They dug canals to drain excess water and used the excavated mud to build raised fields. On steep hillsides they constructed stonewalled terraces to hold water and prevent erosion. In the land around some of the cities, people built complex irrigation webs of canals and ditches. The tourist photos we see today of ruined Maya temples cloaked in wild vegetation may give the impression of remote jungle outposts. In fact, many of these structures formed the cores of densely populated cities surrounded by extensive food-growing suburbs.

Rulers, aristocrats, and rituals.

The social and political class structure of Maya city-states was similar to the hierarchy in Teotihuacán, the Oaxaca valley, and indeed most Afroeurasian states of that era. A minority of aristocratic families stood at the social summit. They enjoyed greater wealth, status, and prestige than other groups and busied themselves keeping civic order and making political and economic decisions. As in other Mesoamerican centers, the Maya elite and their servants and retainers monopolized living space in temple complexes. In some states, a second tier of the elite class also existed, including temple priests, rich merchants, highly skilled artisans, and the managers of lordly estates. Not surprisingly, analysis of skeletal remains indicates that, on the whole, members of elite families lived longer and healthier lives than ordinary folk.

Like monarchs in Afroeurasia, Maya rulers had the tasks of ensuring the security and well-being of their subjects, fighting and winning wars, and negotiating with neighboring states, constantly appealing to the gods to favor those aims. Maya ruling dynasties practiced **primogeniture,** thereby avoiding bloody rivalries among siblings, children, or other relatives for the right to ascend

> **primogeniture** The legal or customary right of the firstborn child, usually the firstborn male, to inherit a family's entire estate, sometimes including a noble title or office, to the exclusion of younger children.

the throne after a monarch's death. Some city-state dynasties endured for several generations. But they could end abruptly if a ruler lost a war or had to yield to a rebel challenger. Most Maya monarchs were men, though the record of ancient inscriptions shows that women occasionally succeeded to power or acted temporarily as regents for child-kings.

Rulers and the officials and priests who served them strove continually through ritual supplication to maintain the harmony of the universe and its three realms: the celestial domain where the sun, moon, and numerous other gods and goddesses dwelt; the earth, which was the back of a giant reptile, sometimes depicted as a turtle; and the soggy underworld, where other deities lurked. The political authorities made sure everyone understood that public disobedience risked not only civil punishment but, worse, the anger of the gods. Contrariwise, flood, drought, military defeat, or other social misfortune signified that the ruler might be failing in his ritual duties and alienating the cosmic powers. Somewhat like the Chinese principle of the Mandate of Heaven, Maya ideology approved withdrawal of support for such a ruler, even violent rebellion. Stone carvings and paintings depict extravagant festivals and intricate ceremonies held to distribute food and gifts to the populace, magnify the glory of the ruler, and please the

Lady Xoc: An Aristocratic Woman in Maya Politics

The royal wife known as Lady Xoc played a key part in the affairs of the Maya city-state of Yaxchilán, which lay along a stretch of the Usumacinta River that today demarcates the border between Mexico and Guatemala. In her youth, Lady Xoc, the daughter of two noble families, married Shield Jaguar, Yaxchilán's crown prince. She was also her husband's cousin. The marriage gave Shield Jaguar the support of powerful elite families within the realm, when in October 681 C.E. he took the throne at the age of thirty-four.

On that day, Lady Xoc celebrated the coronation by performing a blood sacrifice. Clothed in aristocratic robes, she pierced her own tongue with a sharp instrument. Her blood ran downward onto a pile of clean bark paper in a bowl she held before her. The bloodletting induced a hallucinatory state in which she conjured up an ancestral spirit, which emerged from the mouth of a serpent. This spirit was likely the founder of her husband's dynasty, materializing to witness and sanctify the new reign. Years later, Maya artists recorded that day's ritual event in an exquisite image carved into a stone lintel above a doorway in the building identified in Yaxchilán's ruins as Temple 23.

In 709 C.E., more than a quarter-century later, Lady Xoc again shed blood, this time to commemorate a celestial alignment between Saturn and Jupiter. A second image in Temple 23 shows her running a thorn-studded cord through her tongue as Shield Jaguar stands before her holding a long torch. About two months before this ceremony, Shield Jaguar had welcomed a new son, to be named Bird Jaguar. The mother of the child, however, was not Lady Xoc but rather Lady Evening Star, a younger royal wife from an elite family of the city of Calakmul. By marrying Lady Evening Star, Shield Jaguar appears to have sealed an alliance with that powerful city-state. Already sixty-one years old when Bird Jaguar was born, the king groomed the lad to succeed him. When the boy was thirteen, Shield Jaguar dedicated Temple 23, an event that once again featured Lady Xoc taking part in a blood ritual.

Modern scholars have interpreted the visual and textual evidence of Shield Jaguar's reign to suggest that he played an astute political game. He honored his Calakmul allies by choosing the offspring of Lady Evening Star, one of its daughters, as his royal heir. But he also consistently favored Lady Xoc with prestigious ceremonial roles, thereby firming up the support of her influential Yaxchilán family. It seems likely that she had special political status because depictions of women participating in Maya public rituals are extremely rare. Lady Evening Star, by contrast, drops out of the historical record. Shield Jaguar appears to have been such a skilled political dealmaker that he ruled Yaxchilán for sixty-two years, dying in 742 C.E. at the age of ninety-four. Bird Jaguar succeeded him.

Lady Xoc. The queen, represented in stone in the ruins of Temple 23 in Yaxchilán, sheds sacrificial blood from her tongue.

Lady Xoc occupied a place at the center of Yaxchilán's political life for about sixty-five years. But we will never know whether the king's failure to choose a son of hers as heir caused her bitterness or regret.

Thinking Critically

How would you argue for or against the reliability of biographical information about Lady Xoc based on carved images in a Maya temple?

---

gods with offerings and sacrifices. Carvings show aristocratic personages honoring or appeasing the celestial lords with their own blood, women cutting their tongues and men their tongues or penises with sharp obsidian blades or stingray spines. Elaborate public occasions such as the accession of a new ruler called for equally spectacular religious offerings, including ritual murder. The most prized victims were war prisoners of high standing, even defeated and captured kings. Captives of ordinary social class were often enslaved or adopted into families.

The Maya masses. Farmers, artisans, and laborers made up most of the population of Maya states, the majority living in neighborhoods around the city's ceremonial center. Common folk built houses of vertical poles, interlaced sticks, thatched roofs, and sometimes plastered walls. These dwellings sheltered extended families of three generations. Households maintained "kitchen gardens," and family members, very likely women, ground maize to make tortilla flour, wove and embroidered cotton cloth, and fashioned everyday pottery. Commoners paid tribute in food or textiles to both

corvée labor Unpaid labor required by a ruler, an estate lord, or another authority, usually for road work or other construction.

the rulers and the local aristocratic families, and the government typically demanded **corvée labor** to build temples, palaces, canals, or other public structures. Families offered prayers and conducted rituals as part of their everyday routine. Planting a field, harvesting a crop, building a house, or making a ceramic pot were all occasions to supplicate the gods with offerings.

Slaves occupied the bottom rung of the social ladder. Men, women, and children lost their freedom mainly in the heat of war. But criminals could also be enslaved, and destitute people sometimes sold themselves into bondage. As in Egypt and some other Afroeurasian societies, slaves who served aristocrats might be ritually killed when their master died, thus accompanying their owner into the afterlife. People enslaved for theft could regain their liberty after they made restitution to their victim, and the children of slaves typically had free status.

Words, numbers, and calendars. The Maya created a sophisticated writing system, though the deep origins of writing in Mesoamerica remain murky. In the late 1990s a crew building a road near Veracruz in southeastern Mexico discovered a stone block inscribed with sixty-two glyphs. Researchers were astonished when they dated the slab to about 900 B.C.E., pushing the dawn of writing in the ancient Olmec zone along the Gulf coast back several hundred years. The glyphs have not been deciphered, however, and material evidence of writing in Mesoamerica in the following 1,200 years has been tantalizing but meager and scattered. The locations of inscriptions dating mostly to the late centuries B.C.E. suggest that people were simultaneously experimenting with writing in the Olmec zone, the Oaxaca valley, the Valley of Mexico, and the Maya lowlands. The earliest evidence of a developed Maya writing system are glyphs painted on walls in a pyramidal building at San Bartolo in Guatemala. These inscriptions date to as early as 300 B.C.E., but for the following six centuries the evidence of Maya writing remains fragmentary.

The complex system that emerged in the Maya Classic Period represents one of just three cases in world history in which people invented writing independently, that is, without knowing about any external model that would help them go about it. The other two cases were the scripts invented earlier in Mesopotamia and China. The Maya system combined logographic signs, which corresponded to whole words (units of meaning), with phonetic signs, which indicated syllables (units of sound). To this extent the system was similar to ancient Mesopotamian cuneiform writing. Approximately 850 glyphs have been discovered so far, most of them logographs. Maya scholars carved and painted texts on stone monuments, on the walls of buildings, and even on pots and strips of bone. More than 15,000 texts have survived, and linguists have patiently deciphered many of them. Communicating knowledge about religion, mythology, astronomy, royal reigns, wars, the histories of cities, and calendrical computations, the decoded inscriptions have opened wider windows on the Maya past.

Beginning around 200 C.E., Maya writers also produced thousands of books, or codices (singular, *codex*). Scribes painted Maya characters on long strips of bark paper or deerskin, then folded the pages together like an accordion. Probably every city-state had a chief scribe, or "keeper of the royal library." Surviving paintings show him (and sometimes her) as a busy official consulting with the monarch, writing tool in hand. Unfortunately, only four Maya codices have survived from before the sixteenth century C.E. The ravages of time destroyed most of them. In 1562, Diego de Landa, the Spanish bishop of Yucatán, burned more than two dozen Maya books, reporting with satisfaction: "We found a large number of books in these characters and, as they contained nothing in which there were not to be seen superstition and lies of the devil, we burned them all."[1] Ironically, this same priest wrote an extensive account of the Maya as he observed them, including valuable information about their writing system!

Mesopotamians first used writing to keep accounts of goods, Mesoamericans to record dates. Like most ancient societies, Mesoamericans believed that the celestial movements of sun, moon, and stars affected all aspects of life. Heavenly bodies were deities, and sages who recorded their trajectories and cycles also created calendars to indicate when important ceremonies should be held, when the rainy season was likely to start, and what the future might hold.

Several Mesoamerican societies used two intersecting calendars, usually citing dates in both of them. One was an almanac calendar of 260 days that recorded important festivals and religious observances. We do not know the rationale for 260 days, though it might relate to the period of human gestation, or about nine months. The other was a solar calendar of

A Maya scribe. This figure appears on a vase from the Late Classic Maya Period in Guatemala. The scribe holds a paint stylus in his right hand. What different sorts of functions might scribes have performed in Maya society?

365 days. Since the almanac calendar made a complete revolution in a shorter time than the solar calendar, the named dates on the two calendars were not synchronized. So, for example, the two dates that appear on today's calendar would not appear together again for 18,980 days, or approximately fifty-two years. This Calendar Round, as modern scholars call it, permitted precise dating only within a cycle that started over again every fifty-two years. It would be as if 2001 C.E. were recorded as year 1 and 2052 as year 52, but 2053 as year 1 again.

Sometime in the second century C.E., if not earlier, Maya savants rectified the deficiencies of the Calendar Round by inventing the Long Count calendar. This method was based on a much longer cycle of 1,872,000 days, or about 5,128 years. The Maya believed that the world in which human beings lived was a manifestation of one of several Great Cycles of time. They may have reckoned, though on what basis we do not know, that this world came into being on a date equivalent to 3114 B.C.E. On the Long Count calendar, days were counted from that starting date, just as the Christian calendar counts days elapsed from the birth of Jesus. To express dates precisely using the Long Count calendar, Maya scholars broke it down into smaller units of time starting with days, then "months" of 20 days, years of 360 days, and on up to the *bak'tun*, a unit of 144,000 days. The Maya carved or painted Long Count dates on many inscriptions that recorded significant events. Because scholars can now read these dates, they have produced a much more detailed chronology of Maya history than would otherwise have been possible.

Calculating dates using three different calendars (and there were others, as well) almost certainly drove all elements of Maya mathematics, including astronomical calculations, measurement of distances, business accounts, and perhaps performance of higher mathematical operations about which we have no surviving record. As the introduction to this chapter explained, the Maya based their counting system on units of twenty, rather than ten, as our modern system does. They also invented and used several symbols, for example, a picture of a seashell, to represent "zero." This was a major scientific achievement because until the Common Era no other people except the ancient Babylonians incorporated a zero into their numbering system. The Maya appear to have had some concept of zero as a whole number, that is, an integer like 1, 2, or 3. However, they used it mainly in their positional notation scheme to designate a place in a number that has no value, just as we do in our modern system. For example, when we write 900, we show that only the 9 has value. But because we place it in the third position from the right, it must mean 900. We could write this number as 9 , leaving two empty spaces. But that may cause confusion. Inserting one or more zeros shows the exact position each number occupies. The Maya used their zero signs the same way, except that they wrote numbers of vertical columns rather than in horizontal lines.

Maya cultural and commercial connections. We have some idea that Maya merchants kept track of business by writing down numbers. We also know that they engaged in complex trade operations and traveled long distances. In the Classic Period the whole Mayan-speaking region came to constitute a single zone of intense intercommunication, the larger cities serving as the main hubs. In some lowland areas, urbanization sprawled so far from the ceremonial center that the suburbs of one city ran up against those of a neighboring one. City-states fought one another, but diplomats, artisans, and merchants also moved incessantly between them, traveling over roads, trails, and lowland causeways. Aristocratic families of different states intermarried to stabilize regional political relations and seal alliances. Particular cities specialized in certain manufactures, whether painted pottery, obsidian blades, woven baskets, or jade jewelry, encouraging the growth of a sort of Maya common market within which goods circulated. Large-scale urbanization would likely have been impossible if each city had been obliged to rely entirely on its own production rather than trading numerous products with other centers near and far.

The whole Maya zone was also a commercial center of gravity that attracted trade from distant parts of Mesoamerica. Routes that connected Central America with the Valley of Mexico and other northerly population centers all passed through Maya cities and markets. Along the routes in and out of Maya country, merchants carried raw cotton, cotton textiles, dyes, ceramics, obsidian, flint, granite, shell, tobacco, cacao, honey, bark paper, tropical bird feathers, copal resin (for ritual incense), jaguar pelts, and shark teeth. Salt beds on the north coast of the Yucatán provided essential sodium for human consumption throughout Mesoamerica. In the late centuries of Maya prosperity, urban craftspeople began to work gold, silver, and copper, whose ores came mainly from mines north or southeast of the Maya region. Copper bells, cacao beans, and greenstone beads all served as mediums of exchange, that is, as money. Near the end of the first millennium C.E., artisans began to build large canoes carved from hardwood trunks to ship goods around the Yucatán Peninsula between the Gulf of Mexico and the western Caribbean Sea. The cost of moving a particular quantity of salt, cacao beans, or honey by sea from one side of the peninsula to the other was probably significantly less than the cost of transporting the same quantity overland on the backs of porters.

The end of the Maya states. The world is littered with the physical remains of ancient kingdoms, but the disintegration of the Maya urban civilization between 800 and 1200 C.E. is especially intriguing. For one thing, the biggest and most flourishing city-states of the southern lowlands deteriorated first. Some smaller cities of northern Yucatán lasted another two or three centuries. Second, the breakdown happened astonishingly fast in the southern region. The states there all crumbled within a span of about one hundred years. Archaeologists excavating the ruins of the city of Kiuic have found evidence that about 880 C.E. workers suddenly abandoned half-completed public building

A Maya Bible: An Account of Creation in the *Popol Vuh*

Maya societies no doubt produced numerous works of literature, passing them from one generation to the next both orally and in the form of codices, or painted books. Among the few texts to survive the Spanish conquest in the sixteenth century is the renowned Popol Vuh *(paw-pawl vuh), or Book of Counsel, a long poetic narrative illuminating the cosmology, mythology, and history of the Quiché-speaking Maya of the Guatemala highlands. The version we have is the achievement of Maya scribes who sometime in the 1550s* C.E. *wrote out a text in Quiché using a modified Latin script. This work is probably a compilation of stories based on a variety of oral traditions and written sources. This text remained largely unknown until the early eighteenth century, when a Spanish monk named Francisco Ximénez acquired it in Guatemala. He transcribed the Quiché text and added a Spanish translation. Although the sixteenth century work was subsequently lost, the Ximénez text rests today in the Newberry Library in Chicago.*

The Popol Vuh *recounts the creation of the world and the early history of the Quiché Maya in more than nine thousand lines of verse. In the creation story, the gods mourn the fact that there was no one to honor or praise them. So they decided to create animals, only to discover that animals merely "squawked and chattered and roared" and could not speak. So the gods tried to fashion humans out of clay but found that the dolls they created could not turn their heads and tended to dissolve in the rain. Next, the gods carved men and women out of wood, but these were expressionless automatons who had "nothing in their hearts and nothing in their minds." Eventually, the creators tried molding humans out of cornmeal. Corn turned out to be the perfect substance for making animate people who thought and felt. The selection below tells of the final and successful attempt to fashion human beings.*

And here is the beginning of the conception of humans, and of the search for the ingredients for the human body. So they spoke, the Bearer, Begetter, the Makers, Modelers named Sovereign Plumed Serpent [the gods of creation]:

"The dawn has approached, preparations have been made, and morning has come for the provider, nurturer, born in the light, begotten in the light. Morning has come for humankind, for the people of the face of the earth," they said. It all came together as they went on thinking in the darkness, in the night, as they searched and they sifted, they thought and they wondered.

And here their thoughts came out in clear light. They sought and discovered what was needed for human flesh. It was only a short while before the sun, moon, and stars were to appear above the Makers and Modelers. Split Place, Bitter Water Place is the name: the yellow corn [maize], white corn came from there.

And these are the names of the animals who brought the food: fox, coyote, parrot, crow. There were four animals who brought the news of the ears of yellow corn and white corn. They were coming from over there at Split Place [a mountain in modern Guatemala near the border with Mexico], they showed the way to the split.

And this was when they found the staple foods.

And these were the ingredients for the flesh of the human work, the human design, and the water was for the blood. It became human blood, and corn was also used by the Bearer, Begetter.

And so they were happy over the provisions of the good mountain, filled with sweet things, thick with yellow corn, white corn, and thick with . . . cacao, countless zapotes, anonas, jocotes, nances, matasanos [types of tropical fruit], sweets—the rich foods filling up the citadel named Split Place, Bitter Water Place. All the edible fruits were there: small staples, great staples, small plants, great plants. The way was shown by the animals.

And then the yellow corn and the white corn were ground, and Xmucane [the divine grandmother] did the grinding nine times. Food was used, along with the water she rinsed her hands with, for the creation of grease; it became human fat when it was worked by the Bearer, the Begetter, Sovereign Plumed Serpent, as they are called.

After that, they put it into words:

the making, the modeling of our first mother-father,
with yellow corn, white corn alone for the flesh,
food alone for the human legs and arms,
for our first fathers, the four human works.

It was staples alone that made up their flesh. . . . And when they came to fruition, they came out human. They talked and they made words. . . . And then they saw everything under the sky perfectly. After that, they thanked the Maker, Modeler.

Source: Dennis Tedlock, ed. and trans., *Popol Vuh: The Definitive Edition of the Mayan Book of the Dawn of Life and the Glories of Gods and Kings* (New York: Simon & Schuster, 1996).

Thinking Critically

What does this reading suggest about ancient Maya attitudes about both corn and animals? What do you think the *Popol Vuh* implies about the meaning and purpose of human life? Scholars agree that the *Popol Vuh* has characteristics of a myth. What do you think some of those characteristics are? Why do you think that since ancient times societies around the world have told stories of the creation of the earth, animals, and human beings? What creation stories are best known in the United States today?

projects and that families left pots and stone tools in their houses as if they expected to return for dinner. Third, not only states disintegrated but the entire social order. The lowland population, both elites and common folk, fell precipitately after 800 C.E., plunging from as many as 14 million in the Classic Period to 1.8 million within a mere century and a half.[2] The population appears to have been much lower when the Spanish arrived in the early sixteenth century than it had been seven hundred years earlier. Finally, the Maya collapse fascinates us because, as far as the archaeological record shows, no terrible invader put the lowland cities to the torch. Rather people abandoned those centers, and in time tropical forests closed in over the massive temples.

The precise combination of factors that brought on this calamity remains puzzling and controversial. As in the case of the fall of Teotihuacán centuries earlier, we can only consider a range of factors, recognizing that some cities endured longer than others and the causes of collapse almost certainly varied from one place to another. There is no doubt that much of Maya lowland society lived in conditions of serious environmental stress in the eighth and ninth centuries C.E. In both numbers and density, population had followed a general upward trend since the late centuries B.C.E. Farmers worked continuously to increase the productivity of the land, not only to feed their own families but to support the ruling elite and its soldiers, palaces, and temples.

The agricultural possibilities of the Maya region, however, were limited. The water table in the southern lowlands, the most densely populated region, was generally lower than in the north. Whenever a drought cycle arrived, as it inevitably did, problems of finding and storing water became acute. Researchers have discovered from skeletal remains that in densely populated areas malnutrition became widespread, an affliction likely related both to food shortages and to a diet too dependent on maize. This staple has less protein

value than wheat, barley, or the meat of large animal domesticates, none of which Mesoamericans had. The absence of cattle, sheep, or chickens meant that people were spared certain animal-related infectious diseases such as measles, smallpox, or influenza. This does not mean, however, that Maya lowlanders seldom got sick. Energy-draining illnesses such as yellow fever and malaria, as well as syphilis and certain types of heart disease, were endemic. Protein deficiency would have made people generally more susceptible to these maladies.

Farmers in the Yucatán who could not coax higher crop yields from their existing fields tried to open new land. Unfortunately, this meant clearing forests in ever-widening circles around the central city. Because fertile tropical soils tended also to be thin, deforestation aggravated erosion, aggravating soil loss. That in turn caused rivers, reservoirs, and drainage systems to silt up, compounding the problems of both soil and water management.

In the Maya Classic era, intercity conflicts appear to have become more frequent and violent. Maya rulers typically responded to military crises, not by investing heavily in projects to preserve and develop resources, but by concentrating more power at the top of the social pyramid, conscripting larger armies, and building more ostentatious shrines to appease the gods. Projects to save the state by exalting it encouraged megalomania within the lordly class, which pulled more farmers away from their fields to put up grander temples. In Tikal, workers continued to erect splendorous temples even as the government was collapsing. There must have been wise officials in some states who had practical ideas for improving water management or food shortages. But the long-term economic problems resulting from simultaneous population growth and ecological degradation were probably too complex for them to solve.

For hundreds of years, Maya farmers had faced recurring droughts and survived. But climatologists have shown that starting about 760 C.E. and for a century thereafter calamitous droughts occurred every few decades, affecting particular cities at different times but eventually wearing them all down. More frequent droughts on top of chronic ecological problems may have pushed some big cities over the brink, resulting in breakdown of trade, social confusion, and mass flight, which inevitably affected smaller centers in the same region.

Archaeologists have presented evidence that by the ninth century C.E. several southern lowland cities became more vulnerable to both local rebellion and foreign attack. In Piedras Negras, a city west of Tikal, vandals mutilated stone images of rulers, suggesting that people rose up against lords who appeared to have lost the blessing of the gods. Some northern lowlands cities, which generally survived the ninth century in reasonable shape, apparently

Ruins of Kiuic. Archaeologists have been working at Kiuic in recent years to understand why the city was rapidly abandoned in the late ninth century.

took advantage of troubles in the south to launch raids or invasions. Like candles sputtering and finally burning out, Long Count date inscriptions appear less and less frequently in one southern Maya city after another after 800 C.E., finally ceasing altogether in 910 C.E. In the northern lowlands, some cities, for example, Chichén Itzá and Uxmal, endured a century or two longer. Urban centers were smaller there than in the south, which may have eased pressure on land and water. Also, attacks on weakened southern centers may have brought a short-term bonanza of loot and captive labor.

The northern cities, however, soon disintegrated as well, and between about 900 and 1200 C.E. the whole lowland population plummeted. What, then, happened to all the people? This phenomenon remains a subject of debate among scholars. Certainly war, starvation, disease, and flight to other regions played a part; over a longer term, falling birth rates coupled with rising death rates, especially among malnourished young children, could have produced rapid population fall-off. Once farmers abandoned their fields and the elites their fine homes and temples, water systems would have deteriorated quickly and tropical vegetation closed in. Large-scale recovery would have been impossible except over decades, and the much smaller farm communities that remained in the lowlands may have been quite content with village-level independence if it meant freedom from high-handed aristocrats, public bloodlettings, and heavy taxes.

Developments in Upper North America

The North American land mass has the shape of a curved funnel, and a demographic map dated, say, 100 C.E. would show the heaviest clusters of human population at the bottom end of it, that is, in Mesoamerica. Moving up the funnel from the Valley of Mexico, urban centers would have appeared smaller and fewer between and population generally thinner, correlating to progressively drier climate, especially at low elevations. No cities on the scale of Teotihuacán, Monte Albán, or Tikal would be seen anywhere on the map between Mesoamerica and the Arctic Circle (see Map 8.3). Even so, some regions of upper North America had much larger populations than others. On our hypothetical map, the largest concentrations of people who grew crops and lived in villages would have appeared along the Pacific coast of what is today the United States and Canada, in the Eastern Woodlands stretching from the Mississippi River to the Atlantic, and, on a smaller scale, in the Sonoran Desert. They spoke hundreds of languages, and they practiced various combinations of hunting, foraging, fishing, and farming depending on local ecological conditions. In the second millennium B.C.E., people of the Eastern Woodlands began to domesticate and cultivate goosefoot, may grass, and other indigenous plants yielding tiny but nutritious seeds (see Chapter 4). By the end of that millennium, maize cultivation had spread from central Mexico northward to the Sonoran Desert.

The Pacific coast. People who lived along North America's western rim from California to British Columbia did not adopt maize farming on an important scale before the arrival of Europeans, but economies based on acorn and buckeye nut meal, edible grasses, fish, shellfish, and wild game sustained village life. The archaeological record shows that, in the first millennium C.E., some villages along the coast and interior valleys sheltered hundreds of people, and lineages of privileged elites and craft specialists distinguished themselves from ordinary men and women. In the forested coast lands north of California, villagers who consumed salmon and other sea and river life built houses of split timbers, and they carved giant cedar-trunk canoes for coastal fishing and trade. In the same millennium, coastal peoples also began to adopt the bow and arrow. This weapon, which probably diffused from Canada, augmented wild animal protein in the diet but also tended to make intervillage raiding more lethal. Near the end of the millennium, communities along the north coast began to build log-walled forts on high ground, suggesting fiercer warfare over food resources and trade.

The Hohokam of the Sonoran Desert. The U.S. Southwest and far northwestern Mexico represent another area where village societies emerged in the early first millennium C.E. Communities there, known collectively as the Hohokam, a local Indian name for ancestral people, grew maize, squash, cotton, and other crops on river floodplains, constructing canals as much as ten miles long to divert water into fields. Scholars think the people who became the Hohokam migrated into the northern Sonoran Desert from Mexico, perhaps bringing maize technology with them. Their taste for platform mounds, distinctive textile designs, and ball courts attest to material, if indirect connections with Mesoamerica. Discoveries of copper bells and stone figurines at Hohokam suggest trade connections leading south. In contrast to Pacific coast societies, which preferred tar-sealed baskets to pottery, the Hohokam acquired skill at making brown, red-painted ceramic ware. At the site known as Snaketown, south of Phoenix, Hohokam inhabitants built a cluster of villages, which might have formed a local political confederation. The site includes a central plaza, platform mounds, and ball courts where some scholars think village teams competed against one another. The Hohokam were pioneer farmers whose successful adaptation to harsh land prefigured the larger-scale societies that emerged in that region in later centuries.

The Adena and Hopewell societies. A tradition of mound building in the lower Mississippi valley goes back to the mid-fourth millennium B.C.E. (see Chapter 4), but the first sustained wave of it occurred in the Eastern Woodlands starting about 800 B.C.E. The builders known as the Adena flourished in a wide area around the Ohio River valley until about 100 B.C.E. The Hopewell culture, also centered on the

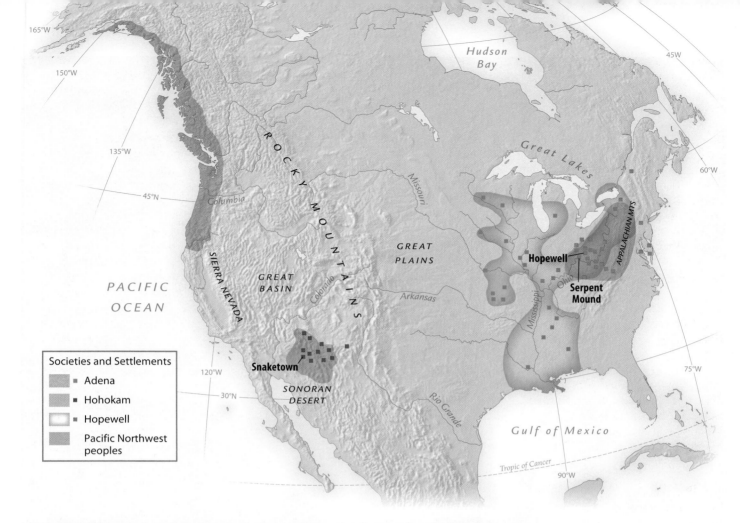

MAP 8.3 Major settlements and societies in upper North America, before 400 C.E.
What geographical factors might help explain why relatively dense societies developed in the areas indicated on the map?

Ohio, existed from then until around 400 C.E. Sites identified as Adena have been discovered as far from Ohio as New England. The Hopewell tradition extends to the Mississippi valley and New York State. We do not know whether the second culture was derived directly from the first, *culture* here meaning a set of distinctive material artifacts and structures discovered on a number of sites. But the two traditions shared several characteristics. Both Adena and Hopewell people practiced a mix of hunting; foraging; and farming of squash, goosefoot, sump weed, and other regional domesticates. Climatic research indicates that Hopewell communities thrived and spread during a prolonged period of relatively mild winters. Farmers knew about maize but did not make it a staple crop. Both cultures include large earthen mounds that in some cases concealed burial chambers richly stocked with goods. The most impressive Hopewell structures take the form of embankments laid out in precisely measured squares and circles. Among the most dramatic is the Serpent Mound, an earthwork in rural southern Ohio that slithers nearly a quarter of a mile along a ridge.

The head of the snake is aligned with the summer solstice. The dating of this mound, however, remains uncertain.

Both traditions suggest a trend toward social complexity. Ordinary families cremated deceased members, but some individuals received privileged treatment. The community buried these special people under mounds in rooms constructed of stout timbers. Others were obliged to accompany them into the afterlife, probably wives, children, servants, or slaves. Goods excavated from elite tombs have included fabrics, copper jewelry, flint blades, freshwater pearl beads, gold nuggets, fine pottery, and tobacco pipes in the shape of birds, otters, and fish. The honored corpses in these tombs were doubtless leaders, but we do not know whether Adena or Hopewell ever organized themselves politically outside the level of the village or village cluster. Nor do we know any details of the religious significance of earthen mounds.

Hopewell burial sites that include copper from the Great Lakes region, carved mica figures from North Carolina, obsidian from Wyoming, and turtle shells from the Atlantic coast dramatically testify to an active network of trade

Serpent Mound. This earthwork in Adams County, Ohio, is an example of an effigy mound, a structure having the shape of a bird or animal. People of the Adena tradition may have built a mound here before 100 B.C.E., though carbon dating of charcoal in the structure suggests that it acquired its present form only in the twelfth century C.E. The mound extends more than 1,300 feet, though no burials or artifacts have been found in it. Does the Serpent Mound deserve listing as a Unesco World Heritage Site along with places like Stonehenge, the Taj Mahal, and the Great Wall of China?

stretching nearly across temperate North America. Oddly, this trade appears to have moved mostly one way, since archaeologists have rarely found Eastern Woodland products beyond the Hopewell cultural zone. Scholars have naturally wondered whether large-scale mound construction means that Eastern Woodlanders made contact with temple-building Mesoamericans, imitating or learning from them. Archaeology, however, has revealed no significant evidence of such interconnection. In any case, communities at the center of the Hopewell cultural zone gave up big mounds and sumptuous burials after about 400 C.E., a decline perhaps linked to the return of colder climate in the Ohio and upper Mississippi valleys.

South America: Complex Societies along the Andean Spine

FOCUS In what ways did changing environmental and ecological conditions in Andean South America influence the development of agrarian societies and states?

At the start of the first millennium B.C.E., the densest agricultural societies in South America clustered on the slopes and interior valleys of the Andes Mountains (see Map 8.4), growing potatoes, maize, beans, squash, peppers, and many

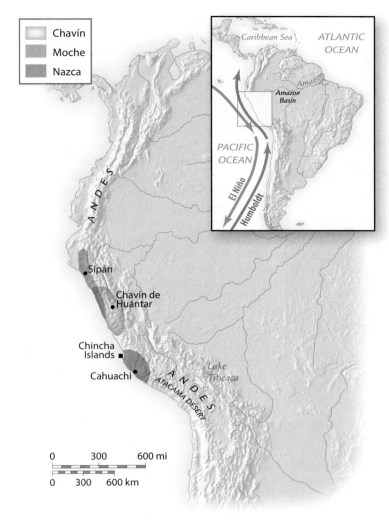

MAP 8.4 Major states in South America, 900 B.C.E.–800 C.E.

Routes of trade running east and west were as important as north–south routes. Why do you think that was the case?

played an important part in human colonization of the Caribbean islands. The earliest humans to reach the islands probably arrived from southern Mesoamerica about six thousand years ago. But later waves of migrants paddling seaworthy canoes departed from the northern South American coasts to settle Caribbean islands one after another. About 200 B.C.E., South American immigrants introduced farming. These people were almost certainly linguistic ancestors of the Arawak-speaking communities that Columbus encountered at the end of the fifteenth century. Archaeological evidence shows that in the first millennium C.E., some islanders kept up trade links with South America, at least much more so than with the Mesoamerican coasts.

Andes Urbanization: The Example of Chavín de Huántar

In the Andes valleys and Pacific coastal plains from Ecuador to southern Peru, steady population growth compelled local societies to organize themselves on larger scales and to compete with neighbors for resources. In the second millennium B.C.E., highland communities built dozens of U-shaped temples around which small urban centers bloomed. These cities may not have had central governments, but shared worship of particular deities expressed in rituals provided a foundation of common identity. Such social glue was necessary because people had to work together to dig canals, transform steep hill slopes into terraced fields, and defend farms against intruders. However, as these centers continued to expand and as the stakes rose to protect generations of investment in complex terraces and irrigation works, elite families that at first provided war leaders, economic managers, and priests began to exert firmer authority over ordinary men and women. A similar process was taking place simultaneously in densely populated regions of Mesoamerica.

Chavín society. Among the ceremonial temple complexes erected in the central highlands, Chavín de Huántar (cha-VEEN deh wan-tar), whose construction started about 900 B.C.E., surpassed them all in size and splendor. At its greatest extent, Chavín's buildings, courtyards, and plazas occupied nearly 125 acres of land. The U-shaped central platform, which archaeologists call the Old Temple, had a cut stone façade that masqueraded as solid rock. But unlike any other platform in the central Andes, the facing concealed an interior labyrinth of passageways, galleries, chambers, and drains kept cool by hundreds of air shafts. Chavín has revealed more than two hundred stone sculptures representing supernatural beings. The center flourished for about seven hundred years, and during the last three hundred of them (500–200 B.C.E.), a huge New Temple was added to the old one. In this later period, at least a few thousand people lived at the site, transforming it from a place of ritual and worship into a lively city.

Chavín occupied a strategic midpoint between the arid north Peruvian coast and high Andes passes leading to

other plant foods. Numerous rivers that plummeted from the highlands also permitted farm communities, even small cities, to flourish in the harsh deserts that paralleled the Pacific shore (see Chapter 4). By the first millennium B.C.E., an elaborate system of trade routes linked together societies up and down this "vertical" sequence of habitation, with traders, for example, carrying sea salt and dried fish far up mountain trails, then returning with sharp obsidian blades from highland mines. On the eastern Andes slopes, routes connected Andean farmers with peoples of the tropical Amazon basin. Only in the far southern cone of South America did communities continue to organize themselves exclusively in small bands of foragers and hunters, generally paralleling the way of life of societies in Canada and Alaska at the opposite end of the Western Hemisphere.

If South Americans had no sustained contact with Mesoamericans across Panama during these millennia, they

Amazonia. Trade routes descended along two mountain river valleys that converged at Chavín, then continued to the coast. Merchants used llama pack trains to move goods from one altitude and ecological zone to another. The center's position as a cultural and commercial node linking the Pacific shore with Amazonia is evident in its buildings and decorations. The temple's U-shaped ground plan, sunken plaza, and bas-relief wall sculptures all relate to coastal architecture of an earlier time. On the other hand, some stone carvings represent animals such as jaguars, monkeys, harpy eagles, and caymans (large reptiles related to alligators) whose natural habitat was the Amazonian forests hundreds of miles to the east.

The residents of Chavín revered an array of deities represented in sculpture as part animal and part human. In the interior of the Old Temple is a free-standing, knife-shaped stone obelisk whose blade sticks into the floor below, the handle into the ceiling overhead. Called the Lanzón, this stele depicts an elegantly robed human whose face is catlike and whose hands and feet have claws. Its thick lips are drawn back into either a smile or a snarl, exposing two large fangs. Archaeologists hypothesize that this divine being was Chavín's chief deity, responsible for keeping all the contradictory forces of the universe in balance. It also may have served as an oracle, that is, a medium that gave responses to the inquiries of worshipers. Material remains of spoons and mortars suggest that priests and ordinary worshipers ingested hallucinogenic snuff or other psychotropic drugs, temporarily leaving their mundane cares behind or transforming themselves into jaguars or birds.

Chavín's later centuries reveal signs of a widening gap between the elite class and the rest of the population. In one part of the site, researchers have found rich collections of expensive and exotic artifacts, such as gold jewelry, fine pottery, imported shells, and cinnabar (a reddish mineral and source of mercury). Families who lived in this zone enjoyed stone houses and augmented their protein diet by consuming the tender meat of young llamas. In other neighborhoods, women and men possessed fewer luxuries, inhabited adobe dwellings, and dined on older, tougher llama meat, when they had meat at all, to supplement their diets of maize, potatoes, and other plant foods.

Chavín's radiating influence. As the center grew in size and population, so did its cultural impact on neighbors near and far. We have no evidence that Chavín had a royal

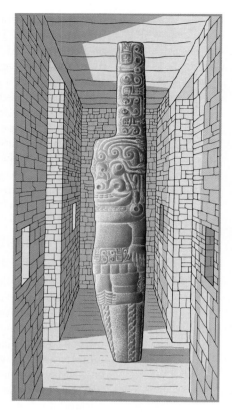

Lanzón stele at Chavín. The Old Temple houses this carved, fifteen-foot pillar of white granite. Why do you suppose the temple builders placed this image of a supernatural being deep in the building's interior?

dynasty, a regular army, or a hierarchy of administrators governing distant districts. It is possible that warriors from the city raided or overran neighboring groups. For example, people in a valley not far from Chavín built twenty-one hilltop forts. Why would they do that if not to defend themselves from external threat? It seems likely, however, that Chavín evolved into a city-state with a governing elite but never into the capital of a military empire to the extent that Teotihuacán did in Mesoamerica.

Chavín's *cultural* power, however, is indisputable. The temple complex may have been the destination of pilgrims who trekked long distances to consult the oracle god, take part in rituals that might invite divine favor, or seek healing from illness. Remains of offerings or residential refuse include objects that originated hundreds of miles from the city, including pieces of pottery and other vessels in styles associated with a number of different coastal and highland societies. From about 500 B.C.E. the evidence grows of a "Chavín cult," a set of religious ideas and practice, gaining popularity across the central Andes. Chavín influence on sculpture, pottery, metalworking, fabric design, and architectural planning has also turned up in the archaeological record of sites far to the north and south. A full explanation of Chavín's cultural brilliance and long reach is beyond the skills of modern archaeology, but it appears to have happened in ways that involved little or no coercion.

Sometime around 200 B.C.E., Chavín was abandoned and partially destroyed. Why this happened is not clear, but the city had never been the only impressive ceremonial center in the Peruvian highlands. Other cities may have competed with it culturally and militarily so that its prestige contracted and pilgrims stopped coming. The soils around Chavín had never yielded bounteous crops, and the reduced population that continued to live near the great temple complex could no longer keep the place up, as it were. It is not that the central Andes suffered an absolute decline of cultural accomplishment. Rather, the scene shifted to other, newer centers, perhaps several of them, though in subsequent centuries no single city quite displayed Chavín's level of grandeur.

Back to the Coast: The Moche Society

Starting in the fourth millennium B.C.E., human communities adapted ingeniously to Peru's intensely arid Pacific coastal plain by damming and diverting the waters of narrow rivers that tumbled down Andes slopes to the sea.

People of the coastal zone called Norte Chico, an area not far north of Peru's modern capital of Lima, built the earliest known urban centers anywhere in the Americas (see Chapter 4). The Norte Chico towns crumbled after about 1800 B.C.E. But other coastal groups improved on that society's irrigated farming technology, and stretches of rainless land continued to bloom.

Farther up the Peruvian coast from Norte Chico, people we call the Moche (or Mochicas) began sometime in the late centuries B.C.E. to build sophisticated dam and canal networks along the valleys of nearly a dozen rivers in order to irrigate fields and support dense populations. Moche urban civilization flourished between about 250 and 800 C.E. Just as the Norte Chico people had done, these riverine societies also exploited the cold, northwestward-flowing Humboldt Current (or Peruvian Current) for fish, shellfish, birds, and sea mammals. Surviving pottery and other objects made in Ecuador to the north, Chile to the south, and Andes valleys to the east show that the Moche conducted a thriving long-distance trade. Fish meal, shells, dried seaweed, and cotton all commanded markets in the Andean highlands. Moche artisans built stout canoes capable of navigating Pacific coastal waters, and we know that crews regularly paddled southward to the tiny Chincha Islands, where they collected heaps of dry seabird droppings, known as guano, to use as fertilizer. (Because almost no rain falls on Peru's coastal islands, the nitrates in bird excrement that accumulated over hundreds of thousands of years did not evaporate or wash away. The ancient Moche could not have understood the fertilizing properties of nitrates, but they knew that guano helped increase crop yields. So did nineteenth-century farmers around the world. Between 1840 and 1880, Peru exported over 20 million tons of bird guano.)

The Moche style. Because of irrigated farming, the Moche valleys, which from north to south bracketed a stretch of coastal plain and Andean foothills about two hundred miles long, could support dense populations. As in Chavín and the Mesoamerican complex societies, families and clans that somehow accumulated and controlled more food resources than others made themselves into a privileged aristocratic class. These elite groups proclaimed that their special status was part of the divine nature of things, and they built great earthen platforms, plazas, and temples to make their own ideology of social class distinction visible to all. Elite families of different valleys appear to have allied and intermarried with one another, evolving a shared culture based on ritual performance, elaborate costumes, and routine cooperation in exercising authority over everyone else. As we know happened in Maya city-states, common people may have paid taxes to

valley lords in the form of corvées on elite farm estates or on irrigation and building projects.

What modern scholars call Moche culture was largely the way of life of the elite minority, including its preferred designs for public buildings and its acquisitions of fine pottery, jewelry, precious metalwork, stone carvings, and mural paintings. Altogether, these material objects revealed a distinct cultural style common to all the Moche valleys. Pots and other vessels depicted animals and vegetables, as well as every conceivable human activity—fighting, working, sleeping, giving birth, and dying. The personalities of Moche individuals seem to reach us across the centuries on pots made in the shape of male or female heads. Sex is a frequent theme in Moche material culture. Drinking from a ceramic vessel's spout, for example, might require enclosing one's lips around a ridiculously large penis. Artisans also used molds to produce everyday pots and other objects, simplifying production and reducing costs. Consequently, distinctive Moche elite styles became more readily available to working families in their small adobe houses. On the other hand, Moche architecture and art tell us much less than we would like to know about the lives of ordinary women and men. Neither the Moche nor any other South American society invented a full writing system. Government officials or couriers carried dried lima beans encoded with glyphs that

Power of the lima bean. This ceramic pot dated to between 100 and 800 C.E. probably represents a woman. She wears a necklace of fruit, and two lima beans adorn her chest. The Moche inserted this vegetable into much of their art and endowed it with spiritual potency.

signaled important information or news, though the meaning of these signs remains unknown.

The cities and their lords. In the early centuries C.E., Moche elites built numerous ceremonial centers, the biggest sheltering 10,000 to 15,000 residents. Physical remains suggest that the grandest of these centers lay in the southerly desert where the Moche River empties into the Pacific. This site displays the remains of two massive adobe brick temple platforms named the Pyramids of the Sun and the Moon (Huaca del Sol and Huaca de la Luna). Archaeologists have estimated that the builders of the Pyramid of the Sun, which covers some thirteen acres, used about 143 million bricks. Extending between the platforms was an urban zone of plazas, residences, and craft shops. The city's governing lords looked out upon their realm from an elaborate building complex perched on the pyramid's summit.

In the northern Moche zone, Sipán was an important center. There, in 1987, looters discovered gold in a burial chamber. In the nick of time a Peruvian archaeologist managed to prevent wholesale pillaging of the tomb, which turned out to be the resting place of a man of the highest social rank, probably the city's chief priest and ruler. The burial dramatically confirmed both the exclusive wealth of the local lordly class and the exquisite quality of objects produced to show off its high status and power. Ornamentation of silver, gold, copper, and semiprecious stones adorned the lord's mummified corpse, and numerous other costly items lay around him. His funeral, which took place about 300 C.E., featured human sacrifices, including his wife, two other women, a military officer, a watchman, a child, and a dog.

The Moche cultural region as a whole probably never constituted a unitary state with a single monarch and government. During Moche's seven-century history, periods of political integration in particular parts of the region alternated with years of greater fragmentation and intervalley wars. The city clustered around the Pyramid of the Sun emerged as the center of a sizable state. Laborers built a network of roads to move both warriors and goods between valleys that paid tribute to the capital. Moche painted pottery garishly depicts warriors triumphing over their enemies. Stripped naked in defeat, hapless captives ascend temple steps to pay homage to a warrior-priest, who then decides their fate. Rulers practiced human sacrifice to some extent. Ceramic objects show priests slitting prisoners' throats and consuming their blood in a gruesome ritual of thanksgiving to the gods. But periods of fighting aside, Moche elites also found it in their long-term interest to work together to preserve and enforce their shared elite status.

The Nazca

A complex society contemporary to Moche emerged about six hundred miles to the south, where the coastal plain was equally dry. Known as Nazca, this society was small in territory and population compared to Moche but nonetheless culturally rich. Eight westward-flowing rivers converge to form the Nazca River, which flows to the sea. In three of these tributary rivers, the water descended underground for some miles, then resurfaced. Nazca farmers initially settled where the streams rose to the surface. Later, they began to construct a diversionary system of subterranean tunnels, surface water tanks, and irrigation canals to elevate the water relative to the descending terrain, then stored it and directed it to land otherwise too dry to cultivate. Irrigated crops and ocean resources supported growing numbers of farmers and construction of the ceremonial center of Cahuachi, which got under way about 200 B.C.E. In contrast to the capital city in the Moche River valley, Cahuachi's remains show little evidence of residential settlement. Rather it appears to have been a place of ritual performance and feasts at special times of the year. People also came from surrounding villages to bury their dead in Cahuachi's cemetery. If an organized Nazca state existed, it was likely a loose federation of clans. The center has more than forty temple platforms, not a big central one, suggesting that various descent groups may have administered many of their own affairs within some type of cooperative framework.

Like the Moche, the Nazca amaze us today with astonishing art. Pots display farmers shooing birds from maize fields, fishermen launching canoes, and a one-man band busily playing a horn, rattle, drum, and pipes. Even more famous are the spectacular animal, plant, and geometric forms that the Nazca cut into local hillsides and plains. Whereas the Moche etched tiny symbols on lima beans, the Nazca created **geoglyphs,** enormous line drawings engraved on more than four hundred square miles of landscape. Some of these geoglyphs, forming outlines of birds, monkeys, whales, and other animals, are plainly visible today on hillsides. The Nazca people also scraped designs on flat terrain, and these are so big that no one can see them whole from the ground. In fact, archaeologists first discovered many of these pictures by studying aerial photographs. Some flat geoglyphs depict trapezoids, triangles, zigzags, and spirals. They also include many miles of straight lines that radiate outward from hills. Workers made these patterns by moving away surface stone to expose lighter colored soil beneath. Centuries of extreme aridity helped preserve images that would otherwise have washed away long ago. Modern observers have speculated that long straight lines represent ritual pathways or maps of fault lines where underground water sources might be found. People also walked along the lines that formed animals, plants, and geometric shapes, perhaps to perform ceremonies. Executing these patterns was perfectly feasible because the artists could figure out ways to keep track of the curves and angles they wanted their lines to trace. Some geoglyphs could be seen clearly from nearby hills. But we discount the several popular books arguing that the formations served as landing beacons for ancient space aliens!

> **geoglyph** An image, character, or set of lines imprinted on a landscape, usually on a large scale, by moving rocks or soil or by cutting into the ground surface.

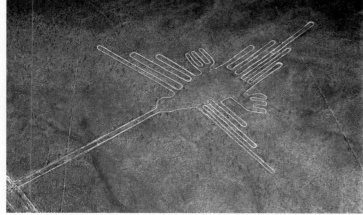

Geoglyph of a hummingbird. Some scholars argue that the geoglyphs served as offerings to the gods of rain and fertility. Others suggest that the Nazca wished to communicate with the heavens above. The dark area in the deep Ingenio River valley on the left side is farmland.

Troubles in the Sixth Century

The Moche and the Nazca complex societies went into decline in the sixth century C.E., the first gradually, the second quite abruptly. Important archaeological clues to this deterioration are the disappearance of particular ceramic and other artistic styles, the abandonment of temple centers, and in the case of the Moche a weakening of the aristocratic culture that had manifested itself in opulent ritual objects and burial practices. By 800 C.E. the Moche no longer gave any ruler the magnificent funeral that had marked the death of the lord of Sipán.

During the sixth and seventh centuries, the western Andes and coastal plains experienced severe climatic instability.

Scholars have related this condition to the El Niño Southern Oscillation (ENSO), alternating periods when the surface temperature of the equatorial Pacific rises above normal, then falls below normal (the phase called La Niña). Extreme ENSO swings could be associated both with drought and torrential rain and with significant reduction of sea life off the South American coast. Glacial core samples from the Andes have revealed wet and dry cycles in the region in the sixth and seventh centuries, including extended periods of drought. An extreme dry period lasted from 563 to 594 C.E. and coincides with archaeological evidence of Moche's weakening and Nazca's full collapse. A drought lasting more than three decades would have radically reduced river water levels in the Andes foothills and coastal plains. As drought dragged on from one year to the next, farmers would have had to abandon fields, irrigation ditches would have clogged with sand, and toxic salt deposits would have built up in soils because mountain runoff was too weak to flush them out. Chronically diminishing harvests would have led to famine, early death, lower birth rates, and greater social tension among clans, social classes, and neighboring populations.

Priests, aristocrats, and farmers must all have prayed fervently to their rain god for relief, but ENSO shifts could suddenly bring such heavy rain and flooding that conditions got far worse. In the Moche valleys, deluges and river torrents very likely ripped apart dams, dikes, and canals and washed away adobe dwellings. Great volumes of soil washed out to sea, but then ocean waves and winds redeposited it on the coast as sand, which buried houses, fields, and canals. People who had built up the irrigation infrastructure and the civic centers over many generations had no hope of restoring them quickly after the rain stopped, perhaps to be succeeded by more drought. When people abandoned the Pyramids of the Sun and Moon about 600 C.E., they were already partially buried.

Weather extremes alone almost certainly do not explain the fall of the Moche and the Nazca political and cultural systems. Scholars have argued that, similarly to the situation in the Maya lands a few centuries later, the ecological possibilities of the Peruvian valleys had by the sixth century nearly reached their limit. In the Moche zone, however, the ruling elites appear to have lived in splendid isolation from the common population and to have insisted on controlling greater and greater shares of wealth from field, sea, and human labor to pay for bigger public structures and larger quantities of precious goods. Social dissension over gross differences in income between lordly families and everyone else may already have been simmering when the first signs of climatic instability appeared. When it grew worse, the population may have suspected that the gods had stopped responding favorably to priestly offerings and performances, signaling that the leaders in the high temples had lost their legitimacy. As in the Maya case, even the best intentioned Moche lords probably found recurring damage to the agricultural infrastructure beyond their technical and managerial powers to fix.

Political and social breakdown affected different Moche regions at different times, and the temples carried on longer in the far northern valleys than in the south. Even though all the big centers collapsed eventually, farming and fishing population did not disappear. Archaeological analysis shows that as the extreme weather alternations tapered off, people set to work rebuilding irrigation works. In some valleys, elite clans simply retreated farther up the valleys, where farmland was more restricted but water more reliable. They built new temples in some places, but the distinctive Moche cultural style was not restored.

• • •

Conclusion

This chapter has accentuated developments in the most populous regions of the Americas, where complex societies rose, and fell, during a span of nearly two thousand years. The final quarter of that period, that is, from about 500 to 900 C.E., appears to have been a time of calamity for all the big societies we have highlighted in both Mesoamerica (Teotihuacán, the Oaxaca valley, the Maya lowlands) and South America (Chavín de Huántar, Moche, and Nazca). All of those societies moved along an arc of change that started with exuberant agricultural production, city building, and artisanship and ended in material ruin—at least the ruin of the splendid public structures that symbolized great imagination and skill. Different factors surely contributed to decline in each case. ENSO-related droughts that went on for years may have weakened all these societies. Similarly, social strains resulted from elites accumulating too large a share of wealth and then, when times got tough, failing to dissuade common people that the gods might be happier if jewel-bedecked aristocrats went away.

In any case the story of collapse in the late first millennium C.E. should not be overstated. First, and as we will see in Chapter 14, new city-states, empires, and brilliant artistic traditions arose to replace those that had crumbled, though not necessarily in exactly the same places. In both the Valley of Mexico and the Andes highlands, new empires came to display more power than any that had come before, but the Maya lowlands remained depleted of population and large temple centers until the coming of Europeans in the sixteenth century. Second, the regions where the most impressive societies arose between 900 B.C.E. and 900 C.E. covered only a small part of the two American continents. In those centuries, humans occupied just about every latitude and ecological niche from the Arctic to the tip of South America. We have no evidence that peoples who practiced village-level farming, foraging, fishing, or hunting on Alaskan tundra, Amazon forest, or Argentine plains experienced any general crisis in the later first millennium C.E. We saw that, in upper North America, the Hopewell people stopped building finely engineered earthen mounds about 400 C.E., but other groups continued to do it in other woodland regions, in a few places on a grander scale than ever before. Trends toward greater social complexity also continued in the Sonoran Desert and the Pacific Northwest.

Finally, on a global scale, the Mesoamerican and South American civilizations had no monopoly on decline and collapse in the first millennium C.E. In Chapter 9 we return to Afroeurasia, where mighty empires had deep troubles of their own.

• • •

Key Terms

Adena society 236
Chavín de Huántar 239
corvée labor 232
geoglyph 242
glyph 226
Hohokam society 236

Hopewell society 236
Maya city-states 224
Moche society 240
Monte Albán 228
Nazca society 242
Popol Vuh 234

primogeniture 230
Serpent Mound 237
Snaketown 236
Teotihuacán 224
Zapotec society 228

Change over Time

ca. 1350 B.C.E.–400 B.C.E.	The Olmecs build Mesoamerica's earliest urban society.
ca. 900–200 B.C.E.	Chavín de Huántar in Andean South America becomes a cultural and commercial node connecting the Pacific shore with Amazonia.
ca. 800 B.C.E.–400 C.E.	Adena and then Hopewell societies flourish in Woodland North America
ca. 500 B.C.E.	Early Maya urban building appears in Mesoamerica.
ca. 200 B.C.E.–750 C.E.	Teotihuacán rises from city-state to empire in Mesoamerica, then falls.
ca. 200 B.C.E.–700 C.E.	Monte Albán becomes the center of a Zapotec state in Mesoamerica.
ca. 200 B.C.E.–550 C.E.	A Nazca cultural style, including giant geoglyphs, develops among the communities along the arid coast of Andean South America.
ca. 1–1450 C.E.	The Hohokam people inhabit the Sonoran Desert of North America.
ca. 200–800 C.E.	Maya city-state construction reaches its peak (Maya Classic Period); the *Popol Vuh* and other codices are written.
ca. 250–800 C.E.	Moche urban society flourishes in Andean South America.
ca. 563–594 C.E.	Extended droughts disrupt life in Andean South America.
ca. 800–1200 C.E.	Maya city-states decline.

Please see end of book reference section for additional reading suggestions related to this chapter.

part 3
Shifting Power, Thickening Webs
Afroeurasia, 200–1000 C.E.

I f in the very long term human history has been a story of more and more people sharing the planet, while inventing increasingly complex of ways of organizing themselves, interacting with one another, and exploiting the earth's energy to their own benefit, this trend has not been entirely steady. Within the overall movement toward greater complexity, there have been cycles in which population has declined and recovered, cities have shrunk and flourished again, and economies have contracted and expanded. These cycles may be merely regional in scope, but they have also had interregional or even global dimensions, as we have seen in modern times when business recessions reverberate quickly around the world. The three chapters in Part 3 encompass approximately eight hundred years in the history of Afroeurasia, an era when the demographic and economic trends of the previous millennium temporarily slowed down or even reversed themselves, before accelerating again at an even faster pace.

The third century C.E., where Part 3 begins, represents a jarring break—in some places violent and destructive—in the prevailing pattern of population and economic growth. Between about 200 and 600, the Han, Kushana, Parthian, and western Roman empires all collapsed. These upheavals occurred partly in connection with the aggressive migrations of peoples from the Inner Eurasian steppes into neighboring agrarian lands. Western Europe, North Africa, northern India, and northern China all experienced serious economic turmoil. Disease epidemics that swept around the Mediterranean rim and across Southwest Asia in the sixth century had similar consequences. Conditions of life in several regions became harsh enough that Afroeurasia's overall population declined by several tens of millions between the third and seventh centuries, perhaps the first significant drop since the invention of agriculture.

A terra-cotta camel and rider from the era of the Tang dynasty in China.

Not all empires fell and not all economies went into deep recession during these centuries. The armies of Sasanid Persia and the eastern Roman empire held back nomad invaders. In South Asia, the kings of the Gupta state united a large part of the subcontinent. Several regions, including southern China, Southeast Asia, and tropical West Africa, generally escaped dismal depressions and continued to prosper, despite regional wars and dynastic changes. Long-distance trade on the Inner Eurasian silk roads and the chain of seas from China to Southwest Asia fell off, but only the western Mediterranean suffered an extended commercial slump.

In the sixth century, the engines of population and economic growth began to rev up nearly everywhere in Afroeurasia:

■ After three and a half centuries of fragmentation, China achieved political unification under the Sui and Tang dynasties (581–907). This development sparked a new round of technical innovation and rapid population growth in the rice-growing south.

■ In South Asia the Gupta empire disintegrated in the mid-sixth century, but this crisis appears to have had little effect on the subcontinent's swelling production of cotton textiles, pepper, and cinnamon, goods that found eager markets across Afroeurasia.

■ In western Africa, merchants who discovered the hardy qualities of the dromedary camel set up commercial operations that connected the Mediterranean lands with West Africa. This pioneering enterprise, well under way by the seventh century, lubricated the whole Afroeurasian exchange system with injections of West African gold.

■ Assaults of Eurasian nomads on China, India, and Southwest Asia tailed off. In the steppes new warrior empires arose in the sixth century, but they also stabilized political conditions and recharged silk road commerce. In the late first millennium, Europe endured an incursion of Magyar warriors from the steppes, but these intruders settled down quickly.

■ Finally, invaders from the Arabian Desert, who proclaimed Islam as a new universalist religion, politically united most of Southwest Asia, a region of agricultural and urban productivity that had been divided between rival states for nearly a thousand years. The cities of Southwest Asia had for millennia funneled commercial goods and new ideas along a corridor that connected the Mediterranean basin with the whole expanse of Asia

and eastern Africa. Following unification under Arab leadership, that corridor became more animated than ever before. From Southwest Asia, Arab soldiers, preachers, and merchants introduced Islam along the routes of conquest and trade. This new expression of monotheistic faith drew on the teachings of both Judaism and Christianity, and it put great emphasis on social cooperation and codes of proper ethical and legal behavior. Thus, Islam joined Buddhism and Christianity as a universalist faith offering the promise of community harmony and individual salvation. Together, these three religions reached just about every part of Afroeurasia in the late millennium.

Between 200 and 1000 C.E. migrant farmers, long-distance merchants, conquering armies, and wandering missionaries brought more of Afroeurasia into a single arena of human interchange. This happened without any revolutionary breakthroughs in communication and transport technology, though artisans and engineers tinkered endlessly with ship designs, navigational tools, and more efficient systems of banking and credit. By the end of the millennium, signs of new economic growth and social complexity were abundant. Afroeurasia's overall population climbed nearly back to where it had been eight hundred years earlier. Interlinked commercial networks operated across the breadth of Afroeurasia. China was moving into an era of unprecedented industrial growth. And after suffering a half-millennium of chronic disorder, western Europeans were building a new urban civilization.

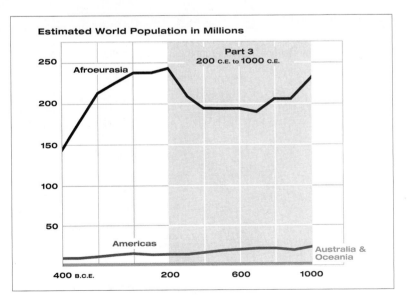

9 Turbulent Centuries
200-600 C.E.

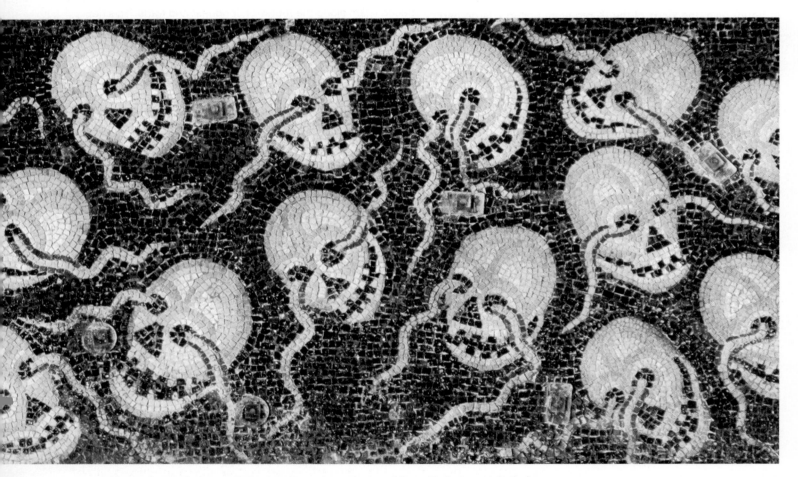

A reminder of mortality in mosaic from the Byzantine cathedral of Santa Maria Assunta in Venice.

hen people come down with flu after flying on an airplane, they often blame the conditions of air travel—the confined space, full flight, and stale air that encourage the spread of infectious germs from one passenger to another. Infected passengers then get off the plane, and before they even know they are sick they may transmit their malady to others at home or work. In this way viral and bacterial ailments may spread from Madrid to Bangkok or Kansas City to Kinshasa in a matter of hours. In today's globalized world, we fear not only annoying contagions but also raging epidemics. Microorganisms mutate constantly into new and possibly deadly forms, and travelers may quickly carry dangerous pathogens to places where people have weak immunological defenses against them. The consequences may be a local disease outbreak or, far worse, a pandemic—an infection that moves quickly from one region to another, possibly affecting millions.

Ancient empires, which made it their business to build good transport networks, were inevitably susceptible to epidemics. Major eruptions of what might have been smallpox, measles, or anthrax spread through parts of the Roman empire in the second and third centuries C.E. A deadlier outbreak, probably bubonic plague, occurred in 541, a time when the emperor Justinian ruled in Constantinople. This infection may have originated somewhere in the upper reaches of the Nile valley, advanced downriver to the Mediterranean, then spread in every direction. Scholars have estimated that within just a few years this pandemic killed one-third to one-half of the population of the Mediterranean region, northern Europe, and perhaps Persia.

The Plague of Justinian, as it was called, caused a demographic and social shock. But it was only one of several disruptions that affected the course of events in Afroeurasia between the third and seventh centuries. In addition to recurring epidemics, the most conspicuous of these disturbances were the movements of armed migrants from Inner Eurasia into densely populated agrarian lands. Persistent political and social tumult connected to these migrations characterized much of Eurasia and northern Africa. Compared to the previous four centuries, when the Roman and Han empires reached their apogees of power, the growth of population, food production, long-distance trade, and urbanization appear to have slowed, though by no means everywhere in Afroeurasia and not all at once.

The first section of this chapter explores major political and economic changes between about 200 and 600 C.E. Here, we emphasize the dramatic interplay between the Inner Eurasian population movements and the critical shifts that took place in the configuration of large states and major centers of economic wealth (see Map 9.1). In this period, the Han, Kushana, and Parthian empires collapsed, and the Roman empire shrank to about half its former size. Powerful new states, however, arose in Persia and South Asia.

In the second section we connect political and economic change to the remarkable growth of Christianity and Buddhism, two multifaceted belief systems that proclaimed a universal message of moral and spiritual deliverance and

Chapter Outline

THE SHIFTING MAP OF EMPIRES

Turbulence in Inner Eurasia
China after the Han Empire: Growth without Unity
The Sasanids: A New Power in Persia
Crisis and Recovery in the Roman Empire
The Huns and the Collapse of the Western Empire
The Mediterranean Fractured
A New Empire in South Asia

RELIGIONS FOR TROUBLED TIMES

The Buddhist Web
The Christian Web

INDIVIDUALS MATTER St. Augustine of Hippo: Christian Theologian

The Manichean Way

TROPICAL AFRICA: FARMERS, TOWNS, AND IRON

The Nok Culture

WEIGHING THE EVIDENCE The Sculptures of Nok

The African East and South
Southeast Asian Contributions to African Society

• • •

that attracted millions of new converts. Both religions became vehicles for the interregional exchange of ideas, people, and goods. We also consider connections between the growth of these two missionary faiths and the fates of other belief systems in that era: Zoroastrianism, Roman polytheism, the South Asian devotional religion that took shape as the Hindu tradition, and Manichaeism.

In the final section, we shift our focus to Africa south of the Sahara Desert. There, the most prominent patterns of change in the early centuries C.E. were the continuing movement of farmers and herders into the continent's southern third and in several places the rise of denser farming populations, bigger towns, and more complex systems of trade. These developments had significant connections to the shifts and disturbances taking place simultaneously in northern Africa and Eurasia.

A Panoramic View

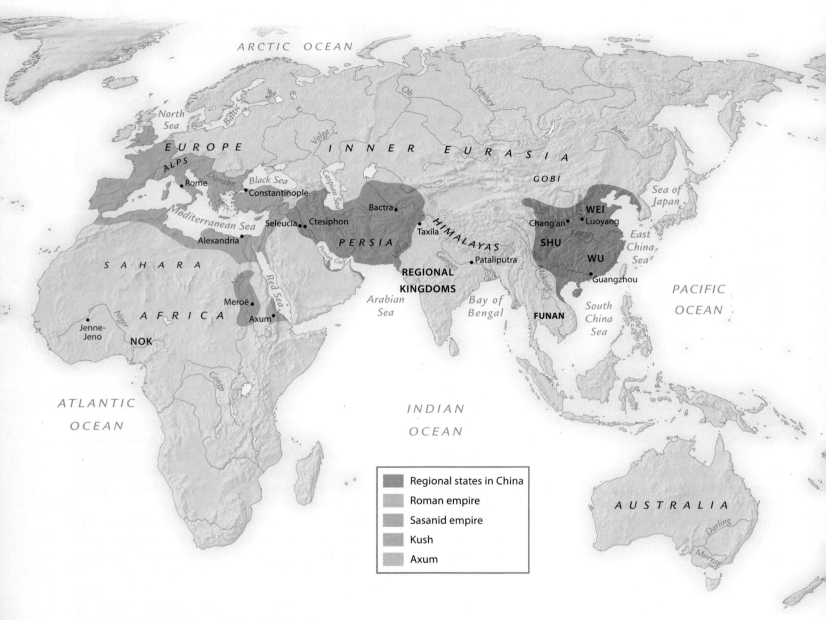

MAP 9.1 Major states of Afroeurasia, 250 C.E.

This map represents Afroeurasia at a moment of impending transformation across the region. Comparing it to Map 7.1, what geopolitical differences do you see?

The Shifting Map of Empires

FOCUS What impact did the armed migrations of pastoral nomads have on political and economic changes in China, Persia, the Mediterranean region, and South Asia?

Empires never last forever, but in the space of little more than two centuries, four enormous states, the largest in world history to that time, either collapsed or splintered: the Han empire in China, the Parthians in Persia, and the Kushanas in Central and South Asia, all in the third century C.E. The western half of the Roman empire fragmented in the fifth century. These crises, however, offered opportunities to new groups to found states or transform old ones. In 224 C.E., the Sasanids (suh-SAH-nids), an Iranian warrior group, eradicated the Parthian dynasty and shortly erected an even bigger Persian empire over its grave. In South Asia the Gupta (GOOP-tah) dynasty, expanding from a base in the Ganges River valley, reunited much of the subcontinent as the Maurya emperors had done five hundred years earlier. The eastern part of the Roman empire, under the new name of Byzantium (BIHZ-ann-tee-um), held firm until after 600 C.E. None of these power shifts took place without upheaval, in large part because of the violent interventions of mounted archers from the Inner Eurasia steppes.

Turbulence in Inner Eurasia

The giant states that existed at the start of the third century formed a curving arc of territories that extended across Eurasia and northern Africa. These territories, rich in food production, supported something like 200 million farmers and city dwellers. Extending north from this arc was Inner Eurasia, whose much sparser population included both cultivators and pastoral nomads. Earlier chapters described the general historical patterns of interaction, whether peaceful or violent, between nomads and densely settled societies. Since the second millennium B.C.E., nomads periodically surged into agrarian lands, sometimes as raiding expeditions and sometimes as migrations of horse archers along with their families, wagons, and livestock.

One of these pulsations started in the third century C.E. and lasted into the sixth. It involved not only attacks on farms and cities but also prolonged disruptions *within* Inner Eurasia, as mounted groups of unequal numbers and power pursued or fled from one another across mountains, deserts, and steppes. Historians have not so far explained with much confidence why this surge took place. They have associated it with various factors: climatic cooling that cut food production in Eurasia's northern latitudes, population growth that put severe pressure on grazing land, steppe wars that forced fleeing groups to push against agrarian neighbors, and weaknesses in big states that left their frontiers vulnerable to nomad attack.

Both the rise and collapse of the Xiongnu, the pastoral nomadic empire that ruled the eastern steppes between the third century B.C.E. and the second century C.E. (see Chapter 7), affected the movements of other herding peoples. In their expansionary phase, Xiongnu warriors attacked not only China but also nomad rivals to the west, provoking peoples that did not wish to be conquered to flee even farther west. The Han campaign that shattered the Xiongnu state sent more tribes westward. In the third and fourth centuries C.E., the Pontic-Caspian region became a vortex of restless herding folk of diverse origins, some of them speaking Mongolian, others Turkic, Iranian, and Germanic languages. The climatic pattern in Inner Eurasia also figured in the tendency for pastoral peoples to push west, since average seasonal rainfall increases progressively in that direction. Migrating herders discovered that the farther west they went, the greener the grazing land was likely to be, especially west of the Black Sea.

China after the Han Empire: Growth without Unity

The Han dynasty (see Chapter 7) endured for nearly four hundred years, with one short interruption. At its height, garrisons secured the borders from northern Korea and Vietnam to oasis towns far out along the Inner Eurasian silk roads. But in the second century, the Han emperors ran into increasing political and financial trouble. Steppe nomads contributed to the dynasty's misfortunes. It collapsed in 220 C.E., and from the third to the sixth centuries, China remained politically fragmented, a time known as the Age of Division.

The end of the Han. The Chinese government faced a particular structural problem that dogged almost all premodern empires. Territorial expansion filled state coffers with booty and new tax revenue. Maintaining control over conquered lands and peoples required large expenditures to pay for garrisons and administration, to suppress uprisings, and to offer lavish gifts in silk and gold to Inner Eurasian nomad leaders, a policy that allowed those chiefs to share in the wealth of China without being tempted to attack it. The great costs of empire, however, strained government resources and aggravated competition for them among China's elite. In the second century C.E., state bureaucrats, military commanders, relatives of the emperor's wife, and royal **eunuchs** all banded into rival political factions and tried to influence state decisions. The imperial corps of eunuchs

> **eunuch** A castrated male who typically served as a functionary in a royal court, especially as an attendant in the female quarters (harem).

moved freely within the palace and were expected to give the emperor unconditional service. Their numbers, however, grew into the thousands, and they increasingly meddled in political affairs to advance their own interests. A string of ineffectual or youthful monarchs made matters worse. More

Han defenses on the northwestern frontier. This remnant of a Han army watchtower stands on the edge of the Tarim Basin near the silk road town of Dunhuang.

than once in the second century, eunuch factions took control of the throne by engineering the succession of a young child and killing or banishing thousands of officials.

Growing disorder at the center inevitably weakened imperial authority throughout the empire. Han generals in distant provinces discovered they could ignore imperial commands and even recruit private armies. The property of landowning (freehold) peasants declined steadily, which meant they paid fewer taxes. This happened partly because of the tradition of families passing land in equal portions to all sons, which forced each man to make a living from a fraction of the father's legacy. But weakening government oversight in the provinces also made it easier for aristocratic estate lords to wheedle land away from peasants, whether legally or not, thereby transforming freeholders into rent-paying tenants or day workers with less taxable wealth. At the same time, rich and influential families found creative ways to escape paying taxes the central government desperately needed.

The Han dynasty's final crisis began in 184 C.E. when the Yellow Turbans, a movement inspired by Daoist ideas of mystical worship, spiritual healing, and social aid to poor people, launched an explosive rebellion against government incompetence and aristocratic land-grabbing. Han forces suppressed the revolt at great cost, but in its aftermath an assortment of warlords and generals competed violently for local power; one private army burned Luoyang, the Han capital. The imperial regime never reestablished order and finally collapsed in 220.

The Age of Division and its trends. During the following 370 years, China remained segmented into several regional kingdoms whose boundaries and relative power shifted. While Chinese elites continued to believe that the country should be unified under a monarch possessing the Mandate of Heaven, none of those states accumulated sufficient resources to dominate all the others. Two trends of this era stand out.

First, large numbers of Chinese migrated from north to south, notably to the Yangzi River valley, which in later centuries emerged as China's economic center. Even before Han times, Chinese farmers had started drifting from the semi-arid Yellow River region to the warmer, rainier south. In the process they exchanged wheat and millet fields for wet-rice farming. To escape the upsurge of fighting that characterized the Age of Division, numerous aristocratic families fled toward the Yangzi, often bringing thousands of peasants with them. Those transplanted elites created new regional states and sped up the south's agricultural development. Landowners set their laborers to building the dams, canals, and dikes required to flood and drain wet-rice fields. More commercial and manufacturing towns sprang up. Landowners also invested heavily in sericulture, the cultivation of mulberry trees to feed silkworms. Peasant women specialized in the meticulous task of unwinding silkworm cocoons, twisting the filaments into thread, and weaving cloth.

Second, the silk trade within China helped revive the commercial economy despite the political disunion. Demand for Chinese silk thread and finished textiles continued to grow in India, Persia, and the Mediterranean lands. The Han collapse coupled with pastoral nomadic wars and migrations almost certainly disrupted the flow of silk on the overland routes west. But those very disturbances coupled with economic growth in southern China stimulated more foreign trade by sea. By the third century, for example, the city of Guangzhou (Canton) on China's southern coast emerged as a window on Afroeurasia, exporting silk, bronzework, and other manufactures as far as East Africa and the eastern Mediterranean. In short, China's political fracturing resulted, not in general economic decline, but rather in an accelerating shift of the territorial center of population and economic activity from north to south.

The Sasanids: A New Power in Persia

The chain of empires that stretched from China to the Mediterranean in the early centuries C.E. included Parthia, whose monarchs ruled Persia and parts of Mesopotamia (see Chapter 7). Somewhat like Han China, the Parthian government weakened in the third century under the strain of incessant struggles among military and aristocratic factions. Whereas Han rulers had to keep Inner Eurasian nomads at bay, the Parthians spent their resources fighting Roman legions for control of Mesopotamian cities. In 224 the Parthian regime collapsed, but in contrast to China, its territories did not fragment. Rather, Ardashir I, a member of a prestigious family of Zoroastrian priests, led a victorious rebellion in southwestern Iran. He had himself proclaimed *Shahanshah*, the King of Kings, and a new imperial dynasty known as the Sasanids quickly replaced the old one.

The Parthian kings, who favored Greek-style art and literature over ancient Persian traditions, had never fully united Iranian aristocratic families in common purpose. The Sasanids, by contrast, zealously boasted their Persian heritage. They represented themselves as the direct heirs of the powerful Persian Achaemenids, the dynasty that had ruled from the sixth to the fourth centuries B.C.E. (see Chapter 6). This strategy brought them aristocratic support. For example, the early Sasanid rulers erected great palaces, temples, tombs, and stone carvings using motifs and images designed to link them historically to the Achaemenid imperial tradition. Ardashir and his son Shapur I, who ruled in succession for nearly half a century (224–272 C.E.), created a more tightly centralized system of government than the Parthians had managed, drawing somewhat on Roman ideas to set up ministries of justice, finance, and military affairs.

Zoroastrian resurgence. The Sasanids also emulated the Achaemenids by patronizing the Zoroastrian religion. Founded on the teachings of the ancient prophet Zoroaster, this faith proclaimed that the long earthly struggle between the supernatural forces of good and evil would inevitably climax in the total triumph of good at the End of Time (see Chapter 6). The Sasanids depicted themselves as servants of Ahura Mazda, the supreme creator god. They sponsored construction of Zoroastrian ritual fire temples throughout the empire, created a hierarchy of temple priests paralleling the political bureaucracy, and permitted particular clerics to exercise great power as political advisers and judges. Periodically, this priesthood moved to suppress rival religions. A

third-century inscription at a Sasanid archaeological site declares that, under orders from the high priest Kartir, "Jews, Sramans (Buddhists), Brahmins, Nasoreans (Christians), . . . and Zandiks (Manichaeans) in the empire were smitten."[1] In the sixth century the government oversaw the codification of the *Avesta*, the compilation of Zoroaster's prophecies and other sacred works. In that period Zoroastrianism achieved its greatest influence as an Asian religion.

Sasanid conquests and wars with Rome. The Parthians had held off nomad intruders and even beat Roman armies a few times by fielding armies of mounted Persian nobles. These aristocratic warriors, called cataphracts, carried lances, and they encased themselves, as well as their large horses, in metal armor. Income from their estates paid the huge expense of raising specially bred horses and manufacturing military gear. Also adopting this style of warfare, the Sasanids persuaded their nobles to fight under central command. They also conscripted infantry and lightly armored horse archers from the wider population. They even took advantage of trade connections with India to import war elephants. This army, combined with talented imperial leadership, transformed the young state into a Southwest Asian power of greater threat to its neighbors than the Parthians had ever been.

Early in his reign, King Ardashir led forces eastward against the Kushana empire, which had been a power in its own right in Central Asia and northern India since the first century B.C.E. (see Chapter 7). He drove the Kushana

King Khosrow II (r. 590–628) ready for battle. The king was among the *cataphracts*, or aristocratic warriors, whose cavalry skills helped make the Sasanid army a powerful force in Southwest Asia. Notice the cylindrical helmet, the shield, and the heavy armor on the horse. This is a detail from a huge relief carved into a rock face along a caravan route in Iran's Zagros Mountains. Why might a long lance be a mounted fighter's preferred weapon?

forces out of all their territories west of the Indus River and seized several important Central Asian commercial cities. Kushana survived into the fourth century C.E. but as a much diminished monarchy.

Starting in 237 Ardashir and Shapur dispatched armies deep into northern Mesopotamia and Syria, catching Roman legions off guard and seizing several cities. They even killed one Roman ruler and captured another, delivering the emperor Valerian to the King of Kings in 257. Shapur kept this hapless potentate in chains, dragging him around with the royal entourage. According to a third-century Christian text, "The king of the Persians, who had made him [Valerian] prisoner, whenever he chose to get into his carriage or to mount on horseback, commanded the Roman to stoop and present his back. . . . Afterward, when [Valerian] had finished this shameful life under so great dishonor, he was flayed, and his skin, stripped from the flesh, was dyed with vermilion, and placed in the temple of the gods of the barbarians."[2]

These defeats and outrages caused shock waves in Rome. By the end of the third century its legions checkmated Sasanid westward expansion; for the next three hundred years, relations between the two powers in Southwest Asia oscillated between peace and war. Both poured immense resources into their chronic struggles, without either side making large territorial gains against the other.

The Sasanid economy.
Persia's well-being depended overwhelmingly on agriculture, and in the large areas of Mesopotamia that the Sasanids controlled, imperial officials launched big projects to expand irrigated farming. Between the third and sixth centuries, they built canals, dams, and levees, as well as several whole cities, in the Tigris-Euphrates valley. Enslaved war prisoners and forcibly resettled peasants from other parts of the empire did the work. In the Sasanid period, if not somewhat earlier, rice, cotton, and cane sugar spread westward from South or Southeast Asia to become important irrigated crops in Southwest Asia.

The Sasanid conquests, especially to the east, meant that the dynasty controlled more cities and longer trade lines than the Parthians had (see Map 9.1). Persian caravans set out from Mesopotamia and western Iran across the deserts north of the Arabian Sea to deliver textiles, perfumes, fine woolen carpets, and Persian Gulf pearls to India. Persian merchants also helped extend imperial influence to port towns on the Arabian side of the gulf. These traders competed with Roman and other shippers on the Arabian Sea routes, founding commercial settlements as far east as Ceylon.

Crisis and Recovery in the Roman Empire

The Persian military threat was just one of the political crises that afflicted Rome in the third century C.E. A variety of troubles compelled the imperial elite to restructure both the government and the army, a challenge that exposed the colossal problems of governing a state that stretched 2,400 miles from Britain to Mesopotamia.

Third-century emergencies.
The absence of clear rules of royal succession, other than the total ineligibility of women, had plagued Rome on and off since the first century C.E. Forceful sovereigns might name the successor they wanted, but if they failed to do that several rival candidates might present themselves for the job, including frontier generals or other ambitious men who could rally support from their troops. Also, a new emperor with only shaky support could provoke civil war among elite factions determined to replace him with their own man. In the half-century between 235 and 284, at least eighteen men occupied the throne with the formal endorsement of the Roman Senate, which by that period had no independent power and generally followed the political wind. Many of those rulers died after short reigns, either in battle or by assassination. This chronic turmoil at the center inevitably disrupted imperial business, especially frontier security, court decisions, and tax-gathering operations.

Third-century emperors also confronted a bundle of economic and social problems. To meet growing expenses, the government allowed mints to cut the silver content in coins, which inevitably reduced their value and caused consumer prices to soar. This inflation mainly affected ordinary men and women, who depended on stable prices for wheat and other basic commodities. Like Chinese peasants in the late Han era, Roman farmers suffered as landowning elites accumulated larger estates at the expense of small freeholders and employed large numbers of renters, day laborers, armed henchmen, and slaves. By the fourth century, a Roman senator, who was almost always a big landowner, could expect to reap an annual income of 120,000 gold pieces or more; a peasant might earn 5. Nevertheless, officials pressured common citizens to pay taxes.

Germanic intruders.
Violent incursions along the empire's frontiers caused serious financial drain, as it did in late Han China. Northeastern Europe, which we may think of as Inner Eurasia's far western edge, was the domain of tribally organized groups that spoke a number of Germanic languages, a branch of the Indo-European language family that also includes ancestral English. In the first and second centuries C.E., when Roman legions advanced into central Europe, Germanic tribes were drifting west toward the Rhine River and south toward the Danube. Germanic peoples raised cattle, sheep, and horses, but they were predominantly farmers, not pastoral nomads. And those tribes living nearest to Roman territory attained a level of social complexity that included village building, iron making, skilled artisanry, and a dominant class of warrior chiefs.

The worlds of Romans and Germanic populations became elaborately intertwined. Trade between them went on nearly all the time. Germanic traders supplied timber, wool, furs, and other raw products to Romans in exchange for textiles, pottery, gold or silver coins, and numerous other items. Roman governors periodically allowed Germanic groups to migrate peacefully into the empire to settle. Germanic

An image of a "barbarian." This scene is a detail from a marble sculpture engraved on the side of a Roman coffin known as the Ludovisi Battle Sarcophagus. The work dates to about 250 C.E., when Germanic and other armed migrants were already assailing the empire's northern frontiers. The artist depicts the captured enemy as a scruffy looking fellow with bulbous nose, long hair, and ragged beard. By contrast, the clean-shaven Roman infantryman projects calm command. What might the Roman soldier intend to do next?

Black Sea, advanced into the Roman-ruled Balkan Peninsula. In 251, Goth intruders killed the emperor Decius in battle and sixteen years later swept far south to pillage Athens and several other venerable Greek cities. Consequently, the Roman government had to spend more than ever on its European legions to defend the empire.

Reforming emperors. Rome's political and economic fortunes recovered under the energetic leadership of Diocletian (reigned 284–305 C.E.) and Constantine I (r. 306–337 C.E.). Both men vowed to address the empire's structural problems. To strengthen the army, Diocletian reorganized its hierarchy of command, increased the number of legions (incorporating more Germanic soldiers), and built up cavalry forces, including Persian-style armored cataphracts. On the eastern frontier, Roman forces halted Sasanid expansion in 298 C.E. Diocletian and Constantine achieved victories over Germanic enemies in Europe and Berber insurgents in North Africa that helped stabilize the empire's western half well into the fourth century.

Diocletian tried to strengthen regional government and reduce imperial succession disputes by dividing the empire into western and eastern sectors, each zone ruled by one of two coemperors. Each of these men had a deputy emperor and designated successor. This system of four collaborating leaders, called the Tetrarchy, worked quite well under Diocletian, but it fell apart in factional quarreling soon after he retired from office. Nevertheless, a tradition of having two corulers, if not four, continued into the fifth century, and the system probably helped prevent civil wars from breaking out more often than they did.

warriors also routinely hired themselves out as Roman soldiers. Like the Han government, the Romans paid large sums to keep the frontier quiet, sending Germanic chiefs gifts in coin or goods. At the same time, most Romans regarded Germanic and all other transfrontier peoples as the cultural opposites of imperial citizens, as "barbarians" of inherently crude, ignorant, and hostile disposition.

Germanic leaders knew what Romans thought of them, and during the third century, some of them played their assigned role eagerly, crossing the frontier to attack settlements and raid farms. Archaeological research has shown that in this period Germanic populations were rising in number, partly owing to improving farming technology: iron plows, manure fertilizing, and crop rotation. Consequently, population pressures may have urged Germanic war bands to push into the rich Roman farmlands beyond the Rhine and Danube. The Germanic group known as Goths, whose territorial base was north and west of the

Rome also became more bureaucratic. In earlier centuries the government had operated largely through personal relations between individuals of status, wealth, and power and subordinate clients who did what they were told in return for money, jobs, and protection (see Chapter 7). The third-century troubles, however, persuaded Diocletian and his successors to create a larger, more formal hierarchy of salaried officers accountable to the state. Between the mid-third and fifth centuries, the number of senior functionaries handling the empire's business grew from about 250 to 6,000.[3] This bureaucracy collected new taxes, curtailed the financial independence of cities, and forced peasants to stay on the land rather than seek urban jobs no matter how impoverished these men and women were. Diocletian also tried to control inflation by fixing prices of essential commodities, though with only partial success. Finally,

Constantine I. The emperor, radiating majestic authority, appears removed from the world of ordinary men and women. This bronze head was once part of a colossal statue. What specific features of the sculpture give it emotional power?

Constantine, Constantinople, and the Christian church. In the fourth and fifth centuries, cities located quite close to the empire's turbulent frontiers served as the nerve centers of imperial government, for example, Milan in Italy, Carthage in North Africa, and Antioch in Syria. Most emperors did not govern from the city of Rome, and some rarely went there. In 313, Constantine established an imperial center on the foundations of Byzantium, an ancient Greek town on a promontory overlooking the western side of the Bosporus, the strait connecting the Black Sea with the Sea of Marmara and the Mediterranean beyond. He renamed the place Constantinople after himself. Protected on three sides by water and on the fourth by walls, the city became the headquarters of imperial security in the eastern and Balkan provinces. Constantine and his successors lavished great sums on public monuments, palaces, libraries, arenas, and waterworks. The population rapidly grew, reaching about half a million in the sixth century. The city of Rome continued to loom large in the historical imagination of all citizens, but its importance to the imperial economy and administration faded gradually, along with its former status as largest city in the world.

The cityscape of fourth-century Constantinople also included churches. Despite periodic persecutions, Christian communities had been sprouting up in towns around the Mediterranean since the first century C.E. (see Chapter 7) In the troubled third century, ordinary people turned to a variety of cults and sects for aid and solace, among them Christianity, a faith whose missionaries preached compassion, generosity, communal love, and the hope of eternal life. Jesus's promise that "the meek shall inherit the earth" appealed deeply to women and men weary of ritual sacrifices to distant and unresponsive gods. The early church devoted itself to charitable giving. When local government authorities failed to distribute food to the poor or care for epidemic victims, church communities rallied round. In the mid-third century, the church in the city of Rome had about 1,500 widows and other poor folk under its care.

Diocletian launched a brutal campaign to harass and jail Christians in 303, but this was the last major Roman persecution. Just a decade later, Constantine decreed free worship for all religions and, according to tradition, accepted Christian baptism when he was near death. In the Edict of Milan of 313, he and Licinius, who was then his coemperor, proclaimed: "We thought it fit to commend these things most fully to your care that you may know that we have given to those Christians free and unrestricted opportunity of religious worship. . . . We have also conceded to other religions the right of open and free observance of their worship for the sake of the peace of our times, that each one may have the free opportunity to worship as he pleases."[4] This act quickly reduced long festering social and political tensions between the growing Christian minority and the adherents of traditional Roman polytheism.

Constantine's edict produced no great outcry from polytheists. Romans believed that divine power sanctified the

Diocletian, Constantine, and several of their successors altered the ideology and style of authoritarian rule. The idea of the emperor as First Citizen, a relic of the old Republic, gave way to a part-Persian, part-Egyptian model of the monarch as absolute, remote, and mysterious, a potentate governing from within multiple protective circles of officials, servants, and bodyguards.

empire, and now the Christian god might substitute for the old ones as a spiritual source of imperial authority. It did not hurt that both Christianity and Roman legal ideals affirmed the equality of all before the law. Growing numbers of aristocrats and senior bureaucrats converted to Christianity, though some did, no doubt, because they thought that Christians would get choicer government posts. Constantine and his successors also asserted leadership over Christian affairs, arbitrating disputes among bishops (the heads of church administrative units), presiding over church councils, and enacting laws regarding Christian faith and practice. Then, in 380 C.E., the Emperor Theodosius made Christianity the official state religion.

Thereafter, the empire became gradually Christianized, though, as one scholar has put it, Christianity was also Romanized.[5] The emperor headed both the state and the church, appointing the Bishop of Rome as one of five **patriarchs.** The other four served in Constantinople, Antioch, Jerusalem, and Alexandria. The structure of the church was set up to mirror the empire's administrative organization.

> **patriarch** In the early Christian centuries, the title of the bishops of Rome, Constantinople, Jerusalem, Antioch, and Alexandria; in later centuries, the title of the highest official of the Greek Orthodox Church, as well as other Asian or African Christian churches.

A Christian woman. In this example of Christian art from about 300 C.E., a woman raises her arms and opens her hands in a gesture of prayer known as the *orans* position, from the Latin word for prayer. The woman appears on a fresco in the Catacomb of Priscilla near Rome. Christian clergy today assume this pose in particular church service rituals.

The church diocese, or seat of a bishop, corresponded to a late Roman political unit of the same name. Rich Roman landowners also got themselves appointed as bishops and, in that office, mimicked the royal court with displays of wealth and pageantry.

The Huns and the Collapse of the Western Empire

The western half of the empire disintegrated in the fifth century C.E., though not mainly because of economic crisis and exhaustion. Rather, most Roman provinces remained economically quite healthy well into the 400s C.E. Archaeological investigation of material consumption and of the size and number of villages has strengthened this argument. Italy and parts of Gaul gradually weakened compared to earlier levels of prosperity, but the inhabitants of eastern North Africa (the area that is today modern Tunisia and part of Algeria and Libya) remained busy producers of wheat, oil, wine, and high-quality pottery for export. The eastern Mediterranean provinces generally enjoyed significant economic growth into the sixth century. Growth, however, did not mean better lives for all. Elite families representing no more than 5 percent of the population owned about 80 percent of the productive land. Diocletian imposed higher taxes on ordinary farmers but exempted senators (whose support he wanted for his reforms) from paying anything. As in China in the post-Han era, freehold peasants continued to decrease in number relative to tenant farmers, low-wage workers, and slaves.

Huns in the saddle. "The Huns fell upon the Alans, the Alans upon the Goths and Taifali, the Goths and Taifali upon the Romans, and this is not yet the end."[6] In this single sentence, Ambrose, the Christian bishop of Milan writing about 378, nicely captured the sequence of events in Europe in the hundred years after he made this observation. In the fourth century, Roman troops were continually forced to defend the Danube and Rhine frontiers not only because of Germanic population buildup but also because of the "bumper-car effect" of wars and migrations in faraway Inner Eurasia. One of the pastoral nomadic groups that spun off from the collapse of the Xiongnu empire was a loose assemblage of migrants that became known as the Huns. This crowd of men, women, children, and animals advanced as far west as the Pontic-Caspian steppes around 360. There Hunnic warriors fought and defeated Iranian-speaking Alan herders, some of whom fled farther west, attacking Goth farmers in southeastern Europe. Bands of Huns followed the Alans, causing even more trouble for Goths. In the summer of 376, thousands of Goths arrived on the north bank of the Danube demanding Roman permission to cross to safety in the Balkan Peninsula. Roman authorities complied, but within a few months the immigrants, running short of food and winter shelter, rose in revolt. This disorder lasted for seven years, the key event taking place in 378, when Goth warriors, joined by freelance bands of Alans and Huns, defeated a Roman army at Hadrianople (Edirne). This town was less than 130 miles from Constantinople. From the Roman perspective the "barbarians" were getting too close for comfort.

Historians have long debated the identity of the Huns, agreeing only that they probably spoke either a Mongolian or a Turkic language. In any case, this horde picked up people of diverse ethnolinguistic origins as they moved west. Romans who wrote about the Huns usually betrayed deep negative prejudice, but the fifth-century scholar Ammianus probably captured their way of life quite accurately:

> Roaming at large amid the mountains and woods, they learn from the cradle to endure cold, hunger, and thirst. When away from their homes they never enter a house unless compelled by extreme necessity; for they think they are not safe when staying under a roof. . . . They are almost glued to their horses, which are hardy, it is true, but ugly, and sometimes they sit on them woman-fashion and thus perform their ordinary tasks. From their horses by night or day every one of that nation buys and sells, eats and drinks, and bowed over the narrow neck of the animal relaxes into a sleep. . . . They are subject to no royal restraint, but they are content with the disorderly government of their important men, and led by them they force their way through every obstacle. . . . No one in their country ever plows a field or touches a plow-handle.[7]

Armed with bow and sword, one large company of Hunnic cavalry advanced from the Pontic-Caspian region southward toward the Caucasus Mountains (see Map 9.2). From there they organized giant raiding expeditions into Mesopotamia and Syria in the 390s, threatening both Roman and Persian cities. Other Huns advanced west, arriving on the grassy plains of Hungary sometime before 420. They set up permanent camps there, pasturing their herds while collecting tribute from local Germanic and the partially Romanized population. They also traded with Roman merchants, and some joined the imperial army as auxiliary cavalry.

The Germanic breakout. When the Huns penetrated central Europe, they triggered more bumper-car migrations.

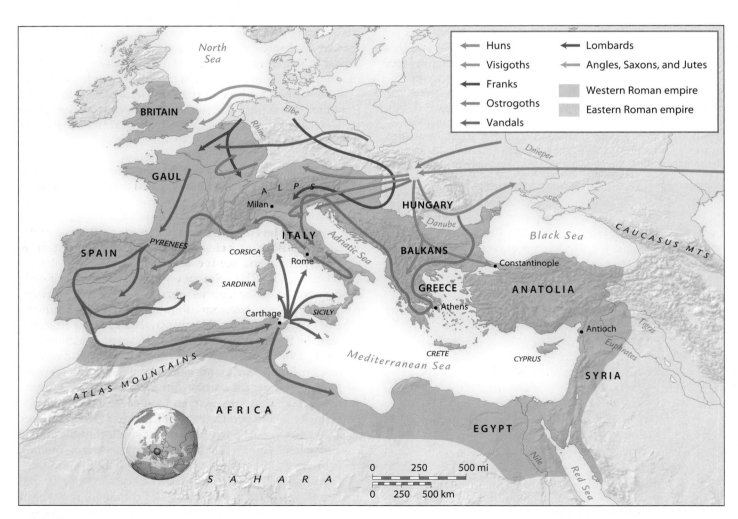

MAP 9.2 Armed migrations, fifth and sixth centuries.
What geographical factors might help explain why Germanic and other invaders advanced westward all the way across Europe?

The skull of a Hunnic woman. Huns were among a number of peoples in world history, including Maya, to practice cranial manipulation. This woman's head was probably tightly wrapped in cloth when she was an infant. What social purpose do you think cranial manipulation of some members of the group might have had?

[Morocco and Algeria], . . . raging with cruelty and barbarity, they completely devastated everything they could by their pillage, murder and varied tortures, conflagrations and other innumerable and unspeakable crimes, sparing neither sex nor age, nor even the priests or ministers of God."[8] The invaders advanced rapidly eastward nearly a thousand miles to Carthage, using good Roman roads most of the way. The fall of North Africa represented a terrible blow to the empire because that region's agriculture was a critical source of military supply.

Attila the Hun. The Huns had at first a mainly indirect impact on fighting in the empire. But shortly before 440, leadership passed to Attila. A Roman envoy described this warrior as "short, with a broad chest and large head; his eyes were small, his beard sparse and flecked with gray, his nose flat and his complexion dark."[9] Coruling with a brother until deciding to murder him, Attila appears to have wanted to found a permanent Hunnic state and to make it a base for extracting gold, goods, and slaves from Roman territory, just as his Xiongnu ancestors had milked Han China's frontiers. Between 442 and 453 he led several major forays into the empire, attacking not only Romans but also Germanic groups that stood in his way. His forces also demonstrated skills at besieging and capturing Roman cities. In 447 an army that included both Huns and Germanic recruits overran the Balkans, crushing two Roman armies and coming close to assaulting the triple line of walls that defended the landward approaches to Constantinople. In 451–452, Attila launched two invasions of what was left of the western empire, first into Gaul and then into Italy. Romans and Germanic Visigoths joined together to turn back the first invasion, and an epidemic helped cut short the second. A Christian chronicler reported that the Hunnic intruders "were victims of divine punishment, being visited with heaven sent disasters: famine and some kind of disease."[10]

The following year Attila died suddenly, and in the absence of decisive leadership from any of his sons, his fledgling empire crumbled quickly. Nevertheless, his campaigns seriously damaged Gaul and Italy, aborted Roman plans to take back North Africa, and, once he was gone, freed Germanic tribes, including Franks, Burgundians, Lombards, and Visigoths, to seize the western empire's remaining pieces. In 476, Odoacer, a leader of Ostrogoth and other Germanic troops, deposed Romulus,

Several Germanic groups, including Visigoths, Vandals, Suevi, and Burgundians, fled the Hunnic approach in the early fifth century. Some headed toward Italy, while others crossed the Rhine into Roman Gaul without invitation. This provocative advance, which also included Iranian-speaking Alans, may have involved 100,000 people or more. In the following several decades, the citizenry of both western Europe and North Africa witnessed growing political disarray, though some Roman commanders made valiant efforts to restore order. The Germanic advance was not a single, methodical invasion but rather involved episodic movements of several separate bands who continued to trade and negotiate with Romans— and to fight one other—as they advanced across Gaul and Iberia. And as territory fell from imperial control, the revenues needed to pay the imperial army to defend cities and provinces steadily shriveled.

In northern Europe, Germanic Saxons and Angles built ships and crossed the North Sea to attack Britain in successive waves. By about 410 C.E. the island effectively dropped out of the Roman empire, though Romanized populations remained. That same year Goth warriors sacked Rome itself, though they avoided wrecking churches because many of the invaders had converted to Christianity. In 429, Vandals and Alans crossed the Strait of Gibraltar into North Africa. The Christian writer Possidius described this event, perhaps with only a little overstatement: "And everywhere through the regions of Mauretania

Skill of the Ostrogoths. Germanic artisans demonstrated extraordinary skill working in gold, enamel, and gemstones. This brooch comes from the Ostrogothic kingdom of Italy. The image of the eagle suggests Roman inspiration.

the last coemperor in Italy, and packed him off to a country estate. Thus, western Rome came rather quietly to an end.

The Mediterranean Fractured

In the next several decades, the western empire fragmented into a number of regional states ruled by kings identified with one Germanic group or another. This particular political division, however, lasted only a few decades because in the sixth century the Roman emperor Justinian (r. 527–565) went on the offensive. The rulers in Constantinople insisted that the loss of the west was temporary, though the eastern empire took on the new name of Byzantium, or the Byzantine empire. Justinian formed a particularly potent partnership with his queen, the strong-minded Theodora, to rule the Roman state with great energy. Together they supervised a new codification of Roman law, the Body of Civil Law (*Corpus Juris Civilis*), which profoundly influenced legal theory and practice in Europe in later centuries. They built lavishly in Constantinople, including the Hagia Sophia (HAH-ya SOH-fee-uh), the city's magnificent Christian cathedral. They made temporary peace with Sasanid Persia and in 533 evicted the Vandal regime from North Africa. In the next few years, Byzantine forces occupied Sicily, seized a large part of Italy from the Ostrogoths, and refortified western Mediterranean coastal points as far west as the Strait of Gibraltar. Byzantine rulers continued to hold on to some of these territories until the eleventh century.

A great depression. Roman reconquests, however, did little for the economies of those lands that Germanic and Hun campaigns had ravaged. Archaeological work has documented the spiraling decline of agrarian production in the western Roman territories. Rural settlements disappeared over wide areas; wood and thatch replaced stone, brick, and roof tiles as building materials, even for the rich; the quality and trade of pottery declined; and the use of money, including copper coins, fell dramatically. A general if gradual process of **deurbanization** took place, as public buildings, including temples, churches, baths, theaters, and elaborate sewer systems fell to pieces. Excavations at the Roman city of Luna on Italy's northwestern coast record that from the fifth-century grand villas were abandoned to ruin, paved roads sank beneath the soil, the major aqueduct dried up, and in time the whole city disappeared. This precipitous drop in material consumption and comfort did not

> **deurbanization** A social process in which cities in a particular region decline or disappear.

The Empress Theodora. Justinian's queen holds out a symbolic offering to Christ in this mosaic from the sixth-century church of San Vitale in Ravenna, the Byzantine provincial capital on the Adriatic coast of Italy. The mosaic largely rejects the naturalistic portrayal of figures and objects characteristic of earlier Roman art. What evidence of that rejection do you see in this picture?

take place everywhere in the west at the same time. Roughly speaking, it started in the northern European provinces, including Britain, and then advanced gradually south.

Volcanic dust and pandemic disease.

In the sixth century a set of natural calamities jolted the wider Mediterranean region. Evidence from sulfate layers in Greenland and Antarctic ice cores, tree rings measurements, and statements by ancient writers indicate that a massive volcanic eruption in 535, probably somewhere near the equator, spewed out sufficient material to cause a world-encircling "dust veil." This layer was probably thick enough to obscure the sun's rays, resulting in a decade of climatic cooling, especially in the northern hemisphere. The sixth-century Byzantine historian Procopius wrote: "The sun gave forth its light without brightness, . . . and it seemed exceedingly like the sun in eclipse, for the beams it shed were not clear nor such as it is accustomed to shed."[11] If this phenomenon lasted more than a year, it could have had serious effects on food production and therefore population levels. Tree-ring and textual evidence also suggest widespread drought in northern China, Inner Eurasia, and northern Europe in the late 530s.

pandemic An infectious disease that moves quickly from one region to another, affecting large numbers of people.

Second, the plague **pandemic** we described in this chapter's introduction struck the Mediterranean in 541. By strict definition, plague refers to a particular ailment having a range of symptoms associated with a type of bacterium, called *Yersinia pestis*, or simply *Y. pestis*. This pathogen, as it is known in modern times, causes bubonic plague, named for the buboes, or dark swellings that typically appear on the victim's body. The principal carriers of this bacterium are fleas that inhabit the fur and feed off the blood of ground-burrowing rodents, including prairie dogs, squirrels, and rats. In certain environmental conditions, *Y. pestis* may accumulate in these animals. When an infected rodent dies, its fleas look for another host. If humans are at hand, bugs may jump to them to get blood meals, transmitting the infection. If the plague entered the Mediterranean from Egypt, which some evidence suggests, human contact with the pathogen may have first occurred far up the Nile River, perhaps in Ethiopia, where plague among rodent populations has been historically endemic.

From Egyptian cities, vessels that sailed relatively short distances from one Mediterranean port to another could easily have transported infected people, along with stowaway rats and fleas, around the rim of the sea in no more than a few years, causing a major pandemic. Plague struck Constantinople in 543 and killed perhaps a third of its population. Then Justinian's troops may have carried it to the western Mediterranean. The disease appears to have reached as far into Europe as Ireland. To the east, it easily crossed the military frontier between Byzantium and Sasanid Mesopotamia, where up to half the population died within a few years.[12] The first epidemic shock wave was

likely the worst, but recurrences every several years continued to take lives in one region or another for another two centuries.

In regions where many people died of plague, labor shortages inevitably caused state revenues to shrink, prices to rise, and the economy generally to weaken. But if a region was prosperous when the plague arrived, which was probably the case in many of the Byzantine and Sasanid provinces, recovery may not have taken long. In the western Mediterranean and Europe, however, the pandemic likely sped up the long-term deterioration that had already set in.

More tempests from the steppes.

Besides plague, the Byzantine and Sasanid empires faced new threats from Inner Eurasia. In the mid-fifth century, a pastoral group probably related in origin to the Huns seized Central Asia's major silk road towns and proclaimed a new dynasty known as the White Huns (or Hephthalites). This ruling group formed a loosely organized empire, and during the following century, White Hun archers invaded northern India. They also repeatedly attacked Persian territory, creating enough trouble to convince Sasanid emperors to pay them off in gold. In the 560s, Khosrow I (r. 531–579), one of the most energetic Sasanid monarchs, allied with other Central Asian nomads to defeat the White Huns, finally ending their depredations.

About the same time that the Sasanids defeated that enemy, the Byzantine emperors faced a dual invasion of Slavs and Avars. Perhaps originating near the Baltic Sea, Slavic migrants (the linguistic ancestors of Russians, Poles, Czechs, Serbians, and other European peoples) advanced south across Europe to the Danube in the sixth century. By contrast, the Avars were Inner Eurasian nomads, probably a motley horde speaking Mongolian, Turkic, and Iranian tongues. Moving west of the Black Sea, Avar bands attacked and subjugated Slavs, pushing some fleeing groups into Byzantine territory. Avar kings founded a state on Attila's old territory, alternately assaulting Byzantine land and collecting large tribute payments in gold. In 626, Avars attacked Constantinople, but when that operation failed, their empire faded quickly.

A New Empire in South Asia

Since the second century B.C.E., when the Maurya empire fell, small regional monarchies shared South Asia. The political map, however, changed dramatically in the early fourth century, when Chandra Gupta I (r. 320–330) founded a powerful new kingdom in the Ganges River valley. Chandra Gupta's son and grandson, Samudra Gupta (r. 330–375) and Chandra Gupta II (r. 375–415), mounted military campaigns that brought most of the northern two-thirds of South Asia under Gupta overlordship (see Map 9.3).

Taking the title Great King of Kings, the Gupta monarchs established firm control over a core territory in the rice-producing middle Ganges. In more distant lands they conquered, they allowed regional kings and aristocratic elites

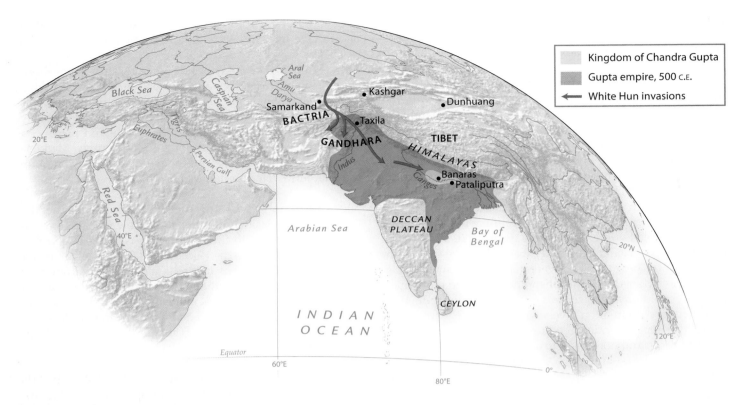

MAP 9.3 South Asia in the Gupta era, 320–550 C.E.
What geographic features may have influenced the expansion and the boundaries of the Gupta empire?

to retain their authority, as long as they paid regular tribute to Pataliputra, the Gupta capital. The emperors kept a close eye on towns and occupational guilds but mostly let them manage their own affairs. In their religious practice, the Gupta monarchs identified with the rituals of the brahmin priests and with a variety of devotions that modern scholars associate with the emerging Hindu tradition.

Textiles and sugar. Fa Xian, a Chinese Buddhist who traveled to South Asia in the fourth century in search of sacred texts, declared that the inhabitants of the towns and cities of the Ganges valley "are rich and prosperous." This characterization probably accurately describes the South Asian economy in that period. Gupta emperors regularly made large grants of land to brahmins, instructing them to organize peasants to work in the fields surrounding temples and monasteries. Spinners and weavers in homes and workshops supplied cotton, silk, linen, and woolen textiles to a large and growing South Asian market. Indeed, India emerged during this era as the single most important supplier of cotton goods to other parts of Afroeurasia.

Indian artisans also figured out how to press out and boil down the juice of sugar cane, a plant introduced from Southeast Asia, to produce crystallized sugar. South Asians were probably the first people in the world to consume sugary foods in quantity. Because this commodity was easy to

store and transport, it quickly commanded markets abroad. Indian merchants traveled the overland roads to Persia and Central Asia, as well as the shipping lanes across the Bay of Bengal to Southeast Asia. Other Indian exports included cotton and silk cloths, pepper and other spices, pearls, indigo, and perfumes. The collapse of the western Roman empire may have cut the Mediterranean market for South Asian luxuries for several centuries, but this had no severe effect, as far as we know, on India's booming commercial ports.

Gupta science and math. Both Buddhist monks and Hindu brahmins founded advanced academic schools linked to monasteries and temples. The Indic language Sanskrit was the principal medium of learning, and scholarly subjects included grammar, logic, composition, poetry, medicine, astronomy, and mathematics, in addition to deep study of religious texts. The brahmin scholar Aryabhata (476–560) accurately calculated *pi* as 3.1416 and the length of the solar year at 365.358 days. He also reasoned correctly that the earth is a sphere rotating on its axis while circling the sun. As described in Chapter 8, Maya thinkers in Mesoamerica in the late centuries B.C.E. invented a positional notation, or place-value system to express numbers, as well as a symbol to represent "zero." Although ancient Mesopotamians had come up with these ideas even earlier, they did not endure in Afroeurasia. Gupta scholars, however, came

Buddhist painting. The artistic achievements of the Gupta period are exemplified in this fresco from the Buddhist monastic caves at Ajanta in central India. Rendered with more naturalism than the Byzantine Christian art of the same era (page 260), this scene portrays a prince piously distributing alms to the poor.

up with a base-10 system for positioning numbers relative to one another, as in 777 meaning 700 + 70 + 7. That system permitted any numerical calculation using just ten signs. Like Maya scholars, Indian sages also elaborated the idea that zero, which they first signified as a dot, worked not only as a filler for an absent value, as in the sequence 707 (700 + nothing + 7), but as a number having the mathematical value of nil. The seventh-century scholar Brahmagupta published a work in 628 C.E. that instructed: "A debt minus zero is a debt; a fortune minus zero is a fortune; zero minus zero is zero."[13] After the seventh century, the Indian numerical system spread both west and east and became the foundation of modern mathematics.

South Asian society. The social system founded on four fundamental varnas, or social castes, distinguished from one another by their relative position on a scale of ritual purity (see Chapter 6), became fully rooted in South Asia in the Gupta era. Sub-castes, or *jatis,* defined by kinship, custom, place, and occupation, also proliferated. Starting in the third century B.C.E., brahmin scholars wrote numerous texts that set forth in exquisite detail the ritual duties and social

obligations of particular castes, as well as the proper behavior of members of different castes toward one another. These codes (*dharma-shastras*) underlay social relations in South Asia until the twentieth century. In the Gupta period the system was fluid enough that some groups, for example, merchants and scribes, managed to pull themselves up the caste ladder, though other groups, such as indigenous forest dwellers, tumbled down. On the whole, women gradually lost social status. The brahmins who set the rules of social rank and behavior, however, had ambivalent views regarding women, urging in some texts that husbands honor their wives and make them happy.

South Asian literature and art generally idealized women as elegant, beautiful, and virtuous. The third-century B.C.E. scholar Manu, on the other hand, declared that "in childhood a female must be subject to her father, in youth to her husband, and when her lord is dead to her sons; a woman must never be independent."[14] Only high caste women had access to any formal education, women had restricted rights to property and inheritance, and families commonly arranged the marriage of girls at very early ages. Some Buddhist women achieved a measure of autonomy by joining monasteries. Simply put, South Asian women occupied all caste ranks but within each one constituted a socially and economically subordinate group.

Gupta decline. In the second half of the fifth century, Gupta territories in northwestern India came under persistent attack from the same White Huns that attacked Sasanid Persia. These raiders never overran the Gupta heartland the way Germanic tribes swarmed across Europe, but they disrupted the Gupta economy and gradually exhausted its defense forces. The Gupta state did not collapse so much as shrink down under the growing burden of rising military costs, rebellious tributary kings, and court intrigues. By the time the Sasanids routed the White Huns in the mid-sixth century, the Gupta empire was already gone. But the framework of Hindu social relations endured.

Religions for Troubled Times

> **FOCUS** What features of Buddhism, Christianity, and Manichaeism made those religions appealing to large numbers of people?

By the third century C.E., Buddhism and Christianity were both attracting millions of people across multiple frontiers of culture, social class, and political rule. Manichaeism (man-ih-KEE-ism), which first appeared in that century, also gained in appeal across its original borders for several centuries. In Chapter 7 we argued that, by the first millennium B.C.E., human interrelations across Afroeurasia reached a level of complexity that demanded new ideas and institutions through which people might bond together and cooperate in greater numbers and over longer distances. Buddhism, Christianity, and Manichaeism served that purpose.

The fundamental characteristic of these universalist religions is that they invited men and women, as human beings rather than as members of particular ethnolinguistic groups, tribes, cities, or kingdoms, to join together in shared morality, devotion, and trust. Moreover, the faithful were encouraged to spread the teachings and bring new followers into the fold. These religions shared several other characteristics as well. All three originated in the public teachings of a single individual—the Buddha, Jesus, Mani—who preached human subordination to divine, transcendent power and devotion to principles of moral behavior, selflessness, and social cooperation. These religions were also salvationist: They assured righteous believers of eventual freedom from care and suffering, whether through release into nonbeing or elevation into heaven. All of them accommodated special individuals, that is, saints in various manifestations, who possessed powers to mediate between believers and transcendent power and to help them along a path to well-being and salvation. All of them offered guiding scriptures, not only core texts, but eventually vast libraries of moral and spiritual writings. Finally, they all addressed both the individual's quest for self-realization through meditation, prayer, study, or self-denial, and the community's need for moral and ethical rules by which people might work together in society, find common meaning in daily events and rituals, and take responsibility for one another's welfare.

As they grew, universalist religions embraced people of differing language, culture, and social status (see Map 9.4). And as distances of time and space widened between communities of believers professing a single tradition, particular beliefs and practices diverged and multiplied. Consequently, each religion also bloomed with distinctive, sometimes conflicting doctrines, devotions, institutions, schools, sects, and denominations.

The Buddhist Web

Starting in the first century C.E., merchants and monks carried the Buddha's moral and salvationist message across Inner Eurasia to China and by sea to Southeast Asia. Missionaries also ventured west into Persia and Syria. The staging area for the Buddhist penetration of Inner Eurasia was the Kushana empire of northern India. In that setting the Mahayana school of Buddhism, called the Greater Vehicle because it held out the promise of salvation to all, differentiated itself from Theravada Buddhism, or the Lesser Vehicle (Hinayana), which esteemed full-time devotion to monastic life. Theravadists believed that to attain nirvana, or escape from the cycle of suffering and reincarnation, meant gaining freedom from all consciousness. Individuals must strive on their own to reach that ultimate release. By contrast, Mahayana thinkers taught that nirvana is a state of total awareness and that people who led ordinary lives might achieve salvation with the assistance of *bodhisattvas*, saintly individuals who stopped short of nirvana to go back and help others along the path. Mahayana teaching also elevated the Buddha from the status of a moral teacher to a god and savior. In that tradition, deified buddhas existed in many different manifestations to encourage and assist the spiritual journeyer. Men and women who lived "in the world" but gave silver, gold, silk, or other gifts to monasteries in dedication to a *bodhisattva* or Buddha might expect to receive spiritual blessings that sped their way to salvation. Consequently, monasteries attracted wealth, and they often contributed to local production and trade.

The Mahayana way transformed Buddhism from a South Asian moral system for the hardiest seekers into a universalist religion available to anyone receptive to its message. It therefore traveled well. Kushana merchants trekked to China to buy silk, and Buddhists among them settled in Luoyang and other Han cities starting in the first century C.E. Monks also came along to found urban monasteries. Initially, Han courtiers and bureaucrats showed little interest in this new religion. Their Confucian values centered on harmonious social and political relations in this life, not on other-worldly desires and monastic privacy. However, the downfall of both

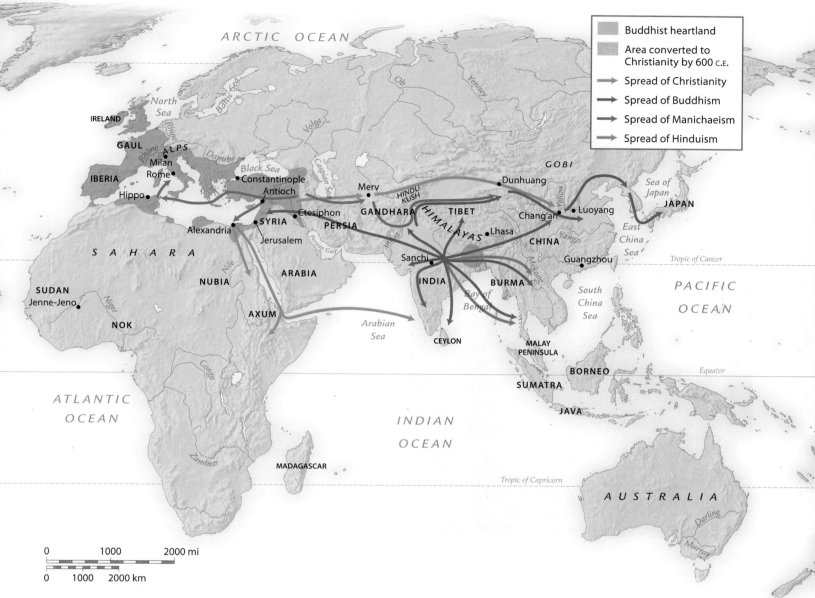

MAP 9.4 Religious diffusion, 200–600 C.E.
Looking at the arrows on the map, in what regions do you think adherents of Buddhism, Christianity, and Manichaeism might all have been found about 600 C.E.?

Legend:
- Buddhist heartland
- Area converted to Christianity by 600 C.E.
- → Spread of Christianity
- → Spread of Buddhism
- → Spread of Manichaeism
- → Spread of Hinduism

the Kushana and the Han empires in the early third century presented nothing but opportunity to Buddhist missionaries offering individual salvation.

Buddhists on the road to China. In China millions more people became receptive to Buddhism during the long Age of Division. Confucian ideals of wise civil government dimmed somewhat as regional states battled one another, refugees took to the road, and peasants lost their land. For poor rural folk, uprooted city artisans, and slaves, the new religion showed the way out of suffering. Imitating the Buddha's spontaneous compassion, monasteries offered food, shelter, and medical care. Even Confucian aristocrats,

many of whom lost their estates or fled south to the Yangzi valley, took up Buddhist studies to find solace and peace. In northwestern China and out on the steppes, many pastoral nomadic chiefs welcomed Buddhist monks, scribes, and merchants and benefited from the spiritual guidance, literacy, and craft skills these newcomers brought from the west. The ex-nomad leaders who founded the Northern Wei kingdom in northwestern China in the fifth century declared themselves to be incarnations of the Buddha and handsomely patronized monasteries that supported this claim. Monarchs of other regional states also identified with Buddhism and patronized monasteries and stupas (structures housing relics of the Buddha). By the early sixth

A Buddhist pagoda. Dating to the early sixth century c.e., this temple located east of Luoyang is the oldest known Buddhist structure in China. There, builders transformed the dome-shaped South Asian stupa into a multilevel tower. This basic form inspired religious architecture across East and Southeast Asia and in fact influenced Hindu temple construction back in India. Why do you think this architectural form had such wide appeal?

century, Luoyang, the Northern Wei capital, had more than a thousand monasteries.

Buddhists and brahmins in Southeast Asia. About the same time that Buddhists traveling on the silk roads reached China, others crossed the Bay of Bengal on the monsoon winds to introduce their faith in Southeast Asia. Buddhist traders and monks probably first established themselves in Funan, a kingdom, or group of small kingdoms, centered on the Mekong River delta in southern Cambodia and Vietnam (see Chapter 7).

Buddhist travelers discovered in Funan and other Southeast Asian states that local populations expected their rulers to demonstrate the rightfulness of their authority less through family descent or force of arms than by displays of both moral leadership and protective supernatural powers. Mahayana Buddhists therefore found ready listeners among aspiring monarchs, offering people stories of the great Buddhist emperor Ashoka (see Chapter 6) as a model of moral virtue and showing how *Bodhisattvas* and buddhas could assist individual progress toward enlightenment. In the first millennium c.e., Buddhist communities multiplied along the Malay Peninsula and on Sumatra and other Indonesian islands, though at first appealing more to princely courts and town dwellers than to rural people. In the seventh century, a Chinese monk named Yijing stopped off in Sumatra after traveling in India. He later wrote:

Many kings and chieftains in the islands of the Southern Ocean admire and believe (Buddhism), and their hearts are set on accumulating good actions. In the fortified city of Bhoga Buddhist priests number more than 1,000 whose minds are bent on learning and good practices. . . . If a Chinese priest [monk] wishes to go to the West in order to hear (lectures) and read (the original), he had better stay here one or two years and practice the proper rules and then proceed to Central India.[15]

Hindu brahmins engaged in trade also traveled from South to Southeast Asia. Many of these high-caste individuals practiced *bhakti,* a devotional faith in the Hindu tradition that, like Buddhism, offered not dry and exhausting ritual sacrifices but intense experience of godly power and love. Originating in southern India, *bhakti* encouraged veneration of the deities Vishnu and Shiva. Southeast Asian elites welcomed *bhakti*'s transcendent worship as well as the possibility that through passionate devotion a ruler might achieve the spiritual rank of *cakravartin,* a king of cosmic moral authority. Buddhist and Hindu ideas and devotions spread through Southeast Asia together, and many new believers did not much care whether they distinguished between them. Historians of religion sometimes refer to the development of a Hindu-Buddhist tradition in that region. For example, temples, stupas, and monasteries that rulers sponsored often blended together symbols and images from both traditions.

One of the historical ironies of the later first millennium c.e. is that as universalist Buddhism continued to spread east of India, it faded gradually as a popular faith in the land of its birth. This happened mainly from the sixth century, when the *bhakti* movement offered spiritual seekers enlightenment through devotion to Vishnu, Shiva, and other gods long worshiped in South Asia. In fact the Hindu tradition absorbed various aspects of Buddhism. For example, by the ninth century the Hindu monastery emerged as a variation on the older Buddhist institution. Numerous Theravada Buddhist monasteries remained in South Asia, though popular Mahayana worship waned, excepting notably on Ceylon.

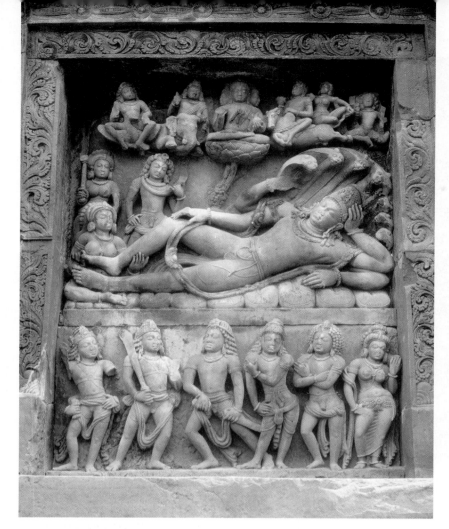

An image of Vishnu. This stone relief decorates a celebrated Gupta temple in the village of Deogarh in central India. The temple is dedicated to the god Vishnu, who in this image reclines gracefully on the serpent deity Ananta Shesha.

The Christian Web

Not long after Jesus preached in Palestine, Christians carried their gospels—the "good news" of his ministry, death, and resurrection—in all directions. As Christian communities sprang up in new social and cultural environments, doctrines, worship, and communal organization took on different hues, just as occurred in Buddhism. Both Buddhists and Christians believed it was critical to their faith to understand the essential nature of their founding teacher. Was he human, was he divine, or was he both? As these religions spread, leading thinkers disagreed over the answers to these questions. In the first four centuries of the Christian era, theologians argued about numerous points of doctrine but especially about the question of who Jesus really was.

Starting in the reign of Constantine, Christian patriarchs and bishops gathered periodically in councils to try to hammer out consensus on this and other questions. Several major schools of thought contended for acceptance. The Byzantine empire officially endorsed the idea of Jesus as God the Son in an equal and indivisible Holy Trinity with God the Father and God the Holy Spirit. A second school, called Arianism, asserted that God created Jesus as a divine being but remained spiritually superior to him. A third school, called Nestorianism after the patriarch Nestorius (386–451 c.e.), declared that Jesus had two distinct natures, one human and one divine, arguing that elemental unity between Jesus the man (who suffered, died, and was resurrected) and God (who could not have had such an experience) was not possible. At the polar opposite of Nestorianism was the Monophysite or Coptic doctrine, which affirmed that Jesus's human nature was fully absorbed into God and therefore disappeared. Finally, Christians known as Gnostics had a mystical view, contending that Jesus possessed a Divine Spark that gave him the power to unite with God, the Divine Spirit. As savior, Jesus showed that all humans have the possibility through spiritual knowledge of an "inner resurrection" and unity with God.

When the Emperor Theodosius made Christianity the official imperial religion, church leaders had the police power of the Byzantine government behind them to successfully outlaw doctrines they regarded as incorrect. Furthermore, they could excommunicate, imprison, or execute individuals charged with **heresy**. In the fourth and fifth centuries, Roman bishops ruled that the Arian, Nestorian, Monophysite, and Gnostic variants were all heretical. But beyond the borders of Byzantine authority, these proclamations could not be enforced.

> **heresy** In Christianity, beliefs or practices that contradict the church's official doctrine.

Working together, state and church also outlawed traditional Roman practices, such as ritual animal sacrifice. Christian communities were permitted to close down pagan temples and destroy statues of the old deities, now regarded as vile demons. Roman polytheism slowly faded out, first in the towns, more slowly in the countryside. Theodosius also abolished legal protections for Jews and refused to punish violent attacks on synagogues.

Monastic Christianity. Some scholars have argued that Buddhist monks who found their way to Persia and Syria inspired the growth of a monastic movement in Christianity. Not only Buddhism and Christianity but the Jewish, Hindu, and, later, Islamic traditions all accommodated men and women who believed that full spiritual devotion requires "leaving the world" to join a secluded spiritual

The sixth-century monastery of Saint Moses the Abyssinian in the desert north of Damascus, Syria. According to legend, Saint Moses was the son of a ruler of Abyssinia (Ethiopia) who renounced wealth and power for the life of a Christian hermit. Why do you think Christians built monasteries in such harsh environments?

community, wander the highways, or take up solitary residence in a forest or desert cave. Those believers adopted

> **asceticism** The principle and practice of renouncing material comforts and pleasures in pursuit of an elevated moral or spiritual state.

asceticism, that is, they renounced the needs of the flesh to one extreme or another and spent their time meditating, praying, begging, worshiping with others, doing useful work, or performing charitable acts. They believed this way of life advanced them toward spiritual enlightenment or eternal life.

Many early Christian ascetics became spiritual hermits in the Egyptian desert. St. Pachomius (d. 346 C.E.) started the first communal home for monks, founding eleven monasteries housing seven thousand monks and nuns who took vows of poverty. Syria was another center of ascetic practice. St. Simeon (d. 459) took bodily renunciation to new heights, as the story goes, by ascending a pillar and refusing to budge from this perch for forty years. Most Christian ascetics renounced material pleasures, and St. Augustine (354–430), the celebrated North African theologian, counseled that if

believers felt compelled to marry, they should try to remain virgins nonetheless. Some male Christian writers claimed that men had a hard time resisting physical temptations because women, having insatiable sexual appetites, would not leave them alone. In this climate Christian theology incorporated the idea that Eve was responsible for Adam's expulsion from the Garden of Eden. Mary, the virgin mother of Jesus, became the model of female virtue.

As in Buddhism, Christian monasteries not only served the needy but also helped advance literacy and learning. In remote rural regions, monks improved farm productivity by clearing land and experimenting with new food crops. The ascetic life did not attract the majority of believers, who preferred to practice their religion while living "in the world." These "lay Christians," however, also needed **clergy** to perform essential rituals in community churches and

> **clergy** In Christianity, people ordained for religious vocations, as distinguished from ordinary worshipers.

look after the moral and physical needs of the members. In the Byzantine church, therefore, the *secular clergy* resided

St. Augustine of Hippo: Christian Theologian

Born to a pagan father and Christian mother in the North African town of Thagaste in present-day Algeria, Augustine of Hippo (354–430 C.E.) grew up in a family that had Berber ancestry but was culturally Romanized. Patrick, Augustine's father, sat on Thagaste's town council, but the family was not wealthy, owning only a few acres of land. Nevertheless, Patrick and his wife Monica wanted to see their clever son educated. They sent him to local schools, and when he was seventeen years old, they secured the patronage of a wealthy landowner to finance his continuing studies in Carthage. There, Augustine became intimate with a servant woman. By law he could not marry her, but the two had a son. Though his mother hoped he would become a Christian, Augustine instead devoted himself to Manichaeism, the religion founded in the previous century that blended Christian beliefs with elements of Zoroastrianism and Buddhism.

After completing his schooling, Augustine became a teacher of rhetoric, first in Carthage and then in Rome. By that time his interest in Manichaeism had cooled, and he turned to Skepticism, a philosophical movement founded on new readings of the ancient Greek texts of Plato. Though Augustine might have been in a state of spiritual flux, his scholarly career continued to advance. When he was thirty, he won the most prominent academic position in the Latin world, the professorship of rhetoric at the Roman imperial court in Milan.

While he lived in that city, however, Augustine began to explore Christian teachings by attending the stirring lectures of Ambrose, the Bishop of Milan. Augustine continued to struggle for a clear spiritual path, when one day he heard a "childlike voice" instructing him, "Take up and read, take up and read." Opening a Bible, his eyes fell on a passage in one of St. Paul's letters that offered him a solution to his spiritual quandary: "Not in revelings and drunkenness, not in sexual indulgence and indecencies, not in contention and rivalry; but put on the Lord Jesus Christ and make no provision for the flesh in lusts."

Shortly after that, Ambrose baptized Augustine. Leaving his professorship in 387, he returned to Thagaste. There, he founded a monastery and gathered together a small community of monks. He wished to lead a life of quiet contemplation and religious writing, but this was not to be. In 391 he traveled to the North African port city of Hippo Regius, where the Christian community persuaded him to join the priesthood. Within five years, he became Bishop of Hippo, an office he held for thirty-four years. Just as Vandal invaders sacked Hippo in 430, he died of an illness, leaving behind a corpus of writings that would inspire Christian thinkers for centuries.

In his numerous letters, sermons, and theological treatises, Augustine emphasized a philosophy of inclusion and sincerity, judging actions more important than words as evidence of Christian faith and virtue. He strove to eliminate pagan elements that had seeped into North African Christianity, but he also welcomed pagan converts. His classic writings include his *Confessions,* which recounted the hedonism of his youth and his conversion to Christianity. In *The City of God,* his monumental work, he explored the relationship between the secular state and the Christian church. In a key doctrine, he declared that all humans are tainted by the original sin of Adam and Eve. Therefore, eternal salvation depends not on individual effort but on God's gift of grace.

A seventh-century fresco of St. Augustine from the Lateran Palace in Rome.

Thinking Critically

In what ways might political and economic conditions in the Mediterranean world in the late fourth and early fifth centuries have affected the course of St. Augustine's life?

among the mass of worshipers, whereas the *regular clergy* lived the monastic life, following a "rule," or special code of conduct for monks and nuns.

Christians beyond the Mediterranean. By the fifth century C.E. the Roman church was well established all around the Mediterranean. In the tumult that attended the collapse of the western empire, bishops and their priests often stepped in to provide local authority and services to the needy. Some Germanic groups had converted to Arian Christianity, partly because they first received Christian teaching from Arian missionaries and partly because they liked the idea of accepting the new faith without having to identify fully with the religion of imperial Rome. As

Christianity in the far north. An early Christian cross characteristic of Celtic society, notably in Ireland.

In the fourth and fifth centuries, Nestorian Christians founded communities in the Sasanid empire, facing persecution if they remained in Roman territory. One distinguishing feature of the Nestorian church was its use of Syriac rather than Greek as the language of its **liturgy,** or formal church worship. Syriac, a written language from the first century C.E., was a dialect of Aramaic, the Semitic language Jesus almost certainly spoke. Operating principally from the city of Ctesiphon on the Tigris, the Nestorian church placed bishops in cities across Persia, and its monasteries multiplied. By the early fifth century, Merv, a major city in northeastern Persia and a gateway to the silk roads, had a Christian community. From Merv, Nestorian monks and merchants traveled to Central Asia and the oasis towns beyond, building their monasteries alongside Buddhist ones. The first Christians reached China early in the seventh century, and the Nestorian church continued to attract congregations in both Inner Eurasia and China for another eight hundred years.

> **liturgy** The established forms of public worship, especially the order of services, including rituals, prayers, readings, and hymns.

According to the Acts of Thomas, a gospel associated with the Gnostic tradition but not included in the Bible of the Roman church, Jesus's apostle Thomas introduced Christianity to South Asia. By the mid-fourth century, communities existed in towns along India's western coast. Cosmas, a fifth-century Egyptian geographer, reports that there were Gnostic churches not only in India but also on Ceylon, including at least one bishop.[16] South Asia had a way of welcoming and then absorbing foreign immigrants and their beliefs into both devotional religion and the Indian social system. Consequently, the Christian community did not grow much, but it maintained its distinct identity as a particular caste within which its families intermarried. Christians subscribed to Indian dietary laws and other customs and represented Jesus Christ as an object of devotional faith parallel to Vishnu and Shiva.

Probably well before the gospels reached western Europe, caravans and ships transported Christian merchants and missionaries along the busy trade corridors of both the Nile River and the Red Sea. In the fifth and sixth centuries, Christians traveled up the Nile to Nubia, the region that corresponds roughly to the modern Republic of the Sudan. By that time the great Nubian kingdom of Kush had disintegrated (see Chapter 7), but rulers of smaller successor states, and eventually most of their populations, converted to either Monophysite (Coptic) or Orthodox Christianity, replacing older polytheistic religions. Archaeological digs in Nubia have uncovered numerous churches, monasteries, and works of Christian art dating to the fifth century and later.

Monophysite Christianity also took root in Axum, the African kingdom and commercial crossroads located in what are today Eritrea and northern Ethiopia (see Chapter 7). Around 350, Ezana, the Axumite king, became a Christian.

the dust of migration and war settled, however, Germanic kings seeking legitimacy transferred their allegiance to the Roman church. Arianism gradually died away.

In the fifth and sixth centuries, monks carried Christianity throughout northwestern Europe and into Britain and Ireland. Missionaries often condemned and destroyed polytheistic beliefs and images, but some found ways to Christianize indigenous religious culture. Locally worshiped gods and goddesses might, for example, be transformed in time into saints. In Celtic Ireland an annual festival to celebrate the goddess Brigid became an occasion to venerate the pious Christian St. Brigit. The sacred rocks, groves, and ponds where spirits dwelled sometimes became Christian holy sites.

Christian communities arose in Mesopotamia and Persia no later than they did in Europe. The kingdom of Armenia in far eastern Anatolia appears to have been the world's first state to adopt Christianity as its official church, about eighty years before Byzantium did. The earliest followers of Jesus to reach the Tigris-Euphrates valley were likely Jewish-Christians, that is, believers who wished to continue to live according to Jewish law. These newcomers made easy contact with the large Jewish communities already established there.

One ancient writer associates this act with Aedesius and Fromentius, two Christian boys who got stranded in a Red Sea port. The queen of Axum recruited these boys, especially the quick-witted Fromentius, to help her govern. He not only did that but also aided Christian merchants in Axum by "providing them with whatever was needed, supplying sites for buildings and other necessaries, and in every way promoting the growth of the seed of Christianity in the country."[17] Missionaries in Axum and eventually a bishop answered to the patriarch of the Monophysite Coptic church in Egypt. Christian scholars translated the Bible from Greek into Ge'ez, a Semitic language that became the medium of the Ethiopian church liturgy. Jewish communities already established in Axum may have also had considerable influence on Ethiopian Christianity. The church emphasized the narratives of the Hebrew Bible (Old Testament), the holiness of the biblical Ark of the Covenant, and the descent of the Axumite royal family from Solomon, the ancient Israelite king.

Manichaeans on the silk road. These Manichaean priests are writing at their desks. The image is from a book dating to the eighth or ninth centuries found at Gaochang, a town on the silk road that skirts the northern edge of the Tarim Basin. What other religions do you think residents of Gaochang practiced in that period?

The Manichean Way

Manichaeism emerged as a third universalist religion in the third century, though after about 1000 C.E., it no longer endured except as scattered sects and communities. Mani (216–272 C.E.), the prophet and founder of this movement, grew up in the Tigris-Euphrates valley. His father may have been a member of a Jewish-Christian sect, and Mani probably came in contact with other faiths as well. He also lived for a time in the Kushana empire, where he may have learned something of both Buddhist and Hindu tradition. The Zoroastrian principle of eternal struggle between the forces of Light and Darkness had already influenced the dualist tendency in Christianity—the struggle of God versus Satan. Mani associated light and goodness with spirit, darkness and evil with matter. He conceived of a universe in which particles of light are ensnared in matter but continually struggle to escape. He also taught that believers devoted to the light should live a rigorously ascetic life, including celibacy. Mani revered Zoroaster, the Buddha, and especially Jesus as prophets but declared himself to be the last and greatest bearer of truth to humankind. If the basis of Mani's teaching was, as some scholars believe, fundamentally Christian, this Christianity incorporated elements of several traditions, including monasticism, vegetarianism, veneration of images, and belief in reincarnation.

At the urging of Zoroastrian priests, the Sasanid regime put Mani in prison, where he died. In the following century, however, his followers carried his message west into the Roman empire and northeast into Central Asia. Manichean communities became well established in many Roman cities about the same time that the western empire was beginning to crack. To the east, white-robed Manichean monks and nuns followed Buddhists and Nestorians along the silk roads. There, Manichean monasteries thrived and converts multiplied, especially among merchants. Manicheans reached China along with Nestorians in the seventh century, though Han Chinese tended to regard them as advocates of one more Buddhist sect. In the following three centuries, the religion attracted many followers among Turkic steppe peoples but after 1000 no longer competed well with the other universalist traditions.

Tropical Africa: Farmers, Towns, and Iron

FOCUS In what ways did interactions with peoples in other parts of Afroeurasia affect patterns of social, cultural, and economic change in tropical Africa?

Africa south of the Saharan Desert makes up nearly 30 percent of the land area of Afroeurasia, but at the start of the Common Era it had only about 5 percent of the supercontinent's population. The fundamental explanation is that farmers began to settle Africa's tropical latitudes in significant numbers only about four thousand years ago, later than dense agricultural populations developed in the irrigated river valleys of Afroeurasia. As farming spread through wet tropical forests and savannas from the second millennium B.C.E., the general pattern was *extensive* agriculture, meaning that when the population of farming or herding communities in an area reached a level that put excessive pressure on land, some groups would move off to open new land where not many people already lived. Consequently, population densities in many areas remained low, especially relative to places like the Nile or Tigris-Euphrates River valleys.

In the early centuries C.E., tropical Africa's population grew gradually as pioneer farmers moved into and through the rainforests of the equatorial zone and out onto the savannas of southern Africa. In some regions, however, more intensive farming and population growth reinforced each other, and this greater density encouraged larger settlements, more occupational specialties, and greater reliance on trade with neighbors.

In the Sudanic belt, the zone of semiarid land (Sahel) and savannas that runs west to east across Africa just south of the Sahara desert, farming and cattle-breeding populations showed signs of increasing social complexity in the first millennium B.C.E. Villages multiplied in the western Sudan, notably among peoples speaking languages in the Mande family. Some villagers specialized in particular crafts, for example, iron smelting, pot making, cotton weaving, or leather working. These artisans formed associations that came to have the characteristics of social castes. Members not only shared religious beliefs and secret rituals but also married exclusively into one another's families. Villages with different specialties grew up in clusters around large settlements where artisans could sell their wares to local farmers and herders or perhaps to merchants from other regions.

Archaeological research has revealed quite a bit about one of these commercial centers, the city of Jenne-Jeno (Old Jenne), a site in the modern Republic of Mali. The town was located in the Niger River's inland delta, a region where in the summer months the river fans out to form a broad alluvial plain of creeks and marshes. The delta teemed with fish, game, and fertile rice-growing land. Settlers founded Jenne-Jeno about 300 B.C.E., and its population may have reached about fifty thousand in the following seven hundred years. Its artisans produced copper ware, gold jewelry, and fine painted ceramics. Iron deposits lay not far from the city, but smelted copper had to be imported from mines in the Sahara about nine hundred miles away. The town became an entrepôt, or transit center, for a variety of metals and manufactures exchanged up and down the Niger or by donkeys to overland destinations. The city and its hinterland may have formed a small state, but we have no evidence of a central government or hierarchy of social classes. Historians have found material remains of comparable towns in Sudanic West Africa, a record showing that urbanization was well under way in this region in the early centuries C.E.

The Nok Culture

Large farming settlements also began to appear near the southern rim of the Sudanic belt, where wooded savannas met tropical forests. In south central Nigeria east of the Niger River, a site named after a village called Nok has yielded iron tools, slag heaps from iron smelting furnaces, fired clay bowls and utensils, and stone carvings of animals and humans. Most remarkable of all are the remains of terra-cotta (ceramic) sculptures of human heads that are life-sized or nearly so and whose features, including triangular-shaped eyes, are naturalistically defined. Historians have speculated that these images, with wooden or ceramic bodies attached, served in rituals linked to the fertility of the land. The material record at Nok, where iron production probably started well before 500 B.C.E., tells us little about the social or political organization of the society. Might the terra-cotta heads be representations of local kings? Or might they be deities? If we can speculate from knowledge of later centuries, Nok people believed in a supreme creator god who did not intervene much in human affairs and in ancestral spirits who communicated more intimately with their living descendants. In any case the sophistication of their art suggests that Nok society had economic resources rich enough to support the work of highly skilled artisans. We also know that the Nok style of sculpture spread widely in the region, indicating the rise of many other iron-working centers.

Change was also taking place rapidly in West Africa's wet forest zone. There, immigrant farmers from the north arrived with iron axes and hoes, but they also had to switch their whole economy from grains, which did not thrive in the wet tropics, to yams and other root crops that did. These cultivators gradually displaced or assimilated small-scale foraging and hunting communities that had lived in the forests for millennia.

The African East and South

In terms of climate and vegetation, the regions of eastern and southern Africa present a more complicated scene. Owing to a north–south belt of highlands on the eastern side of the continent, ecological zones do not form neat east–west bands as they do in West Africa. Grain farmers, forest crop cultivators, cattle herders, and hunter-gatherers therefore shared eastern and southern Africa in an extremely complex mosaic of distinct ecological regions. In the early centuries C.E. Indicopleustes Cosmas, both farmers and cattle herders who spoke a variety of languages, including numerous tongues in the Bantu language family, continued to drift generally southward. Farmers practiced shifting agriculture, working relatively thin tropical soils with both iron and stone tools until nutrients gave out, then moving on to new land. Wherever farm families settled for a time, homesteads, hamlets, or villages sprang up, settlements distinctive for their round, conical-roofed houses of wood and dried mud.

The Sculptures of Nok

In 1928, tin miners working in Nigeria's Jos Plateau region uncovered an unusual object. About four inches high and made of terra cotta, the spherical artifact appeared to be a head. Colonel John Dent-Young, the British co-owner of the mine, donated the find to a nearby museum, unaware that his workers had discovered the first material evidence of an ancient West African cultural tradition.

Fifteen years passed without any more objects surfacing. Then, in 1943, tin miners came across a second terra-cotta head, this one more than twice the size of the first. Bernard Fagg, an archaeologist working in the British colonial administration of Jos Province, began investigating both of these mysterious objects. As he talked with local farmers and miners, he realized that they had been collecting heads and other sculpture fragments for years. Since the first head had been found near the village of Nok, Fagg associated the sculptures with what he called the "Nok culture."

Since Fagg's day, thousands of pieces of Nok sculpture have been excavated on the Jos Plateau. Over half of the objects recovered are terra-cotta heads. Radiocarbon dating and other tests place the earliest sculptures at around 500 B.C.E. and the latest at about 200 C.E. Many of the pieces were sculpted out of blocks of clay, an unusual approach that suggests a wood-carving tradition might also have existed in the Nok culture.

Political conditions in Nigeria have prevented professional archaeologists from conducting systematic excavations in the Jos region. Instead, commercial excavators have taken the initiative to uncover or acquire Nok artifacts, lured by the prices that these pieces fetch from collectors of African art. Because of this trade, forgeries also abound, as does the practice of improperly restoring sculptures by combining many smaller fragments to form a full human figurine. From the pieces that scholars have studied, however, we can surmise that the skilled creators of Nok sculpture worked in an economically and politically complex society that had been developing for centuries. This suggests that similar societies and artistic traditions may yet be discovered in West Africa.

Thinking Critically

What features of the figures stand out to you? Do you see stylistic elements common to both figures? What purpose might these objects have played in Nok society? Formulate hypotheses about the social status or position of the people depicted in these sculptures and about the society in which they lived.

A terracotta head of a whiskered male, Nok Culture, 900 B.C.E.–200 C.E.

A terracotta head and torso of a female, Nok Culture, 500 B.C.E.

In the far south, iron-using, Bantu-speaking immigrants, first arriving sometime before 400 C.E., came in contact with both cattle-herding people known as Khoikhoi (COY-coy) and forager-hunters identified generally as San. These three groups all traded their specialized products with one another, and Khoikhoi animal-breeders taught Bantu farmers much about herding. Over many centuries, however, Bantu peoples came to vastly outnumber the earlier societies, so that Khoikhoi and San survived mainly in drier and more marginal regions, such as along the margins of Namibia's Kalahari Desert.

Southeast Asian Contributions to African Society

Sometime between the first and third centuries C.E., seaborne travelers arrived on the East African coast. Some of these immigrants, whose numbers might have been no more than a few hundred, probably married into existing coastal societies and eventually disappeared as a distinct ethnolinguistic group. Others, however, moved southward along the coast and in the third or fourth centuries crossed the Mozambique Channel to the big island of Madagascar. That land may have been completely uninhabited at the time, and so the newcomers retained the language and some elements of the culture they brought with them. Madagascar's colonizers spoke an early version of Malagasy, which remains the island's principal language today. Malagasy belongs to the Austronesian language family; its closest cousin is a tongue spoken on the island of Borneo in Indonesia.

Just how Austronesian mariners reached East Africa, more than four thousand miles across the Indian Ocean from places like Borneo, remains something of a mystery. We know, however, that Malay merchants and shippers originating in Indonesia and the Malay Peninsula took a large part in the ancient Bay of Bengal and Arabian Sea trade. Malay voyagers founded at least one commercial settlement on the coast of southern Arabia in the late first century B.C.E. Since traders from Axum and the Arabian Peninsula visited the tropical East African coast, Malay venturers may have gone along as well, and perhaps enticed others to follow.

Even though Austronesian speakers who resided on the East African coast disappeared from the historical record, they left a sizable economic footprint. Food plant genetics tell us that these sailors almost certainly introduced Asian yams, taro root, sugar cane, and particular varieties of bananas to Africa. These plants, which thrived in the equatorial climate of Southeast Asia, flourished similarly in equatorial Africa. Farmers there had depended heavily on native varieties of yams and perhaps plantains (a starchy food related to the banana). A highly nutritious staple (cooked in a variety of ways), bananas almost certainly contributed to the growth of agrarian population in the wet tropics. They reached the West African forest sometime before 1000 C.E.

• • •

Conclusion

On the very large scale of history, the long-term trend of rising population, greater social complexity, and expanding economic production and exchange across Afroeurasia leveled off somewhat between the second and seventh centuries. Scholars have estimated that after moving consistently upward for three thousand years, Afroeurasia's overall population dropped from about 245 million to 188 million between 200 and 700 C.E. before starting to climb again.[18] According to another estimate, the number of Afroeurasian cities with populations in the approximate range of 30,000 to 450,000 shrank from seventy-five to forty-seven between 100 and 500 C.E.[19] In western Europe and North Africa, many cities withered or disappeared altogether. Justinian's Plague and recurring epidemics may also have accounted for significant population losses in Europe, North Africa, and Southeast Asia in the sixth and seventh centuries.

Population loss, deurbanization, and economic contraction, however, occurred unevenly in those centuries. The most dramatic negative change almost certainly occurred in Europe and the Mediterranean in connection with Germanic and Hunnic depredations and the breakup of the western Roman empire. Northern China, which was heavily populated and urbanized in the Han era, also appears to have suffered severe depression in the aftermath of that empire's collapse. If silk road trade did not suffer chronic decline after 200, its routes were almost certainly disrupted periodically as power relations among Inner Eurasian pastoral groups became more agitated and unstable.

On the other hand, economic expansion characterized the eastern Roman empire, South Asia in the Gupta era, and especially southern China during the Age of Division.

Tropical Africa had a much lower starting base for demographic and economic growth in 200, compared, say, to India or China. But the *rate* of growth in the following five centuries almost certainly accelerated. Even in the most prosperous Afroeurasian societies in these centuries, agrarian technology did not change much, despite incremental improvements here and there in toolkits and farming methods. Humans continued to rely overwhelmingly on biomass (wood and other vegetation), domestic animal power, human labor, and in some measure wind and water to harness productive energy.

No startling technological breakthroughs occurred in the centuries after 600 either, but the growth trend in Afroeurasia as a whole generally resumed. Several factors contributed to this, among them a new surge of interregional commercial and cultural exchange. This phenomenon was associated with Arabic-speaking peoples, who led the emergence of a zone of political and cultural energy extending from the Mediterranean to India.

• • •

Key Terms

Arianism 267	deurbanization 260	Manichaeism 264
asceticism 268	eunuch 251	Nestorianism 267
Austronesian migrations 274	Gnosticism 267	Nok culture 272
Bantu migrations 274	Gupta empire 251	pandemic 261
bhakti 266	heresy 267	patriarch 257
Byzantine empire (Byzantium) 260	Huns 257	Sasanid empire 251
clergy 268	Jenne-Jeno 272	Theravada Buddhism 264
Coptic (Monophysite)	liturgy 270	White Huns 261
Christianity 267	Mahayana Buddhism 264	

Change over Time

1st century C.E.	Buddhists first arrive in China.
200	Nok culture flourishes in the West African Sudanic region.
216–272	Mani, founder of Manichaeism, teaches in Southwest Asia.
220–581	The Age of Division in China follows the collapse of the Han dynasty.
224–651	The Sasanid empire prospers in Persia.
3rd–4th centuries	Austronesian-speaking migrants colonize Madagascar.
4th century	Bantu-speaking farmers settle in southern Africa.
313	Roman emperor Constantine establishes capital of Constantinople.
320–550	The Gupta empire dominates South Asia.
350	King Ezana of Axum in East Africa converts to Christianity.
378	Germanic Goths defeat the Roman army at Hadrianople.
380	Emperor Theodosius declares Christianity to be Rome's state religion.
400	Germanic groups push into western Roman empire. Population of Jenne-Jeno, a West African entrepôt, reaches around 50,000.
434–453	Attila the Hun leads several major raids into the Roman empire.
527–565	Justinian reigns over the eastern Roman (Byzantine) empire.
541	Bubonic plague breaks out in the eastern Mediterranean region.
7th century	Christians first reach China.

Please see end of book reference section for additional reading suggestions related to this chapter.

10 Afroeurasia in the Era of the Arab Empire

500-800 C.E.

A page from the Quran in Kufic script, Tunisia, tenth century.

Fourteen hundred years ago, Arabic was a relatively minor language spoken in the Arabian Peninsula and parts of Syria and Iraq. Today, it is spoken by somewhere between 200 and 300 million people and is number four on the list of the most widely spoken languages, following Mandarin Chinese, Spanish, and English. It is an official language in twenty-four countries in Southwest Asia and northern Africa. Minority populations speak it in many other countries. Arabic has been a written language since about the fourth century C.E., and today its alphabetic system is used more widely than any other except the Latin alphabet, the one you are reading here.

Like English, Arabic emerged as a major world language because of historical events, in this case the rise of a new empire and the establishment of Islam as a new world religion. In the early seventh century in the desert town of Mecca in western Arabia, Muhammad ibn Abdallah, an Arabic-speaking merchant, began publicly to preach lessons of spiritual and moral reform. According to Muslim tradition, Muhammad received revelations from God in the Arabic language, and his followers eventually set these messages in a body of writings that constituted the Quran (koo-RAHN), Islam's fundamental scripture. Muhammad attracted a group of religious followers, and he also founded a political community to ensure their safety. Following his death in 632, Arab warriors enlarged this state in all directions. Wherever Arabs established their rule, they introduced Arabic, not only as the tongue of a conquering elite, but also as the sacred language of Islam.

The Arab empire grew so large and so fast in the seventh and eighth centuries that it commands attention as a startling world event. In fact, though, this was only one of several large state-building ventures in this period that originated in Afroeurasia's Great Arid Zone, the belt of dry country extending from the African Sahara to East Asia (see Map I-2). The first part of this chapter investigates the rise of these empires and the impact they had on agrarian, densely populated parts of Afroeurasia. We give most detailed attention to the creation of the Arab state. Within a century of its founding in Arabia, it incorporated most of Southwest Asia, northern Africa, and Europe's Iberian Peninsula (Spain and Portugal). The Arabs were also the only empire builders in that era to broadcast a new religious message

Arab-led armies occupied a large part of the Mediterranean rim but not all of it. In the second part of the chapter,

• • •

we investigate the Christian societies that endured both north and south of the Mediterranean. The Byzantine state, heir of the Roman empire, faced an acute crisis in the seventh century as Arab forces took over some of its richest territories and even threatened Constantinople, its great capital. But Byzantium survived as the sanctuary of a distinctive Greek Christian culture. In western and central Europe, the end of the long period of aggressive Germanic and Hunnic migrations left the population seeking a new basis for political stability and economic recovery. There the Christian church played a vital integrating role. South of the Mediterranean, Christian communities continued to flourish in the Nile River valley.

In the final part of the chapter, we turn to China, where the Sui and Tang dynasties ended the region's long Age of Division and reestablished central authority at about the same time that the Arab empire arose. A new period of population and economic growth followed China's reunification. As urbanization, manufacturing, and business surged in both East and Southwest Asia, commercial exchange across Afroeurasia by land and sea accelerated as well.

A Panoramic View

MAP 10.1 Major states of Afroeurasia, 500 C.E.

This map represents Afroeurasia in the aftermath of armed migrations into Europe and North Africa. How has the geopolitical map of the lands around the Mediterranean Sea changed since 250 C.E.? See Map 9.1.

New Empires of Steppe and Desert

FOCUS How were the development of Inner Eurasian empires and the Arab empire similar, and how were they different?

In Chapter 9, we described how several waves of pastoral nomads organized in warrior confederations surged out of the steppes of Inner Eurasia between the third and sixth centuries to disrupt neighboring agrarian societies from India to western Europe and North Africa. These movements, involving Germanic migrants, as well as Alans, Huns, White Huns, Avars, and other bands of mounted archers, precipitated the collapse of the western Roman empire and put eastern Rome, or the Byzantine empire, under prolonged threat. Invaders from the steppes also menaced Persia and northern India. To the east, nomad bands kept up pressure on the northwestern frontiers of China, as they had done off and on for many hundreds of years.

In the seventh and eight centuries, herding peoples continued to factor prominently in Afroeurasia's history, though with two new twists. First, cavalry armies organized large states *within* Inner Eurasia. These groups were not migrating hordes comparable to the Huns. Rather, they aimed to create stable, efficiently organized governments capable of controlling and exploiting large shares of Inner Eurasia's resources in pasture, oasis agriculture, and long-distance trade. Second, the arid Arabian Peninsula emerged for the first time, and quite suddenly, as a new center of political power. In the seventh century, Arabic-speaking nomads and oasis dwellers not only founded a new state but, like the Germanic tribes and the Huns in Europe two centuries earlier, attacked neighboring agrarian lands, overrunning and extinguishing the Sasanid empire of Persia and seizing several of the richest provinces of Byzantium.

Empires along the Silk Roads

After about three hundred years of disturbances and interruptions on the Inner Eurasian caravan routes, traffic picked up again in the later sixth century. This happened in association with the rise of a succession of steppe and mountain empires (see Map 10.2). The principal state-builders were Türks, Tibetans, Uighurs (WEE-goors), and Khazars.

The Türk empires. Warriors known as the Türk (spelled with the letter "ü" as distinct from "u") founded the earliest of the new states to take advantage of silk road recovery and help stimulate it further. The name Türk originally referred to a particular pastoral nomadic tribe that spoke a Turkic languages (spelled without the "ü"). Under talented leaders, Türk cavalry armed with composite bows and steel swords defeated neighboring groups and incorporated their surviving adult males into the Türk ranks to form a larger

confederation of fighters. This more powerful army then conquered more distant tribes, and the Türk war machine snowballed, as it were, across the steppes. As it grew, the state enveloped peoples speaking a number of Inner Eurasian languages, both pastoral nomads and oasis farmers. In addition to tribal and clan organization based on kinship relations, the Türk created a central governing hierarchy. From the top, the supreme leader, or *khagan,* transmitted orders to appointed provincial governors who in turn supervised local tribal and town leaders. The government accumulated wealth to sustain the army and administration by collecting tributes from subject populations and taxing trade.

Two Türk empires rose to power in succession. The first, known as the Eastern Türk, flourished from 552 to 630, then disintegrated in intertribal wars. The Tang imperial government in China played a hand in this violence, using promises of silk cargos and military support to play Türk leaders against one another. The second, or Western Türk empire lasted from 682 to 744. Between them, these states dominated a huge stretch of Inner Eurasia between northwestern China and the Pontic-Caspian steppes north of the Black Sea. In 628, Xuanzang (SHWEN-ZAHNG), a Chinese monk who traveled overland to India to collect Buddhist texts and relics, presented himself before the Türk emperor Tong Yabghu at a western silk road town. Xuanzang confirmed reports of the sumptuousness of the Türk imperial court. The king, he later wrote,

was covered with a robe of green satin, and his hair was loose, only it was bound round with a silken band some ten feet in length, which was twisted around his head and fell down behind. He was surrounded by about 200 officers, who were all clothed in brocade stuff, with their hair braided. On the right and left he was attended by independent troops, all clothed in fur and fine-spun garments; they carried lances and bows and standards, and were mounted on camels and horses. The eye could not estimate their numbers.[1]

To gather trade revenue, the Türk formed a close collaboration with merchants of Sogdiana (SUGG-dee-an-uh), the region of Central Asia that lay between the Amu Darya and Syr Darya Rivers, today Uzbekistan and southern Kazakhstan. Speakers of a language related to Persian (Farsi), the Sogdians became distinguished for their literacy and commercial expertise. Sometime before the Common Era, they began to build a diaspora of trade settlements that radiated out along the silk roads from Samarkand in Sogdiana to cities in China. Under Türk protection, Sogdians shipped silk, linen, wine, jade, and numerous other Chinese luxuries westward in exchange for horses, camels, hides, and the manufactures of Southwest Asia. Many Sogdian merchants practiced Zoroastrianism, others Buddhism, Manichaeism, and Nestorian Christianity. They contributed to the advancement of these religions in China and Inner Eurasia, and Sogdian scholars translated sacred scripture of these faiths into a number of languages, including Chinese.

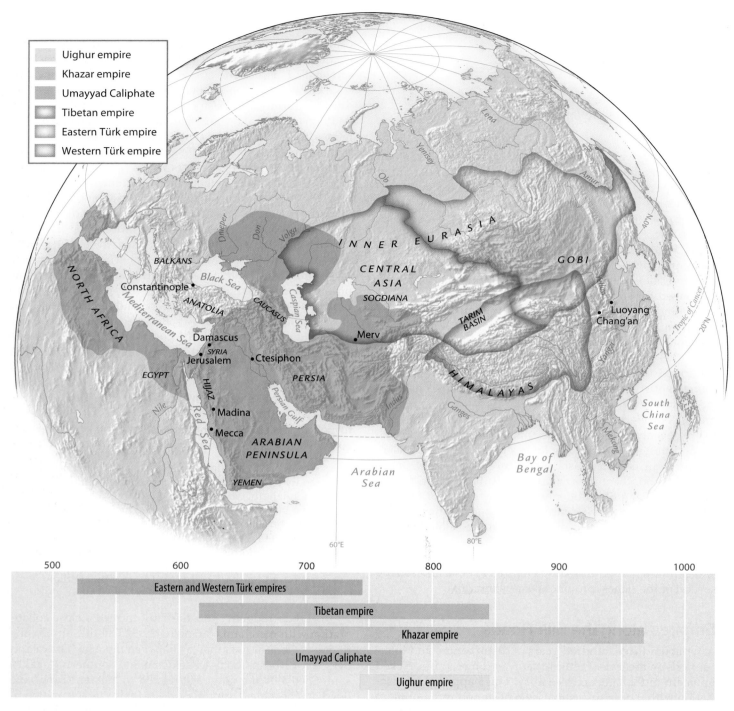

MAP 10.2 Empires of steppe and desert, seventh and eighth centuries.
How would you explain the rise of large and powerful empires in relatively arid regions of Afroeurasia where agriculture was limited?

The Uighur empire. The second Türk empire buckled in the mid-eighth century amid fierce tribal infighting for leadership. However, the Uighurs, a new confederation of Turkic-speaking fighters, quickly expanded their own domain. The Uighur state, which lasted nearly a century (744–840), commanded the eastern end of the silk roads. Uighur cavalry invaded China's Yellow River region several times, seizing urban booty, and withdrawing only when

Chinese officials bought off the intruders with thousands of bolts of silk. Like the Türk, Uighurs were familiar with Buddhism, Zoroastrianism, and Nestorian Christianity, religions that spread along the silk roads. Influenced by monks and merchants from Iran, the Uighur elite converted to Manichaeism, the rigorously ascetic faith preached by the Prophet Mani in the third century (see Chapter 9). Manichean temples and monasteries thrived in both the eastern steppes and China in the later eighth and the ninth centuries. But this religion lost ground to both Buddhism and Nestorian Christianity after the Uighur state disintegrated in 840. That reversal effectively ended Manichaeism's prospects as a major universalist religion.

Tibet. A fourth Inner Eurasian empire arose, not in the steppes, but on the rugged Tibetan plateau, which lies between the Tarim Basin and the great wall of the Himalaya Mountains. Tibetans spoke a language in the family that also includes Chinese, and they practiced a mixed economy of farming and herding. About 618 the Tibetan leader Songtsan Gampo (d. 649) organized local lords under his exclusive command. Accumulating sufficient power to field large armies of horse soldiers outfitted in chain mail armor, Tibetan warriors swooped down from the plateau to the Tarim Basin, capturing many eastern silk road towns and for a time controlling their commercial traffic. All the kings in the Tibetan dynasty patronized Buddhist monks and monasteries. This policy gave the state an aura of religious prestige and laid the foundations for popular conversion to the distinctive set of beliefs and rituals characterized as Tibetan Buddhism. The empire collapsed rather suddenly in 842, but for more than two centuries it played a major part in Inner Eurasian politics, alternately fighting and negotiating with imperial China, Türks, and Uighurs for dominance over cities and trade routes.

The Khazars. The longest lasting Turkic-speaking state of the era was Khazaria (630–965). Arising in the Pontic-Caspian steppes north of the Black and Caspian Seas, the Khazar empire at its height embraced the rich farming valleys of the Volga, Don, and Dnieper Rivers. This state originated as a coalition of disparate Turkic-speaking groups, many of whom had migrated westward in flight from Inner Eurasian wars or droughts. Founding several administrative cities, the Khazar monarchs ruled a diverse population of Indo-European and Turkic farmers, herders, and town dwellers. Khazaria also accumulated wealth by taxing trade on two major commercial arteries, the western silk road that terminated at ports on the Black Sea and the north–south routes that connected the fur-rich temperate forests of Russia with Persia and Syria.

In the eighth century, Judaism spread among the Khazar ruling and commercial classes. We know little of how that happened, though we have evidence that Jewish communities occupied the Caucasus and Black Sea regions long before the arrival of Turkic speakers. Though never converting most of the population, the Khazar kings made Judaism their official religion, inspired mainly by the ancient books of the Hebrew Bible (Old Testament). The political and commercial elite also used the Hebrew alphabet in religious practice, as well as for administrative and commercial communication. When Khazaria broke up in the tenth century, Judaism lost its special position in the region and subsequently declined. Part of the Jewish population, however, may have migrated into eastern and central Europe to form new communities there.

Taken together, the Inner Eurasian empires of the seventh and eighth centuries left an important cultural legacy. Distinctive Turkic styles of artisanry, dress, and cuisine, and especially Turkic languages, spread widely in the region. Today, Turkic tongues are dominant in six Eurasian countries and spoken widely in several others, including China, Russia, and Germany. From this period, moreover, Turkic-speaking peoples came to play an increasingly important part in world history, as we shall see in later chapters.

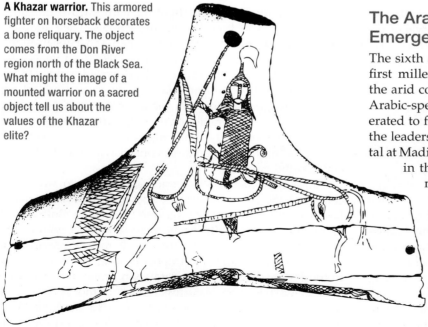

A Khazar warrior. This armored fighter on horseback decorates a bone reliquary. The object comes from the Don River region north of the Black Sea. What might the image of a mounted warrior on a sacred object tell us about the values of the Khazar elite?

The Arab State and the Emergence of Islam

The sixth and by far the largest steppe empire of the later first millennium C.E. arose, not in Inner Eurasia, but in the arid country of the Arabian Peninsula. Starting in 622, Arabic-speaking town dwellers and herding tribes cooperated to found a religious and political community under the leadership of Muhammad ibn Abdallah. From its capital at Madina (Medina), the young Arab state first expanded in the peninsula, a territory nearly twice the size of modern France, Germany, and Spain combined. In contrast to Inner Eurasian empire builders of the same period, however, Arab forces invaded and conquered densely populated and urbanized lands. Within little more than a hundred years, Arab-led armies pushed far to the east and west, carving out a state that stretched from the Indus River valley to Spain.

Also in contrast to the Inner Eurasian imperial ventures, a new religion—a fresh vision

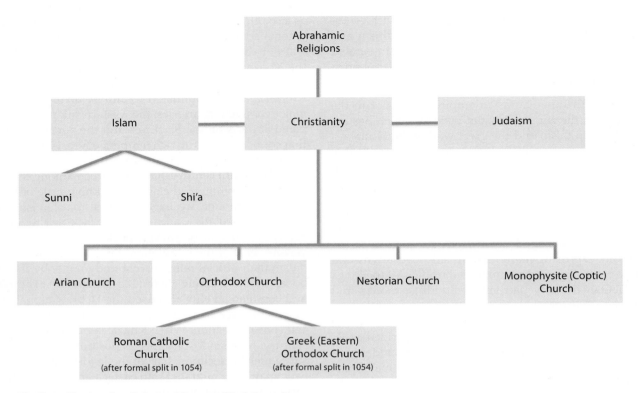

The three Abrahamic religions and some of their branches.

of monotheistic faith based in the tradition of the biblical prophet Abraham, whom Jews and Christians also venerated as an early witness to one, all-powerful god—emerged along with the Arab conquests and founding of the multiethnic Arab state. Although the Arab empire lasted only about a century as a huge unitary state, Islam gradually took root across Southwest Asia and North Africa. Islam thus joined Buddhism and Christianity as a universalist creed directed to all who were prepared to listen to its message. It also offered the religious foundations for a distinctive style of urban civilization.

The Southwest Asian scene in the sixth and seventh centuries. Evidence from ancient texts tell us that Arabic-speaking people, organized in either small states or tribes had participated in greater Southwest Asia's political and cultural life since at least the early first millennium B.C.E. Arab groups that occupied the Arabian Peninsula, Syria, and western Mesopotamia had been allies, political dependents, and trading partners of Rome and of successive Persian empires. The southwestern fringe of the Arabian Peninsula, centered on today's Republic of Yemen, also had a long history of small monarchies drawing wealth from irrigated agriculture and from export trade in incense and other exotic commodities. The peninsula's largest farming population was concentrated in Yemen, whose highlands receive summer monsoon rains.

The Arabian Desert, however, occupies most of the peninsula. Its climate is about the same as that of the eastern Sahara, the two deserts separated only by the Red Sea, a narrow waterway easily crossed in small vessels. Since the domestication of the dromedary, or one-humped camel as early as 2500 B.C.E., pastoral nomads gradually adapted to the harsh Arabian steppes, raising animals wherever oases, wells, and seasonal rainfall provided sufficient grassland and fodder. Like Inner Eurasian herders, Arabia's pastoral tribes lived a mobile way of life, competing with one another for resources and fighting with sword and bow from the backs of both horses and camels. They adopted weaponry and iron armor from Roman and Persian models. From the late centuries B.C.E., they also used the North Arabian saddle, an invention that permitted a rider to sit comfortably astride a dromedary, at the same time toting heavy baggage that hung on the animal's sides. From the fourth century C.E., Arabic-speaking groups advanced more insistently into the agrarian fringes of Syria and Mesopotamia, bringing them into closer contact with the Byzantine and Sasanid empires.

Those two giant states periodically went to war over control of the cities, farmlands, and trade of Syria, Anatolia, and western Mesopotamia (see Chapter 9). Both made pragmatic alliances with Arabs to avoid conflict with them. Both also coveted opportunities to dominate Yemen and the Red Sea commercial entrepôts linking Southwest Asia to the Indian Ocean. By the late sixth century, Byzantium abandoned hopes of restoring Roman authority over the western Mediterranean, where Germanic warrior kings prevailed. Though Byzantium still held scattered territories in

Italy and North Africa, the emperor Heraclius (reigned 610–641) shifted the weight of imperial power to the defense of Egypt, Syria, and Anatolia against the Persians and of the Balkan provinces against encroaching Avar, Slav, or Turkic cavalry. In the early seventh century, fighting between Byzantium and Persia intensified, and for a short time Sasanid forces even occupied northern Egypt. The costs of these wars, plus continuous investment in frontier garrisons and fortifications, strained the treasuries of both states and left them ill prepared to face any new enemies. Moreover, the cycle of plague epidemics that had first struck the eastern Mediterranean in 541 continued throughout the seventh century, causing recurring high mortality and economic setbacks in one region or another.

Muhammad and the preaching of Islam.

The setting for the emergence of both Islam and the new Arab state was western Arabia, or the Hijaz, a region of dry highlands that supported small cities where seasonal rivers or underground water sources could be tapped. These centers included Mecca and Madina. Since Arabia belonged to the same world of commercial and cultural interaction as Byzantium and Persia, it is no surprise that significant numbers of Arabs in Syria and northern Arabia practiced Christianity and that both Christian and Jewish communities were to be found in some Hijaz towns. However, many town dwellers and most pastoral nomads were pagans, that is, polytheists who venerated multiple deities identified with the sun, moon, stars, or sacred trees and rocks. Mecca, a parched Hijaz town nestled among treeless hills, hosted an important pagan shrine centered on a cubic structure called the Ka'ba (KAH-buh). The Meccan gods attracted pilgrim worshipers from across western Arabia.

Muhammad standing before the Ka'ba. This miniature painting is one of 814 in the Siyer-i-Nebi, a multivolume work on the life of the prophet written in the fourteenth century. The painting comes from a sixteenth-century illustrated edition. A tradition developed in Islam of respecting the prophet by veiling his face in visual representations of him. Muhammad is also surrounded by flames. What do you think the flames might signify?

Hijaz towns may have enjoyed rising commercial prosperity in the seventh century in connection with a general upswing in trade across Afroeurasia. Although Mecca's particular importance as a trade center remains historically controversial, historians have argued that growing commercialization encouraged a money-making culture that aggravated social strains among tribes, religious communities, and economic classes.

In these circumstances, Muhammad, a forty-two-year-old man without great social standing, began publicly to preach the power, mercy, and justice of one omnipotent God. Numerous biographies, chronicles, and sacred texts recount the events of his life. As is the case with both Jesus and the Buddha, however, no documents describing his career

and achievements can be dated to his own lifetime. Consequently, historians persistently argue over the reliability and authenticity of early texts that attest to his deeds, utterances, and social milieu. According to Muslim tradition, Muhammad was born into a family of the Quraysh clan in 570. He was orphaned as an infant, raised by an uncle, took up trade, and married Khadija, a successful Meccan businesswoman. In 610 he began to experience visions and hear sounds that he came to acknowledge as messages from God (*Allah* in Arabic). The Angel Gabriel imparted these revelations and instructed Muhammad to share them courageously with his fellow Meccans.

The monotheism of his message was rigorous but compatible with the existing Jewish and Christian traditions.

Human beings, God's supreme creation, must surrender themselves wholeheartedly to his will, bringing him to the center of their consciousness. God is merciful, but he is also just. A day of divine judgment will come when the righteous shall enter heaven, but those who deny God will suffer eternal damnation. Human salvation depends on unconditional devotion to him and to his holy commandments. These laws require all men and women to be pious, compassionate, generous, and respectful of all of divine creation. The willful, egocentric self must be forsaken for the one Self that is God. The Arabic word *Islam* may be translated as "surrender," "submission," or "commitment." An individual who professes Islam is a Muslim, one who surrenders to God's will.

Because Jewish and Christian communities already inhabited western Arabia, Muhammad's preaching was by no means alien. Like Jesus seven centuries earlier, he spoke to popular yearnings for moral assurance, social justice, and divine salvation in an increasingly commercialized and cosmopolitan world. Also like Jesus, he had to struggle to be taken seriously. Only a small part of the Meccan population, including his wife Khadija, listened to him. Most sympathizers were probably poor and downtrodden people, including many women. The majority, and especially the most influential families, did not wish to be told to change their social behavior, share their wealth with the poor, or repudiate the idols that brought the city profitable business.

The Muslim tradition relates that in 622, after eleven years of confronting mostly indifference and persecution, Muhammad and a small band of believers left Mecca, traveling 250 miles north to the city of Yathrib, known from that time forward as Madina. This town had a rich irrigated farming economy, but it suffered from chronic interclan feuding. Consequently, the city accepted Muhammad's moral and political leadership. He demanded only that all the Madinan clans renounce their quarrels and join together in a unified, God-directed community, called in Arabic the *umma*. For Muslims, the prophet's migration to Madina, known as the *hijra*, or flight, is the key event in history. He now had a safe base from which to preach God's word and organize his religious and political society. The year 622 C.E. is year 1 on the Muslim calendar.

In Islamic belief, Muhammad continued to receive divine directives from 610 until 632, when he died. The full body of those revelations formed the Quran (Koran), the "recitation" of God's message to the world. Muhammad transmitted that message orally, and sometime after his death Muslim scribes set it in Arabic script. For Muslims, the Quran is a work of resounding spiritual authority. They affirmed that Muhammad, more faithfully than any other human, thought and lived in accord with God's will. In addition to the Quran, therefore, Muslims also draw inspiration, guidance, and legal precedents from the Traditions of the Prophet (*Hadith*). These sacred texts are reports of Muhammad's exemplary words and deeds, which later scholars corroborated by persuasive testimony. To Muslims, Muhammad was the

"perfect man," though not the Son of God, as the majority of early Christians came to regard Jesus.

The Quran also sets forth the ethical rights and responsibilities that individuals must exercise as God's favored creation. As a guide to moral living, it has much in common with the Hebrew and Christian Bibles. It specifies a body of rules, norms, and rituals, which are anchored in the five "pillars" of the faith: daily prayers, regular donations to the poor, pilgrimage to Mecca, annual fasting, and affirmation of God's oneness and Muhammad's place as His final prophet on earth.

Like the Hebrew Bible, the Quran specifies ethical standards that should govern property transactions, inheritance, commerce, kin relations, slavery, and almost any sphere of social and economic life in seventh-century Arabia. Marriage and the family were particularly important subjects. As in most of the world in the first millennium C.E., Arabian social groups were patriarchal, that is, dominated by adult men. Tribal ideology defined women and children essentially as family property and esteemed honor and loyalty among males above stable marriage relations. Muhammad did not propose radical social equality any more than Christian teachings did. But he deplored Arabian values as antagonistic to God and destructive of social harmony. Rather, all humans are deserving of moral respect, and women and men have identical responsibilities to their creator. The Quran extols stable marriage, discourages divorce, prohibits incest, condemns female infanticide, permits polygamy only under strict conditions, and awards women property and inheritance rights. Slavery was part of Afroeurasia's social fabric almost everywhere, and Muhammad did not oppose its legality. Like the Christian New Testament, the Quran instructs believers to treat slaves with compassion and encourages masters to grant them freedom.

A new Southwest Asian state. In contrast to either Jesus or the Buddha, both of whom rejected worldly leadership, Muhammad built a community that was simultaneously religious, social, and political. After moving to Madina, he organized a federation of oasis-dwelling and pastoral clans primarily to defend the young community and ensure the way of life that he believed God prescribed. He faced stern hostility from both Meccans and other western Arabian groups. Part of Madina's large Jewish minority population accepted his prophecy and political leadership. But political factions that opposed the Muslim community or violated agreements with it, including some Jews, were subjected to exile or execution. Muhammad also organized an armed force, and following a series of clashes with opponents between 622 and 628, he and his troops entered Mecca in 630. After this success, much of Arabia, including both Yemen and northern areas extending into the Syrian Desert, declared their allegiance to the Muslim state. Muhammad cleansed the Ka'ba in Mecca of its idols and, reaffirming the tradition that Abraham had built the structure as a monument to monotheistic faith, he rededicated it to the one God. He also declared that God commanded him to retain the Ka'ba's status as a pilgrimage site and to instruct Muslims to travel there at least once in their lives, if they are able, as one of their five fundamental devotional duties. This journey is named the *hajj*.

From an Afroeurasian perspective, the rise of the Arab Muslim state generally paralleled the trajectory of the Türk, Uighur, and Khazar empires in that it coalesced as an alliance among arid-zone pastoral clans and commercially minded town dwellers. The early success of the Muslim community against all odds, however, appears to have inspired Arabs with a sense of common identity and mission never known before. Scholars generally agree that Muhammad did not intend to found a new religion. He hoped, rather, to persuade Jews, Christians, and all other monotheists to join together in shared faith. Indeed, before Muhammad returned to Mecca in 630, he instructed his followers to pray facing Jerusalem, the holiest of cities for both Jews and Christians. But just as early Christians gradually separated themselves from Judaism, so Muslims, in the years following the prophet's death, increasingly defined themselves as distinct from both of those faiths.

The Arab Muslim Empire

Because Muhammad designated no successor, his death in 632 brought on a crisis of leadership. However, Abu Bakr, one of the prophet's early companions, secured a consensus among Muslim clan leaders that he should take command as **caliph** (KAL-ihf), or "deputy" of Muhammad. During his two years as leader (632–634), Abu Bakr suppressed rebellions and made political contacts with Arab groups in the Syrian Desert to the north. In alliance with them, he launched raids on the Byzantine and Persian frontiers. In these ways, he preserved and energized the young state.

> **caliph** In Sunni Islam, the deputy or successor of the Prophet Muhammad as leader of the Muslim community.

The Arab military triumph. Under the leadership of Abu Bakr and his two successors, Caliph Umar (r. 634–644) and Caliph Uthman (r. 644–656), Arab frontier incursions expanded into all-out invasion of Southwest Asia. Byzantine and Sasanid armies fought back, but militarily off balance, fiscally strained, and still hostile toward each other, they suffered defeat. The Byzantine emperor was forced to abandon Syria, Palestine, and Egypt. To the northeast, Arab forces invaded Iraq (ancient Mesopotamia). In 637 they chased the Persian king from Ctesiphon, his splendid capital on the banks of the Tigris River, and during the following twelve years overran Iraq and much of Iran. In barely more than a decade, Arab armies decisively changed the Southwest Asian political landscape. They eliminated the Persian empire, which had endured under one dynasty of rulers or another for 1,300 years. And they deprived the Byzantines of their rich Syrian and Egyptian provinces. These conquests erased the frontier that for about seven centuries had separated Southwest Asia into two great spheres of power.

Mecca's sacred sanctuary. Twilight descends on Mecca as Muslims gather in the grand mosque to pray facing the Ka'ba. That cubical structure is draped in black fabric. Compare the modern Ka'ba with the one pictured on page 285.

How did they do it? One factor was simply effective use of horse cavalry, supported by camel trains for logistical transport, against the larger but slower Byzantine and Persian armies. Another factor was that neither of those empires commanded the wholehearted loyalty of its subjects. The Byzantine state was largely Christian, but the official, or orthodox church had to compete with, and sometimes persecuted, the Monophysite and Nestorian churches, which were popular in Egypt, Syria, and Mesopotamia. Neither those two communities nor the Jewish minority of Southwest Asia felt much inclined to fight for the Byzantine emperor and his bishops. Also, the Arab conquerors let Christians and Jews continue to practice their own monotheistic faiths. On the Persian side, Christian, Jewish, and Manichean minorities in Mesopotamia and Iran had little cause to defend the Sasanid ruling class, which identified closely with Zoroastrian worship, a religion that most farmers and herders under Persian rule did not follow.

The conquests had two important short-term consequences. One was that an Arab military elite quite suddenly took the place of Byzantine and Persian officials from Egypt to northeastern Iran. Headquartered in Madina, the early caliphs appointed Arab governors in the major cities. They also kept soldiers who were not on campaign confined to military camps, reducing opportunities for ambitious officers to build local power centers of their own.

Rapid conquest also set off a violent struggle among Arab leaders. Though Muhammad would no doubt have lamented it, factional strife may have been inevitable owing to the high political stakes involved in controlling the immense agrarian wealth of Southwest Asia and Egypt. The early caliphs, clan chiefs, imperial governors, and members of Muhammad's family all emerged at one moment or another as poles around which opposing political blocs formed. Major players in the first civil struggle, which lasted from 656 to 661, included Uthman, the third caliph; Ali ibn Abu Talib, the fourth caliph and cousin and son-in-law of the prophet; Aisha, one of the prophet's widows; and Muawiya, the Arab governor of Syria. In the struggle, Uthman and Ali were both assassinated, and Muawiya, whose Meccan family was known as the Umayyads (oo-MEYE-ahds), achieved victory. Supported by a majority of Muslims, he took the title of caliph and moved the imperial capital from Madina to Damascus, an important Syrian city that was much closer to the center of the new empire.

The shift from Madina to Damascus.

The new Arab leaders lost little time in transforming themselves from desert cavaliers living in tents or mud-brick houses into an urban, palace-dwelling elite. The leaders of the Umayyad Caliphate spoke Arabic rather than Greek or Persian, but they governed local populations largely as the Byzantines and Sasanids had done, employing armed officials to keep order and collect taxes. The new state maintained roads and irrigation works, founded a professional army, and, to demonstrate its piety, built religious monuments such as the

The Caliph Ali and his forces in battle. From a thirteenth-century manuscript.

beautiful Dome of the Rock in Jerusalem. The Umayyads also recruited accountants and secretaries from among educated Greek, Syrian, Egyptian, and, eventually, Persian families. Muawiya maintained the fiction that he governed with the consent of the community of believers, the Arabian model of leadership that Abu Bakr, the first caliph, had kept intact. In fact, Muawiya put forward his own son to succeed him and by that stroke founded a hereditary monarchy. Indeed, authoritarian monarchy had been the standard form of government in most of the region for the previous three thousand years.

The Great Mosque of Damascus. The Umayyad caliphs supported major public construction after they established their capital in Damascus. The mosque site is one of the oldest known places of continuous religious worship in the world. As early as 3000 B.C.E. there was an Aramean temple to the god Hadad here. The site was later a Roman temple, then a Christian church dedicated to St. John the Baptist. Why might successive states have used the same religious site?

Under the Umayyad dynasty, which ruled from 661 to 750, Islam began to spread to non-Arab peoples, though this happened slowly at first. The first generation of Arab conquerors, who saw themselves as exclusively chosen by God to fulfill divine prophecy in the world, did not encourage conversion. They largely left Christians, Jews, and other believers to their own worship. One estimate suggests that by 750 (118 years after the prophet's death), fewer than 10 percent of the non-Arab population of the Umayyad empire had become Muslims.[2] Also, diffusion of basic knowledge of Islam took time, partly because the great majority of the people who lived under Arab rule did not speak or read Arabic. In the later eighth century, however, the conversion rate began to accelerate. Zoroastrianism, whose adherents were concentrated in Iran and Central Asia, lost ground to Islam much faster than did Christianity or Judaism. From about 1000 C.E., it faded as a potential world faith, though some communities survive today, notably the Parsis of western India.

Sunni and Shi'a. A second key development in the Umayyad period was continuing debate over the organization and leadership of the Muslim state. According to Muslim tradition, Muhammad and the early caliphs regarded the growth of the political community as inseparable from the mission to establish a God-approved society on earth. That is, Muhammad founded the community to fulfill moral and spiritual ideals and to prepare humans for God's judgment, not just to set up a power hierarchy and send out tax collectors. But opposing factions disputed the proper structure of government during the first civil war (656–661) and on through a second one (683–692).

The Umayyad government in Damascus had majority support for the view that the first four caliphs set Islam on its proper path. According to this model, the caliph was the community's "chief executive" and had the task of defending the state, promoting social justice, and enforcing God's laws—for as long as he had the community's consent. Believers who accepted this ideal came to be known as Sunni (SOON-nee) Muslims, from the Arabic word *sunna*, which refers to the norms established by the prophet and the first four caliphs.

The main challengers of the Sunni view were the Shi'a (SHEE-ah), a name that in Arabic means "party" or "faction," specifically the faction loyal to Ali, the fourth caliph and kinsman of Muhammad. (An alternate version of the name is Shiite.) Shi'a adherents argued that God intended the leader of the community to be chosen exclusively from the family of Ali, who, they said, inherited some of the prophet's extraordinary moral and spiritual qualities. Although political enemies killed both Ali and one of his two sons in the civil conflicts, Muhammad had other blood descendants in Ali's line. Only they, the Shi'a claimed, had the right to rule. Furthermore, those men, who were given the title of **imam,** understood disguised meanings in the Quran that were essential to human salvation.

> **imam** In Islam in general, the individual who leads congregational worship and carries out other duties such as officiating at marriages.

The largest Shi'a group teaches that in the ninth century the twelfth Imam in the family line of Ali went into a hidden state. Since then, he has continued to live concealed from the world but guides the most devoted Shi'a leaders through inspiration. One day he will return to initiate a final era of justice on earth. This doctrine has given the Shi'a tradition a messianic quality, meaning expectation of the coming of a holy savior, or messiah, an idea comparable to the Christian doctrine of the second coming of Christ. In time, Shi'a

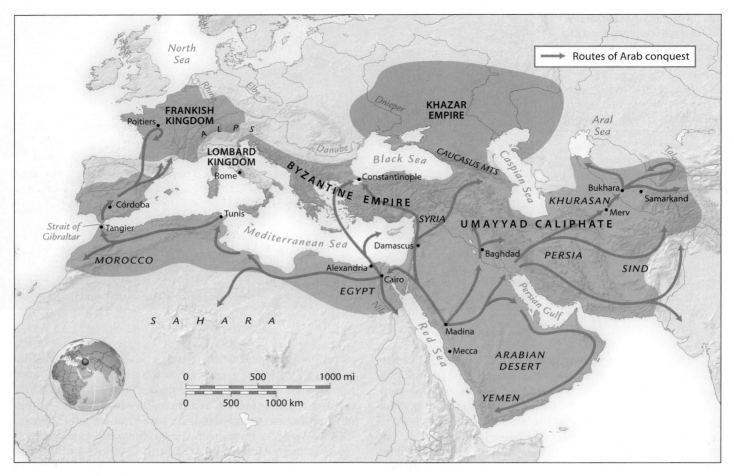

MAP 10.3 The Arab empire at its height, 750.
What geographical factors might help explain the direction of expansion of the Arab empire?

adherents split into a number of branches, each with somewhat different beliefs and practices. Nevertheless, Shi'a doctrines later inspired both religious and political movements, including the founding of a number of Muslim states. Today, upward of 20 percent of the world's Muslim population adhere to one Shi'a group or another, the greatest numbers in Iraq and Iran.

The empire at its zenith. A third development under Umayyad rule was the spectacular territorial expansion of the Arab state (see Map 10.3). Because of big victories over the Byzantines and Sasanids, no major power stood in the way of Arab advance eastward across Iran and westward across North Africa. The Umayyads wanted the revenue that more conquests would bring. They also regarded fresh military operations as a way to direct the energies of Arab soldiers who would otherwise be confined to tedious garrison duty and might become rebellious. Campaigning farther afield also promised booty, including opportunities for soldiers to sell war captives in urban slave markets.

To the west, Arab forces moved along the North African coast, seizing all remaining Byzantine coastal possessions and suppressing local Berber resistance as far as Morocco. As the armies advanced, defeated Berber warriors often joined the cause, some, though not all, converting to Islam. In 711 a large force of Arabs and Berbers crossed the Strait of Gibraltar into Spain. It quickly routed the Germanic kingdom of the Visigoths and occupied most of the Iberian Peninsula, establishing a new Umayyad province that was more than two thousand miles from Damascus.

To the northeast, Arab forces established a major base in Khurasan, previously Sasanid territory that today overlaps northeastern Iran and Turkmenistan. Following conquests there, thousands of Arab families migrated to the region to take advantage of its rich agriculture and urban commercial resources. Operating from Merv and other cities, Arab contingents advanced into Central Asia, crossing the Amu Darya and seizing one western silk road town after another. Numerous Turkic horse soldiers joined the Arab ranks. In 751, Muslim forces confronted a Chinese army at the Talas River in today's Kyrgyzstan Republic. The Muslims were victorious, and in the aftermath of the battle Chinese imperial armies pulled back from Central Asia.

To the east, Arab commanders led troops into Sind, the land neighboring the lower Indus valley, between 711 and 713. That arid region did not have abundant agricultural resources, but it was a hinge of trade between South Asia and Persia. Arab governors appointed from Damascus devoted themselves mainly to controlling and taxing that commerce. In the early eighth century, South Asia was a patchwork of regional monarchies. But states located east of the Indus were strong enough to stop Arab forces from advancing to the Ganges valley or down the western Indian coast.

Back in Southwest Asia, Arab cavalry penetrated Byzantine territory in eastern Anatolia and reached the foothills of the Caucasus Mountains. The Umayyads ordered construction of a Mediterranean navy, using the maritime skills of Christian crews and shipbuilders from Egypt and Syria. As eastern European Avars had done in 626, Arab forces laid siege to Constantinople, the massively defended Byzantine capital. Assaults in 668 and 717 both failed, however, barring Arab advance into the Balkan Peninsula and leaving the Greek emperor a weakened but still important political player in the eastern Mediterranean.

Despite their political and military successes, the Umayyad rulers did not resolve the deep religious and political conflicts that had triggered the first two civil conflicts. Following a third civil war between 747 and 750, the Umayyad government fell to the leaders of a branch of Muhammad's family known as the Abbasids. This new dynasty, the Abbasid Caliphate, solidified its authority over the central lands of the empire and moved the imperial capital from Syria eastward to the Tigris-Euphrates valley. We will return to the Abbasid empire (750–1258) in Chapter 11.

Christian Societies in Europe and Africa

FOCUS In what ways did Christian society change in Europe and the Mediterranean region between the sixth and eighth centuries?

When the Arabs first introduced their alternative monotheistic faith to Southwest Asia, Christianity was well established as the dominant religion throughout the Mediterranean basin. Two centuries later, Christian numbers were declining along the sea's southern rim as more and more people converted to Islam or were born into it. Where Arab invaders did not succeed, however, Christian societies continued to thrive and grow, though specific doctrines and practices varied considerably from one region to another. This does not mean that the Mediterranean basin was rigidly partitioned into religious compartments, each with its own bloc of territory. Christians, Jews, and Muslims shared the region as much as they divided it. They sometimes persecuted and killed one another, but they also lived together in many cities, traded with one another, and exchanged customs and ideas. It is worth pointing out again that Judaism, Christianity, and Islam were all variants of a common monotheistic tradition that collectively distinguished these three religions from Buddhism or Hinduism.

The Byzantine Empire Holds Its Own

In the first three decades of the seventh century, the Greek-speaking rulers of Byzantium, heirs of the eastern half of the Roman Empire, managed to defend Constantinople and at least part of their Balkan territories against the onslaughts of Slavs from northeastern Europe and Avar and Bulgar archers from the Inner Eurasia steppes. In the following two decades, however, Byzantium lost about half its territory and perhaps three-fourths of its agrarian and commercial resources, notably the grain harvests of the Nile valley, to Arab conquerors. In that century, Byzantine land and sea trade contracted, church building nearly ceased, and cities shrank or even disappeared as fighting and hard times persuaded Greek Christians to huddle behind urban walls or flee to fortified country villages. For example, the once-sprawling city of Athens in Greece dwindled to the area of the Acropolis, the town's central hill fort. On the other hand, Arab forces failed to break through Constantinople's stout landward walls, and in western Anatolia local militias of Greek soldier-farmers stood firm against all attacks.

The Byzantine response to these military crises was to restructure the much-reduced empire into an even more tightly centralized state than it already was. The emperors concentrated all bureaucratic power in Constantinople, built more frontier fortifications, closely regulated commerce and manufacturing, and raised taxes on the peasantry. Under Emperor Leo III (717–741), political and economic conditions became more stable. Byzantine gold coins circulated widely again, and Constantinople's population started to grow from a low in the later eighth century of around 300,000. Except for Baghdad after 800 C.E., Constantinople remained probably the biggest Afroeurasian city west of China.

Defensive action against invaders made Byzantine society culturally more uniform and self-contained. After the loss of its Syrian and Egyptian territories, most Christians remaining within the empire practiced Greek Orthodoxy. They believed that the church and its priesthood offered Christians the exclusive path to eternal salvation. They revered Constantinople as a sacred city, venerated the emperor as God's representative on earth, and regarded the security of church and empire as identical. One consequence of this was a deep cultural and religious conservatism that produced superb churches and decorative art but not much intellectual innovation.

The Greek emperors, who were expected to live up to Christian standards in their public moral behavior, exercised tight control over religious officials and institutions. They appointed all bishops, including the patriarch of Constantinople, who was the highest ranking priest. They also closely monitored Byzantium's numerous monasteries,

Constantinople. This map of the great city dates to the early fifteenth century, but it is the earliest one in existence. Set on hills above the Bosporus and the Sea of Marmara and surrounded by thick walls, the Byzantine capital repelled attacks by Avar, Bulgar, and Ummayad Muslim armies in the seventh and eighth centuries. Can you identify on the map the domed cathedral of Hagia Sophia?

whose pious monks safeguarded the accumulated learning of the Roman empire.

In the early ninth century, the Byzantine state had little resemblance to the Rome of old, but it was still an important regional power. It possessed productive farmlands and controlled the strategic maritime route that ran beneath the walls of Constantinople to connect the Black Sea with the Mediterranean. Moreover, periodic wars between the Byzantines and their Muslim neighbors by no means precluded commercial and diplomatic exchanges. We will see in later chapters that Byzantium's day was far from over.

Christian Society in Europe

In the later seventh century, when Arab Muslim forces were advancing westward across North Africa toward the Atlantic, peoples on the northern side of the Mediterranean were still working through the consequences of the armed invasions they had experienced more than two hundred years earlier. The Germanic migrants who overran western Europe in the fifth and sixth centuries finished off all that remained of Roman government, except for the relatively small territories where Byzantine authority held on for a few more hundred years. Once the Germanic populations settled down, they divided the region into several kingdoms. Extensive intermarriage and cultural mixing occurred between Germanic newcomers and previously Romanized populations, many of them descended from more ancient Celtic-speaking peoples. The major exception to this pattern was Spain, where Arab conquerors extinguished the Germanic kingdom of the Visigoths. The Muslim state that succeeded it embraced a diverse population of Germanic, Romanized, and Celtic people, plus Berber immigrants from North Africa and Arabs from as far away as Syria.

Western Europe in pieces. When the Roman imperial administration crumbled in western Europe under Germanic and Hunnic attack, the region's population plummeted, cities shrank or disappeared, and trade withered (see Chapter 9). Imperial coins no longer circulated much in Europe, except in Italy. Even there, the population of the city of Rome declined from as many as a million people in the first century C.E. to about fifty thousand in the seventh. The flow of pottery, spices, and other luxury goods from the eastern Mediterranean contracted, and most trade took place along local networks connecting villages and towns.

The process of cultural Romanization that had characterized western Europe for about four centuries shifted into reverse. For example, Latin remained vital as the language of the church, scholarship, and diplomacy, but it faded as a commonly spoken language. Moreover, Latin gradually spawned several regional variants that eventually evolved into the Romance, or "Roman" languages, including the ancestors of modern Italian, French, Spanish, Portuguese, and Romanian. In northern Europe, Germanic-speaking newcomers became numerous and politically powerful enough to tilt the linguistic balance in their favor, though with wide regional differentiation. English, German, Dutch, and the Scandinavian languages (except for Finnish) all evolved from Germanic grammatical structure and core vocabulary, though they also borrowed thousands of words from Latin or its Romance descendants. In eastern Europe, Slavic languages came to predominate. Today, Europeans speak about forty-five different languages. By stark contrast, the southern and eastern shores of the Mediterranean moved toward greater linguistic homogeneity. The early Arab Muslim empire embraced many tongues, but over several centuries Arabic gradually won out as the premier written and spoken language all the way from Iraq to Morocco.

As Europe's languages multiplied in the post-Roman era, so too did institutions of government and social order. Among the Slavic and Scandinavian populations of eastern Europe, kinship-based clan groups, rather than states, continued for a few more centuries as the basic political and social units. In central and western Europe, including Britain, around two hundred petty kingdoms emerged. These largely Germanic monarchies, however, were all small and weak compared to Byzantium or the Muslim Caliphate.

Germanic kings wore their royal titles proudly, but their authority depended on the sworn oaths and personal loyalties of kinsmen, warrior companions, and local chiefs, not on professional armies and bureaucrats. They had little direct control over local noble families, who carved new estates, or **manors** from Europe's forests, marshes, and abandoned Roman farmlands. Wars among noble families were common. Fighting often involved long sieges against enemies who holed up in hill forts and old Roman bastions.

> **manor** In medieval Europe, a landed estate; also the main house or castle on the estate.

Social inequality and the rise of serfdom.

Between the sixth and eighth centuries, European women and men of peasant status became generally less free. Population decline meant that farm workers were in shorter supply than they had been in Roman times. Needing to secure laborers, landlords coerced local people to work on estates or provide other services for so many days a year. In return, lords offered these men and women physical protection and rights to grow food on private plots. Though social and legal relations varied widely across Europe, many peasants became bound in a tangle of labor obligations that prohibited them from abandoning the estate to look for unoccupied land (of which there was plenty) to farm on their own. The term *serf*, a word derived from the Latin *servus*, originally meaning slave, described their unfree status. Serfdom differed from slavery mainly because serfs could not legally be bought and sold as chattels, that is, mere property. Slavery in fact declined in western Europe, not because kings and estate lords morally disapproved of it but because they lacked the military and administrative resources that the Romans had marshaled to control slaves. The institution remained more prominent in the Byzantine and Arab-ruled lands partly because those states had stronger military and police power. Nevertheless, European merchants continued to acquire and export slaves, many of them non-Christians from northern and eastern Europe, to markets in the Mediterranean.

The social flux that followed the breakup of western Rome did nothing to improve the status of European women. Slavery appears to have declined at a significantly slower rate for women than for men, and peasant women became serfs alongside fathers and husbands. Male members of rich families commonly married women "informally" or kept concubines, depriving these women of the wifely legal status that would otherwise assure them of rights to property. As in most premodern agrarian societies, aristocratic men routinely used marriageable young women as instruments of negotiation and alliance with other powerful families.

The Labors of the Months. Because so much medieval European art is concerned with the spiritual realm, historians prize imagery that reveals aspects of daily rural life. This painting from the era of Charlemagne is one example of a recurring artistic subject—the intimate relationship between earthly life and the changing seasons. How would you identify and interpret the activities depicted in each of the twelve scenes?

On the other hand, the favored wives of kings and nobles might exert significant political influence. Also, because the mortality rate among warrior nobles was high, widows frequently found themselves managing estates and inheriting extensive lands.

The Christian church as unifying force.

From the fifth to the eight centuries, the only social institution in Europe that became larger and more integrated rather than smaller and more fragmented was the Christian church. To establish its predominance in western Europe, it had to prevail over alternative versions of Christian faith. It achieved an important victory in the fifth and sixth centuries when most European kings and nobles renounced Arianism, the Christian variant that many Germanic chiefs had accepted earlier. A second success, which became apparent only gradually in the later first millennium C.E., was the emergence of the Patriarch of Rome as church leader effectively independent of both the Byzantine emperor and the patriarch of Constantinople. Claiming supremacy in the west,

pope The title used from about the ninth century to designate the head of the Christian church in western and central Europe.

this cleric came to assume the title of **pope** (from the Latin *papa,* or "father"). One important factor here was the Arab conquests, which further weakened Byzantine cultural influence in the western Mediterranean.

Like the Greek Christian organization, the Roman church had a hierarchical structure of authority extending from the pope down through regional bishops to village priests. Between the fifth and seventh centuries, bishops frequently provided the only government available in the shrinking towns of western Europe. From **cathedrals,** church officials exercised political as well as religious authority over neighboring areas, often collaborating with regional monarchs. Cathedral towns also became centers where Latin education and preservation of ancient texts continued and from which priests were trained and assigned to minister to local parishes (church districts).

cathedral A church that serves as the seat, or headquarters, of a Christian bishop; typically, a large church that attracts worshipers and pilgrims from a wide surrounding region.

Monasteries numbered in the hundreds in western Europe by 800. Founded as enclosed religious communities whose members devoted themselves to prayer, study, scholarship, and agricultural labor, monasteries were vital to the spread of Christian faith and learning. Popes, bishops, and kings typically allowed monasteries to govern their own affairs. Pious monks and nuns sometimes attained great prestige for their holiness, wisdom, and learning. These communities brought at least a smattering of literate culture to areas where there might be no towns at all. In far northern Europe and east of the Rhine River, the monasteries were the main instruments of Christian conversion. Because these houses aimed to be self-sufficient, monks and nuns not only

grew their own food but sometimes cleared great tracts of woodland and planted large estates that rivaled those of local aristocrats. Like the cathedrals, monasteries served as centers of Latin education, text copying, and artistic creativity, sometimes deep in the forest-bound wilderness. At first, many European monastic communities allowed both men and women, though sexual segregation later became standard.

The monk and missionary Benedict of Nursia (480–550) contributed to Christian expansion by founding a "rule," that is a set of regulations for how monks and nuns should live and worship. The Benedictine rule emphasized, not monkish isolation, but vigorous communal life, scholarship, and missionary enterprise. The Benedictines, headquartered in Italy, established an intercommunicating network of monasteries that extended to the British Isles and eastward into Germany. In the later first millennium C.E., monks and nuns, many of them Benedictines, served as key agents of cultural integration and exchange across Europe. People in Ireland and northern Britain first embraced Christianity owing entirely to the work of monks (there is little early evidence of nuns in those places). The monks built thriving communities and produced gospel manuscripts whose stunning illuminations (elaborate calligraphy, designs, and images) appeared to bear almost no influence of Mediterranean Christian artistic traditions. Some Irish and English monks left their cloisters to become perpetual pilgrims, returning to continental Europe, bringing books with them and founding new communities. In effect, Europe was partially Christianized from north to south.

The rise and fall of the Frankish empire. In the eighth century, Charles the Great, or Charlemagne, made an energetic though short-lived attempt to reunify Europe, drawing on the agricultural resources and warrior power of the kingdom of the Franks centered on the Rhine River valley. A succession of three

Plan for the monastery of St. Gall. This model of a Swiss monastery is based on a building plan that monks drew up under Charlemagne's direction. This self-contained religious community includes a church, library, dormitories, guesthouse, orchard, garden, stables, bakery, brewery, and school. No one knows whether a monastery that looked exactly like this model was ever built.

The Book of Kells. One of the most celebrated works of Celtic Christian art, the wondrously decorated Book of Kells contains the four New Testament gospels in Latin. Created by Irish monks around 800 C.E., the intricate interlaced designs reveal pre-Christian artistic influences. This illustration portrays Christ enthroned.

rulers led this imperial venture, beginning with Charlemagne's grandfather, Charles Martel (r. 714–741). This Germanic aristocrat was not king but rather "mayor of the palace," a position he used to direct state affairs under the Merovingian dynasty, a feeble line of rulers that proved incapable of active governance. After Muslim forces invaded Spain, numerous Arab-led raiding bands crossed the Pyrenees Mountains into Frankish territory. Martel repelled a large Arab force near the city of Tours in France's Loire Valley in 732. Historians have traditionally celebrated Martel for saving European Christendom from Arab Muslim invasion. More recently, historians have questioned whether the Arab forays, including the one against Tours, would ever have escalated into a determined invasion north of the Pyrenees.

In 741 the pope anointed Martel's son Pepin king of the Franks, but the drive for empire accelerated rapidly under the rule of Pepin's son Charlemagne (r. 768–814). These two men founded the new Carolingian dynasty (from the Latin name Carolus, or Charles). From their core territory in the Rhine River valley, Frankish armies conquered almost all of what are today France and Germany, pushing farther east than Roman legions had ever done. Charlemagne's forces also marched across the Alps to take northern Italy, and he extended Carolingian authority beyond the Pyrenees into northern Spain. Advancing into Hungary, Charlemagne destroyed the Turkic Avar state, which had long harassed Byzantium. In these campaigns, Frankish aristocrats weighted both themselves and their horses with iron armor, successfully adopting heavy cavalry, or cataphract techniques introduced from Sasanid Persia by way of Byzantium. The stirrup, an Inner Eurasian invention, also came into wide use in western Europe as a device that gave a rider more stability on horseback, though Carolingian fighters typically galloped into battle, then dismounted to fight with sword and axe.

Pepin and Charlemagne regarded themselves as champions of the church. Their close alliance with it had two important consequences. One was to advance the Christianizing of central Europe. By conquering the pagan Saxons in northeastern Germany, Charlemagne opened that region to rapid conversion, and he encouraged the founding of more monasteries east of the Rhine. He also aimed to raise society's standards of moral behavior and expectation by systematizing church teachings, educating priests, and eliminating such pagan practices as polygamy and "informal marriage" for men. In 800, Pope Leo III crowned Charlemagne Emperor of the Romans, a move that symbolized both revived hopes for a new Christian Roman empire and the growing gap between the Latin and Greek churches. Irene, the Byzantine empress at the time, vigorously objected to the pope's act, but she could do nothing about it.

The second consequence of Carolingian piety was a surge of creative activity in western Europe, especially in the later decades of Charlemagne's reign. In 794 he founded a new capital at Aachen (Aix-la-Chapelle) west of the Rhine and there presided over what scholars have named the "Carolingian renaissance." Though he supported fine architecture and art (and tried without much success to start building a western version of Constantinople), he was interested primarily in the written word. He founded a royal library to collect and preserve Greek, Roman, and Christian texts. He assembled a kind of medieval "think tank" of scholars from around Europe to copy texts accurately and to educate priests, monks, nuns, and young children,

Two Views of the Battle of Tours

Not long after the Battle of Tours (sometimes called the Battle of Poitiers), both European and Arab chroniclers began to record accounts of this contest. These narratives describe the event from different, sometimes contradictory, perspectives. Modern historians have not been able to reconcile all these accounts, but they can analyze them comparatively and make informed judgments about their relative reliability. The first selection below comes from the Chronicle of 754, *a narrative of Spanish history in the seventh and eighth centuries. The author, an anonymous Christian who lived under Muslim rule somewhere in Spain, composed the text in Latin, probably not long after 754. The author of the second selection was an Arabic-speaking Muslim. This individual's identity is also unknown. An early-nineteenth-century Spanish historian quoted this writer anonymously in a work on Muslim Spain based largely on early Arabic documents in Spanish archives.*

Abd al-Rahman Al-Ghafiki, an officer of the Umayyad Caliphate, led the Arab and Berber soldiers that approached Tours in 732. Charles Martel is identified as leader of Franks from Austrasia, a territory that was part of the kingdom of the Franks.

DOCUMENT 1 A Christian View

Then Abd al-Rahman, seeing the land filled with the multitude of his army, crossed the Pyrenees, and traversed the defiles [in the mountains] and the plains, so that he penetrated ravaging and slaying clear into the lands of the Franks. . . . Whereupon Abd al-Rahman . . . destroyed palaces, burned churches, and imagined he could pillage the basilica of St. Martin of Tours. It is then that he found himself face to face with the lord of Austrasia, Charles [Martel], a mighty warrior from his youth, and trained in all the occasions of arms.

For almost seven days the two armies watched one another, waiting anxiously the moment for joining the struggle. Finally they made ready for combat. And in the shock of the battle the men of the North seemed like a sea that cannot be moved. Firmly they stood, one close to another, forming as it were a bulwark of ice; and with great blows of their swords they hewed down the Arabs. . . . At last night sundered the combatants. The Franks with misgivings lowered their blades, and beholding the numberless tents of the Arabs, prepared themselves for another battle the next day. Very early, . . . the men of Europe saw the Arab tents ranged still in order, in the same place where they had set up their camp. . . . In fact, during the night they had fled with the greatest silence, seeking with all speed their home land.

DOCUMENT 2 A Muslim View

The Muslims smote their enemies, and passed the river Garonne, and laid waste the country, and took captives without number. And that army went through all places like a desolating storm. . . . All the nations of the Franks trembled at that terrible army, and they betook them to [Charles Martel], and told him of the havoc made by the Muslim horsemen, and how they rode at their will through all the land of Narbonne, Toulouse, and Bordeaux. . . . Then the king bade them be of good cheer, and offered to aid them. . . . He mounted his horse, and he took with him a host that could not be numbered, and went against the Muslims. And he came upon them at the great city of Tours. . . .

Near the river [Loire], the two great hosts of the two languages and the two creeds were set in array against each other. The hearts of Abd al-Rahman, his captains and his men were filled with wrath and pride, and they were the first to begin to fight. The Muslim horsemen dashed . . . forward against the battalions of the Franks, who resisted manfully, and many fell dead on either side, until the going down of the sun. Night parted the two armies: but in the grey of the morning the Muslims returned to the battle. Their cavaliers had soon hewn their way into the center of the Christian host. But many of the Muslims were fearful for the safety of the spoil which they had stored in their tents; . . . whereupon several squadrons of the Muslim horsemen rode off to protect their tents. . . . And while Abd al-Rahman strove to check their tumult, and to lead them back to battle, the warriors of the Franks came around him, and he was pierced through with many spears, so that he died. Then all the host fled before the enemy, and many died in the flight.

Sources: Chronicle of 754, "Isidore of Beja's Chronicle" (Chronicle of 754), English translation from Internet Medieval Sourcebook, http://www.fordham.edu/halsall/sbook2.asp. The principal edition of the *Chronicle of 754* is J. E. Lopez Perreira, *Estudio critico sobre la Cronica Mozarabe de 754* (Zaragoza: Anubar, 1980). Anonymous Arab chronicler quoted in Jose Antonio Condé, *History of the Dominion of the Arabs in Spain,* trans. Mrs. Jonathan Foster, vol. 1 (London: Henry G. Bohn, 1854), 108–111.

Thinking Critically

What do the selections tell you about why and where the two adversaries fought the Battle of Tours? Which passages in these two selections appear to corroborate each other? Which passages appear to be inconsistent? Which words or phrases suggest religious or political bias on the part of one author or the other? How do the two authors appear to regard the courage and fighting qualities of both armies?

mainly boys and girls from aristocratic families. He even learned to read Latin and a little Greek (though he never got the hang of how to write). Finally, Carolingian scribes, working partly from experiments undertaken in women's monasteries, perfected a clearer, simpler alphabetic system called Caroline script (or Carolingian minuscule), which stimulated written communication in western Europe. This script is close to the "Roman" alphabet we use today.

In the political sphere, Charlemagne made a start at organizing the existing jumble of Roman and Germanic customary law and creating a rudimentary central bureaucracy to collect taxes and enforce royal decrees. As a ruler on the northern periphery of urban civilization, he made a large enough impression on the Abbasid Caliphate that the two states exchanged a number of diplomatic missions, one of them including an albino elephant—a gift from Caliph Harun al-Rashid to the Carolingian court. (The elephant, no doubt miserable in cold Europe, died within a few years.) Recent historical research has shown that in the Carolingian period both regional European and trans-Mediterranean trade began to liven, and it involved growing commercial exchange between Europeans and the subjects of Muslim states. Also, larger numbers of Christians made long pilgrimages to Palestine to visit the holy sites in Jerusalem, which was under Muslim rule. One of the busiest commercial and pilgrimage routes ran from central Europe down the Danube River to the Black Sea and from there to Constantinople and Palestine beyond.

Charlemagne's death in 814 signaled the empire's rapid decline. Whatever grand title the pope gave the monarch, his authority ultimately rested mainly on the personal loyalty of the Frankish nobility. Louis, Charlemagne's son and heir, showed himself to be a much less effective leader. Because he could not perpetuate territorial expansion, he could not ensure aristocratic allegiance by promising booty and new estates. The reunification of Europe was aborted, and the region entered a new period of political and social turbulence.

Dwindling Christian Society in North Africa

Between the fourth and early seventh centuries, Mediterranean Africa may have been on the way to becoming as thoroughly Christian as Europe did. Owing to quarrels over church organization and leadership, however, Christian practice among North Africans tended to be divisive. The Arab invasion in the seventh century further split Christian communities from one another. Islamic conversion accelerated, and within a few centuries Christianity mostly

Pope Leo III crowns Charlemagne Emperor of the Romans. This ceremony, illustrated in an early medieval manuscript, worked to the advantage of both parties. Charlemagne acquired an elevated title, and the pope cast himself as a maker of emperors. How would you identify the other figures in the picture?

disappeared in the regions that are today Tunisia, Algeria, and Morocco. Judaism, on the other hand, did not decline. In fact, the Jewish minority in those regions grew larger, perhaps because Arab unification stimulated Jewish merchants, artisans, and farmers to settle there, as well as in Spain.

Only in Egypt did a sizable Christian population survive on the southern Mediterranean rim. When Arab forces invaded the Nile valley in the mid-seventh century, they expelled the priestly representatives of the Greek Orthodox Church, but they allowed Monophysite Christians, of which there were many, to worship as a protected group. Monophysite doctrine, contrary to Greek Orthodoxy, gave primacy to Christ's spiritual nature over his humanity (see Chapter 9). Under Muslim rule the Egyptian church took on a distinctive identity, anointing its own patriarch and using Coptic, a late version of ancient Egyptian written in a modified Greek alphabet, as its language of worship. In the ensuing centuries, the Coptic community continued to flourish, though shrinking slowly relative to the number of Muslims. Today, Egypt's Christian population is about 9 percent of the total.

Up the Nile valley in Nubia (southern Egypt and northern Sudan), the Christian communities that flourished between

St. Mary's church in Cairo. Built originally in the seventh century, this sanctuary became the residence of the patriarch, or head of the Monophysite Coptic church, in the eleventh century. The building is also called the Hanging Church because it was erected above the gatehouse of a Roman fort.

the fifth and seventh centuries gradually faded away. After the Arabs conquered Egypt, Orthodox Christians in Nubia managed to stay in communication with Constantinople and the Greek church. Muslim traders, preachers, and pastoral nomadic groups, however, entered the region in ever-growing numbers. In the early second millennium C.E., Islam replaced Christianity in Nubia as the faith of the great majority. Southeast of the Nile, however, the Monophysite church in Ethiopia continued to thrive.

East Asia: Return to Unity in China

> **FOCUS** What consequences did the unification of China under the Sui and Tang dynasties have for the region's economic and cultural development?

Paralleling the political unification of Southwest Asia under Muslim rulers, two successive dynasties, the Sui (SWAY) and the Tang, restored strong central government in China, absent since the collapse of the Han empire in the early third century (see Map 10.4). In 581 a military coalition whose leaders were a mix of Chinese and Turkic aristocrats conquered northern China, proclaimed the Sui dynasty (581–618), and then advanced south to the Yangzi valley. Within a decade, northern and southern China were united

once again. The two emperors of the Sui appealed to Chinese Buddhists for support and attempted to extend their authority along the Inner Eurasian frontier, as well as in southwestern China, Vietnam, and the Korean peninsula. When the Sui armies became overextended, however, civil war allowed Li Yuan, an insurgent military officer of both Chinese and Turkic descent, to seize the imperial throne in 618 and proclaim the Tang dynasty. In the more than three centuries of Sui and Tang rule, China experienced periods of both internal struggle and foreign invasion. But the Confucian model of the emperor and his hierarchy of scholar-bureaucrats as the "natural" leaders of a unified China became reality once again.

The Tang State

Up to about 750, the Tang state advanced China's political, economic, and cultural integration. This consolidation occurred mainly under four emperors: Taizong (r. 626–649), Gaozong (r. 649–683), the Empress Wu (r. 690–705), and Xuanzong (r. 712–756). As Gaozong's wife and then ruler in her own right, Wu dominated state affairs for about half a century. Though all these rulers patronized Buddhism to one degree or another, they managed state affairs according to Confucian principles of centralized command exercised through public ministries that reached down to the local level. Ideally, bureaucratic officers were sworn to

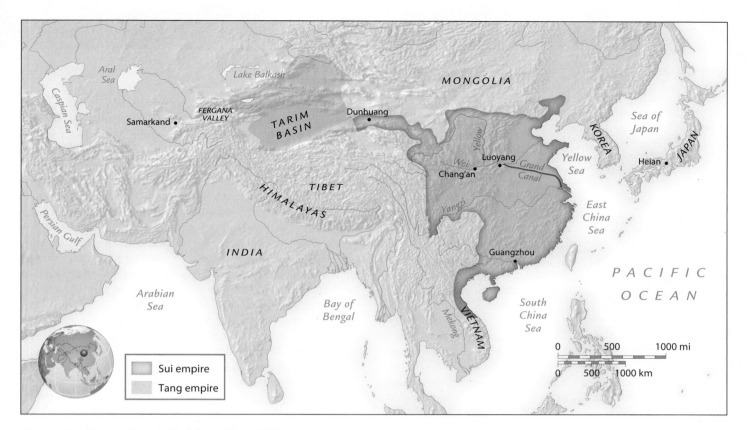

MAP 10.4 Sui and Tang empires, 589–907.
Why do you think the Tang empire narrows to a long neck of territory between northern China and Inner Eurasia?

reasonable, sympathetic administration and selfless service to the state. The government examination system, initiated in the era of the Han dynasty, was expanded greatly to educate prospective officials in the Confucian classics. Students who performed well on the exhausting tests received assignments to imperial administrative posts. The exam takers were mostly sons of wealthy landowning families, but because intelligence, diligence, and ambition were requisite qualifications for service, not simply circumstances of birth, young men who had financial sponsorship might rise from the peasantry to positions of responsibility.

Like the Emperor Justinian in sixth-century Byzantium, the Tang rulers sought to unify the empire by implementing a rational, uniform, and efficient legal system. The Tang Code followed Confucian principles in envisioning society as constituting a hierarchy of three groups: (1) the privileged class of ranking officials and imperial courtiers; (2) commoners, who made up the vast majority of peasants and town folk; and (3) "inferior people," such as slaves and others in a condition of personal bondage. The code also had numerous statutes that perpetuated legal and social inequality between men and women. A man, for example, was legally entitled to beat his wife, but a woman who killed her husband was subject to severe penalty.

Stabilizing the peasantry. The early Tang emperors aimed to put as much arable land as possible to the plow, alleviate insecurity and poverty that might ignite rural protests, and make the huge peasant class productive enough to pay regular taxes. To this end, they adopted an institution known as the **equal-field system,** an idea initiated by an earlier regional dynasty. By this policy, the state allocated arable land to individual peasant families to farm for their lifetime, the amount of acreage depending mainly on the family's size and wealth. In some cases, a family could pass on its property to the next generation, especially if the farm produced silk and therefore had to have mulberry trees that took more than a generation to mature. As for aristocratic families, the state (with varying success) put limits on the amount of land they could own in order to reduce the number of peasants who served as tenants or day workers on giant estates.

Through the equal-field system, the Tang also aimed to build a militia of farmer-soldiers who worked their acreage part of the year and gave military service the rest. Here,

> **equal-field system** The Chinese system for state distribution of land; the state assigned fixed acreages of crop land to families on the basis of labor, both adult males and animals, available to work it.

Individuals MATTER

The Empress Wu: Patron of Buddhism

An eighteenth-century Chinese artist's imagining of the Empress Wu Zetian.

Empress Wu Zetian (625–705), the only woman ever to rule China in her own right, was one of the Tang era's most enthusiastic patrons of Buddhist devotion and art. She entered the Tang imperial court as a concubine of Emperor Taizong. At the time, she was between thirteen and sixteen years old. The young girl's command of literature and history soon earned her the emperor's favor. But his death a decade later left her facing a future as a Buddhist nun, the expected path for a concubine of a deceased monarch.

Instead of retiring to a monastery, however, Wu attracted the attention of Taizong's son, the new Emperor Gaozong. She eventually rose to the position of primary consort, or companion of the emperor, by giving birth to sons. She also bore a daughter, then accused Gaozong's wife, Empress Wang, of murdering the baby. Empress Wang was disgraced and killed, and in 655 Wu became Gaozong's new wife.

Within five years, however, Gaozong suffered a crippling stroke. This crisis offered Wu the opportunity to serve as ruler, first in the name of the incapacitated Gaozong and after his death in 683 as regent for her docile and submissive sons. In 690 she proclaimed herself the legitimate monarch and declared a new dynasty, the Zhou, a name that invoked the long-enduring Zhou dynasty of the first millennium B.C.E.

Traditional Confucian doctrines did not allow for the possibility of a female ruler. But Empress Wu sought to counter that ideology by patronizing Buddhism, which embodied a somewhat less constricted view of women's social roles. She promoted the cult of the Bodhisattva Maitreya, a figure prophesied to return in the body of a woman to rule over a golden age. She supported Buddhist temples and translations of important religious texts into Chinese. Reversing the policy of earlier Tang emperors, she gave Buddhists precedence over Daoists in imperial court rituals. She is best remembered for sponsoring the carving of spectacular statues of the Buddha and other divines in the Longmen Grottoes. These are niches and shallow caves excavated from the limestone cliffs above the Yishui River near Luoyang, where Wu spent her entire reign.

Besides shoring up support for her reign through these cultural avenues, Wu engaged in apparently ruthless palace politics, including possible assassination of a son and recruitment of a secret police force that ferreted out and brutally punished anyone who challenged her authority. It is difficult, however, to accurately assess her actions, since conservative Confucian scholars who wrote about her reign consistently portrayed her as a dangerous woman occupying the imperial throne in opposition to the natural order of the universe. Around 700, in any case, her health deteriorated, and she relied increasingly on the advice of two men who were not only counselors but also lovers. In 705 Wu's son Zhongzong joined a group of court officials who conspired to kill these advisers. Zhongzong then seized the emperorship, declaring the end of the short-lived Zhou dynasty and the restoration of the Tang. Empress Wu gave no resistance and moved to a residence outside the palace, where she died later that year.

Thinking Critically

What strategies were available to Empress Wu to advance her political ambitions?

---

the state wished to fashion an army whose core units were hardy, well-trained, loyal peasants, not nomad mercenaries from the steppe. Many of these soldiers, who clad themselves in iron armor and specialized in archery, did duty on the northern and western frontiers facing Inner Eurasia.

Integrating north and south. The task of militarily and politically integrating the East Asian land mass and its seventh-century population of about 60 million demanded strategic and technical innovation. The unified Roman

empire had had the advantage of the Mediterranean Sea, a giant central "lake" for moving soldiers, supplies, messages, and commercial goods long distances at costs much lower than overland transport allowed. The Tang emperors, by contrast, had no "middle sea" to speed communication. The Yellow and Yangzi Rivers, the two most important transport corridors, flowed generally west to east. The principal grain staple in the north was wheat; in the south it was rice. To encourage greater commercial integration between the two great river valleys, the Tang government undertook construction of the Grand Canal, an enormous, centrally directed engineering project to link the two great river basins by a series of north–south waterways. The state conscripted tens of thousands of laborers to do the digging, and evidence suggests that a majority of those workers were peasant women. The canal functioned primarily to supply the Chinese administration and army, which was concentrated heavily in the north, with the rice and other food products of the warmer, wetter south. Imperial roads ran alongside the canal, and numerous subsidiary channels, rivers, and tracks connected the central line to provincial cities and rural hinterlands.

Tang engineers also built a canal that extended westward to the Tang capital of Chang'an (modern Xian) near the Wei River, a tributary of the Yellow. From this imperial city, whose outer walls of brick and pounded earth extended more than five miles on each side, the royal palace and six major ministries managed affairs of state. The emperor obliged independent-minded aristocrats, especially from the south, to establish residences in Chang'an in order to keep them under close watch. The presence of this elite meant that tens of thousands of farmers, artisans, soldiers, merchants, entertainers, and servants also had to be on hand to meet aristocratic needs. Chang'an also accommodated thousands of non-Chinese residents. Until the later eighth century, the Tang government took a broadminded view of foreigners who came to trade, preach their faith, or enlist in the army or civil service. The estate-owning classes also wanted the luxury imports that merchants brought in on the silk roads or through southern China's seaports, especially Guangzhou (Canton). Consequently, Turks, Sogdians, Persians, Tibetans, Koreans, Japanese, Nestorian Christians, Manicheans, and Jews all circulated in Chang'an's streets and bazaars.

Urban Chinese also acquired enthusiastic tastes for the arts of Inner Eurasia, Persia, and India. Musicians and entertainers traveled the silk roads to seek work in Chang'an and other cities. Distant kingdoms paid tribute to the Tang royal court by sending orchestras and dance troops. These visitors brought with them musical instruments, compositional styles, and dances that influenced more traditional Chinese musical arts. Both noble households and popular urban crowds enjoyed Inner Eurasian lute players, drummers, acrobats, magicians, puppeteers, and fire eaters, as well as a company of girls who danced and twirled on top of large rolling balls. Not all educated Chinese, however, approved of so many foreigners from the "west" crowding into their cities. One Tang poet wrote:

> Ever since the alien horsemen began raising smut and dust,
> Fur and fleece, rank and rancid, have filled Hsien
> [Chang'an] and Luo [Luoyang, another Tang capital]
> Women make themselves western matrons by the study
>   of western makeup,
> Entertainers present western tunes, in their devotion to
>   western music.[3]

Counting both Chinese and expatriate residents, the population of Chang'an in the seventh and eighth centuries may have reached between one and two million, making it the largest city in the world, bigger than either Constantinople or Baghdad.

The Tang imperial thrust. Military campaigns of the first Tang century pushed Chinese imperial power from the Yangzi valley to both the subtropical coastlands of the far south and into Vietnam. For a time, the Tang also dominated part of Korea. The most spectacular campaigns, however, took place to the northwest. Emperor Taizong and the Empress Wu after him triumphed over pastoral nomads on the eastern steppes. Deftly combining military might with aggressive diplomacy, the Tang government helped engineer the collapse of the Eastern Türk empire and forced numerous war chiefs to accept Chinese suzerainty. Like the Han expansion seven hundred years earlier, these offensives aimed to expand the state's control of commerce as far across Inner Eurasia as logistically possible. The army also had an insatiable demand for horses, which the Ferghana valley in modern Tajikistan could steadily supply. Only after

Musicians of the Tang era. These terra-cotta figures from the seventh century represent female entertainers playing a drum and a Chinese lute.

Arab forces vanquished a Chinese army northwest of Ferghana in 751 and after numerous internal problems arose within the empire did the Tang rulers pull back from their extended Inner Eurasian frontiers.

Migrations to the South

In the sphere of demographic and social change, the Tang era witnessed a steady shift of the geographical center of China's population from the Yellow River valley to the Yangzi. Chinese farmers equipped with iron hoes, axes, and plows had already been moving southward for several centuries. Their reasons for migrating included overcrowding on northern grain land, the perennial threat of nomad attack, and the north's fickle climate, which periodically brought drought and famine. As more Han Chinese farmers headed south, ancient local peoples of non-Chinese ethnicity either assimilated to the growing Chinese population through intermarriage and cultural conversion or retreated to inaccessible highlands.

The pioneering Chinese who settled the south had an enormous impact on East Asia's economic development and integration. They drained river valleys and marshes, leveled fields, and constructed dams, dykes, and canals. The draining projects also improved human prospects by reducing mortality from malaria and waterborne diseases. Transforming southern China into the urban, commercialized dynamo it became required generations of peasant labor. From the economic and social perspective, the long-term payoff was rapid population growth in the south and greatly intensified exchange of commodities and manufactures with China.

Cultural Integration

Culturally, China remained a jumble of languages and ethnic groups, but Chinese speakers, generally called Han Chinese, became progressively dominant in the south. There, literate Chinese introduced the written language, and Confucian scholars and officials exercised growing influence. Consequently, at the level of elite culture and manners, north and south fused gradually. In this respect, the Chinese script, purged by this time of most of its regional variants, served the same intellectually unifying purpose as Latin did in western Europe and Arabic in Southwest Asia and North Africa. Chinese poetry, for example, matured as a major form of literary expression throughout the Tang empire.

Tang patronage of Buddhism. Buddhism, which silk road monks and merchants introduced to China in the first century C.E., also became an important unifying force in the Tang era. Recognizing Buddhism's surging popularity and the value of identifying themselves with a universalist

Vairochana Buddha. Chinese Buddhists adopted the Indian tradition of carving images of the Buddha in rock. Caves and niches cut from sandstone cliffs at Longmen, a site on the Yi River near Luoyang, contain more than 100,000 statues of the Buddha of varying sizes. Empress Wu sponsored creation of the cave containing the Vairochana, or Resplendent Buddha, which is about forty-nine feet high. What qualities of character do you think this Buddha displays?

system of morality and worship, the early Tang emperors patronized Buddhist monasteries and convents enthusiastically. They sponsored thousands of new monastic communities, libraries, and stupas (shrines to house relics of the Buddha), as well as rock carvings and cave paintings of the Buddha, Buddhist saints (*bodhisattvas*), and other aesthetic imagery. The emperors liked to represent themselves as models of sacred Buddhist kingship, the Emperor Taizong even identifying himself vaguely with Ashoka, the great monarch and Buddhist patron of India in the third century B.C.E. (see Chapter 6). Chinese monks traveled to India in increasing numbers to visit shrines and collect religious texts. The Chinese cleric Xuanzang (596–664), whose description of the Türk monarch we quoted earlier in this chapter, crossed Inner Eurasia to reach India, returned home after sixteen years to the acclaim of the imperial court, and became a skilled translator of Sanskrit writings into Chinese.

Buddhists meet the Confucian and Daoist traditions. As much as Buddhist statuary and painting impressed ordinary Chinese, monks and scholars still had their work cut out for them putting scriptures in South Asian languages into words that made sense in East Asia. They had to express their religious concepts and moral values in ways that might resonate with Chinese people whose framework of thought and action had a Confucian orientation. Confucians stressed responsibility to family members, so Buddhists argued that *bodhisattvas* would help entire families along the road to salvation. Buddhists linked the Confucian concept of respect for authority to the Indian idea of *karuna,* or all-encompassing compassion. Confucian scholars valued quiet study and contemplation, which Buddhist teachings endorsed warmly.

Daoism, the other major Chinese belief system, shared with Buddhism the yearnings women and men had for health, inner peace, salvation, and immortality. Buddhists found they could connect quite easily with Daoist thought, which encouraged individuals to extricate themselves from worldly affairs and strive for spiritual oneness with cosmic reality. The Daoist tradition offered a private, meditative counterpoint to the incessant Confucian demand to manage and improve society. Buddhists represented themselves as offering Chinese seekers even richer inner experience, complementing more than competing with Daoist beliefs and practices. The Buddhist concept of *dharma,* which means at one level to behave righteously and at another to live in harmony with deepest reality, was linked to the *dao,* the divine principle of being. The state of *nirvana* was associated with *wuwei,* the Daoist concept of "non-action," or utter peace. In the later first millennium C.E., the Buddhist and Daoist traditions became so deeply intermingled that few Chinese thought about the precise differences between them.

Buddhism succeeded brilliantly in demonstrating its universalist appeal in China. Distinctly Chinese schools of Buddhist thought began to emerge. Chinese devotees, both aristocratic families and rural villagers, donated wealth to monasteries, and Chinese styles of Buddhist art and architecture evolved. In the first flush of Buddhist success, Confucian scholarship went into partial eclipse. But neither Buddhism nor Daoism aimed deliberately to contradict or compete with Confucian ideals that promoted harmonious family relations, social order, and good government.

A Chinese traveler. A fourteenth-century portrait of the Chinese monk Xuangzang returning from his journey to India depicts him carrying a bamboo backpack filled with scrolls. He holds a flywhisk to drive away evil spirits in one hand and a prayer scroll in the other.

• • •

Conclusion

A military strategist with a bird's-eye view of Afroeurasia in the mid-eighth century might have predicted that Arab Muslim armies were about to conquer the entire hemisphere north of the tropics. Arab forces reached Chinese-occupied territory on the northern silk route, and according to Muslim tradition, an early caliph offered the governorship of China to whichever of his generals got there first. In the west, military operations in the early eighth century might have looked like a grand pincer operation against Europe, as Arab commanders advanced simultaneously on Constantinople and Spain. As we have seen, however, the Arab Muslim juggernaut faltered, if only because invasions of China and all of Europe were beyond the technological and logistical powers of the new Muslim governments based in Southwest Asia. Nevertheless, for the first time in history, a powerful state and an emerging new religious and cultural tradition encompassed most of Southeast Asia and the eastern Mediterranean. With the Byzantine frontiers pushed back and the Sasanid empire destroyed, the land between Syria and Mesopotamia was no longer a "shatter zone" of chronic conflict between competing empires but the heart of a new and creative civilization.

The political and cultural integration of Southwest Asia under Muslim leadership helped fuel a new surge of urbanization, production, and commerce that stimulated long-distance trade linking that region to the rest of Afroeurasia. Probably even more important for trans-hemispheric exchange, China moved into a new era of economic growth in connection with the Sui and Tang unification. Given its dense population and rich resources, China's agricultural and manufacturing potential far exceeded all other Afroeurasian regions with the exception of India.

In the far west, temperate Europe began, starting in the seventh century, to recover from the wreckage of the western Roman empire and to restructure itself along new economic and political lines. In Spain, Arab conquerors, with help from engineers, architects, and irrigation experts who arrived from Southwest Asia, laid the foundations of a small but flourishing Muslim civilization. To the northeast, the Frankish conqueror Charlemagne tried to pull together a new pan-European state founded on Roman Christian culture. This experiment, however, did not outlast him. Most of Europe remained an aggregate of competing political entities, though this did not stop population and production from starting to rise.

Other forces also helped set the stage for a new era of economic growth and commercial exchange from the Mediterranean to East Asia. South Asia, though divided into a number of states, continued to churn out great quantities of cotton textiles and other products for export. The maritime network of merchants and shippers plying the southern seas from China to East Africa had been growing for centuries and was primed for more traffic. Tang and Arab expansion in Inner Eurasia, plus successful pastoral nomadic state-building there, kept the silk roads in business with few interruptions. Western and central Europe had to face serious new external threats in the ninth century, but within less than two hundred years that region was also poised for a burst of economic activity that would in time far surpass the achievement of western Rome. Finally, after two hundred years of microbial assaults, recurrences of plague faded out about 705 in the Mediterranean and Southwest Asian lands.

In short, Afroeurasia as a whole moved in the sixth century and (in some places somewhat later) into a new growth phase. From a millennial low of less than 190 million in 700 c.e., Afroeurasia's population rose to about 235 million by 1000, an increase correlated broadly with a revival of agrarian production, more vigorous trade, and proliferation in the size and number of cities.[4] This trend would continue with only modest dips for another three centuries.

• • •

Key Terms

Arab empire 281
Benedictines 294
caliph 287
Carolingian renaissance 295
cathedral 294
Eastern and Western Türk empires 301
equal-field system 299

Franks 294
hijra 286
imam 289
Islam 283
Khazar empire 281
manor 293
pope 294
Quran (Koran) 279

serf 293
Shi'a Muslims 289
Sui dynasty 298
Sunni Muslims 289
Tang dynasty 281
Tibetan empire 281
Uighur empire 281
Umayyad dynasty 288

Change over Time

552–744	Eastern and then Western Türk empires dominate steppes of Inner Eurasia.
570–632	The Prophet Muhammad preaches one God and founds a state in Arabia.
581–618	The Sui dynasty restores strong central government to China.
618–842	The Tibetan empire of the Tibetan plateau is a major player in Inner Eurasian politics.
618–907	The Tang dynasty integrates and expands Chinese territory.
622	Muhammad and his followers flee from Mecca to Madina (*hijra*); the Muslim calendar begins.
630–965	The Khazar empire, the longest-lasting Turkic-speaking state of the era, dominates Inner Eurasia.
632–661	The Muslim community is led by the first four caliphs.
661–750	The Umayyad Caliphate centered in Damascus leads a major expansion of the Arab state.
744–840	The Uighur empire in Inner Eurasia commands the eastern end of the silk roads.
750	The Umayyad government falls to Abbasids; the Abbasid Caliphate begins.
768–814	Charlemagne reigns over the kingdom of the Franks; "Carolingian renaissance."

Please see end of book reference section for additional reading suggestions related to this chapter.

11 State Power and Expanding Networks of Exchange

750–1000 C.E.

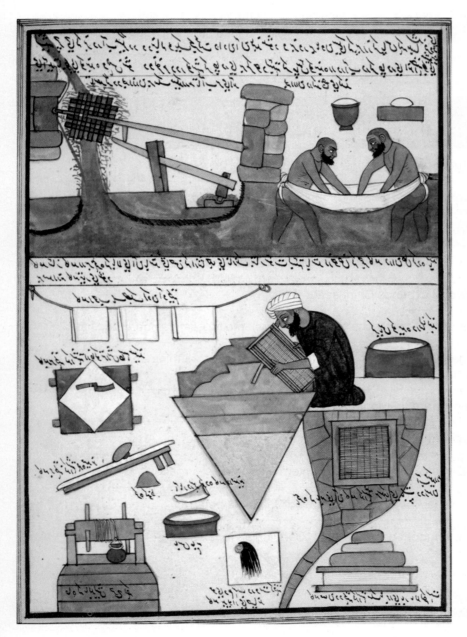

Traditional Muslim paper manufacturing is illustrated in the *Album of Kashmiri Trades,* a text of the mid-nineteenth century.

Not many years ago, some technology experts predicted that the computer revolution would spell the end of paper. So far, that has not happened. The human race continues to consume vast and increasing quantities of paper as a cheap, smooth-surfaced material for inscribing messages. Annual production of paper and paperboard worldwide exceeds 400 million metric tons. In the period we investigate in this chapter, people began to use paper across Afroeurasia on a significant scale. In the second century B.C.E., or perhaps earlier, Chinese artisans invented a way to fabricate paper by suspending pieces of flax, hemp, textile rags, or mulberry tree bark in a mixture of water and lye. This concoction was then cooked and pounded to break up the fibers, leaving a mushy pulp of cellulose. The next steps were to dip a framed fabric screen into a pan of the cellulose, spread the pulp over the surface, and set it out to dry. Finally, the artisan peeled the dried sheet off the screen and cut it into pieces of required size.

The secret of papermaking spread eastward to Korea and Japan in the early centuries C.E. and westward along the Inner Eurasian silk roads a few hundred years later. According to a traditional story, Arab soldiers advancing into Inner Eurasia in the eighth century took several Chinese paper experts prisoner and marched them to Baghdad in Iraq to build a mill. More likely, artisans were already manufacturing paper in Central Asian cities far west of China, and they passed the technology to the Arabs. In any case, paper became common in India, the Mediterranean basin, and Europe in the following three hundred years. Its use began to revolutionize human ability to record, transmit, and store information of all kinds.

The diffusion of paper technology is one example of the upward trend of social, cultural, and economic complexity that characterized Afroeurasia as a whole in these centuries. Around 600 C.E., long-distance commercial and cultural exchange began to pick up across the hemisphere, and this trend continued, with some fluctuations, for the next seven hundred years. Merchants, missionaries, pilgrims, and scholars moved in unprecedented numbers along land and sea routes. By rough estimates, Afroeurasia's overall population appears to have declined slightly between 400 and 700 C.E. but then jumped by nearly 50 percent in the next three hundred years. Demographic growth reflected and in turn stimulated expansion and greater complexity in farming, manufacturing, and technical knowledge, including, for example, the diffusion of paper.

This chapter starts by surveying developments in the central region of Afroeurasia, where Arabic-speaking rulers professing Islam, the youngest of the major religions, united most of Southwest Asia. The first Arab empire, created in the later seventh century under the Umayyad dynasty, extended far beyond that region, but it lasted less than a century. After 750 C.E., the Abbasid Caliphate, the second Muslim royal dynasty, continued to rule Southwest Asia but lost direct control of more distant lands, where new kingdoms multiplied. From Spain to northwestern India, however, these kingdoms were all Muslim.

Following the rise of the Abbasid state, commercial exchange along the chain of seas from the Persian Gulf to the South China Sea intensified dramatically. Farmers and artisans produced commodities that could be sold far and wide, and merchants became more sophisticated, forming larger trading diasporas to connect ports over long distances and inventing better methods for transporting goods and exchanging money. In the second part of the chapter, we take a tour along the chain of seas, stopping to investigate developments in the Arabian Sea basin, maritime Southeast Asia, China, and finally Japan and Korea.

The third section of the chapter introduces a new arena of human interchange, the rim of the Sahara Desert. Merchants who learned how to guide dromedary camels from one side of that wilderness to another without dying along the way blazed the first caravan trails, permanently joining the Mediterranean with tropical West Africa. Agrarian states already existed in West Africa when the trans-Saharan trade got under way, but exchange of gold, slaves, copper, salt, and other commodities inspired larger state-building projects, notably

Chapter Outline

• • •

Ghana, which in the later first millennium C.E. achieved imperial proportions.

The final part of the chapter shifts northward to Europe, where in the eighth century the future looked brighter for ordinary people after three centuries of trouble and decline. However, in the ninth century the Christian empire that King Charlemagne built (see Chapter 10) broke apart. Soon afterward, military bands intruded aggressively into the heart of Europe once again, this time from North Africa, the Inner Eurasia steppes, and the Scandinavian north. These incursions interrupted Europe's return to stability but also obliged its aristocratic leaders to work out new strategies for defending their lands and ensuring social order.

A Panoramic View

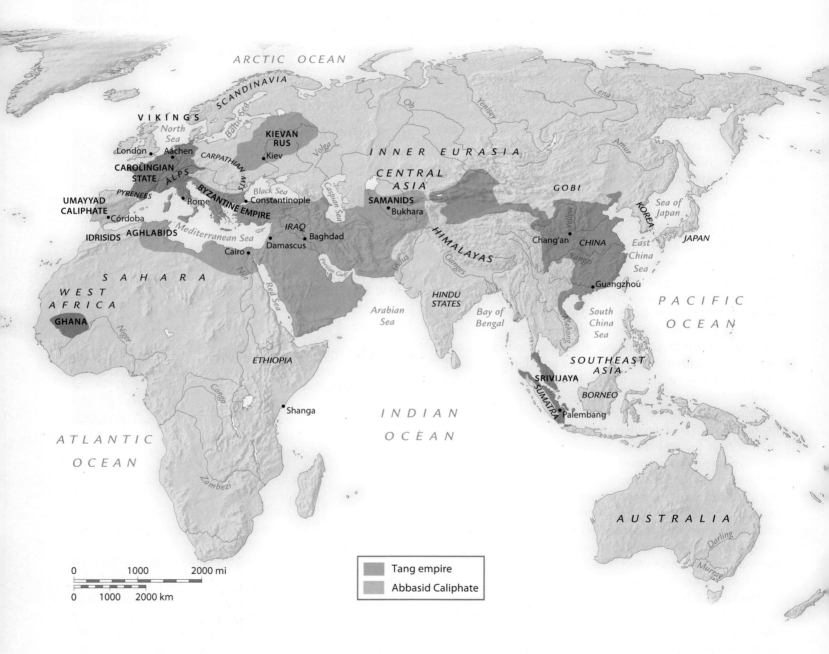

MAP 11.1 Major states in Afroeurasia, 800.

Large empires continued to claim significant portions of Afroeurasia's temperate zones. What geographic features might help account for the frontiers between some of these states?

Muslim Power and Prosperity

FOCUS How did the rise of the Abbasid Caliphate and other Muslim states between the eighth and tenth centuries contribute to the emergence of a new Afroeurasian cultural tradition centered on Islam?

As the eighth century C.E. neared its midpoint, the Arab caliphs (rulers) of the Umayyad dynasty claimed sovereignty over an enormous territory extending from Damascus, the imperial capital in Syria, about 3,000 miles to the west and nearly 2,500 miles to the east. As astonishing as they were, these conquests cost the Muslim Umayyad rulers much treasure. In the 740s, Arab garrisons in the empire's outlying provinces faced a surge of local rebellions, which left the caliphate financially exhausted and militarily enfeebled. In 747 the leaders of the Abbasids, an Arab clan descended from an uncle of the Prophet Muhammad, rose up against the Umayyads and three years later drove them out of Damascus. The Abbasids declared themselves the rightful and universal caliphs, or supreme leaders of Muslims everywhere, though they did not manage to keep the whole Arab empire together. After 750, other new Muslim states appeared from Spain to Central Asia, and the Christian Byzantine monarchy fought persistently to keep control of Anatolia (modern Turkey). But for more than two centuries, the Abbasids taxed the immense agrarian and urban wealth of both Southwest Asia and Egypt, and they witnessed the continuing spread of Islam in all directions.

From Damascus to Baghdad: The Abbasid Empire

As ancient empire builders had often done, the Abbasid rulers advertised their triumph by forsaking the capital of their opponents and founding a new one. They chose Baghdad, a site on the Tigris River in Iraq not far from the former Persian capital of Ctesiphon. This change meant that the center of gravity of the Muslim state in Southwest Asia shifted from Syria eastward to Iraq (see Map 11.1). The Tigris-Euphrates valley and its tens of thousands of irrigated fields became the heartland of the Arab Muslim empire. It also meant that the people of Iran just to the east began to loom larger in Muslim state and cultural affairs.

Abbasid might. Extracting great wealth not only from Iraq but also from Egypt, Syria, and Iran, the early Abbasid caliphs supported

Abbasid artisanship. The refined skill of Abbasid artisans is evident in this exquisitely designed water pitcher. It was among the gifts that Harun al-Rashid sent to the Frankish king Charlemagne.

large armies, a complex and educated bureaucracy, and an imperial household that basked in stupendous luxury. The organization of the caliphate was not radically different from that of earlier Southwest Asian and Mediterranean empires. The Abbasids incorporated various governing methods modeled on Sasanid Persia. In fact their success as Muslim state builders depended on preserving continuity with the former Persian, and to some extent Byzantine, imperial systems. The Abbasids organized a hierarchy of provinces and districts, set up specialized ministries, employed thousands of secretaries and accountants, and appointed a Persian-style vizier, or chief counselor, to direct daily affairs in the caliph's name. The government relied increasingly on the support of Persian aristocratic families and recruited numerous literate Persians to take official jobs.

As in the former Persian and Byzantine empires, Abbasid government rested on collaboration between the royal household and the elite landowning families of the realm to control and tax the men and women who worked the land. The caliphs had no choice except to negotiate political arrangements with wealthy families, tribal groups, and ethnic communities to ensure their allegiance and cooperation.

To the general population, however, the Abbasids projected themselves as the personification of absolute authority and magical, semidivine power. In stark contrast to the first four caliphs after Muhammad, the Abbasids ruled in a distinctly Persian style, cloaking themselves in pomp and secret wonder. The caliph referred to himself as the "Shadow of God on Earth," outfitted himself in the robes and tall conical hat of a Persian potentate, and spoke to petitioners while hidden from view behind a screen. History remembers Caliph Harun al-Rashid (reigned 786–809) less as an able ruler, which he generally was, than as an exalted monarch whose magnificent palaces dazzled all who saw them.

Government communication between Baghdad and distant provinces depended initially on the system of roads and trails built earlier by Persians and Romans. The Abbasid public works ministry gradually improved this network, constructing more highways, bridges, and way stations. The government also built on the old infrastructures to create the *barid,* an elaborate postal and intelligence web. Lacing the empire together along nearly four hundred different routes, the dispatch riders of the *barid,* a sort of pony express, kept the imperial palace closely informed about provincial governors, local notables, and potential troublemakers.

Islam and the caliphate: an uncertain relationship. The Abbasids' fondness for concentrated power and semidivine monarchy had little to do with the ideals of Islam. Most of the rulers tried therefore to project a public image of spiritual humility and worthiness as the "commander of the believers." They took special care to display respect for the Muslim community's religious and legal scholars. This learned class, known in Arabic as the *ulama*, emerged as the guardians and interpreters of Islamic law, or *shari'a* (shah-REE-ah). The caliphs encouraged legal experts among the *ulama* to shape the body of laws into a unified code to regulate religious, social, and economic life throughout the empire.

> *ulama* Muslim religious scholars, judges, teachers, and mosque officials.

> *shari'a* The body of Islamic laws and moral precepts based on the Quran and the sayings and actions of the Prophet Muhammad.

The *ulama*, however, never fully accepted the Abbasids as legitimate successors of the revered caliphs who followed Muhammad. They contended that in the sight of God the caliph was no better than ordinary men and women. The community should therefore accept him only in so far as he was devoted and responsible, not simply powerful. The contradictions between the ideal of a community of equal, decision-making believers and the reality of an authoritarian monarchy were consequently not resolved. On one side was the principle of an egalitarian society in which the caliph, chosen by the leading religious figures, carried out the community's will. On the other was the reality of a Persian-style absolute monarchy that perpetuated itself in alliance with a wealthy class that consumed lavishly and, in the eyes of the righteous, often behaved wickedly. For example, Islamic law specified that an adult male was permitted a maximum of four wives as long as he treated them all equally. The law did not, however, authorize caliphs to keep harems of thousands of women as slaves and concubines. A further complication was that the *ulama* also wanted the social order and military defense that effective monarchs could provide. Consequently, pragmatic cooperation combined with ideological tension between the ruler and the spiritual leaders became part of the fabric of Muslim political life. In times of social distress, popular protesters or rebels could justify their actions on the grounds that the caliph had lost his moral legitimacy.

Political and ecological troubles. Provincial rebellions were just one sort of problem that the Abbasids faced within less than a century of taking power. The monarchy had no clear rules of succession. Despite the fiction that the *ulama*, representing the will of the community, chose each new caliph, various males in the royal family (with the participation of wives, mothers, and sisters) typically plotted against one another following a ruler's death until one of them got the better of the rest. The death of Caliph Harun al-Rashid in 809, for example, triggered civil strife that went on for several years. Rulers also found it increasingly difficult to prevent governors in far-off provinces from withholding tax revenues owed to the state and building their

A Muslim judge hears a case. Members of the educated class trained in jurisprudence settled civil disputes and set penalties according to Islamic law. How does the picture express the elite social status that judges enjoyed in the Abbasid Caliphate?

own power bases. The government in Baghdad could not rule any further than horses, camels, or boats could transport troops. For example, the caliphs spent heavily on summer campaigns to seize land in Anatolia from Christian Byzantium, but they made little headway. Without revenues from fresh conquests, the cost of keeping order in the existing empire increased steadily. Against good economic judgment, the Abbasids also minted huge numbers of gold and silver coins, which caused serious price inflation.

Beneath the visible surface of political and fiscal trouble lay a deeper problem, the accelerating degradation of productive farmland in the southern Tigris-Euphrates valley. Agriculture there was entirely dependent on irrigation, which in turn required a steady workforce to maintain canals, dikes, and dams. Unfortunately, a plague epidemic swept through Iraq in 749, just before the Abbasids came to power. The population of the lower valley fell, producing a serious shortage of labor to control floods and channel water to farmers. In addition, buildup of salt deposits in the soil remained a perennial and worsening problem. The wealth and glitter of Baghdad masked the fact that lower Iraq's resources were shrinking and with them wealth that the state desperately needed.

In the later ninth century, Arab and Persian landlords tried to revitalize agriculture in the valley by draining salt marshes and planting commercial crops, notably sugar cane. To meet the colossal demand for labor that this task required, they brought in thousands of slaves, mostly men and women captured in East Africa and sold to slave merchants who transported them up the Persian Gulf. Imitating the Roman model of slave labor, the landowners worked these captives in large gangs under appalling conditions. The consequence was a massive slave revolt. The Zanj Rebellion, as it was known from the Arab name for the East African coast, took the Abbasid army fifteen years to put down (869–883), cost thousands of lives, and further depleted the Abbasid treasury.

Military slavery. The Abbasids also found another way to use slaves. From the 830s, caliphs tried to strengthen their military forces by recruiting special soldiers, known in Arabic as *mamluks*, who would have no ties either to the regular army or to local families and factions. Many of these recruits were Turkic war prisoners and other captives from Inner Eurasia. Skilled as riders and archers, these "slaves on horses" were converted to Islam and in many cases given their freedom with the understanding that they remained permanently in the caliph's service.[1] As a result of this experiment, **military slavery** became a key political and social institution in the central Muslim lands.

> *mamluk* In Muslim states, a slave or freedman having primarily military or administrative duties.

> **military slavery** The personal bondage of an individual to a ruler or other authority with an obligation to provide military service.

This innovation, however, did not go according to plan. The urbane Persian scholar Jahiz (d. 869) pronounced Turks to be a people "uninterested in craftsmanship or commerce, . . . they care only about raiding, hunting, horsemanship, skirmishing with rival chieftains, taking booty, and invading other countries."[2] Jahiz exaggerated out of his own cultured bias. Nevertheless, as the slave soldiers acquired weapons, armor, horses, and an expanding sense of their own importance, they split into competing factions of their own, joined palace plots, and increasingly manipulated imperial affairs.

Rival Centers of Muslim Power

The Abbasids took power after first starting a rebellion in the northeastern region of Khurasan. But almost as soon as they succeeded, they had to face their own rebels and usurpers, some of whom managed to found independent Muslim monarchies.

The Umayyad state in Spain. The first important region to go its own way was the distant Iberian Peninsula. When in 750 the Abbasids seized Damascus and toppled the Umayyads, a member of that royal family escaped to Spain, gathered an army, and defeated the Abbasid-appointed governor there. In 756 he declared a new Umayyad dynasty with its capital at Córdoba (Cordova).

The fertile alluvial valleys of central and southern Spain, plus a Roman legacy of complex irrigation farming, offered the new Umayyad rulers a sound base for state building. The Christian population (whose rulers had been the Visigoths before the Arab invasion of 711), together with Berber newcomers from North Africa and immigrants from Syria

The Umayyad mosque at Córdoba. Abd al-Rahman I, the prince who founded the Umayyad dynasty of Spain, started constructing a grand mosque for his capital in 784. In the following two centuries, the structure was enlarged three times to produce one of the wonders of Muslim architecture. After capturing the city in the thirteenth century, Christian rulers built a cathedral inside the mosque but retained many of its columns and colorful, double-tiered arches.

and Iraq (some of them skilled in the science and technology of farming), created a prosperous economy. By the ninth century, Córdoba, once a Roman town, emerged as the largest city in the Mediterranean region after Constantinople.

Like the early Abbasid empire, Umayyad Spain benefited from a string of able rulers. No doubt the greatest was Abd al-Rahman III (r. 912–961). From his splendid palace complex near Córdoba, he patronized art and literature and engaged diplomatically with both the Abbasids and the Byzantines. He was far enough away from Baghdad, however, that in 929 he declared himself the rightful, universal leader of the Muslim community in opposition to the Abbasid king, thereby creating a rival caliphate in the western Mediterranean.

The Fatimids: a Shi'a empire. New Muslim power groups also established several states in North Africa in defiance of Abbasid authority. In the region that is now Tunisia and eastern Algeria, a rebellious governor founded an independent dynasty that lasted nearly two hundred years. In 909, however, it fell to revolutionaries who championed Shi'a Islam. This minority sect taught that the Abbasids had no right to rule because God approved only blood descendants of Ali, the fourth of the revered early caliphs, as legitimate leaders of the Muslim community (see Chapter 10). The new Shi'a regime, called the Fatimid dynasty (969–1171), built up its North African power base and then in 969 dispatched an army of Arab and Berber warriors to invade Egypt. This force expelled the Abbasid governor and declared Fatimid rule.

The Fatimids patronized the particular Shi'a branch of Islam known as Ismailism. Like other Shi'a groups, Ismailis believed that a descendant of Muhammad through Ali must be Islam's universal leader (Imam). Ismailis, however, identified that leadership with a different line of descent from what the majority of Shi'a accepted. They also claimed Fatima, the daughter of Muhammad and wife of Ali, as a revered ancestral figure, thus the dynastic name Fatimid. (In modern times the largest Ismaili communities have been in Pakistan and India.)

From its capital at Cairo at the apex of the Nile delta, the Fatimid regime declared itself to be Islam's true caliphate. For two hundred years they ruled a territory that at its zenith extended from Algeria and Sicily to Syria. They tried to overthrow the Abbasids, though without success. In addition to revenue from the Nile valley estates that millions of Egyptian peasants cultivated, the Fatimids benefited from a boost in commercial traffic. Indian Ocean merchants, uneasy about political and economic instability in Abbasid Iraq, increasingly sailed past the Persian Gulf and made for ports near the southern entrance to the Red Sea. This shift directed more Asian cargo up that sea and west to the Nile valley.

The Samanids and the silk roads. More than 1,100 miles northeast of Baghdad, an aristocratic Persian family known as the Samanids dominated both Khurasan and part of Central Asia in the ninth and tenth centuries (819–999). Founding their capital at the commercial city of Bukhara (today in Uzbekistan), these princes built their state on wealth from stock breeding and oasis farming. Also, the region's

Fatimid peacocks. Artists of the Fatimid dynasty created a distinctive Egyptian style of Muslim art. The peacock, perhaps symbolizing long life and good fortune, is a recurring theme. These birds appear on a limestone window screen.

major towns had long served as commercial swinging doors between the Inner Eurasian silk routes and Southwest Asia. As Islam grew in that region, Muslim merchant networks took over most of the long-distance trade through those entrepôts, and Samanid monarchs promoted Muslim missionary activity along the trails to China.

The Abbasid empire fades. In the later ninth century the Abbasid Caliphate deteriorated gradually from a sprawling empire to a patchwork of territories controlled variously by the caliph, provincial governors who professed allegiance but did what they pleased, local dynasties, and independent pastoral nomadic tribes. In 945 an aristocratic Iranian family known as the Buyids seized Baghdad and ruled there for more than a hundred years. Though they were Shi'a Muslims, they passed themselves off as the "protectors" of the caliphate. The Sunni caliph stayed on the job to make the Buyids appear legitimate, but in fact he was no longer more than one influential political figure among many.

The Byzantine Resurgence

The Byzantine state was Christian, but its political and cultural affairs were deeply intertwined with its Muslim neighbors. Despite its loss of critical territories to Arab conquerors in the seventh century, the empire remained a significant power in the eastern Mediterranean and Balkan Peninsula between the eighth and eleventh centuries. After Arab forces failed to capture Constantinople in either

Basil II, the Bulgar Slayer. Angels bestow the imperial crown on Basil II, who appears ready for combat in this depiction from a tenth-century Byzantine manuscript. How might you interpret the figures at the bottom of the image?

the islands of Cyprus and Crete from Muslim governors. That success allowed Byzantine warships to dominate the Aegean Sea as they had three centuries earlier. In the Balkan Peninsula, Basil faced the kingdom of Bulgaria, a loosely organized warrior state of Turkic horse archers that lorded over the majority of Slavic-speaking peasants. Later in history, he acquired the tag "the Bulgar Slayer" because he annexed Bulgaria and pushed the Byzantine frontier all the way to the Danube River. (According to legend, he also blinded nearly 15,000 Bulgarian captives, leaving 150 one-eyed soldiers to lead them home.) This Balkan campaign opened more of southeastern Europe to Greek Orthodox missionary activity. At Basil's death in 1025, Byzantium was a strong member of the club of mostly Muslim Mediterranean states. The rulers that followed him, however, were as inept as he was capable, so imperial expansion came to an end.

Islam on New Frontiers

Even though the unified Arab empire lasted less than a century, societies from Morocco and Spain to Central Asia and the lower Indus valley advanced toward a new cultural integration in which Islam provided an overarching framework of worship, moral ideals, and law. Islam joined Christianity and Buddhism as a universalist religion, that is, a belief system whose message was directed to all human beings, not only people of a particular ethnic or regional identity. The Islam of the Quran and the Traditions of the Prophet urged cooperative, compassionate, and egalitarian behavior among members of the community of believers. Such social collaboration rested on moral trust—between husbands and wives, parents and children, rulers and subjects, buyers and sellers. Devout Christians cherished fundamentally the same values, though with somewhat less emphasis on social cooperation and community behavior and more on individual expression of brotherly and sisterly love.

The Islamic insistence on social trust may have heightened the religion's appeal in the highly urbanized, socially fluid, and **cosmopolitan** environment of Southwest Asia, where individuals and cooperating groups sought opportunities to bind themselves to one another through agreements and contracts for doing business. This set of ethics attracted members of the commercial class and therefore oiled the wheels of exchange across Southwest Asia and far beyond. In short, Islam, like both Christianity and Buddhism in somewhat different ways, answered

> **cosmopolitan** Characteristic of a place where people of diverse origins come together or of an individual who travels widely.

668 or 717, Byzantium and the Abbasids settled into a routine of nearly continuous raid and counter-raid along a fluctuating frontier running across Anatolia. At the same time, however, Christian, Muslim, and Jewish merchants continued to do business in eastern Mediterranean ports.

Then, in the 860s, the rulers in Constantinople launched an extraordinary political comeback. A new line of capable emperors, known collectively as the Macedonian dynasty (867–1056), reorganized the imperial army and sent it on offensive campaigns against Abbasid frontier forts and cities in Anatolia. Under Basil II (r. 976–1025), the empire achieved its political high point. Smart and ruthless, he first suppressed Greek aristocratic families that tried to dodge Constantinople's authority. He then awarded greater power to the capital's salaried, educated bureaucrats, who had always been crucial to Byzantine political stability. He shrewdly avoided attacks against solidly Muslim territories. Instead, he shifted his imperial thrust to the west and north.

In the Mediterranean, Byzantine troops recaptured a substantial part of southern Italy, and Basil's navy took popular needs for coherent systems of trust and honest conduct among peoples of different regions, languages, and ethnicities who nonetheless found themselves thrown together in complex relationships.

In the two centuries following Muhammad's preaching, people in all Muslim-ruled states, including millions who did not speak Arabic or know anything of Arab traditions, accepted Islam at an accelerating rate. According to one scholarly estimate, inhabitants of Iran, who were already familiar with several religions, converted to Islam in large numbers in the late eighth and ninth centuries. By the 860s the Muslim population reached about 80 percent of the total.[3] A similar trajectory may have occurred in other areas where Muslims ruled. **Proselytizing** for Islam was a highly informal and diffuse process. In contrast to the Christian churches, Islam had no formal religious organization, no hierarchy of appointed officials like patriarchs and bishops who helped direct the work of conversion. In contrast to the Christian patriarch in Constantinople or the pope in Rome, the caliph was not the chief administrator of a formal religious organization. Moreover, the *ulama,* the Muslim community's religious scholars, served as spiritual guides, moral counselors, and legal experts. They were not ordained priests who offered prospective converts a path to salvation through baptism or other holy sacraments. In Islam the ultimate spiritual authority was not the church but the Quran, which all believers could hear, study, and recite.

> **proselytize** To convert or attempt to convert an individual or group to one's religion.

Also by the ninth century many more Muslims undertook the sort of missionary activity that had already succeeded for Christians and Buddhists. From that time, Muslim merchants, scholars, and preachers, more and more of them Persians, Turks, and Berbers, as well as Arabs, shared their religious faith with men and women in regions where Muslims did not rule (or at least not yet). Simultaneously, an interregional Muslim cultural network based on shared faith, law, moral expectations, literature, art, and architecture began to fuse together. This "style" of culture was derived in some measure from Arabia—especially the Arabic language—but mainly from Persian, Byzantine, Egyptian, and other older civilized traditions. The centers of this literate cultural life were the cities where Muslim communities became established. Christians and Jews who learned Arabic and to some extent adopted Muslim styles and manners also took part in this network.

A "Green Revolution" in Muslim Lands

Archaeological and written evidence suggests that between 750 and 1000 the Muslim-ruled lands generally experienced population, urban, and economic growth, despite serious environmental problems in the Tigris-Euphrates valley. Scholars have linked these upswings to the spread of new crops and farming technologies. Centuries or millennia earlier, farmers had domesticated rice, sugar cane, citrus fruits,

Water management in an arid climate. Dating to the ancient Achaemenid Persian empire or earlier, *qanats* are gently angled underground channels that lead water from highland slopes to arid areas. This irrigation technology spread from Iran eastward to Afghanistan and westward to North Africa. Vertical shafts to the tunnels provide ventilation and access for upkeep. Why do you think that farmers needed to maintain *qanats* diligently?

melon, mango, sweet peppers, eggplant, spinach, and cotton in the tropical and subtropical climates of southern India and Southeast Asia. Some of these crops reached Southwest Asia before the Arab Muslim conquests; others arrived during the period of expanding Muslim power (see Map 11.2). In any case, Southwest Asian farmers experimented with new crops and irrigation technologies, and Muslim governments and big estate owners encouraged these innovations. As a result, agricultural production intensified.

Farmers successfully cultivated new tropical plants in arid regions by efficiently managing water from rivers, underground sources, or moderate winter rainfall. In earlier centuries they had planted mainly winter crops such as wheat, barley, lentils, and oil seeds, leaving fields to lie fallow in the hot, rainless summers. But now they began to grow abundant quantities of crops that thrived in summer weather as long as water could be supplied. From the Abbasid lands, a veritable seed catalog of crops—oranges, lemons, watermelon, artichokes, bananas, rice, cotton—diffused northeastward into Central Asia, southward to Yemen, and westward across North Africa to Spain. Arabic became a medium for detailed agricultural manuals, and irrigation experts carried new ideas for lifting water, tapping it from underground channels, and building reservoirs. For example, ancient Iranians invented the *qanat,* an underground tunnel that led water from higher to lower elevations. In the early Muslim centuries, *qanat* technology spread from Iran to North Africa and Spain—and after 1500 to Mexico and the American Southwest.

Muslim Urban Society

Bounty from irrigated land and busy long-distance trade supported the proliferation and growth of cities in the Muslim

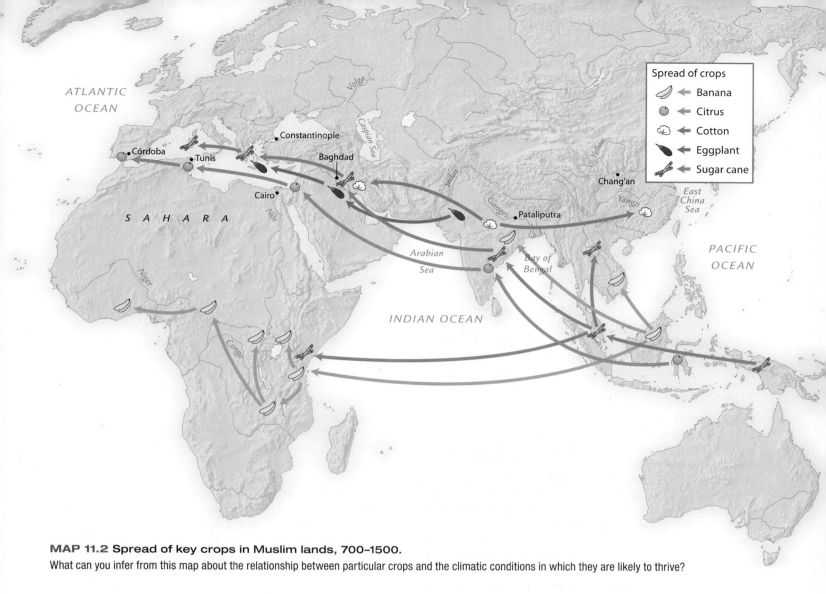

MAP 11.2 Spread of key crops in Muslim lands, 700–1500.
What can you infer from this map about the relationship between particular crops and the climatic conditions in which they are likely to thrive?

lands. The grandest of them was Baghdad. Iraq (Mesopotamia) had supported many magnificent capitals since the third millennium B.C.E., but Baghdad probably grew to metropolitan size faster than any of them. The Abbasid caliph Al-Mansur (r. 754–775) commissioned the city's construction in 762, and by the ninth century it had a population of between 200,000 and 500,000, surpassing that of Constantinople and every other city west of China. It attracted thousands of artisans, merchants, laborers, soldiers, and scholars to serve the royal household, the army, and the homes of the elite. Al-Mansur, the second Abbasid ruler, had his engineers design the city in the shape of a wheel. The royal palace was the hub, and four avenues radiated out from it, symbolically carrying goods and ideas to numerous other cities across Afroeurasia.

Islamic principles obliged Muslims who lived together in cities to worship as equals, obey the same laws, and refrain from publicly flaunting material wealth. Nevertheless, social class distinctions were as evident in Muslim towns as in any other part of Afroeurasia. Indeed, yawning canyons of wealth and prestige separated the governing, estate-owning, and large merchant families from the laboring masses. As cities accumulated wealth from manufacturing and trade, these social divisions only widened.

Urban women of all classes made decisions in their family spheres and probably had great influence on the urban economy by choosing what foods and other goods the family would consume. Adult men dominated public spaces—places of worship, government buildings, plazas, and markets—as they had in ancient times. Research in biographies of notable Muslims compiled by Arab or Persian scholars in the early Islamic period suggests that the number of women recognized for their achievement as writers and legal specialists declined significantly after the first century or two. The cities of Umayyad Spain may have been the exception. There, an unusual number of literate women gained distinction as teachers, jurists, librarians, and copyists.

Slavery was also a part of urban life. Leaving aside the growing numbers of male slaves or ex-slaves in military service, the majority of unfree city residents were probably women, working as domestics, attendants, entertainers, and concubines. From the perspective of the enslaved, there was one slightly encouraging trend. Following the long Zanj Rebellion in southern Iraq in the later ninth century, Muslim landowners mostly abandoned the idea of using slaves in large, unwilling gangs to produce commercial crops. The potential for violent rebellion was too great.

Many Muslim-ruled cities had populations of non-Muslims, especially Jews and Christians. Those groups usually resided in distinct quarters of the city and most of the time lived in peace with their Muslim neighbors. In fact, Muslim governments encouraged such physical separation, not to enforce social segregation, but to give minority groups, who chose their own leaders, official recognition and protection. Multifaith harmony perhaps worked best in Córdoba and other cities of Spain, where, despite occasional outbreaks of conflict or persecution, daily business and intellectual exchange was common among religious communities. There, Jews, Christians, and Muslims all spoke Arabic.

The Stream of Ideas

Big Muslim cities harbored intellectuals and artists, while Islam and the Arabic language provided a matrix for lively cultural interaction among cities from Spain to northern India. Muslims traveled to acquire knowledge, do business, or perform the pilgrimage to Mecca. In the process they developed a cosmopolitan consciousness that they inhabited the Dar al-Islam (House of Islam), the amalgam of lands where Muslim populations predominated or Muslim elites ruled. Christian, Jewish, Hindu, and Buddhist sages traveled the interurban networks as well. For inquisitive men and women, the Dar al-Islam was not so much a mosaic of kingdoms as an interlinked web of cities. The people who moved throughout this web tended to pay as little attention as possible to the frontiers between the territories of one ruler and another.

The Arabic language, both written and spoken, inevitably accompanied Islam wherever it went, because in Muslim belief Arabic was the very medium of God's divine revelation to Muhammad. In much the same way that ancient Han linguists standardized Chinese writing, Muslim academicians in Iraqi cities labored in the eighth and ninth centuries to systematize Arabic script, spelling, and grammar. As a language of both statecraft and scholarship, Arabic gradually displaced Greek, Aramaic, and Latin in the Muslim lands. Persian, or Farsi, a major language of the earlier Persian empires, fared better. So many Persian speakers flocked to Islam that the language emerged in the eastern Muslim lands as the dominant medium of religious and intellectual culture.

Translating ancient texts. The first great intellectual task for scholars in Baghdad and other Southwest Asian cities was to translate scientific, technical, philosophical, and historical documents from Greek, Persian, Syriac, and Sanskrit (the main literary language of India) into Arabic. Texts were scattered in many lands, and Muslims, Christians, and Jews frequently collaborated to assemble them, learning one another's languages and arguing over the meaning and interpretation of documents. With the support of the early Abbasid caliphs, scholars set up translation projects in Baghdad. Caliph al-Ma'mun (r. 813–833) established a research center called the House of Wisdom. Its residents, including some South Asian scholars, investigated mathematical and astronomical ideas that had been formulated in the Gupta empire three hundred years earlier (see Chapter 9). Between the ninth and eleventh centuries, Cairo and Córdoba, as well as Bukhara in Central Asia, also emerged as leading centers of learning.

Producing new knowledge. Translation, however, was only the start. Scholars wanted not only to preserve ancient learning but to correct, reinterpret, and add to it. Among the numerous spheres of knowledge—and none were closed to inquiry—the Muslim religious sciences commanded the highest prestige. They included studies of the Quran,

Model of an automaton. The Egyptian mathematician, engineer, and inventor al-Jaziri (1136–1206) wrote the *Book of Knowledge of Mechanical Devices*, a study of different types of machines, including water clocks and water raising machines. Some of these devices were automata, or self-operating contrivances, made only for amusement.

Abu Bakr al-Razi: Muslim Physician

The Persian polymath Abu Bakr al-Razi (ca. 865–925 C.E.) wrote almost one hundred texts on topics such as astronomy, chemistry, alchemy, philosophy, and Islamic theology. But he gained his greatest fame as a physician and author of medical treatises. Born in Rey, a bustling Iranian commercial center that is today a suburb of Tehran, al-Razi had an early interest in music and achieved a reputation as a master of the stringed instrument called the *ud.* He also received an education in philosophy, metaphysics, logic, and mathematics before deciding to train as a doctor. In addition to practicing medicine and teaching students, he served as director of hospitals in both Rey and Baghdad in the early tenth century.

Al-Razi's most enduring legacy is his dozens of medical books. A careful observer and meticulous note-taker, he pioneered the systematic approach to experimentation that we now call the "scientific method." Working in busy hospitals with large numbers of patients enabled al-Razi to study and write on a variety of medical conditions. In one influential work, he explained how to distinguish clinically between small-pox, chicken pox, and measles. In another book he described why roses cause certain people to suffer from swelled heads, runny noses, and weepy eyes—the first identification of hay fever. He also made important contributions to ophthalmology and pediatrics. Dedicated to improving public health, he composed a home medical manual designed to enable anyone to treat a range of diseases with simple medicines prepared from common ingredients. Like Hippocrates, the ancient Greek medical authority, al-Razi argued that physicians should receive extensive training and hold licenses to practice.

Al-Razi was well versed in classical Greek medical scholarship, though he declared certain of its propositions to be incorrect or incomplete. He respected the work of his Greek

An imaginative woodcut depicts al-Razi studying a learned text.

predecessors, the physician Galen in particular, but he critiqued their findings and encouraged other scholars to do the same in the interest of medical practice. After al-Razi's death, his notebooks were compiled and published as a massive twenty-volume work titled *The Comprehensive Book on Medicine.* These tomes represented an encyclopedia of knowledge about diseases. For each ailment, al-Razi cited the views of Greek, Syrian, Indian, Persian, and Arab writers before adding his own clinical thoughts and observations. Translated into Latin during the thirteenth century and published in Europe, al-Razi's work became a fundamental text for European medical students to the end of the seventeenth century.

Thinking Critically

In what ways did al-Razi both make use of and advance beyond ancient Greek scientific and medical learning?

---

theology, law, grammar, and the methodology of verifying the Traditions of the Prophet. Then there were the "philosophical sciences," which in that era included logic (derived principally from the Greek philosopher Aristotle), cosmology, astrology, physics, chemistry, biology, medicine, agronomy, geography, and mathematics. Thinkers in those fields engaged not only in theoretical reasoning, but also in systematic observation and recording of natural phenomena, describing and classifying plants, for example, or compiling astronomical tables. To accomplish these things, they used an array of improved or newly invented scientific instruments, such as balances, water clocks, and astrolabes (for plotting the movement of heavenly bodies).

The progress of mathematics illustrates the importance of intellectual collaboration across cultural and political frontiers. In cooperation with Christian and Jewish

academicians, Muslims refined and expanded the mathematical knowledge of ancient Mesopotamia, Egypt, and Greece, solving, for example, geometrical problems that Euclid, the renowned Hellenistic Greek mathematician, had not cracked. Drawing also on Indian mathematics, ninth-century scholars formulated the sciences of algebra and trigonometry largely as they are taught in high schools today.

The single most conspicuous scientific development in Abbasid times was the transfer from India of the base-ten positional numerical system that incorporates a sign to indicate "zero." This system was an achievement associated with the Gupta empire. As communication picked up between South Asia and the central Muslim lands, Indian scientific ideas reached scholars in Baghdad and other cities. Among these sages was Muhammad ibn Musa al-Khwarizmi (ca. 780–850), a Persian mathematician who lived and worked in Bukhara in the ninth century. He propagated the Indian system of reckoning and brought it to bear on the study of algebra. In fact, the word *algebra* comes from the Arabic *al-jabr,* meaning "restoration." After his death about 850, other scholars gradually switched from the cumbersome Greek or Roman to the efficient Indian system. Latin Christian scholars who traveled to Muslim Toledo or Córdoba in Spain introduced what came to be called "Arabic numerals" into western Europe, where the new system caught on widely in the thirteenth century. Today, these ten simple signs represent the closest thing the world has to a universal language.

Tension between science and faith. Like ancient Greek and Roman thinkers, scholars of the Abbasid era made no formal distinction between science as we understand it today and philosophy or theology. Their work included both scientific study and speculation on matters of the spirit, that is, the relation between divine revelation and the evidence of reality gathered through the exercise of reason, logic, and observation. Muslim scholars meticulously explored the ancient Greek masters such as Aristotle and Pythagoras and wrote numerous philosophical works.

Other Muslims, however, especially religious leaders more attuned to daily ritual, law, and doctrine, became wary of theoretical speculation about nature and the universe. The early Islamic centuries witnessed much disputation among literate Muslims about faith and reason. For example, does God predetermine the life experience of every individual, or are individuals morally responsible for their own experience? A question like that often pitted theologians who accepted the totality of God's will against rationally oriented believers, who argued for free inquiry and human responsibility. The general trend from about the eleventh century was for leaders who emphasized divine revelation and obedience to sacred law to gain ascendancy in the mosques and colleges where the religious sciences were taught. Theological and philosophical musings on the nature of reality continued, but mainly in private and informal settings.

Cities, Merchants, and Kingdoms along the Chain of Seas

> FOCUS What part did maritime commerce play in the development of states and cities along the chain of seas extending from the Arabian Sea to the Sea of Japan between 750 and 1000 C.E.?

Between the seventh and eleventh centuries, impressive economic growth took place not only in Muslim-ruled lands but also in several kingdoms bordering the chain of seas that extended from the Arabian Sea to the Sea of Japan (see Map 11.3). Hungry for revenue from trade, the rulers of these states cooperated readily with shippers and traders. Sea merchants also contributed to commercial expansion by organizing large networks of mercantile buyers and sellers and by employing increasingly sophisticated commercial tools, such as partnerships, loans, and letters of credit to finance enterprise and speed merchandise on its way.

Trade of the Arabian Sea

Between the sixth and eleventh centuries C.E., shipbuilders, captains, and merchants employed in Arabian Sea trade made incremental improvements in sail and hull design and learned more about the seasonal intricacies of the Indian Ocean monsoon winds. For example, they acquired more precise information about the best times of year to leave a particular port in order to reach a destination in reasonably predictable time. Consequently, mariners gained confidence sailing across open seas, notably between the Red Sea, Persian Gulf, or East Africa and the ports of southern India and Ceylon.

Maritime trade also rose in volume owing to the development of southern India's commercial economy. Because India juts southward into the Indian Ocean and narrows to a point, the inhabitants of the southern third of the subcontinent all lived close to either the Bay of Bengal or the Arabian Sea. Southern India had functioned as a commercial pivot point between the two seas for a thousand years or more. But from the seventh century, the volume of merchandise that passed through these ports increased in tandem with economic growth in the South Asian interior. Among the several monarchies that shared India, the Pallava dynasty dominated much of the south between the sixth and tenth centuries. The Pallavas patronized Hindu devotional religion, or *bhakti,* as well as Sanskrit learning. The great majority of southern India's peasants spoke Tamil, a language of the ancient Dravidian family. Most of them raised rice, a crop that the Pallava kings encouraged by constructing irrigation works and great reservoirs to conserve and distribute water during the dry winter and spring months. Farmers also increased cotton textile production and grew black pepper, both commodities exported throughout South Asia and across the seas. Burgeoning towns and merchant networks linked to coastal ports accompanied this economic prosperity. Further to the northwest, the region of Gujarat also continued to grow as a center of cloth making. Gujarati merchants were to be seen in ports all around the rim of the Arabian Sea.

Commercial towns also multiplied along the African coast south of the Red Sea, in what are now Somalia, Kenya, and Tanzania. Farming populations that lived on those shores and spoke Bantu languages emerged as Swahili, a name derived from the Arabic term for "people of the coast." The Swahili language was fundamentally Bantu in structure and vocabulary, though it absorbed many Arabic and some Persian words. The early Swahili communities were thoroughly sea oriented, selling ivory, gold, animal skins, rock crystal (transparent quartz), and other commodities to Arabian Sea traders. New towns sprang up along the coast,

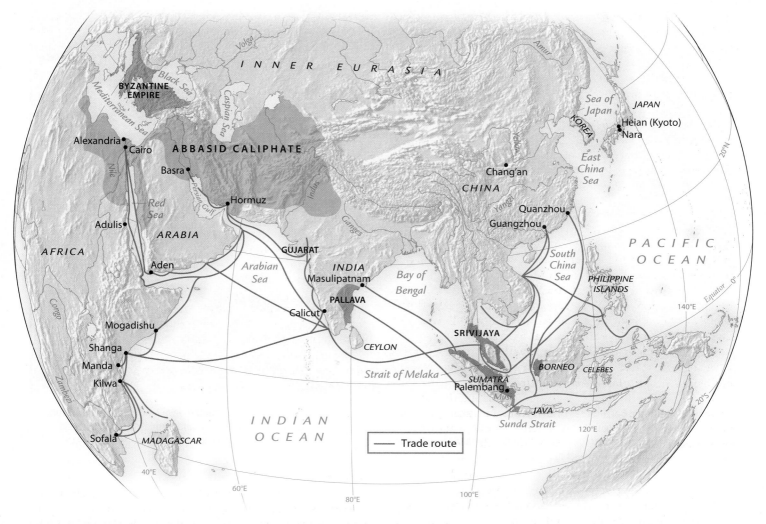

MAP 11.3 Connections along the chain of seas, tenth century.
How might geographical factors have contributed differently to the commercial prosperity of the Abbasid Caliphate and the kingdom of Srivijaya?

including Shanga and Manda, which had populations of 15,000 to 18,000. Swahili merchants also traded in slaves, buying captive men and women from dealers who operated in the deep East African interior and then selling them for transport to Southwest Asia or India.

Arabs and Persians had been Arabian Sea rovers long before the advent of Islam, but the rise of the Umayyad and Abbasid empires and their new urban markets encouraged longer profit-making voyages. Between the eighth and tenth centuries, Muslim traders founded settlements on the coasts of East Africa, India, Ceylon, Sumatra, and even southern China. These outposts formed a trans-hemispheric Muslim commercial diaspora. Arab geographers of that era labeled the Indian Ocean the "Sea of China," a name suggesting the feasibility of voyaging from the Persian Gulf all the way to China and back by timing port departures with the alternating monsoon winds. For nearly two centuries, Muslim

merchants made this eighteen-month round trip regularly. They established a little colony in the Chinese port of Guangzhou (Canton), and some merchants resided there at least temporarily to act as hosts for arriving sailors and as agents for Chinese buyers. If fortune smiled on shippers, they returned to Iraq with cargos of silks, cottons, porcelain, sandalwood, jade, and spices, which Abbasid consumers purchased at huge markups.

The Maritime Empire of Srivijaya

Commercial traffic across the Bay of Bengal between India and Southeast Asia enjoyed a boost from about 700, when the kingdom of Srivijaya (SREE-vih-JAI-yuh) arose on the island of Sumatra at the western end of the Indonesian archipelago. Srivijaya's success as a maritime power for about six hundred years resulted mainly from its domination of

The Temple Mountain. Constructed of about two million stone blocks and rising more than 100 feet above the central Java landscape, the principal temple at Borobudur symbolically represents the three prime elements of the universe: the spheres of desire, form, and formlessness. A pyramid-shaped base of five square terraces constitutes the first and lowest sphere. The second is three circular platforms supporting stupas that house statues of the Buddha. The third is a mammoth stupa, which is empty.

the strategic Malacca and Sunda Straits, the two narrow sea passages that connected the South China Sea with the Bay of Bengal and all points west. Srivijaya arose as a maritime state controlling ports, agricultural hinterlands (inland areas), and sea lanes, rather than extensive territories. In the later first millennium C.E., wet-rice farmers expanded their operations in lowlands and river valleys across Southeast Asia, transforming tropical forests into paddy fields and paying taxes to Srivijayan monarchs or local lords. Centered in the fertile rice-growing Musi River valley near the modern city of Palembang, Srivijaya accumulated sufficient wealth and naval power to collect tribute from smaller states along the northern coasts of Sumatra and Java. The royal court watched over these local princes in a kind of political federation.

Like other Southeast Asian monarchs, Srivijayan kings and aristocrats became eager patrons of Buddhism. They built monasteries, employed Buddhist monks as officials, adopted Sanskrit from India as the region's main written language, and patronized Buddhist learning. Increasing numbers of Malay sailors also took up Mahayana, or popular Buddhism, and carried it from port to port. Srivijaya benefited from a close alliance with the Buddhist Sailendra dynasty, which ruled the interior of Java, where wet-rice cultivation in rich volcanic soils produced bountiful surpluses.

The Sailendra kings accumulated sufficient wealth by the eighth century to build Borobudur, a colossal Buddhist monument and one of the architectural marvels of the world. The Sailendra monarchy unfortunately enmeshed itself in a fatal civil war in the ninth century, though Srivijaya continued to dominate the straits trade for another three hundred years.

Chinese Trade and the Fate of the Tang Dynasty

Malay, Indian, Arab, and Persian merchants all gravitated to China's southern coast owing to that country's remarkable demographic and economic growth following its political unification under the Sui (581–618) and Tang (618–907) dynasties (see Chapter 10). Between 750 and 1100, China's population grew from about 50 to 100 million, and the geographical center of both population and economic production continued to shift toward the rice-growing south. Market towns and ports multiplied, especially from the Yangzi River valley to the southern coasts, where several busy ports, including Guangzhou and Quanzhou flourished handling maritime trade.

Farming, manufacturing, and foreign commerce all prospered in China even as the Tang government progressively lost control over its own imperial administration and finally collapsed. Serious trouble began in 755 when An Lushan, a disaffected general of Turkic origin, built up a personal military force of more than 100,000 soldiers and marched on Chang'an, forcing emperor Xuanzong (r. 712–756), the last of the great Tang monarchs, first to flee his capital and then to abandon his throne to a son.

In the aftermath of the rebellion, which Turkic Uighur cavalry helped put down at the price of huge payments of silk, the weakened regime had to appoint military men, rather than loyal civil bureaucrats, to top provincial posts. These officers, many of whom had supported the An Lushan revolt, set themselves up as virtually independent warlords in several parts of China and refused to send taxes to Chang'an. Buddhist monasteries, of which there may have been thirty thousand in China in the eighth century, enjoyed exemption from taxation. Many of them accumulated large agricultural estates, conducted their own commercial businesses, and even created their own militias. For nearly a century after the An Lushan rebellion, furthermore, forces of the Tibetan and Uighur empires threatened China's northwestern frontiers, ending earlier Tang campaigns to extend imperial power deep into Inner Eurasia. In the late eighth century, emperors tried to recapture the military advantage by organizing eunuchs, castrated males who served the imperial court, into a personally loyal armed force. But palace eunuchs split into feuding factions, took over palace affairs, and in the ninth century started murdering and replacing emperors.

In the later eighth century, the Tang government lost its grip on the Chinese economy; estate owners and entrepreneurs took the opportunity to engage in more freewheeling commercial activity. The Tang equal-field system, whereby the government allotted land to peasants and kept close track of both production and tax payments, gradually fell apart for lack of government funds to manage it. Consequently, big landowners put increasing pressure on peasants to sell their land to get out of debt and then employed tenants and day laborers to produce grain, silk, cotton, and other commodities for the commercial market. Poor men and women continued to stream to the south, many of them finding only low-wage jobs on farm estates. As the Tang government deteriorated, local power holders willingly promoted private business and trade because they could then tax its profits. The Tang dynasty collapsed in 907, and from then until 960 China was once again divided into a number of competing regional states. In the same period, however, exports of silk and other wares from the southern ports continued to grow.

Japan and Korea at the Eastern End of the Chain of Seas

The last links in Afroeurasia's chain of seas were the East China Sea and the Sea of Japan (or East Sea), which extend northeastward into the temperate latitudes. In the first millennium C.E., the lands around those two seas—northern China, the Korean peninsula, and the Japanese archipelago—emerged gradually as a distinct zone of seaborne intercommunication.

Ships had to cross five hundred miles of cyclone-prone waters to reach southern Japan from the Chinese coast, but only one hundred miles of the Korea Strait separated Japan from the southern tip of Korea. That passage became Japan's main link to China and indeed to the whole Afroeurasian world. Between about 400 B.C.E. and 600 C.E., rice farming, weaving technology, iron metallurgy, writing, central governing techniques, and Buddhism all apparently entered Japan by way of Korea.

Both Japan and Korea are lands with mountainous interiors. Only about 16 percent of Japan is suitable for farming, 20 percent of Korea. Japan's mountains include sixty active volcanoes, but the archipelago's volcanic soils are rich and summer rains typically ample. After knowledge of wet-rice cultivation arrived, farm hamlets spread across Japan's coastal plains and inland valleys. In the first six centuries C.E., its population rose from about one million to five million, a huge acceleration of growth. On Honshu, the big, central island, farmer power was sufficient to support a tribute-collecting class of aristocratic families. Some of them recruited enough armed retainers to found small states, which from about the third century warred against one another for control of good land and peasant labor.

In contrast to island Japan, Korea lay within the shadow of successive Chinese empires. The ancient Han dynasty occupied much of the peninsula, and the Tang made it a tributary region. In 668, however, a line of Korean rulers known as the Silla (SHEE-lah) took control of most of the peninsula and kept it unified until after 900.

Commanders of Japan. Between the sixth and eighth centuries, regional chiefs centered on Honshu gradually built up an effective system of central command. Combining cavalry troops with claims of sacred authority, these lords began to refer to themselves as "heavenly sovereigns," or emperors. Known as the Yamato dynasty (from the name of a river), these monarchs, whose line included several female heavenly sovereigns, founded the town of Nara in 710 as a palace and an administrative center. This was Japan's first true city and clear evidence of the dynasty's success at gathering surplus wealth from rice-growing peasants. In 794 the dynasty moved its capital to the even grander imperial center of Heian (pronounced HAY-ahn, later known as Kyoto).

The Yamato kings and queens associated themselves closely with beliefs and rituals that rural Japanese relied on to appease and manipulate the world of spirits. These beings, including the spirits of recent ancestors, pervaded the natural world and had power to ensure health, safety, and rich harvests. This belief system, known as Shinto, included an important role for the Yamato rulers, whose ceremonial offerings aimed to stave off natural or human-induced calamities. Beginning about 850, however, an important power shift occurred. The reigning emperors lost their grip on political affairs to aristocratic families. Nevertheless, these powerful nobles legitimized themselves by governing in the name of the emperor, who retained only ritual duties.

Silla royal tombs. Gyeongju, the city in South Korea that served as the capital of the Silla dynasty, is the site of several tumuli, or burial mounds, containing the remains of Silla rulers. Can you think of other societies in the world where important people were entombed in this way?

Currents of exchange between China and Japan. About the third century c.e., traffic between Japan and the Asian mainland began to intensify. After the Han empire (206 b.c.e.–220 c.e.) broke up, Chinese and Korean exiles and adventurers headed to Japan, a sort of East Asian "land of opportunity." The Japanese elite class, knowing it lacked the refined civilization of its Korean and Chinese neighbors, warmly received educated and skilled immigrants. These newcomers offered the Japanese much new knowledge: advanced metallurgy, writing, sericulture (silk production), textile manufacture, paper making, and techniques of government and warfare. When the Sui and Tang emperors reunified China in the late sixth century, and Silla kings mastered most of Korea, migration to Japan diminished. China's immense power, however, only stimulated Japanese appetites for its culture. Palace aristocrats invited Chinese literary scholars and experienced officials to their courts, as well as boatload after boatload of Buddhist monks and nuns, who offered the Yamato emperors spiritual learning and protection. Ships returning to China carried Japanese intellectuals, who sought out knowledge of Confucian statecraft and sacred Buddhist texts.

Japan did not, however, become a mere cultural satellite of either China or Korea. Rather, a distinctive Japanese style of culture developed out of the complex interplay between, for example, Buddhism and Shinto, Tang city design and traditional Japanese building materials, or Chinese orchestral music and Japanese instruments. Another example was the Japanese system of civil and penal codes (*ritsuryō*

seido). This governmental scheme of administrative ranks, offices, and duties was clearly derived from Chinese Confucian models of political organization, but Japanese rulers tailored it for their much smaller territory and population.

Up to the tenth century, Japanese scholars simply learned Chinese and used it to write government documents and religious texts. A few experimenters, however, devised ways to represent Japanese sounds using Chinese logographic characters. This was a tough job because Japanese had no structural relationship to Chinese. Since aristocratic males regarded Chinese as the language of social prestige, the work of creating an indigenous writing system fell largely to refined and learned women, who did not consider the task beneath them. Buddhist monks and nuns also contributed. By the tenth century these scholars collectively produced a workable script called *wabun,* which was based on simplified forms of Chinese characters.

Several schools of Mahayana Buddhism spread from China and Korea to Japan after about 600. Shrines, temples, and monasteries multiplied on the islands, and in the eighth century Nara became famous for its Buddhist teachers and soaring temples. The Great Buddha Hall (Daibutsu) in Nara remains today the largest wooden building in the world. Buddhist clerics offered common folk hope, health, and salvation, as well as supernatural defense against crop failures. Buddhist and Shinto ideas also mingled much as Buddhist and Daoist beliefs did in China. For example, Shinto nature gods became associated with Buddhist spirits and *bodhisattvas.*

Japan's population and economy continued to grow, with some interruptions, throughout the later first millennium C.E. The islands had about five million people in 700, rising to about seven million by 1200. (China's population in 1200 was about 120 million.)[4] In the 730s, however, waves of smallpox hit the islands, killing both children and adults and reducing the total population by as much as 25 percent.[5] Korean and Chinese visitors appear to have introduced this and other infectious maladies, which had long been endemic in most of Afroeurasia. Later in the eighth century, adult Japanese began to develop partial immunities to these diseases, though recurring epidemics kept the upward demographic trend modest.

Japan's emergence as a complex society owes far more to its agrarian economy, population growth, and contacts

The Great Buddha. Rulers of the Yamato dynasty avidly promoted Buddhist temple construction. The Great Buddha Hall in Nara houses the world's largest bronze statue, an image of the Vairochana Buddha originally cast in the mid-eighth century. The statue is nearly fifty feet tall. The Buddha raises his right hand in the classic gesture of assurance and protection. Compare this image to the limestone Vairochana Buddha carved in China several decades earlier (Chapter 10, page 302).

with China and Korea than to exchanges with more distant lands along the chain of seas. The islands remained culturally bonded to Korea and China, though the eastward flow of ideas diminished after 1000. By that time, however, the Japanese aristocracy was effectively creating a distinctive Japanese form of literate civilization.

The Sahara Rim: A New Zone of Intercommunication

FOCUS How did agrarian peoples living in the Mediterranean region and West Africa become linked together in a network of commercial and cultural exchange between the seventh and tenth centuries?

Japan's connection to the rest of East Asia filled in one of the significant gaps in the networks of exchange that connected peoples of Afroeurasia with one another. Another and much larger gap existing in the early centuries C.E. was the Sahara Desert (see Map 11.4). In that period pastoral peoples introduced the dromedary, or one-humped camel, from the Arabian Peninsula, probably to the semiarid country bordering the southern edge of the Sahara. The dromedary, with its wide feet and tolerance for going without water longer than most mammals, provided the "technological" solution to the problem of crossing the great desert north to south (see Chapter 7). But only later in the millennium did north–south crossings became regular.

Gold and Slaves, Copper and Salt

For merchants, the primary incentive to cross the Sahara was the simple fact that productive agrarian societies existed on both sides of it. Along the northern rim from Egypt to Morocco were young Muslim states, all of them increasingly urbanized after the eighth century and all linked into the trade of the Mediterranean and Southwest Asia. South of the desert were three broad climatic and vegetational zones. The Sahel, a belt of semiarid scrubland, bordered the Sahara. Further south lay open or wooded savannas (grasslands) where farming populations raised rice, millet, sorghum, and cattle, channeling surpluses into a network of trade that connected market towns. This web extended into the wet tropical forests, the third zone, where growing populations harvested yams and other root crops and where small states were beginning to emerge. Arab geographers of North Africa referred to the savanna belt as the *Bilad al-Sudan* ("land of black-skinned people"), or simply the Sudan, a historic region to be distinguished from the modern republics of Sudan and South Sudan.

Sudanic states. By the later first millennium C.E., enough people were producing crop and livestock surpluses in the Sudan to support significant kingdom-building ventures.

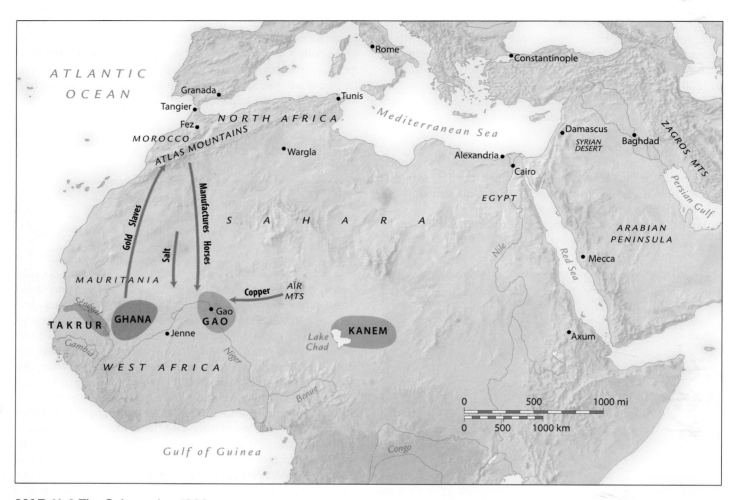

MAP 11.4 The Sahara rim, 1000.
What geographic features and natural resources help account for the location of the Takrur, Ghana, and Gao states?

From Arabic geographical texts and archaeological data, we know a fair amount about a few of the states that flourished between the eighth and eleventh centuries in West Africa—the Subsaharan zones on the western side of the continent. In the far west was Takrur, a monarchy whose economy was based on rice growing and trade in the floodplain of the middle and lower Senegal River valley. A second polity was Gao, a small state whose main city of the same name occupied a commercially strategic spot where the Niger River begins flowing south across all three climatic zones to the Atlantic Ocean. A third state was Kanem, whose founders were probably Saharan pastoral warriors. That kingdom emerged in the eighth century in the grasslands bordering Lake Chad, then a vast wetland and the sixth largest lake in the world (a status it has more recently lost owing to recurring drought).

Modern analysis of long-term climatic cycles in West Africa shows that in the period from approximately 300 to 1100 rainfall was generally higher than in the previous several centuries. During those eight hundred years, farmers were able to plant crops and herders graze cattle in more northerly parts of the Sahel. That permitted population growth and town building in areas that are today bleak deserts. In the later centuries of this "wet phase," Berber merchants in towns located along the northern rim of the Sahara began to organize camel caravans that with growing regularity crossed the desert to the Sudan.

The flow of gold. Sudanic peoples had long been involved in long-distance trade, but the trans-Saharan connection further stimulated their economies. Muslim rulers in both the Mediterranean region and Southwest Asia had an ever-growing appetite for gold, and the richest reachable deposits were in West Africa. They wanted gold mainly to display their authority and encourage commerce by minting gold coins. The chief West African mining centers lay along the upper Senegal and Niger Rivers in the transition zone between woodland and tropical rainforest. West African gold merchants typically spoke Soninke, one language among many in the Niger-Congo family of languages. We

A modern-day caravan. People of the Sahara continue to mine salt in a few places and transport it southward to West African towns. Laborers cut the salt into large slabs and tie them to the sides of camels. Why do you think camels continue to be used in this business?

have no evidence that large states controlled the mines. Rather, Soninke buyers did business with local chiefs independently, then shipped bags of dust and nuggets to the Sudanic caravan centers, where camel merchants shipped some of it northward across the desert. This trade expanded even faster after the turn of the millennium, when merchants from an economically reviving Europe began to frequent North African ports to buy gold. In the ensuing centuries, African bullion moved both northward into Europe and eastward to the central Muslim lands, even to India.

The trans-Saharan slave trade. A second important item in the trade was slaves. Caravan merchants bought slaves in Sudanic markets and force-marched them across the desert, many no doubt dying along the way. We know little of how the slave trade operated in those early centuries. Captives were the unfortunate victims of local wars, famines, social ostracism, or deliberate raiding and kidnapping. Women very likely outnumbered men in the slave caravans. They were taken to serve as domestics, entertainers, and concubines in the households of rulers or affluent families in the Mediterranean and Southwest Asia. As we have seen, Muslim monarchs began in the ninth century to recruit growing numbers of military slaves. They acquired captives from any source they could, though Muslim ethics (not always honored) prohibited enslavement of fellow believers. The majority of the slaves brought into

the central Muslim lands came from Inner Eurasia, India, and Europe. Only a minority came from Africa south of the desert.

Southbound trade. The trans-Saharan trade ran in both directions, of course. To markets in the Sudan, Berber and Arab merchants from North Africa carried products such as textiles, jewelry, ironware, and horses (which did not breed well in the Sudan owing to animal sleeping sickness). They also transported slabs of salt, a commodity with limited West African sources, from mines in the west central desert. From the Sahara's Aïr Mountains they brought copper, a mineral in great demand for making tools, ritual objects, and jewelry. In the towns of the Sahel, the camel merchants transferred their shipments to Sudanic traders and then returned north hauling not only gold and slaves but also ivory, ostrich feathers, animal skins, and grain. The desert journey, barring disastrous experiences with sand storms, bandit pillagers, missed trails, or dried-up wells, took something short of three months.

The Empire of Ghana

Among the early known West African states, Ghana was surely the largest before the turn of the first millennium C.E. Known also as Wagadu, it may have begun to take form as early as the fourth century. At its height in the tenth century,

Ghana dominated a territory extending from the Senegal valley to the great bend of the Niger River. Its heartland lay in the Sahel and its political capital almost certainly in modern Mauritania, though we do not know exactly where. The king, known in Arabic sources as "the Ghana," commanded a large royal household, a hierarchy of officials, and an army made up mainly of infantry archers. Thanks to southbound Saharan trade in horses, cavalry became possible after about 1000 C.E. The ruler did not control gold mines but may have held a monopoly over the trade, thereby enriching

matrilineal succession The practice of tracing descent or the transmission of property or authority primarily through female relatives.

the state. Royal succession was **matrilineal;** that is, a king was succeeded not by his son but by a son of one of his sisters. The ruler enjoyed sacred status, which meant that he possessed special supernatural powers to mediate between humans and supernatural beings and to perform religious rituals necessary to the people's welfare. Like the Abbasid Caliph, he held public audiences from behind a screen and permitted only a privileged few ever to see him. The central administration was loosely organized. As in the case of many ancient empires, territories distant from the capital remained under the authority of local leaders, who periodically paid tribute to royal officers on pain of armed reprisals. The eleventh-century Arab geographer Al-Bakri, who lived in Spain and collected testimony from trans-Saharan travelers, described the royal household as a place festooned with gold:

> The king adorns himself like a woman (wearing necklaces) round his neck and (bracelets) on his forearms, and he puts on a high cap decorated with gold and wrapped in a turban of fine cotton. He sits in audience . . . in a domed pavilion around which stand ten horses covered with gold-embroidered materials. Behind the king stand ten pages holding shields and swords decorated with gold, and on his right are the sons of the (vassal) kings of his country wearing splendid garments and their hair plaited with gold. . . . When the people who profess the same religion as the king approach him they fall on their knees and sprinkle dust on their head, for this is their way of greeting him.[6]

Islam in West Africa. Muslim merchants and other visitors of Saharan or North African origin almost certainly first introduced Islam to West Africa. According to Al-Bakri, the royal capital of Ghana, whose location is not known, was divided into two areas. "One of these towns, which is inhabited by Muslims, is large and possesses twelve mosques, in which they assemble for the Friday prayer. There are salaried imams [prayer leaders] and muezzins [criers who call Muslims to prayer] as well as jurists and scholars. . . . The king's town is six miles distant from this one."[7] In time the Muslim residents of Ghana's capital converted Sudanic merchants, notably people who spoke Soninke. The converts subsequently carried knowledge of the faith deeper into the savanna. Islam's cultural package inevitably included

Arabic, which established itself quickly as the Sudan's alphabetic language for religion, scholarship, and administration. According to Al-Bakri, many of Ghana's royal officials were literate Muslims.

West African kings tended to walk a narrow religious line, encouraging Muslim commercial enterprise and Arabic literacy but serving their non-Muslim majorities as well by performing traditional sacred rituals. Nevertheless, the ruler of Gao converted to Islam about 1000 C.E., and the kings of Ghana and other states not much later. Thus, West Africa became enmeshed in the larger Afroeurasian network of trade and cultural exchange.

Europe's Struggle for Stability

FOCUS How did invasions and migrations between the seventh and ninth centuries affect Europe's struggle for political and economic stability?

With the exception of the Muslim Umayyad state in Spain, Europe west of the Byzantine empire in the ninth and tenth centuries was a scene of small monarchies and dukedoms, despite the effort the Frankish king Charlemagne had made between 768 and 814 to forge a new Christian empire (see Chapter 10). Within a few decades of Charlemagne's death, his kingdom fragmented amid civil struggles among his three grandsons and the subsequent dividing and subdividing of its former territory among numerous aristocratic families. None of them had sufficient military resources to reverse this trend.

Scholars used to write off the whole era of western European history from the fifth to the eleventh centuries as a "dark age" of economic stagnation nearly everywhere except Spain. More recently, historians using both written texts and archaeological data have redrawn this picture. New evidence suggests that in the eighth and early decades of the ninth centuries, including the decades when Charlemagne ruled, Europe was inching along a track of demographic and economic recovery. Evidence of this upward trend includes the movements of travelers such as diplomatic envoys, pilgrims, and merchants; the number of ships plying the Mediterranean; the flow of gold and silver coins from Muslim states and Byzantium into western Europe; the production and distribution of pottery; and amounts of expenditures on church and monastic buildings.

This growth trend used to go unnoticed partly because it faltered temporarily in the later ninth and tenth centuries as new bands of raiders and invaders stormed into western Europe: Arabs from across the Mediterranean, Magyars (MAH-jahrs) from the Inner Eurasian steppes, and Vikings (Norse) from Scandinavia. These aggressions interrupted, if only temporarily, Europe's agrarian recovery as well as its reintegration into the expanding Mediterranean exchange network.

Muslims and Magyars

Muslim states, including the Umayyad kingdom in Spain, dominated the southern and western shores of the Mediterranean. Using their agrarian wealth to build a fleet of warships, the dynasty known as the Aghlabids (800–909), whose center was modern Tunisia, seized the island of Sicily from its Byzantine Greek governors and took command of the crucial sea passages that connected the eastern and western halves of the Mediterranean. Aghlabid forces, plus bands of Muslim pirates, raided the coasts of Italy and France, advanced up the Rhône and other navigable rivers, and built a scattering of forts and trading posts. In 846, for example, the people of Rome watched in dismay as Arab-led raiders sailed up the Tiber River and sacked the city's outer neighborhoods.

The Aghlabid offensive had two important consequences for Europe. First, Muslim soldiers became major players in the politics of southern Italy, competing with Byzantine forces, troops commanded by the Christian pope, and, at times, Frankish armies for control of towns and trade. Consequently, Italy remained in a general state of turmoil and economic uncertainty until the end of the first millennium. Second, because Muslims dominated the central Mediterranean sea lanes, Italian and other Christian European merchants had a hard time breaking into the maritime trade, and therefore into the wider trans-hemispheric system, until the late tenth century.

European traders knew that they could avoid Muslim sea rovers by exporting goods to Byzantium or other points down the Danube River. In the late ninth century, however, the Magyars, a new horde of pastoral nomads, nearly shut down that route. In the typical pattern of Inner Eurasian population movements, the Magyars appear to have moved westward from the steppes north of the Black Sea into central Europe because other aggressive migrants pushed them from behind. Magyar horse culture was similar to that of Turkic pastoralists. However, the Magyar language, which was ancestral to modern Hungarian, belongs along with modern Finnish and Estonian to the Finno-Ugric family, whose origins lie in the eastern steppes.

Putting down a base on the grassy plains of Hungary west of the Carpathian Mountains, Magyar cavalry raided deep into Germany, France, and northern Italy, avoiding well-defended towns but plundering villages, disrupting harvests, and carrying off large numbers of peasant men and women to sell to eastern Mediterranean slave dealers. Fortunately for settled folk, the Magyar whirlwind blew itself out within about fifty years. Defeated by armored German cavalry in the mid-tenth century, surviving Magyar warriors and their families settled on the Hungarian plain, turned to farming, and eventually converted to Christianity.

The Viking Adventure

Arab and Magyar raids disrupted western Europe, but the Vikings, predatory migrants from Scandinavia (Denmark, Norway, and Sweden), changed it profoundly. Ranging over an astonishingly large expanse between the ninth and eleventh centuries, Vikings pillagers, conquerors, merchants, and colonizers operated from the Black Sea in the east to Newfoundland in far-off North America (see Map 11.5).

The ancestors of the Vikings, or Norse, were speakers of North Germanic languages who occupied Scandinavia as part of the westward movement of Indo-European-speaking peoples that also included the Saxons, Franks, Vandals, and other Germanic groups. Viking men and women made their livings as farmers, fishers, and traders on the coastal plains, valley floors, and islands of the Baltic Sea region. In the post-Roman centuries, when Christian culture was implanting itself in Ireland and Britain, Vikings, largely oblivious to the Holy Gospel, worshiped a household of powerful gods and goddesses.

Motives for expansion. Why did Vikings sail forth to plunder distant neighbors, set up trading posts, and found colonial settlements? One factor may have been a climatic warming trend in northern Europe starting around 800 C.E. and lasting until about 1300. Climatologists call this warming cycle the North Atlantic Warm Period (or Medieval Warm Period). This change permitted Scandinavian farmers to grow oats, barley, and wheat at higher elevations and more northerly latitudes than they previously could. Population subsequently grew, eventually outstripping available farmland and forcing some people to seek livings abroad. A second possibility is that as the Scandinavian farming and fishing economy expanded, local leaders tried to create centralized states. This may have happened in Denmark as early as the eighth century. These ventures involved political struggles, prompting independent warrior-farmers who rejected kingly rule to head off on their own. Third, Scandinavians had taken part in European commercial networks in Roman times, exchanging amber, furs, walrus ivory, and other products of the north for urban manufactures. Vikings therefore became practiced sailors and shipbuilders. When their migrations began, they already had seaworthy vessels. These relatively light ships had broad-bottomed hulls of overlapping planks that permitted both easy beaching and movement along shallow coasts and rivers. From the eighth century, oarsmen powered these ships with help from great square sails that Viking women wove from wool. Shipwrights constructed war vessels long and narrow for speed; they built cargo ships shorter and wider for ample carrying capacity. Both types were stout enough to sail on rough northern seas and out of sight of land for many days.

Viking offensives. The Norse assaults on other parts of Europe involved numerous independent campaigns. From what is today Norway, bands attacked northern Britain, Scotland, and Ireland, deliberately targeting churches and monasteries for brutal destruction because these places often had stores of gold. In 793, for example, Viking sea raiders hit the northeastern coast of England, completely demolishing Lindisfarne, the richest center of Christian

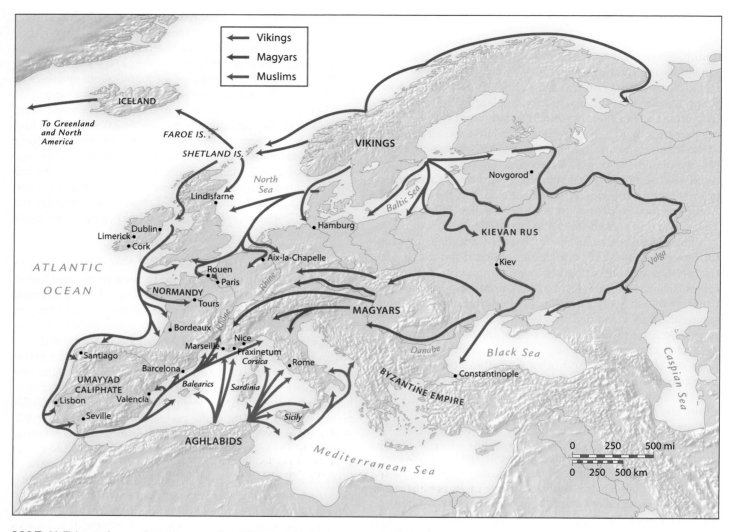

MAP 11.5 Invasion, migration, and settlement in Europe, ninth to eleventh centuries.
Did Vikings, Magyars, and North African Muslims have any similar motivations for attacking or migrating into western Europe?

learning in the British Isles. In some places, Vikings arrived as looters and killers but then stayed on to settle and colonize, founding, for example, the towns of Dublin, Cork, and Limerick in Ireland. From those centers, Norse warriors launched further expeditions, while women, children, and slaves stayed behind to grow crops and expand settlements.

Norwegian Vikings also contributed to the initial human colonization of some places. Seaborne bands very likely founded the earliest settlements on both the Faroe Islands (north of Scotland) and Iceland. Near the end of the tenth century, Viking ships reached the southern edge of ice-capped Greenland—a huge island already frequented by Inuit sea hunters from North America. A few thousand Viking men and women settled fjords along the Greenland coast. There, they scratched out grain fields, though they remained dependent for food on sea links with Iceland and Europe.

Archaeologists have verified that Viking mariners reached North America and lived for part of the eleventh century at L'Anse aux Meadows on the northeastern coast of Newfoundland. We know nothing of their interaction with local American Indians, and after a few decades they abandoned their settlement. Six hundred miles of open North Atlantic water separated L'Anse aux Meadows from Greenland, a distance that even the hardiest Viking sailors could not bridge for long.

While Norwegians prowled the far north, Danish Vikings moved out from Jutland (the peninsula that today is part of Denmark) to assail France and England, skimming along coasts and far up rivers, including the Seine and the Thames. In the ninth century, Danish forces, leaving their ships to fight on foot and horseback, conquered much of England. Anglo-Saxon warriors, whose own Germanic ancestors had

A Viking ship. This graceful vessel, discovered by a Norwegian farmer in 1903, no doubt survived from the ninth century because it was pulled from the water and transformed into a burial structure for two women, probably members of elite families. An array of grave goods accompanied the women, including the corpses of sacrificed horses, dogs, and cows. The mast supported a square sail, and the ship could accommodate thirty rowers. The ship resides in the Viking Ship Museum in Oslo. Why do you think Vikings used vessels as burial chambers?

invaded the island only a few centuries earlier, held on to the southwest and gradually pushed the Danes northward. Many Vikings settled in England, married Anglo-Saxon women, took up farming, and converted to Christianity. Eventually, the Danes of England disappeared as a distinct ethnic and linguistic group.

Viking raiders took full advantage of the disintegration of the Carolingian empire to step up attacks on northern France. They plundered and then colonized the fertile Seine valley. At the end of the tenth century, the king of the Franks, who was then simply a regional lord, ratified Norse control of a large area of northern France, henceforth known as the Duchy of Normandy. These immigrants married into local families and in time became known as the Normans.

Vikings and the rise of Kiev. Swedish-speaking Norse, more merchants than swordsmen at first, pioneered southeastward expansion from Scandinavia. Crossing the Baltic, they voyaged up several northern continental rivers, then down the Dnieper to the Black Sea. With them went furs, honey, amber, wax, and slaves for Abbasid and Byzantine markets. This "northern arc" of sea, river, and overland forest routes joined northeastern Europe with Southwest Asia. Swedish traders strengthened the northern routes by founding settlements at Novgorod, Kiev, and other strategic points already inhabited by Slavic or Turkic peoples. Archaeologists have uncovered hoards of Arab silver coins (more than 50,000 of them) in Scandinavian sites, and even a bronze Buddha dating to the sixth or seventh centuries. These finds testify to the success and long reach of the northern arc trade.

In the ninth century, Kiev, today the capital of Ukraine, emerged as the center of a Viking warrior state that supplanted the power of the Khazar kingdom (see Chapter 10) north of the Black Sea. Viking sea raiders even approached Constantinople three times between 860 and 941, though they probably hoped only to win political and commercial recognition from the Greek emperor. In the Kiev region, as in western Europe, Viking men married local women and gradually took up the ways and speech of the predominantly Slavic population. Arab geographers adopted the name "Rus" to describe this cultural merger of Swedes, Slavs, and Turks.

Bjarni Herjolfsson and the Viking Discovery of America

The discovery of a spindle weight, a ring-headed pin, and a Norwegian coin have provided conclusive archeological evidence for Viking settlement in North America during the eleventh century. In addition, two textual sources, The Saga of the Greenlanders *and* The Saga of Erik the Red, *offer thirteenth-century accounts of Viking expeditions to North America. Known together as* The Vinland Sagas, *these documents set down tales that had circulated in Viking oral traditions for several centuries. Blended with other legends and influenced by stories from Europe,* The Vinland Sagas *are sometimes fanciful. Historians have questioned their veracity and generally regard them as semifictional elaborations of events that actually took place. The selection here comes from* The Saga of the Greenlanders. *It describes the travels of Bjarni Herjolfsson, a Norwegian explorer who in 985 or 986 C.E. appears to have sighted North America but did not anchor his ships there.*

[Bjarni] was a promising young man. While still a youthful age he longed to sail abroad. He soon earned for himself both a good deal of wealth and a good name, and spent his winters alternately abroad and with his father. Soon Bjarni had his own ship making trading voyages. During the last winter Bjarni spent in Norway, [his father] Herjolf decided to accompany Erik the Red to Greenland and left his farm. . . .

Bjarni steered his ship into Eyrar [in Iceland] in the summer of the year that his father had sailed from Iceland. Bjarni was greatly moved by the news and would not have his cargo unloaded. His crew then asked what he was waiting for, and he answered that he intended to follow his custom of spending the winter with his father—"and I want to set sail for Greenland, if you will join me."

All of them said they would follow his counsel.

Bjarni then spoke: "Our journey will be thought an ill-considered one, since none of us has sailed the Greenland Sea."

Despite this they set sail once they had made ready and sailed for three days, until the land had disappeared below the horizon. Then the wind dropped and they were beset by winds from the north and fog; for many days they did not know where they were sailing.

After that they saw the sun and could take their bearings. Hoisting the sail, they sailed for the rest of the day before sighting land. They speculated among themselves as to what land this would be, for Bjarni said he suspected this was not Greenland.

They asked whether he wanted to sail up close into the shore of this country or not. "My advice is that we sail in close to the land."

They did so, and soon saw that the land was not mountainous but did have small hills, and was covered with forests. Keeping it on their port side, they turned their sail-end landwards and angled away from the shore.

They sailed for another two days before sighting the land once again.

They asked Bjarni whether he now thought this to be Greenland.

He said he thought this no more likely to be Greenland than the previous land—"since there are said to be very large glaciers in Greenland."

They soon approached the land and saw that it was flat and wooded. The wind died and the crew members said they thought it advisable to put ashore, but Bjarni was against it. They claimed they needed both timber and water.

"You've no shortage of those provisions," Bjarni said, but he was criticized somewhat by his crew for this.

[Bjarni and his crew then sighted a third land. But they did not land there and sailed back out to sea.]

Upon seeing a fourth land they asked Bjarni whether he thought this was Greenland or not.

Bjarni answered, "This land is most like what I have been told of Greenland, and we'll head for shore here."

This they did and made land along a headland in the evening of the day, finding a boat there. On this point Herjolf, Bjarni's father, lived [. . .] Bjarni now joined his father and ceased his merchant voyages. He remained on his father's farm as long as Herjolf lived and took over the farm after his death.

Following this, Bjarni Herjolfsson sailed from Greenland to Earl Erik, who received him well. . . .

Bjarni became one of the earl's followers and sailed to Greenland the following summer. There was now much talk of looking for new lands.

Source: The Vinland Sagas: The Icelandic Sagas about the First Documented Voyages across the North Atlantic, *trans. Keneva Kunz, intro. and notes by Gisli Sigurdsson (London and New York: Penguin, 2008), pp. 3–5.*

Thinking Critically

What sort of information did Bjarni rely on to guide him to Greenland? Why do you think he refused to stop and explore the first three lands his crew spotted? Should Bjarni be credited with "discovering" America? Why or why not?

The Rus thus became Russians, builders of a state of increasing size and power. Negotiation and trade, as much as conflict, characterized relations between the Rus state and Byzantium. Around 1000 the Russian prince Vladimir (r. 980–1015) converted to Greek Orthodox Christianity. Thereafter, the Russian state and the Christian church became close collaborators. One consequence was a surge of Greek artistic and architectural influence into western Inner Eurasia. In the eleventh and twelfth centuries, towns from Kiev in the south to Novgorod in the cold, forested north acquired stone churches, bishops, and church laws that regulated social and ritual life. The Russian church, however, made itself distinct from its Byzantine parent, adopting, for example, East Slavic, not Greek, as the language of religious literacy and worship.

Kiev may be counted among the most prosperous and beautifully adorned capitals in western Eurasia in those centuries. Even so, the plains and woodlands stretching north of Kiev had relatively poor soils and a short growing season. This limited agrarian base obliged the Russian rulers to press down hard on the farming population, risking local revolt. They also had to compete with other princely families, who had their own provincial power centers beyond Kiev's controlling radius. Consequently, the princes of Kiev never accumulated vast wealth or fully subordinated rival Russian noble families to their authority.

The Changing Shape of Western Europe

In western Europe, local societies experimented with new forms of defense and government in response to Arab, Magyar, and Viking raiders. In the region that is now Belgium and northern France, the crumbling of Charlemagne's empire convinced Frankish aristocratic families, none of whom had much concentrated military power, to fall back on relatively small core territories. There, they built castles and manors (fortified houses) to protect fields, grazing land, and the hamlets where their tenants and serfs lived. From these local bastions, estate holders tried to defend themselves against alien intruders and, much of the time, against one another. The individual who held the title of king in the tenth century was one of these barons and not always the most powerful. Aristocratic men did most of the fighting, adopting a war technology that had antecedents in Byzantium and, before that, Sasanid Persia. Frankish knights heavily armored both themselves and their big horses and did battle with lance and sword, sometimes mounted, sometimes on foot. A relatively small group of knights armed in this way could effectively protect a manor house and the estate around it, though aristocrats generally lacked the resources to transport arms, servants, and horses over long distances. Thus, warfare was mostly defensive and local.

An eleventh-century castle. In that era, northern European nobles and their families needed stout defenses. This replica image of a fortified residence has both a moat and a bailey, or outer wall. Behind the inner wall is the castle proper, called the keep.

Origins of European feudalism. Historians describe the style of political relations among these numerous western

fief An estate of land an individual holds on condition of allegiance and service to the grantor.

European warlords as feudal, which comes from the Latin word *feudum,* meaning landed estate, or **fief.** The key element in relations among aristocratic warriors was personal obligations of military service and responsibility cemented by rituals that all parties were to take very seriously. This system of power was based not on bureaucrats serving a central authority but on associations for mutual benefit between patrons and clients, that is, between militarily strong individuals and

vassal An individual who is subordinate to or dependent on another individual; in feudalism an individual who holds land given by a lord in return for loyal service.

relatively weaker ones. Feudal relations were hierarchical in the sense that one warrior, called the **vassal,** offered service, recognition, and loyalty to a more powerful warrior, the lord. In return, the lord granted protection, rewards, and privileges to his vassals.

In western Europe's still fragile economic conditions, aristocratic lords had little to offer their vassals except agriculturally productive fiefs. Moreover, the most powerful lords—the dukes and barons—needed fighting knights so badly that they granted vassals not only fiefs but also rights to transfer their property to their heirs, thereby creating multigenerational feudal relations. Some vassals became rich enough to recruit vassals of their own, awarding these lesser knights land in return for military service. This practice expanded the hierarchy of obligation and service to three or more levels.

Aristocratic men specialized in fighting, but well-born women fully involved themselves in feudal relations. To operate effectively from one generation to the next, the system required male heirs and family alliances, which meant marriage agreements over which mothers, sisters, and prospective brides exerted great influence. Also, women frequently managed estates, large and small, when sons and husbands went off to battle.

In a strict sense, feudal bonds involved only men and women of the landowning elite, a small minority of western Europe's population. Other forms of patron-client relationship, especially serfdom (see Chapter 10), bound landlords and peasants to one another, the latter farming the lands that provided revenue for war horses, manors, fortifications, and the elite's relatively comfortable lifestyle. At their master's command, peasants also went to war as infantry soldiers, servants, and laborers.

Northern state builders. The struggle for political and social order took significantly different turns in both England

and northern Germany. Those regions also adopted the rituals and institutions of **feudalism,** but state building there was successful earlier than it was in

feudalism A hierarchical system of social and political organization in which an individual gives grants of land to other individuals in return for allegiance and service.

France. In the later ninth century, Alfred the Great (r. 871–899), king of the small Anglo-Saxon state of Wessex in southern England, pushed back Danish invaders and even revived in some measure Latin literacy and scholarship. Dukes and barons continued to exert great power, but in the interests of political stability they more readily accepted the king as paramount than did aristocrats in northern France.

At the end of the tenth century, however, Vikings briefly triumphed once again. This time the militarily gifted and thoroughly Christian king Canute, operating from Jutland, conquered not only England but also Norway and Estonia. From about 1015 to 1035, he ruled a unified state that spanned the Baltic and North Seas. The most important stake in this project was the maritime trade of the two seas, which began to grow dramatically near the end of the first millennium. When Canute died, however, his northern sea empire disintegrated quickly, leaving England to an independent fate.

Central monarchy also succeeded, at least loosely, in northern Germany in the tenth century. There, Otto I (r. 936–973), the ruler of Saxony, managed to subdue the dukes of four other powerful German territories and in 955 crushed the Magyars. He then invaded Italy, and in 962 the pope named him Holy Roman Emperor, the same majestic but exaggerated title Charlemagne had held. Otto allied closely with the church, handing out estates and offices to bishops and the men and women who headed monasteries. He therefore commanded the loyalty of administrators who could not marry and build family power because they were members of the clergy. Otto's successors worked to perpetuate this fledgling central bureaucracy, but aristocratic families continued to press for regional autonomy, exposing the political fragility of the Holy Roman Empire.

Italian city-states. In Italy the southern region remained a land of contention among Byzantine Greeks, Muslims, and Catholic Christians. In the center and north, feudal relations had little relevance. Rather, individuals commonly identified with a particular town or city and the surrounding land it controlled. These city-states were in no way democracies, and many of them were ruled by bishops and their appointed officers. The pope governed Rome and extensive lands around it. Nevertheless, as the economy of the peninsula revived gradually, the landowning and commercial class exerted increasing influence. By the early eleventh century, Europe both north and south of the Alps was set for a burst of economic growth and cultural creativity.

• • •

Conclusion

The world historian Lynda Shaffer has characterized many of the developments discussed in this chapter as part of a larger process that she calls "southernization."[8] The term refers to a historical process whereby a number of ideas, techniques, and products of great importance in human history developed in India and Southeast Asia and then spread to other parts of Afroeurasia. Southernization got under way in the early centuries C.E. and continued as a significant pattern into the modern era. Among the elements of southernization were the thickening of trade routes and networks across the southern seas, growing production and exchange of tropical spices such as pepper, the wide diffusion of South Asian crops such as cotton and sugar, the spread of improved sailing and navigation technologies, and the dissemination of ingenious mathematical concepts. As a result of influences from India and Southeast Asia, other regions, including East Asia, the central Muslim lands, Europe, and tropical Africa, all became in some measure "southernized" in economy and culture.

Not all important ideas of the later first millennium C.E., however, spread outward from southern Asia. We may point to Christianity, Islam, the silk industry, and the invention of paper, among many innovations, that originated in other parts of the hemisphere. In any case, southernization occurred on such a large scale only because available communication and transport technologies allowed it. In the centuries this chapter has addressed, networks of interchange advanced far beyond their range and complexity as of, say, 500 C.E. The hubs in these networks were the ports and inland cities where routes converged and branched out. The era witnessed a remarkable multiplication of these hubs, notably in the lands rimming the southern seas. Traffic moved faster and more efficiently along the trans-hemispheric routes because of ideas and institutions that served the communication system itself. These included the moral and ethical codes of the major religions, which provided standards of right behavior among people who spoke different languages and had mutually unfamiliar customs; the standardizing of written languages and accompanying spread of literacy; the simplifying of commercial accounting with base-ten "Indian" numerals; the production of documents using paper; the organizing of larger, more complex diasporas of professional merchants; and an array of financial techniques for speeding market exchange. In Chapter 12, which focuses on Afroeurasia between 1000 and 1250, we will see that these trends continued, though the centers of most dynamic growth and innovation shifted significantly.

• • •

Key Terms

Abbasid empire 309	Kiev, Rus 329	*shari'a* 310
cosmopolitan 313	Magyars 326	Silla dynasty 321
Fatimid dynasty 312	*mamluk* 311	Srivijaya 319
feudalism 332	matrilineal succession 326	*ulama* 310
fief 332	military slavery 311	vassal 332
Ghana 325	Pallava dynasty 318	Vikings 336
Holy Roman Empire 332	proselytize 314	Yamato dynasty 321
Kanem 324	Samanid dynasty 312	Zanj Rebellion 311

Change over Time

7th–13th centuries	The kingdom of Srivijaya becomes a maritime empire in Southeast Asia.
668–935	The Silla dynasty rules in Korea.
710	The Yamato dynasty founds the town of Nara as a royal center.
750–1258	The Abbasid Caliphate rules from Baghdad, reaching its zenith of power during the reign of Harun al-Rashid (786–809).
756–1031	The Umayyad dynasty, ruling from Córdoba, presides over a prosperous urban economy in Spain.
819–999	Persian aristocrats establish the Samanid dynasty with its capital at Bukhara; the dynasty promotes Muslim missionary activity along silk roads.
869–883	The Abbasids face the Zanj Rebellion in Iraq.
9th century	Vikings assault northern Europe; Magyars invade central Europe; Muslim Aghlabids take control of Mediterranean sea lanes and raid Italy.
10th century	The kingdom of Ghana, the largest state in West Africa, reaches its height of prosperity.
936–973	Otto I reigns over the Holy Roman empire in western Europe.
969–1171	The Shi'a Fatimid dynasty in Egypt declares itself Islam's true caliphate.
976–1025	Byzantine territorial expansion resumes during the reign of Basil II.
ca. 1000	The ruler of Gao in West Africa converts to Islam.
980–1035	Prince Vladimir of Kiev establishes the Russian Orthodox Church.
11th century	Vikings settle in Newfoundland.

Please see end of book reference section for additional reading suggestions related to this chapter.

part 4

Interconnections and Their Consequences

900–1500

A blue-green porcelain vase from China's Song Dynasty.

Looking at the human past through a very wide-angle lens, we might say that the world did not change much between the era we explored in Part 3 and the six centuries we now investigate in Part 4. Between 900 and 1500, the agrarian age continued as before. In other words, agriculture, including both crop and domestic animal raising, remained the economic foundation of both rural villagers and the builders of complex societies with their cities, centralized governments, and grand buildings. The ability of humans to produce food, fiber, and fuel remained as strictly dependent on the soil as it had throughout the agrarian age. Even though people continued to invent practical new tools—better plows, horse harnesses, sails, water-lifting machines—the number of daily calories of useful energy an individual could control barely doubled from the dawn of agriculture to 1000.[1] And that number did not begin to accelerate at a much faster rate until the nineteenth century, when our species devised ways to exploit immense underground stores of energy from coal, oil, and gas.

If we view history through a somewhat narrower lens, we see that several large-scale patterns of change under way in the first millennium C.E. continued into the second. World population, economic output, and interregional trade all continued to increase, while societies fashioned more complex social and economic institutions and accumulated more scientific and technical knowledge. We saw in Part 3 that these trends, all generally characteristic of the agrarian age, could be interrupted by unforeseen slumps in population and economy accompanied by more intense social and political turmoil. This happened between the third and sixth centuries. As we shall see in Part 4, it happened again in the 1300s, a depressive period marked by the great

Afroeurasian disease pandemic we call the Black Death. But as in the first millennium, the downturn was temporary. Recovery took hold in the fifteenth century, and between 900 and 1500, the population of Afroeurasia managed to double.

If we focus even more closely on hemispheric and regional landscapes, we see that the 900–1500 period looks very different from the previous millennium. In Part 4 we explore changes that had broad regional or hemispheric effects in those six hundred years:

■ In China under the Song (960–1276) and Jin (1115–1234) dynasties, manufacturing, commerce, urbanization, and technical innovation all surged forward. China's economic growth outpaced that of all other regions. And because China both exported and imported larger quantities of goods, its prosperity affected the livelihoods and business activities of peoples as far distant as East Africa and western Europe.

■ Pastoral nomads of Inner Eurasia had a greater impact on Afroeurasia's history between 900 and 1500 than in any period before or after. Beginning in the late tenth century, Turkic-speaking nomads migrated in large numbers into densely settled lands of Southwest Asia, and they raided and conquered along an even wider arc of territory. By the twelfth century, Turkic populations, or at least military elites, dominated societies from Egypt to South Asia's Ganges valley. These movements caused social and political upheavals, but the great cities of Southwest Asia and Egypt continued to prosper as centers of manufacturing and commerce.

■ Among Afroeurasia's major belief systems, Islam spread more widely than any other during these centuries. Because Turkic migrants and conquerors were Muslims, they introduced their faith to new regions. Merchants, scholars, and wandering preachers also founded new Muslim communities from West Africa to China.

■ In Europe, improving political stability and new agricultural inventions fueled more towns and trade, a development that paralleled events in Song China on a smaller scale. By the eleventh century, a new center of urban civilization under the moral and cultural guidance of the Catholic Christian church was taking shape. Europeans linked themselves more firmly to the web of hemispheric exchange, a process interrupted but not halted by climatic change and the Black Death.

■ In Africa south of the Sahara Desert, population levels remained lower than in the agrarian lands of Eurasia and northern Africa. Nevertheless, farming and cattle-herding societies continued to grow and with them more inter-regional trade, cities, and large states. In the thirteenth and fourteenth centuries, for example, the West African empire of Mali stimulated Afroeurasian trade by exporting large quantities of gold.

■ Pastoral nomadic conquests resumed on a spectacular scale in the early thirteenth century, when Mongol and Turkic horse cavalry stormed across Eurasia, forging the largest land empire the world had ever seen. The Mongol conquests from China to Hungary were terrifying, but once the victors founded new governments, they rebuilt cities and patronized art and learning. For more than a century, Mongol rulers encouraged the flow of goods, technologies, and religious ideas across Afroeurasia.

■ In the Americas, total population may have been only a fifth of China's as of 1200, but numbers grew as farmers experimented with irrigation and land-reclaiming techniques and as maize cultivation spread more widely. Several new monument-building states appeared, culminating in the fifteenth century with the rise of the Aztec and Inca empires. Those two states demonstrated that human labor and creativity could be mobilized on an enormous scale despite the absence of iron technology or wheeled transport.

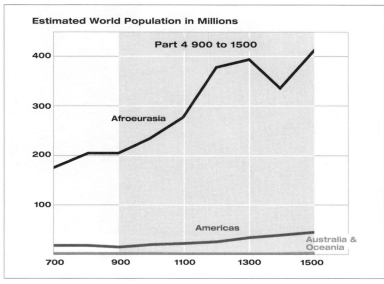

Estimated World Population in Millions

12 Dynamic Centuries across Afroeurasia

1000–1250

Scroll painting of commercial life in Kaifeng, China, in the twelfth century.

very year more than 3,200 state and county fairs are held in North America. Some people go to fairs to compete for blue ribbons for the finest products of farm and home—the best cows, rabbits, quilts, applesauce, and dill pickles. Other people go for the Ferris wheels, Belgian waffles, and country singers. The agricultural fair, where local farmers and artisans sell goods and demonstrate crafts, has been a distinctive American institution since the early nineteenth century. It has its deep origins in the rural or small-town market, an institution that in premodern centuries usually appeared wherever settled populations, workshops, and trade flourished. Rural markets typically sprang up on the borders between different ecological regions or where geography, political conditions, and transport routes encouraged people to meet together in an open space to exchange wares. Sometimes several markets in a region were linked together in a rotation, each one taking place on a particular day of the week or season of the year. To attract merchants and customers, rural markets usually organized some kind of authority to police the grounds, set rules of public behavior, and penalize troublemakers, cheaters, and thieves. If the market also offered food and amusements, it had most of the features of a modern fair.

We have good evidence that both country and town markets were growing in number and size in several parts of Afroeurasia between the eleventh and thirteenth centuries. We know this was happening, for example, in China, the Ganges River valley, southern India, western Europe, and tropical West Africa. Historians generally agree that in most of Afroeurasia's agrarian regions, population, economic production, and commerce started trending upward about the sixth century and that this trend accelerated between 1000 and 1250. Quantitative data to demonstrate this development are very limited. Some societies preserved commercial and financial information more carefully than others did, and in no case has more than a small part of everyday economic records survived to the present. Nevertheless, historians see patterns of growth, not only in the proliferation of local markets, but also in the opening of new trade routes, the numbers of ships plying seas and inland waterways, the circulation of currencies, the invention of new credit and banking techniques, and the size of textile and other manufacturing operations.

China had possessed the largest regional economy in the world throughout most of the first millennium c.e. In the eleventh and twelfth centuries, that economy grew even bigger relative to other Afroeurasian regions, even to India. We begin this chapter with a focus on East Asia because China's Song dynasty (960–1276) presided over an unprecedented rush of industrial and commercial activity, a development

Chapter Outline

THE EAST ASIAN POWERHOUSE IN THE SONG ERA

The Elements of China's Prosperity
Governing China in an Era of Change
China and Its Near Neighbors
Japan within and without the Chinese Sphere
China in the Hemisphere

CONQUERORS AND MIGRANTS IN THE MUSLIM LANDS

Turkic Horse Power
Muslim Ships on the Mediterranean
WEIGHING THE EVIDENCE A Jewish Merchant Writes to His Wife
New Empires in the Western Mediterranean
Cultural Trends in the Muslim Lands

FOUNDATIONS OF URBAN CIVILIZATION IN EUROPE

Warm Weather, Better Plows
New Order in Political Life
INDIVIDUALS MATTER King Philip II: French State-Builder
The Expansion of Western Christendom
European Commercial Power in the Mediterranean
Western Europe's Cultural Style

• • •

that helped stimulate economic growth across Afroeurasia. This section of the chapter also addresses China's close neighbors, especially Japan, an island society that made its own economic gains in the 1000–1250 period and that emerged as a distinctive city-based civilization.

The second part of the chapter highlights the important historical transition that took place in Afroeurasia's middle regions (see Map 12.1). Repeating in some ways the tumultuous pastoral movements of the fourth to seventh centuries, migrants who spoke Turkic languages swept from Central Asia across both Southwest Asia and northern India, replacing old states with new ones and changing the ethnolinguistic identity of wide areas. Despite these political disturbances, however, the numerous cities of Southwest Asia continued to play their accustomed role as centers of manufacturing and commercial exchange. Muslim merchants sailed the Mediterranean as they had done for 350 years, though they faced increasing competition from western European newcomers. Turkic state-builders, already Muslims when they initiated their conquests, became sponsors of Muslim literature and

A Panoramic View

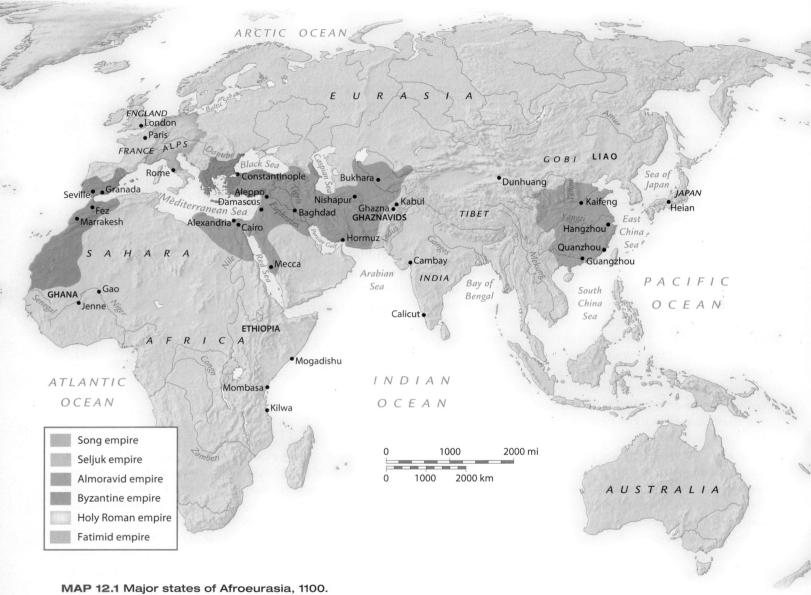

MAP 12.1 Major states of Afroeurasia, 1100.

At the start of the twelfth century, China's Song dynasty presided over Afroeurasia's largest regional economy, while the boundaries of western Christendom expanded. In what regions might you predict pastoral nomadic peoples to emerge as a potent political force?

art, and they energized the continuing spread of Islam. In the far west of the Muslim world, migrating Berber armies mirrored the Turkic invasions by conquering North Africa (modern Morocco, Algeria, and Tunisia) and a large part of Spain.

Western Europe, reduced in population between the fifth and ninth centuries, achieved greater political stability after 900 and entered an era of remarkable economic and cultural renewal. Exploiting the region's agricultural resources with greater efficiency, Europe's farmers and artisans augmented production to the point where towns and the trade routes between them began to multiply. Under the religious and cultural guidance of the Catholic Church, Europeans laid the base of a new urban civilization, pushed out the frontiers of western Christendom east and west, and entered Mediterranean trade on a much larger scale, linking themselves more firmly to the entire trans-hemispheric network.

The East Asian Powerhouse in the Song Era

> **FOCUS** In what ways did China's economy change between the eleventh and thirteenth centuries, and what effects did these economic changes have on other parts of Afroeurasia?

Most world historians agree that China's economic surge in the era of the Song dynasty triggered large commercial and cultural changes in Afroeurasia as a whole. This expansion, centered in the warm, rice-growing latitudes of southern China, involved swelling food production and a stunning acceleration of technical innovation, urbanization, population growth, and both internal and foreign trade. A transhemispheric exchange system already existed at the start of the new millennium. China's boom reverberated all across it.

The Elements of China's Prosperity

Economic and demographic growth got seriously under way in China when the Sui and Tang dynasties unified north and south in the sixth and seventh centuries. That growth continued even after 907, when the Tang regime collapsed and China broke into several rival regional states. Then, starting in 960, Zhao Kuangyin, a military commander from a northern monarchy, consolidated his power in most of the north, conquered the south, and founded the Song dynasty (960–1127). Zhao established his capital at Kaifeng, an interior city not far from the Yellow River.

The Song government accumulated great wealth from taxes on China's prosperity, but it did not, in contrast to its Tang predecessors, push the imperial frontiers deep into the Inner Eurasian steppe. In fact, it faced powerful new states along its grassland frontiers. For example, the farming and pastoral people known as the Kitans (also Qitans), created the Liao (lee-OW) state (916–1125), which stretched across the prairies and forests of Mongolia and Manchuria. The Song government bought decades of reasonable calm with the Liao and other Inner Eurasia kingdoms by sending them annual cargos of silk and silver, as earlier dynasties had done.

A third northern kingdom proved far more dangerous to the Song. Beginning in 1115, the Jurchens, a group native to the forests of Manchuria, destroyed the Liao state and proclaimed the Jin dynasty (1115–1234). The Jurchens made their living more as farmers and hunters than as animal herders, but they were nonetheless masters of cavalry. In 1127 they overran the Yellow River valley and all of northern China. They drove the Song out of their capital of Kaifeng and ascended to power over about forty million Chinese. Meanwhile, the Song governing elite fled south, successfully regrouping in the Yangzi valley and establishing a capital at Hangzhou (hahng-jo). The later Song, or Southern Song, dynasty (1127–1276) was a large regional state more than an empire.

Despite the new political fault line between northern and southern China, both the Jin and the Song thrived. The Jin harvested the huge farm revenues of the Yellow River valley and also took annual payments from the Song in return for peace. Cut off from the immense agricultural revenues of the north, the Song compensated for the loss in part by encouraging farmers in the Yangzi valley and lands farther south to expand production. Some of the same crops that diffused from India and Southeast Asia westward to the Mediterranean also spread to China. These included cotton, sugar cane, and, most important, varieties of quick-ripening, drought-resistant rice. The new rice strains, probably introduced about the tenth century from Vietnam, delivered good harvests not only in wet lowlands but also on terraced hillsides and in relatively dry climates. Farmers could produce two or even three crops a year. Consequently, southern rice production soared. Some scholars have suggested that the North Atlantic Warm Period, the slight rise in Northern Hemispheric temperatures that extended from about 800 to 1300, contributed to larger and more stable food production in China (see Chapter 11). Researchers have linked Song economic growth to higher average temperatures in the southern regions between the ninth and eleventh centuries. There is also evidence that farmers and herders in northern China suffered fewer droughts, floods, and locust infestations than in the immediate earlier or later periods.[1]

Markets, money, and canals. Displaying an unprecedented capitalist mentality, Song economic reformers argued successfully that the state should promote private market activity and tax trade as a major source of revenue. Traditional Confucian economic ideology regarded commerce as a lowly occupation because merchants did not actually *produce* anything. And it idealized peasants as reliable creators of taxable wealth from the land. By contrast, Song policymakers contended that farmers should be encouraged to sell surplus crops, textiles, and handicrafts in local markets for money to further stimulate the commercial economy. These reformers contended that the government could push rural men and women into the market by making them pay taxes in money rather than in grain or other produce. To get money, peasants had to trade. Bronze coins had lubricated the Chinese economy for centuries, but the swelling market, in which individuals, extended families, and private partnerships did business for profit, enhanced the importance of money. The government authorized production of billions of bronze and iron coins and, near the end of the eleventh century, paper money. China's papermaking and printing industries were more than advanced enough to produce large quantities of bills. Eventually, the government backed the value of these bills with reserves of silver.

Also to encourage commerce, the Song extended China's network of canals and deep river channels, already the longest in the world, to more than 30,000 miles of navigable waterways. The north–south Grand Canal linking the Yellow and Yangzi valleys carried tons of grain, iron, copper, pottery, and a thousand other commodities. On narrow

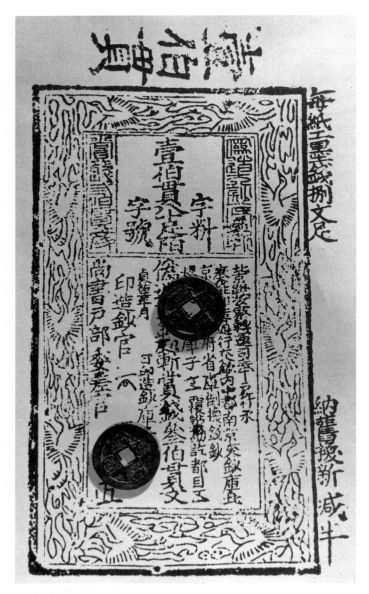

Bronze and paper money. In Song China's prospering economy, the demand for currency, like these two bronze coins, became so great that hundreds of millions, and eventually billions, of coins were minted every year. To ease the problems of making transactions with large quantities of coins, the government began in the eleventh century to issue paper bills. The note shown here would have represented a particular quantity of coins by weight. Why do you think Chinese merchants and consumers had faith in the value of paper money?

fairs were especially popular. A thirteenth-century poet described his arrival at a market in western China:

> Coming in a palanquin [a box-shaped conveyance carried on poles] to visit the Medicine Fair.
> Our bearers' knees are caught in the press of the crowd,
> Little by little we inch our way up to the gate
> Already surrounded by a diversity of goods . . .
> Merchants have buffeted the sea-winds and the waves,
> And foreign merchants crossed over towering crags,
> Drawn onwards by the profits to be made.[2]

Commercialization encouraged new economic habits. Millions of farmers began to produce not only marketable rice and cotton but also new crops such as wine grapes, sugar cane, tea, tangerines, and oil seeds. Rural families manufactured silk thread and cloth, baskets, paper, and charcoal at home. Mounting food production in the countryside meant that cities could support more people engaged full time in industry and commerce. A specialized artisan's best customers were landowners, merchants, and high officials, who had money to spend on silks, lacquered furniture, bronze statuary, and fragile white porcelain.

Wherever metals could be exploited, private mining enterprises flourished. Under the Song and later the Jin rulers, blast furnaces concentrated in great numbers around Kaifeng produced large quantities of iron and steel, a production unmatched anywhere in the world until the nineteenth century. Chinese inventors made several advances in metals technology, notably using coke (made by baking coal to remove impurities) to heat blast furnaces to higher temperatures. The Song army purchased huge quantities of iron arrowheads, swords, and armor, and canal barges shipped iron farm tools, chains for suspension bridges, and millions of nails for the shipbuilding industry in the south.

Technical ingenuity. In the eleventh and twelfth centuries, Chinese inventors and engineers showed remarkable creative spark, a surge related to the pressures of economic growth and opportunities for specialization. Technicians stuffed gunpowder into crude rockets, bombs, and mortars, which Song forces deployed in frontier wars to create noise and confusion, if not great destruction. Woodblock printing became a standard industry, and printed books, including technical and agricultural manuals, circulated widely. Other inventions of the era included the magnetic compass, new techniques for firing porcelain, water-powered bellows for blast furnaces, and spinning wheels for making silk thread. Many of these inventions spread across Afroeurasia in the ensuing centuries.

The period also saw advances in astronomy, chemistry, mathematics, and other scientific fields. Like their counterparts in the central Muslim lands, Chinese mathematicians adopted the Indian place-value system with nine numerals, as well as the zero written as "0." Mathematicians and engineers applied their knowledge mainly to practical problems such as land surveys and construction projects.

canals, rivers, and irrigation channels—the capillaries of the system—farmers and traders transported crops to local markets on boats pushed along with poles.

Local markets and fairs multiplied in the Song period. These gatherings were commonly known as "temple markets" because local people held them in connection with Buddhist or other sacred festivals. Merchants offered the gathered crowd not only candles and other religious paraphernalia but also an array of commercial goods. Medicine

The government encouraged the founding of academies for study of Confucian philosophical and literary texts, though science was pursued outside of those colleges. Scientists, working privately, communicated with one another through letters and printed texts.

The population climb. The elements of economic growth we have described operated against a background of mushrooming population, a phenomenon related to expanding food supplies. Between about 750 and 1300, China's population doubled to around 120 million, representing about a third of the world's total population. Within China, north and south switched places as the center of demographic growth. In 750, about 60 percent of the population lived in the north. By 1200, about 75 percent lived in the Yangzi valley or farther south.

In major cities, populations spilled out beyond defensive walls to make room for shops, fairs, warehouses, and floods of job-seeking rural immigrants. The population of Kaifeng grew to about one million in 1100, making it almost certainly the largest city in the world. Hangzhou, the Southern Song capital in the Yangzi delta, moved toward the million mark in the following century. Southern coastal ports similarly thrived. Quanzhou and its suburbs reached a population of about 500,000.

Rich and poor, powerful and weak. Generally speaking, standards of living rose in the Song era for all of China's traditionally defined social classes—scholars, artisans, farmers, and merchants. The majority of farm families owned land. In contrast, for example, to European serfs, they could sell their property, pass it to their children, and take surplus crops to market. Independent farmers, however, easily slid into debt to money-lenders, and big cities teemed with underemployed rural immigrants. Enterprising merchants

of nonelite origin might accumulate great wealth. Even so, Confucian bureaucrats and landed families took full precedence over merchants in prestige and power.

The speed of economic change significantly altered social relations between men and women. On family farms and in small businesses, mothers, wives, and daughters worked alongside men. Women peddled goods in local markets, and Song laws extended their rights to property. Owing partly to wider availability of printed books, more women in educated families became literate. On the other hand, cities offered a booming market for young women to serve as concubines, entertainers, prostitutes, and domestic laborers. Though legally free, women were commonly bought and sold to do these jobs. Commercialization meant opportunity for some women but drudgery, danger, and despair for many others. Moreover, Confucian leaders tended to confront rapid social change with demands that respectable women belonged at home. Affluent men conceived the idea that small feet and a swaying walk were attractive and stylish in women. Families got the desired effect in their young girls by both binding their toes under and breaking them as they grew. This extreme form of patriarchal domination became all the fashion. Only young women crippled by foot binding could hope to make a good marriage. The practice spread from the upper classes down the social scale. Only at low social levels might girls expect to grow up with normal feet.

Governing China in an Era of Change

In the waning decades of the Tang dynasty, regional army commanders had built up considerable independent power. Zhao Kuangyin, the founder of the Song regime, was himself a military man, but perhaps for that very reason he understood the value of putting the government in civilian

West Lake in Hangzhou. In the Southern Song period, urbanites enjoyed summer boating on the city's picturesque lake.

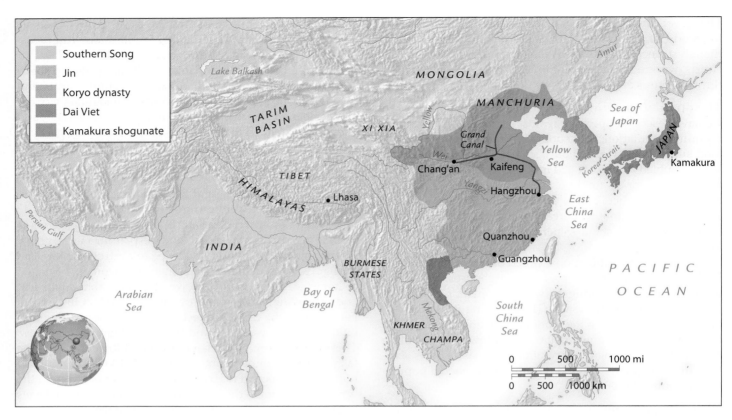

MAP 12.2 East Asia, 1200.
Considering their relative geographical locations, how might the agricultural economies of the Jin and Southern Song states have differed?

hands and keeping the army out of it. Consequently, the traditional elite class of scholar-bureaucrats, championing Confucian ideals of public morality and enlightened statecraft, strongly supported him. They subscribed to an old Chinese saying: "The best iron is not to be used for nails, and the best men are not to be used for soldiers."[3] Both the Northern and Southern Song dynasties fielded large armies to defend their land frontiers (see Map 12.2), but civilian leaders kept a tight rein on potentially unruly or defiant military officers.

Passing the test. The Song made academic success on state civil service examinations, rather than mere membership in an aristocratic family, the entryway to civilian office. The exams assessed knowledge of Confucian classics and literary texts, not accounting or management skills, but they ensured that men who could read, write, and think handled imperial affairs. Thus the Chinese state became more than ever a **meritocracy.** Preparing for the tests, however, required such long and expensive training that almost all examinees had the support of affluent families. Furthermore, male relatives of individuals who already

> **meritocracy** A government or other institution in which individuals are awarded office and responsibility based on their merit—intelligence, talents, or education—rather than merely on their social status or circumstances of birth.

held bureaucratic posts could be given the privilege of taking a somewhat easier exam to qualify for at least a low-level government job. The civil service system contributed to a shared culture and worldview among the thousands of bureaucrats who managed the imperial state, though *within* that bureaucracy factional debates often raged over economic and political policy.

Neo-Confucianism. Song intellectuals also gave fresh thought to China's major belief systems. Daoism, a religion native to China, and Buddhism, one imported from India but thoroughly adapted to Chinese life (see Chapter 7), permeated society from top to bottom. Buddhist monasteries and temples often had large landholdings and political influence, accumulating wealth from agriculture and trade but exempted from taxes. Among the masses, Buddhist and Daoist traditions tended to blur into each other, and both incorporated veneration of local gods, goddesses, and family ancestors. In Song society, both traditions also accommodated themselves quite well to Confucian teachings. Confucian intellectuals had over several centuries absorbed Buddhist and Daoist ideas into their own moral and ethical systems, including meditation, reverence for animal life, and metaphysical inquiry into the meaning of life.

In the twelfth and thirteenth centuries, innovative thinkers wove together several strands of Confucian, Buddhist, and Daoist thought to shape what became known as Neo-Confucianism. The worries and uncertainties that inevitably accompanied life in a commercializing society, together with the loss of northern China to "barbarian" invaders, contributed to a fresh look at Confucian ideals. Intellectual luminaries, notably the brilliant philosopher Zhu Xi (ZHOO-SHEE; 1130–1200), called for a return to the fundamental teachings of Confucius and his early disciples. To him, that meant moral living, disciplined daily ritual, respect for hierarchy, and dedication to families and local communities. A stable social order, he argued, must be built on a base of moral self-improvement. Ethical education and performance of communal service must take priority over the pursuit of imperial office and wealth. "Every day," Zhu wrote, "we must seek some amount of improvement, learning what we do not yet know and changing for the better whatever is not good; thus, we shall improve our virtuous natures. . . . If we pass our days in this fashion, then in three years we might have made a bit of progress."[4] Neo-Confucianism also made wide room for Buddhist-style theorizing on metaphysics and the cosmos, and by the end of the Song era, the Chinese educated class had thoroughly assimilated Neo-Confucian ideas.

China and Its Near Neighbors

Between the eleventh and thirteenth centuries, the Song monarchy occupied the center of a constellation of East Asian states, including island Japan. All these neighbors traded regularly with China and benefited from its economic upswing. In the Korean peninsula, the Silla monarchy (668–935) ruled for 250 years as a tribute-paying junior partner of the Tang dynasty. But the Koryo ruling family that succeeded the Silla in 918 moved out from under China's political shadow. Far to the southwest in Vietnam, local commanders founded the new state of Dai Viet in 938, ending several centuries of Chinese big brotherhood. In the eleventh and twelfth centuries, Dai Viet monarchs built roads, improved rice irrigation in the fertile Red River valley, and otherwise laid the economic foundations of a strong state that remained independent (except for a brief Chinese invasion in the early 1400s) until the late nineteenth century.

Technological and intellectual exchanges prospered between Song China and all its near neighbors. Despite official bans on arms trade, both the Liao and Jin states acquired the catapults, steel weapons, and gunpowder rockets that Chinese masterminds had invented. The Jin elite largely converted to Chinese styles of refined living, embracing Confucian literature and classical learning. In Korea, the Koryo rulers imported the Song civil service exams and used the written Chinese for administration and diplomacy. Korean artisans appear to have been the world's earliest inventors of both woodblock printing and movable type, and these technologies spread quickly to China. In Vietnam, the ruling class continued to revere the Confucian classics, and they imitated Song bureaucratic government. Finally,

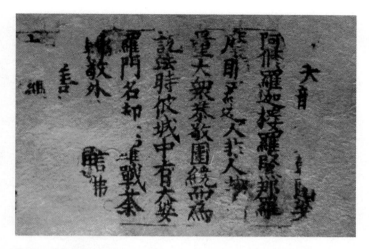

Early printing. The Pure Light Dharani Sutra, a Buddhist scroll, is the world's earliest known printed text. Discovered in a temple in Korea in 1966, the scroll was printed from a woodblock. It dates to the mid-eighth century.

among all of these neighbors, variants of Buddhism, filtered largely through China, became the main popular religion.

Japan within and without the Chinese Sphere

In the later first millennium C.E., Chinese ideas and goods spilled across the Korea Strait and the East China Sea to Japan (see Chapter 11). The Japanese political and intellectual classes sorted through these new things, discarding what they did not like and adapting or modifying what they did. By the eleventh century, a distinctive style of urban civilization was emerging in the archipelago.

Japan's emperor, reigning from Heian (Kyoto) on the island of Honshu, imitated Chinese imperial court ceremony, and he had great religious prestige. But in the later ninth century real power shifted to alliances of aristocratic families, who lived in luxurious Heian mansions and owned great rice-growing estates. Between 850 and 1050, a single aristocratic clan, the Fujiwara, dominated the royal palace, effectively ruling in the name of the emperor. In the twelfth and thirteenth centuries, power shifted again, this time to a much larger elite of rural magnates, who expanded their control over rice land. They gradually supplanted the Heian aristocrats, acquiring title to large rural estates, hiring retinues of armored warriors, and coaxing their tenant farmers to adopt innovative farming techniques. Throughout much of the twelfth century, political disorder reigned across Japan, as rival landlords and coastal pirates competed for territory and loot.

The Kamakura shogunate. In the 1180s the Minamoto, one of the most powerful military clans, founded a new center at Kamakura in the rice-rich Kanto plain. Securing control over central and southern Japan, the clan leader

The *Tale of Genji*. Lady Murasaki's eleventh-century novel of romance and intrigue in the Heian imperial court has numerous characters. This illustration from the story depicts Genji's son Yugiri and his wife Kumoinokari, who leaves him when he brings home a second bride.

system, to form a specifically Japanese religious synthesis. The Buddhist school known as Zen, which emphasized intuitive enlightenment, mental discipline, and meditation, took root in the islands. Toiling rural folk responded warmly to Buddhist teachings that promised personal salvation. Meanwhile, the elegant ladies and gentlemen who lived inside Heian's elite bubble sifted Chinese ideas of fine art and literature through a filter of Japanese language and polished manners. Aristocratic women were more willing than men to write in Japanese rather than the more prestigious Chinese, and they enjoyed greater intellectual freedom than their Song counterparts. Several women blazed creative paths. Sometime between 990 and 1012, Lady Murasaki Shikibu wrote *Tale of Genji*, a complex story of a courtier's life and loves. Some scholars classify this work as the first genuine novel ever created.

China in the Hemisphere

In the Song era, the material impact of China's agricultural and manufacturing economy extended far beyond its near neighbors. China acted as a sort of giant respirator in this period, blowing numerous goods—silks, cottons, porcelain, tea, iron tools, lacquer ware, paper—out across the hemisphere and sucking in foreign products—spices, herbs, resins, aromatic woods, medicines, silver, timber, horses—that growing numbers of Chinese could afford to buy.

The volume and value of foreign trade increased much more rapidly by sea routes than along the overland silk roads. This shift occurred for a number of reasons. First, overland caravan transport was not only more expensive than water shipment but simply inadequate for moving goods in the bulk loads that Chinese merchants wished to handle. The government encouraged private overseas trade, and it built a formidable navy to patrol the coasts and the major inland waterways. Also, goods produced in China's southern provinces had handy access by canal and road to seaports. Finally, the country's commercial expansion attracted growing numbers of foreign merchants—Malays, South Asians, Persians, Arabs, and Jews—to the southern ports. The Song government set up a Seafaring Trade Office to collect customs duties and regulate commerce as closely as it could.

Minamoto no Yoritomo instituted a new government. The emperor, having no real choice in the matter, awarded him the title of shogun, or "great general." The Kamakura shogunate (1185–1333) allowed the emperor and his entourage to reign in Heian. But from this period Japan parted with the Chinese model of central rule by civilian scholar-bureaucrats. Instead, a class of professional fighters of elite status rose to prominence. Some of these warriors, known as samurai, became wealthy landowners. The great majority, however, served powerful families as cavalry soldiers dedicated to a code of courage, honor, solidarity, and military hardihood. In return for their homage and loyalty, samurai fighters typically received food allotments and rights over peasant labor. From Kamakura the shoguns orchestrated the politics of these competing families and their samurai retainers as best they could.

Economic and cultural trends. Japan's population and economy also continued to grow. In the 1100s, farmers began to harvest double crops of rice by adopting quick-ripening varieties from China. From about 1200, population growth accelerated and market towns multiplied, both inland and along the southern and central coasts. The Japanese military elite also coveted fine Chinese manufactures, and cargo vessels carried Japanese silver, copper, steel swords, and timber across the Yellow and East China Seas to the mainland. Chinese coins flooded into the islands, which also helped fuel internal commercialization.

Continuing contact with China stimulated new cultural trends. Buddhism spread more widely among nonelite men and women, and Buddhist practices became thoroughly intertwined with those of Shinto, the ancient indigenous belief

Song naval architects made technical breakthroughs that produced the largest known seagoing ships, or junks, in that era. A medium-sized vessel could carry about 120 tons of cargo and a crew of sixty. The biggest ones accommodated crews of four or five hundred. Shipwrights equipped these craft with as many as six masts, giant sails of bamboo matting, multiple decks, and watertight compartments to contain flooding if the vessel hit an obstruction. They also invented the stern-post rudder, a swinging blade to steer the ship from the stern (the back end). This was an efficient advance over two side rudders. In the twelfth century or earlier, Chinese mariners began to carry compasses, usually a magnetized needle floated on a bowl of water, to help determine the position of a ship relative to the magnetic north or south pole. Indian Ocean sailors adopted this device, and it spread quickly to the Mediterranean. Chinese merchants and landowners with capital banded together to invest in ships. Private traders ventured as far west as the Arabian Sea, though in the Song period Chinese junks typically went no farther than India.

The market for porcelain illustrates the long reach of Chinese commerce. Skilled potters invented the technology to produce white porcelain, what we commonly call "china." It was harder, stronger, and thinner than both earthenware and stoneware because it was made of special clay available in southern China and fired at very high temperatures. Manufacturing centers multiplied to meet rising demand, both internal and overseas, for translucent, snowy-colored porcelain, a much-coveted luxury. Some kilns could fire fifty thousand pieces of porcelain at once, and large seagoing junks could haul tons of it. According to a twelfth-century merchant, vessels left Guangzhou crammed with porcelain, "the small pieces packed in the larger, till there is not a crevice left."[5] In Vietnam, Korea, and Japan, potters eventually learned to imitate Chinese technology and decorative styles. The beauty of East Asian ware also inspired artisans in Persia, Syria, and Egypt to invent new manufacturing, glazing, and painting techniques of their own, often substituting bright colors and bold geometric designs for more muted Chinese decoration. From the Song period, porcelain also began to appear on the tables of wealthy families in Europe.

Conquerors and Migrants in the Muslim Lands

FOCUS What impact did pastoral peoples from both Inner Eurasia and the Sahara Desert have on Afroeurasian agrarian societies between the eleventh and thirteenth centuries?

In the eleventh and twelfth centuries, armed migrants from out of the Great Arid Zone, the band of dry and semiarid lands that extends across Afroeurasia, dramatically altered the course of events in densely populated agrarian lands from China to southwestern Europe. The Jurchen invasion of northern China already described may be counted among these movements. On a larger scale, however, Turkic warriors originating in Inner Eurasia advanced on South and Southwest Asia, founding new military states that within two hundred years ruled from northern India to Egypt. In the same period, confederations of mounted fighters from the Sahara Desert and the mountains of Morocco forged empires that encompassed the western Mediterranean rim. The most potent weapon of these groups was massed cavalry and skill with bows, lances, and swords.

A Song river craft. Chinese naval architects built large seagoing ships, but the smaller vessels that plied the inland waterways powered internal commerce. This replica of a small sailing ship is on display in Millennium City Park in Kaifeng, the Song dynasty's northern capital. Why were rivers and canals so important to the Song economy?

A robe of honor. Muslim rulers wishing to seal bonds of allegiance and loyalty with one another typically exchanged richly designed ceremonial robes. In this illustration from the fourteenth century, the artist depicts the Turkic monarch Mahmud of Ghazni donning a robe sent to him by the Abbasid Caliph. Who might the other figures in the painting be?

raiding parties into South Asia to plunder the Indus River valley, loot Hindu temples, and overthrow regional Hindu monarchs. In the early thirteenth century, more Turkic fighters rode into South Asia, founding the sultanate (kingdom) of Delhi (1206–1526). They settled in as an elite military minority and expanded their reach into the subcontinent, ruling tens of millions of Hindu farmers and city dwellers.

Seljuk empire builders. In the mid-eleventh century, great throngs of Turkic horse archers pushed from Central Asia across Iran and into the densely populated Tigris-Euphrates River valley. These people were not slave soldiers but migrating pastoral nomads, and their numbers included women, children, and enormous herds of horses and sheep. Because of the earlier missionary efforts of Muslim merchants and clerics, these Turks had largely converted to Islam before the invasion of Southwest Asia began. We do not fully understand the conditions that mobilized this movement, but population may have been growing rapidly enough on the Inner Eurasian steppes to cause serious pasture and animal shortages, triggering movements to find better land. The leaders of this migration mass belonged to a clan called the Seljuks, part of a tribal confederation whose members spoke Oghuz Turkish, one of several Turkic languages. In 1055, forces under the command of the Seljuk general Tughril Beg seized Baghdad. In the next twenty-eight years they overran Iraq, northern Syria, and eastern Anatolia. The Great Seljuks, as they became known, assumed power over millions of Arabs and Persians. In the 1080s, their empire sprawled across most of Southwest Asia. Tughril Beg offered fidelity to the caliph, who retained his status as moral and spiritual head of the Muslim community. But Tughril Beg and his successors took the title "sultan" and moved to set up a new military government. They did this with the vital cooperation of numerous educated Persians and Arabs who were skilled administrators, lawyers, and clerks.

All these movements disrupted interregional trade at certain times and places, but the leaders of new kingdoms, once in control, invariably encouraged commerce and urban industry. Turkic migrants and rulers also contributed to the continuing spread of Islam. In the lands that Turks conquered, Islam became either the majority faith of the population, as in Anatolia, or the religion of a governing minority, as in Afghanistan and northern India.

Turkic Horse Power

The Turkic migrants of the eleventh century originated in Central Asia east of the Caspian Sea. They spoke languages at least distantly related to those of Huns, Uighurs, and Khazars, Inner Eurasian peoples that we encountered in earlier chapters. As Chapter 11 pointed out, Turkic soldiers began in the ninth century to serve the Abbasid Caliphate (Abbasid empire) as military slaves, or *mamluks*. Unfortunately, however, for the Abbasid government in Baghdad, this corps splintered into rival factions and began to meddle in political affairs, helping to destabilize rather than strengthen the state to which they had pledged their allegiance.

> **mamluk** In Muslim states, a slave or freedman having primarily military or administrative duties.

In northern Iran and Afghanistan a band of Turkic *mamluk* officers rebelled against Baghdad's authority and succeeded to form their own state with its capital at Ghazna (today Ghazni in Afghanistan). The Ghaznavids, as the new dynasty was called (977–1186), gave theoretical allegiance to the caliph but otherwise ignored him. Ghaznavid cavalry fanned out to conquer both east and west. The ruler Mahmud of Ghazni (reigned 997–1030) dispatched massive

Turks also began to alter the ethnic and linguistic profile of Southwest Asia. Simultaneously with the Seljuk conquests, pastoral groups migrated across northern Iran to the high green valleys of Armenia and eastern Anatolia. The very shape of Anatolia, a long finger of fertile land between the Black and the Mediterranean Seas, channeled the migration westward. At that time, western and central Anatolia were part of the Greek Byzantine state centered on the great city of Constantinople. But at the Battle of Malazgirt (Manzikert) in 1071, Seljuk archers trounced a Greek army. Once the Byzantines lost control of their mountainous eastern frontier, Muslim herders surged across central Anatolia's high plateau. Within a century, the Greek emperors held only their far western area. In the following centuries, Anatolia was transformed gradually into the predominantly Muslim land we now call Turkey. This process involved Turkic newcomers settling in villages, taking up agriculture, and competing with both Greek and Armenian Christian farmers for land. Most Christians who did not leave the region eventually converted to Islam; the Oghuz language, the ancestor of modern Turkish, spread widely. Turkic-speaking peoples also became an important element in the populations of Iraq, Iran, and Afghanistan.

Multiple states in Southwest Asia. Despite the Turkic influx into Southwest Asia, the unified Seljuk empire lasted less than four decades. The irrigation system of the Tigris-Euphrates valley had deteriorated badly in the late Abbasid period, reducing agricultural revenues to much less than the new rulers might have expected. In the Turkic nomad tradition, the most powerful warriors were entitled to compete with one another for top leadership. Consequently, the deaths of the first three sultans ignited feuding among members of the Seljuk clan. Army commanders, who were Sunni Muslims, also had to prepare defenses against the Fatimids, the hostile Shi'a Muslim rulers of Egypt and part of Syria (see Chapter 11). Shi'a revolutionaries repeatedly plotted to assassinate Seljuk officers and otherwise disrupt the Turkic state.

The sultans could hope to stabilize their rule only by giving their sons and officers rights to collect revenues from agricultural lands, but these estates soon became territorial bases for defiance and revolt. By the late eleventh century, the unified Seljuk state splintered into competing local kingdoms ruled by various clan leaders and former governors. By 1200 there were more than a half-dozen Turkic states in Southwest Asia.

The political map became even more complicated following the appearance of Christian crusaders from western Europe. Beginning in 1097, they attacked several points on the coasts of Syria, Palestine, and southern Anatolia. Within about a decade these armored knights and the military retainers, peasant farmers, and Catholic Christian clergy who accompanied them managed to set up four small kingdoms, known as the crusader states, along the eastern Mediterranean coast, including the holy city of Jerusalem. We will come back to the origins of this European initiative later in the chapter. From the Southwest Asian perspective, the crusaders had the good fortune to launch their adventure just when the Great Seljuk empire was breaking up and incapable of mounting a united defense. At first, Muslim leaders tended to regard the crusader states as an unfortunate development, though not a disastrous one. The fact that the intruders were Christians did not in itself cause great alarm. After all, Byzantine Christians continued to dominate part of Anatolia, and

The Tughril Tower. Tughril Beg, founder of the Seljuk empire, is interred in this monumental tomb in the northern Iranian city of Rey.

both Southwest Asia and Egypt had large, long-established Christian minorities.

In the middle decades of the twelfth century, the Turkic rulers of a state centered on the Syrian city of Aleppo consolidated their authority over a wider territory. This kingdom amassed a large enough army to invade Egypt in 1169, defeating the Shi'a Fatimids and ending their two-century rule there. Salah al-Din, or Saladin (r. 1171–1193), a commander of Kurdish ethnic origin and a Sunni Muslim, emerged supreme from this war. He founded the Ayyubid dynasty (1171–1250), which united Egypt with Syria and Iraq (see Map 12.3). From this position of strength, his forces expelled the European knights from Jerusalem in 1187, though crusaders clung to small coastal zones until the late thirteenth century.

The Muslim military kingdoms that ruled most of the region from Egypt to northwestern India generally shared three elements. First, Turkic sultans continued to rely on mounted slave soldiers to defend frontiers and keep order. A ruler typically rewarded worthy officers with rights to rents and taxes from state-owned farmlands worked by local peasant families. Most of these peasants remained legally free, but they suffered poverty and sometimes brutal oppression at the hands of their lords. Also, at the low end of the social scale, nonmilitary slavery continued to be

The citadel of Aleppo. Commanding the old city of Aleppo in northern Syria, this fortified palace is one of the largest castles in the world. Sultans of the Ayyubid dynasty completed major construction in the thirteenth century. The citadel served as a headquarters for war against the Christian crusader states on the eastern Mediterranean coast.

common, especially the use of bonded women as domestic workers, concubines, and entertainers.

A second feature of Turkic military regimes was their pragmatic alliances with the *ulama*, the city-based class of esteemed scholars and lawyers who supervised and regulated Muslim religious life and public behavior. In Southwest Asia and Egypt, Turkic commanders generally left Arab or Persian *ulama* in charge of civic affairs and employed them as judges, professors, secretaries, administrators, and accountants. In turn, the *ulama* accepted the authority of Turkic horse soldiers as preferable to political disorder. Military officers and respectable *ulama* families often sealed their working relationship through marriage. Women in educated families never got to hold public office, but they usually had great influence over marriage arrangements, which determined how the city's network of power took shape.

A third feature was the general prosperity of commerce and urban manufacturing even though little agrarian growth took place, especially compared to Song China. The Turkic movements coincided with the early phase of the North Atlantic Warm Period. This climatic event, which, as we have seen, may have improved crop yields in China, triggered extended droughts in Southwest Asia. Nevertheless, wealth continued to accumulate in the region's great cities, which served as key nodes in the busy exchange networks that linked the land and sea routes running across the hemisphere.

The cities where sultans and governors established their citadels and palaces—Cairo, Damascus, Aleppo, Nishapur, Bukhara, Ghazna (see Map 12.3)—invariably attracted voluminous trade in food, horses, military gear, and luxury wares. The urban artisans in those cities also exported woven textiles, carpets, glassware, ceramics, metalwork, and books. In the twelfth century, Cairo emerged as the greatest Muslim metropolis, owing partly to growing commercial traffic on the Red Sea route between the Indian Ocean and the Mediterranean. By 1300, Cairo's population may have neared 500,000, making it the biggest Afroeurasian city anywhere west of China.

Muslim Ships on the Mediterranean

As of about 1000 C.E., Muslim captains piloted the majority of ships plying the Mediterranean and the Black Seas. Muslim monarchs controlled all the ports of the southern and far eastern Mediterranean as well as the island of Sicily and most of Spain. The Fatimid dynasty built a fleet of war galleys, that is, ships powered by combinations of rowers and sails. These vessels patrolled the eastern Mediterranean and communicated between Fatimid Egypt and Syria. The Byzantine state had a navy as well, though it deteriorated steadily from the eleventh century owing partly to shrinking resources in the face of Turkic military pressures on its territory.

The main artery of Muslim commercial shipping ran along the Mediterranean's African shores, connecting numerous ports from Syria and Egypt to Morocco and Spain. Merchants carried a variety of products—wool, hides, leather goods, grain, and olive oil, as well as gold and slaves from Subsaharan Africa. Muslim and Jewish merchant groups, often working together, controlled trade operations that connected the Mediterranean to the Indian Ocean by way of the Nile valley and the Red Sea. In the eleventh and twelfth centuries, for example, Jewish merchants based in Cairo and as far west as Tunis engaged in both commercial and mining businesses as far away as the western coast of India.

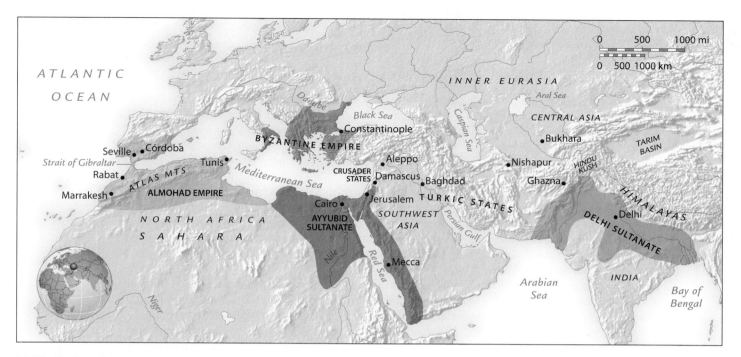

MAP 12.3 Major states in western Afroeurasia, 1200.
What does this map suggest about the historical significance of the Strait of Gibraltar and the Bosporus Strait as dividing lines between Europe and both Africa and Asia?

New Empires in the Western Mediterranean

The first major pastoral nomadic movement to emerge from the Sahara Desert, the western third of Afroeurasia's Great Arid Zone, occurred in the mid-eleventh century. During the previous millennium, Sahara-dwelling people who spoke mainly Berber languages adapted to extremely arid conditions by herding one-humped camels. These beasts fed on seasonal grasses that sprouted in the desert and along its semidry rims. Camels provided caravan transport, as well as meat, milk, and hides. And along with horses, they gave Saharan pastoralists the means of long-range military operations.

The Almoravid empire-builders. The first great military adventure from out of the Sahara started in the far western desert just north of the Senegal River in modern Mauritania. In the ninth and tenth centuries, the region's pastoral peoples began to convert to Islam at the urging of merchants and preachers from North Africa. In the mid-eleventh century, Abdallah ibn Yasin (d. 1059), a passionate Sunni theologian from Morocco, journeyed to the western desert to exhort camel-herding Muslims to raise their standards of worship and moral behavior—regular prayer, no alcoholic drinks, no music, and strict separation of men and women in public. Ibn Yasin also organized a confederation of desert clans and tribes known collectively as the Almoravids (referring loosely in Arabic to "religious warriors").

This coalition seized major trading towns on both the southern and the northern edges of the Sahara. Mounted fighters also raided deep into the West African empire of Ghana (see Chapter 11), seriously weakening it. Bolstered by commercial profits and taxes, an Almoravid army advanced northward, crossing the High Atlas Mountains and capturing the major cities of Morocco and western Algeria. In 1086, shiploads of warriors crossed the Strait of Gibraltar into Spain. They did this at the invitation of local Muslim princes, who faced mounting pressure from Christian crusaders along their northern frontiers. Quickly defeating a Christian force from the kingdoms of León and Castile, the Almoravids united all of Muslim Spain under their authority.

At their zenith, the Almoravids could claim sovereignty over an astonishing realm extending from the Senegal River in West Africa to central Spain. However, Moroccan and Spanish Muslim leaders who at first welcomed these austere Berber reformers soon thought better of it. The Almoravid religious elite not only proved morally rigid and intolerant but also were occupied less with Islamic revival than with power, privilege, and wealth. Almoravid rulers who abandoned their desert tents for magnificent palaces also lost interest in vigorous counter-crusades against the Spanish Christian states.

The Almohads and the oneness of God. Not long into the twelfth century, discontent boiled up. An anti-Almoravid rebellion arose among Berber farmers and herders in the valleys of the High Atlas. Muhammad ibn Tumert

A Jewish Merchant Writes to His Wife

Long-distance marital relationships have never been easy. This is true today, even with our modern communications technology. It was certainly true in the thirteenth century, when couples that had to be apart kept in touch through letters The selection here is an excerpt from a letter that a Jewish merchant residing temporarily in South Asia wrote to his wife in Egypt around the year 1204. The round-trip sea voyage between Egypt and ports on the western coast of India took two years to complete, often longer if merchants encountered bad weather, financial problems, or roving pirates.

In his letter, the merchant reveals that his wife has asked for a divorce. According to Jewish law, this act had to be initiated by the husband. He has decided, however, to place the decision in her hands. He tells her that he knows his time away has placed undue burdens on her but that the separation has been no easier for him. His longing for her has driven him to drink excessively, but he assures her that he has remained faithful, declaring that he has conducted himself "in an exemplary way." Nevertheless, if a divorce is what his wife wants, he writes, he will "set [her] free."

As it turned out, the trader never sent this letter, and the couple did not divorce. He eventually returned to Egypt still in possession of the letter. He placed it in the Cairo Geniza, a special room attached to a synagogue. In the Jewish tradition, papers on which the name of God is written should not be discarded. Synagogues therefore established genizas, *or storerooms, to preserve such documents. Typically, a synagogue would periodically bury the papers in the* geniza, *but in this case the castoff papers were left in storage. In the late nineteenth century, British scholars began exploring the contents of the Cairo Geniza. They carried texts, often just fragments of writing, back to libraries in Britain for careful study. These documents have provided a rich source of knowledge of medieval Jewish life. Though many of the papers are concerned with religious questions, a large portion, like the letter excerpted here, discuss secular issues such as trade, business, legal disputes, and personal affairs. Today, Cairo Geniza documents are to be found in major libraries around the world.*

The Dedicated Husband

In your letters you alternately rebuke and offend me or put me to shame and use harsh words all the time. I have not deserved any of this. I swear by God, I do not believe that the heart of anyone traveling away from his wife has remained like mine, all the time and during all the years—from the moment of our separation to the very hour of writing this letter—so constantly thinking of you and yearning after you. . . . And you write about me as if I had forgotten you and would not remember you had it not been for your rebukes, and as if, had you not warned me that the public would reprove me, I would not have thought of you. Put this out of your mind and do not impute such things to me. . . .

Drunk but Pious

Day and night I was constantly drinking, not of my free will, but I conducted myself in an exemplary way and if anyone poked fun in foul speech in my presence, I became furious with him, until he became silent, he and others. I constantly fulfilled what God knows, and cured my soul by fasting during the days and praying during the nights. The congregations in Aden and in India often asked me to lead them in prayer, and I am regarded by them and regard myself as a pious man. . . .

As to Divorce—the Choice Is Left to the Wife

Now in one of your letters you adjure me to set you free. . . . Now, if this is your wish, I cannot blame you. For the waiting has been long. And I do not know whether the Creator will grant relief immediately so that I can come home, or whether matters will take time, for I cannot come home with nothing. Therefore I resolved to issue a writ which sets you free. Now the matter is in your hand. If you wish separation from me, accept the bill of repudiation and you are free. But if this is not your decision and not your desire, do not lose these long years of waiting: perhaps relief is at hand and you will regret at a time when regret will be of no avail.

And please do not blame me, for I never neglected you from the time when those things happened and made an effort to save you and me from people talking and impairing my honor. . . . All day long I have a lonely heart and am pained by our separation. I feel that pain while writing these lines. But the choice is with you; the decision is in your hand: if you wish to carry the matter through, do so; if you wish to leave things as they are, do so. But do not act after the first impulse. Ask the advice of good people and act as you think will be the best for you. May God inspire you with the right decision.

Source: S. D. Goitein, *Letters of Medieval Jewish Traders* (Princeton, NJ: Princeton University Press, 1973), pp. 222–225.

Thinking Critically

What do you think this letter tells us about the relationship between the trader and his wife? How would you characterize the merchant's attitude toward her? Why might the wife have wanted a divorce, and why is her husband sympathetic to her request? Why do you think the husband never sent the letter? Where is Aden in relation to India, and why would the merchant have been there? What merchandise might the merchant have shipped home from India?

(1080–1130), a Moroccan legal scholar as religiously fervent and charismatic as Ibn Yasin, declared himself to be the Mahdi, or "rightly guided one." The Mahdi, according to popular belief among both Shi'a and Sunni Muslims, was an enlightened, God-chosen individual who would lead the world to a time of peace and justice culminating in the final divine judgment of humankind. Ibn Tumert taught strict piety, and he condemned the Almoravids for betraying their own ideals. In contrast to them, however, he introduced a doctrine that emphasized the absolute spiritual unity of God. That unity prohibited any description of God in terms of human attributes or qualities. Ibn Tumert's disciples thus became known as the Almohads, a term that means "believers in the oneness of God."

In 1147 armed Almohad Berbers swept down from the mountains and within a few years crossed into Spain, overthrowing the already shaky Almoravid government. In 1151 they advanced across Algeria to Tunisia (see Map 12.3). This Berber empire incorporated the entire western Mediterranean basin. But it lasted only a little longer than its predecessor. Like the Almoravids, the second generation of

Almohad leaders lost their religious zeal, and their theologians became reactionary. In contrast to earlier Spanish Muslim rulers, who generally encouraged cooperation among religious groups, the later Almohads harassed and persecuted Jews, obliging many to flee from Spain. In the early thirteenth century, Christian armies from León and Castile, deploying armored knights from several parts of Europe, broke into Almohad territory. Within several decades they overran all of Muslim-ruled Spain with the exception of the mountain-bound kingdom of Granada in the far south and a few strongholds along the Strait of Gibraltar. Later in the century, Almohad authority collapsed in North Africa as well.

The Almoravid and Almohad states, like the Great Seljuk empire, were short-lived. But between them they stimulated intense cultural interchange between Spain and North Africa for nearly two centuries. More urbanized than Morocco, southern Spain (Andalusia) set refined standards for art, craft, cuisine, and refined taste. Muslim and Jewish scholars and artisans moved easily across the strait, diffusing a Spanish cultural style more widely across North Africa. The Christian conquest of southern Spain also persuaded

Almohad mosques in Africa and Europe. Architects of the Almohad dynasty built mosques with massive square minarets in both Morocco and Spain in the late twelfth century. The Hassan Tower (left) in Rabat, Morocco's modern capital, was originally designed to rise even taller but was never completed. The Giralda mosque and minaret in Seville (right) was converted to a church when Christian armies took the city in 1248. In the sixteenth century, Spanish builders added the ornate bell tower above the former minaret. Both structures are austere in form but incorporate finely proportioned carved arches and geometric patterning. Put your hand over the Giralda's bell tower to better see the resemblance between the two buildings.

The Twin Minaret Madrasa. Sunni Muslim scholars and students occupied this college of higher learning in the eastern Anatolian city of Erzurun to study religious and legal subjects. The madrasa dates to the 1260s.

thousands of Muslims and Jews to migrate to North African cities, which subsequently benefited from their talents and skills.

Cultural Trends in the Muslim Lands

The Muslim cavalry captains who took charge from Spain to northern India in the eleventh and twelfth centuries were the sons and grandsons of animal herders. Nevertheless, they adapted quickly to sophisticated city life, and they rivaled one another to patronize creative work in literature, architecture, science, and theology.

College education. One key innovation was the founding of many new Muslim educational institutions dedicated to advanced studies in religion, law, and medicine. In these colleges, called **madrasas** (MAH-drahs-uhs) in Arabic, scholars and students lived and worked together to pursue knowledge. The curriculum centered on the Quran, the traditions of the Prophet Muhammad, theology, logic, rhetoric, grammar, and Sunni Islamic law. Madrasa education, in which white-turbaned professors guided students through religious and legal texts, aimed primarily to preserve and transmit the spiritual and moral truths of the Islamic past. Most madrasas

> **madrasa** A center of higher learning dedicated mainly to the study of Islamic religious and legal subjects.

operated under pious endowments, that is, gifts of rulers or other wealthy individuals. Some colleges were grand monuments to architectural and artistic skill.

Madrasas served as training institutions for judges, lawyers, mosque officials, professors, librarians, and secretaries, that is, the *ulama* class charged with maintaining social and moral stability. Colleges were also intellectual workshops where legal experts interpreted and codified Islamic law (*shari'a*). Finally, the Turkic sultans, all of them Sunni Muslims, conceived the madrasas as centers for combating Shi'a doctrines. Indeed, after the Shi'a Fatimids were driven from Egypt, Cairo emerged as the premier Sunni "university town" in the western Muslim lands.

Science and philosophy. Madrasas did not typically offer humanistic study or inquiries into nature and the cosmos. Many scholars, however, continued to pursue those areas of knowledge informally and privately. In the eleventh through the thirteenth centuries, scholars produced numerous texts in both Arabic and Persian that synthesized and extended knowledge in astronomy, mathematics, optics, medicine, botany, pharmacology, and geography. The Muslim intellectual class of that era had especially cosmopolitan outlooks. They traveled widely, seeking knowledge, books, wealthy patrons, and salaried jobs in governments, legal courts, and religious institutions. Educated Jews and Christians took part in this network as well.

The lives of three great scholars illustrate the intersection of learning and public service. Abu Rayhan al-Biruni (973–1048), born in what is now Uzbekistan, served the sultan Mahmud, the most talented of the Ghaznavid rulers of Afghanistan and northwestern India. Al-Biruni accompanied his sovereign on raiding expeditions into South Asia and from this experience wrote *The Book of India,* an illuminating description of Hindu culture and society. He spoke several languages and published altogether about 150 works on mathematics, astronomy, metallurgy, medicine, history, and philosophy. In the Muslim west, Ibn Rushd (Averroës, 1126–1198) pursued philosophical inquiry in both Spain and Morocco under the patronage of Almohad monarchs. He expanded on a dimension of earlier Islamic thought according to which natural laws, that is, rational and timeless principles, govern the workings of nature and the universe. Moreover, these laws are evidence of God's plan for his creation. Most Muslim theologians in the madrasas opposed this view, arguing that God creates all phenomena, from birds in flight to shining stars, moment by moment according to his will. Ibn Rushd's commentaries on Plato and Aristotle, translated into Latin, had great influence on the development of natural philosophy in Christian Europe. The Jewish thinker Maimonides (Moses ben Maimon, 1135–1204), a contemporary of Ibn Rushd and also a native of Spain, became royal court physician to Salah al-Din in Cairo. He codified Jewish law and wrote theological and philosophical texts that influenced all subsequent Jewish thought.

Sufism and the continuing spread of Islam. Conquerors, scholars, and merchants all contributed to the wider spread of Islam, and so did Sufi saints and devotees. Sufism is the mystical dimension of Islam important to both Sunni and Shi'a believers. Increasingly popular from the eleventh century, Sufi teachings endeavored to guide men and women toward direct experience of God and intuitive understanding of spiritual truths. Christianity and Judaism, the other two monotheistic religions, also incorporated doctrines and practices of **mysticism.** Generally speaking, mystical teachings have less to do with ritual, duty, and public morality than with individual yearnings to transcend the personal self in order to know and merge with ultimate reality, in whatever way the particular religion describes that reality. The historical record suggests that practices such as meditating, joining a monastic community, or living as a hermit in the wilderness were in some measure Islamic adaptations of both Christian and Buddhist traditions that encouraged pursuit of spiritual enlightenment through self-denial and deep devotion.

Two ideas were at the heart of Sufism, a term derived from the Arabic word for the patched woolen garment that spiritual seekers often wore. First, the individual is capable

mysticism The individual pursuit of knowledge or consciousness of spiritual truth or divine reality, through meditation, prayer, study, or ecstatic experience; also, mystical religion, teaching, or practice.

of knowing God in heart as well as mind. Second, the believer walking a path to the divine might benefit from the help of a saintly master, or "friend of God," who radiated divine grace and could transmit it to others. Guided by such holy individuals, Muslims immersed themselves in mystical texts, ecstatic rituals, or special prayers, in order to feel and express God's love.

By the twelfth century, informal associations of saintly teachers and disciples were coalescing into more formal organizations, or religious orders, whose members followed a particular mystical "way" to experience God. Sufi devotional centers—somewhat like monasteries—offered not only congregational devotions but also religious education, charity, and refuge for travelers. By the thirteenth century, Sufi orders and lodges were found across the Muslim lands, and Sufi masters came to exert moral and political influence

Sufi teacher and poet. The spiritual poetry of the thirteenth-century Muslim mystic Jalal al-Din Rumi is still read widely today. In this miniature painting from the late 1500s, Rumi, kneeling at top left, gathers with his disciples.

over rulers. For women, Sufism offered an arena for religious expression and spiritual leadership in a patriarchal world that largely denied them public office or intellectual recognition.

Among Sufi thinkers of the era, the Iranian scholar Abu Hamid al-Ghazali (1058–1111) achieved towering status. He held a law professorship in Baghdad under the Great Seljuks but devoted himself to the Sufi life and to writing theological works. In *The Revival of the Religious Sciences* he offered a guide for pious living. Prayers and rituals were not meant to be sterile, mechanical acts, he wrote, but vehicles for achieving perpetual consciousness of God. In his autobiography, he describes his journey from worldliness to spiritual illumination: "It had already become clear to me that I had no hope of the bliss of the world to come save through a God-fearing life and the withdrawal of myself from vain desire. It was clear to me . . . that this was only to be achieved by turning away from wealth and position and fleeing from all time-consuming entanglements."[6] Al-Ghazali recognized the value of philosophical and scientific inquiry, but he denied that it could help men and women feel the presence of God. He convincingly reconciled mystical practice with public worship and opened the way for Sufism to merge into the mainstream of Muslim life.

Owing to a combination of Sufi energy, new conquests, and the spreading web of Muslim commerce, Islam continued to make headway in the eleventh to thirteenth centuries in Sudanic West Africa, Anatolia, Inner Eurasia, South Asia, and around the Indian Ocean rim. Only in Spain and some Mediterranean islands did Christian soldiers and churchmen force Muslims and their religion to retreat.

Foundations of Urban Civilization in Europe

FOCUS What factors accounted for accelerating economic growth, urbanization, and military power in Europe in the 1000–1250 period?

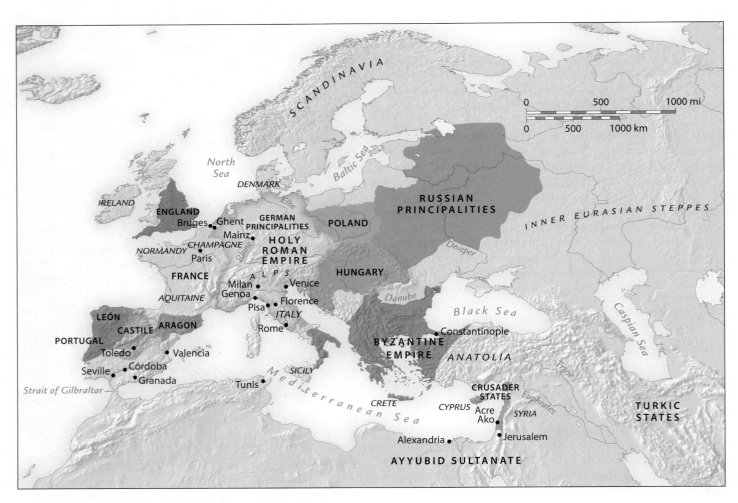

MAP 12.4 Europe and the Mediterranean, 1200.
What factors might account for the proliferation of small states in western Europe compared to relatively larger ones in eastern Europe?

In the mid-eleventh century, Sa'id al-Andalusi, an eminent Muslim scholar of Toledo in central Spain, wrote the *Book of the Categories of Nations* in which he describes the peoples who inhabited northerly parts of Europe. Because they have to endure a cold and cloudy climate, al-Andalusi explained, "their temperament is cool and their behavior is rude. Consequently, their bodies became enormous, their color turned white, and their hair drooped down. . . . They were overcome by ignorance and laziness, and infested by fatigue and stupidity."[7] This unsparing portrait reveals the prejudices of a highly educated urban gentlemen who no doubt received reports of northern Europe as a place of tiny towns and little learning where bands of armored men mostly feuded with one another.

A moldboard plow. In this picture from the twelfth century, a European peasant couple cooperate in plowing a field with two oxen. The parts of the wheeled plow include an iron coulter, or blade that cuts vertically into the soil, an iron share that cuts horizontally to release a strip of soil, and an attached moldboard that forces the soil to lift and turn over. Can you identify these three parts of the plow in the illustration?

To be sure, Europe in 1000 C.E. had a total population of about thirty million, which was around fourteen million *fewer* people than had lived there eight hundred years earlier, when much of the region was part of the Roman empire. There were few cities or strong centralized states. Even so, al-Andalusi's bleak description was not only overstated but out of date. By the later tenth century, western Europeans were experiencing an uneven but hopeful trend toward greater social and political order. The Muslim, Magyar, and Viking marauders who had disrupted Europe in the previous two hundred years had either settled down or gone away, and feudal lords restored relative calm to hundreds of localities (see Chapter 11). Between 1000 and 1300, Europe's population rose from thirty to nearly fifty million. Market towns sprouted up, and some blossomed into cities (see Map 12.4). In those three hundred years, for example, the population of Paris increased tenfold to 200,000.

Warm Weather, Better Plows

Europe's population growth was made possible by a boost in agricultural production having several sources. Greater political stability on the local level meant fewer disruptions to the cycle of planting and harvesting. Several new farming techniques, some of them coming from other parts of Afroeurasia, spread widely in western Europe. These included four-wheeled wagons, improved designs for water-powered mills, iron horseshoes, and an efficient collar-harness that allowed horses to pull heavy loads without being choked. As early as the eighth century, farmers started using a type of plow, perhaps invented in eastern Europe, that could cut into heavy soil and channel the earth into furrows for more efficient seeding and drainage. This tool helped unlock the agricultural potential of parts of Europe where older plows suited to the relatively thin soils of the Mediterranean region had no use. Farmers also took to three-field crop rotation, sowing one plot in the spring and a second in the fall, leaving a third fallow for a year to recover its nutrients. This technique slowed soil exhaustion and permitted planting of a greater variety of crops. Similar to its likely effects in China, the North Atlantic Warm Period brought longer growing seasons and drier summers to northern Europe, allowing farmers to increase production on land already in use. Grain farmers prospered in Scandinavia, and vintners produced drinkable wines in Britain and Poland. Between 800 and 1200, crop yields in western Europe may have doubled, and in good years farmers produced surplus food for market.

As production mounted, so did manufacturing and trade. Europe had neither the labor power nor the engineering knowledge to build a canal network anything like China's. But numerous navigable rivers penetrated far inland from the sea, permitting boat transport of bulk commodities like grain, fish, timber, iron, and stone at low cost. In the ports of the Baltic Sea, the North Sea, and the Atlantic coast, mariners improved ship designs, building vessels with high, rounded hulls that could carry cargos safely across gale-prone waters. Money came into much wider use across Europe. Numerous monarchs and lords minted their own coins, and both Byzantine and Muslim currency circulated as well, especially in Italy.

Two regions in western Europe became thriving centers of urban industry. One was Flanders, where a cluster of towns, including Bruges and Ghent (in modern Belgium) produced woolen cloth for export. London across the North Sea became closely associated with these Flemish towns, its merchants supplying raw English wool to their spinners and weavers. A second cluster of cities sprouted in northern Italy. Venice, Genoa, and Pisa all flourished in the eleventh century as ports linking northern Europe with the Mediterranean sea lanes. The success of these coastal towns stimulated the growth of Florence, Milan, and other interior cities, which developed their own woolen, armor, and other industries for export markets.

In the twelfth and thirteenth centuries, markets held in the Champagne region of north central France became key meeting points of merchants from Italy and northern Europe. The aristocratic rulers of Champagne sponsored six commercial fairs a year, held in rotation in four different towns. These nobles guaranteed market peace, appointed officials to ensure honest dealings, and provided safe conduct along the routes that led to the fairgrounds. In return for these services, they collected tolls, rents, and fees from traders. Flemish merchants brought woolen cloths, tapestries, and furs. From Italy came Mediterranean goods as well as exotic wares from more distant lands. Buyers especially coveted Asian silks, spices, porcelains, and medicines. From a hemispheric perspective, the fairs of Champagne and Song China became linked into a single commercial trade web.

New Order in Political Life

The story of European politics between the eleventh and thirteenth centuries is complicated, partly because numerous power holders competed fiercely for land and resources in a time of economic growth, and partly because kings, queens, princes, barons, popes, and bishops had varying and often conflicting ideas of how western Christendom should be governed.

The limits of the Holy Roman Empire. Three major political experiments were put in play simultaneously. One was the vision of all Christendom united under the leadership of a single devout monarch. King Charlemagne, who ruled the Frankish empire back in the eighth and ninth centuries, had dreamed of such unity (see Chapter 10). It was also the hope of the German king Otto I, on whom the pope bestowed the title Holy Roman Emperor (see Chapter 11). His successors, Otto II and III, held that title but their authority did not extend beyond central Europe and northern Italy. In the generations that followed, German nobles reasserted their independence and central Europe broke into several competing **principalities.** Also, military campaigns to control Italy and Sicily exhausted the emperor's resources and ultimately failed. By 1300 the emperors, elected by German nobles, had little independent power, though the Holy Roman Empire, as it later came to be called, lasted in name to the nineteenth century.

principality A sovereign state or dependent territory, usually relatively small, ruled by a person with a noble title of high rank, for example, prince, princess, duke, or duchess.

The power of the church. Christian popes led the second experiment in European government. The Catholic Church had traditionally argued that it rightly possessed not only spiritual and moral authority but also political preeminence over the emperor and all other monarchs and princes. In the late first millennium C.E., however, the church institution, a pyramidal structure with the pope in

Rome at the top and thousands of parish priests at the bottom, had been weakly organized. Priests were often illiterate and morally lax. Europe's **secular rulers** and powerful aristocratic families had succeeded in exerting much influence over church decisions such as the appointment of bishops and the heads of monasteries.

secular ruler In the Christian tradition a monarch or other ruler who is not an ordained priest and does not formally represent the authority of the church; a temporal, as opposed to spiritual, leader.

Between the eleventh and thirteenth centuries, however, a series of intelligent, strong-willed popes, notably Gregory VII (1073–1085), Urban II (1088–1099), and Innocent III (1198–1216), strove to strengthen the church's decision-making hierarchy and to press the claim that God empowered them to *delegate* authority to secular rulers. In other words, the church sought to collaborate with monarchs and princes, not replace them, but nevertheless asserted that princes held their authority because the pope granted it. The reforming popes strove to recover full power to appoint church officials without kings or nobles interfering. They reorganized the church to ensure greater central control from Rome. They standardized church doctrines and rituals, and they systematized **canon law,** which governed Christian faith, practice, and church administration. They insisted that priests and nuns have good moral and intellectual qualifications. In the twelfth century, priestly councils established the rule that members of the clergy remain celibate (unmarried) and therefore fully dedicated to the service of God and the church.

canon law A code of laws and regulations governing a Christian church or denomination, especially in matters of faith, worship, moral behavior, and church administration.

Centralized monarchies. The third major experiment in government was the emergence of France and England as strong centralized states. Like the German sovereigns, the rulers of these two countries had recurring disputes with Rome. They showed less interest in leading all of Christendom, however, than in building well-organized regional monarchies. These kings (and, in England, one queen) aimed to expand the territories under their direct control and to limit the power of local aristocratic families.

In northern France in the eleventh century, the kings of the Capetian dynasty occupied the top rung in the hierarchy of Frankish lords and vassals but governed only the region around Paris and a few other scattered territories. After 1100, however, they gradually extended their realm through a combination of military action and astute political maneuvering. Because of healthy economic growth in the royal lands, the king's treasury filled up. This permitted recruitment of more armored knights, as well as foot soldiers skilled with iron-piercing crossbows. By 1300 the Capetian monarchy controlled much of what is today France. The kings financed a central administration that depended

The medieval social order in chess pieces. These nine figures carved from walrus ivory are among seventy-eight chess pieces dating to the twelfth century. They were discovered on the Isle of Lewis in northwestern Scotland. The two rooks take the form of soldiers or guards. The two pawns are simple geometric shapes. What characteristics of the other five figures help identify them as king, queen, bishop, and knight?

less on old aristocratic families, who had local political interests that might conflict with royal policy, and more on literate commoners eager to serve the state in return for regular salaries. The king recruited many of these officers from the rising urban, money-making class, or **bourgeoisie.** Somewhat as in Song China, this bureaucracy embraced an ideology of full devotion to the strength and defense of the central state. Beginning in the fourteenth century, the rulers periodically called a council of lords, clergy, and town citizens to Paris to listen to their political and fiscal advice. This body, known as the Estates-General, was no democratic legislature, but it strengthened social and political bonds between the royal palace and the most influential voices in society.

> **bourgeoisie** The social category of town-dwelling artisans, merchants, and bankers who occupied a position between rural peasants and the aristocratic class; in modern usage, the "middle class."

A second strong monarchy arose in England. In 1066 Duke William, ruler of Normandy (northwestern France) and a French-speaking descendant of earlier Viking conquerors, overthrew and replaced the Anglo-Saxon king of England. Subsequently, William awarded his fighting vassals extensive lands on the conquered island. In the next few centuries, this warrior class—which wielded local authority and built great stone castles—intermarried with Anglo-Saxon families and learned to speak English, spawning a distinctive Anglo-Norman elite.

Several twelfth- and thirteenth-century sovereigns, notably Henry II (r. 1154–1189), worked to strengthen central authority partly by building a system of royal law courts and encouraging development of a uniform body of law, or common law, to govern the entire realm. Like the most capable French kings, skillful Anglo-Norman rulers collaborated pragmatically with the great landowning families, the Christian clergy, and the prospering bourgeoisie of growing towns. Even so, kings and nobles had chronically tense relations. In 1215 the great barons of England forced King John, whom they rightly blamed for territorial losses in France, to sign the Magna Carta, or Great Charter. This document ratified the customary rights of the aristocracy against royal power and stipulated that the monarch could levy taxes only with aristocratic consent. The nobles regarded this event as a reaffirmation of the status quo, not a major political change.

As in France, the king periodically convened a council of lords, knights, bishops, and royal officers. In contrast

King Philip II: French State-Builder

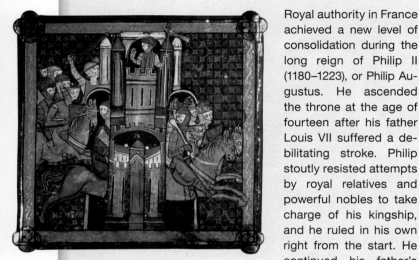

King Philip II of France chases Henry II of England out of Le Mans.

Royal authority in France achieved a new level of consolidation during the long reign of Philip II (1180–1223), or Philip Augustus. He ascended the throne at the age of fourteen after his father Louis VII suffered a debilitating stroke. Philip stoutly resisted attempts by royal relatives and powerful nobles to take charge of his kingship, and he ruled in his own right from the start. He continued his father's mission to centralize royal power and improve the efficiency of government over the lands under royal control.

Philip also extended French territory, partly by incorporating neighboring dukedoms through negotiation and manipulation of noble marriages and partly by attacking territories that the English crown held on the European continent. He warred with England intermittently for two decades, and eventually expelled its troops from all but the region of Aquitaine in southwestern France. He suspended hostilities in 1190–1191 to join England's Richard the Lionheart on the Third Crusade to Syria. A combined force of European knights captured the port of Acre (Ako) from its Muslim rulers, but the two kings soon quarreled. Philip, a more calculating and sober personality than Richard, returned home to advance the interests of the French state.

Philip's personal character—ruthless ambition combined with keen intelligence and diplomatic cunning—served him well. He encouraged agriculture, manufacturing, and trade, and he strengthened royal defenses. He placed his kingdom on a sound financial footing by keeping the royal treasury in the black rather than accumulating debt. Under his direction, the French government took shape as a bureaucratic hierarchy with fixed rules and regulations, standards for record keeping, and professional posts staffed by literate and skilled members of the bourgeois and noble classes rather than by aristocrats with family prestige but little talent. He sought to transform Paris into a worthy capital city, paving a few of its streets and continuing construction of the magnificent Notre Dame cathedral begun during his father's reign. He also granted a **charter** to the University of Paris and established the central market of Les Halles, an institution that operated well into the twentieth century.

> **charter** A document in which a state or other political authority granted specific rights or privileges to an individual, town, guild, or other organization to carry out particular functions.

Like most medieval kings and nobles, Philip married to cement political alliances. But his domestic affairs proved troublesome. After his first wife, Isabelle, died in 1190, he agreed to wed Ingeborg, daughter of the king of Denmark. The two got married on the same day they were introduced to each other, but Philip, for reasons unknown, immediately arranged a divorce with the support of the French Catholic church. He then married the noblewoman Agnes de Méran, with whom he had two children. Pope Innocent II, however, refused to accept the divorce from Ingeborg and placed the kingdom of France under an interdict, which meant that French churches could not legitimately celebrate the mass. Agnes died in 1201, however, and Philip made the pragmatic decision to take Ingeborg back.

Many of Philip's accomplishments can be attributed to his skills as an administrator, diplomat, and military commander. In 1214 he won the Battle of Bouvines in northeastern France, defeating a much larger coalition of British, Flemish, and German troops and confirming French sovereignty over Normandy. He doubled the size of the monarchy and collected far more revenue than his predecessors had ever been able to do, eliminating any doubts of French political dominance in western continental Europe.

Thinking Critically

Taking the example of Philip, what do you think are some of the things that a premodern monarch had to do to create a strong centralized state?

---

to the Estates-General, however, the English Parliament, as it was called, gained authority to approve taxes. In the later thirteenth century, Parliament also began to make new laws. The idea of the monarch ruling in alliance with a permanent assembly of influential males had no precise counterpart anywhere else in the world, even though ruler and Parliament continued to contest the proper balance of power between them for another five hundred years.

The Expansion of Western Christendom

In the same centuries that men and women in the heart of Europe started building a new urban civilization, other Europeans—knights, farmers, artisans, merchants, priests, monks, and nuns—busied themselves doubling the size of the Catholic Christian world. This expansion took place as European conquerors and settlers, operating in different groups, extended Christian frontiers in three major directions: eastward across Germany's Elbe River and around the Baltic Sea, southwestward into Muslim Spain, and southeastward into the Mediterranean basin. In these movements, Christian knights—warrior bands using the technology of heavy cavalry, archery, and the crossbow—seized territory mainly from non-Christian peoples. To secure and develop their holdings, conquering knights typically encouraged peasants and skilled artisans, as well as merchants and Christian clergy, to come in behind them to convert unbelievers and exploit the resources of the land.

Land hunger was indeed the driving motive in all three theaters of expansion. In northwestern Europe, population was growing steadily and unclaimed land vanishing. For young male aristocrats and would-be knights, military adventure abroad offered the chance to seize land that could no longer be had where they were born. The spreading custom of primogeniture, in which an individual's estate passed exclusively to the eldest son—a custom that kept lands from being subdivided and perhaps sold off—whetted the appetites of younger sons for making war far from home and getting lands of their own. For peasant farmers, migration to new territory offered the possibility of escaping serfdom and acquiring larger farms. Business-minded lords encouraged economic growth in conquered territories by granting new towns charters that ensured residents of firm legal rights and a measure of self-government.

Expansion beyond the Elbe.

The Elbe River runs generally northwestward 724 miles across today's Czech Republic and Germany, emptying into the North Sea. It marked a kind of eleventh-century starting line for the advance of German, Flemish, and Frankish heavy cavalry across the plains of central and eastern Europe. Local populations that spoke Slavic or Finno-Ugric languages (Finnish, Estonian, and Hungarian) generally lacked the organization and weaponry needed to prevent this advance. The conquerors built castles, planned new towns, and invited German farmers to move in. In the twelfth century, according to one estimate, about 200,000 German peasants settled east of the Elbe, clearing land and turning fertile soil with heavy plows.[8] The Catholic clergy arrived, too, setting up **bishoprics,** building churches and monasteries, and gradually convincing local peoples to renounce their pagan gods and goddesses.

bishopric In the Catholic Church organization, a district (diocese) under the authority of a bishop.

To the southeast, the once ferocious Magyars, who had earlier invaded Europe from the Inner Eurasian steppes (see Chapter 10), gradually accepted Christ and founded a Hungarian Christian monarchy. Farther south, spiritual agents representing both the Greek Orthodox and Catholic Churches competed for the souls of Slavic princes and their subjects. Before the eleventh century, these missionaries sometimes worked together, despite chronic strains between Constantinople and Rome over authority and doctrine. In 1054, however, a dispute over Catholic claims to the pope's spiritual supremacy independent of the Orthodox Church triggered a formal divorce. Thereafter, rivalry became more intense. Eventually, a religious frontier emerged in eastern Europe that today mainly follows national borders. The populations of Greece, Bulgaria, Romania, Macedonia, and Serbia adhere chiefly to the Orthodox tradition. Croatia, Slovenia, and Hungary are predominantly Roman Catholic.

Crusades in the Iberian Peninsula.

In the early eleventh century, Muslims ruled a large part of Iberia (Spain and Portugal), though the once unified Umayyad state (see Chapter 11) fragmented into several competing kingdoms. In the far northeast of the peninsula, fighting between Muslim armies and the lords of small Christian states had been chronic for three hundred years. We saw earlier in the chapter that the Almoravids and the Almohads, both African Berber powers that preached Islamic reform, successively invaded Spain and reunified the southern region for about 130 years. After 1000, landless knights who recognized the Umayyad breakup for the opportunity it was, formed cavalry bands that, with the blessing of the church, pushed southward. This Iberian crusade paralleled in both chronology and motive the Christian advances into eastern Europe, and both attracted a motley crowd of fighters—Frankish, Flemish, German, English, Italian, and Spanish knights all eager to test their military skills and seize land. Many warriors signed on to serve León-Castile, Aragon, or Portugal, the three most rapidly growing Christian kingdoms on the peninsula.

The conquests took place in two major phases. The first ran from 1080 to 1150, when Christian knights drove Muslim rulers out of central Spain. The second extended from 1212 to 1265, when combined forces of the three large kingdoms made rapid headway against Almohad armies, seizing Córdoba, Valencia, Seville, and other major cities. Only a few Muslim enclaves on the Strait of Gibraltar and the little kingdom of Granada held out longer.

As in the eastern European campaigns, knights who captured Muslim territory in Spain urged Christian farmers to migrate to the new frontier. Rulers rewarded their officers for founding villages and populating them with Christians, and they gave new towns royal charters. Unlike either northern Spain or eastern Europe, however, the southern peninsula was already urbanized when Christian conquerors arrived. In some cities the new overlords expelled Muslim residents, distributing vacated property to nobles, monasteries, and retired foot soldiers. Nevertheless, millions of Muslims and Jews remained in Spain throughout the conquest period. We have abundant evidence of peaceful everyday dealings across religious lines and of Christians learning Arabic and taking up Muslim ways of dress, etiquette, and cuisine. Even after the armies of León-Castile seized central Spain, Toledo and other formerly Muslim cities continued to serve for a time as places where Muslim, Jewish, and Christian scholars sat down together to discuss Greek and Arabic scientific and philosophical texts and translate them into Latin. Nevertheless, Spain's cultural Christianization advanced gradually, marked by Muslims and Jews either converting (or pretending to convert) to Christianity under varying degrees of pressure or else fleeing Spain. This exodus accelerated in the fourteenth century, when Christian rulers adopted harsher religious and political policies toward those minorities.

Crusades in the eastern Mediterranean. Western European crusaders advanced into the eastern Mediterranean basin in 1030, when landless Norman warriors, that is, knights from Normandy in northern France, began arriving in southern Italy. From there, they launched an invasion of Sicily, evicting its Muslim government. Then, in 1095, the reformist Pope Urban II agreed to help the Byzantine emperor resist the Muslim Turks who were just then advancing westward across Anatolia toward Constantinople. In fact, Urban II was interested primarily in capturing Jerusalem, which loomed large in the European imagination as the city where Jesus was crucified and resurrected. An armed crusade to the Holy Land was an opportunity to protect Catholic pilgrims bound for Jerusalem and to firm up Europe's political stability by encouraging landless and unruly knights to seek their fortunes on a new military frontier. Furthermore, despite the pope's show of support for the Byzantines, the Catholic and Greek Orthodox Churches had already split formally. By sponsoring a crusade, the pope saw an opportunity not only to propagate the faith in the core lands of Islam but also to make inroads against the Greek church.

In 1096, between 50,000 and 60,000 people from all over western Christendom, perhaps 6,000 to 7,000 of them mounted knights, marched across southeastern Europe to Constantinople, then on to Syria. In 1099, they took Jerusalem and killed most of its Muslim and Jewish inhabitants. This campaign was the first of seven major crusades that stretched over two hundred years. All of them declared their mission to win and hold the Holy Land, but in reality European knights were eager to capture any Mediterranean territory that offered land and wealth. As we saw earlier, the breakup of the Turkic Seljuk empire allowed Christian forces to implant small crusader states on the coasts of Syria and Palestine. The aristocratic leaders of these European colonies handed out large farm estates to loyal knights. Western European peasants, however, went to Syria or Palestine in small numbers relative to their migrations into eastern Europe or Spain. Southwest Asia was already densely populated, and its semiarid environment and intensely irrigated farming held little attraction for French or German plow farmers.

In the twelfth century, Italian sea merchants operating mainly from Venice, Genoa, and Pisa ferried a steady stream of fighters, pilgrims, war horses, and weaponry to the crusader states. As time went on, the religious fervor that motivated the First Crusade served increasingly as an ideological rationale for straightforward territorial acquisition. In 1191 King Richard I of England seized Cyprus, a Greek Christian island. The Knights Templar and the Knights Hospitaller (Knights of St. John), newly formed religious orders of fighting monks, seized other Greek islands, while European fleets attacked coastal cities in Egypt and North Africa. In 1204 the army of the Fourth Crusade bypassed the Holy Land altogether and assailed Christian Constantinople,

Krak des Chevaliers. The European Knights Hospitaller constructed this mammoth fortress in northwestern Syria in the twelfth century. The castle helped defend the borders of the County of Tripoli, one of the coastal crusader states. The Hospitallers held this citadel from 1142 to 1271, when a Muslim army drove them out.

forcing the Byzantine emperor to flee to Anatolia. A coalition of Christian aristocrats founded a new crusader state there and ruled for about half a century. Byzantine forces regrouped, however, and in 1261 took back the city.

In contrast to the Spanish campaign, the eastern crusades did not fulfill their initial aims. The Europeans did not have sufficient resources to push deep into Southwest Asia, and after 1187, when Muslim cavalry under Salah al-Din retook Jerusalem, the crusader states went on the defensive. In 1291, Muslim forces captured Acre, the last European stronghold on the Syrian coast. Nevertheless, the eastern crusades had long-term political and economic significance. Cyprus, Crete, and other Aegean territories remained in western European hands for hundreds of years. Moreover, the crusader states, like southern Spain, served as conduits for the transmission of knowledge from Muslim lands to western Europe. For example, Italian entrepreneurs learned from Muslims how to grow and process sugar cane for commercial markets, an industry that required building technically sophisticated mills. Europeans first experimented with sugar-making technology in the crusader states. From there, the industry spread westward across the Mediterranean islands to Spain.

European Commercial Power in the Mediterranean

Northern Europe's economic growth and the good business generated by the crusades encouraged Italian merchants to advance aggressively into the Mediterranean, a commercial zone that in the previous several centuries had been a preserve of Muslim and Greek Byzantine shipping. Venice, Genoa, and Pisa, all independent Italian city-states, took the lead. Italian shipwrights built both round-hulled cargo ships and sleek galleys. These port cities became clearinghouses for shipments of Syrian glassware, Indian pepper, Chinese porcelain, and West African gold to northern Europe. The twelfth-century Persian geographer Zakariya al-Qazwini, writing about a city, perhaps Mainz, on northern Europe's Rhine River, observed: "It is astonishing that, although this place is in the Far West, there are spices there which are to be found only in the Far East—pepper, ginger, cloves, spikenard, costus, and galingale [varieties of aromatics], all in enormous quantities."[9] European exports to Mediterranean markets included grain, timber, salt, metals, furs, silver and gold coinage, and, increasingly from the twelfth century, fine woolen cloths manufactured in Flanders or northern Italy.

Genoese and Venetian merchants also led the way in founding communities in both Muslim and Christian ports to serve as hosts and agents for shippers from the home city. A Genoese diaspora, or scattering of trade settlements, spread around the western Mediterranean rim, while Venetian merchants settled in eastern Mediterranean ports. These Italians, however, changed the rules of the game, combining trade with military power in ways largely unfamiliar to Muslims and Greeks. The Venetian government financed commercial enterprises, supported them with military force, seized foreign ports and islands, and pressured Muslim or Byzantine authorities to grant foreign merchants commercial privileges. Venice did not have enough armed might to conquer extensive Mediterranean territories, but it did create an empire of trading posts, protecting them with naval patrols. In Genoa, private entrepreneurs, not the government, organized most mercantile ventures, but the state furnished ships and financial incentives to expand operations. Beginning in the thirteenth century, the two city-states became increasingly violent rivals for Mediterranean trade. Meanwhile, Muslim and Greek merchants had to settle mostly for piracy or local coastal shipping.

Memento of a pilgrimage.
Christian pilgrims commemorated their journeys to holy shrines by purchasing badges, which served as inexpensive souvenirs. This pewter badge shows St. Thomas Becket, Archbishop of Canterbury, returning from France to England shortly before his assassination in 1170. Canterbury Cathedral subsequently became a popular pilgrimage site.

Western Europe's Cultural Style

Europe in the eleventh century was a complex jumble of monarchies, principalities, city-states, languages, and ethnic groups. Nevertheless, in the ensuing three hundred years a distinctive European cultural style, indeed a new Afroeurasian civilization, began to take shape. The invigorated Catholic Church drove western Christendom's early cultural integration. Reform clerics not only encouraged standardized doctrine and canon law but also promoted particular styles of art and architecture. New movements to encourage Christian piety and devotion spread among ordinary women and men. These included pilgrimages to holy shrines within Europe, emotional veneration of Jesus and his mother Mary, and sponsorship of charities. Though Europeans spoke many different tongues, Latin served as the common language of priests, bureaucrats, lawyers, and scholars from Ireland to Hungary.

Efforts to unify Christian life did not, however, bode well for Europe's Jews. The popes formally accepted responsibility for protecting them, but as pious reforms progressed and crusading fervor took hold, social toleration of Jews deteriorated. Under Pope Innocent III, clerics attending the Fourth Lateran Council held in 1215 imposed new discriminatory laws on Jews, obliging them to wear distinctive dress and barring them from public office. Jewish trade diasporas had played an early part in linking Europe to the wider Afroeurasian world. But as economic growth accelerated, Jews steadily retreated from the commercial sphere, except as money lenders.

Another aspect of cultural integration was the founding of more monasteries as centers of vibrant economic and cultural activity. In the twelfth century, for example, the Cistercian monastic order specialized in opening holy houses in rural and remote corners of Europe and devoting themselves to clearing forests and cultivating the land. The Cistercians created a remarkably integrated network of monasteries that by the early thirteenth century numbered in the hundreds and extended from Spain to Norway and the frontiers of Russia. Like the reforming popes, the Cistercian founders aimed to cleanse Christian society of worldliness and spiritual complacency. Life in a monastic house was austere and rigorous—a simple diet, little heat in winter, and a ban on almost all conversation. Even so, Cistercian communities became large-scale producers of food and wool and made significant advances in animal breeding and farm technology.

Monasteries for women also multiplied but much more slowly. The Cisterians and most other male-dominated orders often obstructed their growth, arguing that nuns could pull less economic weight than male members of the community and that pious donors were less inclined to give money to support cloistered women. The male leaders of orders also justified their resistance by reciting, as priests had for centuries, tired truisms about the dangers of women's company. As one abbot pronounced, "We unanimously decree for the safety of our souls no less than that of our bodies and goods, that we will on no account receive any more sisters [into the monastery]."[10]

Christian Europe's cultural integration, especially at elite levels, proceeded hand in hand with population growth, urbanization, and expanding trade. In the thirteenth century the young civilization achieved full bloom manifested in the continuing spread of literacy, the triumph of Gothic architecture, and a remarkable synthesis of Christian, Greek, and Muslim learning. We return to these achievements in Chapter 13.

• • •

Conclusion

Several interrelated developments mark the approximate year 1000 as an important turning point in Afroeurasian history. The weightiest of these was the extraordinary expansion of the Chinese economy under the Song and Jin dynasties. China produced so many goods that other societies wanted, and its internal market expanded so much, that its economy, more than any other single factor, stimulated trans-hemispheric commercial exchange to unprecedented levels.

A second development, paralleling China's economic surge but on a smaller scale, was the political stabilizing and economic revival of Europe. For the first time since the fall of the western Roman empire, the Mediterranean zone of inter-communication expanded outward to the north and north-west to fully incorporate western Europe. Indeed, Europeans not only pressed into the Mediterranean trade networks but in the ensuing two and a half centuries came to dominate them. Moreover, European civilization, shaped primarily by the Catholic Church and the Latin language, expanded ter-ritorially, as mounted knights and migrating peasants ad-vanced into eastern Europe, the Iberian Peninsula, and, with limited success, the eastern Mediterranean.

Third, the central Muslim lands experienced much po-litical turbulence in the eleventh and twelfth centuries as Turkic horse archers with their families, herds, and flocks streamed in. Turkic cavalry captains attempted to found a unitary state on the scale of the great Abbasid empire of the ninth century. But this project failed, and by the end of the twelfth century the whole region from Egypt to northern India was a collage of states, most of them ruled by Turkic military elites. In contrast to Inner Eurasia, the Sahara Desert had never spawned large pastoral confederations capable of overrunning neighboring agrarian lands. But parallel to the Turkic movements, Berber-speaking warriors burst out of the western Sahara in the eleventh century to conquer not only North Africa but also Muslim Spain. The Strait of Gibraltar as a boundary between the African and European land masses had little political or cultural meaning for the next two centuries.

The complex commercial and cultural exchanges of the eleventh and twelfth centuries clearly did not depend on the existence of several giant empires. Across Afroeurasia, in fact, there were a greater number of relatively small states than during the previous several centuries. China became divided, and South Asia already was. Turkic commanders divvied up the central Muslim lands, and no monarch or pope managed to politically unify all of Christian Europe. In West Africa the Ghana empire faded, owing partly to the assaults of the Saharan Almoravids. In the early thirteenth century, however, the largest territorial empire the world has ever known arose abruptly. The Mongolian founder of this state became known as Chingis Khan, the Universal Lord.

• • •

Key Terms

Almohads 353	Jin dynasty 341	principality 358
Almoravids 351	Kamakura shogunate 345	samurai 346
bishopric 361	madrasa 354	secular ruler 358
bourgeoisie 359	Magna Carta 359	Seljuks 349
canon law 358	*mamluk* 348	Song dynasty 350
charter 360	meritocracy 344	Sufism 355
crusades 361	mysticism 355	*Tale of Genji* 346
Dai Viet 345	Neo-Confucian 344	
Ghaznavids 348	North Atlantic Warm Period 341	

Change over Time

9th–13th centuries	The North Atlantic Warm Period is associated with more stable food production in China and Europe.
960–1276	The Song dynasty in China (960–1127, Southern Song, 1127–1276) presides over an unprecedented rush of industrial and commercial activity, stimulating economic growth across Afroeurasia.
977–1186	The Ghaznavid dynasty, founded by Turkic *mamluk* officers, rules in Afghanistan and South Asia.
1054	The Greek Orthodox and Catholic Churches split formally (Great Schism).
1055–1092	The Great Seljuk empire, founded by Turkic migrants from Inner Eurasia, encompasses much of Southwest Asia.
1058–1111	The theologian and mystic al-Ghazali integrates Sufism into Muslim belief and practice.
1062–1147	The Almoravid dynasty, founded by Berber reformers in North Africa, rules in the western Mediterranean.
1066	Normans led by William I invade and conquer England.
1088–1099	Pope Urban II champions armed Christian crusade to the Holy Land.
1099–1291	European crusader states in Syria and Palestine become conduits for the transmission of new knowledge to western Europe.
1115–1234	The Jin dynasty replaces the Song dynasty in northern China.
1120–1269	The Almohad dynasty replaces the Almoravids in the western Mediterranean.
1130–1200	The Chinese philosopher Zhu Xi teaches Neo-Confucianism.
1138–1204	The Jewish philosopher and theologian Maimonides codifies Jewish law.
1169–1250	The Ayyubid dynasty rules in Southwest Asia and Egypt; its founder, Salah al-Din, expels European knights from Jerusalem in 1187.
1185–1333	During the Kamakura shogunate in Japan, the samurai class rises to prominence.
1204–1261	Constantinople becomes a western European crusader state.
1206–1526	The Delhi sultanate, founded by Turkic fighters, rules much of South Asia.
1215	The Magna Carta is signed in England, ratifying the customary rights of the aristocracy against royal power.
1236	Muslim Córdoba falls to Christian crusaders.

Please see end of book reference section for additional reading suggestions related to this chapter.

Afroeurasia in the Era of Mongol Power

1200–1350

Arab travelers arriving in a village, depicted in a miniature painting from a short story collection of Abu Muhammad al-Hariri.

Many people have stories to tell of running into someone they know in an unexpected place far from home. Even though more than seven billion people share the planet, the high-speed mobility of our era means that sudden encounters between acquaintances on airplanes or in restaurants happen all the time. Before the age of fast global transport, most men and women stayed close to home and never had such experiences. But people who did travel long distances by caravan or sailing ship kept to the well-known roads, trails, and shipping lanes. Therefore, chance meetings between acquaintances thousands of miles from their hometown probably occurred more often than we might imagine.

Take the case of Abu Abdallah ibn Battuta, a Muslim legal scholar from Morocco who traveled back and forth across Afroeurasia between 1325 to 1354 and then produced a book about his experience (see Map 13.2). He made several pilgrimages to Mecca, studied with renowned scholars in Southwest Asian cities, and worked for the sultan of Delhi in India. In his narrative he tells us that during his journeys he repeatedly bumped into people he already knew. When he visited China's southern coast in 1346, he encountered a man named al-Bushri. This scholar and merchant came originally from Ceuta, a Moroccan town only forty miles from Tangier, Ibn Battuta's native city. Conversing together, the two men realized that in fact they had already met some years earlier in northern India. Shortly after that happy encounter, Ibn Battuta returned to Morocco. But more than five years later, while visiting a caravan city on the edge of the Sahara Desert (at the opposite end of the hemisphere from China), he met and lodged with a lawyer who turned out to be al-Bushri's brother!

Ibn Battuta was just one of thousands of merchants, scholars, soldiers, pilgrims, and missionaries who traveled widely in Afroeurasia in the 1200–1350 period. During much of that era, wide areas of the supercontinent experienced remarkable political stability, as well as long-distance commercial activity that exceeded in volume and complexity the already expansive scale of interchange that characterized the previous two centuries.

This upsurge in the movement of goods, as well as people and ideas, can be attributed partly to the spectacular state-building venture of the Mongol conqueror Chingis Khan (also, Genghis Khan) in the early thirteenth century. The Mongol era began as a violent military onslaught of Inner Eurasian pastoral nomads, campaigns that engulfed and subjugated the entire region from China to Iran. Chingis (CHEEN-gihs) erected an empire that after the mid-thirteenth century devolved into four major Mongol-ruled states. The combined territories of these states extended from Korea to eastern Europe, and they affected the lives, directly or indirectly, of hundreds of millions of people. Moreover, the Mongol khans, or monarchs, became protectors of trade, builders of cities, and patrons of cultural achievement.

This chapter begins with an account of the Mongol irruption—its beginnings in Mongolia, its extraordinary military triumphs, and the consequences it had for the populations it overpowered. We also describe developments in the four Mongol successor states and their continuing campaigns to bring more territory under the authority of the descendants of Chingis Khan.

The second part of the chapter investigates the period from about 1250 to 1350, when the four big Mongol states, as well as other successful monarchies, encouraged trade and cultural interchange across Afroeurasia. Historians have labeled that century the Mongol Peace (*Pax Mongolica* in Latin). It was hardly free of warfare, but relative political calm over large areas stimulated the movement of goods, ideas, and inventions to distant places where they had previously been unknown. Religious teachings and practices also moved along the busy trade routes, a phenomenon that especially benefited Islam.

Mongol khans presided over a sort of golden age of trade on the ancient silk roads across Inner Eurasia. Nevertheless, maritime commerce on the Afroeurasian seas continued, as it had in the preceding centuries, to far outweigh caravan traffic in volume and value. In the third part of the chapter we focus on the Indian Ocean basin from Southeast Asia to East Africa, a region that largely escaped Mongol attacks and where new and prospering ports, city-states, and monarchies continued to appear.

The fourth section takes us back to Europe, a region that from the tenth century enjoyed rising population, steady

• • •

urbanization, and a rush of cultural innovation. In the Mongol age Europe also played a more energetic part in trans-hemispheric exchange. For the first time since the days of the Roman empire, European merchants were to be seen in at least small numbers in the lands east of the Mediterranean, even in China. And in contrast to both China and Southwest Asia, Europe's western lands did not have to endure Mongol invasions.

In the final part of the chapter, we shift southward to the lands rimming the Sahara Desert. Though Mongol armies never penetrated any part of Africa, the trans-Saharan

A Panoramic View

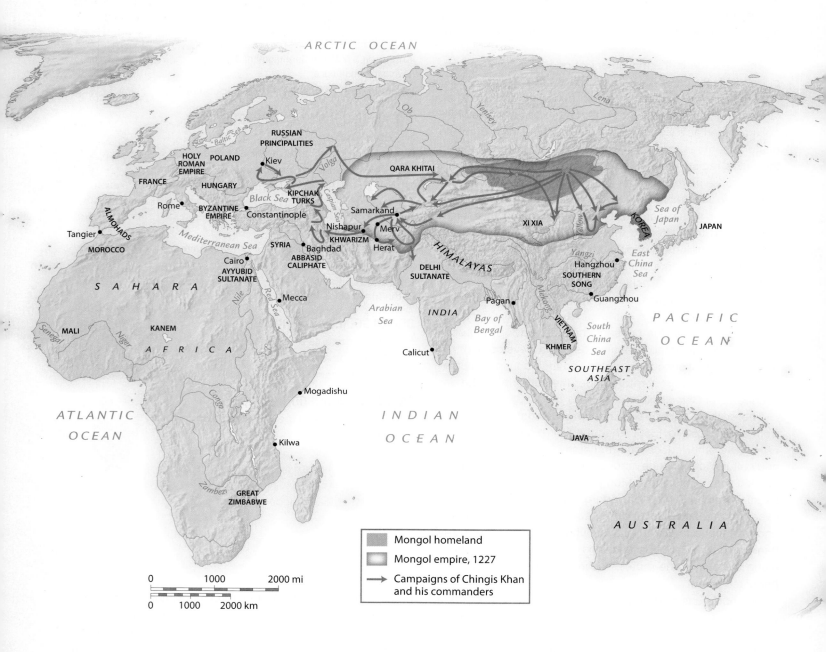

MAP 13.1 Afroeurasia at the death of Chingis Khan, 1227.
Over the course of two decades, Chingis Khan forged the largest empire in world history to that point. What geographic factors contributed to the success of his conquests?

trade network became tied more firmly than ever to Eurasian routes. Several West African states benefited from long-distance trade connections, especially Mali, a Muslim empire of agrarian wealth and sources of gold, which flowed in greater abundance through trans-hemispheric pipelines, further energizing production and commerce.

The Ascendance of the Mongol Empires

FOCUS How did Chingis Khan and his armies succeed in forging a state that extended from Iran to China?

In 1206 Chingis Khan (1167?–1227) united the tribes of Mongolia and in less than two decades forged the largest empire the world had ever seen (see Map 13.1). The conquests were still going strong when Chingis Khan died, and by 1260 the Mongol imperium encompassed an area nearly four times that of the Roman empire at its zenith.[1] This gigantic state lasted less than fifty years. After 1260, it fractured into four competing Mongol kingdoms, or **khanates.** All of them, however, remained under the authority of the great conqueror's descendants—members of the House of Chingis—well into the fourteenth century or later. These four states—centered east-to-west on China, Inner Eurasia, Southwest Asia, and the lands north of the Black and Caspian Seas, including Russia—had the dimensions of empires in their own right, embracing peoples of many languages and cultural traditions.

khanate A state ruled by a khan; a Turkic or Mongol monarchy.

Chingis Khan's Path of Conquest

On the eve of Chingis's rise to power, Mongolia was home to herding peoples numbering somewhere between 700,000 and 1,000,000.[2] Like pastoral societies across Inner Eurasia, the Mongols organized themselves in tribes, that is, groups whose social cohesion was based, not on primary allegiance to a government, but on a claim of shared descent from a single male ancestor who had lived sometime in the distant past. Some Mongol families had noble status, owning large herds, assigning pasture to other groups, and leading mounted fighters into battle. Shamans, or local religious specialists, also wielded great influence. Acting as intermediaries between mortals and numerous deities and nature spirits, these men and women performed purification rituals, read omens, and blessed herds. Mongols generally believed that the highest supernatural authority resided in Blue Heaven, though, much like the Chinese Confucian idea of a supreme power called Heaven, this cosmic force took no concrete form and remained aloof from daily human affairs. Some Mongols also identified with Buddhism, Nestorian Christianity, or Manichaeism, religions that had been present in Inner Eurasia for centuries.

Mongol life revolved around the seasonal movement of herds of horses, sheep, cattle, and camels between highland valley pastures in summer and lowland plateaus in winter.

Mongol sport. This sixteenth-century Chinese painting depicts Mongol horsemen playing a type of polo.

Humble sheep had the greatest value as a source of food and fiber, but only horses, the engines of war, gave their owners social and political prestige. In the division of labor, men took charge of hunting, as well as feuding with enemies and raiding their herds and encampments. Women managed children and the domestic hearth, but they also spent long hours in the saddle, overseeing the care of animal stock. A thirteenth-century European visitor wrote:

> The men do not make anything at all, with the exception of arrows, and they also sometimes tend the flocks, but they hunt and practice archery. . . . Their women make everything, leather garments, tunics, shoes, leggings, and everything made of leather; they also drive the carts and repair them, they load the camels, and in all their tasks they are very swift and energetic. All the women wear breeches and some of them shoot like the men.[3]

The conqueror's early career. We have a version of the early life of Temujin (teh-MU-jihn), the birth name of Chingis Khan, in the *Secret History of the Mongols,* a book written in the Mongolian language sometime in the thirteenth century. Temujin belonged to a noble lineage, but at a young age he lost his father to a political assassination, leaving him and his family without herds or protection. At one point, a group of his rival kinsmen captured and imprisoned him, fastening a cangue, or heavy wooden restraining device around his neck and arms. According to the *Secret History,* he waited until his captors had dispersed after a feast, hit his guard on the head, then slipped away to the nearby Onan River: "Then, telling himself that if he lay down in the forest by the Onan, he would be seen, he reclined on his back in the water's stream and, letting his cangue float with the current, he lay with only his face clear."[4] By this ruse he made his escape.

Feats like this, the *Secret History* declares, revealed Temujin's bravery and cunning. Once free, he attracted a personal following among other young warriors, and he eventually won the allegiance of nearly all the tribes of Mongolia. In 1206 a meeting of clan leaders proclaimed him Chingis Khan, or Universal Ruler. He won this title by overawing his enemies with brilliant battle tactics and sheer ruthlessness, including executions of war prisoners. He also, however, assimilated thousands of defeated warriors into his own ranks, offering them his protection and fair shares of the horses and other booty taken on campaign.

In steppe society, the leader of a large coalition of herding tribes could hope to hold power only as long as he produced opportunities for seizing grazing land, horses, and captives. To keep the Mongol confederation together, Chingis had to find new targets for conquest. In 1209 he led his archers southward against Xi Xia (shi shyah), a pastoral nomadic state of Tibetan origin that dominated the eastern end of the silk roads and the prosperous oases scattered along them. The rulers of Xi Xia were forced to pay tribute, and Chingis incorporated thousands of their fighters into his own cavalry. Two years later, he led his growing army across the

Chingis Khan. The artist who painted this portrait lived a century or more after the conqueror died. Is any particular personality trait of the conqueror evident in this picture?

Gobi Desert to northern China, attracted, as Inner Eurasian nomads long had been, by the prospect of plundering the towns and farms of the Yellow River valley. In 1215 Chingis captured the northern capital of the Jin, the ruling group that had overthrown the Northern Song dynasty back in 1127 (see Chapter 12). Seizure of this city near modern Beijing impelled further campaigns. The Jin had a huge army, but because they themselves had risen to power in northern China as foreign invaders, they inspired little loyalty among the Chinese villagers they dominated. Consequently, the Mongols lured many Chinese to their side, recruiting archers and skilled military engineers. Even with these advantages, the fight for northern China raged on for nearly two decades.

Campaigns to the west. The Mongols were the first steppe conquerors to wage campaigns in both northern China and central Inner Eurasia simultaneously. At the same time that Chingis was fighting the Jin, other Mongol bands advanced west across the steppes to the territory of the Qara Khitai empire, which dominated the Inner Eurasian heartland. Qara Khitai had been founded in 1124 by military refugees who had fled westward in the turmoil surrounding the rise of the Jin. In 1218, Mongol forces eradicated the Qara Khitai state, handing Chingis long stretches of the silk roads and immense expanses of horse pasture. He also absorbed thousands more mounted archers, most of them speakers of Turkic languages, into his western army. In fact, these fighters came to far outnumber ethnic Mongols in the invading forces. We might therefore more accurately refer to the Turko-Mongol invasions, though most of the top commanderships went to Chingis's relatives and close companions.

Victory over Qara Khitai put Chingis on a collision course with the empire of Khwarizm. This state, founded by Turkic military men, dominated the fertile lower valley of the Amu Darya (Amu River) east of the Caspian Sea (modern Turkmenistan and Uzbekistan). In the first two decades of the thirteenth century, the rulers of Khwarizm expanded their territory spectacularly, sending cavalry into Afghanistan and Iran and capturing the Central Asian silk road center of Samarkand.

When Chingis sent three ambassadors to Khwarizm to resolve a dispute, the Turkic ruler Ala al-Din Muhammad (reigned 1200–1220) murdered one of them and humiliated the others by shaving off their beards. To answer this insult, the conqueror led his mounted army against Ala al-Din in 1219, unleashing hellfire on the peoples of Central Asia, Afghanistan, and Khurasan (northeastern Iran). The campaign, which continued for four years, earned the Mongols their enduring reputation for horrific killing. They sacked, plundered, or burned most of the great commercial and manufacturing cities of those regions, including Samarkand, Herat, Merv, and Nishapur. They massacred whole populations, though sparing skilled artisans, young women, and others fit for forced labor or sexual service. They killed or evicted tens of thousands of peasants, converting farm lands into pasture for their countless herds. In a few towns they even killed the dogs and cats. "With one stroke," lamented the Persian scholar Ata Malik Juvaini of the invasion of Khurasan, "a world which billowed with fertility was laid desolate, and the region thereof became a desert, and the greater part of the living dead, and their skin and bones crumbling dust."[5] As for the mighty Ala al-Din, he died a fugitive on an island in the Caspian Sea.

The passing of Chingis. Leaving Central Asia and northern Iran a smoldering ruin, Chingis returned to Mongolia in 1223. In his final campaign he destroyed the Xi Xia state to punish its rulers for failing to pay tribute. He died four years later, at the age of about sixty, and was buried in a secret grave in western Mongolia. Modern explorers have mounted several expeditions to find the tomb, so far without success.

Explaining Mongol Power

Chingis Khan created a gigantic state in less than twenty years, but he did it by relying on many of the same military and political methods that the Seljuk Turks and other Inner Eurasian empire-builders had employed in previous centuries. That is, the Mongol army consisted mostly of horse archers equipped with powerful compound bows, lances, and swords. Some mounted units, called heavy cavalry, outfitted themselves in many pounds of defensive armor. Light cavalry wore less armor to enhance their speed and mobility. And like earlier steppe conquerors, the Mongols financed their army and administration by extracting wealth from herders, farmers, and merchants and, whenever they had sufficient power to do it, from the citizens of the commercial cities that rimmed Inner Eurasia on the east and south.

In other respects, the Mongol empire arose out of the particular circumstances that prevailed in the early thirteenth century. First, the Mongol tribes produced a leader of extraordinary talent. In his path to power, the young Temujin brilliantly combined hard discipline with fulsome generosity, mercilessly punishing failure or betrayal but rewarding even the lowliest soldier for showing loyalty and pluck. He also exploited the fact that the Xi Xia, Qara Khitai, and Khwarizm states all had relatively fragile military governments and shallow reserves of popular support. As for the Jin, a century of chronic warfare between them and the Southern Song dynasty made them vulnerable to attack from the steppes.

Mongol success depended more than anything else on horses. Early victories allowed Chingis and his commanders to corral hundreds of thousands of them, potentially several for every warrior. One historian has estimated from later data that in the 1200s Inner Eurasia had half the horses in the world and that Turko-Mongol fighters came to own most of them.[6] With so much spare horse power, Mongol cavalry could advance thirty miles a day and launch ferocious attacks even when their adversaries outnumbered them.

Chingis also adopted some of the military technology of agrarian states. Owing to silk road connections, knowledge of war machines and tactics used in China, India, and the central Muslim lands had been spreading to Inner Eurasian peoples for centuries. Perhaps more eagerly than any earlier steppe warrior, Chingis borrowed weapons and military know-how from more technologically complex societies. These devices included Chinese battering rams and catapults used for breeching walls that cavalry could not penetrate. Chingis also recruited skilled Chinese and Persian engineers to set up and operate these complicated engines. He almost certainly employed Chinese technicians to set off gunpowder bombs and rockets, though only in the following century did gunpowder weaponry become a significant factor in warfare west of China.

Adapting another Chinese idea, Chingis organized his army in nested units of ten, one hundred, one thousand, and ten thousand fighters in order to create a tight chain of mobilization and command. In Mongol and Turkic societies, political allegiance and economic interests centered on extended families and the clans into which they were grouped. Chingis, however, placed warriors from different kinship groups into each unit at every level, thereby

Mongol assault. In this Persian miniature painting, Hulagu, a grandson of Chingis Khan, lays siege to Baghdad in 1258. The two pyramid-shaped structures in the foreground are catapults.

neutralizing kinship loyalties and ensuring that all soldiers would depend absolutely on their military comrades and devote themselves exclusively to the Mongol imperial cause.

Mongol Expansion after Chingis

In the half-century after Chingis Khan died, the Mongol empire went through two successive transformations. First, his immediate successors invested their inherited wealth and cavalry power in even more conquests, nearly doubling the size of the empire. Chingis chose his third son Ogedei (ERG-uh-day, r. 1229–1241) to succeed him as supreme commander, or Great Khan. According to custom, however, any member of the Chingis lineage could lay claim to that office. Consequently, succession disputes and family feuds became chronic. Nevertheless, Ogedei, who established the Mongol capital at Karakorum in central Mongolia, and Mongke (r. 1251–1259), one of Chingis's grandsons, had the political skill necessary to keep the empire together and to push out its frontiers for another three decades. Toregene, the wife of Ogedei, also played a key role by stepping in as de facto ruler between 1241 and 1246, when family intrigues delayed the election of a Great Khan to succeed her husband.

The second important transformation was the fracturing of the unified empire. By the 1260s, conflict within the House of Chingis over both succession to power and control of particular territories led to the rise of four separate and competing Mongol power centers. These were the Yuan (yoo-AHN) empire (the khanate of China, 1271–1368); the khanate of Chagatai in Central Asia and the eastern steppes (1225–1687); the khanate of Kipchak (the Golden Horde, 1241–1502); and the Ilkhanate of Iran and Iraq (1258–1335). All four states remained under the authority of members of the House of Chingis, and Mongol-ruled territory continued to grow until the late thirteenth century (see Map 13.2). The ideology that Mongols had an unstoppable mission to rule the whole world drove this continuing expansion.

The Yuan empire: Mongol triumph in China. The struggle between the Mongols and the Jin for dominance of northern China continued until 1234. Once the Jin fell, the victors then faced the Song state in the south. Owing to that region's spectacular economic growth in the previous three centuries, the Song monarchs had formidable resources for resisting Mongol invasion. In fact, Mongke, together with his brother and successor Kubilai Khan (r. 1271–1294), spent another forty years bringing all of China under Mongol

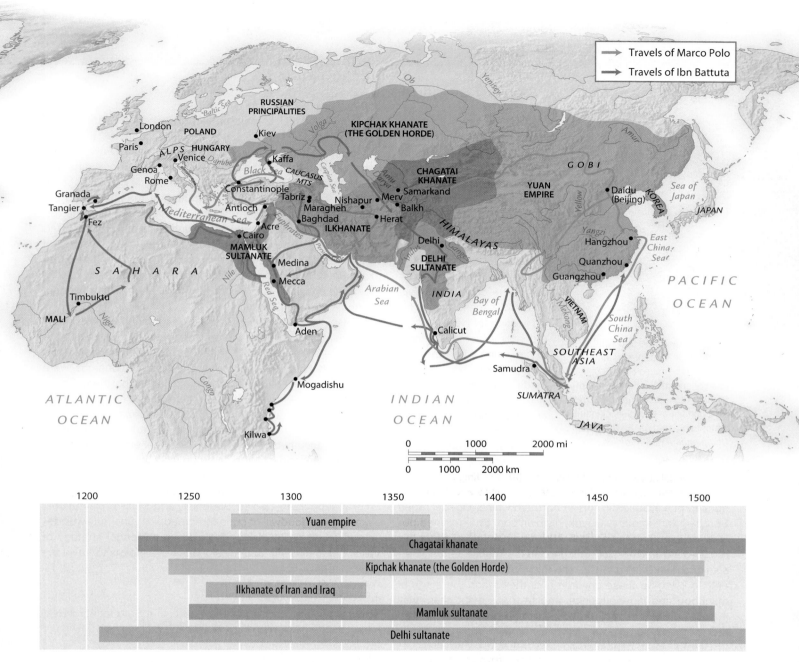

MAP 13.2 Mongol states and their neighbors, 1300.

What geographical or ecological features might help account for the Chagatai khanate being the economically weakest of the four great Mongol states?

authority. Horse archers had to advance into the subtropical south, where open pasture gave way to densely populated rice-growing lands and warm-climate diseases took many Mongol lives. One by one, however, the invaders captured the Song's stout-walled cities, while defecting Chinese sailors helped the Mongols win naval battles on the southern rivers and coasts. The great capital of Hangzhou fell in 1276, and the last Song emperor died three years later.

Kubilai Khan, adopting the dynastic name Yuan, meaning "the origin," united northern and southern China for the first time in a century and a half. But partly to keep up military momentum and to protect his position against family rivals, he campaigned furiously throughout his reign, incorporating the far southwestern region of Yunnan into the Yuan state, attacking Burma, and sending naval expeditions against Vietnam and Java. He also asserted Mongol domination over mountainous Korea, where the rulers of the Koryo dynasty agreed humbly to pay tribute.

Once Korea was subdued, Kubilai looked east across the Korea Strait to Japan, which he and his commanders knew to have a prosperous rice economy, numerous towns, and busy trade with Chinese ports. In the later thirteenth

Sorghaghtani Beki: A Woman of Influence

Sorghaghtani Beki and Tolui. Some of the most historically informative images of the Mongol era, including this one of Sorghaghtani Beki and Tolui, are to be found in Persian physician and historian Rashid al-Din Hamadani's *Compendium of Chronicles.*

Ever since Chingis Khan's rise to power, women linked to the royal household by birth or marriage had taken a strong and visible part in politics. Sorghaghtani Beki was perhaps the most gifted of these women. The niece of a nomad chief that Chingis had defeated, she was given in marriage to Tolui, the youngest of the conqueror's four sons. Tolui spent most of his life fighting for his father and probably seldom went home to his young wife, who very likely managed his lands and herds in his absence.

Tolui died in 1229, just two years after Chingis, leaving Sorghaghtani a widow with four strapping sons. No doubt, she already had political influence because Ogedei, Tolui's older brother and successor to Chingis as Great Khan, awarded her the governorship of a sizable territory in northern China. Ogedei urged Sorghaghtani to marry Guyuk, his own son. She declined politely, arguing that the education and training of her four boys required all her time. According to the fourteenth-century Persian historian Rashid al-Din, she told Ogedei, "[M]y thought is only to bring up these children until they reach the stage of manhood and independence, and to try to make them well mannered and not liable to go apart and hate each other so that, perhaps, some great thing may come of their unity."[7]

Before great things could happen, however, Sorghaghtani had to build her own power base against her rivals. Her toughest foe was Toregene, Ogedei's wife and Guyuk's mother. After Ogedei died, Toregene dominated palace affairs for several years, even during her son's short tenure as Great Khan (1246–1248). Meanwhile, Sorghaghtani bided her time, forging alliances with Mongol generals and the enemies of Guyuk's family.

Her political skills paid off in 1251, when the assembly of Mongol notables made her eldest son, Mongke, the Great Khan. According to Rashid al-Din, "she had always conciliated her kinsfolk and relations by the bestowing of gifts and presents, . . . so that after the death of Guyuk Khan most men were of one mind as to the entrusting of the khanate to her eldest son, Mongke Khan."[8] Unfortunately, she died the following year, never knowing how much three of her sons would achieve. Mongke led the empire effectively for eight years and extended its borders. Her second son, Kubilai, became Great Khan in 1260, completed the conquest of China, and ruled it for three decades. Her third son, Hulagu, founded the Mongol khanate of Iran and Iraq.

Rashid al-Din testified that Sorghaghtani "was extremely intelligent and able and towered above all the women in the world."[9] As an administrator and politician she modeled two policies that her sons, as well as later Mongol monarchs, were well advised to follow. In governing part of northern China, she discouraged conversion of arable land to animal pasture, recognizing that in the long run Chinese farms would generate far more tax revenue than would horse and sheep herding. When he assumed power, Kubilai Khan generally followed her example. Second, she took a broad view of religious practice. Like some other prominent women of the House of Chingis, she was a Nestorian Christian. But she also gave money and moral support to Daoist, Buddhist, and Muslim institutions, winning the goodwill of conquered peoples. She may well deserve credit for initiating the celebrated Mongol strategy of allowing merchants and missionaries of all faiths to travel the silk roads.

Thinking Critically

How would you characterize the skills that Sorghaghtani Beki displayed as a woman involved in Mongol politics?

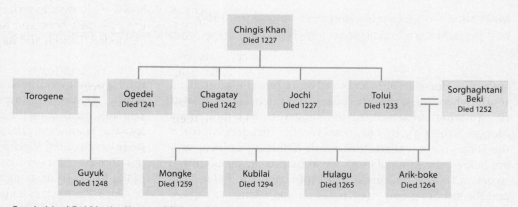

Sorghahtani Beki in the House of Chingis Genealogy.

century, the shoguns (supreme commanders) of the Kama-kura family (1185–1333) claimed to rule Japan, but in fact they progressively lost power to a host of regional land barons and their private armies of samurai warriors. This combination of agrarian wealth and political vulnerability appears to have convinced the restless Kubilai to seize at least part of Japan, rallying Korean forces to help him do the job. He made two seaborne assaults on the islands, the first in 1274, the second in 1281, in each case marshaling thousands of Chinese ships. Both campaigns ended in disaster, however, owing partly to the skill of Japanese archers and partly to storms at sea. In the second offensive, a Pacific typhoon that the Japanese declared a kamikaze, or "divine wind," wrecked much of the invading fleet. Thereafter Japan remained free of Mongol intrusions, though the heavy cost of repelling the invasions contributed to further political disorder in the islands in the next century.

Far western conquests and the founding of the Golden Horde.
Mongol destruction of the Jin dynasty in the mid-1230s freed up troops for a new western offensive into the relatively well-watered steppes west of the Volga River, an invasion route that Huns, Magyars, and other nomads had traced in earlier centuries. The kingdom of Rus (see Chapter 11) offered the invaders an attractive target. Centered in the river valleys north of the Black Sea, this Viking-founded state had flourished in the eleventh and twelfth centuries, transforming the little trading post of Kiev into a splendid Orthodox Christian capital. By 1200, however, Kiev no longer had much authority over regional Russian princes, who competed with one another for territory and the tax revenues extracted from Slavic farmers. Turkic-speaking nomads known as the Kipchaks pastured on the western grasslands, but they had no strong tribal confederation. Taking advantage of these conditions, Batu, a grandson of Chingis, led a huge force across Russia in 1237, sacking towns, burning churches, and murdering peasants. The Russian princes, fatally underestimating the Mongol threat, put up no coordinated resistance. Kiev fell in 1240, and the Kipchak Turks either fled or, hedging their bets, joined the Mongol side.

In 1241, Mongol pursuit of Kipchak enemies escaping into Hungary turned into a full-scale invasion of eastern Europe. One army dashed into Poland, while a second force advanced south of the Carpathian Mountains into the Kingdom of Hungary, at that time a large Catholic Christian monarchy. The region's mounted knights united in defense, but the Mongols annihilated twenty-five thousand Polish fighters while their other cavalry wing destroyed a Hungarian

Bronze seal of a Mongol commander. This relic from Kubilai Khan's lost fleet was retrieved by a Japanese fisherman in the late twentieth century. It is engraved in Chinese and in Phagspa, a written form of Mongolian. Why might an item such as this have been brought onboard a Mongol warship headed for Japan?

force under King Bela IV (r. 1235–1270). In the following weeks, Mongol raiding bands advanced as far west as the Adriatic Sea. News of the Mongol storm caused panicky speculation in Rome and other European capitals. Matthew Paris, an English monk, described the invaders, whom Europeans called Tartars, from reports he received: "Swarming like locusts over the face of the earth . . . , they have razed cities, cut down forests, overthrown fortresses, pulled up vines, destroyed gardens, killed townspeople and peasants. . . . They come with the swiftness of lightning to the confines of Christendom, ravaging and slaughtering, striking everyone with terror and incomparable horror."[10]

Having smashed eastern Europe's best armored knights, the Mongols might then have pushed into Germany and Italy. In 1241, however, the Great Khan Ogedei died, prompting Batu to suspend the campaign and return to Mongolia to deal with the royal succession. Historians have also suggested an ecological reason for the withdrawal: Hungary and Poland had insufficient pasture to support hundreds of thousands of Mongol horses for very long. And far western Europe, wet and forested, offered no ecological base at all for pastoralists and their huge herds.

The Mongols never returned to Hungary and Poland, but they did remain in Russia. There, Batu and his descendants founded the khanate of Kipchak, or, as Russians later called it, the Golden Horde (perhaps a reference to the ruler's camp and his yellow tent). The khans left the Russian Christian principalities intact but considered them political dependencies, sending cavalry to collect annual tributes, intervening in their dynastic affairs, and requiring the princes to make regular appearances at the Mongol court. (Russian nobles were known to write their wills before they went.) After the conquest, however, the Mongol regime left the Russian Orthodox Church and its institutions largely alone.

The Ilkhanate of Iran and Iraq.
Between 1256 and 1260, forces under Hulagu, another grandson of Chingis, swept across Southwest Asia nearly to the shores of the Mediterranean. In this campaign the Mongols faced no great empire but only a cluster of relatively small states ruled by descendants of the Turkic warriors who had invaded the region two centuries earlier. The Sunni Muslim caliph reigned in Baghdad, but soldiers at his disposal controlled very little territory. First crossing Iran's grassy corridors, Turko-Mongol archers swarmed into the Tigris-Euphrates valley, capturing Baghdad in 1258 and killing tens of thousands.[11] According to one Muslim legend, Hulagu arrested the caliph, had him rolled in a carpet, and laid him on a

A relaxed Hulagu. The Mongol conqueror of Iran and Iraq sips from a bowl as he reclines on the ground. He might be drinking *qumizz*, or fermented mare's milk, the Mongols' favorite beverage. This imagined portrayal of Hulagu dates to the sixteenth century. What other objects besides the bowl do you see in the picture?

field for his cavalry to trample. This event marked the end of the Abbasid Caliphate (750–1258).

The Mongols also invaded Syria, but there they met their match. Just a few years earlier, a group of Turkic *mamluks*, or slave soldiers (see Chapter 11) had taken power in Egypt and Syria and proclaimed the Mamluk sultanate (1250–1517). Because they controlled the fertile Nile valley and ruled from Cairo, the biggest city in western Afroeurasia, this regime had deep resources for waging war. In 1260, Mamluk cavalry soundly defeated Mongol intruders at a battlefield in what is today northern Israel, thus limiting their influence in Syria and preventing them from entering Egypt. Mongol forces, however, remained in control of Iran, Iraq, and part of Anatolia. There, Hulagu founded the state known formally as the Ilkhanate (1258–1335), a term referring to the ruler's formally subordinate status to the Great Khan in China. This regime ruled a large part of Southwest Asia assisted by local Muslim scholars and officials literate in Persian or Arabic.

The khanate of Chagatai. The khans of Chagatai, the fourth of the Mongol successor kingdoms, ruled a large part of Central Asia and eastern steppe lands. Revenues from silk road cities, notably Samarkand, accounted for much of the khanate's wealth, as it had a weaker agricultural base than did the other three Mongol states. Chagatai

forces operating from Afghanistan tried several times to add northern India to their realm, but the Turkic-led armies of the sultanate of Delhi (see Chapter 12) forced them out of the Indus valley.

Mongol Murderers: A Deserved Reputation?

Matthew Paris, the English monk quoted earlier, almost certainly never saw a Mongol, but that did not stop him from drawing a lurid picture of them as "inhuman and beastly, rather monsters than men."[12] This frightful image of the Tartar conquerors has endured through the ages. There is no doubt that the Mongols wantonly killed men, women, and children by the hundreds of thousands, severely disrupted economic life in several regions, and destroyed what today would be priceless artworks, buildings, and libraries. But the ravagers also used terror as a deliberate tactic. For example, the Mongol forces that invaded Central Asia in 1219 did not want to besiege walled cities for prolonged periods because they knew local pasture for their tens of thousands of horses would not last long. Therefore, by butchering everyone not useful as workers or slaves in a newly captured city, commanders sometimes convinced the terrified citizens of the next town along the invasion route to open the gates without a fight. If a town surrendered fast enough, the army avoided a siege, horses could be driven to new pasture, and the defeated inhabitants got to live, unless, as sometimes happened, the aggressors decided to kill them anyway. Also, Mongol generals usually called a halt to mass killing and destruction once they achieved control of a region. And later rulers, including Kubilai Khan in China, grasped the fact that long-term political success depended on a steady flow of revenue to the state. This would not happen if most tax-producing farmers and artisans were either dead or hiding in the hills. Therefore, in some places life returned to something like normal fairly quickly.

In northern China, where the invaders demolished more than ninety cities, the economic wounds cut deep. After three centuries of accelerating growth, China's overall population, especially in the north, dropped from as much as 120 million in 1200 to about 85 million a century later.[13] No doubt, warfare, urban destruction, and interruptions of the agricultural cycle all contributed to this precipitous decline. On the other hand, Kubilai ordered his armies to show some restraint in southern China by leaving most cities intact. He permitted cooperative Chinese landlords to keep their estates and peasants to cultivate their rice fields. Therefore, the southern economy survived the conquest fairly intact. In the north, by contrast, the once-flourishing and highly advanced iron industry never recovered from the damage to property and trade.

In Russia, where urbanization, commerce, and Orthodox Christian culture had been advancing, Batu's ferocious assault of 1237–1240 sent the region spiraling into depression. For a century after the conquest, the khans of the Golden Horde continued to pump wealth from Russian princes. These landowning Christian nobles had to pay tribute, but they suffered little themselves, passing most of the financial burden to Slavic peasants who eked out meager livings from the cold northern soil.

In Central and Southwest Asia, the invasions of 1219–1223 and 1256–1260 severely damaged farming. In northern Iran the Mongols killed or scared off so many rural folk that fragile irrigation canals and underground channels silted up, dams collapsed, and salt deposits accumulated. The onslaught transformed a peasantry that had been large and free into one that was for a long time reduced in population and bound to the land by estate lords. In Iraq the Tigris-Euphrates valley's irrigation systems had been deteriorating quite steadily since the ninth century. The Mongol devastation gave it another severe jolt. Nearly a half-century after the conquest, the Persian historian Hamd-Allah Mustawfi predicted "that even if for a thousand years to come no evil befalls the country, yet will it not be possible completely to repair the damage, and bring back the land to the state in which it was formerly."[14]

In short, the Mongol assaults across Eurasia caused immense and long-term damage, but it was also geographically uneven. Some regions that came under Mongol rule suffered much more keenly than others, and all of them recovered at least partially in the following centuries.

The Ambiguous Mongol Peace

> **FOCUS** What consequences did Mongol conquests and state building have for peoples of Eurasia in the thirteenth and fourteenth centuries?

After 1260, when the unified empire splintered, wars among the four successor states became chronic. The khanates of the Golden Horde and Iran-Iraq had consistently bad relations, especially rivalry for control of the trade routes and rich pastures of the Caucasus Mountains. In East Asia, Kubilai Khan spent much of his long reign battling his cousins in neighboring Chagatai. At the same time, however, he formed a close alliance with the Ilkhanate, also an enemy of Chagatai. Therefore, a shaky power balance among the Mongol empires helped keep warfare intermittent and local, and this allowed merchants, missionaries, and scholars to take to the trans-Eurasian highways in much greater numbers than in the time of Chingis. This partial and often fragile Mongol Peace endured well into the fourteenth century.

Silk Road Traffic

Long-distance trade across Inner Eurasia flourished once again. Once in control, Mongol rulers encouraged this commercial renewal in two major ways. First, they and the local elites who agreed to collaborate with them consumed large quantities of luxury goods, some of them transported long distances. Affluent families in Iran and Iraq wanted top-quality ceramics and silks from China. Their counterparts in China coveted carpets, ornamental glass, and other wares from Southwest Asia. Much of the trade that crossed Inner Eurasia in the Mongol era was "official," that is, valuable and exotic goods destined as diplomatic gifts, tribute payments, and political rewards from high-ranking officers to underlings. Moreover, the overland trade reached far beyond the Mongol domains, extending into Southeast Asia, India, North Africa, and western Europe.

Second, the Mongol regimes promoted commerce by creating an effective system of military and political communications. Ogedei Khan probably initiated the military network known as the *yam*, a system of routes, way stations, horses, and supplies used by the army to speed orders, information, and envoys from one part of the empire to another. Mongol governors permitted merchants and other civilians to use this network as long as those travelers had official authorization. This type of passport was often inscribed on a metal or wooden tablet called a *paiza*. Mongol officers also had the cavalry power to help safeguard commercial caravans, deterring local chiefs or bandits from robbing merchants or collecting illicit tolls.

As long as silk-road journeyers carried their *paizas*, commanders paid little attention to their religious or ethnic affiliations. Therefore, after the Mongols withdrew from Poland and Hungary in 1242, Catholic Christian merchants gradually worked up the courage to travel farther east than they ever had before. In the mid-thirteenth century, western Europe was nearing the peak of a three-century curve of strong economic growth. Consequently, aristocratic families and rich town burghers (businesspeople) craved foreign luxuries. Italian shippers, who already dominated the eastern Mediterranean routes, began sailing through the Bosporus strait to the Black Sea. This took them to the very edge of Inner Eurasia to meet and barter with Muslim silk-road traders at northern Black Sea ports such as Kaffa (modern Feodosiya). Small numbers of Italians journeyed as far as China in the later thirteenth and early fourteenth centuries. The Venetian merchant Marco Polo, along with his father and uncle, lived in China from 1275 to 1292. According to his own testimony, he served for a time in the Mongol administration. These Christian visitors, however, numbered far fewer than the thousands of Muslim and Buddhist traders who plied the silk routes.

Slaves, Diplomats, and Career Seekers

People as well as goods were on the move in Mongol times. The four Mongol governments that wielded authority over millions of people depended on tax and accounting skills, diplomatic protocols, and farm and engineering technologies about which Mongolian or Turkic herders knew little. To get the labor and expertise they needed, Mongol officials offered salaries and honors to educated people to serve as clerks, artisans, technicians, and spiritual advisers. The khans of the Golden Horde employed numerous Russian Orthodox Christians as scribes and consultants, while the rulers of the Ilkhanate depended heavily on educated Persians and Arabs to staff state ministries. Across Inner Eurasia, Mongol commanders relied on literate Uighur-speaking Turks, most of them Buddhists or Christians, who lived in the oasis towns. Where the carrots of salary and reward did not work, the stick almost always did. Mongol captains had no more hesitation about forcing people to resettle in some distant land than they had about driving their herds to new pastures. When he invaded Khwarizm, Chingis took along hundreds of Chinese military engineers, whether they wanted to go or not. He also enslaved thousands of Muslim artisans, scholars, and young women and marched them to Mongolia to labor for the army, the royal court, or elite households.

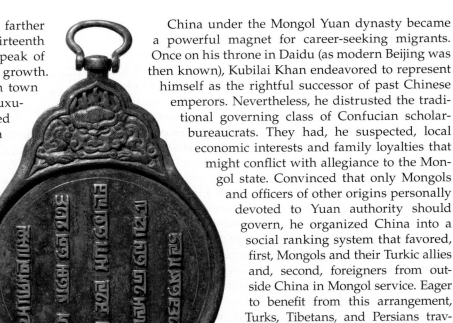

A Mongol safe conduct pass. The silver inscription on this iron passport from Mongol-ruled China reads: "By the strength of Eternal Heaven, an edict of the khan. He who has not respect shall be guilty." The script is Phakpa, named for a Tibetan monk who invented it to write Mongolian. What do you think the phrase "he who has not respect shall be guilty" might mean?

China under the Mongol Yuan dynasty became a powerful magnet for career-seeking migrants. Once on his throne in Daidu (as modern Beijing was then known), Kubilai Khan endeavored to represent himself as the rightful successor of past Chinese emperors. Nevertheless, he distrusted the traditional governing class of Confucian scholar-bureaucrats. They had, he suspected, local economic interests and family loyalties that might conflict with allegiance to the Mongol state. Convinced that only Mongols and officers of other origins personally devoted to Yuan authority should govern, he organized China into a social ranking system that favored, first, Mongols and their Turkic allies and, second, foreigners from outside China in Mongol service. Eager to benefit from this arrangement, Turks, Tibetans, and Persians traveled to China by the thousands to take up jobs as soldiers, scribes, officials, and tax collectors. For example, Christian Alans, an ethnic group from the faraway Caucasus Mountains, traveled to China to take charge of Yuan heavy cavalry.

This influx did not, however, significantly alter China's cultural landscape. The Mongols continued to depend on Chinese clerks, judges, and officials to staff lower levels of government. And as long as civil order prevailed, Kubilai and his hirelings interfered little with Chinese social and cultural life. In fact, he became a patron of Chinese art and literature, and his reign witnessed a flowering of Chinese drama, poetry, painting, and Neo-Confucian philosophy. Moreover, because the Mongols reunified northern and southern China, artists and scholars exchanged ideas more intensively than they had during the previous century and a half.

Cross-Fertilization in Science and Technology

The Mongol regimes in China and Iran-Iraq maintained a particularly firm political alliance. Partly because of that friendship, the links of intellectual communication connecting those two urbanized regions were sophisticated and lively. When Chingis's grandson Hulagu invaded Iraq in 1258, he let his soldiers sack Baghdad and burn its libraries. Within two years, however, he began to rebuild, patronizing scholars and founding an astronomical observatory at Maragheh in northwestern Iran. There, Chinese and Muslim astronomers worked together under Nasir al-Din al-Tusi (1201–1274), a celebrated Persian mathematician, to produce complex astronomical tables, which continued in use for centuries. Paralleling this development, Kubilai Khan set up the Institute for Muslim Astronomy in Beijing. There, Muslim visiting scholars collaborated with Chinese scientists. Like all premodern rulers who sponsored astronomy, the Mongol khans wanted useful information, especially precise readings of the heavens for signs and omens of the future. They also needed accurate calendars to keep track of the agricultural cycle and to predict lunar and solar eclipses—a good way to impress their subjects. Owing to the size of the Mongol domains, rulers commanded scholars to work out complex conversion tables for matching up several different calendar systems in use across Eurasia.

The China–Iran connection also produced key advances in geography, agronomy, and medicine. Chinese maps made in the fourteenth and fifteenth centuries reveal detailed knowledge of India, eastern Africa, and Europe. A Korean chart of 1402 showed identifiable outlines of Europe and the Mediterranean. Owing to plant diffusion from Iran to China, East Asians added carrots, watermelons, and a new variety of lemon to their diet. Conversely, westbound travelers introduced Chinese rhubarb, which people consumed as a digestive aid and purgative, to Southwest Asia and Europe, where the sick swore by its healing properties. Ghazan, the most enlightened Mongol khan of Iran and Iraq (r. 1295–1304), planted a royal garden in the city of Tabriz to experiment with Chinese plants and seeds. According to the Persian scholar Rashid al-Din, the khan gave an order "to bring from all countries seeds of various fruit-bearing trees, aromatic plants, and cereals which were not in Tabriz and which no one there had ever seen before, and to graft these shoots and branches."[15]

The Changing Religious Map

Chingis Khan and his early successors consulted Mongolian shamans on matters of the supernatural. But they also took a cosmopolitan view of celestial truth, believing that Nestorian monks, Tibetan Buddhists, Muslim mystics, and Catholic missionaries might all possess the keys to some part of it. Just as they employed Chinese shipbuilders or Persian siege engineers, Mongol rulers enlisted the spiritual services of any cleric who might bring good fortune to the House of Chingis. It is not that the Mongol khans had a moral ideology of tolerance but that they encouraged whatever devices might work to advance their power, including beneficial rituals and prayers of whatever religion might be at hand.

In the first few generations, no Mongol khan adopted any of the major religions, though Kubilai sponsored palace debates among clerics of different faiths. Tibetan monks attracted the attention of the royal court with their vivid rituals and willingness to declare Kubilai an incarnation of the Buddha. Their influence rose in China in the later thirteenth century, but after 1368, when Mongol power ended, the various Buddhist sects and schools in China retained about the same

Astronomers at work. In this miniature painting from the fifteenth century, Nasir al-Din al-Tusi, the figure on the right, sits at his writing desk in the astronomical observatory at Maragheh. The circular brass objects in this image are astrolabes, instruments used to make astronomical measurements. Al-Tusi persuaded the Mongol khan Hulagu to found this institution.

strength they had had before the invasion. In Mongolia itself, however, Tibetan Buddhism became the dominant faith.

Once the Mongol threat to western Europe receded, Catholic Christian missionaries joined Italian traders on journeys to the territories of the khans. As of the mid-thirteenth century, the Christian crusader states still clung to pieces of the Syrian coast, holding out Catholic hopes of progress against Islam in Southwest Asia. Some Roman leaders speculated that a concerted missionary effort, perhaps in alliance with Nestorian Christians in Asia, might bring pagan Mongols and Turks over to Christ and even facilitate an alliance between European and Mongol states against Muslim kingdoms.

The Qutb Minar. The Muslim Turkic founder of the Delhi sultanate started building this mosque in the late thirteenth century, making use of demolished Hindu temples as building material. The Qutb Minar, the mosque's minaret, rises nearly 238 feet above the Delhi landscape. It is one of the gems of Indo-Muslim architecture, melding Arab, Persian, Afghan, and South Asian elements of design and ornamentation.

The church sponsored several missions to Asia, and European monarchs exchanged diplomatic letters with Mongol khans. In 1245, for example, Pope Innocent IV sent a small mission to Mongolia under the leadership of the Franciscan monk John of Plano Carpini. Far from converting the Mongol leadership, however, John returned home with a letter from the Great Khan Guyuk commanding both the pope and all Christian kings to come to the khan's court to offer their submission. Marco Polo, his father, and his uncle went overland to Beijing in 1271 not only as Venetian merchants but also as representatives of the pope. Beginning in the 1290s, larger parties of Catholic priests and monks went east to convert souls and minister to Christians living in China.

Mongol rulers also made a few initiatives of their own. In 1287, Rabban Sauma, a Nestorian Christian, led a delegation to Europe as representative of the Mongol Ilkhanate. He traveled to Constantinople, then to Rome, Genoa, and France, where he met both the French king Philip IV and the English monarch Edward I. He tried to persuade the Catholic Church to make common cause with the Mongols against the Egyptian Mamluks, though to no avail. He left Europe carrying little more than papal letters, which lectured Nestorian Christian leaders on proper Catholic doctrine.

None of these long-distance contacts between Europeans and Mongols yielded firm results. No khans converted to Catholic Christianity, no anti-Muslim alliance materialized, and in 1291 the Mamluks of Egypt evicted the Christian crusaders from their last stronghold in Syria. When the shaky Mongol Peace disintegrated in the later fourteenth century, the church lost all contact with its missionaries in China.

Among the major religions, Islam achieved the greatest gains during the Mongol era. Between the late thirteenth and early fourteenth centuries, the khans of Iran-Iraq, the Golden Horde, and Chagatai all converted to Sunni Islam, thereby identifying religiously with the majority of their subjects. Turkic-speaking Muslims continued to migrate across Anatolia, some in flight from Mongol armies, others in their ranks. Consequently, Anatolia's Greek Christian population declined steadily. In India, the Delhi sultanate encouraged Muslims of Persian and Arab origin to migrate to India to take official jobs, introduce Islam to Hindu villagers, and settle as farmers in the Indus and Ganges valleys. The Turkic elite promoted mosque building and Muslim education, and Sufi preachers, that is, missionaries of mystical Islam, fanned out across the Hindu countryside performing righteous devotions and showing the way to unity with the divine. Consequently, Islam became established in the fourteenth century as a significant and growing minority faith in South Asia.

Profit and Power in the Southern Seas

FOCUS What factors accounted for the continuing expansion of long-distance exchange in the Indian Ocean and China Seas in the thirteenth and fourteenth centuries?

Historians have sometimes referred to the shipping routes that ran east and west across the Eastern Hemisphere as the "silk roads of the sea." China supplied much of the merchandise that camel caravans carried across Inner Eurasia, but it also pumped great quantities of goods into the sea lanes (see Map 13.3). Marco Polo reported on the trade that passed through the port of Quanzhou in southern China in the late thirteenth century: "I can tell you further that the

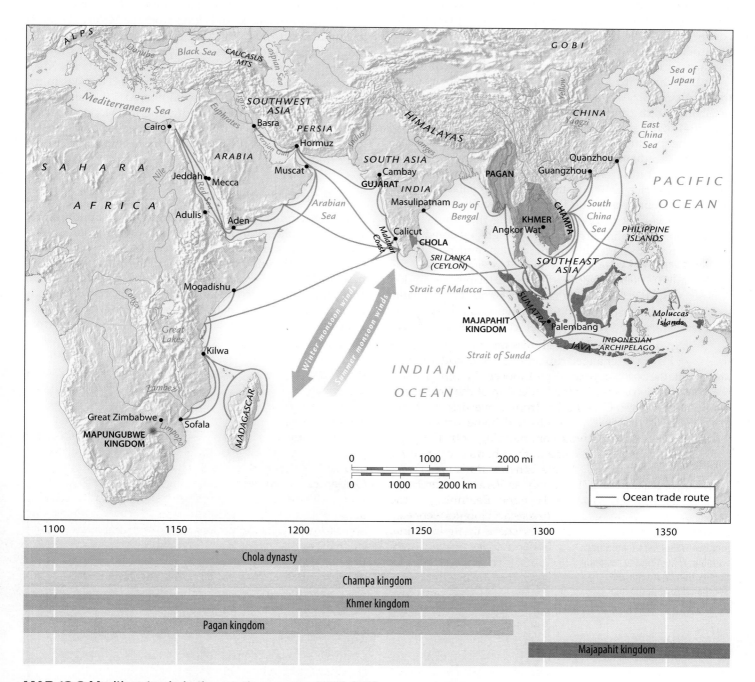

MAP 13.3 Maritime trade in the southern seas, 1200–1350.

Slight annual variations in the shift from one seasonal monsoon wind cycle to the other could affect the price of goods in ports of the southern seas. How would you account for that phenomenon?

revenue accruing to the Great Khan from this city and port is something colossal."[16]

Trade and State Building in Southeast Asia

In the same era that huge Mongol and Turkic states sprawled across Eurasia, many small monarchies, independent city-states, and self-governing merchant organizations rimmed the seas of Southeast Asia. A few states had enough ships and sailors to dominate an entire maritime region for a few decades, and well-organized pirate bands prowled the coasts. Despite the immense value of seaborne trade, however, no state had the fiscal resources to control long sea passages or large numbers of ports.

In Indochina, the long tropical peninsula that separates the South China Sea from the Bay of Bengal, the monarchies of Champa (7th century–1471), Khmer (889–1434), and Pagan (1044–1287) all prospered contemporaneously with Song and Mongol China. Champa had the busiest international waterborne trade because it faced the South China Sea and the routes that ran from East Asia to the Indian Ocean. All three of these rice-growing states had royal palace cultures that blended Hindu and Buddhist ceremony. Theravada Buddhism, the variant of Buddhist teaching that emphasized meditation, self-denial, and spiritual insight, emerged gradually as the dominant faith in the region, and remains so today. The Khmer state reached its peak of prosperity in the twelfth and thirteenth centuries, when its farmers expanded wet-rice irrigated farming to new areas and its merchants exported cardamom, tropical woods, ivory, and vividly colored feathers to the Chinese market. Farm taxes and tens of thousands of slaves permitted the Khmer rulers to build stupendous Hindu and Buddhist temples modeled on Indian architectural forms. The temple complex at Angkor Wat, reclaimed from the rainforest in the nineteenth century, is the largest religious structure in the world, though it represents only a fraction of a complex of temples that covered about 135 square miles.

In the Indonesian archipelago, commercial power in the thirteenth century centered on the island of Java. There, a succession of small naval states amassed revenues trans-shipping nutmeg, mace, and cloves from the Moluccas Islands to China and through the Malacca and Sunda straits to the Indian Ocean. Indeed, Java occupied such a key strategic position in the southern seas trade that in 1292 Kubilai Khan launched a Mongol war fleet southward 2,200 miles to try to seize the island. The force numbered 1,000 ships, but the campaign on land went badly, and the Mongols pulled out. In the aftermath of the war, the kingdom of Majapahit (1295–1527) arose as the pivotal Javanese emporium for the spice trade.

The South Asian Pivot

In southern India, commercialization and town building after 1000 C.E. paralleled, if on a somewhat smaller scale, China's economic florescence. As Indian Ocean traffic grew, southern Indian ports became vital turntables in the trans-hemispheric network. Arabian Sea dhows, Malay ships, and gigantic Chinese junks all dropped anchor in these ports, relaying goods from one group of international merchants to another. Marco Polo, who visited the Malabar Coast on his way home from

Angkor Wat. The twelfth-century Khmer monarch Suryavarman II oversaw construction of this central temple complex in Angkor, his capital. Dedicated to the Hindu deity Vishnu, the temple symbolizes the cosmos. The central tower represents Mt. Meru, the hub of the universe and the home of the gods. By the late thirteenth century, however, Angkor Wat became identified more with Buddhist than Hindu worship, reflecting the religious fluidity that characterized Southeast Asia in the late premodern centuries.

China, observed that visiting ships took on not only Indian products like pepper and cinnamon but also goods that were in transit from other regions:

> When merchants come here from overseas, they load their ships with brass, which they use as ballast, cloth of gold and silk, sendal [sandalwood], gold, silver, cloves, spikenard [an aromatic oil], and other such spices that are not produced here. You must know that ships come here from very many parts, notably from the great province of Manzi [China], and goods are exported to many parts. Those that go [westward] to Aden are carried thence to Alexandria.[17]

A thirteenth-century visitor to crowded southern Indian ports might hear traders speaking Tamil and several other Indian languages, plus Arabic, Persian, Malay, Chinese, and Swahili. The port populations rose and fell in rhythm with the seasonal shifts in the monsoon winds, which dictated the arrival and departure of ships and the prices of goods. In the eleventh and twelfth centuries, merchants of Egyptian and North African origin, including Muslims, Jews, and Coptic Christians, settled in the southern Indian ports. They used Arabic as a common language of trade, but many of them married local Indian women, enriching the ethnic complexity of those towns. Gradually, most coastal rulers converted to Islam, and well-organized Muslim firms pushed the Jewish and Christian merchants to the margins of the commercial economy. By the thirteenth century, the Arabian Sea basin was in commercial terms an almost exclusively Muslim "lake."

In southern India a variety of coastal states, self-governing ports, and agrarian kingdoms competed for territory and resources. In the southeast, the Hindu dynasty of Chola ruled between about 850 and 1279, extracting revenues from peasants who farmed rice in interior river valleys and from Tamil-speaking merchants who sold Indian textiles around the Bay of Bengal. Devotees of the Hindu deity Shiva, the Chola monarchs became rich enough to build numbers of soaring stone temples, whose communities of priests, servants, students, and slaves engaged in artisanry, trade, and banking, contributing significantly to the southern Indian commercial economy. The Chola monarchy, however, had continually to fend off rival states, and in the early thirteenth century it slipped into the lower ranks of South Asian regional powers.

East and Southern Africa in the Indian Ocean World

The Indian Ocean trade network extended far down the East African seaboard, and in the thirteenth century peoples of both the coasts and the deep interior linked themselves to the maritime web on a larger scale. As we have seen in earlier chapters, seaports had been multiplying along East African shores since the early first millennium C.E. As in southern India, merchant princes dominated these towns and collaborated with the leading business families. Most of the coastal town inhabitants were descendants of people who had arrived from East African interior regions many centuries earlier. By the thirteenth century these populations had largely embraced Islam. In addition, Muslim merchants, scholars, and Sufi divines from Arabia and other parts of Southwest Asia constituted significant and influential minorities in the larger towns. At the heart of the region's distinctive cultural identity was Swahili (or Kiswahili), a language of the Bantu family whose vocabulary includes many words of Arabic origin. Swahili emerged from about 1000 C.E., not only as the principal language of the coastal city-states, but also as the primary medium of commercial communication.

In the thirteenth and fourteenth centuries, Mogadishu, today the capital of Somalia, was probably the largest and busiest East African port. The Moroccan traveler Ibn Battuta, who spent a week or two in the city as a guest of its Somali Muslim ruler (see Map 13.2), reports on the business customs that facilitated trade between foreign sea merchants and Somali wholesalers:

> When a ship arrives at the anchorage, the sumbuqs (these are small boats) come out to it. In every sumbuq is a group of young people of the town, and every one of them brings a covered dish with food in it. He offers it to one of the merchants of the ships and says, "This is my guest." Each one of them does similarly. When the merchant disembarks from the ship he goes nowhere but to the house of his host from among these young people. . . . When he lodges with his host, he [the host] sells his goods for him and buys on his behalf.[18]

Kilwa, a second port of great commercial importance, lay farther down the coast on an island off modern Tanzania. The mercantile families of Kilwa prayed in expansive mosques of coral rock, entertained guests in stone houses with sunken courtyards, and dined off Chinese porcelain. Shipwrights, masons, fishers, and artisans led more frugal lives. Male and female slaves brought from the African interior occupied the bottom of the social scale.

The prosperity of the Swahili coast depended not only on seaborne trade but also on traffic with people of the region's interior. Agricultural and herding populations with economies based on grain, bananas, or cattle were growing steadily in the highland region around East Africa's Great Lakes, in the wet forests of the Congo River system, and in the temperate savanna lands of the far south. More towns appeared, and monarchs began to organize political life in more complicated ways. These developments raised the stakes for commercial links with the Indian Ocean coast. In the twelfth century, for example, Mapungubwe, a kingdom of farmers who spoke Bantu languages and the earliest state we know of in southern Africa, amassed wealth partly from exports of ivory and gold. These commodities were carried down the Limpopo River to the shore of what is today Mozambique. There, Swahili merchants bought goods, presumably in return for textiles and other products from the wider world.

The stone enclosure at Great Zimbabwe. Europeans who first saw the ruins of Great Zimbabwe in the late nineteenth century, educated as they were in that era's ideology of white racial superiority, refused to believe that local Africans had constructed this urban complex. They attributed the buildings, rather, to ancient Phoenician or Arab visitors. Archaeological work in the twentieth century proved otherwise, and in fact skilled African artisans built in stone in many places on the Zimbabwe Plateau. The construction at Great Zimbabwe suggests the presence of a strong political authority. How does the site indicate that?

In the thirteenth century a larger stream of gold began to flow from southern Africa into the trans-hemispheric web. The main gold sources were on the Zimbabwe Plateau, a savanna region favorable to grain farming and cattle breeding. The population spoke a Bantu language ancestral to modern Shona, the majority language of modern Zimbabwe. We know that an important state flourished on the plateau from the existing evidence of stone buildings and enclosures that constituted the core of a large town that archaeologists have named Great Zimbabwe. This center, which prospered between the thirteenth and fifteenth centuries, attained a population of perhaps eighteen thousand. Finds of Chinese porcelain reveal Great Zimbabwe's Indian Ocean connection and the affluence of its population, or at least its chiefly families. After about 1430, the city declined, perhaps because an excessive buildup of people and cattle in the region led to ecological crisis. The gold trade, however, simply shifted to new centers somewhat farther north, and the Swahili city-states continued to profit from it into the fifteenth century.

Urban Society in Europe

FOCUS In what ways did Europe manifest the characteristics of a plural society in the thirteenth and fourteenth centuries?

Like Japan and Egypt, western Europe escaped Mongol devastation, if only by the skin of its teeth. Consequently, that region experienced no severe disruption of economic life comparable to what happened in China, Russia, and Southwest Asia. For example, in contrast to China, whose population declined significantly in the thirteenth century, Europe's numbers rose from about thirty-five to seventy million between 1100 and 1300. This growth was concentrated mainly in the temperate northwest from England to Germany. Farming production, commerce, and town building also continued to thrive, as they had been since the late tenth century.

Western Europe's continuing economic expansion took place in conditions of great political variety and flux. In the same era that Mongol khans built giant empires, Europe remained divided into numerous states, both large and small. The Catholic Church arched over them as the preeminent pan-European organization, but by the thirteenth century its authority over kings and princes was limited. In the absence of any single governing power, Europeans achieved remarkable skill at forming private associations devoted to various social, economic, and intellectual enterprises.

The laws, rituals, literature, and art of Catholic Christianity gave Europe its characteristic cultural style as an emerging civilization. In several respects, however, Europe remained remarkably pluralistic, characterized by considerable variety and diversity in politics, language, and social organization.

Many Governments and Languages

As of around 1200 the numerous states of Europe fell into three general categories: independent city-states, whose two principal clusters were in northern Italy and along the rim of the Baltic Sea; small regional kingdoms and principalities, notably the several German states in central Europe; and larger monarchies whose subject populations typically included peoples of varying language and ethnicity (see Map 13.4). Rivalries among these polities made Europe a place of persistent violence, but states also formed alliances, made treaties, and linked themselves to one another through a web of royal marriages.

Despite the political pluralism, several monarchies developed into strong regional states, which reined in the power of local noble families and penetrated remote areas to tax more people. The kings of France built the most efficient power base. Philip IV the Fair (r. 1285–1314) displayed great talent for enlisting loyal, well-educated administrators, who collected revenues on the king's behalf and executed royal commands over wider areas of what is today France. He strengthened ties between the royal court and the prosperous burghers of the growing towns, negotiating shrewdly with them for loans and taxes to advance royal centralization.

The English monarchy paralleled France in fortifying both royal bureaucracy and central legal institutions. King Edward I (r. 1272–1307) conquered mountainous Wales, and he crafted numerous new royal laws, replacing a hodgepodge of local customs. He consulted frequently with Parliament on state affairs, inviting the participation of lower-ranking knights and town leaders, as well as the great barons and bishops. The king had his personal council and secretariat, however, and Parliament remained one of several advisory bodies whose agendas the ruler largely set.

In the Iberian Peninsula, the monarchies of Aragon, Portugal, and Castile (Léon and Castile until they merged in 1230), all gained in centralization and wealth in the thirteenth century following the victory of Christian crusaders over the armies of the Muslim Almohad empire (see Chapter 12). In eastern Europe the kings of Hungary, which had become Catholic Christian in the eleventh century, showed special aptitude for expanding their borders and erecting strong

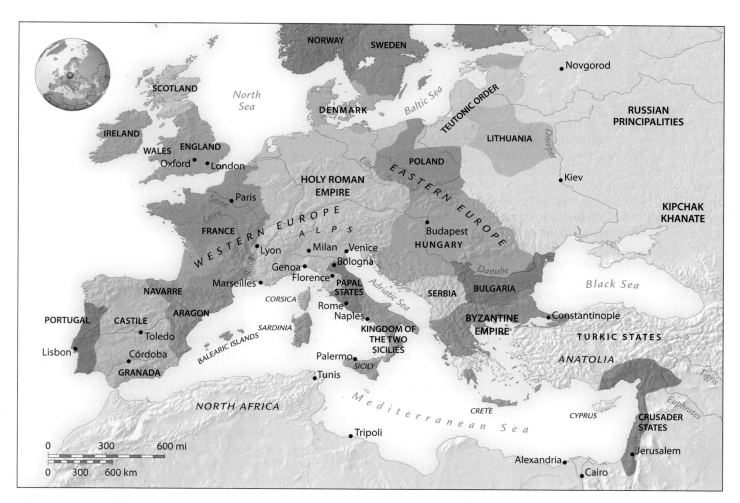

MAP 13.4 Major states in Europe, 1300.

What geographic features may help account for the borders of European states in 1300?

central institutions. The Mongol onslaught of 1241–1242, however, destroyed the Hungarian army and sent the region into several decades of depression.

Western Christendom also became more ethnically and linguistically diverse between the twelfth and fourteenth centuries because frontier expansion brought speakers of Hungarian, Finnish, Estonian, and several Slavic and Germanic languages into the Catholic fold. At the same time that the Roman church embraced a more diverse array of peoples, however, certain **vernacular languages** became dominant. This happened mainly because of the association of these languages with strong monarchies and because poets and essayists began to write in them. English, German, French, Italian, and Castilian Spanish were among the leading vernaculars. Latin, however, remained the premier medium of religion, law, and learning.

> **vernacular language** The native language of a region used by ordinary people.

Carpenters in stained glass. In Europe craft guilds often donated church windows. In this window in Chartres Cathedral in France, two carpenters work on a board resting on three sawhorses. Why do you think guilds wished to depict their professional activities in church windows?

Private Groups and Charters

No single monarch in Europe had the power to monitor or restrict private economic and social activity beyond the regional level. This gave individuals fairly wide latitude to band together privately to start businesses, organize trading ventures, engage in charitable work, or set up learning institutions. Indeed, European rulers, in competition with one another for financial resources, commonly sought alliances with private groups, offering them protections and liberties in return for political loyalty and regular payment of fees and taxes. Increasingly, private groups negotiated with political leaders for corporate status, forming associations of individuals that existed as entities under the law. Legally recognized corporate groups possessed rights and obligations, often spelled out in a charter granted by the king or other political authority. As new towns sprang up and urban businesspeople accumulated wealth, rulers saw advantages in awarding charters of rights and privileges to towns in return for allegiance and promises of revenue. Chartered towns multiplied in Spain and eastern Europe, as conquering knights enticed immigrant farmers and artisans to clear land and build market and manufacturing centers in return for legal incorporation.

Other private groups might seek a charter licensing them to mine silver, build ships, open a bank, or sell woolen cloth. Urban craft guilds—for merchants, goldsmiths, weavers, carpenters, and numerous other professions—secured charters authorizing them to manage their own affairs and to regulate standards. The principal type of corporate association for women was the religious convent. Urban women, however, sometimes participated in guilds and other chartered civic groups. In a few towns women who spun silk or embroidered cloth formed their own chartered guilds but always under some measure of male supervision.

To put Europe's medieval corporatism in comparative perspective, private activity in China took a rather different form. There, business enterprise typically centered on extended families (not just parents and children but also uncles, aunts, and cousins). This tended to restrict the size and resources of those groups, whereas in Europe a corporate venture might invite anyone who could offer talent or money to participate. Moreover, China's imperial government, including the Mongol Yuan dynasty, traditionally initiated and managed commercial, industrial, and cultural projects. A thirteenth-century Confucian civil servant would have been puzzled at the idea of private groups possessing rights in law that inhibited the emperor's officials from regulating their activities.

The Flow of Ideas

Europe's urban wealth, pluralistic politics, and growing access to the accumulated knowledge of the rest of Afroeurasia encouraged technological and intellectual innovation. When the Mongol conquests began, Europe already had strong links to the big Muslim and Greek Christian cities of the eastern Mediterranean, thanks to the initiatives of merchants, pilgrims, and crusaders. Those connections enlarged the stream of useful ideas from Southwest Asia, including new textile weaving methods, papermaking technology, and Syrian secrets for producing glass. Between about 1250 and 1350, western Christendom also benefited from the long-distance technological exchanges of the Mongol age. The magnetic compass, gunpowder, and block printing, all East Asian inventions as far as we know, reached western Europe sometime between the late twelfth and fourteenth centuries. European artisans lost no time tinkering with those novelties to improve them and put them to practical use.

At the same time, European artisans, backed by chartered guilds and affluent patrons, including monarchs, invented numerous new devices and techniques in the spheres of farm technology, cloth manufacture, shipbuilding, weaponry, and the design of churches and fortifications. The grandest innovation of the twelfth century was the Gothic church. Sophisticated mathematical calculations and engineering designs permitted master masons to construct sanctuaries whose stone walls soared as high as forty modern stories. The use of pointed arches, external supports called flying buttresses, and other new devices permitted builders to leave open spaces high up the walls. These were then fitted with colorful stained-glass windows that directed light onto the lofty vaulted ceilings.

Universities. Institutions of advanced learning bloomed across Europe from Spain to Poland in the thirteenth and fourteenth centuries. Universities arose out of western Christendom's expanding need for educated professionals to take jobs in governments, private firms, and the church as administrators, clerks, accountants, secretaries, teachers, lawyers, and priests. The earliest universities were modeled on schools associated with urban cathedrals, where priests offered Latin education to the sons of both aristocrats and townsfolk. The movement that started in Muslim lands a few centuries earlier to found colleges for advanced religious and legal study influenced European ideas of the university as a central place where scholars and students gathered, and often resided, to teach and learn.

Chartres Cathedral. The church of Saint-Denis north of Paris, together with the cathedral at Chartres, a small city forty miles southwest of the capital, provided the primary models for the Gothic style of church building across western Europe. The exterior half arches, or flying buttresses, shown in this view of the cathedral from the south, helped make the construction of high walls and large windows possible.

Class in session. This fourteenth-century painting shows the German monk Henry of Friemar lecturing at the University of Bologna in Italy. He appears to struggle to hold the attention of all of his students. The student third from the near end in the first row appears to be a women. Do you think a female student's presence would have been likely in a medieval European university?

The professors in early European universities, invariably members of the Catholic clergy, organized themselves in guilds and, like urban merchants and artisans, negotiated with political authorities for charters of self-regulation. In 1200, for example, France's King Philip Augustus awarded a "diploma" to the University of Paris by which its teachers and students could largely govern their own affairs subject to the authority of the pope rather than to the local bishop or the king's officers. By 1300 Europe had as many as twenty-three universities. Properly chartered, these institutions brought prestige to rulers but also enjoyed some safeguards against lords or bishops who might be tempted to meddle in the university's finances or curriculum. A university's course of study centered on grammar, rhetoric, and dialectic (logical reasoning and argumentation), and, depending on the particular institution's orientation, on theology, law, astronomy, mathematics, music, and natural philosophy (what we would call "science"). Universities also both stimulated and benefited from other intellectual developments in Europe. These included the spread of literacy beyond the aristocratic and clerical classes, the growing availability of books, and the emergence of new literary forms such as lyric poetry, romance narratives, and travel accounts. For example, Marco Polo's *The Description of the World*, published at the end of the thirteenth century, became a "best seller" among literate Europeans hungry for knowledge of foreign lands.

Scientific awakening. The organization of education in universities, combined with growing awareness of the world beyond Europe, set off intense debates in learned circles over the nature of reason, faith, and free will. The scholars who posed new philosophical and scientific questions started by consulting the existing knowledge available to them. Those sources included the Bible and the classics of Christian theology but also the great stores of learning housed in the cities around the Mediterranean rim. As European merchants and crusaders sent out new communication lines to the cities of Southwest Asia, North Africa, and Spain, Catholic Christian intellectuals gained more access to that knowledge.

Starting in the eighth century, Muslim scholars translated numerous Greek, Persian, and Sanskrit scientific and philosophical texts into Arabic, then corrected, synthesized, and expanded that knowledge. In the twelfth century, European academicians began to acquire linguistic skills to translate this library of manuscripts from Arabic, Greek, or Hebrew into Latin. They did much of this work in Toledo, Córdoba, Palermo (Sicily), and Constantinople, cities that lay along the frontiers between western Christendom and the Byzantine and Muslim spheres. Between about 1140 and 1280, linguists translated all of the surviving texts of the ancient Greek philosopher Aristotle, along with the extensive Arabic commentaries that clarified and expanded on his work.

Translations of scientific treatises gave European thinkers raw material for further innovation. Leonardo Fibonacci (1170–1240), for example, grew up in a port city in North Africa because his father served as an Italian commercial consul. Fibonacci took up the study of mathematics, subsequently traveling far and wide in the Muslim and Greek Mediterranean in search of knowledge. Returning to Italy, he authored several important treatises on geometry and numbers theory, including the first major work explaining the base-ten "Arabic" numerical system. Thanks to him and other scientists, Europe gradually exchanged Roman numerals for the system invented earlier in India that incorporated positional notation and the zero. This shift made possible more advanced mathematical studies.

Another European sage was the English monk Roger Bacon (1214–1294), who lived and worked in both Oxford and Paris and wrote on astronomy, mathematics, optics, alchemy, and numerous other subjects, drawing on Muslim and ancient classical learning. He argued that the key to understanding the universe was not deductive reasoning from general principles but rather inductive reasoning and experimentation, employing useful instruments to observe and measure natural phenomena. "If a man who has never seen fire should prove by adequate reasoning that fire burns and injures things and destroys them," Bacon wrote, "his mind would not be satisfied thereby until he place his hand on some combustible substance in the fire, so that he might prove by experience that which reasoning taught."[19] Bacon was also the first known European to describe the properties of gunpowder.

Scholastic theology. Despite his plea for practical experimentation, Bacon fully accepted the Christian teaching that nature and the cosmos is knowable to us through divine revelation. Muslim scholars had for several centuries been pondering Aristotle's claim that a First Mover (immortal, unchanging being) existed but that humans might also apprehend reality through systematic observation, analysis, and logic. Some Muslim thinkers identified Aristotle's First Mover with the One God and contended that we can understand his creation by exercising the intellectual powers he has given us. Armed with Christian theology, Aristotle's works, and Muslim commentaries, European scholars embarked on fresh philosophical inquiry. The new methodology, called **scholastic theology,** rested on the confidence that the universe might ultimately be understood through systematic questioning. Europe's great thirteenth-century synthesizer was Thomas Aquinas (1225–1274). A lecturer for many years at the University of Paris, he produced about one hundred scholarly works that aimed to harmonize Christian revelation with Aristotle's logic. The writings of Aquinas became the touchstone of all theological and philosophical debate in Europe in the ensuing centuries.

> **scholastic theology** In medieval Europe, systematic investigation of the relations between the authority of spiritual revelation and the claims of human reason; a method of disputation drawing on philosophy, particularly the works of the ancient Greek thinker Aristotle; also, scholasticism.

Trans-Saharan Connections

FOCUS How did trans-Saharan exchange contribute to political, economic, and religious change in societies of North and West Africa in the thirteenth and fourteenth centuries?

Like the silk roads and the routes of the southern seas, the camel trails of the Sahara Desert crossed boundless open spaces to link regions of agrarian population. Those tracks joined ports on the African shores of the Mediterranean with the dense farming societies that inhabited the grassy savannas south of the desert, the region known historically as the West African Sudan. By extension, trails ran farther south to reach states and peoples of the tropical forest zone (see Map 13.5).

The steady development of trans-Saharan camel trade contributed after about 800 C.E. to the rise of Ghana, a West African monarchy that dominated the western Sahel, the semiarid belt wedged between the Sahara proper and the better-watered savannas to the south (see Chapter 11). Ghana weakened slowly in the eleventh and twelfth centuries, but in the mid-thirteenth the kingdom of Mali, a larger and more effectively centralized state than Ghana, emerged to rule over the savanna trade, including the southern desert ports. In the thirteenth and fourteenth centuries, West African miners and merchants supplied a substantial part of the gold that circulated across Afroeurasia.

MAP 13.5 Trans-Saharan connections, 1200–1350.

The map icons locate the sources of important items in the trans-Saharan trade. Why do you think the greatest concentration of routes is in the western part of the Sahara?

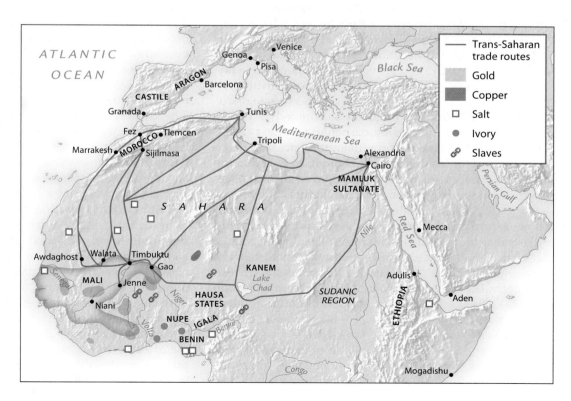

North Africa between the Mediterranean and the Sahara

The Muslim Almohad dynasty, which had unified the lands around the western Mediterranean in the twelfth century, disintegrated in the mid-thirteenth under assault from Christian crusaders (see Chapter 12). Four Muslim states took its place in different parts of the region: the mountain-bound kingdom of Granada in far southern Spain and three kingdoms in North Africa whose territories corresponded roughly to modern Morocco, Algeria, and Tunisia. Also, North Africa's long-established cities continued, despite the Almohad collapse, to prosper as centers of industry and Islamic learning. Tunis, Tlemcen, and Fez were among the most important centers.

North Africa, however, had a much smaller population than Europe did, and its Muslim states lacked the material resources to challenge European domination of western Mediterranean sea trade. Seafaring merchants from Genoa, Venice, Pisa, and the kingdom of Catalonia in Spain appeared in increasing numbers on the North African coast. Their vessels took on cargos of North African wool, leatherwork, grain, and dried fruits, as well as the ivory, ostrich feathers, slaves, and gold that arrived from across the Sahara. In return for these goods, the Europeans sold woolen and cotton textiles, ironware, wine, spices, and weaponry. One product on offer illustrates the hemispheric dimensions of trade. In the waters southwest of India, inhabitants of the Maldive Islands gathered cowrie shells. The harvesters sold the shells by the thousands to Arabian Sea merchants, who relayed them to the Red Sea. Italian shippers acquired them in eastern Mediterranean ports, carried them to North Africa, and sold them to Arab and Berber traders who transported them by camel to West Africa. There, they had scarcity value as both jewelry and a popular form of currency.

The Mali Empire

Mali, whose core area was the upper Niger River valley, emerged about the same time that the Mongol imperial army subjugated Russia and started the conquest of southern China. Mali's rise had no direct connection to Mongol power, but we know that merchants in that era coveted gold as a commodity and medium of exchange. West African mines were rich enough to supply substantial quantities of the metal to Afroeurasian markets. The flow of bullion across the Sahara started growing after the eighth century, in large part because Muslim rulers in the Mediterranean and Southwest Asia preferred to mint gold coins. Then, in the mid-1200s, western European rulers began to produce gold coinage to supplement silver. This happened first in the Italian city-state of Florence, which made the gold coin known as the florin. Since Europe did not have abundant gold resources, demand for African metal shot up. In the fourteenth and fifteenth centuries, West African mines may have produced about two-thirds of Afroeurasia's gold supply.[20] In return for that precious metal, plus ivory, slaves, and other West African items, southbound caravans brought Mali salt and copper from Saharan deposits and a wide range of commodities from North Africa and the wider Mediterranean region.

Mali's ascendancy. The rise of Mali to primacy among Sudanic states is associated with Sunjata (Sundiata), a heroic figure still celebrated in West Africa today. Like Chingis Khan, Sunjata lost his father as a young boy but rose from adversity—in his case, crippled legs—to lead his people to military triumph. Building a powerful state among the savanna people who spoke Malinke, one of West Africa's major languages, Sunjata and his immediate successors forced all rival states to pay tribute. Deploying both infantry and cavalry troops, the Mali kings, or *mansas*, carved out an empire that extended from the semiarid Sahel to the southern savanna woodlands and from the middle Niger to the Atlantic coast.

Environmental historians have hypothesized that Mali's imperial success may have been linked to the end of an eight-hundred-year wet phase in West Africa's climate. Beginning around 1000 C.E., annual rainfall in the Sahel and northern savanna declined gradually, shrinking resources in crops and herds and perhaps contributing to Ghana's disintegration. The region from which Mali expanded, however, was located farther south in better-watered savannas. Also, Mali's military might relied on horses, which were vulnerable to the bite of the tropical tsetse fly. As drier climate set it, the tsetse fly's habitat retreated toward the rainforest, allowing Mali's horse archers to operate over a wider range of savanna than Ghana's army had been able to do. Even without tsetse flies, however, horses did not breed well in tropical West Africa. Mali's emperors had continually to import fresh mounts from the Sahara or North Africa.

The Mali state. Mali belongs in the club of big monarchies that imposed an unusual measure of political order on much of Afroeurasia during the later thirteenth and early fourteenth centuries. The royal court of the *mansa* consisted of his extended family, numerous wives, trusted officers, bodyguards, and slaves. By about 1300 the king also employed a cadre of literate Muslims, some born in Mali, some from North Africa, who served as secretaries, accountants, and administrators and who made Arabic the written language of government and diplomacy. Because of the great wealth the *mansas* accumulated from taxing farming and trans-Saharan trade, some of them exchanged diplomatic missions with the sultans of Morocco and other Muslim states north of the desert. Royal officers directly ruled the upper Niger and Senegal valleys, the empire's core. Beyond there, they collected periodic tribute from local chiefs and princes, much as the Mongol khans of the Golden Horde harvested wealth from Russian nobles. The *mansas* did not

The central mosque in Jenne, Mali. The style of this mosque, originally built in the thirteenth century but reconstructed in 1907, points to architectural influences from southern Morocco on the other side of the Sahara Desert. The structure is constructed of sun-baked mud bricks and mud plaster, the local building material readily at hand in the Niger River's inland delta.

directly control West Africa's two major gold-producing regions, but they closely monitored the Sudanic merchants who transported the metal to the desert ports, and they took for themselves a healthy share of dust and nuggets to embellish the palace and beautify members of the royal family.

Islam in West Africa. At the start of the thirteenth century, some Sudanic rulers, chiefs, and merchant groups practiced Islam, especially those who did business with the Muslim traders who operated the trans-Saharan caravans. Sunjata, Mali's founder, may or may not have been a Muslim, but later rulers practiced the basic rituals and duties of the faith. The political legitimacy of the *mansas,* however, rested on the allegiance of hundreds of local chiefs who did not practice Islam. Rather, those leaders honored the king through beliefs and symbols associated with the idea that he possessed a sacred character linked to the population's health and well-being. Consequently, the *mansas* had to perform a delicate cultural balancing act, upholding traditional standards of royal ceremony—for example, obliging subjects to approach the royal person by prostrating themselves and throwing dust over their heads—and at the same time nurturing their ties to the wider Islamic universe by

attending Friday prayer and in some measure adopting Muslim legal and moral standards.

Mansa Musa (r. 1312–1337) showed particular devotion to Islam by making a pilgrimage to Mecca in 1324–1325, along with an enormous train of notables, soldiers, slaves, camels, and horses. The trip was 3,500 miles each way. He passed through Cairo and while there distributed so much gold that, according to Egyptian chroniclers, the bottom temporarily fell out of the gold market. At home he spent large sums advancing legal and religious education, building mosques, and inviting scholars and architects from abroad. Despite these developments, however, the great majority of people in Sudanic West Africa did not convert to Islam until centuries later.

Mali reached its zenith of power in the mid-fourteenth century. After that, succession disputes within the royal family and revolts in distant tributary kingdoms led to its gradual decline.

Other West African Kingdoms

We know quite a bit about Mali's history, owing in no small measure to Ibn Battuta's first-person account. This state,

Ibn Battuta Assesses the Mali Empire

In 1355, the Muslim lawyer Ibn Battuta, having returned to his Moroccan homeland after twenty-nine years of traveling through much of Afroeurasia, completed preparation of the Rihla, *or "Book of Travels," a lengthy account of his adventures. In collaboration with a young literary scholar proficient in the niceties of Arabic prose, Ibn Battuta composed the* Rihla *in the capital city of Fez at the command of Morocco's ruler. The book circulated in manuscript copies in the western Muslim world, and in the mid-nineteenth century two European scholars translated all of it into French, the first of many translations into Western and Asian languages. The* Rihla *has come down to us as a precious historical document because Ibn Battuta was an eyewitness to events and ways of life in dozens of societies in the second quarter of the fourteenth century, the twilight of the Mongol era.*

When Ibn Battuta set to work on the Rihla, *he had only just returned from the last of his heroic journeys, a trip by camel caravan across the fearsome Sahara to Mali in West Africa (see Map 13.2). Numerous Arab, Mongol, and Turkic potentates had welcomed and rewarded him during his travels, and he makes clear in the* Rihla *that he was seriously annoyed by Mansa Sulayman, the king of Mali, for failing to treat him as a scholar of high distinction. This tepid reception may have influenced his report on Mali, because he gives Mansa Sulayman and his empire a decidedly mixed review. Ibn Battuta's own upbringing in the cosmopolitan city of Tangier as a pious Arab gentleman colors his descriptions of all the Muslim kingdoms he visited in his travels. In the case of Mali, his morally conservative ideas about religious devotion and righteous conduct come through loud and clear.*

In this selection Ibn Battuta sums up what he thinks are the good and not-so-good qualities of the kingdom and its people:

Amongst their good qualities is the small amount of injustice amongst them, for of all people they are the furthest from it. Their sultan does not forgive anyone in any matter to do with injustice. Among these qualities there is also the prevalence of peace in their country, the traveler is not afraid in it nor is he who lives there in fear of the thief or of the robber by violence. They do not interfere with the property of the white man [resident of Saharan or North African background] who dies in their country even though it may consist of great wealth, but rather they entrust it to the hand of someone dependable among the white men until it is taken by the rightful claimant.

Another of the good habits amongst them is the way they meticulously observe the times of the prayers and attendance at them, so also it is with regard to their congregational services and their beating of their children to instill these things in them.

When it is Friday, if a man does not come early to the mosque he will not find a place to pray because of the numbers of the crowd. . . .

Amongst their good qualities is the putting on of good white clothes on Friday. If a man among them has nothing except a tattered shirt, he washes and cleans it and attends the Friday prayer in it. Another of their good qualities is their concern for learning the sublime Quran by heart. They make fetters for their children when they appear on their part to be falling short in their learning of it by heart, and they are not taken off from them till they do learn by heart. . . . One day I passed by a handsome youth from them dressed in fine clothes and on his feet was a heavy chain. I said to the man who was with me, "What has this youth done—has he killed someone?" The youth heard my remark and laughed. It was told me, "He has been chained so that he will learn the Quran by heart."

Among the bad things which they do—their serving women, slave women and little daughters appear before people naked, exposing their private parts. I used to see many of them in this state in Ramadan. . . . Also among their bad customs is the way women will go into the presence of the sultan naked, without any covering; and the nakedness of the sultan's daughters—on the night of the twenty-seventh of Ramadan, I saw about a hundred slave girls coming out of his palace with food, with them were two of his daughters, they had full breasts and no clothes on. Another of their bad customs is their putting dust and ashes on their heads as a sign of respect. And another is the laughing matter I mentioned of their poetic recitals. And another is that many of them eat animals not ritually slaughtered, and dogs and donkeys.

Source: Said Hamdun and Noël King, *Ibn Battuta in Black Africa* (Princeton, NJ: Markus Wiener Publishers, 2005), 58–59.

Thinking Critically

What aspects of Mali's government and society does Ibn Battuta commend? Why do you think he points out these particular conditions and customs for favorable comment? Why do you think he is particularly critical of customs of female dress in Mali's royal court? Do you think he is unjustifiably intolerant, or does he have good reasons for his criticisms? What kind of person, in terms of background and status, do you think Ibn Battuta imagined would read the *Rihla*?

however, was only one of several in West Africa. In the savanna belt east of the Niger River a cluster of city-states arose in the region generally corresponding to the northern half of modern Nigeria. The people of those towns, who spoke a language ancestral to Hausa (the native language of nearly forty-five million people today), prospered from cotton textile manufacture and trans-Saharan exchange of copper, kola nuts, slaves, and numerous products from the rainforests to the south. Further east in the vicinity of Lake Chad, the Kanem empire paralleled Mali as a large tribute-collecting state. Indeed, its ruling dynasty endured much longer than Mali's did, lasting from the eleventh to the nineteenth century.

In West Africa's wooded savannas and rainforests, numerous kingdoms and city-states began to appear from about 800 C.E. By the thirteenth century, small states whose chiefs had mainly ritual functions gave way in some regions to more powerful rulers whose authority rested on the number of troops and retainers they could muster and on the tribute they could collect. Igala, Nupe, and Benin were all states of this type that emerged in the thirteenth or fourteenth centuries in the wooded savannas or rainforests of what is today Nigeria. All of them exchanged kola nuts and other forest products for the grain, horses, and textiles that arrived from the north. The archaeological record shows that Benin, together with several city-states that emerged among the Yoruba-speaking peoples of the forest belt, developed in this period a sophisticated tradition of naturalistic brass sculpture. This work is evidence of long-distance trade links, because the copper used in brass manufacture had to be shipped in from mines located in the south central Sahara.

A Yoruba ruler. A naturalistic brass head of the monarch of a Yoruba state in what is today south central Nigeria. The sculpture dates to between the twelfth and fifteenth centuries.

• • •

Conclusion

In the era of the Mongol empires, nearly every part of Afroeurasia established contact, whether direct or indirect, with every other part, either overland or by sea. People in one region who had money to spend sought the goods of other regions, which might be thousands of miles away. More people traveled longer distances to seek knowledge or share their religion than at any earlier time. And Mongol cavalry operated in a far larger hemispheric arena than an ancient Roman legion could have imagined. Only a small part of the inhabited supercontinent—the frozen Arctic, some deep interior forests or mountain valleys, the arid lands of far southwestern Africa—remained disconnected from the hemispheric communication web.

The existence of elaborate trade networks, however, does not mean that Afroeurasian peoples were moving toward cultural unification. The number of languages spoken ran to the tens of thousands, and interchange among societies could breed suspicion, rivalry, and violence as well as toleration and understanding. On the other hand, cultural homogenizing processes were at work, at least on the regional level. Some languages and cultural styles gained numerous converts while others shrank. In this era, for example, additional millions converted to Buddhism, Christianity, and Islam and in the process learned new languages and accepted new, more uniform life ways. Languages that spread impressively in the Mongol era, along with cultural forms that invariably accompany language, included Chinese, Persian, Arabic, Oghuz Turkish, Swahili, Malinke, German, French, and English. Ironically, Mongolian never caught on much outside its homeland.

Because ship captains of the thirteenth and fourteenth centuries were masters of Afroeurasia's chain of seas, we may imagine that probes into Atlantic waters and Christopher Columbus's landfall on a Caribbean island were events waiting to happen. But even though 1492 was fast approaching, peoples of North and South America continued to explore entirely separate paths of empire building, trade, and cultural creativity. In Chapter 14 we return to the Western Hemisphere to explore developments between 900 and 1500 C.E.

• • •

Key Terms

Angkor Wat 384	guild 388	Mongol Peace (*Pax Mongolica*) 369
Benin 395	Ilkhanate 374	Mongols 371
charter 388	Kanem empire 395	scholastic theology 391
Chola dynasty 385	khanate 371	Swahili coast 385
Golden Horde 374	Khmer kingdom 384	vernacular language 388
Gothic architecture 389	Mali empire 392	Xi Xia 372
Great Zimbabwe 386	Mamluk kingdom 378	Yuan dynasty 374

Change over Time

850–1279	The Chola dynasty rules in southern India; commercial exchange and temple construction intensifies.
889–1434	The Khmer kingdom rules in Southeast Asia and sponsors construction of the Angkor Wat temple complex.
1167?–1227	Chingis Khan conquers far and wide, founding the Mongol empire.
Mid-13th–late 15th centuries	The Mali empire dominates much of West Africa.
1241–1502	The Mongol khanate of Kipchak (the Golden Horde) rules in Inner Eurasia and Russia.
1258–1335	The Mongol Ilkhanate of Iran and Iraq rules in Southwest Asia.
1260	The Mamluk sultanate of Egypt and Syria (1250–1517) repels Mongol forces.
1271–1295	Marco Polo travels from Venice to China and back.
1271–1368	The Mongol Yuan empire, founded by Kubilai Khan (r. 1271–1294), unites northern and southern China.
1272–1307	England becomes a strong regional European state under Edward I.
1274 and 1281	Japan under the Kamakura dynasty (1185–1333) repels two Mongol invasions.
1285–1314	France becomes a strong regional European state under Philip IV the Fair.
1287–1288	The Mongol envoy Rabban Sauma travels in Southwest Asia and Europe.
1291	The last of the European crusader states in Syria falls to the Mamluks of Egypt.
1324–1325	Mansa Musa, emperor of Mali, undertakes pilgrimage to Mecca.
1325–1354	Ibn Battuta travels throughout Afroeurasia.

Please see end of book reference section for additional reading suggestions related to this chapter.

14 Cities and Empires in the Americas

900–1500

In 1978, power company employees working on the Mexico City subway system made a startling discovery. As they were digging a trench for an electrical cable, they unearthed a giant stone disk showing the dismembered body of a woman. Historians identified the woman as Coyolxauhqui, an Aztec goddess who, according to legend, had conspired with her brothers and sisters to murder Huitzilopochtli, their youngest sibling, out of jealousy. When Huitzilopochtli discovered the plot, he took hold of a scepter and stabbed his sister in the heart, then cut off her head. Coyolxauhqui's body fell to the ground and broke into pieces. Huitzilopochtli promptly defeated the rest of his enemies and established himself as the preeminent god.

Recognizing the disk as an Aztec ceremonial object that might signal a major find, archaeologists extended the trench. They found a series of steps—the lower portions of a much larger staircase ascending the steep side of a pyramid. The structure appeared to have been built in five stages during the fifteenth and early sixteenth centuries. Artifacts

The dismembered body of the goddess on the Coyolxauhqui stone disk.

filled the niches under floors and between walls: masks, stone sculptures, and ceramic containers from central and northern Mexico; coral, seashells, and even alligator bones from the coast. Archaeologists theorized that subject peoples of the Aztecs presented many of these items as tribute.

These discoveries confirmed researchers' hunches that the ruins were the foundations of the Great Temple of Tenochtitlán (teh-noach-teet-LAWN), which Spanish conquistadors had destroyed in the sixteenth century. For more than a century before the arrival of Europeans, this sanctuary had been the spiritual and political heart of the largest empire in Mesoamerica. Modeled partially on the older pyramids of Teotihuacán (see Chapter 8), the Great Temple reflected the Aztecs' view of themselves as heirs of earlier Mesoamerican civilizations, divinely destined to surpass their predecessors in wealth and power. Every year, priests sacrificed thousands of human victims to Huitzilopochtli, their patron, who was said to have dismembered his treacherous sister on this very site.

At about the same time that the Aztecs were building their empire in Mesoamerica, the Incas established control over much of the Andes. While both the Inca and Aztec states surpassed earlier civilizations in size, population, and military prowess, they relied heavily on cultural foundations their predecessors had laid. The Aztecs were influenced by the earlier Mesoamerican societies of Toltec, Maya, and Teotihuacán. The Incas extended and improved on the road networks, irrigation technologies, record systems, and fine crafts developed by earlier states and temple centers in the Andean highlands and along the Pacific coast. Meanwhile, complex agrarian societies also emerged in other parts of North and South America and in the Caribbean basin. Although some of these societies built mounds, ball courts, stone temples, and palaces, they left behind more fragmented archaeological records and virtually no oral traditions, making it difficult for us to reconstruct their histories.

This chapter explores the development of large urban centers and imperial states in the Americas over a six-hundred-year period, emphasizing the influence of changing environmental conditions (see Map 14.1). The first part of the chapter surveys a variety of complex societies, moving roughly from north to south along the Western Hemisphere's long axis. Starting in the North American woodlands, we describe the continuing development of the Mississippian mound-building tradition (see Chapter 8), brought to a cultural summit in the urban complex of Cahokia (kuh-HOH-kee-uh). We then shift to the Colorado Plateau region of the southwestern United States. There, Ancestral Puebloans (Anasazi) carried on the irrigated farming technologies of earlier peoples, building remarkable multistory settlements

• • •

in semiarid canyons. Farther south in central Mexico, Toltec migrants rebuilt the city of Tula and presided over a far-reaching trade network extending to the Yucatán Peninsula and Central America. We also investigate the migration of Nahuatl-speaking peoples, ancestors of the Aztecs, into the central Mexican highlands. Finally, we turn to South America, where the Tiwanaku, Wari, and Chimu states came to dominate the central Andes and the arid Pacific coast.

Conflict for control of water, land, and labor led to the emergence of new imperial powers in the early fifteenth century. In the second part of the chapter, we explore the rise of the Aztec and Inca empires. When Spanish soldiers and missionaries arrived after 1500, they encountered complex political societies at the height of their power. The Spanish tore down many of the buildings in the Aztec and Inca capitals, destroying what would have been part of the archaeological record. They also wrote about the people they encountered, however, handing down to us striking if incomplete descriptions of American societies at the moment of European invasions. Perhaps the most enduring legacy of the Aztecs and the Incas is the oral histories they passed from one generation to the next. In the sixteenth and seventeenth centuries, Spanish Catholic missionaries transcribed these stories and taught Native American boys to write their native languages in Latin script. These sources, along with modern archaeological studies, inform our narrative.

A Panoramic View

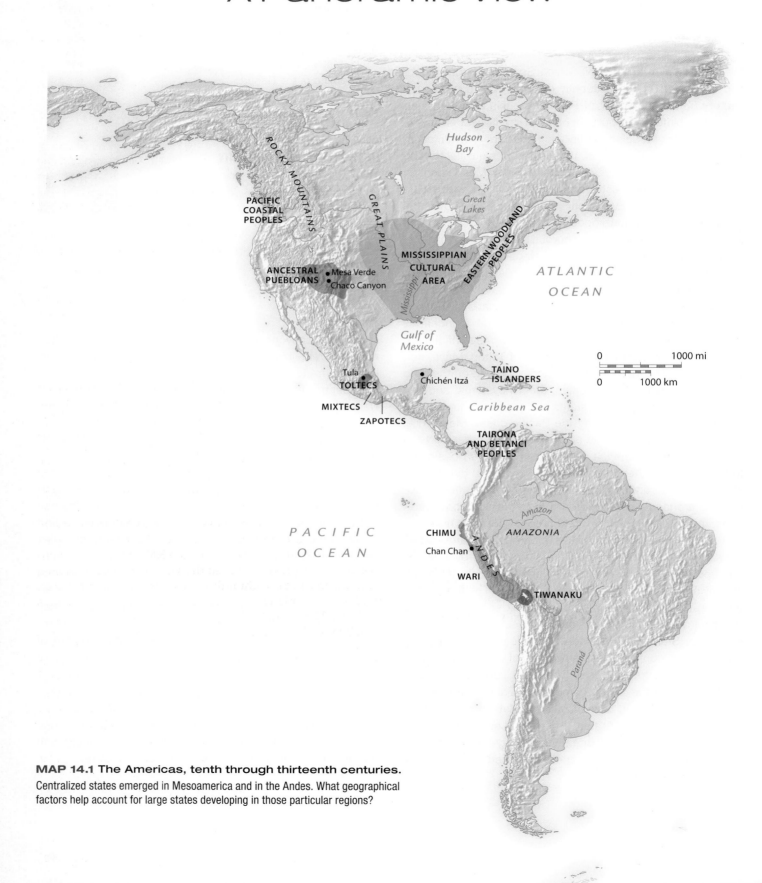

ROCKY MOUNTAINS

Hudson
Bay

Great
Lakes

PACIFIC
COASTAL
PEOPLES

GREAT PLAINS

MISSISSIPPIAN
CULTURAL
AREA

EASTERN WOODLAND PEOPLES

ATLANTIC
OCEAN

ANCESTRAL
PUEBLOANS

• Mesa Verde
• Chaco Canyon

Mississippi

Gulf of
Mexico

0   1000 mi

0   1000 km

Tula
• TOLTECS

• Chichén Itzá

TAINO
ISLANDERS

MIXTECS

ZAPOTECS

Caribbean Sea

TAIRONA
AND BETANCI
PEOPLES

PACIFIC
OCEAN

Amazon

AMAZONIA

CHIMU

Chan Chan •

ANDES

WARI

TIWANAKU

Paraná

MAP 14.1 The Americas, tenth through thirteenth centuries.

Centralized states emerged in Mesoamerica and in the Andes. What geographical
factors help account for large states developing in those particular regions?

American Societies in an Age of Environmental Change

FOCUS In what ways did large-scale environmental change affect historical developments in the Americas between the tenth and fifteenth centuries?

Several interconnected environmental and ecological trends affected peoples of much of the Western Hemisphere between the ninth and thirteenth centuries. The North Atlantic Warm Period, the slight rise in global temperature that occurred during those four hundred years, affected North America as well as the northern regions of Afroeurasia (see Chapter 11). In Andean South America, the climatic wet and dry cycles associated with El Niño Southern Oscillation had a large impact on ecological conditions and therefore on social change. In North America the warming trend appears to have encouraged the spread of farming, especially maize cultivation, to new regions. In western parts of both North and South America, drier conditions limited population growth, encouraging people to move into larger, denser communities with more reliable access to scarce resources. New states emerged in central Mexico and the Andes, only to fall victim to ecological changes similar to those that weakened the Teotihuacán and Moche civilizations of earlier centuries (see Chapter 8).

The uptick in global temperature boosted agricultural production, notably in humid forested areas along rivers, a type of ecological zone common in what is now the United States from the Mississippi River valley to the Atlantic. Peoples of the Eastern Woodlands farmed more productively, extended their fields, and introduced new varieties of beans, squash, and other foodstuffs. Maize production became widespread by 1000 c.e., owing in large part to the introduction of eastern flint corn, a variety of Mesoamerican origin that grew well in relatively cool and moist climatic conditions. Having a higher caloric value than other local staples, maize supported larger numbers of people, especially in the Mississippi and numerous other river valleys. As population grew, more complex social and political systems evolved. Individual leaders and chiefly families accumulated more power to regulate water consumption and protect the food supply.

Between the ninth and thirteenth centuries, the plateaus and desert valleys of what is now the southwestern United States experienced unpredictable cycles of rainfall and drought. In response to those uncertainties, local societies invented ingenious ways to irrigate land, diversify crops, and plant maize in several different places to cut risk, maximize yield, and conserve water. Despite these efforts, delicate **ecosystems**

> **ecosystem** A biological system in which living organisms—plants, animals, microorganisms, humans—interact with one another and with nonliving elements such as air, sunlight, soil, and water.

could support only so many hungry humans. Sudden dry spells could wipe out all the farms in an area in a matter of months. Two major droughts, the first in the middle of the twelfth century and the second in the last quarter of the thirteenth, forced thousands of people to abandon communities in the Sonoran Desert (which overlaps Arizona, California, and northwestern Mexico). Some displaced groups migrated south to the comparatively temperate valleys of central Mexico. Among them were forerunners of the Toltecs and Aztecs.

Like western North America, the Andean highlands experienced fluctuations between wet and dry periods that could determine the fate of human settlements. In addition, the narrow, arid plains separating the mountains from the Pacific shore were subject to occasional yet unpredictable weather events related to El Niño cycles. Torrential rains could destroy crucial irrigation systems, inundate farmland, and disrupt fisheries. Nevertheless, between 900 and 1300, several cities in the region reached population levels in the tens of thousands by expanding the amount of farmland under their control, developing techniques to increase soil fertility, and conquering neighbors. The ability of societies to expand in this fashion depended on their skill at anticipating changing weather conditions and adapting to both deluges and water shortages.

The Mound Builders of Cahokia

Some of the most densely populated areas of North America lay in the valleys of the Mississippi, Missouri, Tennessee, Ohio, and other eastern and midwestern valleys. These rivers and their tributaries were natural conduits of trade. Dense forests provided timber for construction and firewood, as well as wild game for food, fur, hides, and bone. This environment had nurtured farming societies and large settlements since the second millennium b.c.e. (see Chapters 4 and 8).

The confluence of the Mississippi and Missouri Rivers created an eighty-mile floodplain ideal for maize and bean cultivation. Here, sometime between 800 and 1000 c.e., Mississippian peoples established the settlement of Cahokia. Its remains in Illinois eight miles east of St. Louis are listed as a UNESCO World Heritage Site. At its zenith between about 1050 and 1200, Cahokia had perhaps ten to twenty thousand inhabitants. It was probably the largest urban center north of Mexico before the arrival of Europeans. The city was a natural hub of commerce, situated at the meeting point of arteries that connected the Gulf of Mexico to the Great Lakes and the central plains to the Eastern Woodlands. Cahokian pottery and stone tools have been found in Minnesota, Kansas, Arkansas, and Mississippi, along with locally produced imitations of Cahokian wares. The city exported salt and chert (a kind of rock used to make arrowheads and blades) in exchange for copper from Lake Superior, mica from Appalachia, and seashells from the Gulf and Atlantic seaboards.

The most prominent vestiges of Cahokia are earthen mounds, the continuation of a Mississippian tradition going back to the fourth millennium B.C.E. At its height, Cahokia may have had over 120 of these structures, but owing to centuries of erosion and urban development, fewer than 80 are visible. Most of the mounds had flat summits where workers erected wooden structures that functioned as temples, administrative buildings, and residences for elite families. The largest surviving earthwork, called Monks Mound, is located near the center of the archaeological site and has a base width of fourteen acres. It has four ascending terraces, and the modern remains rise to a height of one hundred feet. Built in stages between 900 and 1200, this mound is the largest known earthen structure in North America built before European contact (see Map 14.2). It was probably the residence of Cahokia's ruling family, as well as a ceremonial and administrative center.

Mound 72, half a mile away, is aligned with the sunrise on the winter solstice and the sunset on the summer solstice. This earthwork was an important burial site, enclosing the remains of 272 individuals dating between 1000 and 1050. Some corpses were buried on litters (platforms) or wrapped in blankets, while others were merely tossed into pits, a difference in treatment that suggests social class divisions. One tomb holds the corpse of a forty-year-old man who rests on a platform made of twenty thousand seashell

A Mississippian town. The earthwork known as Monks Mound dominates Cahokia as it looked about 1150 (artist's reconstruction below). The Mississippi River is visible at upper left. Monks Mound looks very different today (photograph at right) but still impresses visitors. When the American congressman Henry M. Brackenridge saw the mound in the early 1800s, he declared: "It is certainly a most stupendous pile of earth, and were it not for the strongest proof, no one would believe it the works of hands."

beads. He may have been an early Cahokian ruler. Several other bodies were buried around him. Nearby, archaeologists have uncovered several mass graves containing more than one hundred females buried in rows along with more than thirty-six thousand shell beads, arrowheads, and broken ceramic containers. Another gravesite contains four men with severed heads and hands. These burials suggest that the Cahokians practiced human sacrifice, as societies did in Mesoamerica. Servants or relatives may have been killed, presumably to accompany their deceased leader into the afterlife.

Around 1150 C.E., the rulers enclosed the city center in a log stockade. From platforms erected against the interior wall, warriors could shoot arrows at attackers and defend gates. The stockade suggests that war menaced Cahokia during the twelfth and thirteenth centuries. Neighboring communities may have challenged its regional hegemony.

Warfare and environmental degradation probably led to the depopulation of Cahokia and its eventual abandonment by about 1400. A city of its size required constant supplies of timber from nearby woodlands. Logging meant

deforestation, which may have ruined the natural habitat of certain plants and animals, depleting part of the local food supply. Deforestation may also have contributed to erosion of farmland and silt buildup in local streams, which increased the risk of flooding. The end of the North Atlantic Warm Period in the 1200s probably caused earlier seasonal frosts and smaller crop yields, especially of maize. Population declined along with the grain supply, while internal feuding over scarce resources may have intensified. Sometime during the thirteenth century, a major earthquake shook the region, liquefying the soft earth near riverbanks and rendering it useless for farming. Gradually, people left Cahokia and migrated to other areas, establishing new, though smaller settlements or assimilating into other Native American groups.

Ancestral Puebloans on the Colorado Plateau

Like the Cahokians, the Pueblo people built spectacular structures between the tenth and twelfth centuries. Most

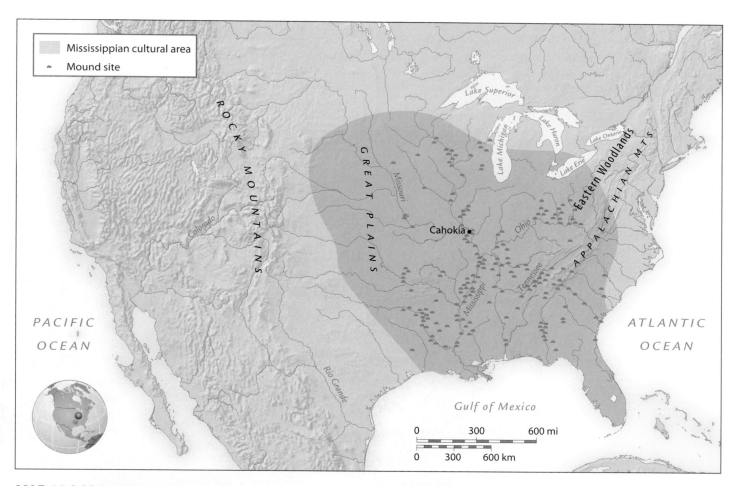

MAP 14.2 Major mounds and earthworks in North America to the fifteenth century.
The region of Mississippian cultural influence encompassed a large part of what is now the United States. What geographical factors might have facilitated trade among communities within the Mississippian area?

of the settlements of this Native American people lay on the Colorado Plateau, a semiarid region that overlaps Utah, Colorado, Arizona, and New Mexico. Initially, Ancestral Puebloans lived in small villages consisting of pit houses similar to those built by the earlier Hohokam people (see Chapter 8). Over time, some of these communities evolved into towns, or **pueblos,** each with five or six stone buildings and a kiva, a large, round, covered pit that served as a meeting place and ceremonial center. Around 900, many communities adopted maize agriculture, and the population began to grow. As pueblos expanded, residents added stories to their structures to accommodate more families.

pueblo A Spanish word meaning "village" or "small town." Spanish colonizers used this term to describe multistory stone or brick compounds that the Ancestral Puebloans (Anasazi) built in the American Southwest.

Chaco Canyon in New Mexico sheltered the densest settlements. The first villages probably appeared around the year 500, as farmers took advantage of increased rainfall to plant corn in the southern part of the canyon. Over several centuries, some of these villages evolved in size and complexity. The largest, Pueblo Bonito, set a general pattern. It began as a small cluster of pit houses and some aboveground storage rooms. During the ninth century the inhabitants constructed stone and adobe rooms in a semicircle. Around 1000, two large kivas were built. At this point, Pueblo Bonito reached five stories high and had more than six hundred rooms, which accommodated between five hundred and one thousand residents.

Inhabitants of Pueblo Bonito belonged to two main groups: the "winter people," who specialized in hunting and gathering, and the "summer people," who farmed. This division of labor shows that the Puebloans could not rely exclusively on agriculture for sustenance in an area prone to droughts and floods. The winter and the summer groups were organized in smaller kinship-based households, each of which had a series of rooms within the pueblo, bound together by a common outer wall. Each kin group had its own small kiva, workshops, storerooms, and communal spaces.

Both trade and migration connected Chaco Canyon to a wide surrounding region. During the late tenth and early eleventh centuries, the population grew faster than the valley's ecosystem could sustain. Probably as a consequence of that, some Ancestral Puebloan kin groups migrated to distant areas on or beyond the Colorado Plateau to found new villages and small pueblos. At the same time, Chaco Canyon became a major center of regional commerce, especially in precious stones and jewelry. Outsiders brought turquoise to the pueblos, where local artisans made ornaments for re-export. Archaeologists have found more than sixty thousand such artifacts.

An impressive yet enigmatic system of roads, still visible today, radiated out from Chaco Canyon like spokes of a wheel (see Map 14.3). Some of these roads are forty feet wide inside the canyon and ten feet wide beyond it. Notably,

Pueblo Bonito. The largest settlement in Chaco Canyon, Pueblo Bonito's buildings rose as many as five stories high. The circular pits are the ruins of kivas, or places of ritual activity. Construction of the town began in 851 and continued for more than two hundred fifty years. The more than six hundred rooms could have accommodated many more than one thousand people. Why do you think the resident population was probably less than it could have been?

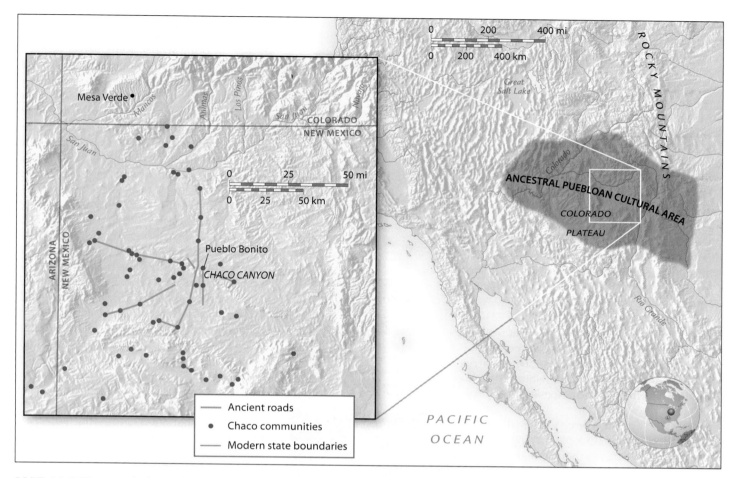

MAP 14.3 The roads from Chaco Canyon.

Ground surveys have marked out some of Chaco Canyon's highways, but other roads are visible only from the air. Referring to the scale on the inset map, estimate the approximate distance from the northernmost to the southernmost Chaco community.

they run straight even over hills and rugged terrain, rather like ancient Roman roads. Scholars have long debated the significance of these highways. One theory suggests that at special times of the year, such as the summer and winter solstices, thousands of pilgrims walked to Chaco Canyon on the roads to participate in ceremonies and to exchange goods. Another theory suggests that the roads were purely symbolic. They may have formed a representation of Puebloan cosmology, wherein Chaco Canyon was the "navel" of the world. A major causeway that heads due north was like an "umbilical cord," connecting the center to a supernatural world beyond civilization. The spirits of the dead traveled along this path to their final resting place in the middle of an uninhabited canyon.

The pueblos of Chaco Canyon declined precipitously after the middle of the twelfth century, not long before Cahokia did. Drought was almost certainly the main reason. A fifty-year dry period between 1130 and 1180 destroyed much of the canyon's farmland and wiped out the previous two centuries of urban development. As the water supply dwindled, inhabitants who survived famine and malnutrition left

to search for fertile land. Refugees migrated from the canyon in different directions, taking with them their techniques of building dams, terraces, and reservoirs. New pueblos sprang up, some of them, notably Mesa Verde in southwestern Colorado, reaching sizes that rivaled the Chaco Canyon settlements. These communities prospered during the thirteenth century but in the end met the same fate as their ancestral home. Another major drought between 1275 and 1299 destroyed the agricultural base of this area, forcing many Puebloan communities once again to disperse.

Maya, Mixtec, and Toltec

The roughly contemporaneous collapse of the Teotihuacán, Zapotec, and Maya states (see Chapter 8) created a power vacuum across much of Mesoamerica. In the Yucatán Peninsula the largest centers of Maya population shifted from the southern highlands to the low-lying north, where freshwater aquifers sustained hundreds of villages and a few large cities. After the collapse of the southern city-states, overland trade routes declined, while seaborne canoe commerce along the rim of the Gulf of Mexico prospered. During the tenth century a Maya group called the Itzá moved into the northern peninsula, where they endeavored to dominate both the canoe trade and coastal production of salt, a valuable export commodity. They established a capital at the lowland Maya city of Chichén Itzá and gradually subordinated nearby communities.

West of Yucatán in the highland valley of Oaxaca, the large Zapotec monarchies that flourished before 700 broke into smaller states (see Chapter 8), which built new fortified centers and warred with one another. After about 800, bands of warriors who spoke the Mixtec language began to invade ancestral Zapotec lands, causing more instability. A ruler named Eight Deer Jaguar Claw (1063–1115) created something close to a Mixtec empire, bringing a number of towns under his control by a combination of military conquest, intermarriage with local noble families, and tribute collection. This state endured until the sixteenth century.

The Toltec ascendancy. During the ninth and tenth centuries, people fleeing drought-ravaged deserts of northern Mexico and the American Southwest traveled long distances to the greener highland regions of central Mexico. The Toltecs were one of the groups that migrated during the ninth century. They settled in Tula, a center in the Valley of Mexico where Mexico City now sprawls. Tula had been a dependency of the great city of Teotihuacán up to the sixth or seventh century. It revived again under Toltec rule, expanding by 1100 C.E. to embrace an area of ten square miles and a population of around thirty-five thousand, plus as many as ninety thousand living in suburban communities.[1] Like Teotihuacán in its time, Tula had two large pyramidal temples surrounded by palaces, priests' residences, and government buildings. The city also had at least five ball courts. We do not understand much about the games played there, but they also certainly had ritual functions, just as these arenas did in other ancient Mesoamerican societies. Toltec monumental building, however, never reached Teotihuacán's grandeur, and the artisanry was noticeably poorer.

Tula never became a large imperial state, but its commercial influence ranged far to the north and south. Local traditions tell us that many different languages could be heard in the city, suggesting that travelers came from all over Mesoamerica to buy and sell. Archaeologists have uncovered ceramics originating in modern Costa Rica, 1,200 miles to the southeast. The Tula region had rich deposits of black and

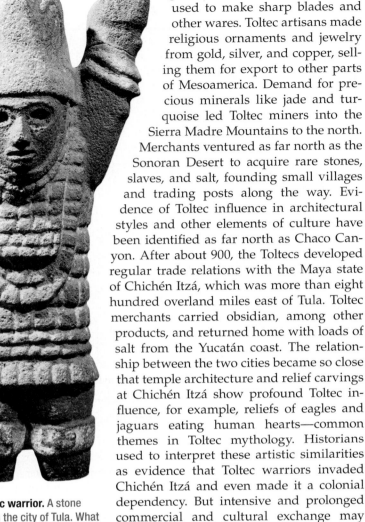

A Toltec warrior. A stone figure from the city of Tula. What material do you think was used to make Toltec body armor, represented here in stone?

green obsidian, the volcanic glass used to make sharp blades and other wares. Toltec artisans made religious ornaments and jewelry from gold, silver, and copper, selling them for export to other parts of Mesoamerica. Demand for precious minerals like jade and turquoise led Toltec miners into the Sierra Madre Mountains to the north. Merchants ventured as far north as the Sonoran Desert to acquire rare stones, slaves, and salt, founding small villages and trading posts along the way. Evidence of Toltec influence in architectural styles and other elements of culture have been identified as far north as Chaco Canyon. After about 900, the Toltecs developed regular trade relations with the Maya state of Chichén Itzá, which was more than eight hundred overland miles east of Tula. Toltec merchants carried obsidian, among other products, and returned home with loads of salt from the Yucatán coast. The relationship between the two cities became so close that temple architecture and relief carvings at Chichén Itzá show profound Toltec influence, for example, reliefs of eagles and jaguars eating human hearts—common themes in Toltec mythology. Historians used to interpret these artistic similarities as evidence that Toltec warriors invaded Chichén Itzá and even made it a colonial dependency. But intensive and prolonged commercial and cultural exchange may have produced the same results.

The end of Toltec power. Droughts in northern Mexico in the twelfth century set off more southward migratory movements into the central highlands, including Tula-controlled areas. Some of these wanderers were Toltecs who abandoned mining and trading colonies. Others were mobile bands, both hunter-foragers and farmers. Tula suffered both water shortages and an influx of desperate and sometimes hostile intruders. Archaeologists have found evidence that invaders sacked the city, looting and defacing temples, burning palaces, and massacring both adults and children. The Toltecs abandoned their capital in the mid-twelfth century and never established another city to call their own.

Chichén Itzá may have suffered a similar fate just a few decades later. The demise of Tula deprived northern Yucatán of valuable trade items, including obsidian weapons. The city lost its regional military supremacy, and, according to traditional Maya histories, a lord from a neighboring city pillaged it. Both the Toltecs and the Itzá deserted the city by the late twelfth century, though several Maya towns regrouped to form a northern confederation that lasted for several generations. This alliance disintegrated in the mid-fifteenth century, and when the Spanish conqueror Hernán Cortés arrived on the Yucatán coast in 1518, he found the peninsula politically splintered.

The Coming of the Nahuas

The collapse of Toltec defenses in the Valley of Mexico encouraged more people from the arid north to infiltrate the region. Many of these newcomers spoke Nahuatl (NAH-watt), a language in the Uto-Aztecan language family that also includes Hopi, Shoshoni, Comanche, and other languages spoken in the central and southwestern United States. These linguistic relationships suggest that Nahuatl speakers, or Nahuas, originated in the Sonoran Desert or a neighboring region and perhaps migrated south in response to the same drought cycle that compelled the Anasazi to disperse from Chaco Canyon.

In the two centuries following the Toltec fall, dozens of city-states inhabited by Nahua and other incoming groups shared the Valley of Mexico and surrounding areas. Each city-state had a defined territory, a patron deity, and a ruler, who served as military commander and high priest to the community's god. In the typical city, a temple, a palace, and other stone buildings were clustered around a central plaza that also functioned as a marketplace. Cities were divided further into wards, neighborhoods, and households of multiple families. Within the households, men and women performed distinct tasks. Men spent most of the day farming or making crafts. When intercity wars broke out, they had to fight. Young boys typically went to school to learn combat. Women, by contrast, spent most of their time at home, raising children, preparing food, and weaving cloth.

A rigid social hierarchy characterized Nahua communities. Commoners did most of the farming, household labor, artisanry, and fighting. Free commoners produced food for their own households and gave the surplus to the leader of their ward. In turn, the wards and the noble families gave tribute to the ruler of the city. Many nobles owned slaves, and during times of drought and resulting famine, people often sold themselves into slavery in order to survive. Debtors and criminals could also be enslaved. The majority of slaves, though, were war captives, who faced either lifelong labor or death as sacrificial victims.

Fertile volcanic soils in the Valley of Mexico supported abundant agriculture. Lakes teemed with fish and waterfowl and supplied salt; rivers brought water from the surrounding mountains. Nahua farmers built and cultivated terraces in the foothills and laid out networks of canals to irrigate fields of maize, beans, and numerous other crops. Perhaps as a result of recurring droughts, farmers adopted a technique, perhaps borrowed from the Maya, of constructing chinampas (chee-NAHM-pahs), or "floating gardens" to extend areas of well-water cropland. Farmers built

Two pyramid temples. The architectural influence of Toltec artisans on distant Chichén Itzá is evident in this comparative view of Pyramid B at Tula (top) and the Temple of the Warriors at Chichén Itzá. The stelas at the summit of Pyramid B and the columns at the base of the Temple of Warriors both portray soldiers. What differences between the two structures do you notice?

up rectangular layers of water plants and soil dredged from shallow or marshy areas along the edges of lakes. In this way they created arable plots. Repeating the process over and over, farmers eventually reclaimed thousands of acres of wetland. Families set up residences on their chinampas and canoed from one to another along networks of canals.

Daily commerce took place in both local and central markets. Ward leaders oversaw local markets where farmers exchanged goods and where women did much of the trading.

Modern *chinampas*. A farmer tends a *chinampa* garden next to a canal in the Valley of Mexico. Why do you think this farming technique has survived to the present in some parts of Mexico?

The city-state ruler regulated the central market, where more valuable exchanges took place. Merchants from surrounding regions hauled in products like cotton, obsidian, feathers, gemstones, and jewelry. Merchants called *pochteca* managed long-distance trade. Forming guild-like organizations within their city, they could become politically powerful, accumulating great wealth and currying favor with the ruler. Some *pochteca* also worked clandestinely as spies, collecting information on rival cities during their travels and using their business contacts as informants.

Trade and agriculture made central Mexico one of the most densely populated regions in the world. By the late fifteenth century, the Valley of Mexico had between 1 and 2.5 million inhabitants; the population of the surrounding areas may have exceeded 6 million. Economic success, however, did not necessarily translate into prosperity for all. During the thirteenth century, population in the valley began to surpass food supplies. Periodic droughts worsened shortages. In bad times many people barely survived. Chronic imbalance between population and productivity also provoked intercity wars over farmland and labor. Sometimes military victors enslaved their neighbors and annexed their lands. More often, they forced defeated city-states to pay tribute, turning them into political satellites. In this way confederations of large and victorious city-states increasingly dominated weaker ones, while smaller cities formed their own alliances to try to preserve their independence. These conditions of violent competition set the stage for the rise of the Aztec empire.

The Caribbean and Amazonia

Maize cultivation spread throughout the Caribbean region and into Amazonia, the vast Amazon River basin, during the North Atlantic Warm Period. Complex societies emerged along the sea's southern rim after about 1000. In the lower Magdalena River valley in modern Colombia, Betanci people constructed mounds that reached up twenty-six feet. These artificial hills supported temples or entire villages. Archaeologists have excavated gold artifacts, painted pottery, and seashells at some Betanci sites. East of the Magdalena valley, the Tairona population grew rapidly from the eleventh century. They created probably the largest and most sophisticated civilization in South America outside the Andes. Archaeologists have excavated stone temples and palaces, as well as large shaft tombs with side chambers filled with gold ornaments. The largest Tairona site has over three thousand structures, including stone bridges.

The Taino, an agricultural, hunting, and fishing people, came to dominate several Caribbean islands after about 1000, moving out from Hispaniola (today Haiti and the Dominican Republic) to populate Cuba, Puerto Rico, Jamaica, and the Virgin Islands. Archaeologists have excavated sites that look like ancient ball courts. Since these ruins resemble structures in Mesoamerica, some scholars have proposed that trade links existed between at least some Caribbean peoples and the continental mainland. The most likely carriers of this trade were Maya canoe merchants who traveled the gulf waterways between Mexico and Panama. Aside from the presumed ball courts, however, there is no evidence that Maya ever journeyed to any Caribbean islands, and the ball courts may have been local inventions.

The population of the Caribbean region probably reached its peak during the thirteenth century, two hundred years before Europeans arrived. After that point, the quality of ceramics and other artifacts diminished noticeably, people built few new stone structures, and settlements shrank. When Christopher Columbus encountered Taino Indians on Hispaniola, he learned that a predatory people from neighboring islands, known as Caribes, had repeatedly raided Taino settlements and forced residents to flee. Little is known about these warrior bands, though by the fifteenth century they were launching attacks on settlements in Puerto Rico and along mainland coasts.

A Tairona pendant. A Tairona artisan living near the Caribbean coast of Colombia displayed extraordinary skill in creating this gold and copper alloy figure. What features of this object suggest that it represents a noble or chief?

A chair with supernatural properties. The Taino of the Caribbean islands used ritual seats like this one to consult with the spirit world. The seat signifies the presence of an ancestor. A supplicant would crouch on top of the chair while under the influence of a mind-altering snuff. The ancestral spirit would offer answers to questions: Will the harvest be good? Whom should my daughter marry?

In Amazonia, farmers adopted maize, as Caribbean peoples did, to supplement long-established crops like manioc, beans, squash, and potatoes. In the 900–1500 period, Amazonians extended trade links with Andes communities to the west, offering gold, coca, medicinal plants, dyes, and slaves in exchange for raw cotton, textiles, sea salt, and dogs. The Amazonian trade network ultimately connected the Andes with both the Caribbean and the Atlantic coast. Amazonian social organization ranged from small hunting and foraging bands to large farming communities with distinct social hierarchies and hereditary rulers. Spanish and Portuguese explorers reported densely settled towns in the region as late as the seventeenth century.

States of the Andes

Cycles of state building along the Pacific coastal plains and Andean slopes of what are today Ecuador, Peru, Bolivia, and Chile continued without interruption from the fourth millennium B.C.E. to the sixteenth century (see Map 14.1). In Chapter 8 we described the rise and fall of the Chavín de Huántar, Moche, and Nazca societies up to the 600s. The latter two peoples succumbed in conditions of severe drought and flooding associated with El Niño oscillations. In the sixth century, however, two new states began to emerge. One was Tiwanaku (Tihuanaco), a kingdom based in the highlands of modern Bolivia; the second was Wari (Huari), in what is now central Peru. In the eighth century, a group known as the Chimu restored part of the old Moche irrigation network along the Pacific coast and built the splendid capital city of Chan Chan.

Tiwanaku. Farming and herding people had been building central plazas and platforms around the shores of Lake Titicaca in modern Bolivia since about 1000 B.C.E. The lake lies at an elevation of 12,500 feet, so farming depended on crops like potatoes and quinoa that would grow at high altitude. Llama and alpaca herds also provided food, wool, and transport. The Tiwanaku state emerged partly in response to climate change. During the drought conditions of the later sixth century, crop production shrank and Lake Titicaca's water level dropped by a third. Consequently, rural villagers had to gather in larger settlements. Tiwanaku city at the southern end of the lake outpaced all other centers in population growth. The aristocratic elite there

acquired great religious prestige and appear to have continually erected new and spectacular temples and other public monuments to attract pilgrims. This elite collected tribute from numerous smaller towns and from distant rural areas, even from peoples on the far side of the Andes crest. We do not know how much of Tiwanaku's imperial expansion depended on military conquest and how much on its talent for inspiring religious fear and wonder.

At its peak in the tenth century, the city may have had about forty thousand residents, while another seventy-five thousand lived in neighboring towns. Two great platforms faced with stone and accessible through massive gateways dominated the Tiwanaku cityscape. The empire's ruling class had residences and administrative offices atop these platforms, but most of the population lived in meager houses. The city appears to have served mainly as a ceremonial and pilgrimage center. There is no evidence at all of marketplaces.

Tiwanaku declined in the tenth century, probably as a result of deteriorating environmental conditions. The water level of Lake Titicaca rose suddenly, inundating farmland. Buildup of salt deposits in irrigated fields may have hindered crop growth. A major drought around 1150 devastated what remained of Tiwanaku civilization. The capital city and its surrounding area were both abandoned, and local populations once under imperial rule reasserted their independence and dispersed into smaller settlements.

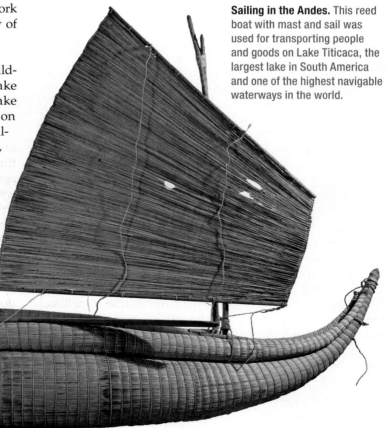

Sailing in the Andes. This reed boat with mast and sail was used for transporting people and goods on Lake Titicaca, the largest lake in South America and one of the highest navigable waterways in the world.

A terraced landscape. Farmers who were the subjects of Wari kings carved terraces out of hillsides in southern Peru's magnificent Colca Canyon. In what ways was terracing likely to improve agricultural productivity in the Andes?

The Wari empire. Like Tiwanaku, the Wari state in the central highlands of Peru emerged in response to the extreme weather events of the sixth century. In Wari's case, successive droughts and downpours impelled small-scale farming communities to shift their most intensive agricultural activities from valley floors to high, steep mountain slopes. There, they undertook stupendous labor to construct numerous stepped terraces, laying out irrigation channels to bring water from Andean snowmelt, and planting potatoes, maize, and other crops that would grow in high, cold places. In this way farmers escaped dearth and flood. However, stronger, more centralized government appears to have been needed to organize and manage this complex infrastructure and to prevent local communities from fighting one another over water and terraced land. Consequently, a minority of noble families rose to political dominance, proclaiming a religious ideology centered on the Staff God, an ancient Andean deity, commonly depicted as a figure having clawed feet and fanged teeth and carrying a staff in each hand.

From the city of Wari, a warren of two- or three-story compounds separated from one another by high walls, the ruling elite dispatched military forces both north and south, colonizing populations and collecting revenue. Wari cultural influences, including terracing technology and pottery styles, followed the armies. At its height in the eighth century, this influence extended along the Andean range about 580 miles, a little more than the distance from Washington, D.C., to Atlanta. To ensure a constant food supply in always unpredictable weather conditions, the rulers founded towns throughout the empire as centers of food collection and storage. They built a network of roads to connect these towns with the capital, and they used *quipus,* or knotted, colored strings as a system for keeping records and sending state messages. Finally, they organized labor drafts, requiring men from communities under their control to give service every year on irrigation, building, and other public projects.

Wari declined about the same time as Tiwanaku, and by 1250 the capital and other imperial towns were abandoned. We cannot explain its demise with any certainty. More drought may be too easy an answer, since Wari had succeeded in the first place by inventing ingenious farming methods that protected it against such disaster.

Chimu. Farmers of Peru's starkly arid coastal plains suffered less from dry cycles than from El Niño events that brought rainfall and flooding severe enough to destroy crops, wipe out irrigation works, and change the course of rivers. Earthquakes also shook canals and reservoirs into ruin from time to time. If anything, urban civilization came harder on the Pacific coast than it did in the cold and rarefied air of the high Andes. Even so, coastal peoples had been building cities for thousands of years, sustaining themselves along the rivers that flowed from the mountains. In the eleventh century the kingdom of Chimu emerged along the northern Peruvian shore.

Chan Chan, the Chimu capital, rose up in the Moche River valley amid the ruins and derelict irrigation works of the older Moche civilization (see Chapter 8). By 1200 the city covered nearly eight square miles and had a population of about thirty-five thousand. The territory under Chimu domination extended along nearly seven hundred miles of coastal plain and inland valleys, embracing a population of at least 250,000. A network of roads connected Chan Chan to numerous vassal cities in neighboring valleys.

The Chimu governing class clearly anticipated extreme weather events and planned for them. To ensure adequate food supplies in all conditions, officials inspected individual households and inventoried the foodstuffs owed to the state as tribute. They were thus prepared to distribute stockpiled food in times of want to prevent mass starvation. The state also resurrected at least part of the old Moche water management system, including canals, reservoirs, hillside terraces, and aqueducts running from one river valley to another. Some canals carried no water to crops but served only as flood channels when they were needed. To collect rainwater and runoff from mountain streams, the Chimu built reservoirs and terraces on steep hills, as well as aqueducts to carry water between cities. To keep up the irrigation network, they implemented a labor draft, similar to the system the rulers of Wari had imposed. Having a ready supply of workers enabled the government to respond quickly to crises. For example, around 1100, a major El Niño storm altered the course of the Moche River, rendering the existing canal network useless. Laborers immediately went to work to build a new one.

Chan Chan consisted of ten large precincts fully enclosed by large adobe walls, some thirty feet high. These enclosures served as the residences, administrative offices, and burial sites of rulers and the governing elite that carried out their commands. Here, Chimu monarchs held public audiences and received tribute in the form of food, wool, cotton textiles, and manufactures. Each precinct had storerooms interspersed among the homes of nobles, officials, and artisans.

Chimu craft. The headgear of this impish-looking man is the spout of a drinking vessel perhaps used for ritual libations. What do you think the man is sitting on?

The city had several royal compounds, not just one, a phenomenon that had to do with a peculiar feature of Chimu kingship. When a ruler died, a single heir assumed the royal title and the powers associated with it. The rest of the royal family, however, took the property of the deceased monarch, including his palace and storerooms and rights to collect tribute. In fact the dead king, regarded as a divine being, was mummified and placed in a special room adjacent to the palace. Archaeologists have found fine textiles, pottery, jewelry, carved wood, and other luxuries in the chambers of these preserved corpses. Several hundred young men might also be sacrificed to accompany the ruler into the afterlife. The royal mummy continued to live on, as it were, in his own palace, and his family and retainers continued to enjoy his wealth. People visited the mummy, rendered homage to it, and asked for favors. Meanwhile, the new king had to build his own compound, establish his own imperial court, and acquire new sources of tribute because he could not touch the income that belonged to his predecessors. He therefore had no choice except to increase the tax burden on his subjects and acquire new tributaries split inheritance The practice of dividing the estate of a person among different heirs.

by conquest. This tradition of **split inheritance,** along with the need to feed growing river valley populations, helps explain Chimu's militaristic expansion.

The empire continued to grow well into the fifteenth century, but its warriors did not push far into mountain valleys. Confined largely to the dry coastal plain, the state had no control over distant sources of its water. When the rising Inca empire seized the highlands, they immediately threatened Chimu's survival.

American Empires in the Fifteenth Century

FOCUS In what ways were the historical development and political and economic institutions of the Aztec and Inca empires similar or different?

During the fifteenth century the Aztec and Inca empires achieved greater size, cohesion, and military success than any earlier states in the Americas. The armies of both empires exercised control over their multiethnic populations from strategically placed fortresses linked together by road networks that speeded messengers and state officials from one locality to another. Wealth generated from conquest, tribute, and trade supported thriving capitals: Tenochtitlán in the Valley of Mexico and Cuzco (Cusco) in southeastern Peru. As the ancient Romans had done, the ruling classes of both empires credited their success to the favor of the gods.

The Aztecs and Incas also displayed some notable differences. The Aztec rulers allowed subjugated groups to retain self-government as long as they paid tribute, which was collected mainly in material goods rather than labor service. The empire resembled a confederation of city-states with one dominant member, the Aztec army, functioning primarily as a deterrent to disorder and rebellion, not as an occupying force. The Inca state, by contrast, evolved a more centralized, bureaucratic government. Subordinate communities could preserve their cultural identities and some local autonomy, but they answered directly to Inca officials, who represented the authority of the divine king. Also in contrast to the Aztecs, the Inca state extracted tribute primarily in labor, mobilizing thousands of men and women for public works projects.

The Aztec Empire

The founding of the Aztec state was the work of the Mexica, one of the numerous Nahuatl-speaking bands that filtered into central Mexico in the twelfth and thirteenth centuries as the Toltec state declined and fell. Many Nahua groups traced their histories to a common origin, a mythic place called Aztlán that lay somewhere to the north. At some point, Nahuas left Aztlán and migrated to the Valley of Mexico. In their origin story, the Mexica claimed to be the last of the Aztlán tribes to enter the valley. The origin of the name *Aztec* in Nahuatl is obscure, and the Mexica who built the empire did not call themselves Aztecs.

According to chronicles compiled in later centuries, the Mexica arrived in the valley around 1250 to find other Nahua groups in possession of cities and most of the fertile land. Consequently, they had to disperse into several different towns and offer their labor in exchange for permission to settle. Nevertheless, Mexica men made a reputation for themselves as skilled and ferocious mercenary fighters. Around 1325 they managed to find a home of their own on two rocky islets in Lake Texcoco in the middle of the valley. Adopting the *chinampa,* or floating garden techniques of their Nahua neighbors, they reclaimed land from the lake and made their little islands much bigger. They also built an aqueduct that brought fresh water from the surrounding mountains, as well as a causeway, or land bridge, connecting their islands to the lake shore. After that, the islands soon became important market centers. In the fourteenth century, the Mexica settlements, once on the margins of Nahua society, blossomed into the thriving cities Tlatelolco (tlah-teh-LOLE-coe) and Tenochtitlán on two ends of a single built-up island.

As the populations of these twin cities grew, they faced the same food insecurities that had troubled other Nahua city-states for two centuries. The two towns could not easily expand their resources because they paid tribute to a larger city named Azcapotzalco. Its rulers prevented them from constructing more *chinampas* and aqueducts. Their survival threatened, the Mexica formed an alliance with the nearby cities of Texcoco and Tlacopan and declared war on Azcapotzalco. They achieved victory around 1428 but then went on to more campaigns of imperial expansion. Over the next six generations, the Triple Alliance (the twin cities and their two collaborators) subjugated the entire Valley of Mexico and most of the surrounding valleys, eventually forging an empire of tribute-paying societies that stretched from the Gulf of Mexico to the Pacific (see Map 14.4). By the early sixteenth century the Triple Alliance, or the Aztecs as they came to be known in modern times, dominated somewhere between 3.3 and 6.4 million people.[2]

Tribute and governance. As a tributary empire, the Triple Alliance permitted the city-states subordinated to it to keep their lands and native rulers, but it collected annual tribute in textiles, clothing, tools, jewels, foodstuffs, animal skins, timber, and slaves. Usually, the city, rather than private households or individuals, surrendered these goods. Special tax collectors toured the empire to enforce tribute obligations. In many parts of the empire, these officials were the only representatives of the Triple Alliance that ordinary people ever saw because there was no centrally directed system of provincial administration or judicial courts. As

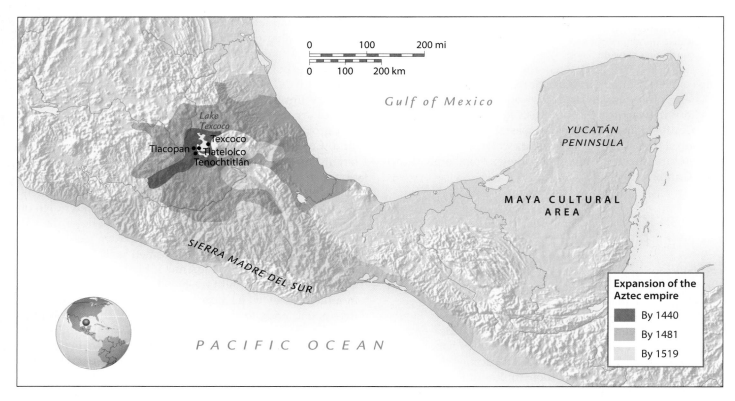

MAP 14.4 Growth of the Aztec empire.

At its height the Aztec empire stretched from the Pacific to the Gulf of Mexico. What geographic factors may help explain why the Aztec state expanded in the directions it did?

a general rule, the degree of communal self-government increased in proportion to the distance from the Valley of Mexico. Communities on the far frontiers paid no tribute at all but simply allied themselves with the Aztecs, serving as a first line of defense against any group that dared to make war on the empire.

The Aztecs ruled by a combination of diplomacy and war. Before sending an army to conquer a city, they dispatched emissaries to offer gifts and other inducements to surrender. In many cases, the targeted community yielded quickly, perhaps after negotiating with the ambassadors for a lower annual tribute. Only if a foreign ruler refused to comply did the Triple Alliance attack. Even then, the conquerors did not aim to annex territory but fought only until the enemy gave in, then ruled by instilling fear of military retaliation. The Triple Alliance built forts and planted garrisons throughout the empire. These posts watched for local rebellions, guarded borders against invasion, and protected long-distance trade routes. An elaborate communication system connected outlying regions with the central cities. Runners stationed at regular intervals along the major routes carried information pony-express-style between the capitals and army commanders in the field.

The twin cities. The influx of tribute and trade brought prosperity to the cities of the Triple Alliance, especially Tenochtitlán and Tlatelolco, the twin capitals of the Mexica. Tlatelolco became the leading commercial center. When the Spanish conquistador Hernán Cortés entered the Valley of Mexico in the early sixteenth century, the two cities were conjoined. In a letter to the king of Spain he described the great Tlatelolco market:

> This city has many public squares, in which are situated the markets and other places for buying and selling. There is one square twice as large as that of the city of Salamanca [a Spanish city], surrounded by porticoes, where are daily assembled more than sixty thousand souls, engaged in buying and selling; and where are found all kinds of merchandise that the world affords, embracing the necessaries of life, as for instance articles of food, as well as jewels of gold and silver, lead, brass, copper, tin, precious stones, bones, shells, snails, and feathers."[3]

Tenochtitlán and Tlatelolco grew rapidly during the fifteenth century, and together their population may have reached as much as 250,000 by the time the Spanish arrived. Mexica rulers sponsored ambitious building projects, adding an aqueduct, increasing the number of causeways, and constructing an elaborate temple complex. Two perpendicular avenues intersected at the central square, dividing Tenochtitlán into four quarters, each with its own sacred precinct. The city's layout reflected Aztec cosmology.

Nezahualcoyotl ("Fasting Coyote"): Political Strategist, Survivor, and Poet

The Aztec empire arose as an alliance of city-states representing distinct Nahua groups. The Mexica were the dominant partner, but their allies were indispensable to imperial success. Texcoco, a Nahua city east of Tenochtitlán and a member of the Triple Alliance, was an especially valuable collaborator under the leadership of Nezahualcoyotl, or Fasting Coyote (1402–1472).

Nezahualcoyotl, whose biography has been pieced together from Spanish chronicles and Nahua codices (singular, **codex**), came of age during a time of food scarcity and regional warfare. When he was fifteen, he marched into battle alongside his father, the king of Texcoco, to defend the city-state from the Tepaneca, a powerful Nahua people. The Texcoco army was annihilated. Nezahualcoyotl, the heir to the Texcoco throne, watched from a tree as enemy soldiers slaughtered his father. The invaders saw the boy, captured him, and made ready to sacrifice him to the Tepaneca patron god. A faithful Texcoco servant, however, slipped into the prison where Nezahualcoyotl was being held, exchanged clothes with him, and volunteered to die in his place. The young prince escaped to Tenochtitlán, where his mother had been born as a member of the ruling family. The Mexica welcomed the fugitive as one of their own.

> **codex** A set of pages of parchment or other material stacked together and bound along one edge or, alternatively, a continuous strip of material folded accordion-style to form pages; a codex is to be distinguished from a scroll.

After eight years in Tenochtitlán, where he was educated, Nezahualcoyotl decided to return to his native city. But Maxtla, the Tepaneca ruler who had conquered Texcoco, put an extravagant price on his head. Once again, the prince had to cheat death. He fled to the mountains where, like a hungry coyote, he hid in ravines and caves. Peasants loyal to his family kept him alive.

Nezahualcoyotl's gritty resistance inspired a larger revolt. Texcoco nobles and mountain villagers formed an army to drive out the hated Tepaneca. The prince led an assault on the city, liberated it, and in the following months joined the rulers of Tenochtitlán and the city-state of Tlacopan in the Triple Alliance. This potent confederation vanquished the Tepaneca and took control of the entire Valley of Mexico.

Nezahualcoyotl became king of Texcoco through violent revolution, but he also excelled at the art of peace. He ordered that laws be codified concerning the sale and inheritance of property. His surveyors measured the plots of both nobles and villagers to settle disputes, and he championed the rights of peasants to stay on their farms no matter which lord owned them. Like all Nahua rulers, he accepted the practice of human sacrifice. The custom, however, appears to have troubled him. As king, he refused to attend the ritual killings.

Nezahualcoyotl embarked on a massive building campaign to improve the lives of his people, constructing new temples, roads, and public gardens. His royal palace compound sprawled across two hundred acres and contained a ball court, a zoo, and a market. He reformed the government, establishing separate councils for war, finance, justice, and the arts. Painters, artisans, and writers flocked to Texcoco. Modern scholars regard poetry attributed to Nezahualcoyotl to be among the finest examples of Nahuatl literature. About a dozen philosophical poems survive thanks to the sixteenth-century historian Juan Bautista de Pomar, the ruler's half-Spanish great grandson. These verses reveal a deep love of nature, an appreciation for life's fragility, and a philosophy best described as *carpe diem*—seize the day. In "The Flower Tree," Nezahualcoyotl writes joyfully about human creativity:

An entirely imagined representation of Nezahualcoyotl on a government building in Mexico City.

> Live here on earth, blossom!
> As you move and shake, flowers fall.
> My flowers are eternal, my songs are forever.
> I raise them,
> I, a singer.
> I scatter them,
> I spill them,
> The flowers become gold,
> They are carried inside the golden place.

Thinking Critically

In terms of his actions, attitudes, and ruling policies, would you say that Nezahualcoyotl is typical or not typical of premodern monarchs?

Residents imagined the world divided into four parts. A large mountain stood at the center. From there a great tree rose into the sky, supporting the ceiling that enveloped the planet. Like medieval Christians, the Aztecs envisaged a multilayered heaven and an underworld. Archaeologists believe that the four quarters of Tenochtitlán symbolized the parts of the earth and that the Great Temple represented the central mountain. The shrine's cavernous interior, which contained numerous artifacts and human bones, stood for the underworld—the residence of the dead.

The lives of Aztec children. Antonio de Mendoza, the first Spanish governor of Mexico in the sixteenth century, may have commissioned local scholars to produce a pictorial account of Aztec history and life. The explanatory text accompanying the pictures is in Spanish. This page of the Codex Mendoza depicts chores and punishments. At the top an adult is punishing a boy (left) and a girl (right) for some infraction by forcing them to breathe the smoke of burning chili peppers. At the bottom a boy is dutifully fishing and a girl is learning to weave cloth. What do you think the children in the middle two scenes might be doing?

The Great Temple had a pyramidal shape and a steep staircase leading up to a platform and two stone huts. Each of these structures was the home of a god. From one of them Tlaloc, the god of rain, presided over the city in summer and fall—the wet months, when crops were planted and harvested. From the other house, Huitzilopochtli, the patron deity of the Mexica, ruled during winter and spring, when the farmers left their fields and went to war. According to tradition, Huitzilopochtli led the Mexica from Aztlán to the Valley of Mexico and later instructed them to found Tenochtitlán.

From their homes atop the Great Temple, the two gods oversaw the central market. It was no coincidence that the market and the temple were in the same place. Like other Mesoamerican peoples, the Mexica believed that the gods, just like human rulers, wanted to be fed, clothed, and indulged with all the material comforts their subjects could offer. The market therefore served as both a bazaar and a sacred place of making offerings to the gods. Commerce and religion were inseparable.

Religion and human sacrifice. Like the Maya of earlier centuries (see Chapter 8), the Mexica believed that blood was the most valuable gift a person could offer the gods, especially human blood and preferably one's own. According to Nahua mythology, the gods created the world and the human race by sacrificing themselves. In one story, the god Nanahuatzin threw himself into a fire and became the sun. When the other deities asked him why he stayed still and refused to move across the sky, he replied, "Because I am asking for their blood, their color, their precious substance."[4] The feathered serpent god Quetzalcoatl promptly cut open the chests of the other gods and held those deities up to Nanahuatzin as an offering. To fulfill their debt to the gods, humans were also expected to offer sacrificial blood, usually by piercing their skin. Slaves, criminals, and especially war captives gave blood by sacrificing their lives. The Mexica ritually killed thousands of people in front of the Great Temple. Most of these victims died under protest, but some perished voluntarily, apparently regarding self-sacrifice as a great honor. In one of the more infamous rituals, the condemned were made to file up the steps of the pyramid. At the top the chief priest brandished a sharp obsidian blade to slice through each victim's rib cage, removing the heart and holding it up to the sky. Other priests then hurled the dead bodies down the steps, covering the side of the temple with trails of blood.

At the bottom, priests cut off the heads of the corpses and put them on display. A rack of skulls from previous victims ringed the base of the pyramid.

Nahua beliefs about sacrifice motivated imperial conquest. Every major event, including childbirth, a battle, the movement of the sun, and the coming of rain and harvest, required some form of sacrifice. Furthermore, tribute had to be collected from as many groups as possible, both to feed urban populations and to satisfy the insatiable hunger of the gods. The armies of the Triple Alliance went to war in part to acquire victims, as did the Aztecs' enemies. In fact, cities sometimes fought prearranged battles in which each side agreed to take a fixed number of captives for ritual killing later on. Sacrifice may also have functioned as a tool of political intimidation. The Mexica were known to invite dependent rulers from distant cities to the Great Temple to watch as warriors from those cities had their hearts ripped out—a reminder that the Triple Alliance wielded the real power.

Some historians have argued that later Spanish conquerors greatly exaggerated Aztec human sacrifice to morally justify their own seizure of Mexico. There might be truth in that claim, though the visual and documentary evidence of the practice is abundant. On the other hand, we can also point to numerous societies in Africa, Asia, and Europe that at one time or another either slaughtered innocents to appease the powers of the universe or performed gruesome public executions on an appalling scale.

Through their religious ceremonies, the Triple Alliance projected confidence in its destiny to rule the earth as the gods' chosen people. Their cosmology also told them, however, that their power would not last forever. They believed that humankind lived in the Fifth Age of the Sun. Like the previous four ages, that one was due to end. In one popular tale, the king sent a group of soldiers north to Aztlán to pay respect to the mother of their patron god. They returned with ominous news. One day, the goddess informed them, the Mexica would lose all their lands to unnamed invaders from out of the eastern sea—the Gulf of Mexico. Another prophecy warned that the god Quetzalcoatl, whose beard was "extremely long and tangled," had long ago set sail in that sea. But he promised to return one day to rule the world."[5] These traditions played nicely into the hands of Cortés, the bearded Spaniard who came ashore in 1519.

A lethal instrument. This Aztec sacrificial stone knife has an ornately carved wooden handle.

The Incas

In the central Andean highlands, a period of political decentralization followed the collapse of the Wari empire in the mid-thirteenth century. Local communities of farmers and llama herders fought intermittently over land, water, and food stores, especially during drought years. These village-dwelling peoples spoke a variety of languages, including dialects of Quechua. The Incas, one small Quechua group, inhabited a number of dispersed villages in the highland area southeast of the old Wari capital. In the 1430s they began to make war on their neighbors, and over the next century they created a bigger and more politically sophisticated empire than South America had ever seen.

Inca beginnings. The Incas traced their origins to an island in Lake Titicaca, not far from where the Tiwanaku civilization had risen and fallen. According to their mythology, a god named Wira Qucha gave birth to the sun, moon, stars, clouds, and lightning—each a god in its own right. Inti the sun god gave birth to human ancestors of the *Incas,* a word that means "children of the sun." Eight of those children—four brothers and four sisters—wandered out of a cave named Pakariq Tampu in search of water and land. During their journey, three of the brothers were turned into stones. The fourth, named Manqu Qhapaq, entered the Cuzco Valley, drove out the inhabitants, and founded the city of Cuzco.

Archaeologists believe that the Incas first occupied that region around 1200 C.E. and over the next two centuries took control of kinship groups already living there. Though subordinating themselves to the Incas, these groups, called *ayllu* in Quechua, managed to preserve their identity and much of their political and social autonomy. Each *ayllu* consisted of extended families that traced descent from a common ancestor, who was often linked to a specific natural object such as a cave, a stream, a rock, or a mountain. Each *ayllu* venerated a particular sacred place, known as a *wak'a,* by making frequent pilgrimages there and offering gold, cloth, seashells, or food. In periods of famine or war, the *ayllu* sometimes also sacrificed animals or even young children, believing that the *wak'a* could bring good or bad fortune depending on how well it was fed. Devotion to the *wak'a* was a major source of the *ayllu*'s common identity.

A ruling family that carried the name Inca presided over hundreds of *ayllu* in the Cuzco Valley. Members of the royal lineage distinguished themselves from the rest of the population by wearing large earrings, a habit that prompted later Spanish colonizers to call them *orejones,* or "big ears." The head of the lineage called Sapa Inca ("Unique Child"), or simply the Inca, ruled as king alongside his wife, who was also his sister. The practice of sibling marriage aimed to uphold the purity of the royal blood line. As a direct descendant of the sun, the king was revered as a living god. According to a Spanish chronicler,

No one was allowed to appear before him with shoes on, no matter how important a lord he might be, not even his brothers; rather, they came barefooted and with their heads bowed all the time they were speaking before him or bringing him a message. He always ate alone, without anyone daring to touch the food he was eating. Lords carried him in a litter on their shoulders. If he went out to the square, he sat on a golden seat under a parasol made of ostrich feathers dyed red. He drank from golden tumblers, and all the other service dishes of his household were of gold. He had a great many women."[6]

Artisans fashioned statues of the king in gold, silver, and other precious materials, and royal servants placed them in specially built houses throughout Cuzco, eventually throughout the empire. The king performed religious rituals vital to the health and well-being of the society. But owing to his divine status, he did not take much part in worldly affairs. Rather, he typically designated brothers or other close relatives to command armies, run state administration, and conduct less important ceremonies.

Like the Chimu, Inca society practiced split inheritance long before they became conquerors. Consequently, by the fifteenth century, Inca society included several dozen royal clans, each venerating the mummified remains of a past ruler and each possessing its own stone compound in Cuzco and its own agricultural lands and tribute rights. When a new Inca came to power, he had to gather his own wealth and find his own tribute payers. As in the Chimu case, split inheritance created a powerful motive for imperial expansion (see Map 14.5).

An empire three thousand miles long. According to oral histories, Inca imperial expansion began around 1425, when a foreign group threatened Cuzco. Out of fear, the reigning Inca and his heir apparent fled the city, while a younger son remained to fight. This lad defeated the invaders and proclaimed himself the new ruler, claiming that his father and elder brother had forfeited the throne on account of their cowardice. Taking the royal name Pachakuti, or World Shaker, the new monarch conquered neighboring peoples north and south along the highland ridges. After his death around 1471, his son Tupac Yupanqui continued the expansion. By the start of the sixteenth century, the Inca empire stretched from the mountains of modern Ecuador to the middle of modern Chile and embraced somewhere between six and thirteen million people.

Like the Mexica, the Incas founded their dominion on skillful combinations of diplomacy and violence. Initially, they lavished local lords with gifts, aiming to get them to submit without a fight. During his victorious war with the Chanka, Pachakuti accumulated rich spoils, including food stores of maize, potatoes, chilies, beans, quinoa, and meat. He hoarded these goods, knowing that harsh

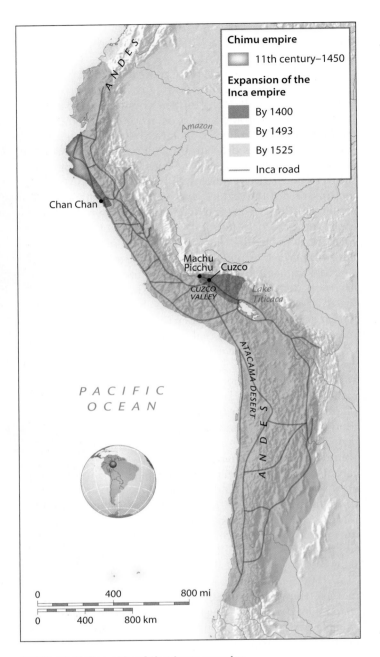

MAP 14.5 Growth of the Inca empire.

The Inca state incorporated a range of altitude from sea level to more than 20,000 feet and therefore a great variety of ecological zones. Why do you think the Inca empire took the territorial shape it did?

and unpredictable Andean weather made them valuable commodities to barter for other goods, favors, and political allegiance. He invited the rulers of neighboring groups to Cuzco, plying them with elaborate feasts and presents of gold, jewels, and other luxuries. These visiting lords brought their own gifts, and both sides exchanged women to serve as concubines, servants, and wives, in that way strengthening bonds of friendship between elite families. Through these strategies, many Andean peoples slipped into dependency on the Incas as weak allies.

Chastity and Marriage in Inca Society

Since Incas did not have a written language, most of our knowledge of their society comes from texts written by Spanish conquistadors. Such books often emphasized the "pagan" and "barbarian" natures of the Incas as justification for Spanish domination. For this reason, Garcilaso de la Vega's Royal Commentaries of the Incas and General History of Peru *stands apart from other early Spanish writings. Garcilaso (1539–1616), son of a conquistador and an Inca noblewoman, was the first* mestizo, *that is, a person of mixed European and indigenous heritage, to write about Andean peoples for a European audience.*

Garcilaso was raised in Cuzco and moved fluidly between Spanish and Inca societies. When he was twenty-one, he used an inheritance from his deceased father to travel to Spain. While there, he under-took to write the Commentaries, *a two-volume history of the Inca state and the Spanish conquest. Part One, published in 1609, is a detailed description of indigenous history, society, and culture, emphasizing the benevolence of the Inca's rule and portraying preconquest Peru as a society of noble and law-abiding pagans, similar to classical Greece or Rome. In Part Two, published the year after he died, he recounted the Spanish conquest. Although Garcilaso approved Spanish rule in Peru, he also tried to persuade readers that Inca civilization was more advanced than Spanish conquistadors wished to admit. In the excerpts below, he describes Inca attitudes toward chastity and some customs surrounding marriage.*

Other women who preserved their virginity, and widows

Besides the virgins who entered monasteries to profess perpetual virginity withdrawn from the world, there were many women of the royal blood who led a similar life in their own homes, having taken a vow of chastity, though not of reclusion. They did not fail to visit their closer relatives in case of sickness or childbirth. . . . Such women were greatly respected for their chastity and high-mindedness, and as a mark of their excellence and divinity they were called *ocllo*, a name held sacred in their idolatry. Their chastity was not feigned, but sincerely preserved, on pain of their being burnt alive as traitors and counterfeiters of their false religion or thrown into the lake of lions, if they were shown to have defiled it. . . .

Nor should one omit to mention the chastity of widows, who usually remained in complete retirement of the whole of the first year of their widowhood. Of those who were childless very few married again. Those who had children never remarried, but lived in continence [abstinence]. This virtue was greatly commended in their laws and ordinances, which prescribed that the fields of widows should be tilled before those of the *curaca* [a class of official] or those of the Inca, apart from many similar privileges.

How they usually married and set up house

It must be explained that every year or every two years, at a certain season, the king ordered all the marriageable maidens and youths of his lineage to gather together in Cuzco. The girls were between eighteen and twenty years old and the youths from twenty-four upwards. They were not allowed to marry earlier, for they said that it was necessary to be old enough and wise enough to rule their houses and estates, and for them to marry earlier would be childish.

The Inca placed himself in the midst of the contracting parties, who were near to one another, and having looked at them, called a youth and a girl, took each by the hand, united them in the bond of matrimony and delivered them to their parents. They then went to the bridegroom's house and solemnized the wedding in the presence of the nearer relatives. The celebrations lasted two, four, or six days, or longer if they wished. These were legitimate wives, and as a mark of greater honor and favor to them they were said in their language to be "given by the Inca's hand." . . .

The houses for the dwellings of bridegrooms who were Incas [members of the royal lineage] . . . were made by Indians from the provinces entrusted with the task according to the division of labor that was set down for everything. The household requirements were provided by the relatives, each bringing a piece. There were no other ceremonies or sacrifices. . . .

For the marriages of the common people the councils of each village were obliged to have houses built for those who were married, and the relatives provided the furniture. It was not lawful for those of different provinces to intermarry, or even those of different towns. All were to marry within their own towns and their own families like the tribes of Israel. . . . All those of one village regarded themselves as relatives, like the sheep of one fold. Even those of the same province did so, if they were all of one tribe and the same language. It was not permitted for them to go from one province and live in another, or from one town to another, or one quarter to another. . . .

Source: Garcilaso de la Vega, *Royal Commentaries of the Incas and General History of Peru,* Part One, trans. Harold V. Livermore (Austin: University of Texas Press, 1966), 204–206.

Thinking Critically

According to Garcilaso, what behavior was expected of widows? What role did the Inca king play in marriage transactions among elites? Why do you think it was unlawful for ordinary people to marry outside their own villages? Why do you think Garcilaso makes reference to the "tribes of Israel"? How does this text challenge sixteenth-century European perceptions of the Incas as primitive or savage?

Groups that resisted Inca entreaties could pay a devastating price, as the Guarco people did. Living in an isolated valley and encasing their city in a stone wall, they thought they could repel an Inca invasion. They threw back four Inca attempts to capture the city but finally gave way. The conquerors proceeded to kill the Guarco warriors, hanging their bodies from the city walls. The Inca ruler confiscated most of the Guarcos' land and redistributed it to colonists brought in from other parts of the empire.

After gaining control of many Andean mountain valleys that channeled snowmelt to the Pacific, the Incas set their sights on the Chimu state and its great capital of Chan Chan. Around 1470, an Inca army moved into the Moche River valley upstream from the city and threatened to obstruct the river and therefore irrigation of the coastal plain. This menace was enough to compel Chan Chan's surrender. The Inca army captured the Chimu king and forced thousands of artisans to relocate to Cuzco. The Chimu state disappeared abruptly, though its art had significant influence on Inca craft and style.

The Inca state. Incas created a more hierarchical and centralized state than the Aztecs did, though they did not stamp out local self-government. They organized the empire into four administrative sectors divided from one another by royal roads that ran outward from Awkaypata, the great public plaza at the center of Cuzco. The four imperial sectors were partitioned further into provinces and smaller districts, each under the authority of a governor drawn from the Cuzco elite. That official supervised tribute collection and presided over state religious ceremonies. The traditional rulers of subject communities kept their titles and local authority unless they resisted or rebelled. They had to recognize Inca sovereignty and surrender a third of their lands to the state. They had to set aside another third to provide tribute to the sun god and other deities, including offerings made at sacred *wak'as* and maintenance of priests and servants who safeguarded those shrines. That left a final third, often the least productive and accessible land, for the farms and pasture of the local population.

Conquered societies paid tribute mainly in labor. Men and women could be drafted into the army or into work gangs that built temples, storehouses, dams, irrigation works, and roads. This labor draft, modeled on those of Wari and Chimu, was called the *mit'a*. The state could also command people to serve in the households of the noble class. Women drafted into service wove garments, cooked, and brewed maize beer, some of which was used in religious rituals. Officials traveling around the empire handpicked girls between the ages of eight and twelve for prestigious service in Cuzco's main temple. When it suited their production and labor needs, the government also forcibly transplanted entire communities from one part of the empire to another. In fact, the state appears to have aimed to homogenize imperial society and culture. When a new area was conquered, officials compelled settlers from other regions to migrate in

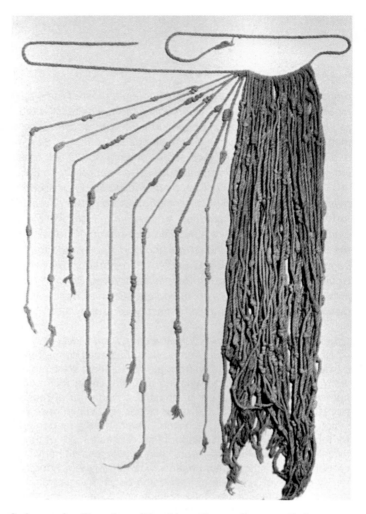

An Inca *quipu*. The colors of the strings, the way they were tied together, the placement of the knots, and the type of wool used all carried specific meanings to those Inca officials who could "read" *quipus*. Only a few hundred *quipus* survive, and modern scholars have never cracked the code to this communication system. Should the *quipu* system be considered a form of writing, or not?

but discouraged them from adopting local speech and customs and obliged the noble families on both the indigenous and the immigrant sides to speak Quechua, the imperial language. If the empire had lasted longer than it did, this grand if fundamentally violent experiment might in time have yielded the most culturally integrated large empire in premodern world history.

Communication and transport. The Incas maintained control over the empire by means of a communication system more tightly organized than the Aztecs had and that rivaled those of the most technically sophisticated Afroeurasian empires. This system had three main components: record keeping, roads, and relay runners.

The Incas recorded messages on *quipus*, a device used in the earlier Wari empire. These were pieces of rope to which secondary cords were attached. Other knotted and colored

principles of linear perspective in action. Titled *The Holy Trinity* (1425), this fresco, a picture made by applying paint to a moist plaster surface, occupies a wall in the church of Santa Maria Novella in Florence. It depicts the crucified Jesus Christ and three other figures as though they were inside a room with an arched ceiling. The illusion of spatial depth is convincing because, in accord with the rules of perspective, all the diagonal lines in the pattern of the ceiling converge at a single point in the picture. Other artists in Florence adopted the new technique, and it subsequently spread throughout Europe. For the next few centuries, the idea that painters should apply rules of perspective so that their canvases appear as "windows" on the natural world became fundamental to European art.

Linear perspective was one of the remarkable innovations in art and architecture that Florentines achieved in the period of European history conventionally called the late Middle Ages. Ironically, the city's cultural flowering, the period that later became known as the Italian Renaissance, took place, not in a time of political and social calm, but when Europe was just beginning to recover from several decades of severe social and economic upheaval. The young Masaccio and numerous other talented Florentines went about their creative labor in a city troubled by disease, war, and poverty.

In fact, Florence was representative of several Afroeurasian cities that sparkled as points of artistic and scholarly light despite repeated episodes of epidemic, violence, and economic disruption. Beginning early in the fourteenth century, the expansionary trend of population, economic output, and long-distance trade that had characterized much of Afroeurasia for about seven hundred years went into reverse. This general downturn, recalling the prolonged economic contraction of the fourth to sixth centuries C.E., involved several crises. One was a serious decline in food production and consequent famine in the Northern Hemisphere linked to climatic change. A second was the outbreak of infectious disease in several parts of Afroeurasia, a pestilence whose initial assault became known in history as the Black Death. A third was a swell of regional wars that reconfigured Afroeurasia's political map. Finally, commercial and cultural exchange along the trans-Eurasian silk roads declined following a century of unprecedented activity. The first part of this chapter explores the environmental catastrophes of the fourteenth century. The second part investigates the economic, political, and social consequences that attended those calamities, focusing here on China, the central Muslim lands, and Europe.

In the third section, we explore how and why demographic and economic motors began to rev up again in the 1400s

• • •

in much of Afroeurasia. Several vigorous new monarchies appeared, some of them eventually to become imperial giants. Silk road traffic picked up again, the shipping lanes along Afroeurasia's chain of seas flourished as never before. The technology of mechanical printing spread along the exchange routes from East Asia to Europe, allowing knowledge to be produced and circulated on a vastly larger scale. The secrets of gunpowder weaponry also spread across the hemisphere, amplifying human capacity to kill and destroy but also enhancing the power of centralized states.

The multiple troubles of the 1300–1500 period, like earlier cycles of retrenchment, revealed humankind's extraordinary talent for adapting to jarring change. Moreover, in the very long term of history, the era represented a short and only partial interruption of the human tendency to devise ever more complex systems of economy, social organization, and cultural exchange.

A Panoramic View

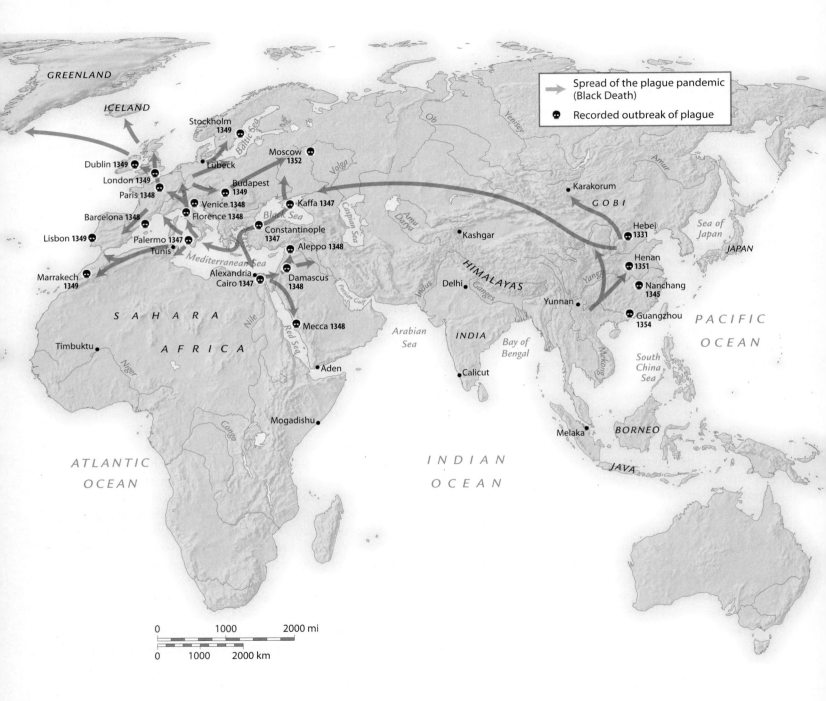

MAP 15.1 Spread of the plague pandemic (Black Death), 1330–1355.
The Black Death was one of several human catastrophes to strike Afroeurasian lands during the fourteenth century. What geographical factors might help explain why the plague pandemic spread in the general directions it did?

Environmental Crises of the Fourteenth Century

FOCUS What historical developments may account for significant population decline in parts of Afroeurasia in the fourteenth century?

After about seven hundred years of steady growth, the population of Afroeurasia as a whole plunged suddenly in the mid-fourteenth century, dropping about 16 percent between 1300 and 1400. This demographic slump did not take place everywhere, nor did it occur all at once. It did not, as far as we know, happen in Subsaharan Africa. In China, Inner Eurasia, and parts of Southwest Asia, on the other hand, numbers started sinking in the 1200s in connection with Mongol destruction, then kept on sinking straight through the 1300s. After three centuries of vigorous growth, Europe's numbers leveled off in about 1300 and then nose-dived between 1340 and 1400. Afroeurasia's overall demographic recovery did not get under way until the second half of the fifteenth century.

The economies of China, Inner Eurasia, the central Muslim lands, and Europe all appear to have slowed significantly in the fourteenth century, especially set against the dramatic growth that had occurred between 1000 and 1200. Subsaharan Africa was almost certainly an exception to this trend. There, towns and trade routes multiplied throughout the crisis decades, though from a lower starting base compared, say, to China.

Monumental changes also took place in the political sphere. Two of the great Mongol states—the Yuan dynasty in China and the khanate of Iran-Iraq (Ilkhanate)—disintegrated before 1370. The other two major Mongol empires—the khanate of Chagatai in the eastern steppes and Central Asia and the Golden Horde in the western steppes and Russia—started imploding before the end of the century as a result of dynastic wars and rebellions. In the Mediterranean basin, the Turkic Mamluk empire of Egypt and Syria had increasing trouble maintaining its economic and financial health, and the three Muslim sultanates that shared North Africa all experienced serious internal troubles after 1350. In West Africa, the Mali empire, the world's most important gold-supplying state as of 1300, also shrank in the later decades of the fourteenth century amid royal succession disputes and provincial revolts.

These economic and political traumas had no single cause, and explanations for stagnancy or upheaval in one region do not necessarily apply in others. We have no index of wars and revolts to prove that the fourteenth century was more violent than any of several previous ages in world history. Russia, for example, certainly suffered more material destruction from the Mongol invasion of 1237–1240 than from any stresses that occurred in the following two hundred years. Nevertheless, we can identify, at least in

northerly parts of Afroeurasia, environmental crises that profoundly disrupted the lives and livelihoods of tens of millions of people in the fourteenth century.

Downpour and Drought

As we saw in earlier chapters, the Northern Hemisphere experienced a small but ecologically significant warming trend, known as the North Atlantic Warm Period, between the ninth and thirteenth centuries. This trend ended sometime after 1200. Temperatures in Arctic and northern temperate latitudes dropped, and this cooling cycle continued erratically to the mid-1800s.

Climatologists have labeled this temperature decline the **Little Ice Age** because of the advance of polar and alpine glaciers that accompanied it. Drawing on evidence from Europe and the North Atlantic, researchers have also suggested three general types of environmental change and accompanying social upheavals centered on the fourteenth century. First, in the Baltic Sea and the North Atlantic, sea ice and colder water temperatures extended farther south, reducing fish stocks and making voyages between Europe and the Norse communities of Iceland and Greenland more dangerous. Second, annual weather patterns became more erratic. Beginning in the 1200s, brutal wind storms and sea floods periodically smashed into the North Atlantic, North Sea, and Baltic Sea coasts, inundating low-lying farmland and in some years killing tens of thousands of people. Third,

> **Little Ice Age** A trend of climatic cooling that affected weather conditions chiefly in the Northern Hemisphere approximately from the late thirteenth to the mid-nineteenth century.

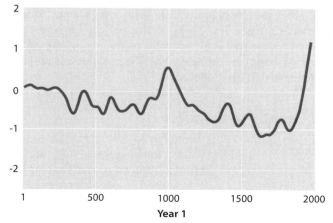

Temperature deviation (°C)

Global temperature changes, 1–2000 C.E. In what one-hundred-year period did the temperature peak of the North Atlantic Warm Period occur? In what one-hundred-year period did the lowest temperature point of the Little Ice Age occur?

summers became generally cooler and wetter all across northern Europe. In northern Britain and Scandinavia, grain farmers had to retreat south, leaving behind hundreds of deserted villages. English vintners found they could no longer produce decent wine.

Between 1315 and 1322 a succession of cool, rainy summers in northern Europe shortened the growing season, hampered crop harvesting, and made sheep and cattle more susceptible to epidemic diseases. Massive famine ensued, disrupting all economic life, expanding the ranks of the destitute, and killing perhaps 5–10 percent of the population. A modern historian, drawing on fourteenth-century chronicles, describes the sufferings of people in the region that is today Belgium during rains that started in May 1315 and continued nearly uninterrupted for a year: "The local harvest was wholly insufficient and the customary imports ceased almost entirely. In Antwerp the moans of the famishing could almost move a stone to pity. . . . They died in large numbers and great pits were dug outside the town into which were cast as many as sixty bodies."[1] Better weather returned after 1322, but climatic conditions remained highly volatile. Regional famines continued to occur throughout the century in both northern and Mediterranean Europe.

The Little Ice Age hit western Europe just when economic growth was leveling off following several centuries of robust expansion. By the later 1200s, farm production could no longer keep pace with population growth. Good cropland in the more densely populated regions of western and central Europe filled up, and the migration of German and other western European farmers to conquered frontier territories in eastern Europe and Spain slowed down (see Chapter 12). Consequently, food prices increased, living standards shrank for all but the very rich, and at the low end of the social scale many serfs and tenant farmers descended into extreme poverty. The famines of 1315 to 1322 made all these problems worse. But even though hunger and disease killed hundreds of thousands, Europe's population appears to have generally recovered in the second quarter of the fourteenth century. The real demographic catastrophe struck in midcentury.

The Great Pestilence

Writing in the late 1370s the North African historian and philosopher Ibn Khaldun recalled the horror he had witnessed two decades earlier: "Civilization both in the East and the West was visited by a destructive plague which devastated nations and caused populations to vanish. It swallowed up many of the good things of civilization and wiped them out. . . . Cities and building were laid waste, roads and way signs were obliterated, settlements and mansions became empty, dynasties and tribes grew weak. The entire inhabited world changed."[2] The infectious disease that Ibn Khaldun described did not in fact affect "the entire inhabited world." But it no doubt seemed that way to him, because

it killed a substantial percentage of North Africa's population and triggered years of economic and political disorder. Next to the massive die-off that American Indians endured when they first came in contact with Afroeurasian pathogens in the sixteenth century, the **Black Death** of 1346 to 1352 stands as the most deadly known

> **Black Death** An infectious disease, probably plague, that caused significant population decline in parts of Afroeurasia in the mid-fourteenth century.

disease crisis up to modern times. It broke upon populations from Inner Eurasia, and perhaps China, to as far west as Greenland (see Map 15.1). Everywhere that it struck, immune systems failed to defend human bodies against the invading microorganism. Millions died after days, or even just hours, of acute suffering from raging fevers, vomiting, and dark painful swellings called buboes. Though as many as 40 percent of infected victims recovered, depending on the locality, people who contracted pneumonic plague, that is, infection of the lungs, almost always died. And before they expired, they often transmitted the pathogen to others by coughing, sneezing, or just breathing. In Afroeurasia the Black Death reached the proportions of a pandemic, a contagion that spread from one region to another, in this case nearly across the hemisphere.

Origins of the Black Death. Since the late nineteenth century, epidemiologists and historians have argued that plague was the infection associated with the Black Death. We sometimes use the word *plague* to characterize any serious epidemic or, metaphorically, any sudden calamity, such as a "plague of locusts." By a stricter definition, however, plague refers to a particular disease having a range of symptoms and biological strains associated with the disease-producing bacterium, or bacillus, called *Yersinia pestis* (*Y. pestis*). For longer than anyone knows, plague has thrived among ground-burrowing rodents that live in certain parts of the world, notably in Inner Eurasia, the Himalayan Mountain foothills, East Africa, and the American Southwest. The principal vector, or carrier, of *Y. pestis* is a type of flea that inhabits the fur of living animals and feeds on their blood. In certain environmental conditions, the bacillus may spread through a large rodent population. Animals infected with *Y. pestis* soon die, forcing equally infected fleas to jump to a living animal to feed, thereby spreading the disease further. If infected animals come into sustained contact with humans, fleas that can find no other hosts may look for blood meals on human bodies, thereby passing *Y. pestis* to them. According to recent research, *Y. pestis* infections caused the first plague pandemic, the Plague of Justinian, which occurred in the mid-sixth century (see Chapter 9).[3]

Some researchers have argued recently that the Black Death had nothing to do with *Y. pestis,* pointing to differences in symptoms and other factors between the fourteenth-century pandemic and modern plague. Nevertheless, current genetic studies, including analysis of DNA from the bones of plague victims buried between 1348 and

1350 in a cemetery in London, have confirmed the presence of *Y. pestis*.[4] This research contends that the Black Death was more virulent than modern plague because infected people were already suffering from malnutrition associated with food shortages linked to the Little Ice Age.

The precise region where the Black Death originated is also debated, but the dominant theory contends that humans mingled with infected rodent communities somewhere in Inner Eurasia in the late thirteenth or early fourteenth century (see Map 15.1). Turkic and Mongol horse soldiers may have been the first to spread the disease widely. Infected rodents and fleas could have infiltrated grain stores in saddlebags and wagons, thus traveling far and wide to contaminate both humans and more rodents. Some scholars have also hypothesized that Little Ice Age conditions helped propel the disease because drier weather on the Inner Eurasian steppes forced rodents to migrate in search of water. As infected creatures moved east or west from areas of sparse to denser human habitation, they set off epidemics.

According to contemporary Chinese reports, a terrible pestilence struck the Hebei region of northern China in 1331, killing nine-tenths of the population. Though we lack a description of symptoms, it is possible that the Black Death enacted its first scene in East Asia. To the west, epidemics occurred in Inner Eurasia in the late 1330s and in the Golden Horde territories north of the Black Sea in the following decade. About 1345, disease erupted in Kaffa (Theodosia) on the Black Sea coast, infecting the resident community of Genoese Italian merchants. Ships leaving the port carried sailors, merchants, and black rats, all infected or soon to be, to other ports around the Black Sea rim. From there the pathogen spread on the sailing ships that linked the Black Sea to the Mediterranean. A ghastly epidemic hit Constantinople in 1347. That same year the contagion spread to Sicily and Egypt, almost certainly carried by Italian seafarers. The Muslim historian al-Maqrizi tells of a ship limping into the port of Alexandria. Out of a company of 332 souls, all had perished of disease at sea except for forty sailors, four merchants, and one slave, and all of those unfortunates died a short time later.[5]

In the grim year of 1348, ships coursing through the Mediterranean deposited their lethal cargo in one port after another. From those towns, caravans and wagon trains distributed the ailment to inland regions of Europe, North Africa, and Southwest Asia. In the spring and summer, epidemics hit dozens of cities—Genoa and Venice, Barcelona and Paris, Damascus and Tunis. An epidemic struck the holy city of Mecca in Arabia in 1348–1349, no doubt carried there by Muslim pilgrims. Florence, already weakened by a succession of famines, may have lost as much as 75 percent of its population of about eighty thousand. Cairo, capital of the Mamluk empire and probably the largest Afroeurasian city west of China, may have lost 300,000 of its estimated 500,000 residents. In his famous collection of stories titled *The Decameron,* the fourteenth-century Florentine writer Boccaccio describes the terrors of the pestilence in both city and countryside:

Fleas in search of blood meals bite rodents infected with plague bacillus.

Bacilli multiply in fleas' gut, causing starvation.

Starving fleas jump from rodent to rodent to try to feed.

Fleas infect healthy rodents with plague bacillus and disease spreads.

When sick rodents die, fleas look for new living hosts.

If infected rats and fleas live near humans, hungry fleas may infect them.

Infected humans become sick; 50 percent or more may die.

If lungs are infected, sick people may transmit bacillus to others through respiration; pneumonic plague is almost always fatal.

How plague spread in the fourteenth century. What are some ways in which humans may have unintentionally transported plague-infected fleas or rats from one village or city to another?

The condition of the common people (and also, in great part, of the middle class) was yet more pitiable to behold, because these . . . fell sick by the thousand daily and being altogether untended and unsuccored, died well-nigh all without recourse. Many breathed their last in the open street, by day and by night, while many others, though they died in their homes, made it known to the neighbors that they were dead rather by the stench of their rotting bodies than otherwise. . . . Throughout the scattered villages and in the fields, the poor miserable peasants and their families without succor of physician or aid of servant, died not like men, but well-nigh like beasts.[6]

In 1349 the pandemic spread like wildfire, advancing simultaneously up the Nile River valley, along the North African coast, and across the English Channel to Britain. It advanced northwestward to Ireland, Iceland, and even Greenland, where it appears to have obliterated one of the

Perspectives on the Black Death

The Black Death spawned innumerable treatises on causes and treatments. Although writers proposed theories and made recommendations that today seem illogical, and perhaps dangerous, these texts help us understand the medical and religious debates that circulated as the epidemic raged. The two selections below discuss the issue of contagion. Document 1 is from a plague tract that a French court physician wrote around 1364. A Swedish bishop republished the text in the mid-fifteenth century under the name Bengt Knutsson. Document 2 is from a work by Lisan al-Din Ibn al-Khatib, a celebrated poet, philosopher, and physician who lived in Granada, Spain, when it was a Muslim-ruled city. Ibn al-Khatib wrote "A Very Useful Inquiry into the Horrible Sickness" about 1349–1352, just when the Black Death was spreading around the Mediterranean rim.

DOCUMENT 1 Bengt Knutsson

I say that pestilence sores are contagious because of infectious humors, and the reek or smoke of such sores is venomous and corrupts the air. And therefore one should flee such persons as are infected. In pestilence time nobody should stand in a great press of people because some man among them may be infected. Therefore wise physicians visiting sick folk stand far from the patient, holding their face towards the door or window, and so should the servants of sick folk stand. . . .

Now it is to be known by what remedies a man may preserve himself from the pestilence. First see the writings of Jeremiah the prophet that a man ought to forsake evil things and do good deeds and meekly confess his sins, for it is the highest remedy in time of pestilence: penance and confession to be preferred to all other medicines. Nevertheless I promise you verily it is a good remedy to void and change the infected place. But some may not profitably change their places. Therefore as much as they can they should eschew every cause of putrefaction and stinking, and namely every fleshly lust with women is to be eschewed. Also the southern wind, which is naturally infective. Therefore spar the windows against the south . . . until the first hour after the middle of the day then open the windows against the north. Of the same cause every foul stench is to be eschewed, of stable, stinking fields, ways or streets, and namely of stinking dead carrion and most of stinking waters where in many places water is kept two days or two nights. . . .

Also let your house be sprinkled especially in summer with vinegar and roses and with the leaves of the vine. Also it is good to wash your hands oft times in the day with water and vinegar and wipe your face with your hands.

Source: Rosemary Horrox, ed. and trans., *The Black Death* (Manchester: Manchester University Press, 1994), 175–177.

DOCUMENT 2 Ibn al-Khatib

If it were asked, how do we submit to the theory of contagion, when already the divine law has refuted the notion of contagion, we will answer: The existence of contagion has been proved by experience, deduction, the senses, observation, and by unanimous reports, and these aforementioned categories are the demonstrations of proof. And it is not a secret to whoever has looked into this matter or has come to be aware of it that those who come into contact with [plague] patients mostly die, while those who do not come into contact survive. Moreover, disease occurs in a household or neighborhood because of the mere presence of a contagious dress or utensil; even a [contaminated] earring has been known to kill whoever wears it and his whole household. And when it happens in a city, it starts in one house and then affects the visitors of the house, then the neighbors, the relatives, and other visitors until it spreads throughout the city. And coastal cities are free of the disease until it comes from the sea through a visitor from another city that has the disease, and thus the appearance of the disease in the safe city coincides with the arrival of this man from the contagious city. And the safety of those who have gone into isolation is demonstrated by the example of the ascetic, Ibn Abu Madyan, who lived in the city of Salé [on the coast of Morocco]. He believed in the contagion, and so he hoarded food and bricked up the door on his family (and his family was large!), and the city was obliterated by the plague and not one soul [except Ibn Abu Madyan] was left in that whole town. And reports were unanimous that isolated places that have no roads to them and are not frequented by people have escaped unscathed from the plague. . . . And it has been confirmed that nomads and tent dwellers in Africa and other nomadic places have escaped unscathed because their air is not enclosed and it is improbable that it can be corrupted.

Source: M. J. Müller, "Ibnulkhatib's Bericht über die Pest," Sitzungsberichte der Königl. Bayerischen Akademie der Wissenschaften, 2 (1863): 2–12. Translated from the Arabic with assistance from Dr. Walid Saleh. In John Aberth, *The First Horseman: Disease in Human History*, 1st Edition, 44–46, © 2007. Reprinted by permission of Pearson Education, Inc., Upper Saddle River, New Jersey.

Thinking Critically

What did Knutsson think caused the deadly disease to spread? How could people avoid contracting it? How does religion figure in Knutsson's list of treatments for the disease? How is Ibn al-Khatib's understanding of contagion similar to or different from Knutsson's? How do the two authors compare in their discussion of "corrupt air" as a cause of epidemic? If fourteenth-century city officials were to consult these two texts, what public health measures might they have taken to combat the spread of the malady?Perspectives on the Black Death

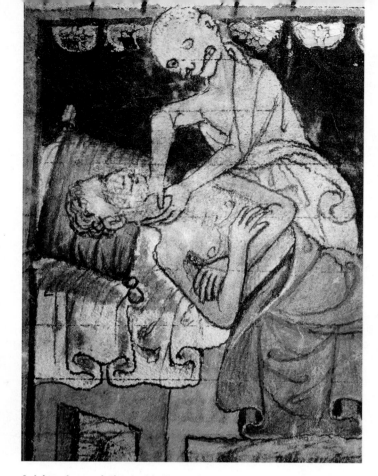

A dying plague victim. In this illustration from a Czech codex (1376), Death, depicted here as a ghoulish demon, strangles a plague sufferer. Why might strangulation be an appropriate image if the victim were suffering from pneumonic plague?

No one understood the biology of contagion, nor was there much agreement about treatment. In both Europe and the Muslim world, learned observers blamed the high mortality on a polluted wind coming from the east, a foul corruption of the air, or a bad alignment of stars. Preventive and curative advice abounded: flee your home, do not flee your home, burn clothes, get fresh air, eat pickled onions, pray, and gather in houses of worship. Christians, Jews, and Muslims all struggled to give the catastrophe divine meaning. Christian doctrine invited the conclusion that the sins of humankind obliged God to teach his creation a lesson it would never forget. In Germany and other European countries, penance-doers, called **flagellants,** tried to expiate the sins of the world by parading through towns while beating themselves savagely with iron-studded leather thongs. Other terrified believers blamed the pandemic on Jews rumored to have "poisoned the wells." In Switzerland and Germany, **pogroms** wiped out Jewish communities in many towns. Thousands of Jews consequently fled eastward to Poland and Russia, where they established new communities that thrived in the following centuries. Despite great social trauma, Muslims interpreted the disaster mostly as a manifestation of the Creator's unknowable plan for his creation. Terror and despair abounded, but this particular catastrophe did not incite significant Muslim maltreatment of Christian or Jewish minorities.

> **flagellants** In Christian Europe in the thirteenth and fourteenth centuries, individuals who whipped, or flagellated, themselves as an act of public penance for sin.

> **pogrom** A violent attack on a minority community characterized by massacre and destruction of property; most commonly refers to assaults on Jews.

Wherever the pandemic hit hard, economic disruption immediately followed. In western Europe, Egypt, and Syria, peasant farmers died or fled their homes in such large numbers that crops rotted in the fields. In hundreds of cities, manufacturing industries temporarily ground to a halt as entire neighborhoods of skilled artisans perished. People who performed vital services—priests, doctors, teachers, lawyers, mule drivers, riverboat crews, even gravediggers—became scarce and expensive. On the brighter side, the plague completely skipped some parts of Europe and Southwest Asia altogether, though the reasons are not clear. We have no sound evidence that the pandemic spread to West Africa, South Asia, or Southeast Asia. We know that severe epidemics occurred in China in 1331, 1333, and 1353–1354, though they could have been outbreaks of diseases other than plague.

two remaining Viking settlements there. To the east, it assaulted Germany, Scandinavia, and the eastern Baltic lands, reaching Moscow, though with declining virulence, in 1352.

Coping with the calamity. Fourteenth-century societies had no effective remedy for either the Black Death or the terrible epidemics that recurred every several years in different localities for another century or more. People suffered not only physical pain but also terror, helplessness, and despair. In both Europe and the Muslim Mediterranean lands, groups who lived in tight communities or administered to the sick endured particularly high mortality rates. Priests, nuns, religious scholars, university faculties, urban artisans, and soldiers living in barracks all proved highly vulnerable. Epidemics swept through armies in Germany and Italy. In southern Spain in 1349–1350, both Muslim and Christian troops battling for control of the city of Gibraltar lost large numbers to the contagion, the Black Death favoring neither side. The pestilence devastated not only crowded cities but also rural hamlets. Peasants who fled their homes to escape the scourge unwittingly passed it on to neighboring villages. A Muslim chronicler who witnessed scenes of flight in Egypt wrote of "those dead who are laid out on the highway like an ambush for others."[7]

Crises in the Political and Social Realms

> FOCUS What evidence indicates that the fourteenth century was a period of unusual crises and instability in several parts of Afroeurasia?

A surge of political and social instability rocked large parts of Afroeurasia in the later fourteenth century. By comparison with the previous hundred years, when the great Mongol empires kept order over much of Eurasia, the century after 1350 looks troubled indeed. Several large states either shrank or collapsed, and in some regions warfare took a particularly vicious turn. We cannot conclude that famine or infectious disease were the primary causes of those upheavals because other known historical factors came into play. Nevertheless, the occurrence of a number of wars, rebellions, and regime changes corresponded with times of food shortage and pestilence, which disrupted the social order.

China: The Collapse of Mongol Rule

The Mongols first invaded China under the great conqueror Chingis Khan in 1211. By 1276 they dominated all of it (see Chapter 13). Kubilai Khan, the grandson of Chingis, founded the Yuan dynasty and ruled China to 1294. Under him and his first few successors, the empire remained unified and generally stable. By the 1320s, however, political factions within the imperial palace at Beijing (known then as Khanbaliq) descended into chronic factional infighting. The Mongol court paid less and less attention to firm administration of the provinces, and emperors lacking Kubilai's backbone became pawns of one power group or another. Togon Temur, the last Mongol emperor, reigned as little more than a figurehead for thirty-six years (1333–1368).

Below the turbulent surface of palace politics, deeper structural shifts helped undermine the Mongol state. The government had allowed military and administrative costs to swell, so that taxes ate up a burdensome portion of people's income. Worse than that, revenues dropped in the fourteenth century, partly because the population kept declining amid successive regional famines and epidemics. An extended cold snap in the second quarter of the century, almost certainly linked to the general global cooling trend, cut both food supplies and tax receipts in the northern provinces. Struggling to finance the regime, Mongol officials churned out more paper money, which accelerated price inflation and pushed down standards of living.

As chains of command broke down, discontented peasants, soldiers, and local warlords felt emboldened to protest poverty and government neglect. In 1351 an uprising flared among tens of thousands of abused and underpaid peasants whom the Mongol regime had drafted to rechannel a section of the Yellow River. Several more insurgencies broke out in the following years, especially in the south. Bandits, smugglers, peasant marauders, and fervent new religious sects all contributed to spreading turmoil. By the 1360s the beleaguered central government had to compete for authority with a dozen or so local rebel groups. Zhu Yuanzhang (JOO yuwen-JAHNG), the leader of one of these insurgent bands, built up a power base in the Yangzi River valley and then sent his army against Beijing. In 1368 he forced the emperor and his entourage to flee to Mongolia. Once in control of the

capital, Zhu Yuanzhang moved vigorously to restore China's unity, this time under Chinese, not foreign, leadership. Suppressing all competing rebel movements, he proclaimed the new Ming dynasty. We return to it later in this chapter.

Political and Economic Troubles in the Central Muslim Lands

The Mongol khanate of Iran-Iraq crumbled in 1335, twelve years before the Black Death even appeared in Southwest Asia. This realm was not economically healthy. Farming in the Tigris-Euphrates valley had been shrinking gradually for several centuries. The Mongol conquest in the previous century did more damage to the economic infrastructure there, as well

Harvest of Victory. Timur, seated on a throne, receives soldiers carrying severed heads. Decapitated enemies lie sprawling in the foreground. The painting comes from a fifteenth century Persian history of the Timurid dynasty. What do you think the structure in the upper center of the picture represents?

as to Iran's irrigated agricultural lands. A few of the khanate's rulers experimented with reforms to improve farm production but made only modest headway. The regime fell, not amid popular revolt as in China, but as a consequence of internal feuding among Mongol and Turkic princes for supreme command. The regime's collapse left the region splintered into several, relatively weak military states.

The Mamluk sultanate of Egypt and Syria, a Turkic state that had defended itself successfully against Mongol assaults, remained intact. But the population plunged in the aftermath of the Black Death and recurring epidemics. As the skilled workforce dwindled, manufacturing became depressed. To take the example of Egypt's once-thriving textile industry, the city of Alexandria had 12,000–14,000 skilled cotton and linen weavers in 1394, but only 800 by 1434.[8] The rural peasant economy suffered as well. Reduced urban populations cut demand for grain; therefore, prices fell. To compensate for their income losses, Turkic and Arab estate lords tightened the screws on peasants, demanding higher rents and taxes. Thus, millions of men and women who farmed the Nile valley and the Syrian plains fell into deeper poverty in the later fourteenth century. On the other hand, the scarcity of labor in the aftermath of the pandemic meant that urban workers who managed to survive, especially those with skills, could command higher wages, at least for a time.

As if the peoples of Southwest Asia did not suffer enough from disease and economic troubles, they also had to endure another episode of massacres and city burnings, a dismal sequel to the Mongol invasions of the previous century.

This time the perpetrator was Timur, also known later in European history as Timur the Lame, or Tamerlane. Born in Central Asia, the young Timur began his career as a local Turkic war captain. Like his role model, Chingis Khan, he bested opposing tribal lords and amassed a large following of mounted archers. He began his ascent to power in Central Asia in the 1360s. His core state embraced vast grazing lands and the fertile valley of the Amu Darya (Amu River), plus Samarkand, Bukhara, and several other silk roads cities. Taxation of these resources paid for his expanding army, and, like Chingis, he ensured the allegiance of fractious warrior clans by continually leading them on huge plundering expeditions. From 1370 to 1405 he kept on the move, incorporating fighters of many origins into his forces as they advanced. Sacking one city after another, he outdid the Mongols in cruelty, raping and enslaving women by the tens of thousands and burying prisoners alive or starving them to death.

Timur led his forces north, east, and west (see Map 15.2). In the early 1390s he advanced north of the Caspian Sea to assault the Mongol khanate of the Golden Horde, destroying several cities in the Volga River valley and seriously weakening Mongol domination of Russia. In 1399 his cavalry rode from Afghanistan to the Indus River valley, where the invaders wrecked the great city of Delhi and permanently crippled the Delhi sultanate, which had once ruled all of northern India. In 1400–1401 he took Damascus, the Mamluk capital in Syria, but then withdrew. Apparently convinced that all great steppe lords should conquer China, he set off in that direction in 1405. But he died just when the expedition was getting under way.

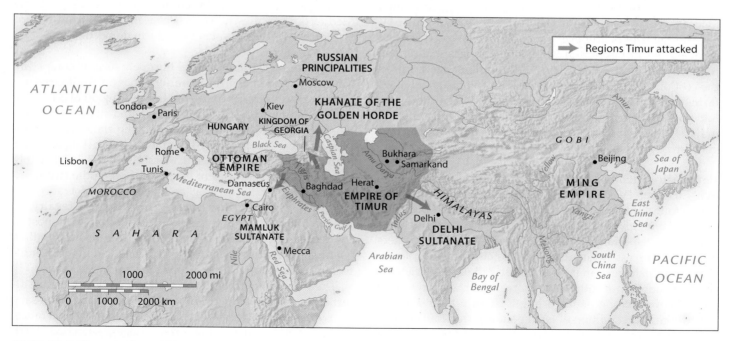

MAP 15.2 The empire of Timur in 1404.
When Timur died in 1405, he was planning to lead an army against China. From a geographical and political perspective, how difficult a task might that have been?

Timur had a genealogy worked up to show, without compelling evidence, that he descended from Chingis Khan and was therefore the right man to fulfill the Mongol ambition to rule the whole world. Though we know little of his thoughts on religion, he professed Islam and appears to have regarded himself as a special agent of God destined to punish both unbelievers and apathetic Muslims. He twice laid waste to the Christian kingdom of Georgia in the Caucasus Mountains and nearly extinguished the Nestorian Christian communities of Inner Eurasia. Muslims who displeased him for one reason or another got no better treatment.

Timur did not, however, match Chingis in the art of empire building. He did little to set up a firm chain of command or administration in conquered cities. He sent thousands of captured artisans and engineers to Samarkand to create a magnificent capital, but he rarely went there himself. He encouraged caravan traffic and thereby won the support of merchants, but his devastating campaigns hampered agriculture and trade. When he died suddenly, power struggles immediately erupted among his four sons and various tribal warlords. The empire soon fell apart, though the most vigorous of his descendants held Central Asia and part of Afghanistan together as a regional state. Timur deserves recognition as the last of the great Inner Eurasian steppe conquerors, but his predations only aggravated Southwest Asia's long-term economic problems.

Europe in the Aftermath of the Black Death

Like the Muslim Mediterranean, western Europe continued to lose population for about a century after 1350. In turn, labor shortages in nearly every occupation slowed economic recovery. As in Egypt and Syria, the demographic plunge reduced the market for grain and simultaneously raised the cost of labor. Land became cheap as people abandoned farms and villages or fell to the pestilence. Like the Mamluk military elite, European aristocrats who owned great manors had a harder time keeping up farm production and generating new wealth.

Population decline and the end of serfdom in western Europe. Peasants lucky enough to escape lethal contagion found that the population fall-off increased the value of their labor, giving them a measure of leverage over their landlords. Especially in northwestern Europe, farmers had some success negotiating with estate owners to lower rents, eliminate customary payments, and ease restrictions on their mobility. In other words, men and women whose labor enjoyed strong demand might bargain their way out of serfdom, the condition of legal bondage that forced them to live and work on a particular estate. Many thousands of serfs simply abandoned their lords and fled to towns, which needed their labor as well. Aristocrats desperate to preserve

their agricultural incomes retaliated by joining with royal governments, notably in France and England, to fight the rising cost of labor and the deterioration of serfdom. These regimes legislated ceilings on wages, imposed new rural taxes, and insisted that peasants meet their manorial obligations, though to little long-term avail.

In some places farmers and landless workers who thought the increased value of their labor deserved more just compensation took up knives and pitchforks in revolt. Rural rebellions flared from England to Hungary in the later fourteenth century. Indeed, these movements paralleled the uprisings that broke out in China in the 1350s and 1360s in similarly unsettled economic conditions. The Jacquerie rebellion in northern France in 1358 and the Peasants' Revolt in England in 1381 were among the most violent insurgencies. Describing the Jacquerie, a disapproving chronicler lamented that "these mischievous people thus assembled without captain or armor, robbed, burnt, and slew all gentlemen that they could lay hands on, and forced and ravished ladies and damosels, and did such shameful deeds that no human creature ought to think on any such."[9] Commanding far better fighters and weapons than the rebels did, landowning elites soon snuffed out these insurgencies. In contrast to what happened in China, none of the rebel groups came close to removing a dynasty.

Nevertheless, serfdom virtually disappeared in western Europe in the fifteenth century. Landowners discovered economic sense in paying wages to workers, collecting money rents from them, or selling them land outright, rather than trying to force labor from aggrieved serfs. Peasants became "free" in the sense that they could legally move from one place to another and to sell their labor for cash. In some Mediterranean cities, however, slaves imported from eastern Europe or Africa continued to perform domestic labor.

Long wars. Warfare among Europe's several competing states may have been no more ferocious in the fourteenth century than in earlier times. But the leveling off of economic growth, followed by famine, disease, and mass die-off, intensified political stresses and raised the stakes for control of resources. The prolonged conflict between England and France known as the Hundred Years' War (1337–1453) merely extended three centuries of hostility between the two monarchies over territories that are today part of France but were then under English rule. At first, English cavalry, as well as infantry troops armed with longbows, won most of the battles, but in the end England had to cede nearly all its continental territory to France, which emerged in the later fifteenth century as western Europe's most powerful state.

The war was marked by episodes of terrible violence alternating with extended lulls, sometimes made necessary by wet summers or epidemics. Fought mostly in France, the conflict involved long urban sieges, scorched earth tactics that destroyed cropland, and deployment on both sides of great bands of hired mercenaries, who sometimes

Ibn Khaldun: A Thinker for Troubled Times

Many scholars from China to Europe wrote narrative descriptions of the tumultuous events of the later fourteenth century. Abd al-Rahman ibn Khaldun (1332–1404) went much further, creating an elegant political theory to explain those wrenching changes. Born of a long line of Muslim scholars who made their mark in both Spain and Tunisia, Ibn Khaldun wrote on subjects as diverse as philosophy, theology, history, law, ethnology, and mathematics.

In his most celebrated work, titled *The Muqaddima* (Introduction to History), Ibn Khaldun theorized that change in human political affairs is not haphazard but follows a pattern of cycles. New dynasties arise when an energetic leader organizes a band of warriors into a sturdy, cohesive military force, which then seizes power. This conquering elite founds a state, but it soon starts to deteriorate because its members become caught up in urban luxury, political squabbling, and selfish oppression of their subject population. Eventually, the dynasty collapses under pressure from a new band of hardy warriors, and a fresh cycle begins. In formulating this theory of change, Ibn Khaldun contended that history has an identifiable shape to it and that finding the underlying pattern depends on close scrutiny of human events. Because he built his theory on concrete observation and research, not simply philosophical conjecture, he foreshadowed the methods of the modern social sciences.

Ibn Khaldun saw enough political and economic instability in the later fourteenth century to hypothesize that Muslim civilization was in jeopardy. In his view the Black Death, which struck his native city of Tunis in 1348, hastened the process of decay, overtaking "the dynasties at the time of their senility." Only a teenager at the time, he lost both of his parents to the pestilence. This personal tragedy, however, drove him to try to explain rationally why social calamities recur.

His learned family provided him with a strong education, and after his parents died he entered a career of public service. Ambitious, a bit snobbish, and sometimes politically meddlesome, he moved in and out of princely favor, holding government posts under several rulers in Tunisia, Morocco, Algeria, and Granada and even going to jail in Morocco for two years for taking part in a court conspiracy. In 1382 he traveled to Egypt, where he accepted posts as judge and law professor in the Mamluk sultanate. His wife and daughters sailed from Tunis to join him in Cairo, but they all died in a shipwreck. He gave brilliant lectures in Cairo's colleges, but he also made enemies. He got fired from every prestigious position he held.

In 1400, after making a pilgrimage to Mecca, Ibn Khaldun traveled to Damascus in Syria in the entourage of the Mamluk sultan. Later, he helped negotiate the city's surrender to Timur. He even got an interview with the conqueror and seems to have regarded Timur as the leader who might restore political unity to the Muslim world. Ibn Khaldun later returned to Cairo, where he continued his academic and legal career until his death in 1406.

Ibn Khaldun is represented as a member of the scholarly class in this modern statue on display in his native city of Tunis.

Ibn Khaldun typified the cosmopolitan spirit among educated Muslims, traveling widely to seek knowledge, serving numerous rulers without giving any of them permanent allegiance, and finding time to observe and write about the human condition. Modern scholars stand in wonder at his immense project to synthesize human history and to discover meaning in the directions it takes.

Thinking Critically

How would you argue that Ibn Khaldun's life and thought might help us better understand the era in which he lived?

---

abandoned the fighting to terrorize country peasants. In short, the brutality of the struggle only aggravated the economic problems that came in the wake of the Black Death.

The Church divided. In the fourteenth century the political authority and moral prestige of the Catholic Church plummeted along with Europe's population. The church had developed into a highly centralized and wealthy organization with its own law courts, diplomatic service, businesses, and vast properties. However, the people who managed these enterprises were generally more interested in worldly affairs than in spiritual ministry. In the political sphere, the pope directly ruled a large part of central Italy from his seat in Rome. But he also continued to press his claim, as divinely appointed shepherd of western Christendom, to supreme authority over all monarchs and princes. In fact, as powerful centralized states arose in western Europe, this assertion no longer had much force. The kings of France and England had particularly strong convictions about their independent authority to tax members of the Christian clergy, require their political allegiance, and prosecute them in royal courts of law, all practices that the pope tried to oppose.

In the fourteenth century the old ideal of Europe as a moral empire under the guiding hand of a benevolent pope perished once and for all. In 1309 the French king Philip IV pressured a newly chosen pope to move his throne from Rome, where it had always been, to Avignon in southern France. There, Philip's officials could make sure that the Holy Father led the church in ways favorable to the French crown. Palace extravagance and financial corruption thrived in Avignon, a state of affairs that appalled ordinary Christians. Moreover, thousands of nuns, monks, and priests died in the Black Death, including many of the best-educated clerics. This led to a chronic shortage of spiritual caregivers, local church leaders, and teachers. In 1378 the church hierarchy fell into near chaos when two popes, one in Avignon and one in Rome, competed for legitimacy. At one point, three men claimed the papal throne. The schism ended finally in 1417 with some church theologians and legal experts leading a reform effort, known as the Conciliar Movement, to transfer supreme church authority from the person of the pope to councils of high clergy. Since the majority of Catholics preferred a strong and morally righteous pope to fractious gatherings of clerics, the movement faded. Nevertheless, the church's prestige continued to suffer, encouraging a new generation of moral critics and reformers to come forward.

Peasants killing nobles. This miniature illustration from the *Chronicles of France* depicts the outbreak of the Jacquerie uprising in France in 1358. Peasants with daggers and swords are making short work of four unarmed aristocrats. Do you think the artist reveals a particular political bias? In favor of which side?

Fifteenth-Century Recuperation

FOCUS What factors may account for a trend of demographic and economic recovery in several parts of Afroeurasia in the fifteenth century?

The population crisis that affected so much of Afroeurasia in the fourteenth century proved to be a short-lived cyclical phenomenon, just as the downturn of the fourth to sixth centuries C.E. had been. By 1500 the supercontinent's overall population reached about 416 million—about 8 million more than the 1340 level. Long-distance trade almost certainly slowed on both land and sea routes in the immediate aftermath of the Black Death. But demand for luxury goods and exotic imports swelled among city dwellers who survived the pandemic and therefore commanded higher incomes. Ironically, cities made smaller by epidemic, famine, and war frequently entered the fifteenth century more important than ever as storehouses of wealth, knowledge, and skill. Several cities emerged as vibrant capitals of new states and dynasties, and in some regions those centers blazed with artistic and literary light.

Technologies for the Future

Both the sources of useful energy—human muscle, animal traction, wind, and water—and the technologies for moving people and goods from place to place remained largely unchanged in most of Afroeurasia between 1300 and 1500. To be sure, entrepreneurs and technicians across Afroeurasia continued to refine mechanical devices and undertake great building projects. In China, for example, engineers expanded the already immense inland waterway system, and shipwrights built ever-larger oceangoing vessels. In Europe, labor shortages and declining land values prompted estate lords and urban manufacturers to improve the technologies of textile production, mining, and wind and water mills. Medical scholars did not learn much about infectious diseases from the Black Death, but European and Muslim physicians gained a little more understanding of the mechanisms of contagion. Two technical advances that spread widely in the fifteenth century were gunpowder weaponry and printing.

Guns. Back in the thirteenth century, Mongol conquerors adopted Chinese techniques for making bombs, rockets, and incendiary weapons by mixing salt peter (potassium nitrate), sulfur, and charcoal to make gunpowder. Mongol and Mamluk armies used explosive devices in the late thirteenth century. About the same time, the gun made its world debut. In elemental form a gun is simply a tube of durable material. A charge of gunpowder is inserted into the tube's base and then ignited to propel a missile out the front end, presumably with destructive, or at least loud, effect. The earliest physical evidence of gun making is a bronze tube that archeologists found in Manchuria (northeastern China) at

the site of a 1288 battle. No doubt, military commanders regarded the earliest firearms merely as new-fangled devices to supplement other types of machines for hurling objects against enemy soldiers or fortifications.

Gunpowder and recipes for making it almost certainly became known in Europe as a result of diffusion westward across Inner Eurasia during the Mongol era. By the 1320s, European soldiers were using gunpowder to propel arrows or stones from pot-shaped metal tubes, though with little force or accuracy. In the following decades, artisans in the employ of princes or towns experimented widely with barrel castings, firing mechanisms, and gunpowder blends. By the end of the century, rulers began using firearms on the battlefield. Some European monarchs had sufficient wealth to cast and deploy rudimentary cannons, which launched stone or iron balls against castle or city walls. In the late phase of the Hundred Years' War, French kings organized Europe's first artillery corps to transport and maintain guns. They used these weapons to help blow the English out of

Early artillery. Near the end of the Hundred Years' War, a French army dislodged the English from the fortress of Cherbourg on the northern coast of France. This fifteenth-century illustration documents French deployment of cannons that fired stone balls. The horse in the foreground is wearing a caparison, or fabric covering, decorated with fleurs-de-lis (lily flowers), a symbol of the French monarchy. How effective do you think artillery of this type might have been in siege warfare compared to the longbows that both sides used?

their remaining continental strongholds. In the same period, rulers in China, India, Southwest Asia, and North Africa all fielded increasing numbers of cannons and handguns. Until the sixteenth century, these weapons had limited military value. Mounted archers with composite bows, as well as infantry carrying crossbows or longbows, could load and fire their weapons much faster than could either hand gunners or artillery crews. Nevertheless, world history's age of gunpowder was well under way by 1450.

Printing. Books printed on paper circulated widely in China during the Song and Yuan (Mongol) dynasties (eleventh to fourteenth centuries) and contributed much to the spread of knowledge across East Asia. The idea of printing words or pictures by pressing sheets of paper onto carved wooden blocks brushed with ink reached Southwest Asia in the later thirteenth century. There, the government of the Mongol khanate of Iran-Iraq tried, and failed, to introduce the Chinese idea of printed paper money. Local merchants wanted no part of it. Neither in India nor in the central Muslim lands did printing for any purpose take hold in the fourteenth or fifteenth century. We should be careful, however, not to equate printing with the hand production of books on paper. In the Muslim world, for example, rulers, religious institutions, colleges, and wealthy families possessed libraries that might contain thousands of hand-copied books, mainly in Arabic or Persian.

Libraries in fifteenth-century Europe were far smaller than in the Muslim lands or China, but Europeans warmed quickly to the idea of printing. By the 1200s, western Europe had a thriving papermaking industry, another technology that originated in China and spread to Europe by way of the Muslim Mediterranean. Italian artisans knew something about block printing images, such as stamping illustrations on playing cards. But the idea of mechanically reproducing books probably reached Europe directly from China, perhaps when Christian travelers returned from Mongol lands carrying Chinese volumes in their packs.

movable type printing A technology in which characters, especially alphabetic letters and punctuation, are individually carved or cast on pieces of wood, ceramic, or metal and then assembled into a text, inked, and printed on paper or other material.

European artisans used block printing for many purposes, but in the fifteenth century they also adopted the technology of **movable type.** Metalsmiths fashioned individual characters; printers arranged them as needed in a frame, inked the frame, and printed a sheet on a press. These individual pieces of type could be used over and over. Chinese printers had invented movable type made of wood or ceramic in the eleventh century, and as early as the thirteenth century Korean artisans discovered the superior durability of metal type produced in molds. In East Asia, however, this technology proved less efficient than block printing because the particular Chinese writing system, which is logographic, not alphabetic, required production of thousands of distinct characters rather than multiple copies of the thirty or fewer signs that make up an alphabet. Nevertheless, East Asia's book industry using block technology continued to expand.

In Europe in the 1440s a team of German craftsmen led by the goldsmith Johannes Gutenberg invented movable metal type for the Latin alphabet, almost certainly independently of the Korean invention a century or more earlier. Gutenberg printed a Latin Bible in 1455 and from that date printing presses multiplied across Europe. Scribes who hunched over desks to copy books could not come close to matching the speed with which a movable type press could produce multiple copies of an absolutely uniform text. In the 1460s, printing presses opened in several cities in Italy, which already led Europe in papermaking technology. In the following decade, printers began to ply their trade in France, the Netherlands, Hungary, Poland, England, and Spain.

A screw press in Hungary. This press, shown here in a woodcut, operated for a short time in the city of Buda (modern Budapest). The man in front on the left is turning the screw to lower the flat surface of the metal platen to press a sheet of paper firmly against a set of inked type. The man in back on the left is holding inking pads. What do you think the worker on the right might be doing?

Ming China: New Prosperity and a Maritime Thrust

After the rebel leader Zhu Yuanzhang expelled the Mongols in 1368, he founded the Ming dynasty (Dynasty of Light), a thoroughly Chinese regime. Ruling for thirty-one years (1368–1398) under the imperial name Taizu, he ordered a torrent of reforms to transform China into a more centralized and efficient monarchy than the Mongols had ever imagined. Under Taizu and his early successors, China's huge economy maintained steady growth. After nearly two centuries of decline, the population recovered as well, rising from about 85 million in 1393 to about 155 million by 1500. By the mid-seventeenth century, when the Ming era ended, about one-third of the world's people lived in China.[10]

The style of early Ming government. As the son of a poor farmer, in fact the first Chinese ruler to come from such humble origins, the emperor Taizu extolled the toiling peasant as the pillar of China's agricultural economy. He aimed to model his imperial government not on the Song dynasties (960–1276), which had given loose rein to business enterprise and technical innovation, but on the more agrarian-oriented Tang empire of the seventh and eighth centuries. He even discouraged the use of paper money, which went largely out of circulation by the mid-fifteenth century. In contrast to what some European kings did in the aftermath of the Black Death, Taizu lowered taxes on ordinary farmers and raised them on the rich. Early in his reign he decreed a comprehensive census of people, occupations, and landholdings to systematize revenue collection. To encourage social stability he prescribed laws that impeded rural people from changing occupations or migrating from village to city—again, contrary to the trend in western Europe. He also encouraged conformity to standards of Neo-Confucian morality, including restrictions on women's social and legal liberties.

Because he improved the state bureaucracy's efficiency and raised living conditions for millions of peasants, Taizu enjoyed broad popular support. Distrusting the landed aristocratic families that had traditionally dominated government offices, he reformed the Neo-Confucian school and examination system to allow talented young men from a wider range of social backgrounds to take up government careers. Also a master of political fear tactics, he created an elaborate apparatus of spies and secret police, and he periodically purged officials who he thought had failed him in one way or another.

The Ming government's policies, which favored a state-regulated, stable agrarian society, ran counter to the interests of private entrepreneurs and merchants, who yearned to pick up where the Song dynasty had left off. Yet despite the state's close supervision of commerce, China became more economically and geographically integrated than ever before. It already had the world's most complex canal and road system, but the Ming extended the Grand Canal so that it ran about a thousand miles from the Yangzi River to Beijing, which after Taizu's death became the imperial capital. The waterway had forty-seven locks, fifteen of them to move barges through hill country. Because Beijing could receive 400 million pounds of grain a year by canal, its population soared in the fifteenth century to over two million.

The Ming and its neighbors. Like the Mongols before them, Taizu and his fifteenth-century successors insisted on government supervision of external trade. Commercial exchange with foreign states had to conform to a protocol that imagined neighboring rulers not as trading partners but as payers of tribute in the form of material goods. In turn, the sublime emperor offered these presumably dependent princes comparable "gifts." China's neighbors often played this ritual game on Ming terms in the interests of profitable commerce. And although the Ming outlawed private overseas trade, Chinese merchants routinely defied this prohibition.

The Ming never tried to conquer deep into Inner Eurasia, as the Tang dynasty had done seven centuries earlier. Even so, early emperors pursued a forceful foreign policy. In Korea the monarchs of the Choson dynasty (1392–1910) accepted a formal tributary relationship with China, while in fact governing independently. They also energetically advanced Chinese Neo-Confucian teachings. Sejong (SAY-johng, reigned 1418–1450), the strongest Korean king of the fifteenth century, patronized Neo-Confucian culture and also inspired the invention of Hangul. This remarkable Korean alphabet used a system of phonetic signs that complemented Chinese logographic writing. In relations with Japan, which was then politically fragmented, the early Ming emperors encouraged diplomatic and cultural exchanges. These initiatives did not last, but private sea trade between the islands and the mainland continued to flourish.

In the subtropical hill country of the far southwest, today Guizhou and Yunnan provinces, landless peasants and discharged soldiers opened a new frontier of Chinese settlement. These lands were by no means empty, however, and non-Chinese ethnic peoples put up stiff though finally unsuccessful resistance. In the longer term, Chinese immigrants and local peoples interacted in complex ways, including marriage. This gave the region a distinct cultural flavor. Further south, a Chinese army invaded the Vietnamese kingdom of Annam in 1407 and occupied it for two decades. Annam's ruling class had already embraced Chinese Confucianism, but it tenaciously fought the intruders. Finally deciding to cut its losses, the Chinese force withdrew in 1427, leaving little to show for the adventure. Similarly to Korea, however, Annam pragmatically accepted the formal role of Chinese tributary by sending annual "gifts" to Beijing.

The Ming government kept a close eye on the northwestern frontiers facing Inner Eurasia, putting three million soldiers under arms to defend the imperial borders. Though the Mongols had retreated to their homeland, they could still command tens of thousands of mounted archers. At

The Great Wall of China. This section of the restored wall near Beijing crosses extremely rugged country. Why do you think historians have characterized the wall as a physical barrier rather than as a series of frontier fortifications?

first, the Ming combined diplomacy and gift giving with military thrusts into pastoral nomad territory. This forward strategy, however, did not go well, and in 1449 Mongol cavalry defeated a huge Chinese army and even captured the reigning emperor. After that humiliation, the state pulled the military frontier further back. It also spent huge sums to extend and connect frontier defensive fortifications, creating most of the 1,500-mile-long Great Wall. Masons reinforced long sections of the barrier to an average height and width of twenty-five feet, and they built guard towers at close intervals to permit soldiers to send signals along the wall at great speed. The project was a stupendous engineering feat, though the northwestern frontier remained turbulent into the next century, causing Ming bureaucrats no end of worry and debate.

The Ming maritime voyages. The Yongle (YAWNG-leh) emperor (r. 1403–1424), Taizu's son and successor, shared his father's grand vision of China as the world's Middle Kingdom surrounded by satellite states. Not only did Yongle attack Mongolia and Vietnam, but he also sought to gather rulers far west of China into the tributary net. In 1405 he placed Zheng He (JUNG-huh), a talented naval officer, in charge of a new seaborne mission to make a show of Ming imperial power and glory in the Indian Ocean (see Map 15.3).

Zheng He was an interesting choice for this project. His life reflected a creative, yet sometimes violent mix of cultural influences. He came from a Muslim family, and his father had made the four-thousand-mile holy pilgrimage to Mecca. Given the name Ma He at birth, he grew up in Yunnan in the southwest, where Ming forces expelled the Mongols when he was about ten years old. Chinese soldiers seized him and other local boys and made him a eunuch to serve in the army as an orderly. The lad, however, distinguished himself as a warrior. He made influential friends in the imperial court and became a trusted member of the corps of eunuchs, which did duty in the palace as bodyguards and administrators, as they had for many centuries. Yongle gave him the new name of Zheng, the name of a battlefield where the young eunuch distinguished himself.

At the emperor's request, Zheng He assembled a massive fleet of 287 junks—62 enormous "treasure ships" and 225 smaller ones. They carried a total crew of about 27,000. The largest vessel may have been more than twice the length of the Santa Maria, the little flagship that Christopher Columbus sailed to America almost a century later.[11] Between 1405 and 1433, Admiral Zheng He commanded seven major expeditions westward, leading his ships into the Indian Ocean and ultimately to the Persian Gulf, the Red Sea, and the East African coast. Many of the common sailors on these ships were recruited from the criminal classes, but the fleets also carried soldiers, doctors, herbalists, astrologers, diplomatic protocol experts, and Arabic and Persian translators.

Zheng He and the ship captains serving under him navigated with compasses, star charts, and coastline maps, as well as ready advice from local Muslim mariners who knew

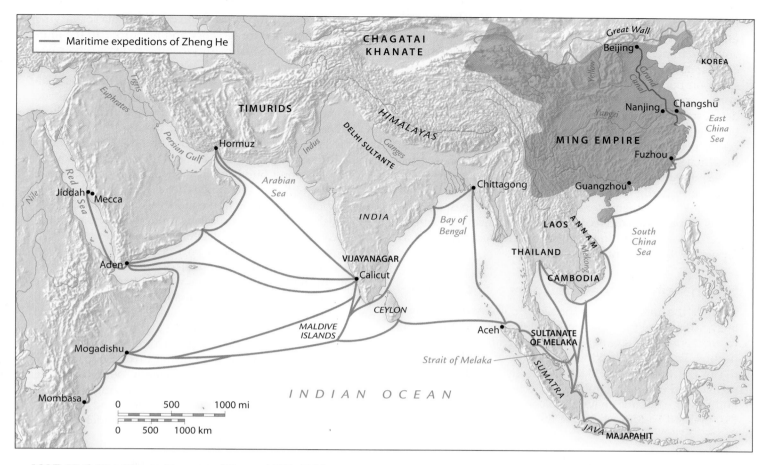

MAP 15.3 The Zheng He expeditions, 1405–1433.
In the fifteenth century, sailors of many Asian and African lands sailed the routes that Zheng He navigated. How would Zheng He and his crews have taken advantage of their knowledge of seasonal monsoon winds in making these long-distance voyages?

the Indian Ocean intimately. He would also have been able to draw on a store of Chinese knowledge. Since the eleventh century or earlier, private traders had been sailing junks from Chinese ports to the coasts of India and possibly farther, accumulating from these journeys a rich fund of navigational and geographic information. About sixty-five years before Zheng He's first expedition, Ibn Battuta, the Moroccan traveler, saw thirteen large Chinese vessels in the port of Calicut on the southwestern Indian coast, ships of four decks, he reports, outfitted with "cabins, suites, and salons for merchants," as well as in-room latrines.[12]

Zheng He's fleet did a good deal of ordinary trading during the expeditions, but their larger mission was to magnify the influence and splendor of the Yongle emperor. The admiral returned from his second voyage with envoys from thirty South and Southeast Asian kingdoms to pay homage to the emperor. On several occasions, violent encounters took place between Chinese visitors and local populations. But Zheng He seized no ports nor founded any imperial colonies.

Not all factions in the royal court supported Yongle's initiative, and when he died in 1424, the chorus of opposition grew louder. Many of the government's scholar-bureaucrats despised palace eunuchs like Zheng He as political opportunists

Zheng He's treasure fleet sets sail. This modern bronze relief depicts the size of the admiral's ships relative to other vessels and to buildings on land. Why might Ming emperors have funded the construction of such enormous vessels? What does their size suggest about the state of Chinese shipbuilding technology in the fifteenth century?

with too much power. These officials reasoned that they might undermine eunuch influence by scuttling any more voyages. Imperial accountants fretted that the expeditions cost far too much and that public money would be better spent on northwestern frontier defenses and internal economic projects. Another factor may have been long-term deforestation in southern China, which made the cost of building more oceangoing ships prohibitive. Yongle's successor permitted a final expedition in 1433, but Zheng He died that same year, perhaps on shipboard. Thereafter, the government dismantled the yards that built the big ships, which eventually rotted away in dry dock. Ming officialdom took no further interest in long sea voyages. As East Asia's population and economy grew, however, Chinese merchants continued to traffic in the China seas at least as far west as the Strait of Malacca.

South Asia: A Steadier Course of Change

Though the international ports of South Asia remained busy throughout the fourteenth and fifteenth centuries, the region appears to have experienced a significant population decline. Evidence is lacking for a massive pandemic in India in the years of the Black Death. It is more likely that people died in larger numbers as a consequence of regional famines or epidemics having no connection to the disease that ravaged Southwest Asia or Europe.

Like Europe, India was a region of many states of varying sizes that competed for territory and resources. In the fourteenth century the Muslim Turkic military lords who ruled the North Indian sultanate of Delhi made a bid to unify the entire subcontinent. Expansion sputtered, however, and after Timur's army pillaged Delhi in 1399, the sultanate carried on as merely one of several monarchies sharing northern and central India. Islam, however, became the dominant faith in both the upper Indus valley and the Ganges watershed, as the sultans encouraged Muslim farmers to move in to clear land and build towns. The Muslim population of Bengal, the region of the Ganges delta, grew steadily, laying the religious foundation of the modern state of Bangladesh. Sufi Muslim clerics and preachers fanned out across central India, converting Hindu villagers in some places.

By contrast, the southern part of the subcontinent became more politically consolidated and remained largely Hindu. In the 1340s a victorious warrior band founded the Vijayanagar (vizh-ah-na-ya-GAR-ah) monarchy in semiarid south central India. In the ensuing decades, this upstart Hindu kingdom conquered or put under tribute several other southern states, recruiting Muslim mercenaries from the north and deploying gunpowder artillery against enemy strongholds. Revenues subsequently poured into Vijayanagar city from both the lush rice-growing valleys of the southeast and the great trade entrepôts along the southern coasts. Gold and silver coins circulated widely, market

Royal elephant stables. Fifteenth-century monarchs of Vijayanagar housed war elephants in the large arched rooms in this grand structure. The open space in front of the stables probably served as a parade ground. Why do you think a ruler would construct such an elaborate and expensive building to keep his elephants?

towns multiplied, and the farming population appears to have enjoyed prosperity.

The Hindu elite also spent great sums building magnificent temples in the capital and other cities. These buildings ingeniously combined southern Indian techniques and styles with architectural elements, including domes and arches, imported from northern India and, more broadly, from Iran. The empire remained quite loosely organized, however, held together on the strength of alliances with local potentates and frequent campaigns against rebels. Nevertheless, Vijayanagar continued to dominate southern India until the mid-1500s.

Astronomy and Empire Building in the Central Muslim Lands

Shortly after his death in 1405, the conqueror Timur's huge but fragile empire broke apart, leaving Central and Southwest Asia in the hands of several competing princes and military lords, as it had been before his rise. Political divisions and economic doldrums persisted across Southwest Asia. Against this background, however, two dynamic developments stand out, one of them artistic and intellectual, the other political.

The Timurids. In the core region of Timur's empire, his offspring managed to preserve a much smaller but nevertheless prosperous state for about a century after 1405. The main urban poles of the Timurid sultanate, as this dynasty was called, were Samarkand in what is now Uzbekistan and Herat in western Afghanistan. Through much of the fifteenth century, these two cities functioned as capitals of largely self-governing northern and southern sections of the kingdom. In both places Timurid princes erected splendid palaces using tax revenues from irrigated farming and trade. In contrast to Timur, most of these rulers cared more about knowledge and literature than military glory, and their capitals attracted scholars from throughout the Muslim world.

In the first half of the fifteenth century, Ulugh Beg (r. 1447–1449) oversaw the transformation of Samarkand into a center of art and intellect. Timur had started to beautify Samarkand with mosques and palaces, and Ulugh Beg added a grand college of advanced learning (madrasa), whose walls inside and out sparkled with the reflected light of millions of multicolored tiles. This institution expanded the traditional Muslim college curriculum from law and the religious sciences to mathematics, astronomy, history, and several other subjects. Ulugh Beg sponsored scientific research and built an imposing observatory. Indeed, Timurid scholars made important advances in algebra, trigonometry, and astronomy. Most

notably, they produced a comprehensive star catalog in the form of astronomical tables, the most advanced gazetteer of the heavens produced anywhere in the world to that point. In the following centuries, scientists in Europe used the catalog as a key research tool.

In the second half of the fifteenth century, Herat took over as the leading cosmopolitan center. Combining Persian with Chinese elements of art and design, Herat's intellectual elite excelled in painting and calligraphy, especially the art of the illustrated book. In both Herat and Samarkand, poets and prose writers composed in Persian and Arabic, as well as Chagatai, a Turkic language. The reputations of Jami and Navai, fifteenth-century Herat's most famous poets, remain very much alive today. Early in the sixteenth century, political troubles and a shift of wealth and power to other capitals sent Samarkand and Herat into cultural eclipse, though they remained important emporia on the trade routes between Southwest Asia and India.

The Ottoman Turkish state. In 1300, Anatolia (modern Turkey) was among the most politically fragmented regions of Southwest Asia. The Mongols based in Iran and Iraq ruled the eastern half of Anatolia with declining competence. Several Turkic principalities shared western Anatolia, and the Christian Byzantine monarchy clung to a chip of territory across the Bosporus from Constantinople, the Greek capital. During the fourteenth century, however, this landscape changed radically. The House of Osman, a line of Muslim warrior sultans later known as the Ottoman dynasty, rose to dominate not only much of Anatolia but also Europe's Balkan Peninsula. The transformation of Anatolia from a Greek-speaking Christian land to a Turkish-speaking

The Observatory in Samarkand. Like many of the other buildings constructed during the rule of Ulugh Beg, the observatory was beautiful as well as functional. The building is now in ruins, but this nineteenth-century watercolor offers a representation of how it might have looked to the leading astronomers of the fifteenth century. Why might this building have been important in the eyes of a European artist four centuries later?

Muslim land, a process that had started with Turkic migrations in the eleventh century (see Chapter 12), accelerated along with the Ottoman expansion.

The Turkish warlord Osman (r. 1281–1324) founded the new state, but his successors Orkhan (r. 1324–1360) and Murad I (r. 1360–1389) made it a regional power by defeating rival sultanates in Anatolia and sending cavalry across the Dardanelles, first to raid, then to occupy Christian territory deep in the Balkans. As Ottoman forces amassed booty and slaves, more warriors joined in, including many from conquered states. As in the case of the early Mongol empire, every military success bred more of the same. By the end of the century, the empire had absorbed Christian Bulgaria and reduced the kingdom of Serbia to dependency. Writing in the later fifteenth century, the Greek chronicler Kritovoulos described the Ottoman advance in Europe: "Thus they came down into the plain, and there nothing was any obstacle to them any more. They occupied the level country, sacked the villages, and captured the cities, overthrew castles, defeated armies, and subdued many peoples."[13]

Boisterous and loosely organized, the young empire kept growing, though more as a result of the sultans' skills negotiating with local chiefs than owing to any well-organized central administration. The Turkic warrior tradition of *ghaza,* a code of military honor having to do with the accumulation and division of plunder, imposed some order on the wars of conquest. Moreover, Greek Christian aristocrats and their mounted knights joined the Ottoman offensive in significant numbers. Turkic warriors, or *ghazis,* coalesced around personal loyalty to the ruler, who promised land and loot. However, *ghazi* frontier fighters tended also to be unruly and opportunistic, too undisciplined for single-minded empire building.

In the late fourteenth century, Murad I addressed this problem by creating a professional standing army. To do this, he adopted a system of drafting healthy boys from Christian families in the Balkans every three to seven years as the need arose. These recruits, called **janissaries,** had the legal status of slaves of the sultan. As sons of Christian peasants, conscripts had, in contrast to members of Turkic warrior families, no stake in Ottoman politics or factional feuding and could be expected to give absolute personal allegiance to the ruler. Moreover, Christian families did not necessarily lament the loss of these children, since at least some lads rose to positions of responsibility and influence within the Ottoman

janissaries An elite infantry corps in the Ottoman Turkish state whose members were conscripted as boys from Christian families in southeastern Europe.

The Ottoman capture of Constantinople. This illustration from a fifteenth-century French chronicle conveys the intensity of the battle to control the city. We see evidence of Ottoman naval power and the infantry using ladders to scale the city walls built by Emperor Theodosius ten centuries earlier. What features communicate the artist's impressions of this battle? Does the painting convey sympathy for the conquering Ottomans or the besieged Byzantines?

state. Young janissaries had to convert to Islam and undergo rigorous training before taking military or administrative posts. About the same time, the Ottoman state began to build powerful cavalry regiments (*sipahis*). These units ensured order in rural provinces, and their commanders received in return rights to collect taxes on their own account from an assigned number of villages.

The capture of Constantinople. For more than a century after crossing the Bosporus and Dardanelles straits to penetrate the Balkans, Ottoman forces either bypassed or failed to penetrate the great Byzantine bastion of Constantinople. They absorbed nearly all other Greek-ruled territories, and by the early fifteenth century, the Byzantine emperor found himself effectively surrounded. Finally, in 1453, Sultan Mehmed II, known as the Conqueror (r. 1451–1481), breached the city's triple walls, deploying gunpowder artillery and handguns. The Greek historian Kritovoulos described the hours preceding the victory:

The day was declining and near evening, and the sun was at the Ottomans' back but shining in the faces of their enemies. . . . First they exchanged fire with the heavier weapons, with arrows from the archers, stones from the slingers, and iron and leaden balls from the cannon and muskets. Then, as they closed with battleaxes and javelins, and spears, hurling them at each other and being hurled at pitilessly in rage and fierce anger. . . . Many on each side were wounded, and not a few died.[14]

Mehmed gave his troops free rein to plunder the city for three days, and they murdered or enslaved much of the Christian population. In imitation of Mongol conquerors before him, however, Mehmed called a halt to the carnage and immediately set to work to restore and repopulate the city as the Ottoman capital. For example, the sultan recruited a diverse team of architects, including Italians, to build his magnificent palace of Topkapi Saray, an architectural complex that blended Muslim, Greek, Roman, and Italian elements. Western European rulers reacted to the fall of the greatest of Christian cities with shock and dismay, but they soon established diplomatic contacts with the new regime. The Ottoman empire would play a key part in the politics of Europe, the Mediterranean basin, and Southwest Asia for the next 450 years.

The Meaning of Recovery in Europe

Although Europe's population began to climb again after about 1450, many of its cities showed new vigor well before that date. Urban dwellers who survived epidemics found they could command higher prices for their labor, products, and professional services. They had more money to spend on food, luxuries, and capital investment in business and property. Consumers demanded a wide range of high-quality goods, stimulating both European industry and import trade. Europe's banking industry, which nearly collapsed during the Black Death, thrived once again. Florence emerged as the leading financial hub. From there, the Medici family and other rich firms built up pan-European commercial and banking empires. In Florence, Venice, Cologne, Paris, Bruges, London, and other cities, socially well-placed families piled up great wealth.

The bourgeoisie, that is, the nonaristocratic propertied

Catherine of Siena. A lay member of a society associated with the Dominican monastic order, Catherine reported numerous mystical experiences, including a spiritual marriage to Christ. She also had political influence, working to end war between Florence and Rome and successfully urging Pope Gregory XI to move the papal court from Avignon, where it had been under French domination for sixty-eight years, back to the Vatican in Rome. How would you describe the way the Italian artist represents Catherine in this painting made around 1462?

class, took advantage of business success to build bigger houses, purchase better educations for their children, and carve out solid social positions between the privileged nobility above and the working masses below. Urban women also gained a measure of social and cultural status following the plague era. Scarce labor meant that male heads of households felt obliged, if grudgingly, to concede more value to women's homemaking and artisanry. In the fifteenth century, both urban and rural women enjoyed somewhat greater freedom to earn money as spinners, weavers, teachers, and business owners. Literary works of the fifteenth century showed a new regard for the cultural worth of motherhood and wifery. As the all-male priesthood lost prestige (especially after the pope decamped to Avignon) and as the psychological gloom of the Black Death persisted, more women emerged as spiritual guides and reformers. Christian practice in the fifteenth century paralleled in some ways Sufi tendencies in Islam, as men and women turned to personal, inward worship centered on adoration of God, Jesus, and the Virgin Mary and on acts of communal service and humble living. Among female mystics, Catherine of Siena (1347–1380) achieved renown across Europe, urging both spiritual renewal and church reform in her writings. A radical ascetic, she practiced self-denial to the point of sleeping and eating as little as possible, a habit that may have cost Catherine her life at the age of thirty-three.

Royal power. Several of Europe's numerous states achieved new strength between 1350 and 1500 (see Map 15.4). The troubles of the church, the declining incomes of local aristocrats, and the renewed economic growth of the fifteenth century offered able and ambitious rulers opportunities to assert their authority in creative ways. Out of Italy's crazy-quilt of princedoms and city-states, five polities emerged in the 1300s to tower over the peninsula: the kingdom of Naples in the south, the papal states centered on Rome, and the northern

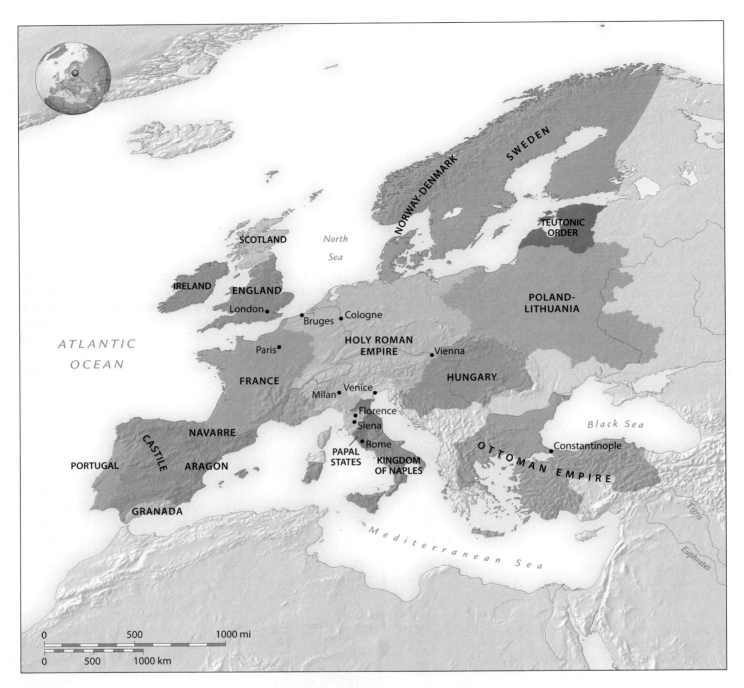

MAP 15.4 Europe in 1455.

The mid-fifteenth century was a time of prosperity in many European states. What geographical factors might help account for lavish financial patronage of the visual arts in cities of the Italian Peninsula in the fifteenth century?

city-states of Milan, Florence, and Venice. Together, these five dominated or absorbed weaker cities and small states.

The kingdoms of France, England, Spain, and Portugal all consolidated royal power. The French and English monarchs invented new taxes to impose on their subjects to pay for larger armies and more officials. Sometimes using cannons to smash castle walls, they subdued local estate lords and put royal bureaucrats directly in charge. France devoted

large sums to a standing professional army, equipping it with artillery units that no unruly duke or rebel leader could hope to afford. England endured a bitter civil war near the end of the fifteenth century (the Wars of the Roses), but Henry VII (r. 1485–1509), the first king of the Tudor dynasty, took the state to new levels of bureaucratic efficiency. In Iberia, Queen Isabella of Castile (r. 1474–1504) and King Ferdinand of Aragon (r. 1479–1516) formed a powerful alliance in 1469, unifying their two kingdoms at the dynastic level through marriage. Along the Atlantic, the kingdom of Portugal also built a sturdy central administration. In all of these states, rulers claimed supreme authority but nonetheless governed in consultation with various advisory bodies made up of aristocrats and bishops, and sometimes town leaders and rich commoners. Only in England, however, did the head of state formally share power with a representative body. In the fourteenth century, Parliament's House of Commons (see Chapter 12) evolved into a genuine legislative body, making many laws and obliging the monarch to get its approval before imposing new taxes.

Poland-Lithuania emerged as Europe's territorially largest monarchy, when in 1385 Queen Jadwiga of Poland married the Grand Duke of Lithuania to merge the two kingdoms. This state claimed sovereignty over a huge area stretching from the Baltic to the grassland frontier of the Mongol Golden Horde. Formerly pagan, Lithuanians moved steadily into the Catholic Christian fold. Especially in Poland, urbanization, commercialization, and higher education developed rapidly, bolstered by a continuing inflow of German migrants, as well as thousands of Jewish families who fled persecution in western Europe during the Black Death. In contrast to the trend in western Europe, however, local

Polish, Lithuanian, and German aristocrats retained much power within the empire. Royal governance in rural areas remained relatively weak, despite the empire's impressive size. Similarly in central Europe, the Holy Roman Empire continued to exist under the sovereignty of the Habsburg dynasty, but the emperor had limited power and functioned mainly to legitimize the regional authority of several German dukes.

The Italian Renaissance. At particular historical moments starting in ancient times, certain cities have shone more brightly than any others. Athens in the fifth century B.C.E., Baghdad in the ninth century C.E., and Hangzhou in the twelfth century produced innovations in art, literature, and science that have endured in the world's imagination. In the fourteenth and fifteenth centuries, Beijing, Vijayanagar, Delhi, Samarkand, and Cairo numbered among Afroeurasia's most creative centers of intellect and skill. In the decades following the Black Death, Florence in north central Italy emerged as Europe's liveliest hub of cultural genius. The movement that began there in the 1300s and that historians later labeled the Renaissance, or "rebirth," spread rapidly to other Italian cities and, in a variety of expressions, to the rest of Europe.

Florence in the late fifteenth century. The Arno River divides the walled city. Locate the Duomo, the cathedral that Filippo Brunelleschi completed.

Located in the Arno River valley amid the rolling hills of Tuscany, Florence had, despite its severe population loss in the later fourteenth century, the right mix of ingredients to achieve cultural distinction. It possessed sufficient wealth from manufacturing, trade, and banking to support ambitious artistic and literary projects. In that era, no city could excel in the arts or sciences without the backing of elite men and women who possessed both surplus wealth and urban cultural refinement. Often, the ruler of a city or state stepped forward as the most generous cultural patron, as in the case of Ulugh Beg in Samarkand. In Florence the eight hundred or so wealthiest families, including the Medici banking family, patronized the arts by offering stipends, commissioning projects, and purchasing sculptures, paintings, and numerous other art objects.

In Florence rich aristocrats and merchants competed with one another to spend money on art and buildings, confident that some of the glory would reflect back on them. As the city's reputation grew, artists and writers flocked there from around Europe. Other important Italian towns, some of them political enemies of Florence, vied for attention. Poets, painters, and fine metalsmiths traveled from one city to another—Milan, Siena, Rome, Venice—to look for books, find patrons, and exchange ideas with like-minded individuals. By the later fifteenth century a network of cultural exchange inspired by Italian ideas spread across Europe to embrace educated men and women from Portugal to Poland.

humanism European movement of the fourteenth to sixteenth centuries dedicated to rediscovering, investigating, and reinterpreting ancient Greek and Roman civilization.

The cultural movement centered on Florence took shape around the multifaceted philosophy called **humanism.** Today, that word is commonly associated with secularism, a human-oriented, nonreligious attitude or way of life. Six hundred years ago, however, humanism was fundamentally a project to search out and retrieve the surviving literary and aesthetic achievements of ancient Rome and, by extension, Greece. Inquisitive Italians could see Rome's physical ruins everywhere, and they knew that more of the record of classical civilization lay moldering in churches, monasteries, and palace cellars. Humanists argued that anyone wishing to restore, analyze, or interpret ancient knowledge should master the *studia humanitatis,* that is, the study of the "humanistic" disciplines of grammar, rhetoric, poetry, moral philosophy, and history. These disciplines, they said, must form the core of young people's education and should be dedicated to recovering ancient wisdom, which humanists regarded as intellectually and morally superior to anything Europe had produced in the intervening centuries. Three of the most important pioneers of this rebirth of classical culture came from Tuscany. The epic poet Dante Alighieri (1265–1321), the lyric poet Petrarch (1304–1374), and the classical scholar and storyteller Boccaccio (1313–1375) all devoted their careers to finding and elucidating ancient literary and philosophical texts and to reviving classical arts.

Humanists put forth numerous ideas. They considered Greek and Roman achievements to be the proper point of reference for moral thought and behavior. Human beings, they argued, had responsibilities not only to perform religious duties but to better themselves as individuals through education and constructive thought. Taking the early Roman republic as their model, humanists also encouraged public service as a moral obligation, though no genuinely democratic republic existed anywhere in Europe. Indeed, the classicist and diplomat Niccolò Machiavelli (1469–1527) argued in his book *The Prince* that rulers who wished to strengthen Italy against foreign invaders should be guided by ruthless pragmatism, not Christian morality. Machiavelli's humanism emphasized political activism, even violent or deceitful measures, to defend the freedom and integrity of the republican city-state.

Renaissance men and women found much to criticize about the dogmatism and corruption they witnessed in the Roman church. Somewhat like Muslim scientists and philosophers in the same era, humanist scholars gravitated mainly to princely courts and aristocratic households for support, not to established centers of learning. They tended to consider Europe's universities as preserves of narrow-minded theologians and lawyers. Eventually though, humanist ideas penetrated the universities.

The Italian Renaissance embraced all expressions of art and craft. Gifted sculptors of the era, such as Donatello (1386–1466) and the relentlessly creative and long-lived Michelangelo (1475–1564), studied classical models to create sublime naturalist images in marble and bronze. As we saw at the beginning of the chapter, early Renaissance painters, such as Masaccio, strove to recreate the "real," three-dimensional world using new techniques of perspective. Artists also depicted not only Christian subjects but also historical, mythological, and everyday secular themes. Architects such as Filippo Brunelleschi (1377–1446) built churches and other monumental structures that combined Roman engineering with clever new techniques. For example, in building a great dome for Florence's cathedral (known as the Duomo), he constructed in effect two domes, one inside the other and connected together, in order to reduce the weight of the structure on the supporting walls.

Brilliant achievements like these gave rise to the modern phrase "Renaissance man" to describe someone of wide-ranging interests and skills. It was indeed a man's world. Humanist ideology made little room for urban women to express themselves except in perfecting the arts of household management and social adornment. However, a few women achieved fame in the arts, several applying their aesthetic talents as painters, calligraphers, and book illuminators. Other upper-class women patronized male artists and scholars from behind the scenes. Among the early humanists, Christine de Pizan (1364–1431) stands out.

Daughter of an Italian astrologer who lived at the court of King Charles V of France, she made a living after the death of her husband writing poetry, biography, and political treatises under the patronage of various aristocrats. Modern historians have paid special attention to her because of her spirited writings challenging medieval male stereotypes of women as slow witted and wanton.

The Renaissance beyond Italy. The movement of Renaissance art and ideas from Italy to the rest of Europe in the later fifteenth century occurred in tandem with the spread of printing technology. The early presses of the fifteenth century put out Bibles, catechisms, and sermons, but literate Europeans soon demanded poetry, stories, histories, classical texts, scientific works, and advertising broadsheets. By 1500, just a half-century after the invention of metal movable type, presses had already turned out somewhere between six and fifteen million books. Many of these volumes appeared in regional vernacular languages, not Latin. By the sixteenth century, therefore, mechanically produced books added a revolutionary new dimension to the collective sharing of wisdom and information.

The early Renaissance evolved from an Italian into a European phenomenon, but we should also think of it as taking place within the larger Mediterranean world. Although the humanists tapped much ancient knowledge that Europeans had forgotten, they also used numerous philosophical and scientific texts that reached Europe owing to contacts with Muslim and Byzantine cities. The works of Plato, Aristotle, the Jewish philosopher Maimonides, and numerous Muslim savants were already part of Europe's intellectual library when humanism appeared. Books in Arabic—as well as Muslim textiles, art objects, and numerous ideas about design, architecture, and fine cuisine—continued to stream into Italy. When Byzantine travelers and Greek Orthodox Church envoys visited Rome, they often brought copies of ancient texts. It is no surprise that images of Muslim philosophers, Egyptian landscapes, decorative Arabic inscriptions, and Syrian textile designs turned up in early Renaissance paintings.

Although Latin Christians bemoaned the fall of Constantinople to the Turks in 1453, the new Ottoman capital quickly became a participant in Renaissance exchange. Sultan Mehmed II collected printed books from Europe to add to existing stores of Arabic and Persian literature, and

An Italian portrait of Sultan Mehmed II. The Venetian painter Gentile Bellini spent a year in Constantinople, where he painted the Ottoman ruler in royal robe and voluminous turban. Can you identify elements of Muslim art in the painting?

he took keen interest in Greek and Roman philosophy. In 1479 the Italian artist Gentile Bellini (1429–1507) painted a Renaissance-style portrait of Mehmed. Sultan Bayezid II (r. 1481–1512) invited both Michelangelo and Leonardo da Vinci (1452–1519) to Istanbul (Constantinople) to undertake commissions, though neither went. The early designs for St. Peter's Basilica in Rome, begun in 1506, emulated Constantinople's Hagia Sophia, even though Mehmed II had turned this great Byzantine church into a mosque. Lively cultural exchange between the Ottoman empire and Renaissance Europe continued into the sixteenth century, even as Turkish and Christian armies fought fiercely for control of southeastern Europe.

• • •

Conclusion

If we take a very long historical perspective, Afroeurasia's fourteenth-century population crisis and all the suffering that attended bad weather, epidemics, and war looks slightly less gloomy. In the past 200,000 years, the world's population increased fairly steadily until about three centuries ago, when it began to grow at a much faster rate. Thus, the demographic and economic decline that started around 1330 fits into the longer trend as just one of many recurring but short-lived downturns.

The fourteenth-century plunge *looks* calamitous partly because we have a richer documentation of it than of any earlier slump. It *was* calamitous because by that century human society in Afroeurasia had become so intermeshed that a demographic shift of that scope inevitably caused great upheaval. In fact, the trans-hemispheric pandemic likely occurred only because the dense exchange network strengthened by Mongol rulers was still in place to transmit infectious microbes from one person to another across steppe, mountain, and sea.

In the fifteenth century, economic growth began to accelerate again in many parts of Afroeurasia. The Zheng He voyages demonstrated spectacularly the prosperity of commerce in the southern seas. The larger classes of Chinese junks were probably seaworthy enough to brave any of the world's oceans, but Chinese officialdom decided after 1433 that it could no longer spend great sums on overseas power displays. Meanwhile, economic conditions in western Europe were improving, and shipbuilders were making incremental changes to small but buoyant sailing craft in order to explore Atlantic fishing grounds, look for new islands, and probe commercial possibilities along the North African and Saharan coast. These Italian, Portuguese, and Spanish mariners, like the crowd of Asian and African merchants who crisscrossed the Indian Ocean, no doubt anticipated that seaborne trade would continue to grow, though within networks already known. Well-traveled, cosmopolitan Afroeurasians thought the world was theirs. They had no inkling of America.

• • •

Key Terms

Black Death 428	janissaries 444	Renaissance 447
Choson dynasty 439	Little Ice Age 427	Timur (Tamerlane) 433
flagellants 431	Ming dynasty 432	Timurid sultanate 443
Great Wall 440	movable type printing 438	Vijayanagar kingdom 442
Gutenberg Bible 438	Ottoman Turks 443	Zheng He expeditions 440
humanism 448	papal schism 436	
Hundred Years' War 434	pogrom 431	

Change over Time

Late 13th–mid-19th century	Temperatures in the Arctic and northern latitudes drop (Little Ice Age), contributing to environmental changes and social upheavals of the 14th century.
1280–1324	Osman rules over the newly created Ottoman Turkish state.
1315–1322	Massive famines hit northern Europe.
1340s–early 17th century	The Vijayanagar state in southern India prospers from agriculture and trade links.
1337–1453	France and England wage the Hundred Years' War over territorial dispute.
1346–1352	The Black Death pandemic hits Inner Eurasia, Southwest Asia, North Africa, and Europe.
1350s and 1360s	Rural rebellions erupt in China and western Europe.
1368–1644	Mongols are expelled from China, ushering in several centuries of rule under the Ming dynasty.
1370–1405	From a Central Asian base, Timur leads conquests to the north, east, and west.
1378–1417	Papal schism disrupts the Catholic Church.
1392–1910	The Choson dynasty rules in Korea; Hangul, a Korean alphabet, is invented under Sejong.
1394–1449	Ulugh Beg rules the Timurid state in Central Asia and Afghanistan.
1405–1433	Zheng He leads Chinese maritime expeditions.
1453	Ottomans capture Constantinople.
1455	Johannes Gutenberg produces a printed Bible.
1474–1516	Queen Isabella of Castile) and King Ferdinand of Aragon create a powerful Christian state in the Iberian Peninsula.

Please see end of book reference section for additional reading suggestions related to this chapter.

Glossary

A

absolutism A political doctrine asserting that in a monarchy the ruler holds sole and unquestionable power by divine authority.

Afroeurasia The land masses of Africa and Eurasia, together with adjacent islands, as a single spatial entity.

agrarian society A society in which agriculture, including both crop production and animal breeding, is the foundation of both subsistence and surplus wealth.

agricultural revolution The transition from collecting food in the wild to domesticating and producing particular plants and animals for human consumption.

Anthropocene The era beginning in the nineteenth century in which human beings have become the primary agents of change in the earth's biosphere.

apartheid The political and legal system in force in South Africa from 1948 to 1994; designed to ensure the domination of the white minority over the majority population.

asceticism The principle and practice of renouncing material comforts and pleasures in pursuit of an elevated moral or spiritual state.

australopithecines Several species of the earliest bipedal hominins, now extinct, whose remains have been found in eastern Africa.

autarky A country that aims to achieve economic independence and self-sufficiency, especially freedom from dependence on external trade or assistance; also autarkic.

authoritarian monarchy A state, headed by a king, a queen, or an emperor, whose ruling class demands strict authority over the rest of the population.

B

baby boom A period of increased birth rates, especially in Western countries, from the end of World War II to about 1957.

biological old regime Human history before the nineteenth century, when economic production depended almost entirely on capturing flows of energy from the sun.

biomass Plant matter, including wood, brush, straw, and animal waste, used especially as a source of fuel.

biosphere The zone of the earth that can support life.

bipedal Walking upright on two legs, one skill among others that distinguishes hominins from apes.

bishopric In the Catholic Church organization, a district (diocese) under the authority of a bishop.

Black Death An infectious disease, probably plague, that caused significant population decline in parts of Afroeurasia in the mid-fourteenth century.

bourgeoisie The social category of town-dwelling artisans, merchants, and bankers who occupied a position between rural peasants and the aristocratic class; in modern usage, the "middle class"; in Marxist thought, the property-owning class that oppresses the working class.

bronze age The era centered on the third and second millennia B.C.E. when bronze making was the most advanced metallurgical technology in the world.

bureaucracy A hierarchy of officials within a government that carries out the laws, decrees, and functions of the state.

business cycle A sequence of economic activity typically characterized by recession, fiscal recovery, growth, and fiscal decline.

C

caliph In Sunni Islam, the deputy or successor of the Prophet Muhammad as leader of the Muslim community.

canon law A code of laws and regulations governing a Christian church or denomination, especially in matters of faith, worship, moral behavior, and church administration.

capitulations International agreements in which one state awarded special privileges within its borders to subjects or citizens of another state.

caravel A type of light, highly maneuverable sailing vessel used by Iberian sailors in the Atlantic in the fifteenth and sixteenth centuries.

carrack An oceangoing ship, larger than a caravel, used extensively by Iberian mariners in the Atlantic and Indian Oceans in the fifteenth and sixteenth centuries.

caste A social class more or less rigidly separated from other classes by distinctions of heredity, occupation, wealth, or degree of ritual purity.

cathedral A church that serves as the seat, or headquarters, of a Christian bishop; typically, a large church that attracts worshipers and pilgrims from a wide surrounding region.

caudillos Autocratic political bosses or dictators, especially in the post-independence period in Latin America.

cavalry The part of a military force trained to fight mounted on horses or camels.

charter A document in which a state or other political authority granted specific rights or privileges to an individual, town, guild, or other organization to carry out particular functions.

chartered company A type of corporation in which the state granted specific rights and obligations to private investors to engage in exploration, commerce, or colonization.

chattel slavery A type of slavery in which the bonded individual has the social and sometimes legal status of a unit of property and therefore no formal rights or privileges in law.

city-state A politically sovereign urban center with adjacent agricultural land.

clan A type of social organization in which a group of people claim shared identity as descendants of a single, usually distant ancestor. Clan organization is common among pastoral nomadic societies.

clergy In Christianity, people ordained for religious vocations, as distinguished from ordinary worshipers.

codex A set of pages of parchment or other material stacked together and bound along one edge or, alternatively, a continuous strip of material folded accordion-style to form pages; a codex is to be distinguished from a scroll.

Cold War The state of antagonism, distrust, and rivalry that existed between the United States and the Soviet Union and their respective allies from the end of World War II to the late 1980s.

collaborationist A government, a group, or an individual who cooperates with foreign enemies, usually an occupying power.

collective learning The process whereby humans accumulate and share complex knowledge and transmit it from one generation to the next.

Columbian Exchange The transfer of living organisms, including plants, animals, microorganisms, and humans, between Afroeurasia and the Americas starting in 1492.

commercial diaspora Merchants who share cultural identity but who live among alien communities to operate networks of trade.

communism A dimension of socialist thought that advocates revolution to eradicate capitalism and establish the universal triumph of the proletariat.

complex society A type of society, also called a "civilization," possessing most of the following features: dense population, an agricultural economy, cities, a complex social hierarchy, complex occupational specialization, a centralized state, monumental building, a writing system, and a dominant belief system.

constitutional monarchy A type of government in which a monarch, usually a member of a family that enjoys hereditary succession, serves as head of state. Under the terms of a constitution or body of laws, however, the monarch surrenders part or all of his or her governing power to a legislature and a judiciary.

consumerism Social and cultural values and practices centered on the continuous accumulation and consumption of material goods.

corvée labor Unpaid labor required by a ruler, an estate lord, or another authority, usually for road work or other construction.

cosmopolitan Characteristic of a place where people of diverse origins come together or of an individual who travels widely.

coup d'état The sudden overthrow of an existing government by a small group. A "stroke of state" in French.

creole A person of African or European descent born in the Americas.

D

debt peon A laborer, usually on a farm or plantation, who works under obligation to repay a loan.

deindustrialization An economic process in which a state or region loses at least part of the capability it previously had to manufacture goods, especially owing to foreign competition or intervention.

demographic transition The stabilization of population level in a society resulting from the decline of both fertility rates and death rates.

deurbanization A social process in which cities in a particular region decline or disappear.

dynasty A sequence of rulers from a single family.

E

ecosystem A biological system in which living organisms—plants, animals, microorganisms, humans—interact with one another and with nonliving elements such as air, sunlight, soil, and water.

El Niño Southern Oscillation (ENSO) A warming of ocean surface temperatures that occurs about every five years in the equatorial Pacific Ocean. An El Niño episode produces unusual, sometimes extreme weather in various parts of the world. A Pacific cooling cycle is called La Niña.

embargo A legal restriction or prohibition imposed on trade.

empire A type of state in which a single political authority, often identified with a particular kinship, linguistic, or ethnic group, rules over peoples of different ethnic or linguistic identities.

encomienda A grant from the Spanish crown to its conquistadors or other Spanish settlers in the Americas, giving them the rights to the labor services and tribute payments of the indigenous people in a particular area.

energy revolution The massive increase of useful heat energy made available to humans by extracting and burning fossil fuels.

entrepôt A port or other urban center where merchants of different origins exchange goods and ship them onward.

equal-field system The Chinese system for state distribution of land; the state assigned fixed acreages of crop land to families on the basis of labor, both adult males and animals, available to work it.

eunuch A castrated male who typically served as a functionary in a royal court, especially as an attendant in the female quarters (harem).

evangelism The practice of propagating the Christian gospel by preaching, personal witnessing, and missionary work.

F

fascism A political ideology that advocates authoritarian leadership, intense national loyalty, cultural renewal, and rejection of both liberal democracy and socialism.

feudalism A hierarchical system of social and political organization in which an individual gives grants of land to other individuals in return for allegiance and service.

fief An estate of land an individual holds on condition of allegiance and service to the grantor.

filial piety The quality in children of showing respect and care for their parents and all ancestors.

fisc The treasury of a sovereign state; a state department concerned with financial matters; also fiscal.

flagellants In Christian Europe in the thirteenth and fourteenth centuries, individuals who whipped, or flagellated, themselves as an act of public penance for sin.

Fordism A system of technology and organization, named after Henry Ford, that aims both to produce goods at minimal cost through standardization and mass production and to pay wage workers rates that allow them to consume the products they make.

fossil fuels Hydrocarbon deposits, especially coal, crude oil, and natural gas, derived from the remains of once-living plant and animal organisms; these deposits are burned to produce heat energy.

free trade An economic doctrine contending that trade among states should be unrestricted, principally by lowering or eliminating tariffs or duties on imported goods; factors of supply and demand should mainly determine price.

freeholders Farmers who own the land they cultivate.

G

galleon A large, multidecked sailing vessel used for both war and commerce from the sixteenth to the eighteenth century.

genocide The premeditated, purposeful killing of large numbers of members of a particular national, racial, ethnic, or religious group.

geoglyph An image, a character, or a set of lines imprinted on a landscape, usually on a large scale, by moving rocks or soil or by cutting into the ground surface.

globalization The process by which peoples around the world have become increasingly interconnected through rapid communication and transport, resulting in both general acceleration of change and endeavors to strengthen the bonds of local community and identity.

glyph A graphic figure or character that conveys information, often a symbol carved or incised in relief.

Great Arid Zone The belt of arid and semiarid land that extends across Afroeurasia from the Sahara Desert in the west to the Gobi Desert in the east. It has been home both to pastoral nomadic communities and to farming societies where sufficient water is available.

Green Revolution Acceleration of world agricultural production, especially from the 1960s, resulting from use of high-yielding varieties of food crops, synthetic fertilizers, pesticides, and expanded irrigation systems.

H

Hellenistic Relating to the interaction between Greek language and culture and the languages and cultural forms of peoples of Southwest Asia, the Nile valley, the western Mediterranean, and the Black Sea region.

heresy In Christianity, beliefs or practices that contradict the church's official doctrine.

hominin The primate subfamily that includes all species of the genus *Homo*. Scientists commonly use "hominid" to refer to the family that includes both the *Homo* and the large ape species.

humanism European movement of the fourteenth to sixteenth centuries dedicated to rediscovering, investigating, and reinterpreting ancient Greek and Roman civilization.

I

ice age Any geological epoch, most recently the **Pleistocene** era (1.6 million to 12,000 years ago), when glaciers covered a large part of the world's surface.

imam In Islam in general, the individual who leads congregational worship and carries out other duties such as officiating at marriages.

import substitution industrialization (ISI) Government economic policies to encourage national industries to produce finished goods that would otherwise be imported.

indirect rule Theory and practice of colonial government favoring the appointment of local leaders as political intermediaries between the colonizer and the indigenous population.

industrial revolution The technological and economic processes whereby industrialization based on fossil-fuel energy, steam engines, and complex machines led to worldwide economic, social, and environmental transformations.

inflation A rise in the level of prices of goods and services over time. Rising inflation means that the purchasing power of a given unit of currency declines.

informal empire A situation in which a powerful state protects its interests in a foreign society by exerting political and economic influence but without assuming the costs of territorial control.

Inner Eurasia The interior land mass of Eurasia, whose dominant features are flat or rolling regions of grassy steppe or forest, interrupted by deserts and highland areas.

insurgency An organized, usually internal rebellion against a government or its policies, sometimes employing guerrilla or terror tactics.

interglacial A period of global warming and retreating glaciers between ice ages. Our current geological epoch, the **Holocene,** is an interglacial.

Internet A global computer network connecting smaller networks, all of which use the same set of communication formats and rules.

Isolationism The national policy or political doctrine of avoiding complex political or economic relations with foreign countries.

J

janissaries An elite infantry corps in the Ottoman Turkish state whose members were conscripted as boys from Christian families in southeastern Europe.

junta A committee or council that seizes control of a local or national government, especially following civil upheaval or revolution.

K

Keynesianism Economic theories of John Maynard Keynes that promote government monetary and financial policies aimed at increasing employment and stimulating economic growth.

khanate A state ruled by a khan; a Turkic or Mongol monarchy.

kinship The quality or state of being related by shared genealogical descent or by marriage. Kinship may also be claimed among a group of people for social or cultural reasons even though no biological relationship exists.

L

language death A process in which the number of native or fluent speakers of a particular language declines over time until no community of speakers remains.

latitude The imaginary east–west lines that circle the earth and that indicate distance in degrees north and south of the equator, which has the value of 0 degrees.

liberalism A set of economic and political doctrines advocating individual freedom, unrestricted market competition, free trade, constitutional government, and confidence in human progress; sometimes called "classical liberalism."

lingua franca A spoken or written language that facilitates commercial or diplomatic communication across cultural frontiers.

Little Ice Age A trend of climatic cooling that affected weather conditions chiefly in the Northern Hemisphere approximately from the late thirteenth to the mid-nineteenth century.

liturgy The established forms of public worship, especially the order of services, including rituals, prayers, readings, and hymns.

longitude The imaginary north–south lines that extend between the North Pole and the South Pole and that run perpendicular to lines of latitude. By international agreement the line with a value of 0 degrees, called the Prime Meridian, passes through Greenwich, England.

M

madrasa A center of higher learning dedicated mainly to the study of Islamic religious and legal subjects.

mamluk In Muslim states, a slave or freedman having primarily military or administrative duties.

manor In medieval Europe, a landed estate; also the main house or castle on the estate.

matrilineal succession The practice of tracing descent or the transmission of property or authority primarily through female relatives.

megalith A large stone sometimes roughly carved and used to build a structure often having religious significance.

megalopolis An extensive and densely urbanized region or chain of urbanized regions.

mercantilism An economic doctrine based on the idea that the world's exploitable wealth could not expand and that a state should therefore erect barriers to keep rival states out of its circuits of trade with its colonies.

meritocracy A government or other institution in which individuals are awarded office and responsibility based on their merit—intelligence, talents, or education—rather than merely on their social status or circumstances of birth.

Mesoamerica The region comprising southern Mexico plus the seven small Central American states.

metropole The colonizer's home country and seat of supreme imperial authority.

microlith A small blade of flaked stone used as a tool.

military slavery The personal bondage of an individual to a ruler or other authority with an obligation to provide military service.

milpa In Mesoamerica a farm plot created by cutting or burning forest and planted with maize, squash, beans, and other crops.

modernism The movement in the arts and humanities that embraces innovation and experimentation and rejects adherence to traditional forms and values.

monotheism The doctrine or belief that there is one supreme and universal deity.

monsoon winds The seasonally reversing winds that governed long-distance sailing in the Indian Ocean and China seas.

movable type printing A technology in which characters, especially alphabetic letters and punctuation, are individually carved or cast on pieces of wood, ceramic, or metal and then assembled into a text, inked, and printed on paper or other material.

mutually assured destruction (MAD) The doctrine aimed at preventing nuclear war between the United States and the Soviet Union by shared knowledge that, if either side attacked, both would suffer mass destruction.

mysticism The individual pursuit of knowledge or consciousness of spiritual truth or divine reality, through meditation, prayer, study, or ecstatic experience; also, mystical religion, teaching, or practice.

N

nation-state A sovereign territorial state whose inhabitants share, or are ideally expected to share, common language, cultural traditions, history, and aspirations for the future.

nationalism An ideology centered on the natural rights of a people or "nation" to constitute a sovereign state.

natural philosophy A method of scientific and moral inquiry founded on the idea that fundamental laws governing nature, including human behavior, may be discovered through the exercise of logic, reason, or careful observation.

natural rights Universal and inherent rights of human beings bestowed by nature or divine power.

neo-Europe A region outside of Europe, predominantly in temperate latitudes, where people of European descent came to make up a large majority of the population.

neoliberalism An economic and political ideology advocating reduced government intervention in economic matters, privatization of state-owned enterprises, free trade, open markets, and deregulation of business.

neolithic era The "new stone age" extending from about 10,000 to 4000 B.C.E. and characterized by refined stone toolmaking and the development of agriculture.

new imperialism The campaigns of colonial empire building that several European powers plus Japan and the United States undertook in the late nineteenth and early twentieth centuries against other societies, especially in Africa and Southeast Asia.

O

Oceania (also, the Island Pacific) The enormous region centered on the tropical Pacific Ocean and its islands. This definition of the region excludes Australia, though not New Zealand.

old regime The political and social system in France and other European monarchies between the sixteenth and eighteenth centuries; characterized by a rigid class hierarchy and rulers' claims to absolute authority.

oligarchy A political system in which a relatively small number of individuals or families control the government.

outsourcing The business practice of reducing costs by transferring work to outside contractors, including foreign companies.

P

paleoanthropologist A scientist concerned with the study of human evolution and the physical and behavioral characteristics of early humans and their biological ancestors.

paleolithic Meaning "old stone age," this period dates from approximately 2.5 million years ago, when hominin species first devised stone tools, to about 12,000 years ago, when humans started experimenting with agriculture.

pandemic An infectious disease that moves quickly from one region to another, affecting large numbers of people.

partition The division of a political entity into two or more separate, autonomous territories.

pastoral nomadism A type of economic and social organization in which livestock raising is the principal means of subsistence. Pastoral nomadic communities typically migrate seasonally in search of pasture and water.

pastoralism A type of economic and social organization involving the breeding and raising of domesticated hoofed animals, or livestock.

patriarch In the early Christian centuries, the title of the bishops of Rome, Constantinople, Jerusalem, Antioch, and Alexandria; in later centuries, the title of the highest official of the Greek Orthodox Church, as well as other Asian or African Christian churches.

patriarchy A society in which males dominate social, political, and cultural life.

patriotism An emotional or sentimental attachment to a place, an ethnic people, or a way of life; in modern times, the attachment is often to one's national homeland.

patron–client system A vertical social and political system in which individuals possessing relative degrees of power, wealth, or social status offer protection or economic benefits to other individuals in return for personal loyalty and services.

peasants The social and economic class of farmers or herders who hold relatively small amounts of productive land as owners, rent-paying tenants, or serfs bound to a particular estate.

phalanx A military formation in which soldiers march and fight in closely packed, disciplined ranks.

pogrom A violent attack on a minority community characterized by massacre and destruction of property; most commonly refers to assaults on Jews.

polis (plural, poleis) The ancient Greek term for a sovereign state centered on a single city; a city-state.

polytheism A belief system that incorporates multiple deities or spirits.

pope The title used from about the ninth century to designate the head of the Christian church in western and central Europe.

popular sovereignty The doctrine that the sovereignty or independence of the state is vested in the people, and that the government is responsible to the will of the citizenry.

price revolution A period of sustained inflation in Europe in the sixteenth and seventeenth centuries.

primogeniture The legal or customary right of the firstborn child, usually the firstborn male, to inherit a family's entire estate, sometimes including a noble title or office, to the exclusion of younger children.

principality A sovereign state or dependent territory, usually relatively small, ruled by a person with a noble title of high rank, for example, prince, princess, duke, or duchess.

proletariat The working class; in Marxist theory, the class that must overthrow the capitalist bourgeoisie to achieve control of the means of production.

proselytize To convert or attempt to convert an individual or group to one's religion.

protectorate A type of colonial relationship in which a foreign power takes control of the top levels of government in the colonized territory but permits it to retain formal, if largely fictional sovereignty.

pueblo A Spanish word meaning "village" or "small town." Spanish colonizers used this term to describe multistory stone or brick compounds that the Ancestral Puebloans (Anasazi) built in the American Southwest.

putting-out system A production method in which employers distributed raw materials to individuals or families, who then made finished goods, typically woolen or cotton yarn or cloth, and returned these goods to the employer for payment.

R

real wages Wages estimated in the amount of goods those wages will buy rather than in the face value of money paid.

regent An individual who administers the affairs of a state when the ruler is absent, is disabled, or has not reached adulthood.

reparations The act of making amends or giving satisfaction for an injustice or injury; payment of compensation by a defeated state for presumed damages inflicted on another state as a result of war between them.

republic A type of government in which supreme power rests with a body of citizens possessing rights to vote to approve laws and to select public officials and representatives.

Romanization The spread within the Roman empire, especially among elite classes, of a style of social and cultural life founded on practice in Roman Italy.

S

satrapy An administrative unit of the Persian empire under the authority of a satrap, or provincial governor.

scholastic theology In medieval Europe, systematic investigation of the relations between the authority of spiritual revelation and the claims of human reason; a method of disputation drawing on philosophy, particularly the works of the ancient Greek thinker Aristotle; also, scholasticism.

secular ruler In the Christian tradition, a monarch or other ruler who is not an ordained priest and does not formally represent the authority of the church; a temporal, as opposed to spiritual, leader.

self-determination The idea put forth during and after World War I that a society sharing common language, history, and cultural traditions should have the right to decide its own political future and govern its own affairs.

serfdom A system of labor in which farmers were legally bound to work for and pay fees to a particular landlord in return for protection.

service nobility A privileged governing class whose members depended entirely on the state rather than on inherited property and titles for their status and income.

shaman A man or woman who the community believes has access to supernatural forces or beings and who can appeal to the spirit world to discern the future, bring good fortune, or perform physical healing.

shari'a The body of Islamic laws and moral precepts principally the Quran and the sayings and actions of the Prophet Muhammad.

shifting agriculture A method of crop production in which a farmer clears and cultivates a plot of land until the soil loses its nutrient value, and then moves on to clear and plant a new field, allowing the first one to lie fallow and recover.

Sinification The spread within East Asia, especially among elite classes, of a style of social and cultural life founded on practice in China.

slavery The social institution in which an individual is held by law, custom, or simply coercion in servitude to another individual, a group, or the state.

social bondage A condition in which an individual or a group holds rights to a person's labor or services, whether for a limited period or for a lifetime. Social bondage may take a variety of forms, including slavery, serfdom, or indentured servitude.

socialism A variety of ideologies that advocate social equality and justice and the community's collective control and management of economic institutions; in Marxist thought, socialism follows capitalism in society's transition to communism.

southern seas The China seas and the Indian Ocean, including the Arabian Sea and the Bay of Bengal.

soviet Revolutionary workers' councils that served during the Russian Revolution as local units of government and civil order. The term was applied later to legislative bodies within the communist regime.

split inheritance The practice of dividing the estate of a person among different heirs.

syncretism In religion, the blending of beliefs or practices from two or more different belief systems; also the incorporation of beliefs or practices of one belief system by another.

T

tax farming A system in which a government awards the right of tax collection to a private individual or group in return for a fee or a percentage of the taxes gathered.

tectonic plates Irregular blocks of solid rock that make up the earth's lithosphere and that constantly shift and change shape.

terra preta A type of nutritionally rich soil that farmers of Amazonia produced by mixing charcoal, organic matter, and pottery shards. Literally, "black earth" in Portuguese.

three estates The principal social classes or orders constituting societies in premodern Europe: the Roman Catholic clergy, the titled nobility, and everyone else.

tribute Wealth in money or material goods paid by one group to another, often a conquered group to its conquerors, as an obligation of submission or allegiance.

total war Warfare, especially characteristic of World Wars I and II, in which the opposing states mobilize their civilian populations and all available resources to achieve victory; also a wartime policy intended to damage or destroy both the enemy's military forces and its economic infrastructure and social fabric.

totalitarianism A political ideology and governing policies that mandate strong central control and regulation of both public and private thought and behavior.

transnational organization An association of individual citizens or private groups that collaborates across national frontiers to carry out particular activities or programs.

treaty ports Sea or river ports in China where, as a consequence of diplomatic and military pressure, foreigners gained special privileges to engage in trade and enjoy exemptions from Chinese laws and courts.

tribe The largest social group in a region whose members claim shared descent.

U

ulama Muslim religious scholars, judges, teachers, and mosque officials.

universal empire A multiethnic state whose ruler claims a right to authority over all of humankind.

universalist religion A religion whose doctrines and practices aim to appeal to all people irrespective of their language, ethnicity, social class, or political affiliation.

V

vassal An individual who is subordinate to or dependent on another individual; in feudalism, an individual who holds land given by a lord in return for loyal service.

vernacular language The native language commonly spoken by ordinary people in a region.

viceroy An official appointed by a monarch to govern a colonial dependency as the sovereign's representative. *Vice* is a Latin prefix meaning "in place of" and *roy* means king. The territory administered by a viceroy is called a viceroyalty.

W

welfare state An approach to government in which the state uses public funds to protect and promote the health and social well-being of all citizens.

Recommended Reading

General Works on World History

Jerry H. Bentley. *Old World Encounters: Cross-Cultural Contacts and Exchanges in Pre-Modern Times.* New York: Oxford University Press, 1993.

Jerry H. Bentley, ed. *The Oxford Handbook of World History.* New York: Oxford University Press, 2011.

Jerry H. Bentley, Renate Bridenthal, and Anand A. Yang, eds. *Interactions: Transregional Perspectives on World History.* Honolulu: University of Hawai'i Press, 2005.

J. M. Blaut. *The Colonizer's Model of the World: Geographical Diffusionism and Eurocentric History.* New York: Guilford Press, 1993.

Cynthia Stokes Brown. *Big History: From the Big Bang to the Present.* New York: New Press, 2007.

Edmund Burke III, David Christian, and Ross E. Dunn. *World History: The Big Eras, A Compact History of Humankind for Teachers and Students.* Los Angeles: National Center for History in the Schools, 2012.

Tertius Chandler. *Four Thousand Years of Urban Growth: An Historical Census.* Lewiston/Queenston, ON: St. David's University Press, 1987.

David Christian. *Maps of Time: An Introduction to Big History.* Berkeley: University of California Press, 2004.

David Christian. *This Fleeting World: A Short History of Humanity.* Great Barrington, VT: Berkshire Publishing, 2007.

Pamela Kyle Crossley. *What Is Global History?* Malden, MA: Polity, 2008.

Ross E. Dunn, ed. *The New World History: A Teacher's Companion.* Boston: Bedford St. Martin's, 2000.

Marnie Hughes-Warrington, ed. *World Histories.* New York: Palgrave Macmillan, 2005.

Neil MacGregor. *A History of the World in 100 Objects.* New York: Viking, 2011.

Angus Maddison. *The World Economy: A Millennial Perspective.* Paris: Organization for Economic Co-operation and Development, 2001.

Patrick Manning. *Navigating World History: Historians Create a Global Past.* New York: Palgrave Macmillan, 2003.

John R. McNeill and William H. McNeill. *The Human Web: A Bird's-Eye View of World History.* New York: Norton, 2003.

William H. McNeill. *The Rise of the West: A History of the Human Community; with a Retrospective Essay.* Chicago: University of Chicago Press, 1992.

Douglas Northrup, ed. *A Companion to World History.* Hoboken, NJ: Wiley-Blackwell, 2012.

Introduction. The Earth: World History's Theater

Jared Diamond. *Guns, Germs, and Steel: The Fates of Human Societies.* New York: Norton, 1993.

Ross E. Dunn. "Afro-Eurasia," in William H. McNeill, ed. *Berkshire Encyclopedia of World History,* 5 vols. Great Barrington, MA: Berkshire Publishing, 2005. 1:44–50.

Marshall G. S. Hodgson. *Rethinking World History: Essays on Europe, Islam, and World History,* ed. Edmund Burke III. Cambridge: Cambridge University Press, 1993.

Martin W. Lewis and Kären E. Wigen. *The Myth of Continents: A Critique of Metageography.* Berkeley: University of California Press, 1997.

Mark Monmonier. *How to Lie with Maps,* 2nd ed. Chicago: Chicago University Press, 1996.

William J. Moseley, David A. Lanegran, and Kavita Pandit, eds. *The Introductory Reader in Human Geography: Contemporary Debates and Classic Writings.* Hoboken, NJ: Wiley-Blackwell, 2007.

John P. Snyder. *Flattening the Earth: Two Thousand Years of Map Projections.* Chicago: Chicago University Press, 1997.

Chapter 1. The Peopling of the World

Elizabeth Wayland Barber. *Women's Work: The First 20,000 Years: Women, Cloth, and Society in Early Times.* New York: Norton, 1994.

L. L. Cavalli-Sforza. *Genes, Peoples, and Languages,* trans. Mark Seielstad. New York: North Point Press, 2000.

Richard Dawkins. *The Greatest Show on Earth: The Evidence for Evolution.* New York: Free Press, 2009.

Margaret Ehrenberg. *Women in Prehistory.* Norman: University of Oklahoma Press, 1989.

Brian Fagan. *Cro-Magnon: How the Ice Age Gave Birth to the First Modern Humans.* London: Bloomsbury Press, 2010.

Clive Gamble. *Timewalkers: The Prehistory of Global Colonization.* Cambridge, MA: Harvard University Press, 1994.

Renée Heatherington. *Living in a Dangerous Climate: Climate Change and Human Evolution.* New York: Cambridge University Press, 2012.

Richard G. Klein. *The Dawn of Human Culture.* New York: Wiley, 2002.

David J. Meltzer. *First Peoples in a New World: Colonizing Ice Age America.* Berkeley: University of California Press, 2010.

Steve Olson. *Mapping Human History: Genes, Race, and Our Common Origins.* Boston: Mariner Books, 2003.

Lauren Ristvet. *In the Beginning: World History from Human Evolution to the First States.* Boston: McGraw-Hill, 2007.

Chris Stringer. *Lone Survivors: How We Came to Be the Only Humans on Earth.* New York: Times Book, 2012.

Chris Stringer and Peter Andrews. *The Complete World of Human Evolution,* 2nd ed. London: Thames & Hudson, 2012.

Ian Tattersall. *Masters of the Planet: The Search for Our Human Origins.* New York: Palgrave Macmillan, 2012.

Bernard A. Wood. *Human Evolution: A Very Short Introduction.* Oxford: Oxford University Press, 2005.

Thomas Wynn and Frederick L. Coolidge. *How to Think Like a Neanderthal.* New York: Oxford University Press, 2011.

Chapter 2. Farms, Cities, and the New Agrarian Age

Guillermo Algaze. *The Uruk World System: The Dynamics of Expansion of Early Mesopotamian Civilization,* 2nd ed. Chicago: University of Chicago Press, 2005.

Peter Bellwood. *First Farmers: The Origins of Agricultural Societies.* Malden, MA: Blackwell, 2005.

Richard W. Bulliet. *Hunters, Herders, and Hamburgers: The Past and Future of Human-Animal Relationships.* New York: Columbia University Press, 2005.

Harriet Crawford. *Sumer and the Sumerians,* 2nd ed. Cambridge: Cambridge University Press, 2004.

Christopher Ehret. *The Civilizations of Africa: A History to 1800.* Charlottesville: University of Virginia Press, 2002.

Barry J. Kemp. *Ancient Egypt: Anatomy of a Civilization,* 2nd ed. New York: Routledge, 2006.

Jonathan Mark Kenoyer. *Ancient Cities of the Indus Valley Civilization.* Oxford: Oxford University Press, 1998.

Jane R. McIntosh. *A Peaceful Realm: The Rise and Fall of the Indus Civilization.* Boulder, CO: Westview Press, 2002.

Steven Mithen. *After the Ice: A Global Human History, 20,000–5000 BC.* Cambridge, MA: Harvard University Press, 2003.

Gregory L. Possehl. *The Indus Civilization: A Contemporary Perspective.* Lanham, MD: AltaMira Press, 2003.

J. N. Postgate. *Early Mesopotamia: Society and Economy at the Dawn of History.* New York: Routledge, 1994.

William F. Ruddiman. *Plows, Plagues, and Petroleum: How Humans Took Control of Climate.* Princeton, NJ: Princeton University Press, 2005.

Ian Shaw. *Exploring Ancient Egypt.* New York: Oxford University Press, 2003.

Ian Tattersall. *The World from Beginnings to 4000 BCE.* Oxford: Oxford University Press, 2008.

Marc Van De Mieroop. *A History of the Ancient Near East ca. 3000–323 BC,* 2nd ed. Malden, MA: Wiley-Blackwell, 2006.

Nicholas Wade. *Before the Dawn: Recovering the Lost History of Our Ancestors.* New York: Penguin Press, 2006.

Chapter 3. Afroeurasia's Moving Frontiers: Farmers, Herders, and Charioteers

David W. Anthony. *The Horse, the Wheel and Language: How Bronze-Age Riders from the Eurasian Steppes Shaped the Modern World.* Princeton, NJ: Princeton University Press, 2007.

Edwin Bryant. *The Quest for the Origins of Vedic Culture: The Indo-Aryan Migration Debate.* Oxford: Oxford University Press, 2001.

Billie Jean Collins. *The Hittites and Their World.* Atlanta, GA: Society of Biblical Literature, 2007.

Barry Cunliffe. *The Ancient Celts.* New York: Oxford University Press, 1997.

Robert Drews. *The Coming of the Greeks: Indo-European Conquests in the Aegean and the Near East.* Princeton, NJ: Princeton University Press, 1988.

Robert Drews. *Early Riders: The Beginnings of Mounted Warfare in Asia and Europe.* New York: Routledge, 2008.

Kairn A. Klieman. *The Pygmies Were Our Compass: Bantu and Batwa in the History of West-Central Africa, Early Times to 1900.* Portsmouth, NH: Heinemann, 2003.

Philip L. Kohl. *The Making of Bronze Age Eurasia.* Cambridge: Cambridge University Press, 2009.

J. P. Mallory. *In Search of the Indo-Europeans: Language, Archaeology and Myth.* London: Thames & Hudson, 1989.

J. P. Mallory and Victor H. Mair. *The Tarim Mummies: Ancient China and the Mystery of the Earliest Peoples from the West.* London: Thames & Hudson, 2008.

James L. Newman. *The Peopling of Africa: A Geographic Interpretation.* New Haven, CT: Yale University Press, 1995.

Amanda H. Podany. *Brotherhood of Kings: How International Relations Shaped the Ancient Near East.* Oxford: Oxford University Press, 2010.

Alicia Sanchez-Mazas et al., eds. *Past Human Migrations in East Asia: Matching Archaeology, Linguistics and Genetics.* New York: Routledge, 2008.

Cynthia W. Shelmerdine, ed. *The Cambridge Companion to the Aegean Bronze Age.* New York: Cambridge University Press, 2008.

Robert L. Thorp. *China in the Early Bronze Age.* Philadelphia: University of Pennsylvania Press, 2006.

Marc Van De Mieroop. *King Hammurabi of Babylon: A Biography.* Hoboken, NJ: Wiley-Blackwell, 2004.

Chapter 4. Early Odysseys in the Americas, Australia, and Oceania

Richard E. W. Adams. *Prehistoric Mesoamerica,* 3rd ed. Norman: University of Oklahoma Press, 2005.

Peter S. Bellwood. *The Polynesians: Prehistory of an Island People,* rev. ed. London: Thames & Hudson, 1987.

I. C. Campbell. *Worlds Apart: A History of the Pacific Islands.* Christchurch, New Zealand: Canterbury University Press, 2011.

Donald Denoon, ed. *The Cambridge History of the Pacific Islanders.* Cambridge: Cambridge University Press, 1997.

Richard A. Diehl. *The Olmecs: America's First Civilization.* London: Thames & Hudson, 2004.

Tim Flannery. *The Eternal Frontier: An Ecological History of North America and Its Peoples.* New York: Grove Press, 2001.

Tim Flannery. *The Future Eaters. An Ecological History of the Australasian Lands and People.* New York: G. Braziller, 1995.

Valerie Hansen. *The Open Empire: A History of China to 1600.* New York: Norton, 2000.

Alice Beck Kehoe. *America Before the European Invasion.* New York: Longman, 2002.

Patrick V. Kirch. *On the Road of the Winds: An Archaeological History of the Pacific Islands before European Contact.* Berkeley: University of California Press, 2000.

Danièle Lavallée. *The First South Americans. The Peopling of a Continent from the Earliest Evidence to High Culture,* trans. Paul G. Bahn. Salt Lake City: University of Utah Press, 1995.

Harry Lourandos. *Continent of Hunter-Gatherers: New Perspectives in Australian Prehistory.* Cambridge: Cambridge University Press, 1997.

Charles C. Mann. *1491: New Revelations of the Americas before Columbus.* New York: Alfred A. Knopf, 2005.

Michael E. Moseley. *The Incas and Their Ancestors: The Archaeology of Peru,* rev. ed. London: Thames & Hudson, 2001.

Christopher A. Pool. *Olmec Archaeology and Early Mesoamerica.* Cambridge: Cambridge University Press, 2007.

Paul S. Ropp. *China in World History.* New York: Oxford University Press, 2010.

Helaine Silverman and William H. Isbell, eds. *Handbook of South American Archaeology.* New York: Springer, 2008.

Chapter 5. Afroeurasia: Centers of Power, Trade, and New Ideas

David Abulafia, ed. *The Mediterranean in History.* Los Angeles: J. Paul Getty Museum, 2003.

María Eugenia Aubet. *The Phoenicians and the West: Politics, Colonies, and Trade,* trans. Mary Turton. New York: Cambridge University Press, 1993.

Barry Cunliffe. *Europe between the Oceans, 9000 BC–AD 1000.* New Haven, CT: Yale University Press, 2008.

Oliver Dickinson. *The Aegean from Bronze Age to Iron Age: Continuity and Change between the Twelfth and Eighth Centuries.* New York: Routledge, 2007.

Robert Drews. *The End of the Bronze Age: Changes in Warfare and the Catastrophe ca. 1200 B.C.* Princeton, NJ: Princeton University Press, 1993.

David N. Edwards. *The Nubian Past: An Archaeology of the Sudan.* New York: Routledge, 2004.

Christopher Ehret. *An African Classical Age: Eastern and Southern Africa in World History, 1000 B.C. to A.D. 400.* Charlottesville: University Press of Virginia, 1998.

A. F. Harding. *European Societies in the Bronze Age.* New York: Cambridge University Press, 2000.

Sybille Haynes. *Etruscan Civilization. A Cultural History.* Los Angeles: J. Paul Getty Museum, 2000.

Cho-yun Hsü and Katheryn M. Linduff. *Western Chou Civilization.* New Haven, CT: Yale University Press, 1988.

Michael Loewe and Edward L. Shaughnessy, eds. *The Cambridge History of Ancient China: From the Origins of Civilization to 221 B.C.* New York: Cambridge University Press, 1999.

Howard N. Lupovitch. *Jews and Judaism in World History.* New York: Routledge, 2010.

Ian Shaw, ed. *The Oxford History of Ancient Egypt.* New York: Oxford University Press, 2004.

Burton Stein. *A History of India.* Malden, MA: Blackwell, 1998.

Romila Thapar. *Early India: From the Origins to AD 1300.* Berkeley: University of California Press, 2003.

Chapter 6. Empire Building and Cultural Exchange from India to the Mediterranean

Karen Armstrong. *Buddha.* New York: Viking, 2001.

Pierre Briant. *Alexander the Great and His Empire: A Short Introduction,* trans. Amélie Kuhrt. Princeton, NJ: Princeton University Press, 2010.

Maria Brosius. *The Persians: An Introduction.* New York: Routledge, 2006.

Glenn R. Bugh, ed. *The Cambridge Companion to the Hellenistic World.* New York: Cambridge University Press, 2006.

Barry W. Cunliffe. *The Extraordinary Voyage of Pytheas the Greek.* New York: Penguin, 2003.

R. Malcolm Errington. *A History of the Hellenistic World.* Malden, MA: Blackwell, 2008.

Richard C. Foltz. *Spirituality in the Land of the Noble: How Iran Shaped the World's Religions.* Oxford: Oneworld, 2004.

Richard N. Frye. *The Heritage of Central Asia: From Antiquity to the Turkish Empire.* Princeton, NJ: Markus Wiener, 1996.

Peter Green. *The Hellenistic Age: A History.* New York: Modern Library, 2007.

Herodotus. *The Histories,* trans. Robin Waterfield, with an introduction and notes by Carolyn Dewald. New York: Oxford University Press, 1998.

Sarah Pomeroy, Stanley M. Burstein, Walter Donlan, and Jennifer Tolbert Roberts. *Brief History of Ancient Greece: Politics, Society, and Culture.* New York: Oxford University Press, 2004.

Joyce E. Salisbury. *Encyclopedia of Women in the Ancient World.* Santa Barbara, CA: ABC-Clio, 2001.

Jean W. Sedlar. *India and the Greek World: A Study in the Transmission of Culture.* Totowa, NJ: Rowman & Littlefield, 1980.

Susan M. Sherwin-White and Amélie Kuhrt. *From Samarkhand to Sardis: A New Approach to the Seleucid Empire.* Berkeley: University of California Press, 1993.

Stanley A. Wolpert. *A New History of India,* 8th ed. New York: Oxford University Press, 2008.

Chapter 7. An Age of Giant Empires

Mary T. Boatwright, Daniel J. Gargola, and Richard J. A. Talbert. *The Romans: From Village to Empire.* New York: Oxford University Press, 2004.

Stanley Burstein, ed. *Ancient African Civilizations: Kush and Axum.* Princeton, NJ: Markus Wiener, 1998.

Nicola Di Cosmo. *Ancient China and Its Enemies: The Rise of Nomadic Power in East Asian History.* New York: Cambridge University Press, 2002.

Patricia Buckley Ebrey. *The Cambridge Illustrated History of China.* New York: Cambridge University Press, 1996.

Richard C. Foltz. *Religions of the Silk Roads: Overland Trade and Cultural Exchange from Antiquity to the Fifteenth Century.* New York: St. Martin's Griffin, 1999.

Peter Garnsey and Richard Saller. *The Roman Empire: Economy, Society and Culture.* London: Duckworth, 1987.

Thomas Harrison, ed. *The Great Empires of the Ancient World.* Los Angeles: J. Paul Getty Museum, 2009.

Donald Johnson and Jean Elliot Johnson. *Universal Religions in World History: The Spread of Buddhism, Christianity, and Islam to 1500.* New York: McGraw-Hill, 2007.

Mark Edward Lewis. *The Early Chinese Empires: Qin and Han.* Cambridge, MA: Harvard University Press, 2007.

Xinru Liu and Lynda Norene Shaffer. *Connections across Eurasia: Transportation, Communication, and Cultural Exchange on the Silk Roads.* New York: McGraw-Hill, 2007.

Victor H. Mair, ed. *Contact and Exchange in the Ancient World.* Honolulu: University of Hawai'i Press, 2006.

Stuart C. Munro-Hay. *Aksum: An African Civilization of Late Antiquity.* Edinburgh: Edinburgh University Press, 1991.

Walter Scheidel, ed. *Rome and China: Comparative Perspectives on Ancient World Empires.* New York: Oxford University Press, 2009.

Tansen Sen and Victor H. Mair. *Traditional China in Asian and World History.* Ann Arbor, MI: Association for Asian Studies, 2012.

Manoj K. Thakur. *India in the Age of Kanishka.* Delhi: Oriental Book Centre, 1998.

Roberta Tomber. *Indo-Roman Trade: From Pots to Pepper.* London: Duckworth, 2008.

Derek A. Welsby. *The Kingdom of Kush: The Napatan and Meroitic Empires.* Princeton, NJ: Markus Wiener, 1998.

Greg Woolf, ed. *Cambridge Illustrated History of the Roman World.* New York: Cambridge University Press, 2003.

Chapter 8. American Complexities

Richard E. W. Adams. *Prehistoric Mesoamerica,* 3rd ed. Norman: University of Oklahoma Press, 2005.

Garth Bawden. *The Moche.* Malden, MA: Blackwell, 1996.

William J. Conklin and Jeffrey Quilter, eds. *Chavín: Art, Architecture, and Culture.* Los Angeles: Cotsen Institute of Archaeology, 2008.

Arthur Demarest. *Ancient Maya: The Rise and Fall of a Rainforest Civilization.* Cambridge: Cambridge University Press, 2004.

Alice Beck Kehoe. *America before the European Invasion.* New York: Longman, 2002.

George R. Milner. *The Moundbuilders: Ancient Peoples of Eastern North America.* London: Thames & Hudson, 2004.

Prudence Rice. *Maya Political Science: Time, Astronomy, and the Cosmos.* Austin: University of Texas Press, 2004.

Frank Salomon and Stuart B. Schwartz, eds. *The Cambridge History of the Native Peoples of the Americas.* Vol. 3: *South America.* New York: Cambridge University Press, 1999.

Linda Schele and David Freidel. *A Forest of Kings: The Untold Story of the Ancient Maya.* New York: William Morrow, 1990.

Lynda Norene Shaffer. *Native Americans before 1492: The Moundbuilding Centers of the Eastern Woodlands.* Armonk, NY: M. E. Sharpe, 1992.

Robert J. Sharer. *Daily Life in Maya Civilization,* 2nd ed. Westport, CT: Greenwood Press, 2009.

Robert J. Sharer with Loa P. Traxler. *The Ancient Maya,* 6th ed. Stanford, CA: Stanford University Press, 2008.

Helaine Silverman and William H. Isbell, eds. *Handbook of South American Archaeology.* New York: Springer, 2008.

Bruce G. Trigger and Wilcomb E. Washburn, eds. *The Cambridge History of the Native Peoples of the Americas.* Vol. 1: *North America, Part I.* New York: Cambridge University Press, 1996.

Chapter 9. Turbulent Centuries

Thomas J. Barfield. *The Perilous Frontier: Nomadic Empires and China.* Malden, MA: Blackwell, 1989.

Peter Brown. *The Rise of Western Christendom: Triumph and Diversity, A.D. 200–1000,* 2nd ed. Malden, MA: Blackwell, 2003.

Averil Cameron. *The Byzantines.* Malden, MA: Blackwell, 2006.

Gert Chesi and Gerhard Merzeder, eds. *The Nok Culture: Art in Nigeria 2,500 Years Ago.* New York: Prestel, 2006.

Peter Christensen. *The Decline of Iranshahr: Irrigation and Environments in the History of the Middle East 500 B.C.E. to A.D. 1500.* Copenhagen: Museum Tusculanum Press, 1993.

David Christian. *A History of Russia, Central Asia and Mongolia.* Vol. 1: *Inner Eurasia from Prehistory to the Mongol Empire.* Malden, MA: Blackwell, 1998.

Graham Connah. *Forgotten Africa: An Introduction to Its Archaeology.* New York: Routledge, 2004.

Joe Cribb and Georgina Hermann, eds. *After Alexander: Central Asia before Islam.* New York: Oxford University Press, 2007.

Touraj Daryaee. *Sasanian Iran (224–651 CE): Portrait of a Late Antique Empire.* Costa Mesa, CA: Mazda Publishers, 2008.

Peter Heather. *The Fall of the Roman Empire: A New History of Rome and the Barbarians.* Oxford: Oxford University Press, 2006.

John Philip Jenkins. *The Lost History of Christianity: The Thousand-Year Golden Age of the Church in the Middle East, Africa, and Asia—and How It Died.* New York: HarperOne, 2008.

Roderick J. McIntosh. *Ancient Middle Niger: Urbanism and the Self-Organizing Landscape.* Cambridge: Cambridge University Press, 2005.

John Moorehead. *The Roman Empire Divided, 400–700.* London: Longman, 2001.

Scott Pearce, Audrey Spiro, and Patricia Ebrey, eds. *Culture and Power in the Reconstitution of the Chinese Realm, 200–600.* Cambridge, MA: Harvard University Press, 2001.

William Rosen. *Justinian's Flea: Plague, Empire, and the Birth of Europe.* New York: Viking, 2007.

Bryan Ward-Perkins. *The Fall of Rome and the End of Civilization.* Oxford: Oxford University Press, 2005.

Chapter 10. Afroeurasia in the Era of Arab Empire

Karen Armstrong. *Islam: A Short History.* New York: Modern Library, 2000.

Christopher I. Beckwith. *The Tibetan Empire in Central Asia.* Princeton, NJ: Princeton University Press, 1993.

Jonathan P. Berkey. *The Formation of Islam: Religion and Society in the Near East, 600–1800.* Cambridge: Cambridge University Press, 2003.

Fred M. Donner. *The Early Islamic Conquests.* Princeton, NJ: Princeton University Press, 1981.

Fred M. Donner. *Narrative of Islamic Origins: The Beginnings of Islamic Historical Writing.* Princeton, NJ: Darwin Press, 1998.

John Esposito. *Islam: The Straight Path,* 4th ed. New York: Oxford University Press, 2010.

Jacques Gernet. *Buddhism in Chinese Society: An Economic History from the Fifth to the Tenth Centuries,* trans. Franciscus Verellen. New York: Columbia University Press, 1995.

Peter B. Golden. *Central Asia in World History.* Oxford: Oxford University Press, 2011.

Albert Hourani. *A History of the Arab Peoples.* Cambridge: Belknap Press of Harvard University Press, 1991.

Mark Edward Lewis. *China's Cosmopolitan Empire: The Tang Dynasty.* Cambridge, MA: Belknap Press of Harvard University Press, 2009.

Michael McCormick. *Origins of the European Economy: Communications and Commerce, A.D. 300–900.* Cambridge: Cambridge University Press, 2001.

Thomas Sizgorich. *Violence and Belief in Late Antiquity: Militant Devotion in Christianity and Islam.* Philadelphia: University of Pennsylvania Press, 2008.

Chris Wickham. *Framing the Early Middle Ages: Europe and the Mediterranean, 400–800.* Oxford: Oxford University Press, 2005.

Irving M. Zeitlin. *The Historical Muhammad.* Malden, MA: Polity Press, 2007.

Chapter 11. State Power and Expanding Networks of Exchange

Jonathan M. Bloom. *Paper before Print: The History and Impact of Paper in the Islamic World.* New Haven, CT: Yale University Press, 2001.

Philip D. Curtin. *Cross-Cultural Trade in World History.* New York: Cambridge University Press, 1984.

Thomas F. Glick. *Islamic and Christian Spain in the Early Middle Ages.* Boston: Brill, 2005.

Kenneth R. Hall. *Maritime Trade and State Development in Early Southeast Asia.* Honolulu: University of Hawai'i Press, 1985.

Ahmed Y. al-Hassan and Donald R. Hill. *Islamic Technology: An Illustrated History.* Cambridge: Cambridge University Press, 1986.

Mark Horton and John Middleton. *The Swahili: The Social Landscape of a Mercantile Society.* Malden, MA: Blackwell, 2000.

Hugh Kennedy. *When Baghdad Ruled the Muslim World: The Rise and Fall of Islam's Greatest Dynasty.* Cambridge, MA: Da Capo Press, 2005.

Donald F. Logan, *The Vikings in History.* London: Routledge, 2005.

Seyyed Hossein Nasr. *Islamic Science: An Illustrated Study.* London: World Festival of Islam Publishing, 1976.

Joan R. Piggott. *The Emergence of Japanese Kingship.* Stanford, CA: Stanford University Press, 1997.

Alexandre Popovic. *The Revolt of African Slaves in Iraq in the 3rd/9th Century,* trans. Léon King, with a new introduction by Henry Louis Gates, Jr. Princeton, NJ: Markus Wiener, 1999.

David Robinson. *Muslim Societies in African History.* Cambridge: Cambridge University Press, 2004.

Edward H. Schafer. *The Golden Peaches of Samarkand: A Study of Tang Exotics.* Berkeley: University of California Press, 1963.

Lynda Norene Shaffer. *Maritime Southeast Asia to 1500.* Armonk, NY: M. E. Sharpe, 1996.

J. M. Wallace-Hadrill. *The Barbarian West, 400–1000,* rev. ed. Malden, MA: Blackwell, 1997.

Andrew Watson. *Agricultural Innovation in the Early Islamic World: The Diffusion of Crops and Farming Techniques, 700–1100.* Cambridge: Cambridge University Press, 1983.

Chapter 12. Dynamic Centuries across Afroeurasia

Thomas S. Asbridge. *The Crusades: The Authoritative History of the War for the Holy Land.* New York: Ecco Press, 2010.

Robert Bartlett. *The Making of Europe: Conquest, Colonization and Cultural Change, 950–1350.* Princeton, NJ: Princeton University Press, 1993.

Aziz Basan. *The Great Suljuqs: A History.* New York: Routledge, 2010.

Beverly J. Bossler. *Powerful Relations: Kinship, Status, and the State in Sung China (960–1279).* Cambridge, MA: Council on East Asian Studies, Harvard University, 1998.

Anne-Marie Eddé. *Saladin,* trans. Jane Marie Todd. Cambridge, MA: Belknap Press, 2011.

Carter Vaughn Findley. *The Turks in World History.* Oxford: Oxford University Press, 2005.

Robert Finlay. *The Pilgrim Art: The Culture of Porcelain in World History.* Berkeley: University of California Press, 2010.

Jacques Gernet. *Daily Life in China on the Eve of the Mongol Invasion, 1250–76,* trans. H. M. Wright. Stanford, CA: Stanford University Press, 1962.

Thomas F. Glick, Steven J. Livesey, and Faith Wallis, eds. *Medieval Science, Technology and Medicine: An Encyclopedia.* New York: Routledge, 2005.

C. Warren Hollister and Judith M. Bennett. *Medieval Europe: A Short History,* 10th ed. Boston: McGraw-Hill, 2005.

Dieter Kuhn. *The Age of Confucian Rule: The Song Transformation of China.* Cambridge, MA: Belknap Press of Harvard University Press, 2009.

Angeliki E. Laiou and Roy Parviz Mottahedeh, eds. *The Crusades from the Perspective of Byzantium and the Muslim World.* Washington, DC: Dumbarton Oaks Research Library and Collection, 2001.

J. R. S. Phillips. *The Medieval Expansion of Europe,* 2nd ed. Oxford: Oxford University Press, 1998.

Pierre Souyri. *The World Turned Upside Down: Medieval Japanese Society.* New York: Columbia University Press, 2001.

Richard von Glahn. *Fountain of Fortune: Money and Monetary Policy in China, 1000–1700.* Berkeley: University of California Press, 1996.

Chapter 13. Afroeurasia in the Era of Mongol Power

Ralph A. Austen. *Trans-Saharan Africa in World History.* Oxford: Oxford University Press, 2010.

David C. Conrad, trans. and ed. *Sunjata: A West African Epic of the Mande People,* narrated by Djanka Tassey Condé. Indianapolis: Hackett Publishing, 2004.

Ross E. Dunn. *The Adventures of Ibn Battuta, A Muslim Traveler of the 14th Century,* rev. ed. Berkeley: University of California Press, 2012.

Steven A. Epstein. *An Economic and Social History of Later Medieval Europe, 1000–1500.* New York: Cambridge University Press, 2009.

William W. Fitzhugh, Morris Rossabi, and William Honeychurch, eds. *Genghis Khan and the Mongol Empire.* Media, PA: Dino Don: Mongolian Preservation Foundation; Washington, DC: Arctic Studies Center, Smithsonian Institution; Seattle: Distributed by University of Washington Press, 2009.

Peter B. Golden. *Central Asia in World History.* Oxford: Oxford University Press, 2011.

Charles J. Halperin. *Russia and the Golden Horde: The Mongol Impact on Medieval Russian History.* Indianapolis: Indiana University Press, 1985.

Mark Horton and John Middleton. *The Swahili: The Social Landscape of a Mercantile Society.* Malden, MA: Blackwell, 2000.

Peter Jackson. *The Mongols and the West, 1221–1410.* New York: Pearson Longman, 2005.

Nehemiah Levtzion. *Ancient Ghana and Mali.* London: Methuen, 1973.

George Makdisi. *The Rise of Colleges: Institutions of Learning in Islam and the West.* Edinburgh: Edinburgh University Press, 1981.

Timothy May. *The Mongol Art of War: Chinggis Khan and the Mongol Military System.* Yardley, PA: Westholme Publishing, 2007.

David Morgan. *The Mongols,* 2nd ed. Malden, MA: Wiley-Blackwell, 2007.

Barbara H. Rosenwein. *A Short History of the Middle Ages.* Toronto: University of Toronto Press, 2009.

Morris Rossabi. *Voyager from Xanadu: Rabban Sauma and the First Journey from China to the West.* New York: Kodansha International, 1992.

Chapter 14. Cities and Empires in the Americas

Richard E. W. Adams. *Ancient Civilizations of the New World.* Boulder, CO: Westview Press, 1997.

Richard E. W. Adams and Murdo J. MacLeod, eds. *The Cambridge History of the Native Peoples of the Americas.* Vol. 2: *Mesoamerica.* New York: Cambridge University Press, 1996.

John Bierhorst. *The Hungry Woman: Myths and Legends of the Aztecs.* New York: Quill/William Morrow, 1993.

Inga Clendinnen. *Aztecs: An Interpretation.* Cambridge: Cambridge University Press, 1991.

Thomas E. Emerson. *Cahokia and the Archaeology of Power.* Tuscaloosa: University of Alabama Press, 1997.

John Hyslop. *The Inka Road System.* Orlando, FL: Academic Press, 1984.

James Lockhart. *The Nahuas after the Conquest: A Social and Cultural History of the Indians of Central Mexico, Sixteenth through Eighteenth Centuries.* Stanford, CA: Stanford University Press, 1992.

George R. Milner. *The Moundbuilders: Ancient Peoples of Eastern North America.* London: Thames & Hudson, 2004.

Michael E. Moseley. *The Incas and Their Ancestors: The Archaeology of Peru,* 2nd rev. ed. London: Thames & Hudson, 2001.

Stephen Plog. *Ancient Peoples of the American Southwest.* New York: Thames & Hudson, 2008.

María Rostworowski de Diez Canseco. *History of the Inca Realm.* New York: Cambridge University Press, 1999.

Frank Salomon and Stuart B. Schwartz, eds. *The Cambridge History of the Native Peoples of the Americas.* Vol. 3: *South America.* New York: Cambridge University Press, 1996.

Michael E. Smith. *The Aztecs,* 2nd ed. Malden, MA: Blackwell, 2003.

Dirk R. Van Tuerenhout. *The Aztecs: New Perspectives.* Santa Barbara, CA: ABC-CLIO, 2005.

Chapter 15. Calamities and Recoveries across Afroeurasia

John Aberth. *The First Horseman: Disease in Human History.* Upper Saddle River, NJ: Pearson Prentice Hall, 2007.

Timothy Brook. *The Troubled Empire: China in the Yuan and Ming Dynasties.* Cambridge, MA: Belknap Press of Harvard University Press, 2010.

Peter Burke, *The Renaissance,* 2nd ed. New York: St. Martin's Press, 1997.

Norman F. Cantor. *In the Wake of the Plague: The Black Death and the World It Made.* New York: Free Press, 2001.

Kenneth Chase. *Firearms: A Global History to 1700.* New York: Cambridge, 2003.

Samuel K. Cohn, Jr. *The Black Death Transformed: Disease and Culture in Early Renaissance Europe.* London: Arnold, 2002.

John W. Dardess. *Ming China, 1368–1644: A Concise History of a Resilient Empire.* Lanham, MD: Rowman & Littlefield, 2012.

Brian Fagan. *The Little Ice Age: How Climate Made History, 1300–1850.* New York: Basic Books, 2000.

George Holmes. *Europe: Hierarchy and Revolt, 1320–1450,* 2nd ed. Medford, MA: Blackwell, 2000.

Lisa Jardine. *Worldly Goods: A New History of the Renaissance.* New York: Norton, 1996.

William Chester Jordan. *The Great Famine: Northern Europe in the Early Fourteenth Century.* Princeton, NJ: Princeton University Press, 1996.

H. H. Lamb. *Climate, History and the Modern World,* 2nd ed. New York: Routledge, 1995.

Heath W. Lowry. *The Nature of the Early Ottoman State.* Albany: State University of New York Press, 2003.

Beatrice Forbes Manz. *The Rise and Rule of Tamerlane.* Cambridge: Cambridge University Press, 1989.

D. R. SarDesai. *India: The Definitive History.* Boulder, CO: Westview Press, 2008.

References

introduction

1. Martin W. Lewis and Kären E. Wigen, *The Myth of Continents: A Critique of Metageography* (Berkeley: University of California Press, 1997), 27.

chapter 1

1. Robert J. Wenke, *Patterns in Prehistory: Humankind's First Three Million Years*, 5th ed. (New York: Oxford University Press, 1990), 103.
2. Richard Leakey, *The Making of Mankind* (New York: Dutton, 1981), 117.
3. David Christian, *Maps of Time: An Introduction to Big History* (Berkeley: University of California Press, 2004), 146–148.
4. Christopher Stringer and Robin McKie, *African Exodus: The Origins of Modern Humanity* (New York: Holt, 1996), 117.
5. Elizabeth Wayland Barber, *Women's Work: The First 20,000 Years: Women, Cloth, and Society in Early Times* (New York: Norton, 1994).

chapter 2

1. Richard W. Bulliet, *Hunters, Herders, and Hamburgers: The Past and Future of Human-Animal Relationships* (New York: Columbia University Press, 2005).
2. Miriam Lichtheim, ed., *Ancient Egyptian Literature*, 3 vols. (Berkeley: University of California Press, 1973), 1:25–27.
3. Cyril Aldred, *The Egyptians*, rev. ed. (London: Thames and Hudson, 1984), 102.

chapter 3

1. David Christian, *Maps of Time: An Introduction to Big History* (Berkeley: University of California Press, 2004), 143.
2. Robert Hughes, *The Fatal Shore: The Epic of Australia's Founding* (New York: Alfred A. Knopf, 1987), 9.
3. David W. Anthony, *The Horse, the Wheel, and Language: How Bronze-Age Riders from the Eurasian Steppes Shaped the Modern World* (Princeton, NJ: Princeton University Press, 2007), 197–200.
4. Andrew Sherratt, *Economy and Society in Prehistoric Europe: Changing Perspectives* (Princeton, NJ: Princeton University Press, 1997).
5. Ibid.
6. Anthony, *The Horse, the Wheel, and Language*, 222.
7. Quoted in Billie Jean Collins, *The Hittites and Their World* (Atlanta, GA: Society of Biblical Literature, 2007), 93.
8. Quoted in J. P Mallory, *In Search of the Indo-Europeans: Language, Archaeology and Myth* (London: Thames and Hudson, 1989), 38.

chapter 4

1. Quoted in Colin M. MacLachlan and James E. Rodriguez O., *The Forging of the Cosmic Race: A Reinterpretation of Colonial Mexico* (Berkeley: University of California Press, 1980), 22–23.
2. Andrew Lawler, "Beyond the Family Feud: After Decades of Debate Are Younger Scholars Finally Asking the Right Questions about the Olmecs?" *Archaeology* 60 (Mar/April 2007): 20–25.
3. Terrence Kaufman, Running translation of La Mojarra Stele. Accessed September 19, 2012. http://anthropology.pitt.edu/faculty/kaufman.html.

chapter 5

1. Theodore A. Wertime, "The Pyrotechnologic Industries and Mediterranean Deforestation in Antiquity," *Journal of Field Archaeology* 10 (Winter 1983): 452.
2. Plato, *Critias*, trans. Benjamin Jowett. The Internet Classic Archive, http://classics.mit.edu/Plato/critias.html.
3. Both letters quoted in Marc Van de Mieroop, *A History of the Ancient Near East, ca. 3000–323 BC*, 2nd ed. (Malden, MA: Blackwell, 2007), 194.
4. Mark W. Chavalas, ed., *The Ancient Near East: Historical Sources in Translation* (Malden, MA: Blackwell, 2006), 288.
5. Holy Bible: New International Version, Genesis 12:1–5, BibleGateway.com.
6. Isaiah 37:10 (King James Version).
7. James Henry Breasted, trans., *Ancient Records of Egypt*, Part 4 (Chicago: University of Chicago Press, 1906), 861–883.
8. Population estimate compiled by David Christian in *Maps of Time: An Introduction to Big History* (Berkeley: University of California Press, 2004), 143.
9. Ibid., 326.

chapter 6

1. Herbert Cushing Tolman, *Ancient Persian Lexicon* (Nashville, TN: Vanderbilt University Press, 1908), 51.
2. Ibid., 51.
3. Roland G. Kent, *Old Persian*, 2nd ed. rev. (New Haven, CT: American Oriental Society, 1953), 140.
4. Quoted in Amélie Kuhrt, *The Ancient Near East, c. 3000–330 BC*, Vol. 2 (London: Routledge, 1995), 602.
5. Quoted in Ibid., 670.
6. Aristotle, *Politics*, trans. Benjamin Jowett (New York: Modern Library, 1943), 57.
7. Aristotle, *Metaphysics*, trans. Hippocrates G. Apostle (Bloomington: Indiana University Press, 1966), 14.
8. Margaret C. Miller, *Athens and Persia in the Fifth Century BC: A Study in Cultural Receptivity* (Cambridge: Cambridge University Press, 1997).
9. Rock Edict 13, *The Edicts of King Ashoka*, an English rendering by Ven. S. Dhammika (Kandy, Sri Lanka: Buddhist Publication Society, 1993), DharmaNet Edition, *Access to Insight*, June 5, 2010, http://www.accesstoinsight.org/lib/authors/dhammika/wheel386.html.
10. Pillar Edict 7, *The Edicts of King Ashoka*.
11. Herodotus, *The Histories*, trans. Robin Waterfield, with an introduction and notes by Carolyn Dewald (New York: Oxford University Press, 1998), 256.
12. Hippocrates, *Hippocratic Writings*, edited with an introduction by G.E.R. Lloyd, translated by J. Chadwick and W.N. Mann (New York: Penguin, 1983), 162.

chapter 7

1. Flavius Josephus, *The Great Roman-Jewish War: A.D. 66–70*, trans. William Whiston as revised by D. S. Margoliouth, ed., with an introduction by William R. Farmer (Gloucester, MA: Peter Smith, 1970), 248.

2. Cassius Dio Cocceianus, *Dio's Roman History,* trans. Earnest Cary (New York: Macmillan, 1914–27), 8:85.

3. Quoted in Richard Hingley and Christina Unwin, *Boudica: Iron Age Warrior Queen* (New York: Hambledon Continuum, 2005), 47.

4. Peter Garnsey and Richard Saller, *The Roman Empire: Economy, Society and Culture* (London: Duckworth, 1987), 20.

5. Confucius, *The Analects,* trans. Burton Watson (New York: Columbia University Press, 2007), 34.

6. Laozi, *Daodejing: The Book of the Way,* trans. Moss Roberts (Berkeley: University of California Press, 2001), 91.

7. Quoted in Stanley Burstein, ed., *Ancient African Civilizations: Kush and Axum* (Princeton, NJ: Markus Wiener, 1998), 99–100.

8. Wilfred H. Schoff, ed. and trans., *The Periplus of the Erythraean Sea: Travel and Trade in the Indian Ocean by a Merchant of the First Century* (New York: Longman, Green, 1912), 37–38.

9. Gary Keith Young, *Rome's Eastern Trade: International Commerce and Imperial Policy, 31 BC–AD 305* (London: Routledge, 2001), 181–189.

chapter 8

1. Diego de Landa, *Landa's Relación de las cosas de Yucatán: A translation,* ed. Alfred M. Tozzer (Cambridge, MA: Peabody Museum, 1941). Quoted in Robert J. Sharer with Loa P. Traxler, *The Ancient Maya,* 6th ed. (Palo Alto, CA: Stanford University Press, 2006), 126.

2. Richard E. W. Adams, *Prehistoric Mesoamerica,* 3rd ed. (Norman: University of Oklahoma Press, 2005), 290.

chapter 9

1. "Royal inscription found on the Kabah of Zartusht," Avesta—Zoroastrian Archives, http://www.avesta.org/mp/kz.html.

2. Lactantius, *Of the Manner in Which the Persecutors Died* (Whitefish, MT: Kessinger Publishing, 2004), 6.

3. Peter Heather, *The Fall of the Roman Empire: A New History of Rome and the Barbarians* (Oxford: Oxford University Press, 2006), 28.

4. "Edict of Milan (313 A.D.)," quoted in Paul Halsall, Internet Medieval Sourcebook, http://www.fordham.edu/halsall/sbook.html.

5. Heather, *Fall of the Roman Empire,* 126.

6. Quoted in ibid., 190.

7. Marcellinus Ammianus, *Marcellinus Ammianus,* with an English translation by John C. Rolfe (Cambridge, MA: Harvard University Press, 1958–1963), Book 31: 383–385.

8. Possidius, *Life of St. Augustine,* trans. and with an introduction by Herbert T. Weiskotten (Merchantville, NJ: Evolution Publishing, 2008), 40–41.

9. Jordanes, quoted in Heather, *Fall of the Roman Empire,* 319.

10. Hydatius, *The Chronicle of Hydatius and the Consularia Constantinopolitana,* trans. and ed. R. W. Burgess (New York: Oxford University Press, 1993), 103.

11. Procopius, *Procopius Works,* trans. Henry B. Dewing, Vol. 2 (Cambridge, MA: Harvard University Press, 1936), 329.

12. Peter Christensen, *The Decline of Iranshahr: Irrigation and Environments in the History of the Middle East, 500 B.C. to A.D. 1500* (Copenhagen: Museum Tusculanum Press, 1993), 81.

13. Brahmagupta, *Brahmasphutasiddhanta,* quoted in Ronald Green, *Nothing Matters: A Book about Nothing* (Arlesford, UK: John Hunt, 2011), 7.

14. Quoted in Burton Stein, *A History of India* (Malden, MA: Blackwell, 1998), 93.

15. I-Tsing (Yijing), *A Record of the Buddhist Religion as Practised in India and the Malay Archipelago (A.D. 671–695),* trans. J. Takakusu (Oxford: Clarendon Press, 1896), xxxiv.

16. Indicopleustes Cosmas, *The Christian Topography of Cosmas, an Egyptian Monk,* trans. and ed. J. W. McCrindle (London: Hakluyt Society, 1897).

17. Tyrannius Rufinus (ca. 344–410), quoted in Stanley Burstein, ed., *Ancient African Civilizations: Kush and Axum* (Princeton, NJ: Markus Wiener, 1998), 94–96.

18. Data adapted from David Christian, *Maps of Time: An Introduction to Big History* (Berkeley: University of California Press, 2004), 344–345.

19. Stephen K. Sanderson, "Expanding World Commercialization: The Link between World-Systems and Civilizations," in Stephen K. Sanderson, ed., *Civilizations and World Systems: Studying World-Historical Change* (Walnut Creek, CA: AltaMira Press, 1995), 267.

chapter 10

1. Samuel Beal, trans. and ed., *The Life of Hiuen-Tsiang,* 2nd ed. (Delhi: Manshiram Manoharlal, 1973), 41, quoted in Sally Hovey Wriggins, *The Silk Road Journey with Xuanzang* (Boulder, CO: Westview Press, 2004), 32.

2. Richard W. Bulliet, *Islam: The View from the Edge* (New York: Columbia University Press, 1994), 40.

3. Edward F. Schafer, *The Golden Peaches of Samarkand: A Study of Tang Exotics* (Berkeley: University of California Press, 1963), 28.

4. Population estimates for the first millennium C.E. adapted from David Christian, *Maps of Time: An Introduction to Big History* (Berkeley: University of California Press, 2004), 344–345; Massimo Live-Bacci, *A Concise History of World Population* (Cambridge, MA: Blackwell, 1992), 31; Colin McEvedy and Richard Jones, *Atlas of World Population History* (New York: Penguin, 1978), 345–347.

chapter 11

1. Patricia Crone, *Slaves on Horses, the Evolution of the Islamic Polity* (Cambridge: Cambridge University Press, 1980).

2. Jahiz, *The Life and Works of Jahiz: Translations of Selected Texts by Charles Pellat,* trans. D. M. Hawke (Berkeley: University of California Press, 1969), quoted in Francis Robinson, ed., *The Cambridge Illustrated History of the Islamic World* (Cambridge: Cambridge University Press, 1996), 38.

3. Richard W. Bulliet, *Islam: The View from the Edge* (New York: Columbia University Press, 1994), 38–39.

4. Conrad Totman, *A History of Japan* (Oxford: Blackwell, 2000), 110; Akira Hayami, *The Historical Demography of Pre-modern Japan* (Toronto: University of Toronto Press, 1997), 41–42.

5. Ibid., 84.

6. Al-Bakri, *The Book of Routes and Realms,* quoted in N. Levtzion and J. F. P. Hopkins, *Corpus of Early Arabic Sources for West African History* (Cambridge: Cambridge University Press, 1981), 79–81.

7. Ibid., 79–81.

8. Lynda Shaffer, "Southernization," *Journal of World History* 5 (Spring 1994): 1–21.

part 4

1. I. G. Simmons, *Changing the Face of the Earth: Culture, Environment, History* (Hoboken, NJ: Wiley-Blackwell, 1996), 27.

chapter 12

1. Zhibin Zhang et al., "Periodic Climate Cooling Enhanced National Disasters and Wars in China during AD 10–1900," *Proceedings of the Royal Society* 277 (2010): 3745–3753; Pingzhong Zhang et al., "A Test of Climate, Sun, and Culture Relationships from an 1810-Year Chinese Cave Record," *Science* 322 (Nov. 2008): 940–942.

2. Tu Cheng, quoted in Yoshinobu Shiba, *Commerce and Society in Song China*, Michigan Abstracts of Chinese and Japanese Works in Chinese History, no. 2 (Ann Arbor: Center for Chinese Studies, University of Michigan, 1970), 162–163.

3. Quoted in Charles O. Hucker, *China's Imperial Past: An Introduction to Chinese History and Culture* (Stanford, CA: Stanford University Press, 1975), 324.

4. Zhu Xi, quoted in Hucker, *China's Imperial Past*, 371. See also Allen Wittenborn translation of *Further Reflections on Things at Hand* (Lanham, MD: University Press of America, 2002).

5. Quoted in Robert Finlay, "The Pilgrim Art: The Culture of Porcelain in World History," *Journal of World History* 9 (Fall 1998): 152.

6. Al-Ghazali, *The Faith and Practice of al-Ghazali* by W. Montgomery Watt (London: Allen and Unwin, 1953), 56.

7. Sa'id al-Andalusi, *Science in the Medieval World: Book of the Categories of Nations*, trans. and ed. Sema'an I. Salem and Alok Kumar (Austin: University of Texas Press, 1991), 7.

8. Robert Bartlett, *The Making of Europe: Conquest, Colonization and Cultural Change, 950–1350* (Princeton, NJ: Princeton University Press, 1993), 144. [Citing here work of Walter Kuhn.]

9. Zakariya ibn Muhammad al-Qazwini, *Athar al-Bilad wa-Akhbar al-'Ibad* (Beirut, n.d.). Translated and quoted in Tim Mackintosh-Smith, *Travels with a Tangerine: A Journey in the Footnotes of Ibn Battutah* (London: John Murray, 2001), 126.

10. Quoted in Vern L. Bullough, Brenda Shelton, and Sarah Slavin, *The Subordinated Sex: A History of Attitudes toward Women* (Athens: University of Georgia Press, 1988), 126.

chapter 13

1. Rein Taagepera, "Size and Duration of Empires: Systematics of Size," *Social Science Research* 7 (1978): 108–127.

2. Thomas T. Allsen, *Culture and Conquest in Mongol Eurasia* (Cambridge: Cambridge University Press, 2001), 5.

3. John of Plano Carpini, "History of the Mongols," in *The Mongol Mission*, ed. and with an introduction by Christopher Dawson (London: Sheed and Ward, 1955), 18.

4. Igor de Rachewiltz, trans. and ed., *The Secret History of the Mongols: A Mongolian Epic Chronicle of the Thirteenth Century*, 2 vols. (Leiden: Brill, 2004), 1:23.

5. Ata Malik Juvaini, *The History of the World Conqueror*, trans. J. A. Boyle, 2 vols. (Cambridge, MA: Harvard University Press, 1958), 1:152.

6. S. A. M. Adshead, *Central Asia in World History* (New York: St. Martin's Press, 1993), 61.

7. Rashid al-Din, *The Successors of Genghis Khan*, trans. John Andrew Boyle (New York: Columbia University Press, 1971), 169.

8. Ibid., 199–200.

9. Ibid., 168, 199.

10. Quoted in John Andrew Boyle, *The Mongol World Empire, 1206–1370* (London: Variorum Reprints, 1977), 6–7.

11. David Morgan, *The Mongols* (New York: Blackwell, 1986), 151.

12. Quoted in Boyle, *Mongol World Empire*, 6.

13. F. W. Mote, *Imperial China, 900–1800* (Cambridge, MA: Harvard University Press, 1999), 504.

14. Hamd-Allah Mustawfi, *The Geographical Part of the Nuzhat al-Qulub*, trans. G. Le Strange (Leiden: Brill, 1919), 34.

15. Rashid al-Din, *Ta'rikh-i mubarak-i Ghazani*, ed. Karl Jahn (London: Luzac, 1940). Quoted in Allsen, *Culture and Conquest*, 121.

16. Ronald Latham, trans. and ed., *The Travels of Marco Polo* (New York: Penguin Books, 1958), 237.

17. Ibid., 290.

18. Ibn Battuta, quoted in Said Hamdun and Noël King, eds., *Ibn Battuta in Black Africa* (Princeton, NJ: Markus Wiener, 2005), 16.

19. Roger Bacon, *Opus Majus*, trans. Robert Belle Burke (Philadelphia: University of Pennsylvania Press, 1928), 2:583.

20. Nehemia Levtzion, *Ancient Ghana and Mali* (London: Methuen 1973), 131–133.

chapter 14

1. Richard E. W. Adams, *Prehistoric Mesoamerica*, 3rd ed. (Norman: University of Oklahoma Press, 2005), 299, 304.

2. Dirk R. Van Tuerenhout, *The Aztecs: New Perspectives* (Santa Barbara, CA: ABC-CLIO, 2005), 147.

3. Hernán Cortés, From Second Letter to Charles V, 1520, Modern History Sourcebook, http://www.fordham.edu/halsall/mod/1520cortes.asp.

4. Quoted in Michael E. Smith, *The Aztecs*, 2nd ed. (Malden, MA: Blackwell, 2003), 195.

5. Quoted in John Bierhorst, ed., *The Hungry Woman: Myths and Legends of the Aztecs* (New York: Morrow, 1984), 38, 99–111.

6. Juan de Betanzos, *Narrative of the Incas*, trans. and ed. Roland Hamilton and Dana Buchanan (Austin: University of Texas Press, 1996), 28–29.

7. Pedro Cieza de Leon, *Crónica del Perú*, quoted in María Rostworowski and Craig Morris, "The Fourfold Domain: Inka Power and Its Social Foundations," in *The Cambridge History of the Native Peoples of the Americas*, ed. Frank Salomon and Stuart Schwartz. Vol. 3, Part 1 (Cambridge: Cambridge University Press, 1999), 787.

chapter 15

1. Henry S. Lucas, "The Great European Famine of 1315, 1316, and 1317," *Speculum* 5 (1930): 365–366.

2. Ibn Khaldun, *The Muqaddimah: An Introduction to History*, trans. Franz Rosenthal, 3 vols. (Princeton, NJ: Princeton University Press, 1958), 1:64.

3. Giovanna Morelli et al., "*Yersinia Pestis* Genome Sequencing Identifies Patterns of Global Phylogenetic Diversity," *Nature Genetics* 42 (Dec. 2010): 1140–1145.

4. Ewen Callaway, "Plague Genome: The Black Death Decoded," *Nature* 478 (2011). Retrieved from http://www.nature.com/news/2011/111025/full/478444a.html.

5. Michael Dols, *The Black Death in the Middle East* (Princeton, NJ: Princeton University Press, 1977), 69.

6. Giovanni Boccaccio, *Decameron*, trans. John Payne, revised and annotated by Charles S. Singleton (Berkeley: University of California Press, 1982), 1:14–15.

7. Ibn Abi Hajalah, quoted in Dols, *Black Death in the Middle East*, 238.

8. Dols, *Black Death in the Middle East*, 265.

9. *The Chronicles of Jean Froissart*, trans. Lord Berners, selected, edited, and introduced by Gillian and William Anderson (Carbondale: Southern Illinois University Press, 1963), 138.

10. F. W. Mote, *Imperial China, 900–1800* (Cambridge, MA: Harvard University Press, 1999), 744–745.

11. Sally K. Church, "Zheng He: An Investigation into the Plausibility of 450-Ft Treasure Ships," *Monumenta Serica* 53 (2005): 1–43.

12. H. A. R. Gibb, trans. and ed., *The Travels of Ibn Battuta*, A.D. 1325–1354, Vol. 4, translation completed with annotations by C. F. Beckingham (London: Hakluyt Society, 1994), 814.

13. Kritovoulos, *History of Mehmed the Conqueror*, trans. Charles T. Riggs (Princeton, NJ: Princeton University Press, 1954), 25.

14. Kritovoulos, *History of Mehmed the Conqueror*, 66–67.

Credits

LINE ART/TEXT

Chapter 2

p. 68: Miriam Lichtheim, *Ancient Egyptian Literature,* Volume I: *The Old and Middle Kingdoms,* pp. 118–120. © 1973, 2006 by the Regents of the University of California. Reprinted by permission of the University of California Press.

Chapter 3

p. 98: *Letters from Mesopotamia,* trans. A. Leo Oppenheim, pp. 122ff. Copyright © 1967 by The University of Chicago. Reprinted by permission of The University of Chicago Press.

Chapter 6

pp. 184, 185: "The Edicts of King Ashoka," an English rendering by Ven. S. Dhammika (Kandy, Sri Lanka: Buddhist Publication Society, 1993). © 1993 Buddhist Publication Society. Reprinted with permission.

Chapter 7

p. 204: Laozi, *Dao De Jing: The Book of the Way,* trans. Moss Roberts, p. 90. © 2001 by the Regents of the University of California. Reprinted by permission of the University of California Press.

Chapter 8

p. 234: Reprinted with the permission of Simon & Schuster, Inc. and The Ward & Balkin Agency, Inc. from *Popol Vuh* translated by Dennis Tedlock. Copyright © 1985, 1996 Dennis Tedlock; p. 240: Gordon R. Willey, *Introduction to American Archaeology,* vol. 2: *South America* (Englewood Cliffs, NJ: Prentice-Hall, 1971), Figure 3-38. © 1971 Gordon R. Willey.

Chapter 11

p. 330: *The Vinland Sagas: The Icelandic Sagas about the First Documented Voyages across the North Atlantic,* trans. Keneva Kunz (London and New York: Penguin, 2008), pp. 3–5. Translation copyright © Leifur Eiriksson, 1997. Reprinted by permission of Leifur Eiriksson Publishing Ltd.

Chapter 12

p. 342: Tu Cheng, quoted in Yoshinobu Shiba, *Commerce and Society in Sung China,* trans.

Mark Elvin. Michigan Abstracts of Chinese and Japanese Works in Chinese History, no. 2 (Ann Arbor: Center for Chinese Studies, University of Michigan, 1970), pp. 162–163. Reprinted by permission of Center for Chinese Studies, University of Michigan; p. 352: *Letters of Medieval Jewish Traders,* trans. from the Arabic by S. D. Goitein, pp. 222–225. © 1973 Princeton University Press, copyright renewed 2001 by Princeton University Press. Reprinted by permission of Princeton University Press.

Chapter 13

pp. 385 ("When a ship . . ."), 394: Said Hamdun and Noël King, ed. and trans., *Ibn Battuta in Black Africa,* pp. 16, 58–59. Copyright © 1975 by Said Hamdun and Noël King. Reprinted by permission of Markus Wiener Publishers, Princeton, NJ.

Chapter 14

p. 415: Nezahualcoyotl, "The Flower Tree" in *Ancient American Poets,* trans. John Curl. Bilingual Press, 2005; p. 419: Garcilaso de la Vega, *Royal Commentaries of the Incas and General History of Peru,* Part One, trans. Harold V. Livermore (Austin, TX: University of Texas Press, 1966), pp. 204–206. Copyright © 1966 by The University of Texas Press.

Chapter 15

p. 431: M. J. Müller, "Ibnulkhatib's Bericht über die Pest," Sitzungsberichte der Königl. Bayerischen Akademie der Wissenschaften, 2 (1863): pp. 2–12. Translated from the Arabic with assistance from Dr. Walid Saleh. In John Aberth, *The First Horseman: Disease in Human History,* 1st Edition, pp. 44–46, © 2007. Reprinted by permission of Pearson Education, Inc., Upper Saddle River, New Jersey.

PHOTOS

Front Matter

Page vii(top): Photo by Jordan Catapano; p. vii(bottom): © Graham Proctor; p. ix: © The Metropolitan Museum of Art. Image source: Art Resource, NY; p. x: © Dea/ G Dagli Orti/Age Fotostock; p. xii: © Leo Hol; p. xiii: © akg-images; p. xiv: © The Trustees of the British Museum/Art

Resource, NY; p. xv: © SSPL/Science Museum/Art Resource, NY; p. xvii: © eye35.pix/Alamy.

Introduction

Opener: NASA Earth Observatory image by Robert Simmon, using Suomi NPP VIIRS data provided courtesy of Chris Elvidge (NOAA National Geophysical Data Center). Suomi NPP is the result of a partnership between NASA, NOAA, and the Department of Defense; I-3: © Stock Connection/SuperStock; I-5: © The Granger Collection, New York; I-8(left): © SuperStock/Age Fotostock; I-8(right): © Stock Connection/SuperStock; I-9: © Mark Horn/Getty Images; I-11: © Veronique Durruty/Gamma-Rapho via Getty Images; I-13: © VisitBritain/Britain on View/ Getty Images.

Chapter 1

Part Opener: © The Metropolitan Museum of Art. Image source: Art Resource, NY; p. 20: © John Reader/Science Source; p. 21(1): © Dave Einsel/Getty Images; p. 21(2): © Francesco d'Errico and Marian Van-Haeren; p. 21(3): © Elaine Thompson/AP Photo; p. 21(4): © Jeff Pachoud/AFP/Getty Images; p. 24: © Dave Einsel/Getty Images; p. 25: © CDA/Guillemot/akg-images; p. 26: © Sayyid Azim/AP Photo; p. 30: © Max Planck Institute for Evolutionary Anthropology; p. 31: Engraved ochre—Courtesy of Prof. Christopher Henshilwood; p. 32: © Francesco d'Errico and Marian VanHaeren; p. 34: © The Natural History Museum/The Image Works; p. 35: Elaine Thompson/AP Photo; p. 37: Courtesy Michael R. Waters; p. 38(left, right): Courtesy American Museum of Natural History Library; p. 42: © RIA Novosti/Science Source; p. 43: © Prehistoric/The Bridgeman Art Library/Getty Images; p. 44: © Jeff Pachoud/AFP/Getty Images; p. 45: © Berthold Steinhilber/laif/Redux.

Chapter 2

Opener: © The Trustees of the British Museum/Art Resource, NY; p. 49(top): © Francois Ducasse/Science Source; p. 49(bottom): © Harappan/National Museum of Karachi, Karachi, Pakistan/ The Bridgeman Art Library; p. 53: © Francois Ducasse/Science Source; p. 55: © Sakamoto Photo Research Laboratory/ Corbis; p. 56: © Dorling Kindersley/Getty

Images RF; p. 57: © Martin Shields/ Science Source; p. 62: © Middle Eastern/ The Bridgeman Art Library/Getty Images; p. 63: © The Metropolitan Museum of Art. Image source: Art Resource, NY; p. 64: © Réunion des Musées Nationaux/ Art Resource, NY; p. 65: © The Trustees of the British Museum; p. 67: © Scala/ Art Resource, NY; p. 69: © Ravi Tahilramani/Getty Images RF; p. 70: © Werner Forman/Universal Images Group/Getty Images; p. 71: © Harappan/National Museum of Karachi, Karachi, Pakistan/ The Bridgeman Art Library; p. 73: © bpk, Berlin/Aegyptisches Museum, Staatliche Museen, Berlin, Germany/Art Resource, NY.

Chapter 3

Opener: © Helmut Corneli/imageb/Age Fotostock; p. 79(1): © Werner Foreman Archive/Art Resource, NY; p. 79(2): © The Trustees of the British Museum/Art Resource, NY; p. 79(3): © DEA Picture Library/Getty Images; p. 79(4): © Nigel Pavitt/JAI/Corbis; p. 81: © The Metropolitan Museum of Art. Image source: Art Resource, NY; p. 83: Nimatallah/Art Resource, NY; p. 84: © Photographer Chris Archinet/Getty Images; p. 85: © Kenneth Garrett/National Geographic Creative; p. 86: © Cultural Relics Publishing House, Beijing; p. 87: © Werner Foreman Archive/ Art Resource, NY; p. 89: © The Trustees of the British Museum/Art Resource, NY; p. 91: © akg/Bildarchiv Steffens/ Newscom; p. 93: © Funkystock/Age Fotostock; p. 95: © The Gallery Collection/ Corbis; p. 96: © DEA Picture Library/ Getty Images; p. 97: © The Trustees of The British Museum/Art Resource, NY; p. 101: © Kontos Photo Stock; p. 102: © Jae C. Hong/AP Photo; p. 104: © Nigel Pavitt/ JAI/Corbis.

Chapter 4

Opener: © John Webber/The Bridgeman Art Library/Getty Images; p. 109(1): © Francesco Palermo/Alamy; p. 109(2): © Lemaire Stephane/hem/Age Fotostock; p. 109(3): © Stephan Alvarez/National Geographic Creative; p. 112: © John Doebley; p. 113: © Kevin Schafer/Getty Images; p. 115: © George Steinmetz/Corbis; p. 116: © Werner Forman/Universal Images Group/Getty Images; p. 117: © Scala/Art Resource, NY; p. 119(left): © Francesco Palermo/Alamy; p. 119(right): © Rick Strange/Photoshot; p. 121: © Bill Pogue/ Mira.com; p. 123: Painting by Martin Pate, Newnan, GA. Courtesy of Southeastern Archeological Center, NPS and the State of Louisiana; p. 125: © Lemaire Stephane/ hem/Age Fotostock; p. 127: © Stephan Alvarez/National Geographic Creative.

Chapter 5

Part Opener: © Dea/G Dagli Orti/Age Fotostock; p. 134: © Z. Radovan/Lebrecht/ The Image Works; p. 135(1): © DEA/A. Dagli Orti/Getty Images; p. 135(2): © Clara Amit, Israel Antiquities Authority, HO/AP Photo; p. 135(3): © V&A Images, London/Art Resource, NY; p. 135(4): Ritual Disc with Dragon Motifs (Bi), Chinese, from Jincun, Henan Province, Eastern Zhou Dynasty (771–256 B.C.E.). Jade (nephrite), diameter: 6 1/2 inches (16.5 cm). The Nelson-Atkins Museum of Art, Kansas City, Missouri. Purchase: William Rockhill Nelson Trust, 33–81. Photo: John Lamberton; p. 138: © DEA/A. Dagli Orti/Getty Images; p. 139: © Panoramic Images/Getty Images; p.141: © Erich Lessing/Art Resource, NY; p. 144: © Werner Forman/Universal Images Group/Getty Images; p. 145: © The Granger Collection, New York; p. 146: © The Trustees of the British Museum/Art Resource, NY; p. 147: © Clara Amit, Israel Antiquities Authority, HO/AP Photo; p. 148(left): © Photos 12/Alamy; p. 148(right): © Erich Lessing/Art Resource, NY; p. 149: © Doug McKinlay/Getty Images; p. 151: © Scala/Art Resource, NY; p. 152: © British Museum/Art Resource, NY; p. 154: © V&A Images, London/Art Resource, NY; p. 155: Ritual Disc with Dragon Motifs (Bi), Chinese, from Jincun, Henan Province, Eastern Zhou Dynasty (771–256 B.C.E.). Jade (nephrite), diameter: 6½ inches (16.5 cm). The Nelson-Atkins Museum of Art, Kansas City, Missouri. Purchase: William Rockhill Nelson Trust, 33–81. Photo: John Lamberton.

Chapter 6

Opener: © Werner Forman/Corbis; p. 161(1): © The Granger Collection, New York; p. 161(2): © nagelestock.com/Alamy; p. 161(3): © Araldo de Luca/Corbis; p 161(4): © Luca Tettoni/Corbis; p. 161(5): © Hermitage, St. Petersburg, Russia/ The Bridgeman Art Library; p. 165: © Leemage/Universal Images Group/Getty Images; p. 166(top): © DEA/W. Buss/De Agostini/Getty Images; p. 166(bottom): © The Granger Collection, New York; p. 168: Courtesy of the Oriental Institute of the University of Chicago; p. 169: © Stock Connection Blue/Alamy; p. 170: © Erich Lessing/Art Resource, NY; p. 171: © nagelestock.com/Alamy; p. 172: © akg-images/Andrea Baguzzi/The Image Works; p. 175: © Araldo de Luca/Corbis; p. 177: © Scala/Art Resource, NY; p. 178: © The Metropolitan Museum of Art. Image source: Art Resource, NY; p. 180(left): © DEA/G. Sioen/Getty Images; p. 180(right): © Vanni/Art Resource, NY; p. 182: © Luca Tettoni/Corbis; p. 183: © Dinodia/Age

Fotostock; p. 186: © Hermitage, St. Petersburg, Russia/The Bridgeman Art Library.

Chapter 7

Opener: © Imagebroker.net/Photoshot; p. 191(1): © Araldo de Luca/Corbis; p. 191(2): © Spectrum Colour Library/ Heritage-Images; p. 191(3): © MJ Photography/Alamy; p. 191(4): © Rupert Hansen/Alamy; p. 193: © Araldo de Luca/ Corbis; p. 196: © Vanni/Art Resource, NY; p. 197: © Alinari/Art Resource, NY; p. 198: © View Pictures Ltd/Alamy; p. 199: © Patrick Syder/Getty Images; p. 200: © LatitudeStock/Alamy; p. 202: © Spectrum Colour Library/Heritage-Images; p. 203: © Bettmann/Corbis; p. 204: Ronald Sheridan@Ancient Art & Architecture Collection Ltd.; p. 206: © Henry Arvidsson/Alamy; p. 207: © The Trustees of the British Museum/Art Resource, NY; p. 209: © MJ Photography/Alamy; p. 212: © Rupert Hansen/Alamy; p. 215: © Trustees of the National Museums of Scotland 2010; p. 216: © Canali Photobank, Milan, Italy.

Chapter 8

Opener: © JurriaanBrobbel/Age Fotostock; p. 221(top): © Anne Lewis/Alamy; p. 221(bottom): © Nathan Benn/Corbis; p. 225: © 1998 Copyright IMS Communications Ltd./Capstone Design. All Rights Reserved; p. 226: © Anne Lewis/ Alamy; p. 227: © Courtesy of the Penn Museum, image #60.4.358; p. 228: © Age Fotostock/Robert Harding; p. 228(inset): Photo by Andrew Demarest, Courtesy of Arthur Demarest; p. 231: Reproduced by courtesy of the Trustees of the British Museum, London; p. 232: Photograph © Justin Kerr; p. 235: © Kenneth Garrett/ National Geographic Creative; p. 238: © Tom Till/Alamy; p. 241: © Nathan Benn/ Corbis; p. 243: © George Steinmetz/ National Geographic Creative; p. 243(inset): © Stockfolio(r)/Alamy.

Chapter 9

Part Opener: © Leo Hol; p. 248: © Araldo de Luca/Corbis; p. 249(1): © Ostrogothic/ The Bridgeman Art Library/Getty Images; p. 249(2): © Lowell Georgia/ Corbis; p. 249(3): © akg-images/Werner Forman/Newscom; p. 252: © Dennis Mark Mulhall; p. 253: © Prisma/UIG/ Getty Images; p. 255: © Werner Forman/ Universal Images Group/Getty Images; p. 256: © imagebroker/Alamy; p. 257: © Scala/Art Resource, NY; p. 259(top): © akg-images; p. 259(bottom): © Ostrogothic/ The Bridgeman Art Library/Getty Images; p. 260: © Scala/Art Resource, NY; p. 263: © akg-images/Jean-Louis Nou/The Image Works; p. 266: © Lowell Georgia/Corbis;

p. 267: © Jean-Louis Nou/akg-images; p. 268: © imagebroker/Alamy; p. 269: © The Granger Collection, New York; p. 270: © Philip Coblentz/Brand X Pictures/PictureQuest RF; p. 271: © bpk, Berlin/Museum fuer Asiatische Kunst, Staatliche Museen zu Berlin, Ber/Jürgen Liepe/Art Resource, NY; p. 273(top): © akg-images/Werner Forman/Newscom; p. 273(bottom): © The Glassell Collection of African Gold gift of Alfred C. Glassell, Jr./The Bridgeman Art Library.

Chapter 10

Opener: © V&A Images, London/Art Resource, NY; p. 279(1): © photoaisa; p. 279(2): © Eric Lessing/Art Resource, NY; p. 279(3): © Archives Charmet/The Bridgeman Art Library; p. 285: © Turkish School/The Bridgeman Art Library/Getty Images; p. 287: © Reza/Getty Images; p. 288: © photoaisa; p. 289: © Bruno Morandi/Hemis/Corbis; p. 292: © The Bridgeman Art Library/Getty Images; p. 293: © Harper Collins Publishers/The Art Archive at Art Resource, NY; p. 294: Photo by Wim Cox, Cologne; p. 295: © Classic Image/Alamy; p. 297: © Eric Lessing/Art Resource, NY; p. 298: © Jack Malipan Travel Photography/Alamy; p. 300: © Archives Charmet/The Bridgeman Art Library; p. 301: © RMN-Grand Palais/Art Resource, NY; p. 302: Courtesy of Ross Dunn; p. 303: © Lebrecht/The Image Works.

Chapter 11

Opener: © akg-images/British Library/The Image Works; p. 307(1): © Scala/Art Resource, NY; p. 307(2): © Brian Brake/Science Source; p. 307(3): © Images & Stories/Alamy; p. 307(4): © Archives Larousse, Paris, France/Giraudon/The Bridgeman Art Library; p. 309: © The Bridgeman Art Library/Alamy; p. 310: © Scala/White Images/Art Resource, NY; p. 311: © Scala/Art Resource, NY; p. 312: © Werner Forman Archive/Corbis; p. 313: © North Wind Picture Archives/The Image Works; p. 314: © Georg Gerster/Science Source; p. 316: © Heritage Images/Corbis; p. 317: © Science Source ; p. 320: © Brian Brake/Science Source; p. 322: © Steve Vidler/Iberfoto/The Image Works; p. 323: © Alex Ramsay/Alamy; p. 325: © Images & Stories/Alamy; p. 329: © Robert Harding World Imagery/Alamy; p. 331: © Archives Larousse, Paris, France/Giraudon/The Bridgeman Art Library.

Chapter 12

Part Opener: © akg-images; p. 338: © The Granger Collection, New York; p. 339(1): © TAO Images/SuperStock; p. 339(2): © Edinburgh University Library (Or. Ms. 20, fol. 121); p. 339(3): © The Trustees of the British Museum/Art Resource, NY; p. 342: © The Granger Collection, New York; p. 343: © Mark Harris/Getty Images RF; p. 345: Courtesy of Ross Dunn; p. 346: © Iberfoto/The Image Works; p. 347: © TAO Images/SuperStock; p. 348: © Edinburgh University Library (Or. Ms. 20, fol. 121); p. 349: © Christophe Boisvieux/Age Fotostock; p. 350: © Sami Sarkis/Age Fotostock RF; p. 353(left): © Vincenzo Lombardo/Robert Harding World Imagery/Corbis; p. 353(right): © Slow Images/Getty Images; p. 354: © Jane Sweeney/Age Fotostock; p. 355: © The Pierpont Morgan Library/Art Resource, NY; p. 357: © Biblioteca Medicia Lorenziana, Florence/Index S.A.S.; p. 359: © The Trustees of the British Museum/Art Resource, NY; p. 360: © The Granger Collection, New York; p. 362: © Robert Preston Photography/Alamy; p. 363: © Museum of London/The Art Archive at Art Resource, NY.

Chapter 13

Opener: © Art Resource, NY; p. 369(1): © Bridgeman Art Library/Getty Images; p. 369(2): © The Metropolitan Museum of Art. Image source: Art Resource, NY; p. 369(3): © Digital Vision/Punchstock; p. 369(4): © Sonia Halliday and Laura Lushington/Sonia Halliday Photographs; p. 369(5): © Dirk Bakker/The Bridgeman Art Library; p. 371: © V&A Images, London/Art Resource, NY; p. 372: © The Bridgeman Art Library/Getty Images; p. 374: The Art Archive at Art Resource, NY; p. 376: © akg-images/Newscom; p. 377: Courtesy Wataru Ishihara, ARIUA; p. 378: © The Trustees of the British Museum/Art Resource, NY; p. 380: © The Metropolitan Museum of Art. Image source: Art Resource, NY; p. 381: © R. & S. Michaud/akg-images; p. 382: © dbimages/Alamy; p. 384: © Digital Vision/Punchstock RF; p. 386: © Georg Gerster/Science Source; p. 388: © Sonia Halliday and Laura Lushington/Sonia Halliday Photographs; p. 389: © Prisma Bildagentur AG/Alamy; p. 390: © Kharbine-Tapabor/The Art Archive at Art Resource, NY; p. 393: © Michel Uyttebroeck/Age Fotostock RF; p. 395: © Dirk Bakker/The Bridgeman Art Library.

Chapter 14

Opener: Photograph © Justin Kerr, K 4440; p. 399(1): © De Agostini/Getty Images; p. 399(2): © Photo Researchers/Photoshot; p. 402: © William R. Iseminger/Cahokia Mounds State Historic Site; p. 402(inset): © Ira Block/National Geographic Creative/Corbis; p. 404: © Walter Rawlings/Robert Harding World Imagery/Corbis; p. 406: © De Agostini/Getty Images; p. 407(top): © Ogphoto/Getty Images RF; p. 407(bottom): © Steve Allen/Getty Images RF; p. 408: © National Geographic Creative/Alamy; p. 409(top): © The Metropolitan Museum of Art. Image source: Art Resource, NY; pp. 409(bottom), 410: © The Trustees of the British Museum/Art Resource, NY; p. 411: © Nigel Pavitt/JAI/Corbis; p. 412: © UIG via Getty Images; p. 415: © David R. Frazier Photolibrary, Inc./Alamy; p. 416: © Spanish School/The Bridgeman Art Library/Getty Images; p. 417: © CarverMostardi/Alamy; p. 421(top): © The Granger Collection, New York; p. 421(bottom): © Photo Researchers/Photoshot.

Chapter 15

Opener: © Erich Lessing/Art Resource, NY; p. 425(1): ©Werner Forman/HIP/The Image Works; p. 425(2): © British Library Board/Robana/Art Resource, NY; p. 425(3): © ullstein bild/The Image Works; p. 429(top): John Montenieri/CDC; p. 429(bottom): © Getty Images/Digital Vision RF; p. 430: © Werner Forman/HIP/The Image Works; p. 432: © British Library Board/Robana/Art Resource, NY; p. 435: © Michael Klinec/Alamy; p. 436: © British Library Board/Robana/Art Resource, NY; p. 437: © The Art Archive at Art Resource, NY; p. 438: © Interfoto/Alamy; p. 440: © Robert Harding Picture Library/SuperStock; p. 441: © Imaginechina/Corbis; p. 442: © Dinodia Stock Connection Worldwide/Newscom; p. 443: © Roland and Sabrina Michaud/akg/The Image Works; p. 444: © ullstein bild/The Image Works; p. 445: © Fogg Art Museum, Harvard University Art Museums, USA/Gift of Sir Joseph Duveen/The Bridgeman Art Library; p. 447: © Italian School, (15th century)/Museo de Firenze Com'era, Florence, Italy/The Bridgeman Art Library; p. 449: © National Gallery, London, UK/The Bridgeman Art Library.

Index

Sejong (Korean king), 439
Selam, 24
Seleucia, 177
Seleucid empire, 175, 176, 177, 181, 206
Seljuk empire, 348–349, *349*, 362, 373
Semitic languages, 95, 150, 168, 211
Septuagint, 181
Serbia, 444
serfdom, 156, 293, 361, 434
sericulture. *See* silk
Serpent Mound, 237, *238*
Sesostris I (Egyptian pharaoh), 68
Sesostris III (Egyptian pharaoh), 68
Seville, *353*
Shaffer, Lynda, 333
shamanism, 87–88, 371, 381
Shang dynasty (China), 86–88, 91, 101–102, 135
Shapur I (Sasanid emperor), 253, 254
shari'a, 310, *310*, 354
Shield Jaguar (Maya king), 231
shifting (swidden) agriculture, 105, 272
Shi Huangdi (Chinese emperor), 200–202, 212
Shi'ism, 289–290, 312, 349
Shinto, 321, 346
shipbuilding. *See* maritime technology
Shiva, 155
Shudra class, 154, 185
Sicily, 362
Siddartha Gautama (Buddha), 181–182
Sierra Mountains, 14
silk, 88, 205, 213, 252
silk road trade
    600–200 B.C.E., 187
    300 B.C.E.–300 C.E., 212
    500–800 C.E., 281, 282, 283, 290
    1200–1350 C.E., 369, 373
    and China, 205
    and Mongol campaigns, 373
    and Mongol khanates, 378, 379–380, *380*
Silla dynasty (Korea), 321, 322, *322*, 345
Sima Qian, 155
Simeon, Saint, 268
Sind, 291
Sinification, 205
Sintashta site, 90–91
sipahis, 444
Sipán, 242
slavery
    Abbasid Caliphate, 310–311, 315–316
    Achaemenid empire, 165, 172
    Africa, 319
    ancient Greece, 170, 171, 172
    defined, 65
    early complex societies, 65
    empires, 133
    Europe, 434
    Hellenistic world, 181
    and Islam, 286, 325
    military slavery, 311, 325, 348, 378, 444
    pre-Columbian Mesoamerica, 232, 407
    resistance, 370
    Roman empire, 194, 196, *196*
    and serfdom, 293
    trans-Saharan trade, 325
    Turkic military kingdoms, 349–350
Slavic languages, 292
Slavs, 261
Snaketown, 236
social complexity. *See* complex societies
social equality, 71, 90, 116, 151
social hierarchy. *See* social inequality
social inequality
    Abbasid Caliphate, 315
    Afroeurasia (3000–1000 B.C.E.), 82, 83, 86
    and agricultural revolution, 55, 57
    ancient Greece, 170, 173
    Andean societies, 410
    Babylonian empire, 95–96
    caste system, 135, 153–154, 181, 185, 263
    China, 86, 201–202, 205, 321, 343
    early complex societies, 64–65, *65*
    Europe (500–800 C.E.), 293
    Indic migrants, 101
    Mesoamerica, 118, 120, 230, 235, 407
    Neolithic large villages, 56, 57
    North America, 237
    pastoral nomads, 89–90
    patron-client systems, 194, 198–199
    Roman empire, 193–194, 254, 257
    South America, 240, 241, 242, 244
    and writing, 63
    See also slavery

society types, 59
Socrates, 173, 179
Sogdiana, 281
Solomon Islands, 126
Solomon (king of Israel), 147
Solon, 170
Song dynasty (China), 337, *338*, 339, 341–345, *342*, *343*, 346–347, *347*, 374–375
Songtsan Gampo (Tibetan leader), 283
Soninke language, 324, 326
Sorghaghtani Beki, 376, *376*
South America
    agricultural revolution, 113
    agriculture, 411, *411*, 412
    Amazonia, 410
    Andean societies (900–1500 C.E.), 410–413
    Chimu state, 411–413, 420
    complex societies (900 B.C.E.–900 C.E.), 223, 238–244, *240*
    early complex societies, 116–117, *116*
    geography/climate, 114–115, 243–244, 401, 410, 411
    Inca empire, 399, 417–422, *418*
    maps, *239*, *418*
    Norte Chico, 114–116, 241
    Spanish invasion, 419, 422
    Tiwanaku, 410
    Wari empire, 411, 417
South Asia
    1200–600 B.C.E., 152–155
    Achaemenid empire, 164, 173
    agriculture, 152, 185, 318
    Alexander the Great, 174
    Brahmanism, 133, 135, 154–155, 181, 263
    Buddhism, 133, 181–183, 185, 214, 266, 302
    caste system, 135, 153–154, 181, 185, 263
    Chola dynasty, 385
    Christianity, 270
    Delhi sultanate, 348, 378, 382, 433, 442
    Gupta empire, 247, 251, 261–264, 317
    Harappan civilization, 69–71, 74, 75, 101, 152
    Hinduism, 262, 266, *267*, 318, 385
    Indic migrations, 100–101
    Islam, 382, 385
    Jainism, 183
    Kushana empire, 191, 207–208, 215, 251, 253–254, 264, 271
    maps, *153*, *176*, *262*
    Maurya dynasty, 163, 173, *176*, 181, 183–185, 214, 266
    nomad migrations/invasions, 264
    Pallava dynasty, 318
    Sufism, 442
    textile industry, 318
    trade, 185, 213, 262, 318, 384–385
    Turkic invasions, 348
    and Umayyad Caliphate, 291
    Vijayanagar monarchy, 442–443, *442*
    writing, 150
    See also southern seas
South China Sea, 10
Southeast Asia
    3000–1000 B.C.E., 79–80, *103*, 105–106
    and Africa, 274
    Austronesian migrations, 105–106, 127
    Buddhism, 266, 320, 384
    Hinduism, 266, 384
    monarchies (1200–1350 C.E.), 384, *384*
    and Near Oceania, 126
    and southern seas trade, 213
    Srivijaya state, 319–320
southernization, 333
southern seas, 10
    Chinese maritime exploration (fifteenth century), 440–442, *441*
    trade, 212–213, 312, 318–320, *319*, 369, 383–386, *383*
Southwest Asia
    agricultural revolution, 51, 55–57
    Arab empire, 287–288
    and Arabs, 284–285
    crusader states, 349, 350, 362, 363, 381, 382
    iron technology, 137
    Islam, 247
    Mongol campaigns, 377–378
    Neo-Assyrian empire, *134*, 135, 142–144, 147, 150
    Neo-Babylonian empire, 144, *145*, 146, 147
    relations with ancient Egypt, 98

religion, 133
    Seleucid empire, 175, 176, 177, 181, 206
    Seljuk empire, 348–349, 362, 373
    Timur's empire, *432*, 433–434, 443
    See also Achaemenid empire; Anatolia; Mediterranean basin; Mesopotamia; Muslim lands; Persia
Spain, 399, 407, 409, 417, 422. *See also* Iberian peninsula
Sparta, 169–170, 171, 173
Spartacus, 196
specialization, 60
sphinx, *69*
split inheritance, 413, 418
Sri Lanka (Ceylon), 213
Srivijaya state, 319–320
Staff God, 411
Standard of Ur, *65*
states, 61, *61*. *See also* city-states; early complex societies; government; *specific states*
Stele of Hammurabi, *95*
steppes. *See* Inner Eurasia; nomad migrations/invasions; pastoral nomads
St. Gall, monastery of, *294*
stirrups, 295
St. Mary's Church (Cairo), *298*
Stoicism, 179–180, 204
Stonehenge, 84
stone tools
    and agricultural revolution, 52
    Australia, 125
    Clovis, 41, 43
    and early human colonization, 34, *34*
    Homo sapiens, 32
    Neanderthals, 39
    Neolithic era, 53
    Oceania, 127
    related hominin species, 25, *25*, 27, 28
    upper Paleolithic, 41, 43
string revolution, 42
stupas, *182*, 183
Subsaharan Africa
    3000–1000 B.C.E., 103–105, *103*, *104*
    200–600 C.E., 271–274
    agricultural revolution, 79–80
    Bantu migrations, 105, 138, 272, 274
    geography/climate, 104, 272
    Ghana empire, 307, 325–326, 351, 391
    Great Zimbabwe, 386, *386*
    iron technology, 137–138, 208, 272
    Islam, 326, 393
    Kanem empire, 395
    Mali empire, 370, 391, 392–393, 394, 427
    maps, *103*
    Nok culture, 272, 273, *273*
    Sudanic states (750–1000 C.E.), 323–324
    West African kingdoms (1200–1350 C.E.), 393, 395
    women, 138
Sudan, 104, 272. *See also* Subsaharan Africa
Sudanic states, 323–324, 392
Suez Canal, 10
Sufism, 355–356, *355*, 442
sugar, 262, 363
Sui dynasty (China), 247, 279, 298, *299*
Sumer, 60–62, 64, 72, 75, 81
Sunjata (Sundiata), 392, 393
Sunni Muslims, 289, 349
Suryavarman II (Khmer king), 384
sutras, 214
Swahili language, 318–319, 385
swidden (shifting) agriculture, 105, 272
symbolic expression. *See* art; culture; language
Syria
    crusader states, 349, *350*, 362, *362*, 363, 381, 382
    Mamluk sultanate, 378, 382, 427, 433
Syriac language, 270
Syrian Desert, 8

T

Tacitus, 198
Tadu-Heba (princess of Mittani), 99
Taharqo (Egyptian pharaoh), *152*
Taino people, 408–409, *409*
Tairona people, 408, *409*
Taiwan, 105
Taizong (Chinese emperor), 298, 302
Taizu (Zhu Yuanzhang) (Chinese emperor), 432, 439
Takrur, 324

Tale of Genji (Murasaki), 346, *346*
Tamerlane (Timur), *432*, 433–434, *433*
Tamil language, 318, 385
Tang dynasty (China), *246*, 247, 279, 283, 298–303, *299*, 301, 320–321, 322
Taq-i-Kisra, *206*
Tarim Basin, 102, 205, *252*, 283
technology
    Afroeurasia (3000–1000 B.C.E.), 81–82, *81*
    Afroeurasia (1300–1500 C.E.), 436–438, *437*, 438
    ancient Egypt, 97
    Australia, 125
    bronze, 81, *81*, *86*
    China, 204–205, *204*, 342
    early complex societies, 65
    Etruscans, 151
    Europe (1200–1350 C.E.), 388–389
    fire, 27–28
    iron, 132–133, 137–139, *138*, 152, 156, 208, 342
    Mesopotamia, 65
    Neolithic era, 53
    Oceania, 126, 127
    paper, *204*, 205, 306–307, *306*
    plows, 82, 204–205, 357, *357*
    printing, 345, *345*, 438, *438*, 449
    Teotihuacán, 225
    timeline, 54
    upper Paleolithic, 42–43, *42*
    wagons, 89
    See also communication/transportation systems; pottery; stone tools
tectonic plates, 4–5, *4*
temperate latitudes, 9, 14
temperature. *See* geography/climate
temples, 62
Temujin. *See* Chingis Khan
Ten Commandments, 145
Tenochtitlán, 398–399, 413, 414, 416
teosinte, *112*, 112
Teotihuacán, *132*, 133, 221, 224–228, *225*, 226, 227, 229, 406
Tepe Yahya, 73
terra preta, 113
textile industry, 318, 357
Thebes, 173, 174–175
Theodora (Byzantine empress), 260, *260*
Theodosius (Roman emperor), 257, 267
Thera (Santorini), 99
Theravada Buddhism, 264, 384
Thomas Aquinas, 391
Thule Ultima, 161
Thutmose I (Egyptian pharaoh), 97
Thutmose III (Egyptian pharaoh), 97
tian, 156
Tibet, 283, 321, 381
Tigris-Euphrates River, 8, 58. *See also* Mesopotamia; Southwest Asia
Tikal (Mutal), 227, 230
timelines
    Afroeurasia (3000–1000 B.C.E.), 107
    Afroeurasia (1200–600 B.C.E.), 159
    Afroeurasia (600–200 B.C.E.), 189
    Afroeurasia (300 B.C.E.–300 C.E.), 196, 200, 218
    Afroeurasia (200–600 C.E.), 276
    Afroeurasia (500–800 C.E.), 305
    Afroeurasia (750–1000 C.E.), 334
    Afroeurasia (1000–1250 C.E.), 366
    Afroeurasia (1200–1350 C.E.), 397
    Afroeurasia (1300–1500 C.E.), 451
    agricultural revolution, 51, 77
    American complex societies (900 B.C.E.–900 C.E.), 223, 230, 245
    Americas, 130
    Americas (900–1500 C.E.), 423
    ancient Egypt, 67
    Australia, 130
    China, 156, 200
    early complex societies, 67, 77
    human ancestors, 26, 27, 39, 47
    Maya, 230
    Oceania, 130
    Roman empire, 196
    technology, 54
Timgad, 199, *199*
Timurid sultanate, 443, *443*
Timur's empire, *432*, 433–434, *433*, 443
tin, 81–82
Titus (Roman emperor), *197*
Tiwanaku, 410
Tlatelolco, 413, 414
Tlatilco site, 117–118